"THE GREATEST REPOSITORY OF FIRSTHAND TESTIMONY BY THE ACTUAL CONTENDERS, THIS FAMOUS WORK . . . STANDS UNIQUE IN BREADTH AND DEPTH OF INFORMATION."

—*Atlantic Monthly*

"BECAUSE THE STORIES ARE SO ABLY DONE AND BEAR SO UNMISTAKABLY THE IMPRIMATUR OF THE NOISE OF BATTLE, THE BOOK IS A GENUINE CLASSIC."

—*Saturday Review*

NED BRADFORD, former editor-in-chief of Little, Brown & Company, combined his knowledge of publishing with his interest in Civil War history to compile this edition of *Battles and Leaders of the Civil War.*

Battles

of the

SELECTED AND EDITED BY

and Leaders

Civil War

NED BRADFORD

BOOKS ARE AVAILABLE AT QUANTITY DISCOUNTS WHEN USED
TO PROMOTE PRODUCTS OR SERVICES. FOR INFORMATION PLEASE
WRITE TO PREMIUM MARKETING DIVISION, PENGUIN BOOKS USA INC.,
375 HUDSON STREET, NEW YORK, NEW YORK 10014.

This is an authorized reprint of a hardcover edition published by E. P. Dutton. and
consists of selections from the original four-volume edition edited by R. U. Johnson
and C. C. Buel, published in 1887-88.

 REGISTERED TRADEMARK—MARCA REGISTRADA

Library of Congress Cataloging-in-Publication Data

Battles and leaders of the Civil War / selected and edited by Ned
  Bradford.
      p.   cm.
   Reprint. Originally published: [New York?] : Dutton, c1956.
   ISBN 0-452-01004-7
   1. United States—History—Civil War, 1861–1865—Campaigns.
   2. United States—History—Civil War, 1861–1865—Personal
  narratives.   I. Bradford, Ned, 1911–1979.
E470.B3325   1989
973.7′3—dc20   89-12684
                                                                       CIP

First Meridian Printing, December, 1989

          5   6   7   8   9

PRINTED IN THE UNITED STATES OF AMERICA

Contents

CONTENTS

CONTENTS

CONTENTS

CONTENTS

CONTENTS

"*Lee . . . facing Grant*"

"*An affectionate farewell*"

Preface

THE History of the Civil War has been told and told again. But still new books flow from the presses, demonstrating that a growing popular interest in the subject is keeping pace with literary production in some satisfying ratio. For obvious reasons there is room, and more, for these new books—besides which, it has been observed, every generation must rewrite the story of the past. Yet the whole basic history of the war was written in a definitive way in the 1880's, principally by the men who fought it, and collected into four large, fascinating volumes near the end of that decade under the title *Battles and Leaders of the Civil War.*

With the guidance of the editors of the old *Century Magazine,* and beginning less than twenty years after the conclusion of the war, the commanders on both sides were persuaded to describe their campaigns and individual battles, emphasizing their strategy and tactics and their results, but not neglecting the intimate, personal details which often make truth stranger and more rewarding than fiction.

These articles—by the Grants and the McClellans, the Longstreets and the Beauregards—were then arranged by theaters of operations and as strictly as possible in chronological order, so that cumulatively they became nothing less than a comprehensive history of the war. To be sure, by the 80's a few of the key commanders who had survived the war were dead—Robert E. Lee had died in 1870, causing the greatest lack among contributions from the Southern side—and a few, like General Sheridan, declined to contribute because they had recently published or were planning to publish separate memoirs. Yet even in these circumstances, subordinate officers produced such excellent articles from their commanders' points of view that no single gap was left in the continuous story of the war. And interspersed with all these articles by participants in or directors of the war were others by on-the-spot observers whose recollections were illuminating, humorous or charming, and always evocative of the essential flavor of the period.

The four volumes of *Battles and Leaders,* then, totaled over 350 selections by some 230 contributors, with hundreds of accompanying maps and illustrations—altogether a harvest which could be offered today only at a prohibitive cost to most book buyers. So it is a selection of these articles which comprise this new one-volume edition, together with many of the maps and illustrations which originally supplemented them.

A collection never satisfies everybody. It is even doubtful that it satisfies anybody, especially in such a field as the Civil War where the *aficionados* are so numerous and so well informed. Reducing four volumes of *Battles and Leaders* to one has obviously required some drastic surgery. It would serve no useful purpose to explain in detail what kinds of selections were dropped from the original books in the making of this one; but perhaps it will be sufficient to say that the articles which survived should make it possible for the general reader to follow the main currents of the war from Fort Sumter to Appomattox, to live almost continuously with the armies, to see battles through the eyes of the men who directed them, and to become conscious—perhaps as never before—of the over-all rhythm of the contest. Some of the articles have been cut internally to eliminate overtechnical passages not essential to the action, and brief introductions have been added to round out the general military history and to give the selections the maximum of coherence and continuity.

Finally, it might be well to sketch briefly the organization of the two military establishments, North and South. On both sides the smallest unit with any significant fighting power was the infantry company, the artillery battery or the cavalry troop, headed by a captain. Several companies comprised a regiment, of roughly a thousand men, commanded by a colonel. A brigade, made up of varying numbers of regiments, was commanded by a brigadier general. Several brigades, usually two to five, made a division, commanded by a brigadier or major general. And two or more divisions constituted an army corps, with a major general or lieutenant general in command. Now this table of organization was theoretical and must be somewhat qualified. As the war took its toll, these units got to be commanded by officers of lower grades. Thus lieutenants often commanded companies, majors commanded regiments, and so on down. Too, in the Confederate service there was a tendency for officers of higher grade to command smaller units than in the Union armies. The comparison of the importance of similarly designated units on both sides is complicated, moreover, by the fact that the Confederates simply added reinforcements to already existing regiments, while the Federals more often, and quite illogically, let regiments run down and eventually disappear, using fresh conscripts to form entirely new ones. The Northern army corps, after 1862, were identified by numbers, while the Southern corps (and divisions and brigades as well) were known by the names of their first commanders, even after those commanders had been killed, incapacitated, or assigned to command elsewhere.

Otherwise the opposed armies differed only in details. Both were officered to a considerable extent on the higher levels by West Pointers who had held commissions in the old Army (although of these the South had by far the higher proportion), many of whom had gained valuable experience in the Mexican War. Both, too, had an abundance of political generals and colonels, men who had no previous military experience whatever but who did have influence in Washington or Richmond or simply the wherewithal to raise and equip a regiment—and some of them performed remarkably well in the field in spite of that beginning. In the ranks, the Southern soldier was more of an individualist, less amenable to discipline, but perhaps more willing if not more able to endure war's hardships. The Northern soldier learned more quickly to put a high value on teamwork; he was also more mechanically inclined and so was the first to grasp the importance of new and more scientific methods of warfare. Both were equally devoted to a cause. But the ideal for which one fought was false, based on a social system which even in 1861 was economically outmoded and on moral grounds was becoming impossible to defend. So an ideal perished and the North won. In the process the nation became politically mature, a new power of the first class henceforth to be reckoned with in the foreign ministries of all the countries of the world.

NED BRADFORD

Battles and Leaders
of the Civil War

As the tension rose between North and South in the winter of 1860–1861, the detachments of United States troops garrisoning the various forts and stations of the Gulf and South Atlantic coasts found themselves in equivocal not to say hazardous positions. For the most part these companies were composed of men loyal to the Union. But they were now besieged from an unexpected quarter, surrounded by a population whose hostility to them and their occupation grew stronger every day. Furthermore, their commander in Washington until the end of '61, John B. Floyd, was an outspoken Southern advocate whose policy, in the latter months of his administration of the War Department, seemed to be to see that military supplies were placed in arsenals in the South where they would eventually do the Confederacy the most good, but to withhold supplies from those forts and military units which held strategic points along the coasts and were most likely to thwart the designs of the Confederacy. Fort Sumter was not the only such stronghold lost to the South early in 1861, but it was the first. It received the first shot fired in the War, became a symbol of outrage, and in defeat shocked the North into coöperation and action. Captain Abner Doubleday, later to become famous as the father of baseball, took his men from Fort Moultrie and its exposed position on Sullivan's Island to the yet unfinished but infinitely less vulnerable Fort Sumter on December 26th, 1860. This is his report of that transfer and of the tense months that followed.

"I aimed the first gun"

BY ABNER DOUBLEDAY, BREVET MAJOR-GENERAL, U. S. A., RETIRED

AS SENIOR captain of the 1st Regiment of United States Artillery, I had been stationed at Fort Moultrie, Charleston Harbor, two or three years previous to the outbreak of 1861. There were two other forts in the harbor. Of these, Fort Sumter was unoccupied, being in an unfinished state, while Castle Pinckney was in charge of a single ordnance sergeant. The garrison of Fort Moultrie consisted of 2 companies that had been reduced to 65 men, who with the band raised the number in the post to 73. Fort Moultrie had no strength; it was merely a sea battery. No one ever imagined it would be attacked by our own people; and if assailed by foreigners, it was supposed that an army of citizen-soldiery would be there to defend it. It was very low, the walls having about the height of an ordinary room. It was little more, in fact, than the old fort of Revolutionary time of which the father of Major Robert Anderson had been a defender. The sand had drifted from the sea against the wall, so that cows would actually scale the ramparts. In 1860 we applied to have the fort put in order, but the quartermaster-general, afterward the famous Joseph E. Johnston, said the matter did not pertain to his department. We were then apprehending trouble, for

3

the signs of the times indicated that the South was drifting toward secession, though the Northern people could not be made to believe this, and regarded our representation to this effect as nonsense. I remember that at that time our engineer officer, Captain J. G. Foster, was alone, of the officers, in thinking there would be no trouble. We were commanded by a Northern man of advanced age, Colonel John L. Gardner, who had been wounded in the war of 1812 and had served with credit in Florida and Mexico. November 15th, 1860, Mr. Floyd, the Secretary of War, relieved him and put in command Major Robert Anderson of Kentucky, who was a regular officer. Floyd thought the new commander could be relied upon to carry out the Southern programme, but we never believed that Anderson took command with a knowledge of that programme or a desire that it should succeed. He simply obeyed orders; he had to obey or leave the army. Anderson was a Union man and, in the incipiency, was perfectly willing to chastise South Carolina in case she should attempt any revolutionary measures. His feeling as to coercion changed when he found that all the Southern States had joined South Carolina, for he looked upon the conquest of the South as hopeless.

Soon after his arrival, which took place on the 21st of November, Anderson wanted the sand removed from the walls of Moultrie, and urged that it be done. Suddenly the Secretary of War seemed to adopt this view. He pretended there was danger of war with England, with reference to Mexico, which was absurd; and under this pretext was seized with a sudden zeal to put the harbor of Charleston in condition—to be turned over to the Confederate forces. He appropriated $150,000 for Moultrie and $80,000 to finish Sumter. There was not much to be made out of Fort Moultrie, with all our efforts, because it was hardly defensible; but Major Anderson strove to strengthen it. He put up heavy gates to prevent Charleston secessionists from entering, and made a little man-hole through which visitors had to crawl in and out.

We could get no additional ammunition, but Colonel Gardner had managed to procure a six months' supply of food from the North before the trouble came. The Secretary of War would not let us have a man in the way of reënforcement, the plea being that reënforcements would irritate the people. The secessionists could hardly be restrained from attacking us, but the leaders kept them back, knowing that our workmen were laboring in their interests, at the expense of the United States. When Captain Truman Seymour was sent with a party to the United States arsenal in Charleston to get some friction primers and a little ammunition, a crowd interfered and drove his men back. It became evident, as I told Anderson, that we could not defend the fort, because the houses around us on Sullivan's Island looked down into Moultrie, and could be occupied by our enemies. At last it was rumored that two thousand riflemen had been detailed to shoot us down from the tops of those houses. I proposed to anticipate the enemy and burn the dwellings, but Anderson would not take so decided a step at a time when the North did not believe there was going to be war. It was plain that the only thing to be done was to slip over the water to Fort Sumter, but Anderson said he had been assigned to Fort Moultrie, and that he must stay there. We were then in a very peculiar position. It was commonly believed that we would not be supported even by the North, as the Democrats had been bitterly opposed to the election of Lincoln; that at the first sign of war twenty thousand men in sympathy with the South would rise in New York. Moreover, the one to whom we soldiers always looked up as to a father—the Secretary of War, seemed to be devising arrangements to have us made away with. We believed that in the event of an outbreak from Charleston few of us would survive; but it did not greatly concern us, since that risk was merely a part of our business, and we intended to make the best fight we could. The officers, upon talking the matter over, thought they might control any demonstration at Charleston by throwing shells into the city from Castle Pinckney. But, with only sixty-four soldiers and a brass band, we could not detach any force in that direction.

Finally, Captain Foster, who had misapprehended the whole situation, and who had orders to put both Moultrie and Sumter in perfect order, brought several hundred workmen from Baltimore. Unfortunately, these were nearly all in sympathy with the Charlestonians, many even wearing secession badges.

Bands of secessionists were now patrolling near us by day and night. We were so worn out with guard-duty—watching them—that on one occasion my wife and Captain Seymour's relieved us on guard, all that was needed being some one to give the alarm in case there was an attempt to break in. Foster thought that out of his several hundred workmen he could get a few Union men to drill at the guns as a garrison in Castle Pinckney, but they rebelled the moment they found they were expected to act as artillerists, and said that they were not there as warriors. It was said that when the enemy took possession of the castle, some of these workmen were hauled from under beds and from other hiding-places.

The day before Christmas I asked Major Anderson for wire to make an entanglement in front of my part of the fort, so that any one who should charge would tumble over the wires and could be shot at our leisure. I had already caused a sloping picket fence to be projected over the parapet on my side of the works so that scaling ladders could not be raised against us. The discussion in Charleston over our proceedings was of an amusing character. This wooden *fraise* puzzled the Charleston militia and editors; one of the latter said, "Make ready your sharpened stakes, but you will not intimidate freemen."

When I asked Anderson for the wire, he said I should have a mile of it, with a peculiar smile that puzzled me for the moment. He then sent for Hall,

5

the post quartermaster, bound him to secrecy, and told him to take three schooners and some barges which had been chartered for the purpose of taking the women and children and six months' supply of provisions to Fort Johnson, opposite Charleston. He was instructed when the secession patrols should ask what this meant, to tell them we were sending off the families of the officers and men to the North because they were in the way. The excuse was plausible, and no one interfered. We were so closely watched that we could make no movement without demands being made as to the reason of it. On the day we left—the day after Christmas—Anderson gave up his own mess, and came to live with me as my guest. In the evening of that day I went to notify the major that tea was ready. Upon going to the parapet for that purpose, I found all the officers there, and noticed something strange in their manner. The problem was solved when Anderson walked up to me and said: "Captain, in twenty minutes you will leave this fort with your company for Fort Sumter." The order was startling and unexpected, and I thought of the immediate hostilities of which the movement would be the occasion. I rushed over to my company quarters and informed my men, so that they might put on their knapsacks and have everything in readiness. This took about ten minutes. Then I went to my house, told my wife that there might be fighting, and that she must get out of the fort as soon as she could and take refuge behind the sand-hills. I put her trunks out of the sally-port, and she followed them. Then I started with my company to join Captain Seymour and his men. We had to go a quarter of a mile through the little town of Moultrieville to reach the point of embarkation. It was about sunset, the hour of the siesta, and fortunately the Charleston militia were taking their afternoon nap. We saw nobody, and soon reached a low line of sea-wall under which were hidden the boats in charge of the three engineers, for Lieutenants Snyder and Meade had been sent by Floyd to help Captain Foster do the work on the forts. The boats had been used in going back and forward in the work of construction, manned by ordinary workmen, who now vacated them for our use. Lieutenant Snyder said to me in a low tone: "Captain, those boats are for your men." So saying, he started with his own party up the coast. When my thirty men were embarked I went straight for Fort Sumter. It was getting dusk. I made slow work in crossing over, for my men were not expert oarsmen. Soon I saw the lights of the secession guard-boat coming down on us. I told the men to take off their coats and cover up their muskets, and I threw my own coat open to conceal my buttons. I wished to give the impression that it was an officer in charge of laborers. The guard-ship stopped its paddles and inspected us in the gathering darkness, but concluded we were all right and passed on. My party was the first to reach Fort Sumter.

We went up the steps of the wharf in the face of an excited band of secession workmen, some of whom were armed with pistols. One or two Union men among them cheered, but some of the others said angrily: "What are these soldiers doing here? What is the meaning of this?" Ordering my men to charge bayonets, we drove the workmen into the center of the fort. I took possession of the guard-room commanding the main entrance and placed sentinels. Twenty minutes after, Seymour arrived with the rest of the men. Meantime Anderson had crossed in one of the engineer boats. As soon as the troops were all in we fired a cannon, to give notice of our arrival to the quartermaster, who had anchored at Fort Johnson with the schooners carrying the women and children. He immediately sailed up to the wharf and landed his passengers and stores. Then the workmen of secession sympathies were sent aboard the schooners to be taken ashore.

Lieutenant Jefferson C. Davis of my company had been left with a rear-guard at Moultrie. These, with Captain Foster and Assistant-Surgeon Crawford, stood at loaded columbiads during our passage, with orders to fire upon the guard-boats and sink them if they tried to run us down. On withdrawing, the rear-guard spiked the guns of the fort, burned the gun-carriages on the front looking toward Sumter, and cut down the flag-staff. Mrs. Doubleday first took refuge at the house of the post sutler, and afterward with the family of Chaplain Harris, with whom she sought shelter behind the sand-hills. When all was quiet they paced the beach, anxiously watching Fort Sumter. Finding that the South Carolinians were ignorant of what had happened, we sent the boats back to procure additional supplies.

The next morning Charleston was furious. Messengers were sent out to ring every door-bell and convey the news to every family. The governor sent two or three of his aides to demand that we return to Moultrie. Anderson replied in my hearing that he was a Southern man, but that he had been assigned to the defense of Charleston Harbor, and intended to defend it. . . .

From December 26th until April 12th we busied ourselves in preparing for the expected attack, and our enemies did the same on all sides of us. Anderson apparently did not want reënforcements, and he shrank from civil war. He endured all kinds of hostile proceedings on the part of the secessionists, in the hope that Congress would make some compromise that would save slavery and the Union together.

Soon after daylight on the 9th of January, with my glass I saw a large steamer pass the bar and enter the Morris Island Channel. It was the *Star of the West,* with reënforcements and supplies for us. When she came near the upper part of the island the secessionists fired a shot at her. I hastened to Major Anderson's room, and was ordered by him to have the long roll beaten and to post the men at the barbette guns. By the time we reached the parapet the transport coming to our relief had approached so near that Moultrie opened fire. Major Anderson would not allow us to return the fire, so the transport turned about and steamed seaward. Anderson asked for an explanation of the firing from Governor Pickens, and announced that he

7

would allow no vessel to pass within range of the guns of Sumter if the answer was unsatisfactory. Governor Pickens replied that he would renew the firing under like circumstances. I think Major Anderson had received an intimation that the *Star of the West* was coming, but did not believe it. He thought General Scott would send a man-of-war instead of a merchant vessel. Great secrecy was observed in loading her, but the purpose of the expedition got into the newspapers, and, of course, was telegraphed to Charleston. Bishop Stevens of the Methodist Church stated in a speech made by him on Memorial Day in the Academy of Music, New York, that he aimed the first gun against the *Star of the West*. I aimed the first gun on our side in reply to the attack on Fort Sumter. . . .

We have not been in the habit of regarding the signal shell fired from Fort Johnson as the first gun of the conflict, although it was undoubtedly aimed at Fort Sumter. Edmund Ruffin of Virginia is usually credited with opening the attack by firing the first gun from the iron-clad battery on Morris Island. The ball from that gun struck the wall of the magazine where I was lying, penetrated the masonry, and burst very near my head. As the smoke from this explosion came in through the ventilators of the magazine, and as the floor was strewn with powder where the flannel cartridges had been filled, I thought for a moment the place was on fire.

When it was fully light we took breakfast leisurely before going to the guns, our food consisting of pork and water.

The first night after the bombardment we expected that the naval vessels outside would take advantage of the darkness to send a fleet of boats with reënforcements of men and supplies of provisions, and as it was altogether probable that the enemy would also improvise a fleet of small boats to meet those of the navy, it became an interesting question, in case parties came to us in this way, to decide whether we were admitting friends or enemies. However, the night passed quietly away without any demonstration.

As the fire against us came from all directions, a shot from Sullivan's Island struck near the lock of the magazine, and bent the copper door, so that all access to the few cartridges we had there was cut off. Just previous to this the officers had been engaged, amid a shower of shells, in vigorous efforts to cut away wood-work which was dangerously near the magazine.

After the surrender we were allowed to salute our flag with a hundred guns before marching out, but it was very dangerous and difficult to do so; for, owing to the recent conflagration, there were fire and sparks all around the cannon, and it was not easy to find a safe place of deposit for the cartridges. It happened that some flakes of fire had entered the muzzle of one of the guns after it was sponged. Of course, when the gunner attempted to ram the cartridge down it exploded prematurely, killing Private Daniel Hough instantly, and setting fire to a pile of cartridges underneath, which also exploded, seriously wounding five men. Fifty guns were fired in the salute.

With banners flying, and with drums beating "Yankee Doodle," we marched on board the transport that was to take us to the steamship *Baltic*, which drew too much water to pass the bar and was anchored outside. We were soon on our way to New York.

With the first shot against Sumter the whole North became united. Mobs went about New York and made every doubtful newspaper and private house display the Stars and Stripes. When we reached that city we had a royal reception. The streets were alive with banners. Our men and officers were seized and forced to ride on the shoulders of crowds wild with enthusiasm. When we purchased anything, merchants generally refused all compensation.

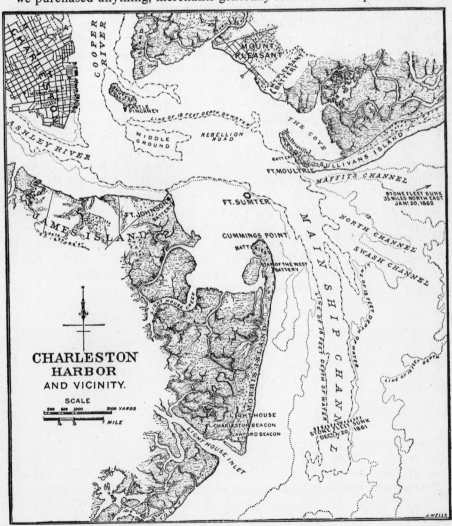

CHARLESTON HARBOR AND VICINITY.

9

On November 6, 1860, Abraham Lincoln was elected President of the United States, carrying seventeen states. (His three opponents divided the remaining sixteen.) Lincoln would not take office until the following March and meanwhile, on December 3rd, Congress met to hear a message from President Buchanan arguing against the right of secession, but expressing doubt about the constitutional power of the central government to make war upon a state. On December 20th, a formal Ordinance of Secession was adopted in South Carolina by a convention called by the state legislature. The day after Christmas a handful of Federal troops stationed at Fort Moultrie at the entrance to Charleston harbor, under the command of Major Robert Anderson, were transferred to the safer shelter of Fort Sumter, on a minuscule island in the harbor's mouth. The following day the United States Revenue Cutter *William Aiken* surrendered to the authorities of South Carolina. On the same day, Messrs. Barnwell, Orr, and Adams, Commissioners from South Carolina, arrived in Washington confidently prepared to treat with the Administration for the evacuation of Sumter (they were rebuffed). On December 29th John B. Floyd of Virginia, anticipating war between North and South, resigned as Secretary of War; and to cap the disasters of the month, on the last day of the year, the sovereign republic of South Carolina seized the United States Arsenal at Charleston. Reflecting the attitude of the Administration, Washington's officialdom was generally stunned into inaction by these events. But below the surface of government fantastic rumors spread, suspicions developed, alarms were sent out and recalled, tension mounted. The octogenarian General Winfield Scott—who had come to Washington on December 12th to advise the President on the condition of the regular army (lamentable)—said to Inspector-General Stone, "A dog fight now might cause the gutters to run with blood."

"Without them Lincoln would never have been inaugurated"

WASHINGTON ON THE EVE OF THE WAR

BY CHARLES P. STONE, BRIGADIER-GENERAL, U.S.V.

ALL WHO knew Washington in the days of December, 1860, know what thoughts reigned in the minds of thinking men. Whatever their daily occupations, they went about them with their thoughts always bent on the possible disasters of the near future. The country was in a curious and alarming condition: South Carolina had already passed an ordinance of secession, and other States were preparing to follow her lead. The only regular troops near the capital of the country were 300 or 400 marines at the marine barracks, and 3 officers and 53 men of ordnance at the Washington arsenal. The old militia system had been abandoned (without being legally abolished), and Congress had passed no law establishing a new one. The only armed volunteer organizations in the District of Columbia were: The Potomac Light Infantry, 1 company, at Georgetown; the National Rifles, 1 company, in Washington; the Washington Light Infantry, of about 160 men, and another small organization called the National Guard Battalion. It had been evident for months that, on assembling in December, Congress would have far different work to consider than the organization of the District of Columbia militia. Nor in the delicate position of affairs would it be the policy of President Buchanan, at the outset of the session, to propose

11

the military organization of the Federal District. It was also evident that, should he be so disposed, the senators and representatives of the Southern States would oppose and denounce the project.

What force, then, would the Government have at its disposal in the Federal District for the simple maintenance of order in case of need? Evidently but a handful; and as to calling thither promptly any regular troops, that was out of the question, since they had already all been distributed by the Southern sympathizers to the distant frontiers of the Indian country—Texas, Utah, New Mexico, Oregon, and Washington Territory. Months would have been necessary to concentrate at Washington, in that season, a force of three thousand regular troops. Even had President Buchanan been desirous of bringing troops to the capital, the feverish condition of the public mind would, as the executive believed, have been badly affected by any movement of the kind, and the approaching crisis might have been precipitated. I saw at once that the only force which could be readily made of service was a volunteer force raised from among the well-disposed men of the District, and that this must be organized, if at all, under the old law of 1799. By consultation with gentlemen well acquainted with the various classes of Washington society, I endeavored to learn what proportion of the able-bodied population could be counted on to sustain the Government should it need support from the armed and organized citizens.

On the 31st of December, 1860, Lieutenant-General Scott, General-in-Chief of the army (who had his headquarters in New York), was in Washington. The President, at last thoroughly alarmed at the results of continued concessions to secession, had summoned him for consultation. On the evening of that day I went to pay my respects to my old commander, and was received by him at Wormley's hotel. He chatted pleasantly with me for a few minutes, recalling past service in the Mexican War, etc.; and when the occasion presented itself, I remarked that I was glad to see him in good spirits, for that proved to me that he took a more cheerful view of the state of public affairs than he had on his arrival—more cheerful than we of Washington had dared to take during the past few days.

"Yes, my young friend," said the general, "I feel more cheerful about the affairs of the country than I did this morning; for I believe that a safer policy than has hitherto been followed will now be adopted. The policy of entire conciliation, which has so far been pursued, would soon have led to ruin. We are now in such a state that a policy of pure force would precipitate a crisis for which we are not prepared. A mixed policy of force and conciliation is now necessary, and I believe it will be adopted and carried out." He then looked at his watch, rose, and said: "I must be with the President in a quarter of an hour," and ordered his carriage. He walked up and down the dining-room, but suddenly stopped and faced me, saying: "How is the feeling in the

District of Columbia? What proportion of the population would sustain the Government by force, if necessary?"

"It is my belief, General," I replied, "that two-thirds of the fighting stock of this population would sustain the Government in defending itself, if called upon. But they are uncertain as to what can be done or what the Government desires to have done, and they have no rallying-point."

The general walked the room again in silence. The carriage came to the door, and I accompanied him toward it. As he was leaving, he turned suddenly, looked me in the face, placed his hand on my shoulder, and said:

"These people have no rallying-point. Make yourself that rallying-point!"

The next day I was commissioned by the President colonel in the staff and Inspector-General of the District of Columbia. I was mustered into the service of the United States from the 2d day of January, 1861, on the special requisition of the General-in-Chief, and thus was the first of two and a half millions called into the military service of the Government to defend it against secession.

I immediately entered upon my duties, commencing by inspections in detail of the existing organizations of volunteers. The Potomac Light Infantry company, of Georgetown, I found fairly drilled, well armed, and, from careful information, it seemed to me certain that the majority of its members could be depended upon in case of need, but not all of them.

On the 2d of January, I met, at the entrance of the Metropolitan Hotel, Captain Schaeffer, of the "National Rifles" of Washington, and I spoke to him about his company, which was remarkable for drill. Schaeffer had been a lieutenant in the Third United States Artillery, and was an excellent drillmaster.

He had evidently not yet heard of my appointment as Inspector-General, and he replied to my complimentary remarks on his company:

"Yes, it is a good company, and I suppose I shall soon have to lead it to the banks of the Susquehanna!"

"Why so?" I asked.

"Why! To guard the frontier of Maryland and help to keep the Yankees from coming down to coerce the South!"

I said to him quietly that I thought it very imprudent in him, an employee of the Department of the Interior and captain of a company of District of Columbia volunteers, to use such expressions. He replied that most of his men were Marylanders, and would have to defend Maryland. I told him that he would soon learn that he had been imprudent, and advised him to think more seriously of his position, but did not inform him of my appointment, which he would be certain to learn the following morning from the newspapers.

It must be admitted that this was not a very cheerful beginning.

13

On inspecting the "National Rifles," I found that Schaeffer had more than 100 men on his rolls, and was almost daily adding to the number, and that he had a full supply of rifles with 200 rounds of ball cartridges, two mountain howitzers with harness and carriages, a supply of sabers and of revolvers and ammunition, all drawn from the United States arsenal. I went to the Chief of Ordnance, to learn how it was that this company of riflemen happened to be so unusually armed; and I found at the Ordnance Office that an order had been given by the late Secretary of War (John B. Floyd) directing the Chief of Ordnance to cause to be issued to Captain Schaeffer "all the ordnance and ordnance stores that he might require for his company!" I ascertained also that Floyd had nominated Captain Schaeffer to the President for the commission of major in the District of Columbia militia, and that the commission had already been sent to the President for his signature.

I immediately presented the matter to the new Secretary of War (Joseph Holt), and procured from him two orders—one, an order to the Chief of Ordnance to issue no arms to any militia or volunteers in the District of Columbia unless the requisition should be countersigned by the Inspector-General; the other, an order that all commissions issued to officers of the District of Columbia should be sent to the Inspector-General for delivery....

Having thus studied the ground, and taken the first necessary steps toward security, I commenced the work of providing a force of volunteers. I addressed individual letters to some forty well-known and esteemed gentlemen of the District, informing each one that it would be agreeable to the Government should he in his neighborhood raise and organize a company of volunteers for the preservation of order in the District. To some of these letters I received no replies; to some I received replies courteously declining the service; to some I received letters sarcastically declining; but to many I received replies enthusiastically accepting the service. In about six weeks thirty-three companies of infantry and riflemen and two troops of cavalry were on the lists of the District volunteer force; and all had been uniformed, equipped, and put under frequent drill.

The Northern Liberties fire companies brought their quota; the Lafayette Hose Company was prompt to enroll; the masons, the carpenters, the stonecutters, the painters, and the German turners responded: each corporation formed its companies and drilled industriously. Petty rivalries disappeared, and each company strove to excel the others in drill and discipline. While the newly organized companies thus strove to perfect themselves, the older organizations resumed their drills and filled their ranks with good recruits.

The National Rifles company (Captain Schaeffer's) was carefully observed, and it was found that its ranks received constant accessions, including the most openly declared secessionists and even members of Congress from the Southern States. This company was very frequently drilled in its armory, and its recruits were drilled nearly every night.

Having, as Inspector-General, a secret service force at my disposition, I placed a detective in the company, and had regular reports of the proceedings of its captain. He was evidently pushing for an independent command of infantry, artillery, and cavalry, having his rifles, cannon, sabers, and revolvers stored in his armory. He also began to prepare for action, ordering his men to take their rifles and equipments home with them, with a supply of ammunition, so that even should his armory be occupied, they could assemble on short notice, ready for action. Meantime, his commission as major was signed by the President and sent to me.

I reported these matters to General Scott, who ordered me to watch these proceedings carefully, and to be ready to suppress any attempt at violence; but to avoid, if possible, any shock, for, said he, "We are now in such a state that a dog-fight might cause the gutters of the capital to run with blood."

While the volunteer force for the support of the Government was organizing, another force with exactly the opposite purpose was in course of formation. I learned that the great hall over Beach's livery stable was nightly filled with men who were actively drilled. Doctor B——, of well-known secession tendencies, was the moving spirit of these men, and he was assisted by other citizens of high standing, among whom was a connection of Governor Letcher of Virginia. The numbers of these occupants of Beach's hall increased rapidly, and I found it well to have a skillful New York detective officer, who had been placed at my disposition, enrolled among them. These men called themselves "National Volunteers," and in their meetings openly discussed the seizure of the national capital at the proper moment. They drilled industriously, and had regular business meetings, full reports of which were regularly laid before me every following morning by "the New York member." In the meeting at which the uniform to be adopted was discussed, the vote was for gray Kentucky jeans, with the Maryland button. A cautious member suggested that they must remember that, in order to procure arms, it would be "necessary to get the requisition signed by 'Old Stone,' and if he saw that they had adopted the Maryland button, and not that of the United States, he might suspect them and refuse the issue of arms!" Doctor B—— supported the idea of the Maryland button, and said that, if Stone refused the arms, the Governor of Virginia would see them furnished, etc. These gentlemen probably little thought that a full report of their remarks would be read the next morning by "Old Stone" to the General-in-Chief.

The procuring of arms was a difficult matter for them, for it required the election of officers, the regular enrolling of men, the certificate of elections, and the muster-rolls, all to be reported to the Inspector-General. The subject was long discussed by them, and it was finally arranged that, out of the 360 men, a pretended company should be organized, officers elected, and the demand for arms made. This project was carried out, and *my* member brought to me early the next morning the report of the proceedings, inform-

15

ing me that Doctor B—— had been elected captain, and would call on the Inspector-General for arms. Sure enough Doctor B—— presented himself in my office and informed me that he had raised a company of volunteers, and desired an order for arms. He produced a certificate of election in due form. I received him courteously, and informed him that I could not give an order for arms without having a muster-roll of his men, proving that a full one hundred had signed the rolls. It was desirable to have the names of men holding such sentiments and nursing such projects as were known to be theirs.

He returned, I think, on the following day, with a muster-roll in due form, containing the names of one hundred men. This was all that I wanted. I looked him full in the face, smiled, and locked the muster-roll in a drawer of my desk, saying:

"Doctor B——, I am very happy to have obtained this list, and I wish you good-morning."

The gallant doctor evidently understood me. He smiled, bowed, and left the office, to which he never returned. He subsequently proved the sincerity of his principles by abandoning his pleasant home in Washington, his large and valuable property, and giving his earnest service to the Confederate cause. The "National Volunteer" organization broke up without further trouble.

Next came the turn of Captain Schaeffer. He entered my office one day with the air of an injured man, holding in his hand a requisition for arms and ammunition, and saying, that, on presenting it at the Ordnance Office, he had been informed that no arms could be issued to him without my approval. I informed him that that was certainly correct, and that the order of the Secretary of War was general. I told him that he had already in his possession more rifles than were required for a company, and that he could have no more. He then said, sulkily, that with his company he could easily *take* the arms he wanted. I asked him, "Where?" and he replied:

"You have only four soldiers guarding the Columbian armory, where there are plenty of arms, and those four men could not prevent my taking them."

"Ah!" I replied, "in what part of the armory are those arms kept?" He said they were on the upper floor, which was true.

"Well," said I, "you seem to be well informed. If you think it best, just try taking the arms by force. I assure you that if you do you shall be fired on by 150 soldiers as you come out of the armory."

The fact was, that only two enlisted men of ordnance were on duty at the Columbian armory, so feeble was the military force at the time. But Barry's battery had just arrived at the Washington arsenal, and on my application General Scott had ordered the company of sappers and miners at West Point to come to Washington to guard the armory; but they had not yet arrived. The precautions taken in ordering them were thus clearly proved advisable.

The time had evidently come to disarm Captain Schaeffer; and when he reached his office after leaving mine, he found there an order directing him to deposit in the Columbian armory, before sunset on that day, the two howitzers with their carriages which he had in his possession, as well as the sabers and revolvers, as these weapons formed no part of the proper armament of a company of riflemen. He was taken by surprise, and had not time to call together men enough to resist; so that nothing was left to him but to comply with the order. He obeyed it, well knowing that if he did not I was prepared to take the guns from his armory by means of other troops.

Having obeyed, he presented himself again in my office, and before he had time to speak I informed him that I had a commission of major for his name. He was much pleased, and said: "Yes, I heard that I had been appointed." I then handed him a slip of paper on which I had written out the form of oath which the old law required to be taken by officers, that law never having been repealed, and said to him:

"Here is the form of oath you are to take. You will find a justice of the peace on the next floor. Please qualify, sign the form in duplicate, and bring both to me. One will be filed with your letter of acceptance, the other will be filed in the clerk's office of the Circuit Court of the District."

He took the paper with a sober look, and stood near my table several minutes looking at the form of oath and turning the paper over, while I, apparently very busy with my papers, was observing him closely. I then said:

"Ah, Schaeffer, have you already taken the oath?"

"No," said he.

"Well, please be quick about it, as I have no time to spare."

He hesitated, and said slowly:

"In ordinary times I would not mind taking it, but in these times—"

"Ah!" said I, "you decline to accept your commission of major. Very well!" and I returned his commission to the drawer and locked it in.

"Oh, no," said Schaeffer, "I want the commission."

"But, sir, you cannot have it. Do you suppose that, in these times, which are not, as you say, 'ordinary times,' I would think of delivering a commission of field-officer to a man who hesitates about taking the oath of office? Do you think that the Government of the United States is stupid enough to allow a man to march armed men about the Federal District under its authority, when that man hesitates to take the simple oath of office? No, sir, you cannot have this commission; and more than that, I now inform you that you hold no office in the District of Columbia volunteers."

"Yes, I do; I am captain, and have my commission as such, signed by the President and delivered to me by the major-general."

"I am aware that such a paper was delivered to you, but you failed legally to accept it."

"I wrote a letter of acceptance to the adjutant-general, and forwarded it through the major-general."

"Yes, I am aware that you did; but I know also that you failed to inclose in that letter, according to law, the form of oath required to accompany all letters of acceptance; and on the register of the War Department, while the issuance of your commission is recorded, the acceptance is not recorded. You have never legally accepted your commission, and it is now too late. The oath of a man who hesitates to take it will not now be accepted."

So Captain Schaeffer left the "National Rifles," and with him left the secession members of the company. I induced quite a number of true men to join its ranks; a new election was ordered, and a strong, loyal man (Lieutenant Smead of the 2d Artillery) was elected its captain. Smead was then on duty in the office of the Coast Survey, and I easily procured from the War Department permission for him to accept the position.

If my information was correct, the plan had been formed for seizing the public departments at the proper moment and obtaining possession of the seals of the Government. Schaeffer's part, with the battalion he was to form, was to take possession of the Treasury Department for the benefit of the new Provisional Government. Whatever may have been the project, it was effectually foiled. With the breaking up of the "National Volunteers"; with the transformation of the secession company of "National Rifles" into a thoroughly faithful and admirably drilled company ready for the service of the Government; with the arrival from West Point of the company of sappers and miners, and, later, the arrival of the Military Academy battery under Griffin; and with the formation in the District of thirty new companies of infantry and riflemen from among the citizens of Washington and Georgetown, the face of things in the capital had much changed before the 4th of March.

I must now go back a little in time, to mention one fact which will show in how weak and dangerous a condition our Government was in the latter part of January and the early part of February, 1861. The invitations which I had issued for the raising of companies of volunteers had, as already stated, been enthusiastically responded to, and companies were rapidly organized. The preparatory drills were carried on every night, and I soon found that the men were sufficiently advanced to receive their arms. I began to approve the requisitions for arms; but, to my great astonishment, the captains who first received the orders came back to me, stating that the Ordnance Department had refused to issue any arms! On referring to the Ordnance Office, I was informed by the Chief of Ordnance that he had received, the day before, an order not to issue any arms to the District of Columbia troops, and that this order had come from the President!

I went immediately to the Secretary of War (Mr. Holt) and informed him of the state of affairs, telling him at the same time that I did not feel disposed to be employed in child's play, organizing troops which could not be armed, and that unless the order in question should be immediately revoked there was no use for me in my place, and that I must at once resign. Mr. Holt told me that I was perfectly right; that unless the order should be revoked there was no use in my holding my place, and he added, with a smile, "and I will also say, Colonel, there will be no use in my holding my place any longer. Go to the President, Colonel, and talk to him as you have talked to me."

I went to the White House, and was received by Mr. Buchanan. I found him sitting at his writing-table, in his dressing-gown, wearied and worried.

I opened at once the subject of arms, and stated the necessity of immediate issue, as the refusal of arms would not only stop the instruction of the volunteers, which they needed sadly, but would make them lose all confidence in the Government and break up the organizations. I closed by saying that, while I begged his pardon for saying it, in case he declined to revoke his order I must ask him to accept my resignation at once.

Mr. Buchanan was evidently in distress of mind, and said:

"Colonel, I gave that order acting on the advice of the District Attorney, Mr. Robert Ould."

"Then, Mr. President," I replied, "the District Attorney has advised your Excellency very badly."

"But, Colonel, the District Attorney is an old resident of Washington, and he knows all the little jealousies which exist here. He tells me that you have organized a company from the Northern Liberty Fire Company."

"Not only one, but two excellent companies in the Northern Liberty, your Excellency."

"And then, the District Attorney tells me you have organized another company from among the members of the Lafayette Hose Company."

"Yes, your Excellency, another excellent company."

"And the District Attorney tells me, Colonel, that there is a strong feeling of enmity between those fire companies, and, if arms are put in their hands, there will be danger of bloodshed in the city."

"Will your Excellency excuse me if I say that the District Attorney talks nonsense, or worse, to you? If the Northern Liberties and the Lafayette Hose men wish to fight, can they not procure hundreds of arms in the shops along the avenue? Be assured, Mr. President, that the people of this District are thinking now of other things than old ward feuds. They are thinking whether or not the Government of the United States is to allow itself to crumble out of existence by its own weakness. And I believe that the District Attorney knows that as well as I do. If the companies of volunteers are not armed, they will disband, and the Government will have nothing to protect it in case of even a little disturbance. Is it not better for the public peace, your Excellency, even if the bloody feud exists (which I believe is forgotten in a greater question)—is it not better to have these men organized and under the discipline of the Government?"

The President hesitated a moment, and then said:

"I don't know that you are not right, Colonel; but you must take the responsibility on you that no bloodshed results from arming these men."

I willingly accepted this responsibility. The prohibitory order was revoked. My companies received their arms, and made good use of them, learning the manual of arms in a surprisingly short time. Later, they made good use of them in sustaining the Government which had furnished them against the faction which soon became its public enemy, including Mr. Robert Ould, who, following his convictions (no doubt as honestly as I was following mine), gave his earnest services to his State against the Federal Government.

I think that the country has never properly appreciated the services of those District of Columbia volunteers. It certainly has not appreciated the difficulties surmounted in their organization. Those volunteers were citizens of the Federal District, and therefore had not at the time, nor have they ever had since, the powerful stimulant of State feeling, nor the powerful support of a State government, a State's pride, a State press to set forth and make much of their services. They did their duty quietly, and they did it well and faithfully. Although not mustered into the services and placed on pay until after the fatal day when the flag was fired upon at Sumter, yet they rendered great service before that time in giving confidence to the Union men, to members of the national legislature, and also to the President in the knowledge that there was at least a small force at its disposition ready to respond at any moment to his call. It should also be remembered of them, that the first troops mustered into the service were sixteen companies of these volunteers; and that, during the dark days when Washington was cut off from communication with the North, when railway bridges were burned and tracks torn up, when the Potomac was blockaded, these troops were the only reliance of the Government for guarding the public departments, for preserving order and for holding the bridges and other outposts; that these were the troops which recovered possession of the railway from Washington to Annapolis Junction and made practicable the reopening of communications. They also formed the advance guard of the force which first crossed the Potomac into Virginia and captured the city of Alexandria.

Moreover, these were the troops which insured the regular inauguration on the steps of the Capitol of the constitutionally elected President. I firmly believe that without them Mr. Lincoln would never have been inaugurated. I believe that tumults would have been created, during which he would have been killed, and that we should have found ourselves engaged in a struggle, without preparation, and without a recognized head at the capital. In this I may be mistaken, of course, as any other man may be mistaken; but it was then my opinion, when I had many sources of information at my command, and it remains my opinion now, when, after the lapse of many years and a somewhat large experience, I look back in cool blood upon those days of political madness. . . .

"Without them Lincoln would never have been inaugurated"

I received daily numerous communications from various parts of the country, informing me of plots to prevent the arrival of the President-elect at the capital. These warnings came from St. Louis, from Chicago, from Cincinnati, from Pittsburgh, from New York, from Philadelphia, and especially from Baltimore. Every morning I reported to General Scott on the occurrences of the night and the information received by the morning's mail; and every evening I rendered an account of the day's work and received instructions for the night. General Scott also received numerous warnings of danger to the President-elect, which he would give me to study and compare. Many of the communications were anonymous and vague. But, on the other hand, many were from calm and wise men, one of whom became, shortly afterward, a cabinet minister; one was a railway president, another a distinguished ex-governor of a State, etc. In every case where the indications were distinct, they were followed up to learn if real danger existed.

So many clear indications pointed to Baltimore, that three good detectives of the New York police force were constantly employed there. These men reported frequently to me, and their statements were constantly compared with the information received from independent sources.

Doubtless, Mr. Lincoln, at his home in Springfield, Ill., received many and contradictory reports from the capital, for he took his own way of obtaining information. One night, between 11 o'clock and midnight, while I was busy in my study over the papers of the day and evening, a card was brought to me, bearing the name "Mr. Leonard Swett," and upon it was written in the well-known hand of General Scott, "Colonel Stone, Inspector-General, may converse freely with Mr. Swett." Soon a tall gentleman of marked features entered my room. At first I thought it was Mr. Lincoln himself, so much, at first glance, did Mr. Swett's face resemble the portraits I had seen of Mr. Lincoln, and so nearly did his height correspond with that attributed to the President-elect. But I quickly found that the gentleman's card bore his true name, and that Mr. Swett had come directly from Mr. Lincoln, having his full confidence, to see for him the state of affairs in Washington, and report to him in person. . . .

As President Lincoln approached the capital, it became certain that desperate attempts would be made to prevent his arriving there. To be thoroughly informed as to what might be expected in Baltimore, I directed a detective to be constantly near the chief of police and to keep up relations with him; while two others were instructed to watch, without the knowledge and independent of the chief of police. The officer who was near the chief of police reported regularly, until near the last, that there was no danger in Baltimore; but the others discovered a band of desperate men plotting for the destruction of Mr. Lincoln during his passage through the city, and by affiliating with them, these detectives obtained the details of the plot.

Mr. Lincoln passed through Baltimore in advance of the time announced for the journey (in accordance with advice given by me to Mr. Seward and which was carried by Mr. Frederick W. Seward to Mr. Lincoln), and arrived safe at Washington on the morning of the day he was to have passed through Baltimore. But the plotting to prevent his inauguration continued; and there was only too good reason to fear that an attempt would be made against his life during the passage of the inaugural procession from Willard's hotel, where Mr. Lincoln lodged, to the Capitol.

On the afternoon of the 3d of March, General Scott held a conference at his headquarters, there being present his staff, General Sumner, and myself, and then was arranged the programme of the procession. President Buchanan was to drive to Willard's hotel, and call upon the President-elect. The two were to ride in the same carriage, between double files of a squadron of the District of Columbia cavalry. The company of sappers and miners were to march in front of the presidential carriage, and the infantry and riflemen of the District of Columbia were to follow it. Riflemen in squads were to be placed on the roofs of certain commanding houses which I had selected, along Pennsylvania Avenue, with orders to watch the windows on the opposite side and to fire upon them in case any attempt should be made to fire from those windows on the presidential carriage. The small force of regular cavalry which had arrived was to guard the side-street crossings of Pennsylvania Avenue, and to move from one to another during the passage of the procession. A battalion of District of Columbia troops were to be placed near the steps of the Capitol, and riflemen in the windows of the wings of the Capitol. On the arrival of the presidential party at the Capitol, the troops were to be stationed so as to return in the same order after the ceremony.

To illustrate the state of uncertainty in which we were at that time concerning men, I may here state that the lieutenant-colonel, military secretary of the General-in-Chief, who that afternoon recorded the conclusions of the General in conference, and who afterward wrote out for me the instructions regarding the disposition of troops, resigned his commission that very night, and departed for the South, where he joined the Confederate army.

During the night of the 3d of March, notice was brought me that an attempt would be made to blow up the platform on which the President would stand to take the oath of office. I immediately placed men under the steps, and at daybreak a trusted battalion of District troops (if I remember rightly, it was the National Guard, under Colonel Tait) formed in a semicircle at the foot of the great stairway, and prevented all entrance from without. When the crowd began to assemble in front of the portico, a large number of policemen in plain clothes were scattered through the mass to observe closely, to place themselves near any person who might act suspiciously, and to strike down any hand which might raise a weapon.

At the appointed hour, Mr. Buchanan was escorted to Willard's hotel, which he entered. There I found a number of mounted "marshals of the

22

day," and posted them around the carriage, within the cavalry guard. The two Presidents were saluted by the troops as they came out of the hotel and took their places in the carriage. The procession started. During the march to the Capitol I rode near the carriage, and by an apparently clumsy use of my spurs managed to keep the horses of the cavalry in an uneasy state, so that it would have been very difficult for even a good marksman to get an aim at one of the inmates of the carriage between the prancing horses.

After the inaugural ceremony, the President and the ex-President were escorted in the same order to the White House. Arrived there, Mr. Buchanan walked to the door with Mr. Lincoln, and there bade him welcome to the House and good-morning. The infantry escort formed in line from the gate of the White House to the house of Mr. Ould, whither Mr. Buchanan drove, and the cavalry escorted his carriage. The infantry line presented arms to the ex-President as he passed, and the cavalry escort saluted as he left the carriage and entered the house. Mr. Buchanan turned on the steps, and gracefully acknowledged the salute. The District of Columbia volunteers had given to President Lincoln his first military salute and to Mr. Buchanan his last.

In April 1861, Harper's Ferry, in what was to be the new state of West Virginia, fell to a Confederate force, the United States Armory there yielding some valuable parts for military arms, and the Confederates' position giving them, temporarily at least, control of the main east-west trunk line of the Baltimore & Ohio Railroad. In June and July, General George B. McClellan fought some minor actions in West Virginia against indifferent opposition and wrote such flamboyant reports of these victories that the Northern newspapers and public, hungry for claims of early successes, began then and there to endow him with the attributes of another Napoleon. But these were mere preludes to the first grand battle of the war—Bull Run, a battle into which green Union troops were pushed by public clamor for a victory (Horace Greeley's New York Tribune carried the permanent running head FORWARD TO RICHMOND!) *and the universal opinion which insisted that one decisive defeat for the Confederacy would bring its leaders to their senses, at least as soon as Richmond fell. So General Irwin McDowell —whom the writer of the following article describes with unconscious humor as a commander "of unexceptional habits"—was placed at the head of the Union army south of the Potomac and propelled forward. Facing him a few miles away, and drawn up along the south bank of a small stream called Bull Run, was an equally inexperienced army under the conqueror of Sumter, General Pierre Gustave Toutant Beauregard—an army which was just as confident as its opponent that when its superior fighting qualities were tested and found invincible by the Yankees, the war would be over and the southern sisters free to go their way in peace.*

At Bull Run, on July 21st, the men of both sides revised their preconception of the fighting qualities of their opponents. But in the process McDowell suffered a painful defeat. The army he had brought from its camps around Washington, as carefree as if it were going to a picnic and accompanied by hundreds of civilian sightseers and their ladies, reeled back in the wildest disorder. A young government clerk named Walt Whitman watched them return to the city "baffled, humiliated, panic struck," and rhetorically he said to them, "Where are the vaunts and the proud boasts with which you went forth? Where are your banners, and your bands of music, and your ropes to bring back your prisoners? Well, there isn't a band playing—and there isn't a flag but clings ashamed and lank to its staff."

"The South triumphant, the North disappointed"

McDOWELL'S ADVANCE TO BULL RUN

BY JAMES B. FRY, BREVET MAJOR-GENERAL, U. S. A.

W HEN the news of the firing upon Sumter reached Washington, President Lincoln prepared a proclamation, and issued it April 15th, convening Congress and calling forth 75,000 three-months militia to suppress combinations against the Government. The Federal situation was alarming. Sumter fell on the 13th of April, and was evacuated on the 14th. Virginia seceded on the 17th, and seized Harper's Ferry on the 18th and the Norfolk Navy Yard on the 20th. On the 19th a mob in Baltimore assaulted the 6th Massachusetts volunteers as it passed through to Washington, and at once bridges were burned and railway communication was cut off between Washington and the North.

Lincoln had had no experience as a party leader or executive officer, and was without knowledge of military affairs or acquaintance with military men. Davis at the head of the Confederacy was an experienced and acknowledged

25

Southern leader; he was a graduate of the Military Academy; had commanded a regiment in the Mexican war; had been Secretary of War under President Pierce, and had been chairman of the Military Committee in the United States Senate up to the time he left Congress to take part with the South. He was not only well versed in everything relating to war, but was thoroughly informed concerning the character and capacity of prominent and promising officers of the army. There was nothing experimental in his choice of high military commanders. With but few exceptions, those appointed at the beginning retained command until they lost their lives or the war closed.

The Southern States, all claiming to be independent republics after secession, with all their governmental machinery, including militia and volunteer organizations, in complete working order, transferred themselves as States from the Union to the Confederacy. The organization of a general government from such elements, with war as its immediate purpose, was a simple matter. Davis had only to accept and arrange, according to his ample information and well-matured judgment, the abundant and ambitious material at hand in the way that he thought would best secure his purposes. Lincoln had to adapt the machinery of a conservative old government, some of it unsuitable, some unsound, to sudden demands for which it was not designed. The talents of Simon Cameron, his first Secretary of War, were political, not military. He was a kind, gentle, placid man, gifted with powers to persuade, not to command. Shrewd and skilled in the management of business and personal matters, he had no knowledge of military affairs, and could not give the President much assistance in assembling and organizing for war the earnest and impatient, but unmilitary people of the North.

Officers from all departments of the Federal civil service hurried to the Confederacy and placed themselves at the disposal of Davis, and officers from all the corps of the regular army, most of them full of vigor, with the same education and experience as those who remained, went South and awaited assignment to the duties for which Davis might regard them as best qualified. All Confederate offices were vacant, and the Confederate President had large if not absolute power in filling them. On the other hand, the civil offices under Lincoln were occupied or controlled by party, and in the small regular army of the Union the law required that vacancies should as a rule be filled by seniority. There was no retired list for the disabled, and the army was weighed down by longevity; by venerated traditions; by prerogatives of service rendered in former wars; by the firmly tied red-tape of military bureauism, and by the deep-seated and well-founded fear of the auditors and comptrollers of the treasury. Nothing but time and experience—possibly nothing but disaster—could remove from the path of the Union President difficulties from which the Confederate President was, by the situation, quite free. In the beginning of the war, the military advantage was on the side of the Confederates, notwithstanding the greater resources of the North, which produced their effect only as the contest was prolonged.

After the firing of the first gun upon Sumter, the two sides were equally active in marshaling their forces on a line along the border States from the Atlantic coast of Virginia in the east to Kansas in the west. Many of the earlier collisions along this line were due rather to special causes or local feeling than to general military considerations. The prompt advance of the Union forces under McClellan to West Virginia was to protect that new-born free State. Patterson's movement to Hagerstown and thence to Harper's Ferry was to prevent Maryland from joining or aiding the rebellion, to re-open the Baltimore and Ohio railroad, and prevent invasion from the Shenandoah Valley. The Southerners having left the Union and set up the Confederacy upon the principle of State rights, in violation of that principle invaded the State of Kentucky in opposition to her apparent purpose of armed neutrality. That made Kentucky a field of early hostilities and helped to anchor her to the Union. Missouri was rescued from secession through the energy of General F. P. Blair and her other Union men, and by the indomitable will of Captain Lyon of the regular army, whose great work was accomplished under many disadvantages. In illustration of the difficulty with which the new condition of affairs penetrated the case-hardened bureauism of long peace, it may be mentioned that the venerable adjutant-general of the army, when a crisis was at hand in Missouri, came from a consultation with the President and Secretary Cameron, and with a sorry expression of countenance and an ominous shake of the head exclaimed, "It's bad, very bad; we're giving that young man Lyon a great deal too much power in Missouri."

Early in the contest another young Union officer came to the front. Major Irvin McDowell was appointed brigadier-general May 14th. He was forty-three years of age, of unexceptional habits and great physical powers. His education, begun in France, was continued at the United States Military Academy, from which he was graduated in 1838. Always a close student, he was well informed outside as well as inside his profession. Distinguished in the Mexican war, intensely Union in his sentiments, full of energy and patriotism, outspoken in his opinions, highly esteemed by General Scott, on whose staff he had served, he at once secured the confidence of the President and the Secretary of War, under whose observation he was serving in Washington. Without political antecedents or acquaintances, he was chosen for advancement on account of his record, his ability, and his vigor.

Northern forces had hastened to Washington upon the call of President Lincoln, but prior to May 24th they had been held rigidly on the north side of the Potomac. On the night of May 23d-24th, the Confederate pickets being then in sight of the Capitol, three columns were thrown across the river by General J. K. F. Mansfield, then commanding the Department of Washington, and a line from Alexandria below to chain-bridge above Washington was intrenched under guidance of able engineers. On the 27th Brigadier-General Irvin McDowell was placed in command south of the Potomac.

By the 1st of June the Southern Government had been transferred from Montgomery to Richmond, and the capitals of the Union and of the Confederacy stood defiantly confronting each other. General Scott was in chief command of the Union forces, with McDowell south of the Potomac, confronted by his old classmate, Beauregard, hot from the capture of Fort Sumter.

General Patterson, of Pennsylvania, a veteran of the war of 1812 and the war with Mexico, was in command near Harper's Ferry, opposed by General Joseph E. Johnston. The Confederate President, Davis, then in Richmond, with General R. E. Lee as military adviser, exercised in person general military control of the Southern forces. The enemy to be engaged by McDowell occupied what was called the "Alexandria line," with headquarters at Manassas, the junction of the Orange and Alexandria with the Manassas Gap railroad. The stream known as Bull Run, some three miles in front of Manassas, was the line of defense. On Beauregard's right, 30 miles away, at the mouth of Aquia Creek, there was a Confederate brigade of 3000 men and 6 guns under General Holmes. The approach to Richmond from the Lower Chesapeake, threatened by General B. F. Butler, was guarded by Confederates under Generals Huger and Magruder. On Beauregard's left, sixty miles distant, in the Lower Shenandoah Valley and separated from him by the Blue Ridge Mountains, was the Confederate army of the Shenandoah under command of General Johnston. Beauregard's authority did not extend over the forces of Johnston, Huger, Magruder, or Holmes, but Holmes was with him before the battle of Bull Run, and so was Johnston, who, as will appear more fully hereafter, joined at a decisive moment.

Early in June Patterson was pushing his column against Harper's Ferry, and on the 3d of that month McDowell was called upon by General Scott to submit "an estimate of the number and composition of a column to be pushed toward Manassas Junction and perhaps the Gap, say in 4 or 5 days, to favor Patterson's attack upon Harper's Ferry." McDowell had then been in command at Arlington less than a week, his raw regiments south of the Potomac were not yet brigaded, and this was the first intimation he had of offensive operations. He reported, June 4th, that 12,000 infantry, 2 batteries, 6 or 8 companies of cavalry, and a reserve of 5000 ready to move from Alexandria would be required. Johnston, however, gave up Harper's Ferry to Patterson, and the diversion by McDowell was not ordered. But the public demand for an advance became imperative—stimulated perhaps by the successful dash of fifty men of the 2d United States Cavalry, under Lieutenant C. H. Tompkins, through the enemy's outposts at Fairfax Court House on the night of June 1st, and by the unfortunate result of the movement of a regiment under General Schenck toward Vienna, June 17th, as well as by a disaster to some of General Butler's troops on the 10th at Big Bethel, near Fort Monroe. On the 24th of June, in compliance with verbal instructions from General Scott, McDowell submitted a "plan of operations and the composition of the force required to carry it into effect." He estimated the Confederate force at Manassas Junction and its dependencies at 25,000 men, assumed that his movements could not be kept secret and that the enemy would call up additional forces from all quarters, and added: "If General J. E. Johnston's force is kept engaged by Major-General Patterson, and Major-General Butler occupies the force now in his vicinity, I think they will not be able to bring up more than 10,000 men, so we may calculate upon having to do with about 35,000 men." And as it turned out, that was about the number he "had to do with." For the advance, McDowell asked "a force of 30,000 of all arms, with a reserve of 10,000." He knew that Beauregard had batteries in position at several places in front of Bull Run and defensive works behind the Run and at Manassas Junction. The stream being fordable at many places, McDowell proposed in his plan of operations to turn the enemy's position and force him out of it by seizing or threatening his communications. Nevertheless, he said in his report:

Believing the chances are greatly in favor of the enemy's accepting battle between this and the Junction and that the consequences of that battle will be of the greatest importance to the country, as establishing the prestige in this contest, on the one side or the other—the more so as the two sections will be fairly represented by regiments from almost every State—I think it of great consequence that, as for the most part our regiments are exceedingly raw and the best of them, with few exceptions, not over steady in line, they be organized into as many small fixed brigades as the number of regular colonels will admit, . . . so that the men may have as fair a chance as the nature of things and the comparative inexperience of most will allow.

This remarkably sound report was approved, and McDowell was directed to carry his plan into effect July 8th. But the government machinery worked slowly and there was jealousy in the way, so that the troops to bring his army up to the strength agreed upon did not reach him until the 16th.

Beauregard's Army of the Potomac at Manassas consisted of about 23,000 men. Johnston's army from the Shenandoah consisted of about 8340. McDowell's army comprised approximately 35,000 men.

There was an ill-suppressed feeling of sympathy with the Confederacy in the Southern element of Washington society; but the halls of Congress resounded with the eloquence of Union speakers. Martial music filled the air, and war was the topic wherever men met. By day and night the tramp of soldiers was heard, and staff-officers and orderlies galloped through the streets between the headquarters of Generals Scott and McDowell. Northern en-

thusiasm was unbounded. "On to Richmond" was the war-cry. Public sentiment was irresistible, and in response to it the army advanced. It was
a glorious spectacle. The various regiments were brilliantly uniformed according to the æsthetic taste of peace, and the silken banners they flung to
the breeze were unsoiled and untorn. The bitter realities of war were nearer
than we knew.

McDowell marched on the afternoon of July 16th, the men carrying three
days' rations in their haversacks; provision wagons were to follow from Alexandria the next day. On the morning of the 18th his forces were concentrated
at Centreville, a point about 20 miles west of the Potomac and 6 or 7 miles
east of Manassas Junction. Beauregard's outposts fell back without resistance. Bull Run, flowing south-easterly, is about half-way between Centreville
and Manassas Junction, and, owing to its abrupt banks, the timber with
which it was fringed, and some artificial defenses at the fords, was a formidable obstacle. The stream was fordable, but all the crossings for eight
miles, from Union Mills on the south to the Stone Bridge on the north, were
defended by Beauregard's forces. The Warrenton Turnpike, passing through
Centreville, leads nearly due west, crossing Bull Run at the Stone Bridge. The
direct road from Centreville to Manassas crosses Bull Run at Mitchell's Ford,
half a mile or so above another crossing known as Blackburn's Ford. . . .

McDowell was compelled to wait at Centreville until his provision wagons
arrived and he could issue rations. His orders having carried his leading division under Tyler no farther than Centreville, he wrote that officer at 8:15 A. M.
on the 18th, "Observe well the roads to Bull Run and to Warrenton. Do not
bring on an engagement, but keep up the impression that we are moving on
Manassas." McDowell then went to the extreme left of his line to examine
the country with reference to a sudden movement of the army to turn the
enemy's right flank. The reconnoissance showed him that the country was
unfavorable to the movement, and he abandoned it. While he was gone to
the left, Tyler, presumably to "keep up the impression that we were moving
on Manassas," went forward from Centreville with a squadron of cavalry
and two companies of infantry for the purpose of making a reconnoissance
of Mitchell's and Blackburn's fords along the direct road to Manassas.
Reaching the crest of the ridge overlooking the valley of Bull Run and a
mile or so from the stream, the enemy was seen on the opposite bank, and
Tyler brought up Benjamin's artillery, 2 20-pounder rifled guns, Ayres's field
battery of 6 guns, and Richardson's brigade of infantry. The 20-pounders
opened from the ridge and a few shots were exchanged with the enemy's batteries. Desiring more information than the long-range cannonade afforded,
Tyler ordered Richardson's brigade and a section of Ayres's battery, supported by a squadron of cavalry, to move from the ridge across the open
bottom of Bull Run and take position near the stream and have skirmishers
"scour the thick woods" which skirted it. Two regiments of infantry, 2 pieces

of artillery, and a squadron of cavalry moved down the slope into the woods and opened fire, driving Bonham's outpost to the cover of intrenchments across the stream. The brigades of Bonham and Longstreet, the latter being reënforced for the occasion by Early's brigade, responded at short range to the fire of the Federal reconnoitering force and drove it back in disorder. Tyler reported that having satisfied himself "that the enemy was in force," and ascertained "the position of his batteries," he withdrew. This unauthorized reconnoissance, called by the Federals the affair at Blackburn's Ford, was regarded at the time by the Confederates as a serious attack, and was dignified by the name of the "battle of Bull Run," the engagement of the 21st being called by them the battle of Manassas. The Confederates, feeling that they had repulsed a heavy and real attack, were encouraged by the result. The Federal troops, on the other hand, were greatly depressed. The regiment which suffered most was completely demoralized, and McDowell thought that the depression of the repulse was felt throughout his army and produced its effect upon the Pennsylvania regiment and the New York battery which insisted (their terms having expired) upon their discharge, and on the 21st, as he expressed it, "marched to the rear to the sound of the enemy's cannon." Even Tyler himself felt the depressing effect of his repulse, if we may judge by his cautious and feeble action on the 21st when dash was required.

The operations of the 18th confirmed McDowell in his opinion that with his raw troops the Confederate position should be turned instead of attacked in front. Careful examination had satisfied him that the country did not favor a movement to turn the enemy's right. On the night of the 18th the haversacks of his men were empty, and had to be replenished from the provision wagons, which were late in getting up. Nor had he yet determined upon his point or plan of attack. While resting and provisioning his men, he devoted the 19th and 20th to a careful examination by his engineers of the enemy's position and the intervening country. His men, not soldiers, but civilians in uniform, unused to marching, hot, weary, and footsore, dropped down as they had halted and bivouacked on the roads about Centreville. Notwithstanding Beauregard's elation over the affair at Blackburn's Ford on the 18th, he permitted the 19th and 20th to pass without a movement to follow up the advantage he had gained. During these two days, McDowell carefully examined the Confederate position, and made his plan to manœuvre the enemy out of it. Beauregard ordered no aggressive movement until the 21st, and then, as appears from his own statement, through miscarriage of orders and lack of apprehension on the part of subordinates, the effort was a complete *fiasco,* with the comical result of frightening his own troops, who, late in the afternoon, mistook the return of one of their brigades for an attack by McDowell's left, and the serious result of interfering with the pursuit after he had gained the battle of the 21st.

31

But Beauregard, though not aggressive on the 19th and 20th, was not idle within his own lines. The Confederate President had authorized Johnston, Beauregard's senior, to use his discretion in moving to the support of Manassas, and Beauregard, urging Johnston to do so, sent railway transportation for the Shenandoah forces. But, as he states, "he at the same time submitted the alternative proposition to Johnston that, having passed the Blue Ridge, he should assemble his forces, press forward by way of Aldie, north-west of Manassas, and fall upon McDowell's right rear," while he, Beauregard, "prepared for the operation at the first sound of the conflict, should strenuously assume the offensive in front." "The situation and circumstances specially favored the signal success of such an operation," says Beauregard. An attack by two armies moving from opposite points upon an enemy, with the time of attack for one depending upon the sound of the other's cannon, is hazardous even with well-disciplined and well-seasoned troops, and is next to fatal with raw levies. Johnston chose the wiser course of moving by rail to Manassas, thus preserving the benefit of "interior lines," which, Beauregard says, was the "sole military advantage at the moment that the Confederates possessed."

The campaign which General Scott required McDowell to make was undertaken with the understanding that Johnston should be prevented from joining Beauregard. With no lack of confidence in himself, McDowell was dominated by the feeling of subordination and deference to General Scott which at that time pervaded the whole army, and General Scott, who controlled both McDowell and Patterson, assured McDowell that Johnston should not join Beauregard without having "Patterson on his heels." Yet Johnston's army, nearly nine thousand strong, joined Beauregard, Bee's brigade and Johnston in person arriving on the morning of the 20th, the remainder about noon on the 21st. Although the enforced delay at Centreville enabled McDowell to provision his troops and gain information upon which to base an excellent plan of attack, it proved fatal by affording time for a junction of the opposing forces. On the 21st of July General Scott addressed a dispatch to McDowell, saying: "It is known that a strong reënforcement left Winchester on the afternoon of the 18th, which you will also have to beat. Four new regiments will leave to-day to be at Fairfax Station to-night. Others shall follow to-morrow—twice the number if necessary." When this dispatch was penned, McDowell was fighting the "strong reënforcement" which left Winchester on the 18th. General Scott's report that Beauregard had been reënforced, the information that four regiments had been sent to McDowell, and the promise that twice the number would be sent *if necessary,* all came too late—and Patterson came not at all.

During the 19th and 20th the bivouacs of McDowell's army at Centreville, almost within cannon range of the enemy, were thronged by visitors, official and unofficial, who came in carriages from Washington, bringing their own supplies. They were under no military restraint, and passed to and fro among the troops as they pleased, giving the scene the appearance of a monster military picnic. Among others, the venerable Secretary of War, Cameron, called upon McDowell. Whether due to a naturally serious expression, to a sense of responsibility, to a premonition of the fate of his brother who fell upon the field on the 21st, or to other cause, his countenance showed apprehension of evil; but men generally were confident and jovial.

McDowell's plan of battle promulgated on the 20th, was to turn the enemy's left, force him from his defensive position, and, "if possible, destroy the railroad leading from Manassas to the Valley of Virginia, where the enemy has a large force." He did not know when he issued this order that Johnston had joined Beauregard, though he suspected it. Miles's Fifth Division, with Richardson's brigade of Tyler's division, and a strong force of artillery was to remain in reserve at Centreville, prepare defensive works there and threaten Blackburn's Ford. Tyler's First Division, which was on the turnpike in advance, was to move at 2:30 A. M., threaten the Stone Bridge and open fire upon it at daybreak. This demonstration was to be vigorous, its first purpose being to divert attention from the movements of the turning column. As soon as Tyler's troops cleared the way, Hunter's Second Division, followed by Heintzelman's Third Division, was to move to a point on the Warrenton Turnpike about 1 or 2 miles east of Stone Bridge and there take a country road to the right, cross the Run at Sudley Springs, come down upon the flank and rear of the enemy at the Stone Bridge, and force him to open the way for Tyler's division to cross there and attack, fresh and in full force.

Tyler's start was so late and his advance was so slow as to hold Hunter and Heintzelman 2 or 3 hours on the mile or two of the turnpike between their camps and the point at which they were to turn off for the flank march. This delay, and the fact that the flank march proved difficult and some 12 miles instead of about 6 as was expected, were of serious moment. The flanking column did not cross at Sudley Springs until 9:30 instead of 7, the long march, with its many interruptions, tired out the men, and the delay gave the enemy time to discover the turning movement. Tyler's operations against the Stone Bridge were feeble and ineffective. By 8 o'clock Evans was satisfied that he was in no danger in front, and perceived the movement to turn his position. He was on the left of the Confederate line, guarding the point where the Warrenton Turnpike, the great highway to the field, crossed Bull Run, the Confederate line of defense. He had no instructions to guide him in the emergency that had arisen. But he did not hesitate. Reporting his information and purpose to the adjoining commander, Cocke, and leaving 4 companies of infantry to deceive and hold Tyler at the bridge, Evans before 9 o'clock turned his back upon the point he was set to guard, marched a mile

33

away, and, seizing the high ground to the north of Young's Branch of Bull Run, formed line of battle at right angles to his former line, his left resting near the Sudley Springs road, by which Burnside with the head of the turning column was approaching, thus covering the Warrenton Turnpike and opposing a determined front to the Federal advance upon the Confederate left and rear. In his rear to the south lay the valley of Young's Branch, and rising from that was the higher ridge or plateau on which the Robinson house and the Henry house were situated, and on which the main action took place in the afternoon. Burnside, finding Evans across his path, promptly formed line of battle and attacked about 9:45 A. M. Hunter, the division commander, who was at the head of Burnside's brigade directing the formation of the first skirmish line, was severely wounded and taken to the rear at the opening of the action. Evans not only repulsed but pursued the troops that made the attack upon him. Andrew Porter's brigade of Hunter's division followed Burnside closely and came to his support. In the mean time Bee had formed a Confederate line of battle with his and Bartow's brigades of Johnston's army on the Henry house plateau, a stronger position than the one held by Evans, and desired Evans to fall back to that line; but Evans, probably feeling bound to cover the Warrenton Turnpike and hold it against Tyler as well as against the flanking column, insisted that Bee should move across the valley to his support, which was done.

After Bee joined Evans, the preliminary battle continued to rage upon the ground chosen by the latter. The Confederates were dislodged and driven back to the Henry house plateau, where Bee had previously formed line and where what Beauregard called "the mingled remnants of Bee's, Bartow's, and Evans's commands" were re-formed under cover of Stonewall Jackson's brigade of Johnston's army.

The time of this repulse, as proved by so accurate an authority as Stonewall Jackson, was before 11:30 A.M., and this is substantially confirmed by Beauregard's official report made at the time. . . . Thus, after nearly two hours' stubborn fighting with the forces of Johnston, which General Scott had promised should be kept away, McDowell won the first advantage; but Johnston had cost him dearly.

During all this time Johnston and Beauregard had been waiting near Mitchell's Ford for the development of the attack they had ordered by their right upon McDowell at Centreville. The gravity of the situation upon their left had not yet dawned upon them. What might the result have been if the Union column had not been detained by Tyler's delay in moving out in the early morning, or if Johnston's army, to which Bee, Bartow, and Jackson belonged, had not arrived?

But the heavy firing on the left soon diverted Johnston and Beauregard from all thought of an offensive movement with their right, and decided them, as Beauregard has said, "to hurry up all available reënforcements, including the reserves that were to have moved upon Centreville, to our left, and fight the battle out in that quarter." Thereupon Beauregard ordered "Ewell, Jones, and Longstreet to make a strong demonstration all along their front on the other side of Bull Run, and ordered the reserves to move swiftly to the left," and he and Johnston set out at full speed for the point of conflict, which they reached while Bee was attempting to rally his men about Jackson's brigade on the Henry house plateau. McDowell had waited in the morning at the point on the Warrenton Turnpike where his flanking column turned to the right, until the troops, except Howard's brigade, which he halted at that point, had passed. He gazed silently and with evident pride upon the gay regiments as they filed briskly but quietly past in the freshness of the early morning, and then, remarking to his staff, "Gentlemen, that is a big force," he mounted and moved forward to the field by way of Sudley Springs. He reached the scene of actual conflict somewhat earlier than Johnston and Beauregard did, and, seeing the enemy driven across the valley of Young's Branch and behind the Warrenton Turnpike, at once sent a swift aide-de-camp to Tyler with orders to "press the attack" at the Stone Bridge. Tyler acknowledged that he received this order by 11 o'clock. It was Tyler's division upon which McDowell relied for the decisive fighting of the day. He knew that the march of the turning column would be fatiguing, and when by a sturdy fight it had cleared the Warrenton Turnpike for the advance of Tyler's division, it had, in fact, done more than its fair proportion of the work. But Tyler did not attempt to force the passage of the Stone Bridge, which, after about 8 o'clock, was defended by only four companies of infantry, though he admitted that by the plan of battle, when Hunter and Heintzelman had attacked the enemy in the vicinity of the Stone Bridge, "he was to force the passage of Bull Run at that point and attack the enemy in flank." Soon after McDowell's arrival at the front, Burnside rode up to him and said that his brigade had borne the brunt of the battle, that it was out of ammunition, and that he wanted permission to withdraw, refit and fill cartridge-boxes. McDowell in the excitement of the occasion gave reluctant consent, and the brigade, which certainly had done nobly, marched to the rear, stacked arms, and took no further part in the fight. Having sent the order to Tyler to press his attack and orders to the rear of the turning column to hurry forward, McDowell, like Beauregard, rushed in person into the conflict, and by the force of circumstances became for the time the commander of the turning column and the force actually engaged, rather than the commander of his whole army. With the exception of sending his adjutant-general to find and hurry Tyler forward, his subsequent orders were mainly or wholly to the troops under his own observation. Unlike Beauregard, he had no Johnston in rear with full authority and knowledge of the situation to throw forward reserves and reënforcements. It was not until 12 o'clock that Sherman received orders from Tyler to cross the stream, which he did at a

35

ford above the Stone Bridge, going to the assistance of Hunter. Sherman reported to McDowell on the field and joined in the pursuit of Bee's forces across the valley of Young's Branch. Keyes's brigade, accompanied by Tyler in person, followed across the stream where Sherman forded, but without uniting with the other forces on the field, made a feeble advance upon the slope of the plateau toward the Robinson house, and then about 2 o'clock filed off by flank to its left and, sheltered by the east front of the bluff that forms the plateau, marched down Young's Branch out of sight of the enemy and took no further part in the engagement. McDowell did not know where it was, nor did he then know that Schenck's brigade of Tyler's division did not cross the Run at all.

The line taken up by Stonewall Jackson upon which Bee, Bartow, and Evans rallied on the southern part of the plateau was a very strong one. The ground was high and afforded the cover of a curvilinear wood with the concave side toward the Federal line of attack. According to Beauregard's official report made at the time, he had upon this part of the field, at the beginning, 6500 infantry, 13 pieces of artillery, and 2 companies of cavalry, and this line was continuously reënforced from Beauregard's own reserves and by the arrival of the troops from the Shenandoah Valley.

To carry this formidable position, McDowell had at hand the brigades of Franklin, Willcox, Sherman, and Porter, Palmer's battalion of regular cavalry, and Ricketts's and Griffin's regular batteries. Porter's brigade had been reduced and shaken by the morning fight. Howard's brigade was in reserve and only came into action late in the afternoon. The men, unused to field service, and not yet over the hot and dusty march from the Potomac, had been under arms since midnight. The plateau, however, was promptly assaulted, the northern part of it was carried, the batteries of Ricketts and Griffin were planted near the Henry house, and McDowell clambered to the upper story of that structure to get a glance at the whole field. Upon the Henry house plateau, of which the Confederates held the southern and the Federals the northern part, the tide of battle ebbed and flowed as McDowell pushed in Franklin's, Willcox's, Sherman's, Porter's, and at last Howard's brigades, and as Beauregard put into action reserves which Johnston sent from the right and reënforcements which he hurried forward from the Shenandoah Valley as they arrived by cars. On the plateau, Beauregard says, the disadvantage of his "smooth-bore guns was reduced by the shortness of range." The short range was due to the Federal advance, and the several struggles for the plateau were at close quarters and gallant on both sides. The batteries of Ricketts and Griffin, by their fine discipline, wonderful daring, and matchless skill, were the prime features in the fight. The battle was not lost till they were lost. When in their advanced and perilous position, and just after their infantry supports had been driven over the slopes, a fatal mistake occurred. A regiment of infantry came out of the woods on Griffin's

right, and as he was in the act of opening upon it with canister, he was de-
terred by the assurance of Major Barry, the chief of artillery, that it "was
a regiment sent by Colonel Heintzelman to support the battery." A moment
more and the doubtful regiment proved its identity by a deadly volley, and,
as Griffin states in his official report, "every cannoneer was cut down and a
large number of horses killed, leaving the battery (which was without support
excepting in name) perfectly helpless." The effect upon Ricketts was equally
fatal. He, desperately wounded, and Ramsay, his lieutenant, killed, lay in the
wreck of the battery. Beauregard speaks of his last advance on the plateau a
"leaving in our final possession the Robinson and Henry houses, with mo
of Ricketts's and Griffin's batteries, the men of which were mostly shot do
where they bravely stood by their guns." Having become separated f
McDowell, I fell in with Barnard, his chief engineer, and while togeth
observed the New York Fire Zouaves, who had been supporting G
battery, fleeing to the rear in their gaudy uniforms, in utter confusion,
upon I rode back to where I knew Burnside's brigade was at rest, an
to Burnside the condition of affairs, with the suggestion that he
move his brigade to the front. Returning, I again met Barnard,
battle seemed to him and me to be going against us, and not kno
McDowell was, with the concurrence of Barnard, I immediately
to Miles, telling him to move two brigades of his reserve up
Bridge and telegraph to Washington to send forward all the tro
be spared.

After the arrival of Howard's brigade, McDowell for the
up the slope to the plateau, forced back the Confederate l
possession of the Henry and Robinson houses and of the
there were no longer cannoneers to man or horses to m
had done so much. By the arrival upon this part of the
serves and Kirby Smith's brigade of Johnston's army ab
regard extended his left to outflank McDowell's sha
disconnected line, and the Federals left the field a
then they had fought wonderfully well for raw troo
forces on the field to support or encourage them,
be seized simultaneously by the conviction that it
more and they might as well start home. Cohesion
with some exceptions being disintegrated, and
There was no special excitement except that ar
of officers to stop men who paid little or no a
said. On the high ground by the Matthews h
taken position in the morning to check Bu
aided by other officers, made a desperate bu
and form them into line. There, I went to A
advised that he unlimber and make a stan

37

saying he was in fair condition and ready to fight as long as there was any fighting to be done. But all efforts failed. The stragglers moved past the guns, in spite of all that could be done, and Arnold at my direction joined Sykes's battalion of infantry of Porter's brigade and Palmer's battalion of cavalry, all of the regular army, to cover the rear, as the men trooped back in great disorder across Bull Run. There were some hours of daylight for the Confederates to gather the fruits of victory, but a few rounds of shell and canister checked all the pursuit that was attempted, and the occasion called for no sacrifices or valorous deeds by the stanch regulars of the rear-guard. There [was] no panic, in the ordinary meaning of the word, until the retiring soldiers, guns, wagons, congressmen, and carriages were fired upon, on the road near Bull Run. Then the panic began, and the bridge over Cub Run being [rendered] impassable for vehicles by a wagon that was upset upon it, utter [confusion] set in: pleasure-carriages, gun-carriages, and ammunition wagons [that could] not be put across the Run were abandoned and blocked the way; stragglers broke and threw aside their muskets and cut horses from [... and] rode off upon them. In leaving the field the men took the [... in] a general way, by which they had reached it. Hence when the [...]'s and Heintzelman's divisions got back to Centreville, they [...] 25 miles. That night they walked back to the Potomac, an [... distance] of 20 miles; so that these undisciplined and unseasoned [...] walked fully 45 miles, besides fighting from about 10 A.M. [... hours] on a hot and dusty day in July. McDowell in person reached [...] before sunset, and found there Miles's division with [...] and 3 regiments of Runyon's division, and Hunt's, [...] Greene's batteries and 1 or 2 fragments of batteries, [...] It was a formidable force, but there was a lack of [...] army was completely demoralized. Beauregard had [...] had not been in the fight, consisting of Ewell's, [... br]igades and some troops of other brigades. Mc- [...] n and brigade commanders who were at hand [...] stand or retreating. The verdict was in favor [... o]fficers one way or the other was of no mo- [...] d for themselves and were streaming away [...] be done. They had no interest or treasure [...] not there. Their tents, provisions, bag- [...] on the banks of the Potomac, and no [...] of the camps they had left less than [... o]f them were sovereigns in uniform, [...] d the army, a disorganized mass, [...] the men pleased away from the [...] the march from Centreville was as barren of opportunities for the rear-guard as the withdrawal from the field of battle had been. When McDowell reached Fairfax Court House in the night, he was in communication with Washington and exchanged telegrams with General Scott, in one of which the old hero said, "We are not discouraged"; but that dispatch did not lighten the gloom in which it was received. McDowell was so tired that while sitting on the ground writing a dispatch he fell asleep, pencil in hand, in the middle of a sentence. His adjutant-general aroused him; the dispatch was finished, and the weary ride to the Potomac resumed. When the unfortunate commander dismounted at Arlington next forenoon in a soaking rain, after 32 hours in the saddle, his disastrous campaign of 6 days was closed.

The first martial effervescence of the country was over. The three-months men went home, and the three-months chapter of the war ended—with the South triumphant and confident; the North disappointed but determined.

Here is Bull Run from the Confederate point of view. In it General Beauregard, the colorful little Creole, does not underestimate his military abilities or the part he played in blunting the first large Union offensive of the war. Yet he must be given his due: on the whole he had done a good day's work and his report of it is a fair one. Beauregard's attitude toward President Jefferson Davis later changed. Davis had a talent for alienating his commanders, and Beauregard was no exception.

"Look at Jackson's brigade! It stands there like a stone wall!"

THE FIRST BATTLE OF BULL RUN

BY G. T. BEAUREGARD, GENERAL, C. S. A.

SOON after the first conflict between the authorities of the Federal Union and those of the Confederate States had occurred in Charleston Harbor, by the bombardment of Fort Sumter—which, beginning at 4:30 A. M. on the 12th of April, 1861, forced the surrender of that fortress within thirty hours thereafter into my hands—I was called to Richmond, which by that time had become the Confederate seat of government, and was directed to "assume command of the Confederate troops on the Alexandria line." Arriving at Manassas Junction, I took command on the 2d of June, forty-nine days after the evacuation of Fort Sumter.

Although the position at the time was strategically of commanding importance to the Confederates, the mere *terrain* was not only without natural defensive advantages, but, on the contrary, was absolutely unfavorable. Its strategic value was that, being close to the Federal capital, it held in ob-

41

servation the chief army then being assembled near Arlington by General McDowell, under the immediate eye of the commander-in-chief, General Scott, for an offensive movement against Richmond; and while it had a railway approach in its rear for the easy accumulation of reënforcements and all the necessary munitions of war from the southward, at the same time another (the Manassas Gap) railway, diverging laterally to the left from that point, gave rapid communications with the fertile valley of the Shenandoah, then teeming with live stock and cereal subsistence, as well as with other resources essential to the Confederates. There was this further value in the position to the Confederate army: that during the period of accumulation, seasoning, and training, it might be fed from the fat fields, pastures, and garners of Loudoun, Fauquier, and the Lower Shenandoah Valley counties, which otherwise must have fallen into the hands of the enemy. But, on the other hand, Bull Run, a petty stream, was of little or no defensive strength; for it abounded in fords, and although for the most part its banks were rocky and abrupt, the side from which it would be approached offensively in most places commanded the opposite ground.

At the time of my arrival at Manassas, a Confederate army under General Joseph E. Johnston was in occupation of the Lower Shenandoah Valley, along the line of the Upper Potomac, chiefly at Harper's Ferry, which was regarded as the gateway of the valley and of one of the possible approaches to Richmond; a position from which he was speedily forced to retire, however, by a flank movement of a Federal army, under the veteran General Patterson, thrown across the Potomac at or about Martinsburg. On my other or right flank, so to speak, a Confederate force of some 2500 men under General Holmes occupied the position of Aquia Creek on the lower Potomac, upon the line of approach to Richmond from that direction through Fredericksburg. The other approach, that by way of the James River, was held by Confederate troops under Generals Huger and Magruder. Establishing small outposts at Leesburg to observe the crossings of the Potomac in that quarter, and at Fairfax Court House in observation of Arlington, with other detachments in advance of Manassas toward Alexandria on the south side of the railroad, from the very outset I was anxiously aware that the sole military advantage at the moment to the Confederates was that of holding the *interior lines*. On the Federal or hostile side were all material advantages, including superior numbers, largely drawn from the old militia organizations of the great cities of the North, decidedly better armed and equipped than the troops under me, and strengthened by a small but incomparable body of regular infantry as well as a number of batteries of regular field artillery of the highest class, and a very large and thoroughly organized staff corps, besides a numerous body of professionally educated officers in command of volunteer regiments—all precious military elements at such a juncture.

Happily, through the foresight of Colonel Thomas Jordan—whom General Lee had placed as the adjutant-general of the forces there assembled before my arrival—arrangements were made which enabled me to receive regularly, from private persons at the Federal capital, most accurate information, of which politicians high in council, as well as War Department clerks, were the unconscious ducts. . . .

In these several ways, therefore, I was almost as well advised of the strength of the hostile army in my front as its commander, who, I may mention, had been a classmate of mine at West Point. Under those circumstances I had become satisfied that a well-equipped, well-constituted Federal army at least 50,000 strong, of all arms, confronted me at or about Arlington, ready and on the very eve of an offensive operation against me, and to meet which I could muster barely 18,000 men with 29 field-guns.

Previously—indeed, as early as the middle of June—it had become apparent to my mind that through only one course of action could there be a well-grounded hope of ability on the part of the Confederates to encounter successfully the offensive operations for which the Federal authorities were then vigorously preparing in my immediate front, with so consummate a strategist and military administrator as Lieutenant-General Scott in general command at Washington, aided by his accomplished heads of the large General Staff Corps of the United States Army. This course was to make the most enterprising, warlike use of the interior lines which we possessed, for the swift concentration at the critical instant of every available Confederate force upon the menaced position, at the risk, if need were, of sacrificing all minor places to the one clearly of major military value—there to meet our adversary so offensively as to overwhelm him, under circumstances that must assure immediate ability to assume the general offensive even upon his territory, and thus conquer an early peace by a few well-delivered blows.

My views of such import had been already earnestly communicated to the proper authorities; but about the middle of July, satisfied that McDowell was on the eve of taking the offensive against me, I dispatched Colonel James Chestnut, of South Carolina, a volunteer aide-de-camp on my staff who had served on an intimate footing with Mr. Davis in the Senate of the United States, to urge in substance the necessity for the immediate concentration of the larger part of the forces of Johnston and Holmes at Manassas, so that the moment McDowell should be sufficiently far detached from Washington, I would be enabled to move rapidly round his more convenient flank upon his rear and his communications, and attack him in reverse, or get between his forces, then separated, thus cutting off his retreat upon Arlington in the event of his defeat, and insuring as an immediate consequence the crushing of Patterson, the liberation of Maryland, and the capture of Washington.

This plan was rejected by Mr. Davis and his military advisers (Adjutant-General Cooper and General Lee), who characterized it as "brilliant and comprehensive," but essentially impracticable. Furthermore, Colonel Chestnut came back impressed with the views entertained at Richmond—as he communicated at once to my adjutant-general—that should the Federal army soon move offensively upon my position, my best course would be to retire behind the Rappahannock and accept battle there instead of at Manassas. In effect, it was regarded as best to sever communications between the two chief Confederate armies, that of the Potomac and that of the Shenandoah, with the inevitable immediate result that Johnston would be forced to leave Patterson in possession of the Lower Shenandoah Valley, abandoning to the enemy so large a part of the most resourceful sections of Virginia, and to retreat southward by way of the Luray Valley, pass across the Blue Ridge at Thornton's Gap and unite with me after all, but at Fredericksburg, much nearer Richmond than Manassas. These views, however, were not made known to me at the time, and happily my mind was left free to the grave problem imposed upon me by the rejection of my plan for the immediate concentration of a materially larger force—*i. e.,* the problem of placing and using my resources for a successful encounter behind Bull Run with the Federal army, which I was not permitted to doubt was about to take the field against me.

It is almost needless to say that I had caused to be made a thorough reconnoissance of all the ground in my front and flanks, and had made myself personally acquainted with the most material points, including the region of Sudley's Church on my left, where a small detachment was posted in observation. Left now to my own resources, of course the contingency of defeat had to be considered and provided for. Among the measures of precaution for such a result, I ordered the destruction of the railroad bridge across Bull Run at Union Mills, on my right, in order that the enemy, in the event of my defeat, should not have the immediate use of the railroad in following up their movement against Richmond—a railroad which could have had no corresponding value to us eastward beyond Manassas in any operations on our side with Washington as the objective, inasmuch as any such operations must have been made by the way of the Upper Potomac and upon the rear of that city.

Just before Colonel Chestnut was dispatched on the mission of which I have spoken, a former clerk in one of the departments at Washington, well known to him, had volunteered to return thither and bring back the latest information of the military and political situation from our most trusted friends. His loyalty to our cause, his intelligence, and his desire to be of service being vouched for, he was at once sent across the Potomac below Alexandria, merely accredited by a small scrap of paper bearing in Colonel Jordan's cipher the two words, "Trust bearer," with which he was to call at a certain house in Washington within easy rifle-range of the White House, ask for the lady of the house, and present it only to her. This delicate mission was as fortunately as it was deftly executed. In the early morning, as the newsboys were crying in the empty streets of Washington the intelligence that the order was given for the Federal army to move at once upon my position, that scrap of paper reached the hands of the one person in all that city who could extract any meaning from it. With no more delay than was necessary for a hurried breakfast and the writing in cipher by Mrs. G—— of the words, "Order issued for McDowell to march upon Manassas to-night," my agent was placed in communication with another friend, who carried him in a buggy with a relay of horses as swiftly as possible down the eastern shore of the Potomac to our regular ferry across that river. Without untoward incident the momentous dispatch was quickly delivered into the hands of a cavalry courier, and by means of relays it was in my hands between 8 and 9 o'clock that night. Within half an hour my outpost commanders, advised of what was impending, were directed, at the first evidence of the near presence of the enemy in their front, to fall back in the manner and to positions already prescribed in anticipation of such a contingency in an order confidentially communicated to them four weeks before, and the detachment at Leesburg was directed to join me by forced marches. Having thus cleared my decks for action, I next acquainted Mr. Davis with the situation, and ventured once more to suggest that the Army of the Shenandoah, with the brigade at Fredericksburg or Aquia Creek, should be ordered to reënforce me—suggestions that were at once heeded so far that General Holmes was ordered to carry his command to my aid, and General Johnston was given discretion to do likewise. After some telegraphic discussion with me, General Johnston was induced to exercise this discretion in favor of the swift march of the Army of the Shenandoah to my relief; and to facilitate that vital movement, I hastened to accumulate all possible means of railway transport at a designated point on the Manassas Gap railroad at the eastern foot of the Blue Ridge, to which Johnston's troops directed their march. However, at the same time, I had submitted the alternative proposition to General Johnston, that, having passed the Blue Ridge, he should assemble his forces, press forward by way of Aldie, north-west of Manassas, and fall upon McDowell's right rear; while I, prepared for the operation, at the first sound of the conflict, should strenuously assume the offensive in my front. The situation and circumstances specially favored the signal success of such an operation. The march to the point of attack could have been accomplished as soon as the forces were brought ultimately by rail to Manassas Junction; our enemy, thus attacked so nearly simultaneously on his right flank, his rear, and his front, naturally would suppose that I had been able to turn his flank while attacking him in front, and therefore, that I must have an overwhelming superiority of numbers; and his forces, being new troops, most of them under fire for the first time, must have soon fallen into a disastrous panic. Moreover, such an operation must have resulted advantageously to the Confederates, in the event that McDowell should, as might have been anticipated, attempt to strike the Manassas Gap railway to my left, and thus cut off railway communications between Johnston's forces and my own, instead of the mere effort to strike my left flank which he actually essayed.

It seemed, however, as though the deferred attempt at concentration was to go for naught, for on the morning of the 18th the Federal forces were massed around Centreville, but three miles from Mitchell's Ford, and soon were seen advancing upon the roads leading to that and Blackburn's Ford. My order of battle, issued in the night of the 17th, contemplated an offensive return, particularly from the strong brigades on the right and right center. The Federal artillery opened in front of both fords, and the infantry, while demonstrating in front of Mitchell's Ford, endeavored to force a passage at Blackburn's. Their column of attack, Tyler's division, was opposed by Longstreet's forces, to the reënforcement of which Early's brigade, the reserve line at McLean's Ford, was ordered up. The Federals, after several attempts to force a passage, met a final repulse and retreated. After their infantry attack had ceased, about 1 o'clock, the contest lapsed into an artillery duel, in which the Washington Artillery of New Orleans won credit against the renowned batteries of the United States regular army. A comical effect of this artillery fight was the destruction of the dinner of myself and staff by a Federal shell that fell into the fire-place of my headquarters at the McLean House.

Our success in this first limited collision was of special prestige to my army of new troops, and, moreover, of decisive importance by so increasing General McDowell's caution as to give time for the arrival of some of General Johnston's forces. But while on the 19th I was awaiting a renewed and general attack by the Federal army, I received a telegram from the Richmond military authorities, urging me to withdraw my call on General Johnston on account of the supposed impracticability of the concentration—an abiding conviction which had been but momentarily shaken by the alarm caused by McDowell's march upon Richmond. As this was not an order in terms, but an urgency which, notwithstanding its superior source, left me technically free and could define me as responsible for any misevent, I preferred to keep both the situation and the responsibility, and continued every effort for the prompt arrival of the Shenandoah forces, being resolved, should they come before General McDowell again attacked, to take myself the offensive. General McDowell, fortunately for my plans, spent the 19th and 20th in reconnoissances; and, meanwhile, General Johnston brought 8340 men from the Shenandoah Valley, with 20 guns, and General Holmes 1265 rank and file, with 6 pieces of artillery, from Aquia Creek. As these forces arrived (most of them in the afternoon of the 20th) I placed them chiefly so as to strengthen my left center and left, the latter being weak from lack of available troops. . . .

"Look at Jackson's brigade! It stands there like a stone wall!"

The preparation, in front of an ever-threatening enemy, of a wholly volunteer army, composed of men very few of whom had ever belonged to any military organization, had been a work of many cares not incident to the command of a regular army. These were increased by the insufficiency of my staff organization, an inefficient management of the quartermaster's department at Richmond, and the preposterous mismanagement of the commissary-general, who not only failed to furnish rations, but caused the removal of the army commissaries, who, under my orders, procured food from the country in front of us to keep the army from absolute want—supplies that were otherwise exposed to be gathered by the enemy. . . .

There was much in this decisive conflict about to open, not involved in any after battle, which pervaded the two armies and the people behind them and colored the responsibility of the respective commanders. The political hostilities of a generation were now face to face with weapons instead of words. Defeat to either side would be a deep mortification, but defeat to the South must turn its claim of independence into an empty vaunt; and the defeated commander on either side might expect, though not the personal fate awarded by the Carthaginians to an unfortunate commander, at least a moral fate quite similar. . . .

General Johnston was the ranking officer, and entitled, therefore, to assume command of the united forces; but as the extensive field of operations was one which I had occupied since the beginning of June, and with which I was thoroughly familiar in all its extent and military bearings, while he was wholly unacquainted with it, and, moreover, as I had made my plans and dispositions for the maintenance of the position, General Johnston, in view of the gravity of the impending issue, preferred not to assume the responsibilities of the chief direction of the forces during the battle, but to assist me upon the field. Thereupon, I explained my plans and purposes, to which he agreed.

SUNDAY, July 21st, bearing the fate of the new-born Confederacy, broke brightly over the fields and woods that held the hostile forces. My scouts, thrown out in the night toward Centreville along the Warrenton Turnpike, had reported that the enemy was concentrating along the latter. This fact, together with the failure of the Federals in their attack upon my center at Mitchell's and Blackburn's fords, had caused me to apprehend that they would attempt my left flank at the Stone Bridge, and orders were accordingly issued by half-past 4 o'clock to the brigade commanders to hold their forces in readiness to move at a moment's notice, together with the suggestion that the Federal attack might be expected in that quarter. Shortly afterward the enemy was reported to be advancing from Centreville on the Warrenton Turnpike, and at half-past 5 o'clock as deploying a force in front of Evans. As their movement against my left developed the opportunity I desired, I immediately sent orders to the brigade commanders, both front and reserves, on my right and center to advance and vigorously attack the Federal left flank and rear at Centreville, while my left, under Cocke and Evans with their supports, would sustain the Federal attack in the quarter of the Stone Bridge, which they were directed to do to the last extremity. The center was likewise to advance and engage the enemy in front, and directions were given to the reserves, when without orders, to move toward the sound of the heaviest firing. The ground in our front on the other side of Bull Run afforded particular advantage for these tactics. Centreville was the apex of a triangle—its short side running by the Warrenton Turnpike to Stone Bridge, its base Bull Run, its long side a road that ran from Union Mills along the front of my other Bull Run positions and trended off to the rear of Centreville, where McDowell had massed his main forces; branch roads led up to this one from the fords between Union Mills and Mitchell's. My forces to the right of the latter ford were to advance, pivoting on that position; Bonham was in advance from Mitchell's Ford, Longstreet from Blackburn's, D. R. Jones from McLean's, and Ewell from Union Mills by the Centreville road. Ewell, as having the longest march, was to begin the movement, and each brigade was to be followed by its reserve. In anticipation of this method of attack, and to prevent accidents, the subordinate commanders had been carefully instructed in the movement by me, as they were all new to the responsibilities of command. They were to establish close communication with each other before making the attack. About half-past 8 o'clock I set out with General Johnston for a convenient position—a hill in rear of Mitchell's Ford—where we waited for the opening of the attack on our right, from which I expected a decisive victory by midday, with the result of cutting off the Federal army from retreat upon Washington.

Meanwhile, about half-past 5 o'clock, the peal of a heavy rifled gun was heard in front of the Stone Bridge, its second shot striking through the tent of my signal-officer, Captain E. P. Alexander; and at 6 o'clock a full rifled battery opened against Evans and then against Cocke, to which our artillery remained dumb, as it had not sufficient range to reply. But later, as the Federal skirmish-line advanced, it was engaged by ours, thrown well forward on the other side of the Run. A scattering musketry fire followed, and meanwhile, about 7 o'clock, I ordered Jackson's brigade, with Imboden's and five guns of Walton's battery, to the left, with orders to support Cocke as well as Bonham; and the brigades of Bee and Bartow, under the command of the former, were also sent to the support of the left.

At half-past 8 o'clock Evans, seeing that the Federal attack did not increase in boldness and vigor, and observing a lengthening line of dust above the trees to the left of the Warrenton Turnpike, became satisfied that the attack in his front was but a feint, and that a column of the enemy was moving around through the woods to fall on his flank from the direction of Sudley Ford. Informing his immediate commander, Cocke, of the enemy's movement, and of his own dispositions to meet it, he left 4 companies under cover at the Stone Bridge, and led the remainder of his force, 6 companies of Sloan's 4th South Carolina and Wheat's battalion of Louisiana Tigers, with 2 6-pounder howitzers, across the valley of Young's Branch to the high ground beyond it. Resting his left on the Sudley road, he distributed his troops on each side of a small copse, with such cover as the ground afforded, and looking over the open fields and a reach of the Sudley road which the Federals must cover in their approach. His two howitzers were placed one at each end of his position, and here he silently awaited the enemy now drawing near.

The Federal turning column, about 18,000 strong, with 24 pieces of artillery, had moved down from Centreville by the Warrenton Turnpike, and after passing Cub Run had struck to the right by a forest road to cross Bull Run at Sudley Ford, about 3 miles above the Stone Bridge, moving by a long circuit for the purpose of attacking my left flank. The head of the column, Burnside's brigade of Hunter's division, at about 9:45 A.M. debouched from the woods into the open fields, in front of Evans. Wheat at once engaged their skirmishers, and as the Second Rhode Island regiment advanced, supported by its splendid battery of 6 rifled guns, the fronting thicket held by Evans's South Carolinians poured forth its sudden volleys, while the 2 howitzers flung their grape-shot upon the attacking line, which was soon shattered and driven back into the woods behind. Major Wheat, after handling his battalion with the utmost determination, had fallen severely wounded in the lungs. Burnside's entire brigade was now sent forward in a second charge, supported by 8 guns; but they encountered again the unflinching fire of Evans's line, and were once more driven back to the woods, from the cover of which they continued the attack, reënforced after a time by the arrival of 8 companies of United States regular infantry, under Major Sykes, with 6 pieces of artillery, quickly followed by the remaining regiments of Andrew Porter's brigade of the same division. The contest here lasted fully an hour; meanwhile Wheat's battalion, having lost its leader, had gradually lost its organization, and Evans, though still opposing these heavy odds with undiminished firmness, sought reënforcement from the troops in his rear.

General Bee, of South Carolina, a man of marked character, whose command lay in reserve in rear of Cocke, near the Stone Bridge, intelligently applying the general order given to the reserves, had already moved toward the neighboring point of conflict, and taken a position with his own and Bartow's brigades on the high plateau which stands in rear of Bull Run in the quarter of the Stone Bridge, and overlooking the scene of engagement upon the stretch of high ground from which it was separated by the valley of Young's Branch. This plateau is inclosed on three sides by two small watercourses, which empty into Bull Run within a few yards of each other, a half mile to the south of the Stone Bridge. Rising to an elevation of quite 100 feet above the level of Bull Run at the bridge, it falls off on three sides to the level of the inclosing streams in gentle slopes, but furrowed by ravines of irregular directions and length, and studded with clumps and patches of young pine and oaks. The general direction of the crest of the plateau is oblique to the course of Bull Run in that quarter and to the Sudley and turnpike roads, which intersect each other at right angles. On the north-western brow, overlooking Young's Branch, and near the Sudley road, as the latter climbs over the plateau, stood the house of the widow Henry, while to its right and forward on a projecting spur stood the house and sheds of the free Negro Robinson, just behind the turnpike, densely embowered in trees and shrubbery and environed by a double row of fences on two sides. Around the eastern and southern brow of the plateau an almost unbroken fringe of second-growth pines gave excellent shelter for our marksmen, who availed themselves of it with the most satisfactory skill. To the west, adjoining the fields that surrounded the houses mentioned, a broad belt of oaks extends directly across the crest on both sides of the Sudley road, in which, during the battle, the hostile forces contended for the mastery. General Bee, with a soldier's eye to the situation, skillfully disposed his forces. His two brigades on either side of Imboden's battery—which he had borrowed from his neighboring reserve, Jackson's brigade—were placed in a small depression of the plateau in advance of the Henry house, whence he had a full view of the contest on the opposite height across the valley of Young's Branch. Opening with his artillery upon the Federal batteries, he answered Evans's request by advising him to withdraw to his own position on the height; but Evans, full of the spirit that would not retreat, renewed his appeal that the forces in rear would come to help him hold his ground. The newly arrived forces had given the Federals such superiority at this point as to dwarf Evans's means of resistance, and General Bee, generously yielding his own better judgment to Evans's persistence, led the two brigades across the valley under the fire of the enemy's artillery, and threw them into action—1 regiment in the copse held by Colonel Evans, 2 along a fence on the right, and 2 under General Bartow on the prolonged right of this line, but extended forward at a right angle and along the edge of a wood not more than 100 yards from that held by the enemy's left, where the contest at short range became sharp and deadly, bringing many casualties to both sides. The Federal infantry, though still in superior numbers, failed to make any headway against this sturdy van, notwithstanding Bee's whole line was hammered also by the enemy's powerful batteries, until Heintzelman's division of 2 strong brigades, arriving from Sudley Ford, extended the fire on the Federal right, while its battery of 6 10-pounder rifled guns took an immediately effective part from a position behind the Sudley road. Against these odds the Confederate force was still endeavoring to hold its ground, when a new enemy came into the field upon its right. Major Wheat, with characteristic daring and restlessness, had crossed Bull Run alone by a small ford above the Stone Bridge, in order to reconnoiter, when he and Evans had first moved to the left, and, falling on some Federal scouts, had shouted a taunting defiance and withdrawn, not, however, without his place of crossing having been observed. This disclosure was now utilized by Sherman's (W. T.) and Keyes's brigades of Tyler's division; crossing at this point, they appeared over the high bank of the stream and moved into position on the Federal left. There was no choice now for Bee but to retire—a movement, however, to be accomplished under different circumstances than when urged by him upon Evans. The three leaders endeavored to preserve the steadiness of the ranks as they withdrew over the open fields, aided by the fire of Imboden's guns on the plateau and the retiring howitzers; but the troops were thrown into confusion, and the greater part soon fell into rout across Young's Branch and around the base of the height in the rear of the Stone Bridge.

Meanwhile, in rear of Mitchell's Ford, I had been waiting with General Johnston for the sound of conflict to open in the quarter of Centreville upon the Federal left flank and rear (making allowance, however, for the delays possible to commands unused to battle), when I was chagrined to hear from General D. R. Jones that, while he had been long ready for the movement upon Centreville, General Ewell had not come up to form on his right, though he had sent him between 7 and 8 o'clock a copy of his own order which recited that Ewell had been already ordered to begin the movement. I dispatched an immediate order to Ewell to advance; but within a quarter of an hour, just as I received a dispatch from him informing me that he had received no order to advance in the morning, the firing on the left began to increase so intensely as to indicate a severe attack, whereupon General Johnston said that he would go personally to that quarter.

After weighing attentively the firing, which seemed rapidly and heavily increasing, it appeared to me that the troops on the right would be unable to get into position before the Federal offensive should have made too much progress on our left, and that it would be better to abandon it altogether, maintaining only a strong demonstration so as to detain the enemy in front of our right and center, and hurry up all available reënforcements—including the reserves that were to have moved upon Centreville—to our left and fight the battle out in that quarter. Communicating this view to General Johnston, who approved it (giving his advice, as he said, for what it was worth, as he was not acquainted with the country), I ordered Ewell, Jones, and Longstreet to make a strong demonstration all along their front on the other side of the Run, and ordered the reserves below our position, Holmes's brigade with 6 guns, and Early's brigade, also 2 regiments of Bonham's brigade, near at hand, to move swiftly to the left. General Johnston and I now set out at full speed for the point of conflict. We arrived there just as Bee's troops, after giving way, were fleeing in disorder behind the height in rear of the Stone Bridge. They had come around between the base of the hill and the Stone Bridge into a shallow ravine which ran up to a point on the crest where Jackson had already formed his brigade along the edge of the woods. We found the commanders resolutely stemming the further flight of the routed forces, but vainly endeavoring to restore order, and our own efforts were as futile. Every segment of line we succeeded in forming was again dissolved while another was being formed; more than two thousand men were shouting each some suggestion to his neighbor, their voices mingling with the noise of the shells hurtling through the trees overhead, and all word of command drowned in the confusion and uproar. It was at this moment that General Bee used the famous expression, "Look at Jackson's brigade! It stands there like a stone wall"—a name that passed from the brigade to its immortal commander. The disorder seemed irretrievable, but happily the thought came to me that if their colors were planted out to the front the men might rally on them, and I gave the order to carry the standards forward some forty yards, which was promptly executed by the regimental officers, thus drawing the common eye of the troops. They now received easily the orders to advance and form on the line of their colors, which they obeyed with a general movement; and as General Johnston and myself rode forward shortly after with the colors of the 4th Alabama by our side, the line that had fought all morning, and had fled, routed and disordered, now advanced again into position as steadily as veterans. The 4th Alabama had previously lost all its field-officers; and noticing Colonel S. R. Gist, an aide to General Bee, a young man whom I had known as adjutant-general of South Carolina, and whom I greatly esteemed, I presented him as an able and brave commander to the stricken regiment, who cheered their new leader, and maintained under him, to the end of the day, their previous gallant behavior. We had come none too soon, as the enemy's forces, flushed with the belief of accomplished victory, were already advancing across the valley of Young's Branch and up the slope, where they had encountered for a while the fire of the Hampton Legion, which had been led forward toward the Robinson house and the turnpike in front, covering the retreat and helping materially to check the panic of Bee's routed forces.

As soon as order was restored I requested General Johnston to go back to Portici (the Lewis house), and from that point—which I considered most favorable for the purpose—forward me the reënforcements as they would come from the Bull Run lines below and those that were expected to arrive from Manassas, while I should direct the field. General Johnston was disinclined to leave the battle-field for that position. As I had been compelled to leave my chief-of-staff, Colonel Jordan, at Manassas to forward any troops arriving there, I felt it was a necessity that one of us should go to this duty, and that it was his place to do so, as I felt I was responsible for the battle. He considerately yielded to my urgency, and we had the benefit of his energy and sagacity in so directing the reënforcements toward the field, as to be readily and effectively assistant to my pressing needs and insure the success of the day.

As General Johnston departed for Portici, I hastened to form our line of battle against the on-coming enemy. I ordered up the 49th and 8th Virginia regiments from Cocke's neighboring brigade in the Bull Run lines. Gartrell's 7th Georgia I placed in position on the left of Jackson's brigade, along the belt of pines occupied by the latter on the eastern rim of the plateau. As the 49th Virginia rapidly came up, its colonel, ex-Governor William Smith, was encouraging them with cheery word and manner, and, as they approached, indicated to them the immediate presence of the commander. As the regiment raised a loud cheer, the name was caught by some of the troops of Jackson's brigade in the immediate wood, who rushed out, calling for General Beauregard. Hastily acknowledging these happy signs of sympathy and confidence, which reënforce alike the capacity of commander and troops, I placed the 49th Virginia in position on the extreme left next to Gartrell, and as I paused to say a few words to Jackson, while hurrying back to the right, my horse was killed under me by a bursting shell, a fragment of which carried away part of the heel of my boot. The Hampton Legion, which had suffered greatly, was placed on the right of Jackson's brigade, and Hunton's 8th Virginia, as it arrived, upon the right of Hampton; the two latter being drawn somewhat to the rear so as to form with Jackson's right regiment a reserve, and be ready likewise to make defense against any advance from the direction of the Stone Bridge, whence there was imminent peril from the enemy's heavy forces, as I had just stripped that position almost entirely of troops to meet the active crisis on the plateau, leaving this quarter now covered only by a few men, whose defense was otherwise assisted solely by the obstruction of an abatis.

With 6500 men and 13 pieces of artillery, I now awaited the onset of the enemy, who were pressing forward 20,000 strong, with 24 pieces of superior artillery and 7 companies of regular cavalry. They soon appeared over the farther rim of the plateau, seizing the Robinson house on my right and the Henry house opposite my left center. Near the latter they placed in position the two powerful batteries of Ricketts and Griffin of the regular army, and pushed forward up the Sudley road, the slope of which was cut so deep below the adjacent ground as to afford a covered way up to the plateau. Supported by the formidable lines of Federal musketry, these 2 batteries lost no time in making themselves felt, while 3 more batteries in rear on the high ground beyond the Sudley and Warrenton cross-roads swelled the shower of shell that fell among our ranks.

Our own batteries, Imboden's, Stanard's, five of Walton's guns, reënforced later by Pendleton's and Alburtis's (their disadvantage being reduced by the shortness of range), swept the surface of the plateau from their position on

53

the eastern rim. I felt that, after the accidents of the morning, much depended on maintaining the steadiness of the troops against the first heavy onslaught, and rode along the lines encouraging the men to unflinching behavior, meeting, as I passed each command, a cheering response. The steady fire of their musketry told severely on the Federal ranks, and the splendid action of our batteries was a fit preface to the marked skill exhibited by our artillerists during the war. The enemy suffered particularly from the musketry on our left, now further reënforced by the 2d Mississippi—the troops in this quarter confronting each other at very short range. Here two companies of Stuart's cavalry charged through the Federal ranks that filled the Sudley road, increasing the disorder wrought upon that flank of the enemy. But with superior numbers the Federals were pushing on new regiments in the attempt to flank my position, and several guns, in the effort to enfilade ours, were thrust forward so near the 33d Virginia that some of its men sprang forward and captured them, but were driven back by an overpowering force of Federal musketry. Although the enemy were held well at bay, their pressure became so strong that I resolved to take the offensive, and ordered a charge on my right for the purpose of recovering the plateau. The movement, made with alacrity and force by the commands of Bee, Bartow, Evans, and Hampton, thrilled the entire line, Jackson's brigade piercing the enemy's center, and the left of the line under Gartrell and Smith following up the charge, also, in that quarter, so that the whole of the open surface of the plateau was swept clear of the Federals.

Apart from its impressions on the enemy, the effect of this brilliant onset was to give a short breathing-spell to our troops from the immediate strain of conflict, and encourage them in withstanding the still more strenuous offensive that was soon to bear upon them. Reorganizing our line of battle under the unremitting fire of the Federal batteries opposite, I prepared to meet the new attack which the enemy were about to make, largely reënforced by the troops of Howard's brigade, newly arrived on the field. The Federals again pushed up the slope, the face of which partly afforded good cover by the numerous ravines that scored it and the clumps of young pines and oaks with which it was studded, while the sunken Sudley road formed a good ditch and parapet for their aggressive advance upon my left flank and rear. Gradually they pressed our lines back and regained possession of their lost ground and guns. With the Henry and Robinson houses once more in their possession, they resumed the offensive, urged forward by their commanders with conspicuous gallantry.

The conflict now became very severe for the final possession of this position, which was the key to victory. The Federal numbers enabled them so to extend their lines through the woods beyond the Sudley road as to outreach my left flank, which I was compelled partly to throw back, so as to meet the attack from that quarter; meanwhile their numbers equally enabled them to outflank my right in the direction of the Stone Bridge, imposing anxious watchfulness in that direction. I knew that I was safe if I could hold out till the arrival of reënforcements, which was but a matter of time; and, with the full sense of my own responsibility, I was determined to hold the line of the plateau, even if surrounded on all sides, until assistance should come, unless my forces were sooner overtaken by annihilation.

It was now between half-past 2 and 3 o'clock; a scorching sun increased the oppression of the troops, exhausted from incessant fighting, many of them having been engaged since the morning. Fearing lest the Federal offensive should secure too firm a grip, and knowing the fatal result that might spring from any grave infraction of my line, I determined to make another effort for the recovery of the plateau, and ordered a charge of the entire line of battle, including the reserves, which at this crisis I myself led into action. The movement was made with such keeping and dash that the whole plateau was swept clear of the enemy, who were driven down the slope and across the turnpike on our right and the valley of Young's Branch on our left, leaving in our final possession the Robinson and Henry houses, with most of Ricketts's and Griffin's batteries, the men of which were mostly shot down where they bravely stood by their guns. Fisher's 6th North Carolina, directed to the Lewis house by Colonel Jordan from Manassas, where it had just arrived, and thence to the field by General Johnston, came up in happy time to join in this charge on the left. Withers's 18th Virginia, which I had ordered up from Cocke's brigade, was also on hand in time to follow and give additional effect to the charge, capturing, by aid of the Hampton Legion, several guns, which were immediately turned and served upon the broken ranks of the enemy by some of our officers. . . .

That part of the enemy who occupied the woods beyond our left and across the Sudley road had not been reached by the headlong charge which had swept their comrades from the plateau; but the now arriving reënforcements were led into that quarter. Kemper's battery also came up, preceded by its commander, who, while alone, fell into the hands of a number of the enemy, who took him prisoner, until a few moments later, when he handed them over to some of our own troops accompanying his battery. A small plateau, within the south-west angle of the Sudley and turnpike cross-roads, was still held by a strong Federal brigade—Howard's troops, together with Sykes's battalion of regulars; and while Kershaw and Cash, after passing through the skirts of the oak wood along the Sudley road, engaged this force, Kemper's battery was sent forward by Kershaw along the same road, into position near where a hostile battery had been captured, and whence it played upon the enemy in the open field.

Quickly following these regiments came Preston's 28th Virginia, which, passing through the woods, encountered and drove back some Michigan troops, capturing Brigadier-General Willcox. It was now about 3 o'clock, when another important reënforcement came to our aid—Elzey's brigade, 1700 strong, of the Army of the Shenandoah, which, coming from Piedmont by railroad, had arrived at Manassas station, 6 miles in rear of the battle-field, at noon, and had been without delay directed thence toward the field by Colonel Jordan, aided by Major T. G. Rhett, who that morning had passed from General Bonham's to General Johnston's staff. Upon nearing the vicinity of the Lewis house, the brigade was directed by a staff-officer sent by General Johnston toward the left of the field. As it reached the oak wood, just across the Sudley road, led by General Kirby Smith, the latter fell severely wounded; but the command devolved upon Colonel Elzey, an excellent officer, who was now guided by Captain D. B. Harris of the Engineers, a highly accomplished officer of my staff, still farther to the left and through the woods, so as to form in extension of the line of the preceding reënforcements. Beckham's battery, of the same command, was hurried forward by the Sudley road and around the woods into position near the Chinn house; from a well-selected point of action, in full view of the enemy that filled the open fields west of the Sudley road, it played with deadly and decisive effect upon their ranks, already under the fire of Elzey's brigade. Keyes's Federal brigade, which had made its way across the turnpike in rear of the Stone Bridge, was lurking along under cover of the ridges and a wood in order to turn my line on the right, but was easily repulsed by Latham's battery, already placed in position over that approach by Captain Harris, aided by Alburtis's battery, opportunely sent to Latham's left by General Jackson, and supported by fragments of troops collected by staff-officers. Meanwhile, the enemy had formed a line of battle of formidable proportions on the opposite height, and stretching in crescent outline, with flanks advanced, from the Pittsylvania (Carter) mansion on their left across the Sudley road in rear of Dogan's and reaching toward the Chinn house. They offered a fine spectacle as they threw forward a cloud of skirmishers down the opposite slope, preparatory to a new assault against the line on the plateau. But their right was now severely pressed by the troops that had successively arrived; the force in the south-west angle of the Sudley and Warrenton cross-roads were driven from their position, and, as Early's brigade, which, by direction of General Johnston, had swept around by the rear of the woods through which Elzey had passed, appeared on the field, his line of march bore upon the flank of the enemy, now retiring in that quarter.

This movement by my extreme left was masked by the trend of the woods from many of our forces on the plateau; and bidding those of my staff and escort around me raise a loud cheer, I dispatched the information to the several commands, with orders to go forward in a common charge. Before the full advance of the Confederate ranks the enemy's whole line, whose right was already yielding, irretrievably broke, fleeing across Bull Run by every available direction. Major Sykes's regulars, aided by Sherman's brigade, made a steady and handsome withdrawal, protecting the rear of the routed forces, and enabling many to escape by the Stone Bridge. Having ordered in pursuit all the troops on the field, I went to the Lewis house, and, the battle being ended, turned over the command to General Johnston. Mounting a fresh horse—the fourth on that day—I started to press the pursuit which was being made by our infantry and cavalry, some of the latter having been sent by General Johnston from Lewis's Ford to intercept the enemy on the turnpike. I was soon overtaken, however, by a courier bearing a message from Major T. G. Rhett, General Johnston's chief-of-staff on duty at Manassas railroad station, informing me of a report that a large Federal force, having pierced our lower line on Bull Run, was moving upon Camp Pickens, my depot of supplies near Manassas. I returned, and communicated this important news to General Johnston. Upon consultation it was deemed best that I should take Ewell's and Holmes's brigades, which were hastening up to the battle-field, but too late for the action, and fall on this force of the enemy, while reënforcements should be sent me from the pursuing forces, who were to be recalled for that purpose. To head off the danger and gain time, I hastily mounted a force of infantry behind the cavalrymen then present, but, on approaching the line of march near McLean's Ford, which the Federals must have taken, I learned that the news was a false alarm caught from the return of General Jones's forces to this side of the Run, the similarity of the uniforms and the direction of their march having convinced some nervous person that they were a force of the enemy. It was now almost dark, and too late to resume the broken pursuit; on my return I met the coming forces, and, as they were very tired, I ordered them to halt and bivouac for the night where they were. After giving such attention as I could to the troops, I started for Manassas, where I arrived about 10 o'clock, and found Mr. Davis at my headquarters with General Johnston. Arriving from Richmond late in the afternoon, Mr. Davis had immediately galloped to the field, accompanied by Colonel Jordan. They had met between Manassas and the battle-field the usual number of stragglers to the rear, whose appearance belied the determined array then sweeping the enemy before it, but Mr. Davis had the happiness to arrive in time to witness the last of the Federals disappearing beyond Bull Run. The next morning I received from his hand at our breakfast-table my commission, dated July 21st, as General in the Army of the Confederate States, and after his return to Richmond the kind congratulations of the Secretary of War and of General Lee, then acting as military adviser to the President.

It was a point made at the time at the North that, just as the Confederate troops were about to break and flee, the Federal troops anticipated them by doing so, being struck into this precipitation by the arrival upon their flank

57

of the Shenandoah forces marching from railroad trains halted *en route* with that aim—errors that have been repeated by a number of writers, and by an ambitious but superficial French author.

There were certain sentiments of a personal character clustering about this first battle, and personal anxiety as to its issue, that gladly accepted this theory. To this may be added the general readiness to accept a sentimental or ultra-dramatic explanation—a sorcery wrought by the delay or arrival of some force, or the death or coming of somebody, or any other single magical event—whereby history is easily caught, rather than to seek an understanding of that which is but the gradual result of the operation of many forces, both of opposing design and actual collision, modified more or less by the falls of chance. The personal sentiment, though natural enough at the time, has no place in any military estimate, or place of any kind at this day. The battle of Manassas was, like any other battle, a progression and development from the deliberate counter-employment of the military resources in hand, affected by accidents, as always, but of a kind very different from those referred to. My line of battle, which twice had not only withstood the enemy's attack, but had taken the offensive and driven him back in disorder, was becoming momentarily stronger from the arrival, at last, of the reënforcements provided for; and if the enemy had remained on the field till the arrival of Ewell and Holmes, they would have been so strongly outflanked that many who escaped would have been destroyed or captured.

Though my adversary's plan of battle was a good one as against a passive defensive opponent, such as he may have deemed I must be from the respective numbers and positions of our forces, it would, in my judgment, have been much better if, with more dash, the flank attack had been made by the Stone Bridge itself and the ford immediately above it. The plan adopted, however, favored above all things the easy execution of the offensive operations I had designed and ordered against his left flank and rear at Centreville. His turning column—18,000 strong, and presumably his best troops —was thrown off by a long ellipse through a narrow forest road to Sudley Ford, from which it moved down upon my left flank, and was thus dislocated from his main body. This severed movement of his forces not only left his exposed left and rear at Centreville weak against the simultaneous offensive of my heaviest forces upon it, which I had ordered, but the movement of his returning column would have been disconcerted and paralyzed by the early sound of this heavy conflict in its rear, and it could not even have made its way back so as to be available for manœuvre before the Centreville fraction had been thrown back upon it in disorder. A new army is very liable to panic, and, in view of the actual result of the battle, the conclusion can hardly be resisted that the panic which fell on the Federal army would thus have seized it early in the day, and with my forces in such a position as wholly to cut off its retreat upon Washington. But the commander of the front line on my right, who had been ordered to hold himself in readiness to initiate the offensive at a moment's notice, did not make the move expected of him because through accident he failed to receive his own immediate order to advance. The Federal commander's flanking movement, being thus uninterrupted by such a counter-movement as I had projected, was further assisted through the rawness and inadequacy of our staff organization through which I was left unacquainted with the actual state of affairs on my left. The Federal attack, already thus greatly favored, and encouraged, moreover, by the rout of General Bee's advanced line, failed for two reasons: their forces were not handled with concert of masses (a fault often made later on both sides), and the individual action of the Confederate troops was superior, and for a very palpable reason. That one army was fighting for union and the other for disunion is a political expression; the actual fact on the battle-field, in the face of cannon and musket, was that the Federal troops came as invaders, and the Southern troops stood as defenders of their homes, and further than this we need not go. The armies were vastly greater than had ever before fought on this continent, and were the largest volunteer armies ever assembled since the era of regular armies. The personal material on both sides was of exceptionally good character, and collectively superior to that of any subsequent period of the war. The Confederate army was filled with generous youths who had answered the first call to arms. For certain kinds of field duty they were not as yet adapted, many of them having at first come with their baggage and servants; these they had to dispense with, but, not to offend their susceptibilities, I then exacted the least work from them, apart from military drills, even to the prejudice of imporant field-works, when I could not get sufficient Negro labor; they "had come to fight, and not to handle the pick and shovel," and their fighting redeemed well their shortcomings as intrenchers. Before I left that gallant army, however, it had learned how readily the humbler could aid the nobler duty.

As to immediate results and trophies, we captured a great many stands of arms, batteries, equipments, standards, and flags, one of which was sent to me, through General Longstreet, as a personal compliment by the Texan "crack shot," Colonel B. F. Terry, who lowered it from its mast at Fairfax Court House, by cutting the halyards by means of his unerring rifle, as our troops next morning reoccupied that place. We captured also many prisoners, including a number of surgeons, whom (the first time in war) we treated not as prisoners, but as guests. Calling attention to their brave devotion to their wounded, I recommended to the War Department that they be sent home without exchange, together with some other prisoners, who had shown personal kindness to Colonel Jones, of the 4th Alabama, who had been mortally wounded early in the day.

Begun in the East, the war was spreading to the West, even beyond the Mississippi where the fate of the important border state of Missouri and the chief city of the West in those days, St. Louis, hung in the balance between slaveholding and non-slaveholding elements. This, from the days of the Kansas-Nebraska troubles in the fifties, had been "dark and bloody ground." Both sides claimed Missouri and both sides needed her. In August 1861, a Union army was defeated at Wilson's Creek in southwestern Missouri and the casualties amounted to over 23 per cent of all engaged, among them the stalwart Unionist General Nathaniel Lyon. The following March came the Battle of Pea Ridge in northwestern Arkansas. This was the first clear and decisive victory gained by the North in a pitched battle west of the Mississippi River, and until 1864 the last effort of the South to carry the war into Missouri except by abortive raids. More importantly perhaps, its result made it possible for veterans of a long series of minor engagements west of the Mississippi to reinforce the armies in the mid-South under Buell, Rosecrans, Sherman, and Grant.

In this area the object of the Federal armies was, of course, to cut the Confederacy in half by clearing the Mississippi from St. Louis all the way to the Gulf and to stab at the heart of the Confederacy via the Tennessee and Cumberland rivers. If successful, these maneuvers would cut Texas off from the main body of the South, hold Kentucky firmly in the Union, and make it difficult for Tennessee to coöperate with her sister states.

In February 1862, Fort Henry, commanding the Tennessee River, was captured with support from gunboats on the river by a taciturn, rumpled, cigar-smoking (some said whisky-drinking) character named Ulysses Simpson Grant of Illinois. Ten days later, Fort Donelson, eleven miles away on the Cumberland River and a very much stronger position for the Confederates, followed suit. The North was beside itself, reveling in the victory and in Grant's memorable answer to Buckner, the Confederate commander who had asked for terms. "No terms except unconditional and immediate surrender can be accepted," said Grant. "I propose to move immediately upon your works." Apparently Mr. Lincoln had at last found a fighting general in Unconditional Surrender Grant.

"It was not possible for brave men to endure more"

THE CAPTURE OF FORT DONELSON

BY LEW WALLACE, MAJOR-GENERAL, U. S. V.

IT IS of little moment now who first enunciated the idea of attacking the rebellion by way of the Tennessee River; most likely the conception was simultaneous with many minds. The trend of the river; its navigability for large steamers; its offer of a highway to the rear of the Confederate hosts in Kentucky and the State of Tennessee; its silent suggestion of a secure passage into the heart of the belligerent land, from which the direction of movement could be changed toward the Mississippi, or, left, toward Richmond; its many advantages as a line of supply and of general communication, must have been discerned by every military student who, in the summer of 1861, gave himself to the most cursory examination of the map. It is thought better and more consistent with fact to conclude that its advantages as a strategic line, so actually obtrusive of themselves, were observed about the same time by thoughtful men on both sides of the contest. With every problem of attack there goes a counter problem of defense. . . .

When General Johnston assumed command of the Western Department, the war had ceased to be a new idea. Battles had been fought. Preparations for battles to come were far advanced. Already it had been accepted that the North was to attack and the South to defend. The Mississippi River was a central object; if opened from Cairo to Fort Jackson (New Orleans), the Confederacy would be broken into halves, and good strategy required it to be broken. The question was whether the effort would be made directly or by turning its defended positions. Of the national gun-boats afloat above Cairo, some were formidably iron-clad. Altogether the flotilla was strong enough to warrant the theory that a direct descent would be attempted; and to meet the movement the Confederates threw up powerful batteries, notably at Columbus, Island Number Ten, Memphis, and Vicksburg. So fully were they possessed of that theory that they measurably neglected the possibilities of invasion by way of the Cumberland and Tennessee rivers. Not until General Johnston established his headquarters at Nashville was serious attention given to the defense of those streams. A report to his chief of engineers of November 21st, 1861, establishes that at that date a second battery on the Cumberland at Dover had been completed; that a work on the ridge had been laid out, and two guns mounted; and that the encampment was then surrounded by an abatis of felled timber. Later, Brigadier-General Lloyd Tilghman was sent to Fort Donelson as commandant, and on January 25th he reports the batteries prepared, the entire field-works built with a trace of 2900 feet, and rifle-pits to guard the approaches were begun. The same officer speaks further of reënforcements housed in four hundred log-cabins, and adds that while this was being done at Fort Donelson, Forts Henry and Heiman, over on the Tennessee, were being thoroughly strengthened. January 30th, Fort Donelson was formally inspected by Lieutenant-Colonel Gilmer, chief engineer of the Western Department, and the final touches were ordered to be given it.

It is to be presumed that General Johnston was satisfied with the defenses thus provided for the Cumberland River. From observing General Buell at Louisville, and the stir and movement of multiplying columns under General U. S. Grant in the region of Cairo, he suddenly awoke determined to fight for Nashville at Donelson. To this conclusion he came as late as the beginning of February; and thereupon the brightest of the Southern leaders proceeded to make a capital mistake. The Confederate estimate of the Union force at that time in Kentucky alone was 119 regiments. The force at Cairo, St. Louis, and the towns near the mouth of the Cumberland River was judged to be about as great. It was also known that we had unlimited means of transportation for troops, making concentration a work of but few hours. Still General Johnston persisted in fighting for Nashville, and for that purpose divided his thirty thousand men. Fourteen thousand he kept in observation of Buell at Louisville. Sixteen thousand he gave to defend Fort Donelson.

The latter detachment he himself called "the best part of his army." It is difficult to think of a great master of strategy making an error so perilous.

Having taken the resolution to defend Nashville at Donelson, he intrusted the operation to three chiefs of brigade—John B. Floyd, Gideon J. Pillow, and Simon B. Buckner. Of these, the first was ranking officer, and he was at the time under indictment by a grand jury at Washington for malversation as Secretary of War under President Buchanan, and for complicity in an embezzlement of public funds. As will be seen, there came a crisis when the recollection of the circumstance exerted an unhappy influence over his judgment. The second officer had a genuine military record; but it is said of him that he was of a jealous nature, insubordinate, and quarrelsome. His bold attempt to supersede General Scott in Mexico was green in the memories of living men. To give pertinency to the remark, there is reason to believe that a personal misunderstanding between him and General Buckner, older than the rebellion, was yet unsettled when the two met at Donelson. All in all, therefore, there is little doubt that the junior of the three commanders was the fittest for the enterprise intrusted to them. He was their equal in courage; while in devotion to the cause and to his profession of arms, in tactical knowledge, in military bearing, in the faculty of getting the most service out of his inferiors, and inspiring them with confidence in his ability—as a soldier in all the higher meanings of the word—he was greatly their superior.

The 6th of February, 1862, dawned darkly after a thunder-storm. Pacing the parapets of the work on the hill above the inlet formed by the junction of Hickman's Creek and the Cumberland River, a sentinel, in the serviceable butternut jeans uniform of the Confederate army of the West, might that day have surveyed Fort Donelson almost ready for battle. In fact, very little was afterward done to it. There were the two water-batteries sunk in the northern face of the bluff, about thirty feet above the river; in the lower battery 9 32-pounder guns and 1 10-inch Columbiad, and in the upper another Columbiad, bored and rifled as a 32-pounder, and 2 32-pounder carronades. These guns lay between the embrasures, in snug revetment of sand in coffee-sacks, flanked right and left with stout traverses. The satisfaction of the sentry could have been nowise diminished at seeing the backwater lying deep in the creek; a more perfect ditch against assault could not have been constructed. The fort itself was of good profile, and admirably adapted to the ridge it crowned. Around it, on the landward side, ran the rifle-pits, a continuous but irregular line of logs, covered with yellow clay. From Hickman's Creek they extended far around to the little run just outside the town on the south. If the sentry thought the pits looked shallow, he was solaced to see that they followed the coping of the ascents, seventy or eighty feet in height, up which a foe must charge, and that, where they were weakest, they were strengthened by trees felled outwardly in front of them, so that the inter-

63

lacing limbs and branches seemed impassable by men under fire. At points inside the outworks, on the inner slopes of the hills, defended thus from view of an enemy as well as from his shot, lay the huts and log-houses of the garrison. Here and there groups of later comers, shivering in their wet blankets, were visible in a bivouac so cheerless that not even morning fires could relieve it. A little music would have helped their sinking spirits, but there was none. Even the picturesque effect of gay uniforms was wanting. In fine, the Confederate sentinel on the ramparts that morning, taking in the whole scene, knew the jolly, rollicking picnic days of the war were over.

To make clearer why the 6th of February is selected to present the first view of the fort, about noon that day the whole garrison was drawn from their quarters by the sound of heavy guns, faintly heard from the direction of Fort Henry, a token by which every man of them knew that a battle was on. The occurrence was in fact expected, for two days before a horseman had ridden to General Tilghman with word that at 4:30 o'clock in the morning rocket signals had been exchanged with the picket at Bailey's Landing, announcing the approach of gun-boats. A second courier came, and then a third; the latter, in great haste, requesting the general's presence at Fort Henry. There was quick mounting at headquarters, and, before the camp could be taken into confidence, the general and his guard were out of sight. Occasional guns were heard the day following. Donelson gave itself up to excitement and conjecture. At noon of the 6th, as stated, there was continuous and heavy cannonading at Fort Henry, and greater excitement at Fort Donelson. . . . At exactly midnight the gallant Colonel Heiman marched into Fort Donelson with two brigades of infantry rescued from the ruins of Forts Henry and Heiman. The officers and men by whom they were received then knew that their turn was at hand; and at daybreak, with one mind and firm of purpose, they set about the final preparation.

Brigadier-General Pillow reached Fort Donelson on the 9th; Brigadier-General Buckner came in the night of the 11th; and Brigadier-General Floyd on the 13th. The latter, by virtue of his rank, took command.

The morning of the 13th—calm, spring-like, the very opposite of that of the 6th—found in Fort Donelson a garrison of 28 regiments of infantry: 13 from Tennessee, 2 from Kentucky, 6 from Mississippi, 1 from Texas, 2 from Alabama, 4 from Virginia. There were also present 2 independent battalions, 1 regiment of cavalry, and artillerymen for 6 light batteries, and 17 heavy guns, making a total of quite 18,000 effectives.

General Buckner's division—6 regiments and 2 batteries—constituted the right wing, and was posted to cover the land approaches to the water-batteries. A left wing was organized into six brigades. Four batteries were distributed amongst the left wing. General Bushrod R. Johnson, an able officer, served the general commanding as chief-of-staff. Dover was converted into a depot of supplies and ordnance stores. These dispositions made, Fort Donelson was ready for battle.

It may be doubted if General Grant called a council of war. The nearest approach to it was a convocation held on the *New Uncle Sam,* a steamboat that was afterward transformed into the gun-boat *Blackhawk.* The morning of the 11th of February, a staff-officer visited each commandant of division and brigade with the simple verbal message: "General Grant sends his compliments, and requests to see you this afternoon on his boat." Minutes of the proceedings were not kept; there was no adjournment; each person retired when he got ready, knowing that the march would take place next day, probably in the forenoon.

There were in attendance on the occasion some officers of great subsequent notability. Of these Ulysses S. Grant was first. The world knows him now; then his fame was all before him. A singularity of the volunteer service in that day was that nobody took account of even a first-rate record of the Mexican War. The battle of Belmont, though indecisive, was a much better reference. A story was abroad that Grant had been the last man to take boat at the end of that affair, and the addendum that he had lingered in face of the enemy until he was hauled aboard with the last gang-plank, did him great good. From the first his silence was remarkable. He knew how to keep his temper. In battle, as in camp, he went about quietly, speaking in a conversational tone; yet he appeared to see everything that went on, and was always intent on business. He had a faithful assistant adjutant-general, and appreciated him; he preferred, however, his own eyes, word, and hand. His aides were little more than messengers. In dress he was plain, even negligent; in partial amendment of that his horse was always a good one and well kept. At the council—calling it such by grace—he smoked, but never said a word. In all probability he was framing the orders of march which were issued that night.

Charles F. Smith, of the regular army, was also present. . . . At the time of the meeting on the *New Uncle Sam* he was a brigadier-general, and commanded the division which in the land operations against Fort Henry had marched up the left bank of the river against Fort Heiman.

Another officer worthy of mention was John A. McClernand, also a brigadier. By profession a lawyer, he was in his first of military service. Brave, industrious, methodical, and of unquestioned cleverness, he was rapidly acquiring the art of war.

There was still another in attendance on the *New Uncle Sam* not to be passed—a young man who had followed General Grant from Illinois, and was seeing his first of military service. No soldier in the least familiar with headquarters on the Tennessee can ever forget the slender figure, large black eyes, hectic cheeks, and sincere, earnest manner of John A. Rawlins, then as-

65

sistant adjutant-general, afterward major-general and secretary of war. He had two special devotions—to the cause and to his chief. He lived to see the first triumphant and the latter first in peace as well as in war. Probably no officer of the Union was mourned by so many armies.

Fort Henry, it will be remembered, was taken by Flag-Officer Foote on the 6th of February. The time up to the 12th was given to reconnoitering the country in the direction of Fort Donelson. Two roads were discovered: one of twelve miles direct, the other almost parallel with the first, but, on account of a slight divergence, two miles longer.

By 8 o'clock in the morning, the First Division, General McClernand commanding, and the Second, under General Smith, were in full march. The infantry of this command consisted of twenty-five regiments in all, or three less than those of the Confederates. Against their six field-batteries General Grant had seven. In cavalry alone he was materially stronger. The rule in attacking fortifications is five to one; to save the Union commander from a charge of rashness, however, he had also at control a fighting quality ordinarily at home on the sea rather than the land. After receiving the surrender of Fort Henry, Flag-Officer Foote had hastened to Cairo to make preparation for the reduction of Fort Donelson. With six of his boats, he passed into the Cumberland River; and on the 12th, while the two divisions of the army were marching across to Donelson, he was hurrying, as fast as steam could drive him and his following, to a second trial of iron batteries afloat against earth batteries ashore. The *Carondelet,* Commander Walke, having preceded him, had been in position below the fort since the 12th. By sundown of the 12th, McClernand and Smith reached the point designated for them in orders.

On the morning of the 13th of February General Grant, with about twenty thousand men, was before Fort Donelson. We have had a view of the army in the works ready for battle; a like view of that outside and about to go into position of attack and assault is not so easily to be given. At dawn the latter host rose up from the bare ground, and, snatching bread and coffee as best they could, fell into lines that stretched away over hills, down hollows, and through thickets, making it impossible for even colonels to see their regiments from flank to flank.

Pausing to give a thought to the situation, it is proper to remind the reader that he is about to witness an event of more than mere historical interest; he is about to see the men of the North and North-west and of the South and South-west enter for the first time into a strife of arms; on one side, the best blood of Tennessee, Kentucky, Alabama, Mississippi, and Texas, aided materially by fighting representatives from Virginia; on the other, the best blood of Illinois, Ohio, Indiana, Iowa, Missouri, and Nebraska.

We have now before us a spectacle seldom witnessed in the annals of scientific war—an army behind field-works erected in a chosen position waiting quietly while another army very little superior in numbers proceeds at leisure to place it in a state of siege. Such was the operation General Grant had before him at daybreak of the 13th of February. Let us see how it was accomplished and how it was resisted.

In a clearing about two miles from Dover there was a log-house, at the time occupied by a Mrs. Crisp. As the road to Dover ran close by, it was made the headquarters of the commanding general. All through the night of the 12th, the coming and going was incessant. Smith was ordered to find a position in front of the enemy's right wing, which would place him face to face with Buckner. McClernand's order was to establish himself on the enemy's left, where he would be opposed to Pillow.

A little before dawn Birge's sharp-shooters were astir. Theirs was a peculiar service. Each was a preferred marksman, and carried a long-range Henry rifle, with sights delicately arranged as for target practice. In action each was perfectly independent. They never manœuvred as a corps. When the time came they were asked, "Canteens full?" "Biscuits for all day?" Then their only order, "All right; hunt your holes, boys." Thereupon they dispersed, and, like Indians, sought cover to please themselves behind rocks and stumps, or in hollows. Sometimes they dug holes; sometimes they climbed into trees. Once in a good location, they remained there the day. At night they would crawl out and report in camp. This morning, as I have said, the sharp-shooters dispersed early to find places within easy range of the breastworks.

The movement by Smith and McClernand was begun about the same time. A thick wood fairly screened the former. The latter had to cross an open valley under fire of two batteries, one on Buckner's left, the other on a high point jutting from the line of outworks held by Colonel Heiman of Pillow's command. Graves commanded the first (Kentucky), Maney the second (Tennessee); both were of Tennessee. As always in situations where the advancing party is ignorant of the ground and of the designs of the enemy, resort was had to skirmishers, who are to the main body what antennæ are to insects. Theirs it is to unmask the foe. Unlike sharp-shooters, they act in bodies. Behind the skirmishers, the batteries started out to find positions, and through the brush and woods, down the hollows, up the hills the guns and caissons were hauled. Nowadays it must be a very steep bluff in face of which the good artillerist will stop or turn back. At Donelson, however, the proceeding was generally slow and toilsome. The officer had to find a vantage-ground first; then with axes a road to it was hewn out; after which, in many instances, the men, with the prolongs over their shoulders, helped the horses along. In the gray of the dawn the sharp-shooters were deep in their deadly game; as the sun came up, one battery after another opened fire, and was instantly and gallantly answered; and all the time behind the hidden sharp-shooters, and behind the skirmishers, who occasionally stopped to take a hand in the fray, the regiments marched, route-step, colors flying, after their colonels.

About 11 o'clock Commander Walke, of the *Carondelet*, engaged the water-batteries. The air was then full of the stunning music of battle, though as yet not a volley of musketry had been heard. Smith, nearest the enemy at starting, was first in place; and there, leaving the fight to his sharp-shooters and skirmishers and to his batteries, he reported to the chief in the log-house, and, like an old soldier, calmly waited orders. McClernand, following a good road, pushed on rapidly to the high grounds on the right. The appearance of his column in the valley covered by the two Confederate batteries provoked a furious shelling from them. On the double-quick his men passed through it; and when, in the wood beyond, they resumed the route-step and saw that nobody was hurt, they fell to laughing at themselves. The real baptism of fire was yet in store for them.

When McClernand arrived at his appointed place and extended his brigades, it was discovered that the Confederate outworks offered a front too great for him to envelop. To attempt to rest his right opposite their extreme left would necessitate a dangerous attenuation of his line and leave him without reserves. Over on their left, moreover, ran the road passing from Dover on the south to Charlotte and Nashville, which it was of the highest importance to close hermetically so that there would be no communication left General Floyd except by the river. If the road to Charlotte were left to the enemy, they might march out at their pleasure.

The insufficiency of his force was thus made apparent to General Grant, and whether a discovery of the moment or not, he set about its correction. He knew a reënforcement was coming up the river under convoy of Foote; besides which a brigade, composed of the 8th Missouri and the 11th Indiana infantry and Battery A, Illinois, had been left behind at Forts Henry and Heiman under myself. A courier was dispatched to me with an order to bring my command to Donelson. I ferried my troops across the Tennessee in the night, and reported with them at headquarters before noon the next day. The brigade was transferred to General Smith; at the same time an order was put into my hand assigning me to command the Third Division, which was conducted to a position between Smith and McClernand, enabling the latter to extend his line well to the left and cover the road to Charlotte.

Thus on the 14th of February the Confederates were completely invested, except that the river above Dover remained to them. The supineness of General Floyd all this while is to this day incomprehensible. A vigorous attack on the morning of the 13th might have thrown Grant back upon Fort Henry. Such an achievement would have more than offset Foote's conquest. The *morale* to be gained would have alone justified the attempt. But with McClernand's strong division on the right, my own in the center, and C. F. Smith's on the left, the opportunity was gone. On the side of General Grant, the possession of the river was all that was wanting; with that Grant could force the fighting, or wait the certain approach of the grimmest enemy of the besieged—starvation.

It is now—morning of the 14th—easy to see and understand with something more than approximate exactness the oppositions of the two forces. Smith is on the left of the Union army opposite Buckner. My division, in the center, confronts Colonels Heiman, Drake, and Davidson, each with a brigade. McClernand, now well over on the right, keeps the road to Charlotte and Nashville against the major part of Pillow's left wing. The infantry on both sides are in cover behind the crests of the hills or in thick woods, listening to the ragged fusillade which the sharp-shooters and skirmishers maintain against each other almost without intermission. There is little pause in the exchange of shells and round shot. The careful chiefs have required their men to lie down. In brief, it looks as if each party were inviting the other to begin.

These circumstances, the sharp-shooting and cannonading, ugly as they may seem to one who thinks of them under comfortable surroundings, did in fact serve a good purpose the day in question in helping the men to forget their sufferings of the night before. It must be remembered that the weather had changed during the preceding afternoon: from suggestions of spring it turned to intensified winter. From lending a gentle hand in bringing Foote and his iron-clads up the river, the wind whisked suddenly around to the north and struck both armies with a storm of mixed rain, snow, and sleet. All night the tempest blew mercilessly upon the unsheltered, fireless soldier, making sleep impossible. Inside the works, nobody had overcoats; while thousands of those outside had marched from Fort Henry as to a summer fête, leaving coats, blankets, and knapsacks behind them in the camp. More than one stout fellow has since admitted, with a laugh, that nothing was so helpful to him that horrible night as the thought that the wind, which seemed about to turn his blood into icicles, was serving the enemy the same way; they, too, had to stand out and take the blast. Let us now go back to the preceding day, and bring up an incident of McClernand's swing into position.

About the center of the Confederate outworks there was a V-shaped hill, marked sharply by a ravine on its right and another on its left. This Colonel Heiman occupied with his brigade of five regiments—all of Tennessee but one. The front presented was about 2500 feet. In the angle of the V, on the summit of the hill, Captain Maney's battery, also of Tennessee, had been planted. Without protection of any kind, it nevertheless completely swept a large field to the left, across which an assaulting force would have to come in order to get at Heiman or at Drake, next on the south.

Maney, on the point of the hill, had been active throughout the preceding afternoon, and had succeeded in drawing the fire of some of McClernand's guns. The duel lasted until night. Next morning it was renewed

69

with increased sharpness, Maney being assisted on his right by Graves's battery of Buckner's division, and by some pieces of Drake's on his left.

McClernand's advance was necessarily slow and trying. This was not merely a logical result of unacquaintance with the country and the dispositions of the enemy; he was also under an order from General Grant to avoid everything calculated to bring on a general engagement. In Maney's well-served guns he undoubtedly found serious annoyance, if not a positive obstruction. Concentrating guns of his own upon the industrious Confederate, he at length fancied him silenced and the enemy's infantry on the right thrown into confusion—circumstances from which he hastily deduced a favorable chance to deliver an assault. For that purpose he reënforced his Third Brigade, which was nearest the offending battery, and gave the necessary orders.

Up to this time, it will be observed, there had not been any fighting involving infantry in line. This was now to be changed. . . .

Down the hill the three regiments went, crashing and tearing through the undergrowth. Heiman, on the lookout, saw them advancing. Before they cleared the woods, Maney opened with shells. At the foot of the descent, in the valley, Graves joined his fire to Maney's. There Morrison reported to Haynie, who neither accepted nor refused the command. Pointing to the hill, he merely said, "Let us take it together." Morrison turned away, and rejoined his own regiment. Here was confusion in the beginning, or worse, an assault begun without a head. Nevertheless, the whole line went forward. On a part of the hillside the trees were yet standing. The open space fell to Morrison and his 49th, and paying the penalty of the exposure, he outstripped his associates. The men fell rapidly; yet the living rushed on and up, firing as they went. The battery was the common target. Maney's gunners, in relief against the sky, were shot down in quick succession. His first lieutenant (Burns) was one of the first to suffer. His second lieutenant (Massie) was mortally wounded. Maney himself was hit; still he staid, and his guns continued their punishment; and still the farmer lads and shop boys of Illinois clung to their purpose. With marvelous audacity they pushed through the abatis and reached a point within forty yards of the rifle-pits. It actually looked as if the prize were theirs. The yell of victory was rising in their throats. Suddenly the long line of yellow breastworks before them, covering Heiman's five regiments, crackled and turned into flame. The forlorn-hope stopped—staggered—braced up again—shot blindly through the smoke at the smoke of the new enemy, secure in his shelter. Thus for fifteen minutes the Illinoisans stood fighting. The time is given on the testimony of the opposing leader himself. Morrison was knocked out of his saddle by a musket-ball, and disabled; then the men went down the hill. At its foot they rallied round their flags and renewed the assault. Pushed down again, again they rallied, and a third time climbed to the enemy. This time the battery set fire to the dry leaves on the ground, and the heat and smoke became stifling. It was not possible for brave men to endure more. Slowly, sullenly, frequently pausing to return a shot, they went back for the last time; and in going their ears and souls were riven with the shrieks of their wounded comrades, whom the flames crept down upon and smothered and charred where they lay.

Considered as a mere exhibition of courage, this assault, long maintained against odds—twice repulsed, twice renewed—has been seldom excelled. One hundred and forty-nine men of the 17th and 49th were killed and wounded. Haynie reported 1 killed and 8 wounded.

There are few things connected with the operations against Fort Donelson so relieved of uncertainty as this: that when General Grant at Fort Henry became fixed in the resolution to undertake the movement, his primary object was the capture of the force to which the post was intrusted. To effect their complete environment, he relied upon Flag-Officer Foote and his gun-boats, whose astonishing success at Fort Henry justified the extreme of confidence.

Foote arrived on the 14th, and made haste to enter upon his work. The *Carondelet* (Commander Walke) had been in position since the 12th. Behind a low output of the shore, for two days, she maintained a fire from her rifled guns, happily of greater range than the best of those of the enemy.

At 9 o'clock on the 14th, Captain Culbertson, looking from the parapet of the upper battery, beheld the river below the first bend full of transports, landing troops under cover of a fresh arrival of gun-boats. The disembarkation concluded, Foote was free. He waited until noon. The captains in the batteries mistook his deliberation for timidity. The impinging of their shot on his iron armor was heard distinctly in the fort a mile and a half away. The captains began to doubt if he would come at all. But at 3 o'clock the boats took position under fire: the *Louisville* on the right, the *St. Louis* next, then the *Pittsburgh,* then the *Carondelet,* all iron-clad.

Five hundred yards from the batteries, and yet Foote was not content! In the Crimean war the allied French and English fleets, of much mightier ships, undertook to engage the Russian shore batteries, but little stronger than those at Donelson. The French on that occasion stood off 1800 yards. Lord Lyons fought his *Agamemnon* at a distance of 800 yards. Foote forged ahead within 400 yards of his enemy, and was still going on. His boat had been hit between wind and water; so with the *Pittsburgh* and *Carondelet.* About the guns the floors were slippery with blood, and both surgeons and carpenters were never so busy. Still the four boats kept on, and there was great cheering; for not only did the fire from the shore slacken; the look-outs reported the enemy running. It seemed that fortune would smile once more upon the fleet, and cover the honors of Fort Henry afresh at Fort Donelson. Unhappily, when about 350 yards off the hill a solid shot plunged through the pilot-house of the flag-ship, and carried away the wheel. Near the same time the tiller-ropes of the *Louisville* were disabled. Both vessels became unmanageable and began floating down the current. The eddies turned them round like logs. The *Pittsburgh* and *Carondelet* closed in and covered them with their hulls.

Seeing this turn in the fight, the captains of the batteries rallied their men, who cheered in their turn, and renewed the contest with increased will and energy. A ball got lodged in their best rifle. A corporal and some of his men took a log fitting the bore, leaped out on the parapet, and rammed the missile home. "Now, boys," said a gunner in Bidwell's battery, "see me take a chimney!" The flag of the boat and the chimney fell with the shot.

When the vessels were out of range, the victors looked about them. The fine form of their embrasures was gone; heaps of earth had been cast over their platforms. In a space of twenty-four feet they had picked up as many shot and shells. The air had been full of flying missiles. For an hour and a half the brave fellows had been rained upon; yet their losses had been trifling in numbers. Each gunner had selected a ship and followed her faithfully throughout the action, now and then uniting fire on the *Carondelet*. The Confederates had behaved with astonishing valor. Their victory sent a thrill of joy through the army. The assault on the outworks, the day before, had been a failure. With the repulse of the gun-boats the Confederates scored success number two, and the communication by the river remained open to Nashville. The winds that blew sleet and snow over Donelson that night were not so unendurable as they might have been.

The night of the 14th of February fell cold and dark, and under the pitiless sky the armies remained in position so near to each other that neither dared light fires. Overpowered with watching, fatigue, and the lassitude of spirits which always follows a strain upon the faculties of men like that which is the concomitant of battle, thousands on both sides lay down in the ditches and behind logs and whatever else would in the least shelter them from the cutting wind, and tried to sleep. Very few closed their eyes. Even the horses, after their manner, betrayed the suffering they were enduring.

That morning General Floyd had called a council of his chiefs of brigades and divisions. He expressed the opinion that the post was untenable, except with fifty thousand troops. He called attention to the heavy reënforcements of the Federals, and suggested an immediate attack upon their right wing to reopen land communication with Nashville, by way of Charlotte. The proposal was agreed to unanimously. General Buckner proceeded to make dispositions to cover the retreat, in the event the sortie should be successful. Shortly after noon, when the movement should have begun, the order was countermanded at the instance of Pillow. Then came the battle with the gunboats.

In the night the council was recalled, with general and regimental officers in attendance. The situation was again debated, and the same conclusion reached. According to the plan resolved upon, Pillow was to move at dawn with his whole division, and attack the right of the besiegers. General Buckner was to be relieved by troops in the forts, and with his command to support Pillow by assailing the right of the enemy's center. If he succeeded, he was to take post outside the intrenchments on the Wynn's Ferry road to cover the retreat. He was then to act as rear-guard. Thus early, leaders in Donelson were aware of the mistake into which they were plunged. Their resolution was wise and heroic. Let us see how they executed it.

Preparations for the attack occupied the night. The troops for the most part were taken out of the rifle-pits and massed over on the left to the number of ten thousand or more. The ground was covered with ice and snow; yet the greatest silence was observed. It seems incomprehensible that columns mixed of all arms, infantry, cavalry, and artillery, could have engaged in simultaneous movement, and not have been heard by some listener outside. One would think the jolting and rumble of the heavy gun-carriages would have told the story. But the character of the night must be remembered. The pickets of the Federals were struggling for life against the blast, and probably did not keep good watch.

Oglesby's brigade held McClernand's extreme right. Here and there the musicians were beginning to make the woods ring with reveille, and the numbed soldiers of the line were rising from their icy beds and shaking the snow from their frozen garments. As yet, however, not a company had "fallen in." Suddenly the pickets fired, and with the alarm on their lips rushed back upon their comrades. The woods on the instant became alive.

The regiments formed, officers mounted and took their places; words of command rose loud and eager. By the time Pillow's advance opened fire on Oglesby's right, the point first struck, the latter was fairly formed to receive it. A rapid exchange of volleys ensued. The distance intervening between the works on one side and the bivouac on the other was so short that the action began before Pillow could effect a deployment. His brigades came up in a kind of echelon, left in front, and passed "by regiments left into line," one by one, however; the regiments quickly took their places, and advanced without halting. Oglesby's Illinoisans were now fully awake. They held their ground, returning in full measure the fire that they received. The Confederate Forrest rode around as if to get in their rear, and it was then give and take, infantry against infantry. The semi-echelon movement of the Confederates enabled them, after an interval, to strike W. H. L. Wallace's brigade, on Oglesby's left. Soon Wallace was engaged along his whole front, now prolonged by the addition to his command of Morrison's regiments. The first charge against him was repulsed; whereupon he advanced to the top of the rising ground behind which he had sheltered his troops in the night. A fresh assault followed, but, aided by a battery across the valley to his left, he repulsed the enemy a second time. His men were steadfast, and clung to the brow of the hill as if it were theirs by holy right. An hour passed, and yet another hour, without cessation of the fire. Meantime the woods rang with a monstrous clangor of musketry, as if a million men were beating empty barrels with iron hammers.

Buckner flung a portion of his division on McClernand's left, and supported the attack with his artillery. The enfilading fell chiefly on W. H. L. Wallace. McClernand, watchful and full of resources, sent batteries to meet Buckner's batteries. To that duty Taylor rushed with his Company B; and McAllister pushed his three 24-pounders into position and exhausted his ammunition in the duel. The roar never slackened. Men fell by the score, reddening the snow with their blood. The smoke, in pallid white clouds, clung to the underbrush and tree-tops as if to screen the combatants from each other. Close to the ground the flame of musketry and cannon tinted everything a lurid red. Limbs dropped from the trees on the heads below, and the thickets were shorn as by an army of cradlers. The division was under peremptory orders to hold its position to the last extremity, and Colonel Wallace was equal to the emergency.

It was now 10 o'clock, and over on the right Oglesby was beginning to fare badly. The pressure on his front grew stronger. The "rebel yell," afterward a familiar battle-cry on many fields, told of ground being gained against him. To add to his doubts, officers were riding to him with a sickening story that their commands were getting out of ammunition, and asking where they could go for a supply. All he could say was to take what was in the boxes of the dead and wounded. At last he realized that the end was come. His right companies began to give way, and as they retreated, holding up their empty cartridge-boxes, the enemy were emboldened, and swept more fiercely around his flank, until finally they appeared in his rear. He then gave the order to retire the division.

W. H. L. Wallace from his position looked off to his right and saw but one regiment of Oglesby's in place, maintaining the fight, and that was John A. Logan's 31st Illinois. Through the smoke he could see Logan riding in a gallop behind his line; through the roar in his front and the rising yell in his rear, he could hear Logan's voice in fierce entreaty to his "boys." Near the 31st stood W. H. L. Wallace's regiment, the 11th Illinois, under Lieutenant-Colonel Ransom. The gaps in the ranks of the two were closed up always toward the colors. The ground at their feet was strewn with their dead and wounded; at length the common misfortune overtook Logan. To keep men without cartridges under fire sweeping them front and flank would be cruel, if not impossible; and seeing it, he too gave the order to retire, and followed his decimated companies to the rear. The 11th then became the right of the brigade, and had to go in turn. Nevertheless, Ransom changed front to rear coolly, as if on parade, and joined in the general retirement. Forrest charged them and threw them into a brief confusion. The greater portion clung to their colors, and made good their retreat. By 11 o'clock Pillow held the road to Charlotte and the whole of the position occupied at dawn by the First Division, and with it the dead and all the wounded who could not get away.

Pillow's part of the programme, arranged in the council of the night before, was accomplished. The country was once more open to Floyd. Why did he not avail himself of the dearly bought opportunity, and march his army out?

Without pausing to consider whether the Confederate general could now have escaped with his troops, it must be evident that he should have made the effort. Pillow had discharged his duty well. With the disappearance of W. H. L. Wallace's brigade, it only remained for the victor to deploy his regiments into column and march into the country. The road was his. Buckner was in position to protect Colonel Head's withdrawal from the trenches opposite General Smith on the right; that done, he was also in position to cover the retreat. Buckner had also faithfully performed his task.

On the Union side the situation at this critical time was favorable to the proposed retirement. My division in the center was weakened by the dispatch of one of my brigades to the assistance of General McClernand; in addition to which my orders were to hold my position. As a point of still greater importance, General Grant had gone on board the *St. Louis* at the request of Flag-Officer Foote, and he was there in consultation with that officer, presumably uninformed of the disaster which had befallen his right. It would take a certain time for him to return to the field and dispose his forces for pursuit. It may be said with strong assurance, consequently, that Floyd could have put his men fairly *en route* for Charlotte before the Federal commander could have interposed an obstruction to the movement. The real difficulty was in the hero of the morning, who now made haste to blight his laurels. General Pillow's vanity whistled itself into ludicrous exaltation. Imagining General Grant's whole army defeated and fleeing in rout for Fort Henry and the transports on the river, he deported himself accordingly. He began by ignoring Floyd. He rode to Buckner and accused him of shameful conduct. He sent an aide to the nearest telegraph station with a dispatch to Albert Sidney Johnston, then in command of the Department, asseverating, "on the honor of a soldier," that the day was theirs. Nor did he stop at that. The victory, to be available, required that the enemy should be followed with energy. Such was a habit of Napoleon. Without deigning even to consult his chief, he ordered Buckner to move out and attack the Federals. There was a gorge, up which a road ran toward our central position, or rather what had been our central position. Pointing to the gorge and the road, he told Buckner that was his way and bade him attack in force. There was nothing to do but obey; and when Buckner had begun the movement, the wise programme decided upon the evening before was wiped from the slate.

When Buckner reluctantly took the gorge road marked out for him by

75

Pillow, the whole Confederate army, save the detachments on the works, was virtually in pursuit of McClernand, retiring by the Wynn's Ferry road—falling back, in fact, upon my position. My division was now to feel the weight of Pillow's hand; if they should fail, the fortunes of the day would depend upon the veteran Smith.

When General McClernand perceived the peril threatening him in the morning, he sent an officer to me with a request for assistance. This request I referred to General Grant, who was at the time in consultation with Foote. Upon the turning of Oglesby's flank, McClernand repeated his request, with such a representation of the situation that, assuming the responsibility, I ordered Colonel Cruft to report with his brigade to McClernand. Cruft set out promptly. Unfortunately a guide misdirected him, so that he became involved in the retreat, and was prevented from accomplishing his object.

I was in the rear of my single remaining brigade, in conversation with Captain Rawlins, of Grant's staff, when a great shouting was heard behind me on the Wynn's Ferry road, whereupon I sent an orderly to ascertain the cause. The man reported the road and woods full of soldiers apparently in rout. An officer then rode by at full speed, shouting, "All's lost! Save yourselves!" A hurried consultation was had with Rawlins, at the end of which the brigade was put in motion toward the enemy's works, on the very road by which Buckner was pursuing under Pillow's mischievous order. It happened also that Colonel W. H. L. Wallace had dropped into the same road with such of his command as staid by their colors. He came up riding and at a walk, his leg over the horn of his saddle. He was perfectly cool, and looked like a farmer from a hard day's plowing. "Good-morning," I said. "Good-morning," was the reply. "Are they pursuing you?" "Yes." "How far are they behind?" That instant the head of my command appeared on the road. The colonel calculated, then answered: "You will have about time to form line of battle right here." "Thank you. Good-day." "Good-day."

At that point the road began to dip into the gorge; on the right and left there were woods, and in front a dense thicket. An order was dispatched to bring Battery A forward at full speed. Colonel John M. Thayer, commanding the brigade, formed it on the double-quick into line; the 1st Nebraska and the 58th Illinois on the right, and the 58th Ohio, with a detached company, on the left. The battery came up on the run and swung across the road, which had been left open for it. Hardly had it unlimbered, before the enemy appeared, and firing began. For ten minutes or thereabouts the scenes of the morning were reënacted. The Confederates struggled hard to perfect their deployments. The woods rang with musketry and artillery. The brush on the slope of the hill was mowed away with bullets. A great cloud arose and shut out the woods and the narrow valley below. Colonel Thayer and his regiments behaved with great gallantry, and the assailants fell back in confusion and returned to the intrenchments. W. H. L. Wallace and Oglesby re-formed their commands behind Thayer, supplied them with ammunition, and stood at rest waiting for orders. There was then a lull in the battle. Even the cannonading ceased, and everybody was asking, What next?

Just then General Grant rode up to where General McClernand and I were in conversation. He was almost unattended. In his hand there were some papers, which looked like telegrams. Wholly unexcited, he saluted and received the salutations of his subordinates. Proceeding at once to business, he directed them to retire their commands to the heights out of cannon range, and throw up works. Reënforcements were *en route,* he said, and it was advisable to await their coming. He was then informed of the mishap to the First Division, and that the road to Charlotte was open to the enemy.

In every great man's career there is a crisis exactly similar to that which now overtook General Grant, and it cannot be better described than as a crucial test of his nature. A mediocre person would have accepted the news as an argument for persistence in his resolution to enter upon a siege. Had General Grant done so, it is very probable his history would have been then and there concluded. His admirers and detractors are alike invited to study him at this precise juncture. It cannot be doubted that he saw with painful distinctness the effect of the disaster to his right wing. His face flushed slightly. With a sudden grip he crushed the papers in his hand. But in an instant these signs of disappointment or hesitation—as the reader pleases—cleared away. In his ordinary quiet voice he said, addressing himself to both officers, "Gentlemen, the position on the right must be retaken." With that he turned and galloped off.

Seeing in the road a provisional brigade, under Colonel Morgan L. Smith, consisting of the 11th Indiana and the 8th Missouri Infantry, going, by order of General C. F. Smith, to the aid of the First Division, I suggested that if General McClernand would order Colonel Smith to report to me, I would attempt to recover the lost ground; and the order having been given, I reconnoitered the hill, determined upon a place of assault, and arranged my order of attack. . . . These dispositions filled the time till about 2 o'clock in the afternoon, when heavy cannonading, mixed with a long roll of musketry, broke out over on the left, whither it will be necessary to transfer the reader.

The veteran in command on the Union left had contented himself with allowing Buckner no rest, keeping up a continual sharp-shooting. Early in the morning of the 14th he made a demonstration of assault with three of his regiments, and though he purposely withdrew them, he kept the menace standing, to the great discomfort of his *vis-à-vis.* With the patience of an old soldier, he waited the pleasure of the general commanding, knowing that when the time came he would be called upon. During the battle of the gunboats he rode through his command and grimly joked with them. He who never permitted the slightest familiarity from a subordinate, could yet indulge in fatherly pleasantries with the ranks when he thought circumstances justified them. He never for a moment doubted the courage of volunteers; they were not regulars—that was all. If properly led, he believed they would storm the gates of his Satanic Majesty. Their hour of trial was now come.

From his brief and characteristic conference with McClernand and myself, General Grant rode to General C. F. Smith. What took place between them is not known, further than that he ordered an assault upon the outworks as a diversion in aid of the assault about to be delivered on the right. General Smith personally directed his chiefs of brigade to get their regiments ready. Colonel John Cook by his order increased the number of his skirmishers already engaged with the enemy.

Taking Lauman's brigade, General Smith began the advance. They were under fire instantly. The guns in the fort joined in with the infantry who were at the time in the rifle-pits, the great body of the Confederate right wing being with General Buckner. The defense was greatly favored by the ground, which subjected the assailants to a double fire from the beginning of the abatis. The men have said that "it looked too thick for a rabbit to get through." General Smith, on his horse, took position in the front and center of the line. Occasionally he turned in the saddle to see how the alignment was kept. For the most part, however, he held his face steadily toward the enemy. He was, of course, a conspicuous object for the sharp-shooters in the rifle-pits. The air around him twittered with minie-bullets. Erect as if on review, he rode on, timing the gait of his horse with the movement of his colors. A soldier said: "I was nearly scared to death, but I saw the old man's white mustache over his shoulder, and went on."

On to the abatis the regiments moved without hesitation, leaving a trail of dead and wounded behind. There the fire seemed to get trebly hot, and there some of the men halted, whereupon, seeing the hesitation, General Smith put his cap on the point of his sword, held it aloft, and called out, "No flinching now, my lads?—Here—this is the way! Come on!" He picked a path through the jagged limbs of the trees, holding his cap all the time in sight; and the effect was magical. The men swarmed in after him, and got through in the best order they could—not all of them, alas! On the other side of the obstruction they took the semblance of re-formation and charged in after their chief, who found himself then between the two fires. Up the ascent he rode; up they followed. At the last moment the keepers of the rifle-pits clambered out and fled. The four regiments engaged in the feat—the 25th Indiana, and the 2d, 7th, and 14th Iowa—planted their colors on the breastwork. Later in the day, Buckner came back with his division; but all his efforts to dislodge Smith were vain.

We left my division about to attempt the recapture of the hill, which had been the scene of the combat between Pillow and McClernand. . . .

Riding to my old regiments—the 8th Missouri and the 11th Indiana—I asked them if they were ready. They demanded the word of me. Waiting a moment for Morgan L. Smith to light a cigar, I called out, "Forward it is, then!" They were directly in front of the ascent to be climbed. Without stopping for his supports, Colonel Smith led them down into a broad hollow, and catching sight of the advance, Cruft and Ross also moved forward. As the two regiments began the climb, the 8th Missouri slightly in the lead, a line of fire ran along the brow of the height. The flank companies cheered while deploying as skirmishers. Their Zouave practice proved of excellent service to them. Now on the ground, creeping when the fire was hottest, running when it slackened, they gained ground with astonishing rapidity, and at the same time maintained a fire that was like a sparkling of the earth. For the most part the bullets aimed at them passed over their heads and took effect in the ranks behind them. Colonel Smith's cigar was shot off close to his lips. He took another and called for a match. A soldier ran and gave him one. "Thank you. Take your place now. We are almost up," he said, and, smoking, spurred his horse forward. A few yards from the crest of the height the regiments began loading and firing as they advanced. The defenders gave way. On the top there was a brief struggle, which was ended by Cruft and Ross with their supports.

The whole line then moved forward simultaneously, and never stopped until the Confederates were within the works. There had been no occasion to call on the reserves. The road to Charlotte was again effectually shut, and the battle-field of the morning, with the dead and wounded lying where they had fallen, was in possession of the Third Division, which stood halted within easy musket-range of the rifle-pits. It was then about half-past 3 o'clock in the afternoon. I was reconnoitering the works of the enemy preliminary to charging them, when Colonel Webster, of General Grant's staff, came to me and repeated the order to fall back out of cannon range and throw up breastworks. "The general does not know that we have the hill," I said. Webster replied: "I give you the order as he gave it to me." "Very well," said I, "give him my compliments, and say that I have received the order." Webster smiled and rode away. The ground was not vacated, though the assault was deferred. In assuming the responsibility, I had no doubt of my ability to satisfy General Grant of the correctness of my course; and it was subsequently approved.

When night fell, the command bivouacked without fire or supper. Fatigue parties were told off to look after the wounded; and in the relief given there was no distinction made between friend and foe. The labor extended through the whole night, and the surgeons never rested. By sunset the conditions of the morning were all restored. The Union commander was free to order a general assault next day or resort to a formal siege.

A great discouragement fell upon the brave men inside the works that night. Besides suffering from wounds and bruises and the dreadful weather, they were aware that though they had done their best they were held in a close grip by a superior enemy. A council of general and field officers was held at headquarters, which resulted in a unanimous resolution that if the position in front of General Pillow had not been reoccupied by the Federals in strength, the army should effect its retreat. A reconnoissance was ordered to make the test. Colonel Forrest conducted it. He reported that the ground was not only reoccupied, but that the enemy were extended yet farther around the Confederate left. The council then held a final session.

General Simon B. Buckner, as the junior officer present, gave his opinion first; he thought he could not successfully resist the assault which would be made by daylight by a vastly superior force. But he further remarked, that as he understood the principal object of the defense of Donelson was to cover the movement of General Albert Sidney Johnston's army from Bowling Green to Nashville, if that movement was not completed he was of opinion that the defense should be continued at the risk of the destruction of the entire force. General Floyd replied that General Johnston's army had already reached Nashville, whereupon General Buckner said that "it would be wrong to subject the army to a virtual massacre, when no good could result from the sacrifice, and that the general officers owed it to their men, when further resistance was unavailing, to obtain the best terms of capitulation possible for them."

Both Generals Floyd and Pillow acquiesced in the opinion. Ordinarily the council would have ended at this point, and the commanding general would have addressed himself to the duty of obtaining terms. He would have called for pen, ink, and paper, and prepared a note for dispatch to the commanding general of the opposite force. But there were circumstances outside the mere military situation which at this juncture pressed themselves into consideration. As this was the first surrender of armed men banded together for war upon the general government, what would the Federal authorities do with the prisoners? This question was of application to all the gentlemen in the council. It was lost to view, however, when General Floyd announced his purpose to leave with two steamers which were to be down at daylight, and to take with him as many of his division as the steamers could carry away.

General Pillow then remarked that there were no two persons in the Confederacy whom the Yankees would rather capture than himself and General Floyd (who had been Buchanan's Secretary of War, and was under indictment at Washington). As to the propriety of his accompanying General Floyd, the latter said, coolly, that the question was one for every man to decide for himself. Buckner was of the same view, and added that as for himself he regarded it as his duty to stay with his men and share their fate, whatever it might be. Pillow persisted in leaving. Floyd then directed General Buckner to consider himself in command. Immediately after the council was concluded, General Floyd prepared for his departure. His first move was to have his brigade drawn up. The peculiarity of the step was that, with the exception of one, the 20th Mississippi regiment, his regiments were all

Virginians. A short time before daylight the two steamboats arrived. Without loss of time the general hastened to the river, embarked with his Virginians, and at an early hour cast loose from the shore, and in good time, and safely, he reached Nashville. He never satisfactorily explained upon what principle he appropriated all the transportation on hand to the use of his particular command.

Colonel Forrest was present at the council, and when the final resolution was taken, he promptly announced that he neither could nor would surrender his command. The bold trooper had no qualms upon the subject. He assembled his men, all as hardy as himself, and after reporting once more at headquarters, he moved out and plunged into a slough formed by backwater from the river. An icy crust covered its surface, the wind blew fiercely, and the darkness was unrelieved by a star. There was fearful floundering as the command followed him. At length he struck dry land, and was safe. He was next heard of at Nashville.

General Buckner, who throughout the affair bore himself with dignity, ordered the troops back to their positions and opened communications with General Grant, whose laconic demand of "unconditional surrender," in his reply to General Buckner's overtures, became at once a watchword of the war.

The Third Division was astir very early on the 16th of February. The regiments began to form and close up the intervals between them, the intention being to charge the breastworks south of Dover about breakfast-time. In the midst of the preparation a bugle was heard and a white flag was seen coming from the town toward the pickets. I sent my adjutant-general to meet the flag half-way and inquire its purpose. Answer was returned that General Buckner had capitulated during the night, and was now sending information of the fact to the commander of the troops in this quarter, that there might be no further bloodshed. The division was ordered to advance and take possession of the works and of all public property and prisoners. . . .

I found General Buckner with his staff at breakfast. He met me with politeness and dignity. Turning to the officers at the table, he remarked: "General Wallace, it is not necessary to introduce you to these gentlemen; you are acquainted with them all." They arose, came forward one by one, and gave their hands in salutation. I was then invited to breakfast, which consisted of corn bread and coffee, the best the gallant host had in his kitchen. We sat at the table about an hour and a half, when General Grant arrived and took temporary possession of the tavern as his headquarters. Later in the morning the army marched in and completed the possession.

General Albert Sidney Johnston, in command of the Confederacy's armies west of the Alleghanies (except the Gulf Coast), was the very beau ideal of a soldier. Physically imposing, stainless in character, with an enviable record in the cavalry of the old army, he was the South's acknowledged best before Shiloh. But after Donelson fell, even he had no alternative but to leave Nashville to the Federals under Don Carlos Buell and retreat into Mississippi. Grant's army pushed into Tennessee and Johnston marched again to check him. They met, somewhat to Grant's surprise, near Shiloh Church at Pittsburg Landing. In one of the great battles of the war, and with timely reinforcements from Buell, Grant turned an apparent Sunday defeat into a Monday victory, driving the Confederates back into Mississippi. They retreated under Beauregard, for Johnston had been killed the first day, another serious blow to the hopes of the South. In her inimitable diary, when she heard the news, Mrs. Mary Chesnut wrote, "There is grief enough for Albert Sidney Johnston now. We begin to see what we have lost. We were pushing them in the river when he was wounded. Without him there is no head to our western army."

"Regiments broke at the first fire"

THE BATTLE OF SHILOH

BY ULYSSES S. GRANT, GENERAL, U. S. A.

THE BATTLE of Shiloh, or Pittsburg Landing, fought on Sunday and Monday, the 6th and 7th of April, 1862, has been perhaps less understood, or, to state the case more accurately, more persistently misunderstood, than any other engagement between National and Confederate troops during the entire rebellion. Correct reports of the battle have been published, notably by Sherman, Badeau, and, in a speech before a meeting of veterans, by General Prentiss; but all of these appeared long subsequent to the close of the rebellion, and after public opinion had been most erroneously formed.

Events had occurred before the battle, and others subsequent to it, which determined me to make no report to my then chief, General Halleck, further than was contained in a letter, written immediately after the battle, informing him that an engagement had been fought, and announcing the result. The occurrences alluded to are these: After the capture of Fort Donelson, with over fifteen thousand effective men and all their munitions of war, I believed much more could be accomplished without further sacrifice of life.

Clarksville, a town between Donelson and Nashville, in the State of Tennessee, and on the east bank of the Cumberland, was garrisoned by the enemy. Nashville was also garrisoned, and was probably the best-provisioned depot at the time in the Confederacy. Albert Sidney Johnston occupied Bowling Green, Ky., with a large force. I believed, and my information justified the belief, that these places would fall into our hands without a battle, if threatened promptly. I determined not to miss this chance. But being only a district commander, and under the immediate orders of the department commander, General Halleck, whose headquarters were at St. Louis, it was my duty to communicate to him all I proposed to do, and to get his approval, if possible. I did so communicate, and, receiving no reply, acted upon my own judgment. The result proved that my information was correct, and sustained my judgment. What, then, was my surprise, after so much had been accomplished by the troops under my immediate command between the time of leaving Cairo, early in February, and the 4th of March, to receive from my chief a dispatch of the latter date, saying: "You will place Major-General C. F. Smith in command of expedition, and remain yourself at Fort Henry. Why do you not obey my orders to report strength and positions of your command?" I was left virtually in arrest on board a steamer, without even a guard, for about a week, when I was released and ordered to resume my command.

Again: Shortly after the battle of Shiloh had been fought, General Halleck moved his headquarters to Pittsburg Landing, and assumed command of the troops in the field. Although next to him in rank, and nominally in command of my old district and army, I was ignored as much as if I had been at the most distant point of territory within my jurisdiction; and although I was in command of all the troops engaged at Shiloh, I was not permitted to see one of the reports of General Buell or his subordinates in that battle, until they were published by the War Department, long after the event. In consequence, I never myself made a full report of this engagement.

When I was restored to my command, on the 13th of March, I found it on the Tennessee River, part at Savannah and part at Pittsburg Landing, nine miles above, and on the opposite or western bank. I generally spent the day at Pittsburg, and returned by boat to Savannah in the evening. I was intending to remove my headquarters to Pittsburg, where I had sent all the troops immediately upon my reassuming command, but Buell, with the Army of the Ohio, had been ordered to reënforce me from Columbia, Tenn. He was expected daily, and would come in at Savannah. I remained, therefore, a few days longer than I otherwise should have done, for the purpose of meeting him on his arrival.

General Lew Wallace, with a division, had been placed by General Smith at Crump's Landing, about five miles farther down the river than Pittsburg, and also on the west bank. His position I regarded as so well chosen that he was not moved from it until the Confederate attack in force at Shiloh.

The skirmishing in our front had been so continuous from about the 3d of April up to the determined attack, that I remained on the field each night until an hour when I felt there would be no further danger before morning. In fact, on Friday, the 4th, I was very much injured by my horse falling with me and on me while I was trying to get to the front, where firing had been heard. The night was one of impenetrable darkness, with rain pouring down in torrents; nothing was visible to the eye except as revealed by the frequent flashes of lightning. Under these circumstances I had to trust to the horse, without guidance, to keep the road. I had not gone far, however, when I met General W. H. L. Wallace and General (then Colonel) McPherson coming from the direction of the front. They said all was quiet so far as the enemy was concerned. On the way back to the boat my horse's feet slipped from under him, and he fell with my leg under his body. The extreme softness of the ground, from the excessive rains of the few preceding days, no doubt saved me from a severe injury and protracted lameness. As it was, my ankle was very much injured; so much so, that my boot had to be cut off. During the battle, and for two or three days after, I was unable to walk except with crutches.

On the 5th General Nelson, with a division of Buell's army, arrived at Savannah, and I ordered him to move up the east bank of the river, to be in a position where he could be ferried over to Crump's Landing or Pittsburg Landing, as occasion required. I had learned that General Buell himself would be at Savannah the next day, and desired to meet me on his arrival. Affairs at Pittsburg Landing had been such for several days that I did not want to be away during the day. I determined, therefore, to take a very early breakfast and ride out to meet Buell, and thus save time. He had arrived on the evening of the 5th, but had not advised me of the fact, and I was not aware of it until some time after. While I was at breakfast, however, heavy firing was heard in the direction of Pittsburg Landing, and I hastened there, sending a hurried note to Buell, informing him of the reason why I could not meet him at Savannah. On the way up the river I directed the dispatch boat to run in close to Crump's Landing, so that I could communicate with General Lew Wallace. I found him waiting on a boat, apparently expecting to see me, and I directed him to get his troops in line ready to execute any orders he might receive. He replied that his troops were already under arms and prepared to move.

Up to that time I had felt by no means certain that Crump's Landing might not be the point of attack. On reaching the front, however, about 8 A. M., I found that the attack on Shiloh was unmistakable, and that nothing more than a small guard, to protect our transports and stores, was needed at

Crump's. Captain A. S. Baxter, a quartermaster on my staff, was accordingly directed to go back and order General Wallace to march immediately to Pittsburg, by the road nearest the river. Captain Baxter made a memorandum of his order. About 1 P. M., not hearing from Wallace, and being much in need of reënforcements, I sent two more of my staff, Colonel James B. McPherson and Captain W. R. Rowley, to bring him up with his division. . . .

Shiloh was a log meeting-house, some two or three miles from Pittsburg Landing, and on the ridge which divides the waters of Snake and Lick creeks, the former entering into the Tennessee just north of Pittsburg Landing, and the latter south. Shiloh was the key to our position, and was held by Sherman. His division was at that time wholly raw, no part of it ever having been in an engagement, but I thought this deficiency was more than made up by the superiority of the commander. McClernand was on Sherman's left, with troops that had been engaged at Fort Donelson, and were therefore veterans so far as Western troops had become such at that stage of the war. Next to McClernand came Prentiss, with a raw division, and on the extreme left, Stuart, with one brigade of Sherman's division. Hurlbut was in rear of Prentiss, massed, and in reserve at the time of the onset. The division of General C. F. Smith was on the right, also in reserve. General Smith was sick in bed at Savannah, some nine miles below, but in hearing of our guns. His services on those two eventful days would no doubt have been of inestimable value had his health permitted his presence. The command of his division devolved upon Brigadier-General W. H. L. Wallace, a most estimable and able officer —a veteran, too, for he had served a year in the Mexican war, and had been with his command at Henry and Donelson. Wallace was mortally wounded in the first day's engagement, and with the change of commanders thus necessarily effected in the heat of battle, the efficiency of his division was much weakened.

The position of our troops made a continuous line from Lick Creek, on the left, to Owl Creek, a branch of Snake Creek, on the right, facing nearly south, and possibly a little west. The water in all these streams was very high at the time, and contributed to protect our flanks. The enemy was compelled, therefore, to attack directly in front. This he did with great vigor, inflicting heavy losses on the National side, but suffering much heavier on his own.

The Confederate assaults were made with such disregard of losses on their own side, that our line of tents soon fell into their hands. The ground on which the battle was fought was undulating, heavily timbered, with scattered clearings, the woods giving some protection to the troops on both sides. There was also considerable underbrush. A number of attempts were made by the enemy to turn our right flank, where Sherman was posted, but every effort was repulsed with heavy loss. But the front attack was kept up so vigorously that, to prevent the success of these attempts to get on our flanks, the National troops were compelled several times to take positions to the rear, nearer Pittsburg Landing. When the firing ceased at night, the National line was all of a mile in rear of the position it had occupied in the morning.

In one of the backward moves, on the 6th, the division commanded by General Prentiss did not fall back with the others. This left his flanks exposed, and enabled the enemy to capture him, with about 2200 of his officers and men. General Badeau gives 4 o'clock of the 6th as about the time this capture took place. He may be right as to the time, but my recollection is that the hour was later. General Prentiss himself gave the hour as half-past five. I was with him, as I was with each of the division commanders that day, several times, and my recollection is that the last time I was with him was about half-past four, when his division was standing up firmly, and the general was as cool as if expecting victory. But no matter whether it was four or later, the story that he and his command were surprised and captured in their camps is without any foundation whatever. If it had been true, as currently reported at the time, and yet believed by thousands of people, that Prentiss and his division had been captured in their beds, there would not have been an all-day struggle with the loss of thousands killed and wounded on the Confederate side.

With the single exception of a few minutes after the capture of Prentiss, a continuous and unbroken line was maintained all day from Snake Creek or its tributaries on the right to Lick Creek or the Tennessee on the left, above Pittsburg. There was no hour during the day when there was not heavy firing and generally hard fighting at some point on the line, but seldom at all points at the same time. It was a case of Southern dash against Northern pluck and endurance.

Three of the five divisions engaged on Sunday were entirely raw, and many of the men had only received their arms on the way from their States to the field. Many of them had arrived but a day or two before, and were hardly able to load their muskets according to the manual. Their officers were equally ignorant of their duties. Under these circumstances, it is not astonishing that many of the regiments broke at the first fire. In two cases, as I now remember, colonels led their regiments from the field on first hearing the whistle of the enemy's bullets. In these cases the colonels were constitutional cowards, unfit for any military position. But not so the officers and men led out of danger by them. Better troops never went upon a battle-field than many of these officers and men afterward proved themselves to be who fled panic-stricken at the first whistle of bullets and shell at Shiloh.

During the whole of Sunday I was continuously engaged in passing from one part of the field to another, giving directions to division commanders. In thus moving along the line, however, I never deemed it important to stay long with Sherman. Although his troops were then under fire for the first time, their commander, by his constant presence with them, inspired a confidence in officers and men that enabled them to render services on that bloody battle-field worthy of the best of veterans. McClernand was next to Sherman, and the hardest fighting was in front of these two divisions. Mc-Clernand told me on that day, the 6th, that he profited much by having so able a commander supporting him. A casualty to Sherman that would have taken him from the field that day would have been a sad one for the troops engaged at Shiloh. And how near we came to this! On the 6th Sherman was shot twice, once in the hand, once in the shoulder, the ball cutting his coat and making a slight wound, and a third ball passed through his hat. In addition to this he had several horses shot during the day.

The nature of this battle was such that cavalry could not be used in front; I therefore formed ours into line, in rear, to stop stragglers, of whom there were many. When there would be enough of them to make a show, and after they had recovered from their fright, they would be sent to reënforce some part of the line which needed support, without regard to their companies, regiments, or brigades. . . .

The situation at the close of Sunday was as follows: Along the top of the bluff just south of the log-house which stood at Pittsburg Landing, Colonel J. D. Webster, of my staff, had arranged twenty or more pieces of artillery facing south, or up the river. This line of artillery was on the crest of a hill overlooking a deep ravine opening into the Tennessee. Hurlbut, with his division intact, was on the right of this artillery, extending west and possibly a little north. McClernand came next in the general line, looking more to the west. His division was complete in its organization and ready for any duty. Sherman came next, his right extending to Snake Creek. His command, like the other two, was complete in its organization and ready, like its chief, for any service it might be called upon to render. All three divisions were, as a matter of course, more or less shattered and depleted in numbers from the terrible battle of the day. The division of W. H. L. Wallace, as much from the disorder arising from changes of division and brigade commanders, under heavy fire, as from any other cause, had lost its organization, and did not occupy a place in the line as a division; Prentiss's command was gone as a division, many of its members having been killed, wounded, or captured. But it had rendered valiant service before its final dispersal, and had contributed a good share to the defense of Shiloh.

There was, I have said, a deep ravine in front of our left. The Tennessee River was very high, and there was water to a considerable depth in the ravine. Here the enemy made a last desperate effort to turn our flank, but was repelled. The gun-boats *Tyler* and *Lexington,* Gwin and Shirk commanding, with the artillery under Webster, aided the army and effectually checked their further progress. Before any of Buell's troops had reached the west bank of the Tennessee, firing had almost entirely ceased; anything like an attempt on the part of the enemy to advance had absolutely ceased. There was some artillery firing from an unseen enemy, some of his shells passing beyond us; but I do not remember that there was the whistle of a single musket-ball heard.

As his troops arrived in the dusk, General Buell marched several of his regiments part way down the face of the hill, where they fired briskly for some minutes, but I do not think a single man engaged in this firing received an injury; the attack had spent its force.

General Lew Wallace, with 5000 effective men, arrived after firing had ceased for the day, and was placed on the right. Thus night came, Wallace came, and the advance of Nelson's division came, but none—unless night—in time to be of material service to the gallant men who saved Shiloh on that first day, against large odds. Buell's loss on the 6th of April was two men killed and one wounded, all members of the 36th Indiana Infantry. The Army of the Tennessee lost on that day at least 7000 men. The presence of two or three regiments of his army on the west bank before firing ceased had not the slightest effect in preventing the capture of Pittsburg Landing.

So confident was I before firing had ceased on the 6th that the next day would bring victory to our arms if we could only take the initiative, that I visited each division commander in person before any reënforcements had reached the field. I directed them to throw out heavy lines of skirmishers in the morning as soon as they could see, and push them forward until they found the enemy, following with their entire divisions in supporting distance, and to engage the enemy as soon as found. To Sherman I told the story of the assault at Fort Donelson, and said that the same tactics would win at Shiloh. Victory was assured when Wallace arrived even if there had been no other support. The enemy received no reënforcements. He had suffered heavy losses in killed, wounded, and straggling, and his commander, General Albert Sidney Johnston, was dead. I was glad, however, to see the reënforcements of Buell and credit them with doing all there was for them to do. During the night of the 6th the remainder of Nelson's division, Buell's army, crossed the river, and were ready to advance in the morning, forming the left wing. Two other divisions, Crittenden's and McCook's, came up the river from Savannah in the transports, and were on the west bank early on the 7th. Buell commanded them in person. My command was thus nearly doubled in numbers and efficiency.

During the night rain fell in torrents, and our troops were exposed to the storm without shelter. I made my headquarters under a tree a few hundred yards back from the river-bank. My ankle was so much swollen from the fall of my horse the Friday night preceding, and the bruise was so painful, that I could get no rest. The drenching rain would have precluded the possibility of sleep, without this additional cause. Some time after midnight, growing restive under the storm and the continuous pain, I moved back to the log-house on the bank. This had been taken as a hospital, and all night wounded men were being brought in, their wounds dressed, a leg or an arm amputated, as the case might require, and everything being done to save life or alleviate suffering. The sight was more unendurable than encountering the enemy's fire, and I returned to my tree in the rain.

89

The advance on the morning of the 7th developed the enemy in the camps occupied by our troops before the battle began, more than a mile back from the most advanced position of the Confederates on the day before. It is known now that they had not yet learned of the arrival of Buell's command. Possibly they fell back so far to get the shelter of our tents during the rain, and also to get away from the shells that were dropped upon them by the gun-boats every fifteen minutes during the night.

The position of the Union troops on the morning of the 7th was as follows: General Lew Wallace on the right, Sherman on his left; then McClernand, and then Hurlbut. Nelson, of Buell's army, was on our extreme left, next to the river; Crittenden was next in line after Nelson, and on his right; McCook followed, and formed the extreme right of Buell's command. My old command thus formed the right wing, while the troops directly under Buell constituted the left wing of the army. These relative positions were retained during the entire day, or until the enemy was driven from the field.

In a very short time the battle became general all along the line. This day everything was favorable to the Federal side. We had now become the attacking party. The enemy was driven back all day, as we had been the day before, until finally he beat a precipitate retreat. The last point held by him was near the road leading from the landing to Corinth, on the left of Sherman and right of McClernand. About 3 o'clock, being near that point and seeing that the enemy was giving way everywhere else, I gathered up a couple of regiments, or parts of regiments, from troops near by, formed them in line of battle and marched them forward, going in front myself to prevent premature or long-range firing. At this point there was a clearing between us and the enemy favorable for charging, although exposed. I knew the enemy were ready to break, and only wanted a little encouragement from us to go quickly and join their friends who had started earlier. After marching to within musket-range, I stopped and let the troops pass. The command, *Charge,* was given, and was executed with loud cheers, and with a run, when the last of the enemy broke. . . .

After the rain of the night before and the frequent and heavy rains for some days previous, the roads were almost impassable. The enemy, carrying his artillery and supply trains over them in his retreat, made them still worse for troops following. I wanted to pursue, but had not the heart to order the men who had fought desperately for two days, lying in the mud and rain whenever not fighting, and I did not feel disposed positively to order Buell, or any part of his command, to pursue. Although the senior in rank at the time, I had been so only a few weeks. Buell was, and had been for some time past, a department commander, while I commanded only a district. I did not meet Buell in person until too late to get troops ready and pursue with effect; but, had I seen him at the moment of the last charge, I should have at least requested him to follow. . . .

Shiloh was the severest battle fought at the West during the war, and but few in the East equaled it for hard, determined fighting. I saw an open field, in our possession on the second day, over which the Confederates had made repeated charges the day before, so covered with dead that it would have been possible to walk across the clearing, in any direction, stepping on dead bodies, without a foot touching the ground. On our side National and Confederate were mingled together in about equal proportions; but on the remainder of the field nearly all were Confederates. On one part, which had evidently not been plowed for several years, probably because the land was poor, bushes had grown up, some to the height of eight or ten feet. There was not one of these left standing unpierced by bullets. The smaller ones were all cut down.

Contrary to all my experience up to that time, and to the experience of the army I was then commanding, we were on the defensive. We were without intrenchments or defensive advantages of any sort, and more than half the army engaged the first day was without experience or even drill as soldiers. The officers with them, except the division commanders, and possibly two or three of the brigade commanders, were equally inexperienced in war. The result was a Union victory that gave the men who achieved it great confidence in themselves ever after.

The enemy fought bravely, but they had started out to defeat and destroy an army and capture a position. They failed in both, with very heavy loss in killed and wounded, and must have gone back discouraged and convinced that the "Yankee" was not an enemy to be despised.

After the battle I gave verbal instructions to division commanders to let the regiments send out parties to bury their own dead, and to detail parties, under commissioned officers from each division, to bury the Confederate dead in their respective fronts, and to report the numbers so buried. The latter part of these instructions was not carried out by all; but they were by those sent from Sherman's division, and by some of the parties sent out by McClernand. The heaviest loss sustained by the enemy was in front of these two divisions.

The criticism has often been made that the Union troops should have been intrenched at Shiloh; but up to that time the pick and spade had been but little resorted to at the West. I had, however, taken this subject under consideration soon after reassuming command in the field. McPherson, my only military engineer, had been directed to lay out a line to intrench. He did so, but reported that it would have to be made in rear of the line of encampment as it then ran. The new line, while it would be nearer the river, was yet too far away from the Tennessee, or even from the creeks, to be easily supplied with water from them; and in case of attack, these creeks would be in the hands of the enemy. Besides this, the troops with me, officers and men, needed discipline and drill more than they did experience with the pick, shovel, and axe. Reënforcements were arriving almost daily, composed of troops that had been hastily thrown together into companies and regiments —fragments of incomplete organizations, the men and officers strangers to each other. Under all these circumstances I concluded that drill and discipline were worth more to our men than fortifications. . . .

General Albert Sidney Johnston, who commanded the Confederate forces at the beginning of the battle, was disabled by a wound in the afternoon of the first day. His wound, as I understood afterward, was not necessarily fatal, or even dangerous. But he was a man who would not abandon what he deemed an important trust in the face of danger, and consequently continued in the saddle, commanding, until so exhausted by the loss of blood that he had to be taken from his horse, and soon after died. The news was not long in reaching our side, and, I suppose, was quite an encouragement to the National soldiers. I had known Johnston slightly in the Mexican war, and later as an officer in the regular army. He was a man of high character and ability. His contemporaries at West Point, and officers generally who came to know him personally later, and who remained on our side, expected him to prove the most formidable man to meet that the Confederacy would produce. Nothing occurred in his brief command of an army to prove or disprove the high estimate that had been placed upon his military ability.

General Beauregard was next in rank to Johnston, and succeeded to the command, which he retained to the close of the battle and during the subsequent retreat on Corinth, as well as in the siege of that place. His tactics have been severely criticised by Confederate writers, but I do not believe his fallen chief could have done any better under the circumstances. Some of these critics claim that Shiloh was won when Johnston fell, and that if he had not fallen the army under me would have been annihilated or captured. *Ifs* defeated the Confederates at Shiloh. There is little doubt that we would have been disgracefully beaten *if* all the shells and bullets fired by us had passed harmlessly over the enemy, and *if* all of theirs had taken effect. Commanding generals are liable to be killed during engagements; and the fact that when he was shot Johnston was leading a brigade to induce it to make a charge which had been repeatedly ordered, is evidence that there was neither the universal demoralization on our side nor the unbounded confidence on theirs which has been claimed. There was, in fact, no hour during the day when I doubted the eventual defeat of the enemy, although I was disappointed that reënforcements so near at hand did not arrive at an earlier hour.

The Confederates fought with courage at Shiloh, but the particular skill claimed I could not, and still cannot, see; though there is nothing to criticise except the claims put forward for it since. But the Confederate claimants for superiority in strategy, superiority in generalship, and superiority in dash and prowess are not so unjust to the Union troops engaged at Shiloh as are many Northern writers. The troops on both sides were American, and united they need not fear any foreign foe. It is possible that the Southern man started in with a little more dash than his Northern brother; but he was correspondingly less enduring.

The endeavor of the enemy on the first day was simply to hurl their men against ours—first at one point, then at another, sometimes at several points at once. This they did with daring and energy, until at night the rebel troops were worn out. Our effort during the same time was to be prepared to resist assaults wherever made. The object of the Confederates on the second day was to get away with as much of their army and material as possible. Ours then was to drive them from our front, and to capture or destroy as great a part as possible of their men and material. We were successful in driving them back, but not so successful in captures as if further pursuit could have been made. As it was, we captured or recaptured on the second day about as much artillery as we lost on the first; and, leaving out the one great capture of Prentiss, we took more prisoners on Monday than the enemy gained from us on Sunday. On the 6th Sherman lost 7 pieces of artillery, McClernand 6, Prentiss 8, and Hurlbut 2 batteries. On the 7th Sherman captured 7 guns, McClernand 3, and the Army of the Ohio 20.

At Shiloh the effective strength of the Union force on the morning of the 6th was 33,000. Lew Wallace brought five thousand more after nightfall. Beauregard reported the enemy's strength at 40,955. According to the custom of enumeration in the South, this number probably excluded every man enlisted as musician, or detailed as guard or nurse, and all commissioned officers—everybody who did not carry a musket or serve a cannon. With us everybody in the field receiving pay from the Government is counted. Excluding the troops who fled, panic-stricken, before they had fired a shot, there was not a time during the 6th when we had more than 25,000 men in line. On the 7th Buell brought twenty thousand more. Of his remaining two divisions, Thomas's did not reach the field during the engagement; Wood's arrived before firing had ceased, but not in time to be of much service.

Our loss in the two-days fight was 1754 killed, 8408 wounded, and 2885 missing. Of these 2103 were in the Army of the Ohio. Beauregard reported a total loss of 10,699, of whom 1728 were killed, 8012 wounded, and 959 missing. This estimate must be incorrect. We buried, by actual count, more of the enemy's dead in front of the divisions of McClernand and Sherman alone than here reported, and four thousand was the estimate of the burial parties for the whole field. Beauregard reports the Confederate force on the 6th at over 40,000, and their total loss during the two days at 10,699; and at the same time declares that he could put only 20,000 men in battle on the morning of the 7th.

The navy gave a hearty support to the army at Shiloh, as indeed it always did, both before and subsequently, when I was in command. The nature of the ground was such, however, that on this occasion it could do nothing in

93

aid of the troops until sundown on the first day. The country was broken and heavily timbered, cutting off all view of the battle from the river, so that friends would be as much in danger from fire from the gun-boats as the foe. But about sundown, when the National troops were back in their last position, the right of the enemy was near the river and exposed to the fire of the two gun-boats, which was delivered with vigor and effect. After nightfall, when firing had entirely ceased on land, the commander of the fleet informed himself, proximately, of the position of our troops, and suggested the idea of dropping a shell within the lines of the enemy every fifteen minutes during the night. This was done with effect, as is proved by the Confederate reports.

Up to the battle of Shiloh, I, as well as thousands of other citizens, believed that the rebellion against the Government would collapse suddenly and soon if a decisive victory could be gained over any of its armies. Henry and Donelson were such victories. An army of more than 21,000 men was captured or destroyed. Bowling Green, Columbus, and Hickman, Ky., fell in consequence, and Clarksville and Nashville, Tenn., the last two with an immense amount of stores, also fell into our hands. The Tennessee and Cumberland rivers, from their mouths to the head of navigation, were secured. But when Confederate armies were collected which not only attempted to hold a line farther south, from Memphis to Chattanooga, Knoxville and on to the Atlantic, but assumed the offensive, and made such a gallant effort to regain what had been lost, then, indeed, I gave up all idea of saving the Union except by complete conquest. Up to that time it had been the policy of our army, certainly of that portion commanded by me, to protect the property of the citizens whose territory was invaded, without regard to their sentiments, whether Union or Secession. After this, however, I regarded it as humane to both sides to protect the persons of those found at their homes but to consume everything that could be used to support or supply armies. Protection was still continued over such supplies as were within lines held by us, and which we expected to continue to hold. But such supplies within the reach of Confederate armies I regarded as contraband as much as arms or ordnance stores. Their destruction was accomplished without bloodshed, and tended to the same result as the destruction of armies. I continued this policy to the close of the war. Promiscuous pillaging, however, was discouraged and punished. Instructions were always given to take provisions and forage under the direction of commissioned officers, who should give receipts to owners, if at home, and turn the property over to officers of the quartermaster or commissary departments, to be issued as if furnished from our Northern depots. But much was destroyed without receipts to owners when it could not be brought within our lines, and would otherwise have gone to the support of secession and rebellion. This policy, I believe, exercised a material influence in hastening the end.

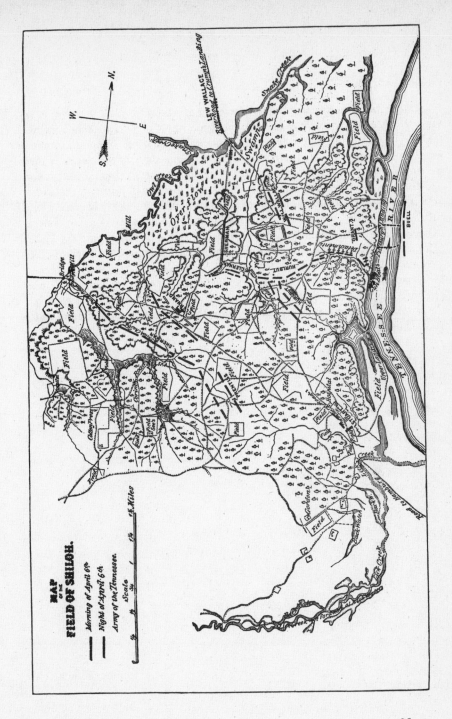

95

In three and a half hours on the afternoon of March 8, 1862, every navy in the world became obsolete. The instrument was the Confederate ship Virginia *(the old frigate* Merrimac *rebuilt with four inches of armor plate all around) which in Hampton Roads destroyed two U.S. Navy ships of the line as if they were toy boats in a washtub and caused three others to run aground. But action and reaction. The next day when the* Virginia *moved out to finish off the Union vessels, she was confronted by John Ericsson's* Monitor—*the "cheesebox on a raft," the "tin can on a shingle"—which had arrived from the north in the tow of a tug during the night. The engagement that ensued lasted some six hours. Militarily it was a draw; but it blighted the South's hopes that* Virginia *and later similar craft would break the Northern blockade that was slowly strangling her economy and depriving her armies of the means of making war. She desperately needed salt, niter, quinine, and a long list of vital materials, but once again the promise of them was snatched away by the superior mechanical ingenuity of the Yankees.*

"The battle was a drawn one"

THE FIRST FIGHT OF IRON-CLADS

BY JOHN TAYLOR WOOD, COLONEL, C. S. A.

THE engagement in Hampton Roads on the 8th of March, 1862, between the Confederate iron-clad *Virginia,* or the *Merrimac* (as she is
known at the North), and the United States wooden fleet, and that on
the 9th between the *Virginia* and the *Monitor,* was, in its results, in some respects the most momentous naval conflict ever witnessed. No battle was ever
more widely discussed or produced a greater sensation. It revolutionized the
navies of the world. Line-of-battle ships, those huge, overgrown craft, carrying from eighty to one hundred and twenty guns and from five hundred to

97

twelve hundred men, which, from the destruction of the Spanish Armada to our time, had done most of the fighting, deciding the fate of empires, were at once universally condemned as out of date. Rams and iron-clads were in future to decide all naval warfare. In this battle old things passed away, and the experience of a thousand years of battle and breeze was forgotten. The naval supremacy of England vanished in the smoke of this fight, it is true, only to reappear some years later more commanding than ever. The effect of the news was best described by the London "Times," which said: "Whereas we had available for immediate purposes one hundred and forty-nine first-class war-ships, we have now two, these two being the *Warrior* and her sister *Ironside.* There is not now a ship in the English navy apart from these two that it would not be madness to trust to an engagement with that little *Monitor.*" The Admiralty at once proceeded to reconstruct the navy, cutting down a number of their largest ships and converting them into turret or broadside iron-clads.

The same results were produced in France, which had but one sea-going iron-clad, *La Gloire,* and this one, like the *Warrior,* was only protected amidships. The Emperor Napoleon promptly appointed a commission to devise plans for rebuilding his navy. And so with all the maritime powers. In this race the United States took the lead, and at the close of the war led all the others in the numbers and efficiency of its iron-clad fleet. It is true that all the great powers had already experimented with vessels partly armored, but very few were convinced of their utility, and none had been tried by the test of battle, if we except a few floating batteries, thinly clad, used in the Crimean War.

In the spring of 1861 Norfolk and its large naval establishment had been hurriedly abandoned by the Federals, why no one could tell. It is about twelve miles from Fort Monroe, which was then held by a large force of regulars. A few companies of these, with a single frigate, could have occupied and commanded the town and navy yard and kept the channel open. However, a year later, it was as quickly evacuated by the Confederates, and almost with as little reason. But of this I will speak later.

The yard was abandoned to a few volunteers, after it was partly destroyed, and a large number of ships were burnt. Among the spoils were upward of twelve hundred heavy guns, which were scattered among Confederate fortifications from the Potomac to the Mississippi. Among the ships burnt and sunk was the frigate *Merrimac* of 3500 tons and 40 guns, afterward rechristened the *Virginia,* and so I will call her. During the summer of 1861 Lieutenant John M. Brooke, an accomplished officer of the old navy, who with many others had resigned, proposed to Secretary Mallory to raise and rebuild this ship as an iron-clad. His plans were approved, and orders were given to carry them out. She was raised and cut down to the old berth-deck. Both ends for seventy feet were covered over, and when the ship was in fighting trim were just awash. On the midship section, 170 feet in length, was built at an angle of

45 degrees a roof of pitch-pine and oak 24 inches thick, extending from the water-line to a height over the gun-deck of 7 feet. Both ends of the shield were rounded so that the pivot-guns could be used as bow and stern chasers or quartering. Over the gun-deck was a light grating, making a promenade about twenty feet wide. The wood backing was covered with iron plates, rolled at the Tredegar works, two inches thick and eight wide. The first tier was put on horizontally, the second up and down—in all to the thickness of four inches, bolted through the wood-work and clinched. The prow was of cast-iron, projecting four feet, and badly secured, as events proved. The rudder and propeller were entirely unprotected. The pilot-house was forward of the smoke-stack, and covered with the same thickness of iron as the sides. The motive power was the same that had always been in the ship. Both of the engines and boilers had been condemned on her return from her last cruise, and were radically defective. Of course, the fire and sinking had not improved them. We could not depend upon them for six hours at a time. A more ill-contrived or unreliable pair of engines could only have been found in some vessels of the United States navy.

Lieutenant Catesby ap R. Jones was ordered to superintend the armament, and no more thoroughly competent officer could have been selected. To his experience and skill as her ordnance and executive officer was due the character of her battery, which proved so efficient. It consisted of 2 7-inch rifles, heavily reënforced around the breech with 3-inch steel bands, shrunk on. These were the first heavy guns so made, and were the bow and stern pivots. There were also 2 6-inch rifles of the same make, and 6 9-inch smooth-bore broadside—10 guns in all.

During the summer and fall of 1861 I had been stationed at the batteries on the Potomac at Evansport and Aquia Creek, blockading the river as far as possible. In January, 1862, I was ordered to the *Virginia* as one of the lieutenants, reporting to Commodore French Forrest, who then commanded the navy yard at Norfolk. Commodore Franklin Buchanan was appointed to the command—an energetic and high-toned officer, who combined with daring courage great professional ability, standing deservedly at the head of his profession. In 1845 he had been selected by Mr. Bancroft, Secretary of the Navy, to locate and organize the Naval Academy, and he launched that institution upon its successful career. Under him were as capable a set of officers as ever were brought together in one ship. But of man-of-war's men or sailors we had scarcely any. The South was almost without a maritime population. In the old service the majority of officers were from the South, and all the seamen from the North.

Every one had flocked to the army, and to it we had to look for a crew. Some few seamen were found in Norfolk, who had escaped from the gunboat flotilla in the waters of North Carolina, on their occupation by Admiral Goldsborough and General Burnside. In hopes of securing some men from the army, I was sent to the headquarters of General Magruder at Yorktown, who was known to have under his command two battalions from New Orleans, among whom might be found a number of seamen. The general, though pressed for want of men, holding a long line with scarcely a brigade, gave me every facility to secure volunteers. With one of his staff I visited every camp, and the commanding officers were ordered to parade their men, and I explained to them what I wanted. About 200 volunteered, and of this number I selected 80 who had had some experience as seamen or gunners. Other commands at Richmond and Petersburg were visited, and so our crew of three hundred was made up. They proved themselves to be as gallant and trusty a body of men as any one would wish to command, not only in battle, but in reverse and retreat.

Notwithstanding every exertion to hasten the fitting out of the ship, the work during the winter progressed but slowly, owing to delay in sending the iron sheathing from Richmond. At this time the only establishment in the South capable of rolling iron plates was the Tredegar foundry. Its resources were limited, and the demand for all kinds of war material most pressing. And when we reflect upon the scarcity and inexperience of the workmen, and the great changes necessary in transforming an ordinary iron workshop into an arsenal in which all the machinery and tools had to be improvised, it is astonishing that so much was accomplished. The unfinished state of the vessel interfered so with the drills and exercises that we had but little opportunity of getting things into shape. It should be remembered that the ship was an experiment in naval architecture, differing in every respect from any then afloat. The officers and the crew were strangers to the ship and to each other. Up to the hour of sailing she was crowded with workmen. Not a gun had been fired, hardly a revolution of the engines had been made, when we cast off from the dock and started on what many thought was an ordinary trial trip, but which proved to be a trial such as no vessel that ever floated had undergone up to that time. From the start we saw that she was slow, not over five knots; she steered so badly that, with her great length, it took from thirty to forty minutes to turn. She drew twenty-two feet, which confined us to a comparatively narrow channel in the Roads; and, as I have before said, the engines were our weak point. She was as unmanageable as a water-logged vessel.

It was at noon on the 8th of March that we steamed down the Elizabeth River. Passing by our batteries, lined with troops, who cheered us as we passed, and through the obstructions at Craney Island, we took the south channel and headed for Newport News. At anchor at this time off Fort Monroe were the frigates *Minnesota, Roanoke,* and *St. Lawrence,* and several gunboats. The first two were sister ships of the *Virginia* before the war; the last was a sailing frigate of fifty guns. Off Newport News, seven miles above, which was strongly fortified and held by a large Federal garrison, were anchored the frigate *Congress,* 50 guns, and the sloop *Cumberland,* 30. The day was calm, and the last two ships were swinging lazily by their anchors. [The tide was at its height about 1:40 P. M.] Boats were hanging to the lower booms, washed clothes in the rigging. Nothing indicated that we were expected; but when we came within three-quarters of a mile, the boats were dropped astern, booms got alongside, and the *Cumberland* opened with her heavy pivots, followed by the *Congress,* the gun-boats, and the shore batteries.

We reserved our fire until within easy range, when the forward pivot was pointed and fired by Lieutenant Charles Simms, killing and wounding most of the crew of the after pivot-gun of the *Cumberland.* Passing close to the *Congress,* which received our starboard broadside, and returned it with spirit, we steered direct for the *Cumberland,* striking her almost at right angles, under the fore-rigging on the starboard side. The blow was hardly perceptible on board the *Virginia.* Backing clear of her, we went ahead again, heading up the river, helm hard-a-starboard, and turned slowly. As we did so, for the first time I had an opportunity of using the after-pivot, of which I had charge. As we swung, the *Congress* came in range, nearly stern on, and we got in three raking shells. She had slipped her anchor, loosed her foretop-sail, run up the jib, and tried to escape, but grounded. Turning, we headed for her and took a position within two hundred yards, where every shot told. In the meantime the *Cumberland* continued the fight, though our ram had opened her side wide enough to drive in a horse and cart. Soon she listed to port and filled rapidly. The crew were driven by the advancing water to the spar-deck, and there worked her pivot-guns until she went down with a roar, the colors still flying. No ship was ever fought more gallantly. The *Congress* continued the unequal contest for more than an hour after the sinking of the *Cumberland.* Her losses were terrible, and finally she ran up the white flag.

As soon as we had hove in sight, coming down the harbor, the *Roanoke, St. Lawrence,* and *Minnesota,* assisted by tugs, had got under way, and started up from Old Point Comfort to join their consorts. They were under fire from the batteries at Sewell's Point, but the distance was too great to effect much. The first two, however, ran aground not far above Fort Monroe, and took but little part in the fight. The *Minnesota,* taking the middle or swash channel, steamed up half-way between Old Point Comfort and Newport News, when she grounded, but in a position to be actively engaged.

Previous to this we had been joined by the James River squadron, which had been at anchor a few miles above, and came into action most gallantly, passing the shore batteries at Newport News under a heavy fire, and with some loss. It consisted of the *Yorktown* (or *Patrick Henry*), 12 guns, Captain John R. Tucker; *Jamestown,* 2 guns, Lieut.-Commander J. N. Barney; and *Teaser,* 1 gun, Lieut.-Commander W. A. Webb.

As soon as the *Congress* surrendered, Commander Buchanan ordered the gun-boats *Beaufort,* Lieut.-Commander W. H. Parker, and *Raleigh,* Lieut.-Commander J. W. Alexander, to steam alongside, take off her crew, and set fire to the ship. Lieutenant Pendergrast, who had succeeded Lieutenant Smith, who had been killed, surrendered to Lieutenant Parker, of the *Beaufort.* Delivering his sword and colors, he was directed by Lieutenant Parker to return to his ship and have the wounded transferred as rapidly as possible. All this time the shore batteries and small-arm men were keeping up an incessant fire on our vessels. Two of the officers of the *Raleigh,* Lieutenant Tayloe and Midshipman Hutter, were killed while assisting the Union wounded out of the *Congress.* A number of the enemy's men were killed by the same fire. Finally it became so hot that the gun-boats were obliged to haul off with only thirty prisoners, leaving Lieutenant Pendergrast and most of his crew on board, and they all afterward escaped to the shore by swimming or in small boats. While this was going on, the white flag was flying at her mainmast-head. Not being able to take possession of his prize, the commodore ordered hot shot to be used, and in a short time she was in flames fore and aft. While directing this, both himself and his flag-lieutenant, Minor, were severely wounded. The command then devolved upon Lieutenant Catesby Jones.

It was now 5 o'clock, nearly two hours of daylight, and the *Minnesota* only remained. She was aground and at our mercy. But the pilots would not attempt the middle channel with the ebb tide and approaching night. So we returned by the south channel to Sewell's Point and anchored, the *Minnesota* escaping, as we thought, only until morning.

Our loss in killed and wounded was twenty-one. The armor was hardly damaged, though at one time our ship was the focus on which were directed at least one hundred heavy guns, afloat and ashore. . . .

But at daybreak we discovered, lying between us and the *Minnesota,* a strange-looking craft, which we knew at once to be Ericsson's *Monitor,* which had long been expected in Hampton Roads, and of which, from different sources, we had a good idea. She could not possibly have made her appearance at a more inopportune time for us, changing our plans, which were to destroy the *Minnesota,* and then the remainder of the fleet below Fort Monroe. She appeared but a pigmy compared with the lofty frigate which she guarded. But in her size was one great element of her success. I will not attempt a description of the *Monitor;* her build and peculiarities are well known.

After an early breakfast, we got under way and steamed out toward the enemy, opening fire from our bow pivot, and closing in to deliver our starboard broadside at short range, which was returned promptly from her 11-inch guns. Both vessels then turned and passed again still closer. The *Monitor* was firing every seven or eight minutes, and nearly every shot struck. Our ship was working worse and worse, and after the loss of the smoke-stack, Mr.

Ramsey, chief engineer, reported that the draught was so poor that it was with great difficulty he could keep up steam. Once or twice the ship was on the bottom. Drawing 22 feet of water, we were confined to a narrow channel, while the *Monitor,* with only 12 feet immersion, could take any position, and always have us in range of her guns. Orders were given to concentrate our fire on the pilot-house, and with good result, as we afterward learned. More than two hours had passed, and we had made no impression on the enemy so far as we could discover, while our wounds were slight. Several times the *Monitor* ceased firing, and we were in hopes she was disabled, but the revolution again of her turret and the heavy blows of her 11-inch shot on our sides soon undeceived us.

Coming down from the spar-deck, and observing a division standing "at ease," Lieutenant Jones inquired:

"Why are you not firing, Mr. Eggleston?"

"Why, our powder is very precious," replied the lieutenant; "and after two hours' incessant firing I find that I can do her about as much damage by snapping my thumb at her every two minutes and a half."

Lieutenant Jones now determined to run her down or board her. For nearly an hour we manœuvred for a position. Now "Go ahead!" now "Stop!" now "Astern!" The ship was as unwieldy as Noah's ark. At last an opportunity offered. "Go ahead, full speed!" But before the ship gathered headway, the *Monitor* turned, and our disabled ram only gave a glancing blow, effecting nothing. Again she came up on our quarter, her bow against our side, and at this distance fired twice. Both shots struck about half-way up the shield, abreast of the after pivot, and the impact forced the side in bodily two or three inches. All the crews of the after guns were knocked over by the concussion, and bled from the nose or ears. Another shot at the same place would have penetrated. While alongside, boarders were called away; but she dropped astern before they could get on board. And so, for six or more hours, the struggle was kept up. At length, the *Monitor* withdrew over the middle ground where we could not follow, but always maintaining a position to protect the *Minnesota.* To have run our ship ashore on a falling tide would have been ruin. We awaited her return for an hour; and at 2 o'clock P. M. steamed to Sewell's Point, and thence to the dockyard at Norfolk, our crew thoroughly worn out from the two days' fight. Although there is no doubt that the *Monitor* first retired—for Captain Van Brunt, commanding the *Minnesota,* so states in his official report—the battle was a drawn one, so far as the two vessels engaged were concerned. But in its general results the advantage was with the *Monitor.* Our casualties in the second day's fight were only a few wounded.

This action demonstrated for the first time the power and efficiency of the ram as a means of offense. The side of the *Cumberland* was crushed like an egg-shell. The *Congress* and *Minnesota,* even with our disabled bow, would have shared the same fate but that we could not reach them on account of our great draught.

It also showed the power of resistance of two iron-clads, widely differing in construction, model, and armament, under a fire which in a short time would have sunk any other vessel then afloat.

The *Monitor* was well handled, and saved the *Minnesota* and the remainder of the fleet at Fort Monroe. But her gunnery was poor. Not a single shot struck us at the water-line, where the ship was utterly unprotected, and where one would have been fatal. Or had the fire been concentrated on any one spot, the shield would have been pierced; or had larger charges been used, the result would have been the same. Most of her shot struck us obliquely, breaking the iron of both courses, but not injuring the wood backing. When struck at right angles, the backing would be broken, but not penetrated. We had no solid projectiles, except a few of large windage, to be used as hot shot, and, of course, made no impression on the turret. But in all this it should be borne in mind that both vessels were on their trial trip, both were experimental, and both were receiving their baptism of fire.

On our arrival at Norfolk, Commodore Buchanan sent for me. I found him at the Naval Hospital, badly wounded and suffering greatly. He dictated a short dispatch to Mr. Mallory, Secretary of the Navy, stating the return of the ship and the result of the two days' fight, and directed me to proceed to Richmond with it and the flag of the *Congress,* and make a verbal report of the action, condition of the *Virginia,* etc.

I took the first train for Petersburg and the capital. . . .

The news of our victory was received everywhere in the South with the most enthusiastic rejoicing. Coming, as it did, after a number of disasters in the south and west, it was particularly grateful. Then again, under the circumstances, so little was expected from the navy that this success was entirely unlooked for. So, from one extreme to the other, the most extravagant anticipations were formed of what the ship could do. For instance: the blockade could be raised, Washington leveled to the ground, New York laid under contribution, and so on. At the North, equally groundless alarm was felt. As an example of this, Secretary Welles relates what took place at a Cabinet meeting called by Mr. Lincoln on the receipt of the news. " 'The *Merrimac,*' said Stanton, 'will change the whole character of the war; she will destroy, *seriatim,* every naval vessel; she will lay all the cities on the seaboard under contribution. I shall immediately recall Burnside; Port Royal must be abandoned. I will notify the governors and municipal authorities in the North to take instant measures to protect their harbors.' He had no doubt, he said, that the monster was at this moment on her way to Washington; and, looking out of the window, which commanded a view of the Potomac for many miles, 'Not unlikely, we shall have a shell or cannon-ball from one of her guns in the White House before we leave this room.' Mr. Seward, usually buoyant and self-reliant, overwhelmed with the intelligence, listened in responsive sympathy to Stanton, and was greatly depressed, as, indeed, were all the members."

I returned the next day to Norfolk, and informed Commodore Buchanan that he would be promoted to be admiral, and that, owing to his wound, he would be retired from the command of the *Virginia.* Lieutenant Jones should have been promoted, and should have succeeded him. He had fitted out the ship and armed her, and had commanded during the second day's fight. However, the department thought otherwise, and selected Commodore Josiah Tattnall; except Lieutenant Jones he was the best man. He had distinguished himself in the wars of 1812 and with Mexico. . . .

Tattnall took command on the 29th of March. In the meantime the *Virginia* was in the dry dock under repairs. The hull four feet below the shield was covered with 2-inch iron. A new and heavier ram was strongly secured to the bow. The damage to the armor was repaired, wrought-iron port-shutters were fitted, and the rifle-guns were supplied with steel-pointed solid shot. These changes, with 100 tons more of ballast on her fan-tails, increased her draught to 23 feet, improving her resisting powers, but correspondingly decreasing her mobility and reducing her speed to 4 knots. The repairs were not completed until the 4th of April, owing to our want of resources and the difficulty of securing workmen. On the 11th we steamed down the harbor to the Roads with six gun-boats, fully expecting to meet the *Monitor* again and other vessels; for we knew their fleet had been largely reënforced, by the *Vanderbilt,* among other vessels, a powerful side-wheel steamer fitted as a ram. We were primed for a desperate tussle; but to our surprise we had the Roads to ourselves. We exchanged a few shots with the Rip-Raps batteries, but the *Monitor* with the other vessels of the fleet remained below Fort Monroe, in Chesapeake Bay, where we could not get at them except by passing between the forts.

The day before going down, Commodore Tattnall had written to Secretary Mallory, "I see no chance for me but to pass the forts and strike elsewhere, and I shall be gratified by your authority to do so." This freedom of action was never granted, and probably wisely, for the result of an action with the *Monitor* and fleet, even if we ran the gauntlet of the fire of the forts successfully, was more than doubtful, and any disaster would have exposed Norfolk and James River, and probably would have resulted in the loss of Richmond. For equally good reasons the *Monitor* acted on the defensive; for if she had been out of the way, General McClellan's base and fleet of transports in York River would have been endangered. . . .

A few days later we went down again to within gun-shot of the Rip-Raps, and exchanged a few rounds with the fort, hoping that the *Monitor* would come out from her lair into open water. Had she done so, a determined effort would have been made to carry her by boarding. Four small gun-boats were ready, each of which had its crew divided into parties for the performance of certain duties after getting on board. Some were to try to wedge the turret, some to cover the pilot-house and all the openings with tarpaulins, others to scale with ladders the turret and smoke-stack, using shells, hand-grenades, etc. Even if but two of the gun-boats should succeed in grappling her, we were confident of success. Talking this over since with Captain S. D. Greene, who was the first lieutenant of the *Monitor*, and in command after Captain Worden was wounded in the pilot-house, he said they were prepared for anything of this kind and that it would have failed. Certain it is, if an opportunity had been given, the attempt would have been made.

A break-down of the engines forced us to return to Norfolk. Having completed our repairs on May 8th, and while returning to our old anchorage, we heard heavy firing, and, going down the harbor, found the *Monitor*, with the iron-clads *Galena, Naugatuck,* and a number of heavy ships, shelling our batteries at Sewell's Point. We stood directly for the *Monitor*, but as we approached they all ceased firing and retreated below the forts. We followed close down to the Rip-Raps, whose shot passed over us, striking a mile or more beyond the ship. We remained for some hours in the Roads, and finally the commodore, in a tone of deepest disgust, gave the order: "Mr. Jones, fire a gun to windward, and take the ship back to her buoy."

During the month of April, 1862, our forces, under General J. E. Johnston, had retired from the Peninsula to the neighborhood of Richmond to defend the city against McClellan's advance by way of the Peninsula, and from time to time rumors of the possible evacuation of Norfolk reached us. On the 9th of May, while at anchor off Sewell's Point, we noticed at sunrise that our flag was not flying over the batteries. A boat was sent ashore and found them abandoned. Lieutenant Pembroke Jones was then dispatched to Norfolk, some miles distant, to call upon General Huger, who was in command, and learn the condition of affairs. He returned during the afternoon, reporting, to our great surprise, the town deserted by our troops and the navy yard on fire. This precipitate retreat was entirely unnecessary, for while the *Virginia* remained afloat, Norfolk was safe, or, at all events, was not tenable by the enemy, and James River was partly guarded, for we could have retired behind the obstructions in the channel at Craney Island, and, with the batteries at that point, could have held the place, certainly until all the valuable stores and machinery had been removed from the navy yard. Moreover, had the *Virginia* been afloat at the time of the battles around Richmond, General McClellan would hardly have retreated to James River; for, had he done so, we could at any time have closed it and rendered any position on it untenable.

Norfolk evacuated, our occupation was gone, and the next thing to be decided upon was what should be done with the ship. Two courses of action were open to us: we might have run the blockade of the forts and done some damage to the shipping there and at the mouth of the York River, provided they did not get out of our way—for, with our great draught and low rate of speed, the enemy's transports would have gone where we could not have followed them; and the *Monitor* and other iron-clads would have engaged us with every advantage, playing around us as rabbits around a sloth, and the end would have been the certain loss of the vessel. On the other hand, the pilots said repeatedly, if the ship were lightened to eighteen feet, they could take her up James River to Harrison's Landing or City Point, where she could have been put in fighting trim again, and have been in a position to assist in the defense of Richmond. The commodore decided upon this course. Calling all hands on deck, he told them what he wished done. Sharp and quick work was necessary; for, to be successful, the ship must be lightened five feet, and we must pass the batteries at Newport News and the fleet below before daylight next morning. The crew gave three cheers, and went to work with a will, throwing overboard the ballast from the fan-tails, as well as that below—all spare stores, water, indeed everything but our powder and shot. By midnight the ship had been lightened three feet, when, to our amazement, the pilots said it was useless to do more, that with the westerly wind blowing, the tide would be cut down so that the ship would not go up even to Jamestown Flats; indeed, they would not take the responsibility of taking her up the river at all. This extraordinary conduct of the pilots rendered some other plan immediately necessary.

The ship had been so lifted as to be unfit for action; two feet of her hull below the shield was exposed. She could not be sunk again by letting in water without putting out the furnace fires and flooding the magazines. Never was a commander forced by circumstances over which he had no control into a more painful position than was Commodore Tattnall. But coolly and calmly he decided, and gave orders to destroy the ship; determining if he could not save his vessel, at all events not to sacrifice three hundred brave and faithful men; and that he acted wisely, the fight at Drewry's Bluff, which was the salvation of Richmond, soon after proved. She was run ashore near Craney Island, and the crew landed with their small-arms and two days' provisions. Having only two boats, it took three hours to disembark. Lieutenant Catesby Jones and myself were the last to leave. Setting her on fire fore and aft, she was soon in a blaze, and by the light of our burning ship we pulled for the shore, landing at daybreak. We marched 22 miles to Suffolk and took the cars for Richmond.

The news of the destruction of the *Virginia* caused a most profound feeling of disappointment and indignation throughout the South, particularly as so much was expected of the ship after our first success. On Commodore Tattnall the most unsparing and cruel aspersions were cast. He promptly demanded a court of inquiry, and, not satisfied with this, a court-martial, whose unanimous finding, after considering the facts and circumstances, was: "Being thus situated, the only alternative, in the opinion of the court, was to abandon and burn the ship then and there; which, in the judgment of the court, was deliberately and wisely done by order of the accused. Wherefore, the court do award the said Captain Josiah Tattnall an honorable acquittal."

It only remains now to speak of our last meeting with the *Monitor.* Arriving at Richmond, we heard that the enemy's fleet was ascending James River, and the result was great alarm; for, relying upon the *Virginia,* not a gun had been mounted to protect the city from a water attack. We were hurried to Drewry's Bluff, the first high ground below the city, seven miles distant. Here, for two days, exposed to constant rain, in bottomless mud and without shelter, on scant provisions, we worked unceasingly, mounting guns and obstructing the river. In this we were aided by the crews of small vessels which had escaped up the river before Norfolk was abandoned. The *Jamestown* and some small sailing-vessels were sunk in the channel, but, owing to the high water occasioned by a freshet, the obstructions were only partial. We had only succeeded in getting into position three thirty-twos and two sixty-fours (shell guns) and were without sufficient supply of ammunition, when on the 15th of May the iron-clad *Galena,* Commander John Rodgers, followed by the *Monitor* and three others, hove in sight. We opened fire as soon as they came within range, directing most of it on the *Galena.* This vessel was handled very skillfully. Coming up within six hundred yards of the battery, she anchored, and, with a spring from her quarter, presented her broadside; this under a heavy fire, and in a narrow river with a strong current. The *Monitor,* and others anchored just below, answered our fire deliberately; but, owing to the great elevation of the battery, their fire was in a great measure ineffectual, though two guns were dismounted and several men were killed and wounded. While this was going on, our sharp-shooters were at work on both banks. . . . Finding they could make no impression on our works, the *Galena,* after an action of four hours, returned down the river with her consorts.

This was one of the boldest and best-conducted operations of the war, and one of which very little notice has been taken. Had Commander Rodgers been supported by a few brigades, landed at City Point or above on the south side, Richmond would have been evacuated. The *Virginia's* crew alone barred his way to Richmond; otherwise the obstructions would not have prevented his steaming up to the city, which would have been as much at his mercy as was New Orleans before the fleet of Farragut.

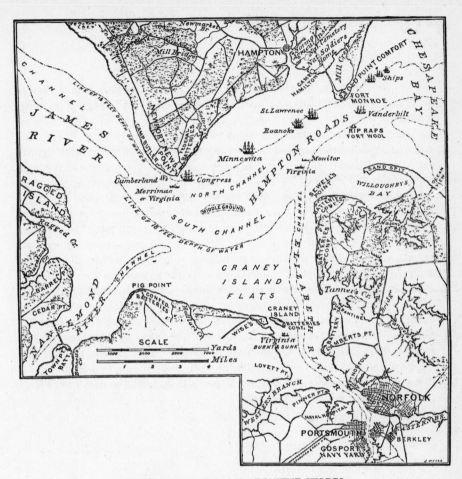

HAMPTON ROADS AND ADJACENT SHORES

109

The inventor of the Monitor, *John Ericsson, was a Swede who had come to this country in 1839. Both in Sweden and America he had designed and built a wide variety of mechanical devices, and in 1861 he offered a Naval Board his plans for "an impregnable steam-battery of light draught, suitable to navigate the shallow rivers and harbors of the Confederate States." Somewhat to the inventor's surprise, since his idea had previously been rejected when brought to the Board by a friend, he was permitted "to present a theoretical demonstration concerning the stability of the new structure." Gustavus V. Fox, the Assistant Secretary of the Navy, championed his proposal and even Lincoln, at a later meeting of the Naval Board, examining Ericsson's pasteboard model, commented, "All I have to say is what the girl said when she put her foot into the stocking. It strikes me there's something in it." So the Navy Department accepted Ericsson's proposal, issued a contract for its construction, and he immediately set to work. The new ship was completed in a hundred days.*

Ericsson himself selected the name Monitor *and his choice was a subtle one. Writing to Fox on the subject, he said his ship would "admonish the leaders of the Southern Rebellion that the batteries on the banks of their rivers will no longer present barriers to the entrance of the Union forces. The iron-clad intruder will thus prove a severe monitor to those leaders." As, he added, it would to certain other leaders. "'Downing Street' will hardly view with indifference this last Yankee notion, this monitor."*

"We thought we had gained a great victory"

IN THE "MONITOR" TURRET

BY S. DANA GREENE, COMMANDER, U. S. N., EXECUTIVE OFFICER OF THE "MONITOR"

THE KEEL of the most famous vessel of modern times, Captain Ericsson's first iron-clad, was laid in the ship-yard of Thomas F. Rowland, at Greenpoint, Brooklyn, in October, 1861, and on the 30th of January, 1862, the novel craft was launched. On the 25th of February she was commissioned and turned over to the Government, and nine days later left New York for Hampton Roads, where, on the 9th of March, occurred the memorable contest with the *Merrimac*. On her next venture on the open sea she foundered off Cape Hatteras in a gale of wind (December 29th). During her career of less than a year she had no fewer than five different commanders; but it was the fortune of the writer to serve as her only executive officer, standing upon her deck when she was launched, and leaving it but a few minutes before she sank.

So hurried was the preparation of the *Monitor* that the mechanics worked

111

upon her day and night up to the hour of her departure, and little opportunity was offered to drill the crew at the guns, to work the turret, and to become familiar with the other unusual features of the vessel. The crew was, in fact, composed of volunteers. Lieutenant Worden, having been authorized by the Navy Department to select his men from any ship-of-war in New York harbor, addressed the crews of the *North Carolina* and *Sabine,* stating fully to them the probable dangers of the passage to Hampton Roads and the certainty of having important service to perform after arriving. The sailors responded enthusiastically, many more volunteering than were required. Of the crew Captain Worden said, in his official report of the battle, "A better one no naval commander ever had the honor to command."

We left New York in tow of the tug-boat *Seth Low* at 11 A. M. of Thursday, the 6th of March. On the following day a moderate breeze was encountered, and it was at once evident that the *Monitor* was unfit as a sea-going craft. Nothing but the subsidence of the wind prevented her from being shipwrecked before she reached Hampton Roads. The berth-deck hatch leaked in spite of all we could do, and the water came down under the turret like a waterfall. It would strike the pilot-house and go over the turret in beautiful curves, and it came through the narrow eye-holes in the pilot-house with such force as to knock the helmsman completely round from the wheel. The waves also broke over the blower-pipes, and the water came down through them in such quantities that the belts of the blower-engines slipped, and the engines consequently stopped for lack of artificial draught, without which, in such a confined place, the fires could not get air for combustion. Newton and Stimers, followed by the engineer's force, gallantly rushed into the engine-room and fire-room to remedy the evil, but they were unable to check the inflowing water, and were nearly suffocated with escaping gas. They were dragged out more dead than alive, and carried to the top of the turret, where the fresh air gradually revived them. The water continued to pour through the hawse-hole, and over and down the smoke-stacks and blower-pipes, in such quantities that there was imminent danger that the ship would founder. The steam-pumps could not be operated because the fires had been nearly extinguished, and the engine-room was uninhabitable on account of the suffocating gas with which it was filled. The hand-pumps were then rigged and worked, but they had not enough force to throw the water out through the top of the turret—the only opening—and it was useless to bail, as we had to pass the buckets up through the turret, which made it a very long operation. Fortunately, toward evening the wind and the sea subsided, and, being again in smooth water, the engine was put in operation. But at midnight, in passing over a shoal, rough water was again encountered, and our troubles were renewed, complicated this time with the jamming of the wheel-ropes, so that the safety of the ship depended entirely on the strength of the hawser which connected her with the tug-boat. The hawser, being new, held fast; but during the greater part of the night we were constantly engaged in fighting the leaks, until we reached smooth water again, just before daylight.

It was at the close of this dispiriting trial trip, in which all hands had been exhausted in their efforts to keep the novel craft afloat, that the *Monitor* passed Cape Henry at 4 P. M. on Saturday, March 8th. At this point was heard the distant booming of heavy guns, which our captain rightly judged to be an engagement with the *Merrimac,* twenty miles away. He at once ordered the vessel stripped of her sea-rig, the turret keyed up, and every preparation made for battle. As we approached Hampton Roads we could see the fine old *Congress* burning brightly, and soon a pilot came on board and told of the arrival of the *Merrimac,* the disaster to the *Cumberland* and the *Congress,* and the dismay of the Union forces. The *Monitor* was pushed with all haste, and reached the *Roanoke* (Captain Marston), anchored in the Roads, at 9 P. M. Worden immediately reported his arrival to Captain Marston, who suggested that he should go to the assistance of the *Minnesota,* then aground off Newport News. As no pilot was available, Captain Worden accepted the volunteer services of Acting Master Samuel Howard, who earnestly sought the duty. An atmosphere of gloom pervaded the fleet, and the pygmy aspect of the new-comer did not inspire confidence among those who had witnessed the destruction of the day before. Skillfully piloted by Howard, we proceeded on our way, our path illumined by the blaze of the *Congress.* Reaching the *Minnesota,* hard and fast aground, near midnight, we anchored, and Worden reported to Captain Van Brunt. Between 1 and 2 A. M. the *Congress* blew up—not instantaneously, but successively. Her powder-tanks seemed to explode, each shower of sparks rivaling the other in its height, until they appeared to reach the zenith—a grand but mournful sight. Near us, too, at the bottom of the river, lay the *Cumberland,* with her silent crew of brave men, who died while fighting their guns to the water's edge, and whose colors were still flying at the peak.

The dreary night dragged slowly on; the officers and crew were up and alert, to be ready for any emergency. At daylight on Sunday the *Merrimac* and her consorts were discovered at anchor near Sewell's Point. At about half-past 7 o'clock the enemy's vessels got under way and steered in the direction of the *Minnesota.* At the same time the *Monitor* got under way, and her officers and crew took their stations for battle. Captain Van Brunt, of the *Minnesota,* officially reports, "I made signal to the *Monitor* to attack the enemy," but the signal was not seen by us; other work was in hand, and Commander Worden required no signal.

The pilot-house of the *Monitor* was situated well forward, near the bow; it was a wrought-iron structure, built of logs of iron nine inches thick, bolted through the corners, and covered with an iron plate two inches thick, which was not fastened down, but was kept in place merely by its weight. The

113

sight-holes or slits were made by inserting quarter-inch plates at the corners between the upper set of logs and the next below. The structure projected four feet above the deck, and was barely large enough inside to hold three men standing. It presented a flat surface on all sides and on top. The steering-wheel was secured to one of the logs on the front side. The position and shape of this structure should be carefully borne in mind.

Worden took his station in the pilot-house, and by his side were Howard, the pilot, and Peter Williams, quartermaster, who steered the vessel throughout the engagement. My place was in the turret, to work and fight the guns; with me were Stodder and Stimers and sixteen brawny men, eight to each gun. John Stocking, boatswain's mate, and Thomas Lochrane, seaman, were gun-captains. Newton and his assistants were in the engine and fire rooms, to manipulate the boilers and engines, and most admirably did they perform this important service from the beginning to the close of the action. Webber had charge of the powder division on the berth-deck, and Joseph Crown, gunner's-mate, rendered valuable service in connection with this duty.

The physical condition of the officers and men of the two ships at this time was in striking contrast. The *Merrimac* had passed the night quietly near Sewell's Point, her people enjoying rest and sleep, elated by thoughts of the victory they had achieved that day, and cheered by the prospects of another easy victory on the morrow. The *Monitor* had barely escaped shipwreck twice within the last thirty-six hours, and since Friday morning, forty-eight hours before, few if any of those on board had closed their eyes in sleep or had anything to eat but hard bread, as cooking was impossible. She was surrounded by wrecks and disaster, and her efficiency in action had yet to be proved.

Worden lost no time in bringing it to test. Getting his ship under way, he steered direct for the enemy's vessels, in order to meet and engage them as far as possible from the *Minnesota*. As he approached, the wooden vessels quickly turned and left. Our captain, to the "astonishment" of Captain Van Brunt (as he states in his official report), made straight for the *Merrimac,* which had already commenced firing; and when he came within short range, he changed his course so as to come alongside of her, stopped the engine, and gave the order, "Commence firing!" I triced up the port, ran out the gun, and, taking deliberate aim, pulled the lockstring. The *Merrimac* was quick to reply, returning a rattling broadside (for she had ten guns to our two), and the battle fairly began. The turrets and other parts of the ship were heavily struck, but the shots did not penetrate; the tower was intact, and it continued to revolve. A look of confidence passed over the men's faces, and we believed the *Merrimac* would not repeat the work she had accomplished the day before.

The fight continued with the exchange of broadsides as fast as the guns could be served and at very short range, the distance between the vessels frequently being not more than a few yards. Worden skillfully manœuvred his quick-turning vessel, trying to find some vulnerable point in his adversary. Once he made a dash at her stern, hoping to disable her screw, which he thinks he missed by not more than two feet. Our shots ripped the iron of the *Merrimac,* while the reverberation of her shots against the tower caused anything but a pleasant sensation. While Stodder, who was stationed at the machine which controlled the revolving motion of the turret, was incautiously leaning against the side of the tower, a large shot struck in the vicinity and disabled him. He left the turret and went below, and Stimers, who had assisted him, continued to do the work.

The drawbacks to the position of the pilot-house were soon realized. We could not fire ahead nor within several points of the bow, since the blast from our own guns would have injured the people in the pilot-house, only a few yards off. Keeler and Toffey passed the captain's orders and messages to me, and my inquiries and answers to him, the speaking-tube from the pilot-house to the turret having been broken early in the action. They performed their work with zeal and alacrity, but, both being landsmen, our technical communications sometimes miscarried. The situation was novel: a vessel of war was engaged in desperate combat with a powerful foe; the captain, commanding and guiding, was inclosed in one place, and the executive officer, working and fighting the guns, was shut up in another, and communication between them was difficult and uncertain. It was this experience which caused Isaac Newton, immediately after the engagement, to suggest the clever plan of putting the pilot-house on top of the turret, and making it cylindrical instead of square; and his suggestions were subsequently adopted in this type of vessel.

As the engagement continued, the working of the turret was not altogether satisfactory. It was difficult to start it revolving, or, when once started, to stop it, on account of the imperfections of the novel machinery, which was now undergoing its first trial. Stimers was an active, muscular man, and did his utmost to control the motion of the turret; but, in spite of his efforts, it was difficult, if not impossible, to secure accurate firing. The conditions were very different from those of an ordinary broadside gun, under which we had been trained on wooden ships. My only view of the world outside of the tower was over the muzzles of the guns, which cleared the ports by only a few inches. When the guns were run in, the port-holes were covered by heavy iron pendulums, pierced with small holes to allow the iron rammer and sponge handles to protrude while they were in use. To hoist these pendulums required the entire gun's crew and vastly increased the work inside the turret.

The effect upon one shut up in a revolving drum is perplexing, and it is not a simple matter to keep the bearings. White marks had been placed upon the stationary deck immediately below the turret to indicate the direction

115

of the starboard and port sides, and the bow and stern; but these marks were obliterated early in the action. I would continually ask the captain, "How does the *Merrimac* bear?" He replied, "On the starboard-beam," or "On the port-quarter," as the case might be. Then the difficulty was to determine the direction of the starboard-beam, or port-quarter, or any other bearing. It finally resulted, that when a gun was ready for firing, the turret would be started on its revolving journey in search of the target, and when found it was taken "on the fly," because the turret could not be accurately controlled. Once the *Merrimac* tried to ram us; but Worden avoided the direct impact by the skillful use of the helm, and she struck a glancing blow, which did no damage. At the instant of collision I planted a solid 180-pound shot fair and square upon the forward part of her casemate. Had the gun been loaded with thirty pounds of powder, which was the charge subsequently used with similar guns, it is probable that this shot would have penetrated her armor; but the charge being limited to fifteen pounds, in accordance with peremptory orders to that effect from the Navy Department, the shot rebounded without doing any more damage than possibly to start some of the beams of her armor-backing. . . .

The battle continued at close quarters without apparent damage to either side. After a time, the supply of shot in the turret being exhausted, Worden hauled off for about fifteen minutes to replenish. The serving of the cartridges, weighing but fifteen pounds, was a matter of no difficulty; but the hoisting of the heavy shot was a slow and tedious operation, it being necessary that the turret should remain stationary, in order that the two scuttles, one in the deck and the other in the floor of the turret, should be in line. Worden took advantage of the lull, and passed through the port-hole upon the deck outside to get a better view of the situation. He soon renewed the attack, and the contest continued as before.

Two important points were constantly kept in mind: first, to prevent the enemy's projectiles from entering the turret through the port-holes—for the explosion of a shell inside, by disabling the men at the guns, would have ended the fight, as there was no relief gun's crew on board; second, not to fire into our own pilot-house. A careless or impatient hand, during the confusion arising from the whirligig motion of the tower, might let slip one of our big shot against the pilot-house. For this and other reasons I fired every gun while I remained in the turret.

Soon after noon a shell from the enemy's gun, the muzzle not ten yards distant, struck the forward side of the pilot-house directly in the sight-hole, or slit, and exploded, cracking the second iron log and partly lifting the top, leaving an opening. Worden was standing immediately behind this spot, and received in his face the force of the blow, which partly stunned him, and, filling his eyes with powder, utterly blinded him. The injury was known only to those in the pilot-house and its immediate vicinity. The flood of light

116

rushing through the top of the pilot-house, now partly open, caused Worden, blind as he was, to believe that the pilot-house was seriously injured, if not destroyed; he therefore gave orders to put the helm to starboard and "sheer off." Thus the *Monitor* retired temporarily from the action, in order to ascertain the extent of the injuries she had received. At the same time Worden sent for me, and leaving Stimers the only officer in the turret, I went forward at once, and found him standing at the foot of the ladder leading to the pilot-house.

He was a ghastly sight, with his eyes closed and the blood apparently rushing from every pore in the upper part of his face. He told me that he was seriously wounded, and directed me to take command. I assisted in leading him to a sofa in his cabin, where he was tenderly cared for by Doctor Logue, and then I assumed command. Blind and suffering as he was, Worden's fortitude never forsook him; he frequently asked from his bed of pain of the progress of affairs, and when told that the *Minnesota* was saved, he said, "Then I can die happy."

When I reached my station in the pilot-house, I found that the iron log was fractured and the top partly open; but the steering gear was still intact, and the pilot-house was not totally destroyed, as had been feared. In the confusion of the moment resulting from so serious an injury to the commanding officer, the *Monitor* had been moving without direction. Exactly how much time elapsed from the moment that Worden was wounded until I had reached the pilot-house and completed the examination of the injury at that point, and determined what course to pursue in the damaged condition of the vessel, it is impossible to state; but it could hardly have exceeded twenty minutes at the utmost. During this time the *Merrimac,* which was leaking badly, had started in the direction of the Elizabeth River; and, on taking my station in the pilot-house and turning the vessel's head in the direction of the *Merrimac,* I saw that she was already in retreat. A few shots were fired at the retiring vessel, and she continued on to Norfolk. I returned with the *Monitor* to the side of the *Minnesota,* where preparations were being made to abandon the ship, which was still aground. Shortly afterward Worden was transferred to a tug, and that night he was carried to Washington.

The fight was over. We of the *Monitor* thought, and still think, that we had gained a great victory. This the Confederates have denied. But it has never been denied that the object of the *Merrimac* on the 9th of March was to complete the destruction of the Union fleet in Hampton Roads, and that she was completely foiled and driven off by the *Monitor;* nor has it been denied that at the close of the engagement the *Merrimac* retreated to Norfolk, leaving the *Monitor* in possession of the field. . . .

The subsequent career of the *Monitor* needs but a few words.

On the day after the fight I received the following letter from Mr. Fox, Assistant Secretary of the Navy:

117

U. S. Steamer *Roanoke*, Old Point, March 10th, 1862

My Dear Mr. Greene: Under the extraordinary circumstances of the contest of yesterday, and the responsibilities devolving upon me, and your extreme youth, I have suggested to Captain Marston to send on board the *Monitor,* as temporary commanding, Lieutenant Selfridge, until the arrival of Commodore Goldsborough, which will be in a few days. I appreciate your position, and you must appreciate mine, and serve with the same zeal and fidelity. With the kindest wishes for you all, most truly,   G. V. Fox

For the next two months we lay at Hampton Roads. Twice the *Merrimac* came out of the Elizabeth River, but did not attack. We, on our side, had received positive orders not to attack in the comparatively shoal waters above Hampton Roads, where the Union fleet could not manœuvre. The *Merrimac* protected the James River, and the *Monitor* protected the Chesapeake. Neither side had an iron-clad in reserve, and neither wished to bring on an engagement which might disable its only armored vessel in those waters.

With the evacuation of Norfolk and the destruction of the *Merrimac,* the *Monitor* moved up the James River with the squadron under the command of Commander John Rodgers, in connection with McClellan's advance upon Richmond by the Peninsula. We were engaged for four hours at Fort Darling, but were unable to silence the guns or destroy the earth-works.

Probably no ship was ever devised which was so uncomfortable for her crew, and certainly no sailor ever led a more disagreeable life than we did on the James River, suffocated with heat and bad air if we remained below, and a target for sharp-shooters if we came on deck.

With the withdrawal of McClellan's army, we returned to Hampton Roads, and in the autumn were ordered to Washington, where the vessel was repaired. We returned to Hampton Roads in November, and sailed thence (December 29th) in tow of the steamer *Rhode Island,* bound for Beaufort, N. C. Between 11 P. M. and midnight on the following night the *Monitor* went down in a gale, a few miles south of Cape Hatteras. Four officers and twelve men were drowned, forty-nine people being saved by the boats of the steamer. It was impossible to keep the vessel free of water, and we presumed that the upper and lower hulls thumped themselves apart.

No ship in the world's history has a more imperishable place in naval annals than the *Monitor.* Not only by her providential arrival at the right moment did she secure the safety of Hampton Roads and all that depended on it, but the idea which she embodied revolutionized the system of naval warfare which had existed from the earliest recorded history. The name of the *Monitor* became generic, representing a new type; and, crude and defective as was her construction in some of its details, she yet contained the idea of the turret, which is to-day the central idea of the most powerful armored vessels.

118

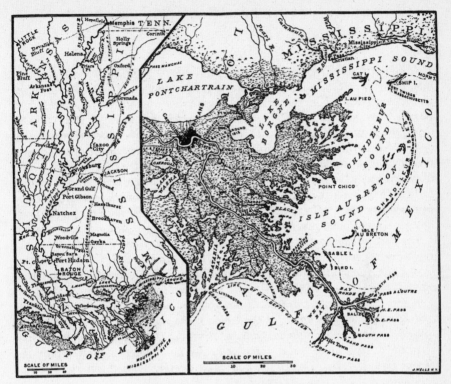

MAPS OF THE LOWER MISSISSIPPI

The Mississippi River was controlled primarily by fortified Confederate positions below New Orleans and at Vicksburg, Memphis, and Island Number Ten. Grant's capture of Fort Henry and Donelson made both Memphis and Island Number Ten accessible to Union armies, to which they soon fell. But New Orleans, the most important city of the South, could only be reached practicably by a Union naval expedition sailing up the river. The importance of its capture was obvious. It would expose Vicksburg to attack from the river, release Union blockading ships at the river's mouth for duty elsewhere, disrupt transportation facilities between Texas, Arkansas, most of Louisiana and the rest of the Confederacy east of the Mississippi, deprive the enemy of some useful manufactures, and have a profound psychological effect both in North America and abroad.

The commander of the expedition against New Orleans which began to assemble at the mouth of the Mississippi early in March 1862, was Flag Officer (soon to be Admiral) David G. Farragut, a Virginian who, although he had been offered the command of the rebel navy, remained loyal to the Union. (Lincoln, Kentucky-born, never seems to have harbored any suspicions of men like Thomas and Farragut who declared for the Union.) The choice of commander proved to be a sound one for in the last days of April the Union ships, which had survived the terrible fire of ships, forts, and other land batteries, anchored off the city of New Orleans. The Union had made another "thrust into the vitals of the Confederacy."

"Our cake is all dough"

THE OPENING OF THE LOWER MISSISSIPPI

BY DAVID D. PORTER, ADMIRAL, U. S. N.

T HE MOST important event of the War of the Rebellion, with the exception of the fall of Richmond, was the capture of New Orleans and the forts Jackson and St. Philip, guarding the approach to that city. To appreciate the nature of this victory, it is necessary to have been an actor in it, and to be able to comprehend not only the immediate results to the Union cause, but the whole bearing of the fall of New Orleans on the Civil War, which at that time had attained its most formidable proportions.

Previous to fitting out the expedition against New Orleans, there were eleven Southern States in open rebellion against the Government of the United States, or, as it was termed by the Southern people, in a state of secession. Their harbors were all more or less closed against our ships-of-war, either by the heavy forts built originally by the General Government for their protection, or by torpedoes and sunken vessels. Through four of these seceding States ran the great river Mississippi, and both of its banks, from Memphis to its mouth, were lined with powerful batteries. On the west side

121

of the river were three important States, Louisiana, Arkansas, and Texas, with their great tributaries to the Mississippi—the White, the Arkansas, and the Red—which were in a great measure secure from the attacks of the Union forces. These States could not only raise half a million soldiers, but could furnish the Confederacy with provisions of all kinds, and cotton enough to supply the Rebel Government with the sinews of war. New Orleans was the largest Southern city, and contained all the resources of modern warfare, having great workshops where machinery of the most powerful kind could be built, and having artisans capable of building ships in wood or iron, casting heavy guns, or making small arms. The people of the city were in no way behind the most zealous secessionists in energy of purpose and in hostility to the Government of the United States.

The Mississippi is thus seen to have been the backbone of the Rebellion, which it should have been the first duty of the Federal Government to break. At the very outset of the war it should have been attacked at both ends at the same time, before the Confederates had time to fortify its banks or to turn the guns in the Government forts against the Union forces. A dozen improvised gun-boats would have held the entire length of the river if they had been sent there in time. The efficient fleet with which Du Pont, in November, 1861, attacked and captured the works at Port Royal could at that time have steamed up to New Orleans and captured the city without difficulty. Any three vessels could have passed Forts Jackson and St. Philip a month after the commencement of the war, and could have gone on to Cairo, if necessary, without any trouble. But the Federal Government neglected to approach the mouth of the Mississippi until a year after hostilities had commenced, except to blockade. The Confederates made good use of this interval, putting forth all their resources and fortifying not only the approaches to New Orleans, but both banks of the river as far north as Memphis. . . .

This was the position of affairs on May 31st, 1861, only forty-nine days after Fort Sumter had been fired on.

On the 9th of November, 1861, I arrived at New York with the *Powhatan* and was ordered to report to the Navy Department at Washington, which I did on the 12th. In those days it was not an easy matter for an officer, except one of high rank, to obtain access to the Secretary of the Navy, and I had been waiting nearly all the morning at the door of his office when Senators Grimes and Hale came along and entered into conversation with me concerning my service on the Gulf Coast. During this interview I told the senators of a plan I had formed for the capture of New Orleans, and when I had explained to them how easily it could be accomplished, they expressed surprise that no action had been taken in the matter, and took me in with them at once to see Secretary Welles. I then gave the Secretary, in as few words as possible, my opinion on the importance of capturing New Orleans, and my plan for doing so. Mr. Welles listened to me attentively, and when

I had finished what I had to say he remarked that the matter should be laid before the President at once; and we all went forthwith to the Executive Mansion, where we were received by Mr. Lincoln.

My plan, which I then stated, was as follows: To fit out a fleet of vessels-of-war with which to attack the city, fast steamers drawing not more than 18 feet of water, and carrying about 250 heavy guns; also a flotilla of mortar-vessels, to be used in case it should be necessary to bombard Forts Jackson and St. Philip before the fleet should attempt to pass them. I also proposed that a body of troops should be sent along in transports to take possession of the city after it had been surrendered to the navy. When I had outlined the proposed movement the President remarked:

"This should have been done sooner. The Mississippi is the backbone of the Rebellion; it is the key to the whole situation. While the Confederates hold it they can obtain supplies of all kinds, and it is a barrier against our forces. Come, let us go and see General McClellan."

At that time General McClellan commanded the Army of the Potomac, and was in the zenith of his power. He held the confidence of the President and the country, and was engaged in organizing a large army with which to guarantee the safety of the Federal seat of Government, and to march upon Richmond.

Our party was now joined by Mr. Seward, the Secretary of State, and we proceeded to McClellan's headquarters, where we found that officer diligently engaged in the duties of his responsible position. He came to meet the President with that cheery manner which always distinguished him, and, seeing me, shook me warmly by the hand. We had known each other for some years, and I always had the highest opinion of his military abilities.

"Oh," said the President, "you two know each other! Then half the work is done."

He then explained to the general the object of his calling at that time, saying:

"This is a most important expedition. What troops can you spare to accompany it and take possession of New Orleans after the navy has effected its capture? It is not only necessary to have troops enough to hold New Orleans, but we must be able to proceed at once toward Vicksburg, which is the key to all that country watered by the Mississippi and its tributaries. If the Confederates once fortify the neighboring hills, they will be able to hold that point for an indefinite time, and it will require a large force to dislodge them."

In all his remarks the President showed a remarkable familiarity with the state of affairs. Before leaving us, he said:

"We will leave this matter in the hands of you two gentlemen. Make your plans, and let me have your report as soon as possible."

General McClellan and myself were then left to talk the matter over and draw up the plan of operations. With a man of McClellan's energy, it did not take long to come to a conclusion; and, although he had some difficulty in finding a sufficient number of troops without interfering with other important projects, he settled the matter in two days, and reported that his men would be ready to embark on the 15th of January, 1862.

The plan of the campaign submitted to the President was as follows: A naval expedition was to be fitted out, composed of vessels mounting not fewer than two hundred guns, with a powerful mortar-flotilla, and with steam transports to keep the fleet supplied. The army was to furnish twenty thousand troops, not only for the purpose of occupying New Orleans after its capture, but to fortify and hold the heights about Vicksburg. The navy and army were to push on up the river as soon as New Orleans was occupied by our troops, and call upon the authorities of Vicksburg to surrender. Orders were to be issued to Flag-Officer Foote, who commanded the iron-clad fleet on the upper Mississippi, to join the fleet above Vicksburg with his vessels and mortar-boats.

The above plans were all approved by the President, and the Navy Department immediately set to work to prepare the naval part of the expedition, while General McClellan prepared the military part. The officer selected to command the troops was General B. F. Butler, a man supposed to be of high administrative ability, and at that time one of the most zealous of the Union commanders.

The Assistant-Secretary of the Navy, Mr. G. V. Fox, selected the vessels for this expedition, and to me was assigned the duty of purchasing and fitting out a mortar-flotilla, to be composed of twenty large schooners, each mounting one heavy 13-inch mortar and at least two long 32-pounders. It was not until December, 1861, that the Navy Department got seriously to work at fitting out the expedition. Some of the mortar-vessels had to be purchased; the twenty mortars, with their thirty thousand bomb-shells, had to be cast at Pittsburg and transported to New York and Philadelphia, and the mortar-carriages made in New York. It was also necessary to recall ships from stations on the coast and fit them out; also to select officers from the few available at that time to fill the various positions where efficiency was required—especially for the mortar-flotilla, the operation of which imposed unfamiliar duties.

By the latter part of January the mortar-flotilla got off. In addition to the schooners, it included seven steamers (which were necessary to move the vessels about in the Mississippi River) and a store-ship. Seven hundred picked men were enlisted, and twenty-one officers were selected from the merchant marine to command the mortar-schooners.

An important duty now devolved on the Secretary of the Navy, viz., the selection of an officer to command the whole expedition. Mr. Fox and myself had often discussed the matter. He had had in his mind several officers of high standing and unimpeachable loyalty; but, as I knew the officers of the navy better than he did, my advice was listened to, and the selection fell upon Captain David Glasgow Farragut.

I had known Farragut ever since I was five years old. He stood high in the navy as an officer and seaman, and possessed such undoubted courage and energy that no possible objection could be made to him. On the first sign of war Farragut, though a Southerner by birth and residence, had shown his loyalty in an outspoken manner. The Southern officers had used every argument to induce him to desert his flag, even going so far as to threaten to detain him by force. His answer to them has become historical: "Mind what I tell you: You fellows will catch the devil before you get through with this business." . . .

I continually urged Farragut's appointment, and finally the department directed me to go on to New York, and ascertain in a personal interview whether he would accept the command and enter warmly into the views of the Government. I found him, as I had expected, loyal to the utmost extent; and, although he did not at that time know the destination of the expedition, he authorized me to accept for him the Secretary's offer, and I telegraphed the department: "Farragut accepts the command, as I was sure he would."

In consequence of this answer he was called to Washington, and on the 20th of January, 1862, he received orders to command the expedition against New Orleans. In the orders are included these passages: "There will be attached to your squadron a fleet of bomb-vessels, and armed steamers enough to manage them, all under command of Commander D. D. Porter, who will be directed to report to you. As fast as these vessels are got ready they will be sent to Key West to await the arrival of all and the commanding officers, who will be permitted to organize and practice with them at that port.

"When these formidable mortars arrive, and you are completely ready, you will collect such vessels as can be spared from the blockade, and proceed up the Mississippi River, and reduce the defenses which guard the approaches to New Orleans, when you will appear off that city and take possession of it under the guns of your squadron, and hoist the American flag therein, keeping possession until troops can be sent to you. If the Mississippi expedition from Cairo shall not have descended the river, you will take advantage of the panic to push a strong force up the river to take all their defenses in the rear."

As soon as possible Farragut proceeded to his station and took command of the West Gulf Blockading Squadron. In the meantime the Confederates had not been idle. They had early been made acquainted with the destination of the expedition, and had put forth all their energies in strengthening Forts Jackson and St. Philip, obstructing the river, and preparing a naval force with which to meet the invaders. The ram *Manassas* was finished and placed in commission, and the iron-clad *Louisiana,* mounting sixteen heavy guns and heavily armored, was hurried toward completion. Besides these vessels there was another powerful iron-clad, building at New Orleans, which was expected to sweep the whole Southern coast clear of Union vessels. Two iron-clad rams, the *Arkansas* and *Tennessee,* were building at Memphis, and several other iron-clad vessels were under construction at different points on the tributaries.

This energy and forethought displayed by the South seems marvelous when compared with what was done by the North during the same period of time; for among all the ships that were sent to Farragut there was not one whose sides could resist a twelve-pound shot. Considering the great resources of the Northern States, this supineness of the Government appears inexcusable. Up to the time of the sailing of the expedition, only three iron-clads, the *Monitor, Galena,* and *New Ironsides,* had been commenced, in addition to the gun-boats on the Upper Mississippi; and it was only after the encounter of the *Monitor* with the *Merrimac* that it was seen how useful vessels of this class would be for the attack on New Orleans, particularly in contending with the forts on the banks of the Mississippi.

Flag-Officer Farragut did not arrive at Ship Island with the *Hartford* until the 20th of February, 1862, having been detained for some time at Key West, where he began to arrange his squadron for the difficult task that lay before him.

The vessels which had been assigned to his command soon began to arrive, and by the middle of March all had reported, together with six steamers belonging to the mortar-flotilla: the *Harriet Lane, Owasco, Clifton, Westfield, Miami, Jackson;* besides the mortar-schooners. The frigate *Colorado,* mounting fifty guns, had arrived, but Flag-Officer Farragut and Captain Bailey both came to the conclusion that she could not be lightened sufficiently to cross the bar.

On the 18th of March all the mortar-schooners crossed the bar at Pass à l'Outre, towed by the steamers *Harriet Lane, Owasco, Westfield,* and *Clifton.* They were ordered by Farragut to proceed to South-west Pass.

As yet the only ships that had crossed the bar were the *Hartford* and *Brooklyn.* The Navy Department had made a mistake in sending vessels of too great draught of water, such as the *Colorado, Pensacola,* and *Mississippi.* The two latter succeeded in crossing with great difficulty, but the whole fleet was delayed at least twelve days.

The first act of Farragut was to send Captain Henry H. Bell, his chief-of-staff, up the river with the steamers *Kennebec* and *Wissahickon,* to ascertain, if possible, what preparations had been made by the enemy to prevent the passage of the forts. This officer reported that the obstructions seemed formidable. Eight hulks were moored in line across the river, with heavy chains extending from one to the other. Rafts of logs were also used, and the passage between the forts was thus entirely closed.

The Confederates had lost no time in strengthening their defenses. They had been working night and day ever since the expedition was planned by the Federal Government. Forts Jackson and St. Philip were strong defenses, the former on the west and the latter on the east bank of the Mississippi. As they are to hold an important place in the following narration of events, it will be well to give a description of them.

Fort Jackson was built in the shape of a star, of stone and mortar, with heavy bomb-proofs. It set back about one hundred yards from the levee, with its casemates just rising above it. I am told that the masonry had settled somewhat since it was first built, but it was still in a good state of preservation. Its armament consisted of 42 heavy guns in barbette, and 24 in casemates; also 2 pieces of light artillery and 6 guns in water-battery—in all, 74 guns. The last was a very formidable part of the defenses, its heavy guns having a commanding range down the river. The main work had been strengthened by covering its bomb-proofs and vulnerable parts with bags of sand piled five or six feet deep, making it proof against the projectiles of ordinary guns carried by ships-of-war in those days. The fort was also well supplied with provisions and munitions of war, which were stowed away in a heavily built citadel of masonry situated in the center of the works. Altogether, it was in a very good condition to withstand either attack or siege. Fort Jackson was under the immediate command of Lieutenant-Colonel Edward Higgins, formerly an officer of the United States navy, and a very gallant and intelligent man.

Fort St. Philip was situated on the other side of the river, about half a mile above Fort Jackson, and, in my opinion, was the more formidable of the two works. It covered a large extent of ground, and although it was open, without casemates, its walls were strongly built of brick and stone, covered with sod. The guns were mounted in barbette, and could be brought to bear on any vessel going up or down the river. There were in all 52 pieces of ordnance. One heavy rifled gun bore on the position of the mortar-fleet, and caused us considerable disturbance until the second or third day after the bombardment commenced, when it burst.

Each of the forts held a garrison of about seven hundred men, some of whom were from the Northern States, besides many foreigners (Germans or Irish). The Northern men had applied for duty in the forts to avoid suspicion, and in the hope that they would not be called upon to fight agai$_\text{\ }$ the Federal Government. In this hope they had been encouraged b$_\text{\ }$ officers, all of whom, including the colonel in command, were of t$_\text{\ }$ that no naval officer would have the hardihood to attac$_\text{\ }$ positions.

All of the land defenses were under Brigadier-General Johnson K. Duncan, who showed himself to be an able and gallant commander.

The best passage up the river was near the west bank close under the guns of Fort Jackson, where the current was not very rapid and few eddies existed. Across this channel the Confederates had placed a raft of logs, extending from the shore to the commencement of a line of hulks which reached to the other side of the river. These hulks were anchored and connected to each other by chains. The raft was so arranged that it could be hauled out of the way of passing vessels, and closed when danger threatened. Although this plan of blocking the river was better than the first one tried by the Confederates, viz., to float a heavy chain across on rafts, it was not very formidable or ingenious.

In addition to the defenses at the forts, the Confederates worked with great diligence to improvise a fleet of men-of-war, using for this purpose a number of heavy tugs that had been employed in towing vessels up and down the river, and some merchant steamers. These, with the ram *Manassas* and the iron-clad *Louisiana,* made in all twelve vessels. The whole naval force was nominally under the control of Commander John K. Mitchell, C. S. N.

The iron-clad *Louisiana,* mounting 16 heavy guns, with a crew of 200 men, was a powerful vessel, almost impervious to shot, and was fitted with a shot-proof gallery from which her sharp-shooters could fire at an enemy with great effect. Her machinery was not completed, however, and during the passage of the Union fleet she was secured to the river-bank and could only use one broadside and three of her bow guns. At this time she was under the immediate command of Commander Charles F. McIntosh, formerly of the United States navy. The *McRae,* Lieutenant Thomas B. Huger, was a sea-going steamer mounting 6 32-pounders and 1 9-inch shell-gun; the steamer *Jackson,* Lieutenant F. B. Renshaw, mounting 2 32-pounders; the iron-clad ram *Manassas,* Lieutenant A. F. Warley, mounting 1 32-pounder (in the bow); and two launches, mounting each one howitzer. Two steamers had been converted into Louisiana State gun-boats, with pine and cotton barricades to protect the machinery and boilers: the *Governor Moore,* Commander Beverley Kennon, and the *General Quitman,* Captain Grant. "All the above steamers, being converted vessels," says Commander Mitchell, "were too slightly built for war purposes."

The River Defense gun-boats, consisting of six converted tow-boats under the command of a merchant captain named Stephenson, were also ordered to report to Commander Mitchell; but they proved of little assistance to him owing to the insubordination of their commander. "All of the above vessels," says Commander Mitchell, "mounted from one to two pivot 32-pounders each, some of them rifled. Their boilers and machinery were all more or less protected by thick, double pine barricades, filled in with compressed cotton."

128

They were also prepared for ramming by flat bar-iron casings around their bows.

The Confederate fleet mounted, all told, 40 guns, of which 25 were 32-pounders, and one-fourth of them rifled.

It is thus seen that our wooden vessels, which passed the forts carrying 192 guns, had arrayed against them 126 guns in strongly built works, and 40 guns on board of partly armored vessels.

In addition to the above-mentioned defenses, Commodore Mitchell had at his command a number of fire-rafts (long flat-boats filled with pine-knots, etc.), which were expected to do good service, either by throwing the Union fleet into confusion or by furnishing light to the gunners in the forts. On comparing the Confederate defenses with the attacking force of the Union fleet, it will be seen that the odds were strongly in favor of the former. It is generally conceded by military men that one gun in a fort is about equal to five on board of a wooden ship, especially when, as in this case, the forces afloat are obliged to contend against a three-and-a-half knot current in a channel obstructed by chains and fire-rafts. Our enemies were well aware of their strength, and although they hardly expected us to make so hazardous an attack, they waited impatiently for Farragut to "come on," resting in the assurance that he would meet with a disastrous defeat. They did not neglect, however, to add daily to the strength of their works during the time that our ships were delayed in crossing the bar and ascending the river.

Farragut experienced great difficulty in getting the larger vessels over the bar. The *Hartford* and *Brooklyn* were the only two that could pass without lightening. The *Richmond* stuck fast in the mud every time she attempted to cross. The *Mississippi* drew two feet too much water, and the *Pensacola,* after trying several times to get over, ran on a wreck a hundred yards away from the channel. There she lay, with her propeller half out of water, thumping on the wreck as she was driven in by the wind and sea. Pilots had been procured at Pilot Town, near by; but they were either treacherous or nervous, and all their attempts to get the heavy ships over the bar were failures. Farragut felt extremely uncomfortable at the prospect before him, but I convinced him that I could get the vessels over if he would place them under my control, and he consented to do so. I first tried with the *Richmond* (Commander Alden), and, although she had grounded seven times when in charge of a pilot, I succeeded at the first attempt, crossed the bar, and anchored off Pilot Town. The next trial was with the frigate *Mississippi.* The vessel was lightened as much as possible by taking out her spars, sails, guns, provisions, and coal. All the steamers of the mortar-fleet were then sent to her assistance, and after eight days' hard work they succeeded in pulling the *Mississippi* through. To get the *Pensacola* over looked even more difficult. I asked Captain Bailey to lend me the *Colorado* for a short time, and with this vessel

I went as close as possible to the *Pensacola,* ran out a stream-cable to her stern, and, by backing hard on the *Colorado,* soon released her from her disagreeable position. The next day at 12 o'clock I passed her over the bar and anchored her off Pilot Town.

The U. S. Coast Survey steamer *Sachem,* commanded by a very competent officer, Mr. F. H. Gerdes, had been added to the expedition for the purpose of sounding the bar and river channel, and also to establish points and distances which should serve as guides to the commander of the mortar-flotilla. Mr. Gerdes and his assistants selected the positions of the bomb-vessels, furnished all the commanders of vessels with reliable charts, triangulated the river for eight miles below the forts, and planted small poles with white flags on the banks opposite the positions of the different vessels, each flag marked with the name of a vessel and the distance from the mouth of its mortar to the center of the fort. The boats of the surveyors were frequently attacked by sharp-shooters, who fired from concealed positions among the bushes of the river bank. During the bombardment the Coast Survey officers were employed day and night in watching that the vessels did not move an inch from their places, and the good effect of all this care was shown in the final result of the mortar practice.

Having finished the preliminary work, on the 16th of April Farragut moved up with his fleet to within three miles of the forts, and informed me that I might commence the bombardment as soon as I was ready. The ships all anchored as they came up, but not in very good order, which led to some complications.

The place which I had selected for the first and third divisions of the mortar-vessels was under the lee of a thick wood on the right bank of the river, which presented in the direction of the fort an almost impenetrable mass. The forts could be plainly seen from the mast-heads of the mortar-schooners, which had been so covered with brush that the Confederate gunners could not distinguish them from the trees. The leading vessel of the first division, of seven vessels, under Lieutenant-Commanding Watson Smith, was placed at a point distant 2850 yards from Fort Jackson and 3680 yards from Fort St. Philip. The third division, commanded by Lieutenant Breese, came next in order, and the second division, under Lieutenant Queen, I placed on the east side of the river, the head of the line being 3680 yards from Fort Jackson.

The vessels now being in position, the signal was given to open fire; and on the morning of the 18th of April the bombardment fairly commenced, each mortar-vessel having orders to fire once in ten minutes.

The moment that the mortars belched forth their shells, both Jackson and St. Philip replied with great fury; but it was some time before they could obtain our range, as we were well concealed behind our natural rampart. The enemy's fire was rapid, and, finding that it was becoming rather hot, I sent Lieutenant Guest up to the head of the line to open fire on the forts with his 11-inch pivot. This position he maintained for one hour and fifty minutes, and only abandoned it to fill up with ammunition. In the meantime the mortars on the left bank (Queen's division) were doing splendid work, though suffering considerably from the enemy's fire.

I went on board the vessels of this division to see how they were getting on, and found them so cut up that I considered it necessary to remove them, with Farragut's permission, to the opposite shore, under cover of the trees, near the other vessels, which had suffered but little. They held their position, however, until sundown, when the enemy ceased firing.

At 5 o'clock in the evening Fort Jackson was seen to be on fire, and, as the flames spread rapidly, the Confederates soon left their guns. There were many conjectures among the officers of the fleet as to what was burning. Some thought that it was a fire-raft, and I was inclined to that opinion myself until I had pulled up the river in a boat and, by the aid of a night-glass, convinced myself that the fort itself was in flames. This fact I at once reported to Farragut.

At nightfall the crews of the mortar-vessels were completely exhausted; but when it became known that every shell was falling inside of the fort, they redoubled their exertions and increased the rapidity of their fire to a shell every five minutes, or in all two hundred and forty shells an hour. During the night, in order to allow the men to rest, we slackened our fire, and only sent a shell once every half hour. Thus ended the first day's bombardment, which was more effective than that of any other day during the siege.

Next morning the bombardment was renewed and continued night and day until the end. . . .

I was not ignorant of the state of affairs in the fort; for, on the third day of the bombardment, a deserter presented himself and gave us an account of the havoc created by our shells, although I had doubts of the entire truth of his statements. He represented that hundreds of shells had fallen into the fort, breaking in the bomb-proofs, setting fire to the citadel, and flooding the interior by cutting the levees. He also stated that the soldiers were in a desperate and demoralized condition. This was all very encouraging to us, and so stimulated the crews of the mortar-boats that they worked with unflagging zeal and energy. I took the deserter to Farragut, who, although impressed by his statement, was not quite prepared to take advantage of the opportunity; for at this time the line of hulks across the river was considered an insurmountable obstruction, and it was determined to examine and, if possible, remove it before the advance of the fleet.

On the night of the 20th an expedition was fitted out for the purpose of breaking the chain which was supposed to extend from one shore to the other. Two steamers, the *Pinola*, Lieutenant Crosby, and *Itasca*, Lieutenant Caldwell, were detailed for the purpose and placed under the direction of Captain Bell, chief-of-staff. Although the attempt was made under cover of darkness, the sharp eyes of the Confederate gunners soon discovered their enemies, and the whole fire of Fort Jackson was concentrated upon them. I had been informed of the intended movement by Farragut, so was ready to redouble the fire of the mortars at the proper time with good effect. In Farragut's words: "Commander Porter, however, kept up such a tremendous fire on them from the mortars that the enemy's shot did the gun-boats no injury, and the cable was separated and their connection broken sufficiently to pass through on the left bank of the river."

The work of the mortar-fleet was now almost over. We had kept up a heavy fire night and day for nearly 5 days—about 2800 shells every 24 hours; in all about 16,800 shells. The men were nearly worn out for want of sleep and rest. The ammunition was giving out, one of the schooners was sunk, and although the rest had received little actual damage from the enemy's shot, they were badly shaken up by the concussion of the mortars.

On the 23d instant I represented the state of affairs to the flag-officer, and he concluded to move on past the works, which I felt sure he could do with but little loss to his squadron. He recognized the importance of making an immediate attack, and called a council of the commanders of vessels, which resulted in a determination to pass the forts that night. The movement was postponed, however, until the next morning, for the reason that the carpenters of one of the larger ships were at work down the river, and the commander did not wish to proceed without them. The iron-clad *Louisiana* had now made her appearance, and her commander was being strongly urged by General Duncan to drop down below the forts and open fire upon the fleet with his heavy rifle-guns. On the 22d General Duncan wrote to Commander Mitchell from Fort Jackson:

It is of vital importance that the present fire of the enemy should be withdrawn from us, which you alone can do. This can be done in the manner suggested this morning under the cover of our guns, while your work on the boat can be carried on in safety and security. Our position is a critical one, dependent entirely on the powers of endurance of our casemates, many of which have been completely shattered, and are crumbling away by repeated shocks; and, therefore, I respectfully but earnestly again urge my suggestion of this morning on your notice. Our magazines are also in danger.

Fortunately for us, Commander Mitchell was not equal to the occasion, and the *Louisiana* remained tied up to the bank, where she could not obstruct the river or throw the Union fleet into confusion while passing the forts.

While Farragut was making his preparations, the enemy left no means untried to drive the mortar-boats from their position. A couple of heavy guns in Fort St. Philip kept up a continual fire on the head of the mortar column, and the Confederates used their mortars at intervals, but only succeeded in sinking one mortar-schooner and damaging a few others. A body of rifle-men was once sent out against us from the forts, but it was met by a heavy fire and soon repulsed.

Two o'clock on the morning of the 24th instant was fixed upon as the time for the fleet to start, and Farragut had previously given the necessary orders to the commanders of vessels, instructing them to prepare their ships for action by sending down their light spars, painting their hulls mud-color, etc.; also to hang their chain-cables over the sides abreast the engines, as a pro-tection against the enemy's shot. He issued the following "General Order":

UNITED STATES FLAG-SHIP *Hartford,* MISSISSIPPI RIVER, April 20th, 1862

The flag-officer, having heard all the opinions expressed by the different com-manders, is of the opinion that whatever is to be done will have to be done quickly, or we shall be again reduced to a blockading squadron, without the means of carrying on the bombardment, as we have nearly expended all the shells and fuses, and material for making cartridges. He has always entertained the same opin-ions which are expressed by Commander Porter; that is, there are three modes of attack, and the question is, which is the one to be adopted? His own opinion is that a combination of two should be made, viz.: the forts should be run, and when a force is once above the forts, to protect the troops, they should be landed at quarantine from the gulf side by bringing them through the bayou, and then our forces should move up the river, mutually aiding each other as it can be done to advantage.

When, in the opinion of the flag-officer, the propitious time has arrived, the signal will be made to weigh and advance to the conflict. If, in his opinion, at the time of arriving at the respective positions of the different divisions of the fleet, we have the advantage, he will make the signal for close action, No. 8, and abide the result, conquer or to be conquered, drop anchor or keep under way, as in his opinion is best.

Unless the signal above mentioned is made, it will be understood that the first order of sailing will be formed after leaving Fort St. Philip, and we will proceed up the river in accordance with the original opinion expressed. The programme of the order of sailing accompanies this general order, and the commanders will hold themselves in readiness for the service as indicated. Very respectfully, your obedient servant,

D. G. FARRAGUT, Flag-Officer West Gulf Blockading Squadron

Farragut's first plan was to lead the fleet with his flag-ship, the *Hartford,* to be closely followed by the *Brooklyn, Richmond, Pensacola,* and *Mississippi,* thinking it well to have his heavy vessels in the van, where they could im-mediately crush any naval force that might appear against them. This plan was a better one than that afterward adopted; but he was induced to change the order of his column by the senior commanders of the fleet, who repre-sented to him that it was unwise for the commander-in-chief to take the brunt of the battle. They finally obtained his reluctant consent to an arrangement by which Captain Bailey was to lead in the gun-boat *Cayuga,* commanded by Lieutenant N. B. Harrison—a good selection, as it afterward proved, for these officers were gallant and competent men, well qualified for the position. Captain Bailey had volunteered for the service, and left nothing undone to overcome Farragut's reluctance to give up what was then considered the post of danger, though it turned out to be less hazardous than the places in the rear.

The mortar-flotilla steamers under my command were directed to move up before the fleet weighed anchor, and to be ready to engage the water-batteries of Fort Jackson as the fleet passed. These batteries mounted some of the heaviest guns in the defenses, and were depended upon to do efficient work.

The commanders of vessels were informed of the change of plan, and instructed to follow in line according to the order of attack.

At 2 o'clock on the morning of April 24th all of the Union vessels began to heave up their anchors. It was a still, clear night, and the click of the capstans, with the grating of the chain-cables as they passed through the hawse-holes, made a great noise, which we feared would serve as a warning to our enemies. This conjecture proved to be correct, for the Confederates were on the alert in both forts and steamers to meet the invaders. One fact only was in our favor, and that was the division of their forces under three different heads, which prevented unanimity of action. In every other respect the odds were against us.

Before Farragut ascended the river, the French admiral and Captain Preedy, of the English frigate *Mersey,* had both been up as far as the forts and had communicated with the military commanders. On their return, they gave discouraging accounts of the defenses, and pronounced it impossible for our fleet to pass them. This, of course, did not tend to cheer our sailors. There were some in the fleet who were doubtful of success, and there was not that confidence on our side that should have existed on such an occasion; but when it was seen that the river obstructions and rafts had been washed away by the currents, and that there appeared to be an open way up the river, every one became more hopeful.

The entire fleet did not get fully under way until half-past 2 A. M. The current was strong, and although the ships proceeded as rapidly as their steampower would permit, our leading vessel, the *Cayuga,* did not get under fire until a quarter of 3 o'clock, when both Jackson and St. Philip opened on her at the same moment. Five steamers of the mortar-flotilla took their position below the water-battery of Fort Jackson, at a distance of less than two hundred yards, and, pouring in grape, canister, and shrapnel, kept down the fire of that battery. The mortars opened at the same moment with great fury, and the action commenced in earnest.

Captain Bailey, in the *Cayuga,* followed by the other vessels of his division in compact order, passed the line of obstructions without difficulty. He had no sooner attained this point, however, than he was obliged to face the guns of Fort St. Philip, which did him some damage before he was able to fire a shot in return. He kept steadily on, however, and, as soon as his guns could be brought to bear, poured in grape and canister with good effect and passed safe above. He was here met by the enemy's gun-boats, and, although he was beset by several large steamers at the same time, he succeeded in driving them off. The *Oneida* and *Varuna* came to the support of their leader, and by the rapid fire of their heavy guns soon dispersed the enemy's flotilla. This was more congenial work for our men and officers than that through which they had just passed, and it was soon evident that the coolness and discipline of our navy gave it a great advantage over the fleet of the enemy. Bailey dashed on up the river, followed by his division, firing into everything they met; and soon after the head of the flag-officer's division had passed the forts, most of the river craft were disabled, and the battle was virtually won. This was evident even to Lieutenant-Colonel Higgins, who, when he saw our large ships pass by, exclaimed, "Better go to cover, boys; our cake is all dough!"

In the meantime the *Varuna,* being a swift vessel, passed ahead of the other ships in the division, and pushed on up the river after the fleeing enemy, until she found herself right in the midst of them. The Confederates, supposing in the dark that the *Varuna* was one of their own vessels, did not attack her until Commander Boggs made himself known by delivering his fire right and left. One shot exploded the boiler of a large steamer crowded with troops, and she drifted ashore; three other vessels were driven ashore in flames. At daylight the *Varuna* was attacked by the *Governor Moore,* a powerful steamer, fitted as a ram, and commanded by Lieutenant Beverley Kennon, late of the U. S. Navy. This vessel raked the *Varuna* with her bow-gun along the port gangway, killing 5 or 6 men; and while the Union vessel was gallantly returning this fire, her side was pierced twice by the iron prow of the ram. The Confederate ram *Stonewall Jackson* also attacked the *Varuna,* ramming her twice about amidships; the *Varuna* at the same moment punished her severely with grape and canister from her 8-inch guns, and finally drove her out of action in a disabled condition and in flames. But the career of the *Varuna* was ended; she began to fill rapidly, and her gallant commander was obliged to run her into shoal water, where she soon went to the bottom. Captain Lee, of the *Oneida,* seeing that his companion needed assistance, went to his relief, and rescued the officers and men of the *Varuna.* The two Confederate rams were set on fire by their crews and abandoned. Great gallantry was displayed on both sides during the conflict of these smaller steamers, which really bore the brunt of the battle, and the Union commanders showed great skill in managing their vessels.

Bailey's division may be said to have swept everything before it. The *Pensa-*

cola, with her heavy batteries, drove the men from the guns at Fort St. Philip, and made it easier for the ships astern to get by. Fort St. Philip had not been at all damaged by the mortars, as it was virtually beyond their reach, and it was from the guns of that work that our ships received the greatest injury.

As most of the vessels of Bailey's division swept past the turn above the forts, Farragut came upon the scene with the *Hartford* and *Brooklyn*. The other ship of Farragut's division, the *Richmond*, Commander James Alden, got out of the line and passed up on the west side of the river, near where I was engaged with the mortar-steamers in silencing the water-batteries of Fort Jackson. At this moment the Confederates in Fort Jackson had nearly all been driven from their guns by bombs from the mortar-boats and the grape and canister from the steamers. I hailed Alden, and told him to pass close to the fort and in the eddy, and he would receive little damage. He followed this advice, and passed by very comfortably.

By this time the river had been illuminated by two fire-rafts, and everything could be seen as by the light of day. I could see every ship and gun-boat as she passed up as plainly as possible, and noted all their positions.

It would be a difficult undertaking at any time to keep a long line of vessels in compact order when ascending a crooked channel against a three-and-a-half-knot current, and our commanders found it to be especially so under the present trying circumstances. The *Iroquois*, Commander De Camp, as gallant an officer as ever lived, got out of line and passed up ahead of her consorts; but De Camp made good use of his opportunity by engaging and driving off a ram and the gun-boat *McRae*, which attacked him as soon as he had passed Fort Jackson. The *McRae* was disabled and her commander (Huger) mortally wounded. The *Iroquois* was much cut up by Fort St. Philip and the gun-boats, but did not receive a single shot from Fort Jackson, although passing within fifty yards of it.

While the events above mentioned were taking place, Farragut had engaged Fort St. Philip at close quarters with his heavy ships, and had driven the men from their guns. He was passing on up the river, when his flag-ship was threatened by a new and formidable adversary. A fire-raft in full blaze was seen coming down the river, guided toward the *Hartford* by a tug-boat, the *Mosher*. It seemed impossible to avoid this danger, and as the helm was put to port in the attempt to do so, the flag-ship ran upon a shoal. While in this position the fire-raft was pushed against her, and in a minute she was enveloped in flames half-way up to her tops, and was in a condition of great peril. The fire department was at once called away, and while the *Hartford's* batteries kept up the fight with Fort St. Philip, the flames were extinguished and the vessel backed off the shoal into deep water—a result due to the coolness of her commander and the good discipline of the officers and men. While the *Hartford* was in this perilous position, and her entire destruction was threatened, Farragut showed all the qualities of a great commander. He walked up and down the poop as coolly as though on dress-parade, while Commander Wainwright directed the firemen in putting out the flames. At times the fire would rush through the ports and almost drive the men from the guns.

"Don't flinch from that fire, boys," sang out Farragut; "there's a hotter fire than that for those who don't do their duty! Give that rascally little tug a shot, and don't let her go off with a whole coat!" The *Mosher* was sunk.

While passing the forts the *Hartford* was struck thirty-two times in hull and rigging, and had 3 men killed and 10 wounded.

The *Brooklyn,* Captain Thomas T. Craven, followed as close after the flag-ship as the blinding smoke from guns and fire-rafts would admit, and the garrison of the fort was again driven to cover by the fire of her heavy battery. She passed on with severe punishment, and was immediately attacked by the most powerful vessel in the Confederate fleet, excepting the *Louisiana* —the ram *Manassas,* commanded by Lieutenant Warley, a gallant young officer of the old service. The blow that the *Manassas* struck the *Brooklyn* did but little apparent injury, and the ram slid off in the dark to seek other prey. (It must be remembered that these scenes were being enacted on a dark night, and in an atmosphere filled with dense smoke, through which our commanders had to grope their way, guided only by the flashes of the guns in the forts and the fitful light of burning vessels and rafts.) The *Brooklyn* was next attacked by a large steamer, which received her broadside at the distance of twenty yards, and drifted out of action in flames. Notwithstanding the heavy fire which the *Brooklyn* had gone through, she was only struck seventeen times in the hull. She lost 9 men killed and 26 wounded.

When our large ships had passed the forts, the affair was virtually over. Had they all been near the head of the column, the enemy would have been crushed at once, and the flag-ship would have passed up almost unhurt. As it was, the *Hartford* was more exposed and imperiled than any of her consorts, and that at a time when, if anything had happened to the commander-in-chief, the fleet would have been thrown into confusion.

The forts had been so thoroughly silenced by the ships' guns and mortars that when Captain Bell came along in the little *Sciota,* at the head of the third division, he passed by nearly unharmed. All the other vessels succeeded in getting by, except the *Itasca,* Lieutenant Caldwell, the *Winona,* Lieutenant Nichols, and the *Kennebec,* Lieutenant Russell. The first two vessels, having kept in line, were caught at daylight below the forts without support, and, as the current was swift and they were slow steamers, they became mere targets for the Confederates, who now turned all that was left of their fighting power upon them. Seeing their helpless condition, I signaled them to retire, which they did after being seriously cut up. . . .

While these events were taking place, the mortar-steamers had driven the men from the water-batteries and had kept up a steady fire on the walls of Fort Jackson. Although at first sight my position in front of these batteries, which mounted six of the heaviest guns in the Confederate works (1 10-inch and 2 8-inch Columbiads, 1 10-inch sea-coast mortar, and 2 rifled 32-pounders), seemed a very perilous one, it was not at all so. I ran the steamers close alongside of the levee just below the water-batteries, and thus protected their hulls below the firing-decks. I got in my first broadside just as the middle of Bailey's column was opened upon by Fort Jackson. The enemy responded quickly, but our fire was so rapid and accurate that in ten minutes the water-battery was deserted. I had 25 8-inch and 32-pounders on one side and 2 11-inch pivot-guns. During the remainder of the action I devoted most of my attention to the battlements of the main fort, firing an occasional shot at the water-battery. The *Harriet Lane* had two men killed, but the only damage done to the vessels was to their masts and rigging, their hulls having been well protected by the levees.

While engaged on this duty I had an excellent opportunity of witnessing the movements of Farragut's fleet, and, by the aid of powerful night-glasses, I could almost distinguish persons on the vessels. The whole scene looked like a beautiful panorama. From almost perfect silence—the steamers moving slowly through the water like phantom ships—one incessant roar of heavy cannon commenced, the Confederate forts and gun-boats opening together on the head of our line as it came within range. The Union vessels returned the fire as they came up, and soon the guns of our fleet joined in the thunder, which seemed to shake the very earth. A lurid glare was thrown over the scene by the burning rafts, and, as the bomb-shells crossed each other and exploded in the air, it seemed as if a battle were taking place in the heavens as well as on the earth. It all ended as suddenly as it had commenced. In one hour and ten minutes after the vessels of the fleet had weighed anchor, the affair was virtually over, and Farragut was pushing on toward New Orleans, where he was soon to crush the last hope of Rebellion in that quarter by opening the way for the advance of the Union army.

Descriptions of campaigns by high military leaders are numerous, partly perhaps because they can be fairly sure of a public audience. While an unknown fellow in the ranks, if he can find time and place to put down his observations at all, usually must want to do so only for the family or friends back home. When he does, though, the result often gives the reader a rare opportunity for participation at the level on which the actual fighting takes place. Such a report follows.

The writer's brief glimpse of McClellan under sudden fire quietly knocking the ashes from his cigar while the French Prince jumped is an admiring one, and typical of one of McClellan's men. They loved him because he loved them. He was the Little Father, tireless in looking to their needs. Sometimes he was in the saddle as long as nine hours a day, prancing through their camps or along their lines, and they thought him the very picture of a great commander. They even had a song:

> *"For McClellan's our leader; he is gallant and strong.*
> *For God and our Country we are marching along."*

But unfortunately for the Union, he hated to make them fight.

"Why don't you get behind a tree?"

YORKTOWN AND WILLIAMSBURG

BY WARREN LEE GOSS, PRIVATE, U. S. A.

IT WAS with open-eyed wonder that, as part of McClellan's army, we arrived at Old Point Comfort and gazed upon Fort Monroe, huge and frowning. Negroes were everywhere, and went about their work with an air of importance born of their new-found freedom. These were the "contrabands" for whom General Butler had recently invented that sobriquet. We pitched our tents amid the charred and blackened ruins of what had been the beautiful and aristocratic village of Hampton. The first thing I noticed about the ruins, unaccustomed as I was to Southern architecture, was the absence of cellars. The only building left standing of all the village was the massive old Episcopal church. Here Washington had worshiped, and its broad aisles had echoed to the footsteps of armed men during the Revolution. In the church-yard the tombs had been broken open. Many tombstones were broken and overthrown, and at the corner of the church a big hole showed that some one with a greater desire for possessing curiosities than reverence for ancient landmarks had been digging for the corner-stone and its buried mementos.

Along the shore which looks toward Fort Monroe were landed artillery, baggage-wagons, pontoon trains and boats, and the level land back of this

141

was crowded with the tents of the soldiers. Here and there were groups frying hard-tack and bacon. Near at hand was the irrepressible army mule, hitched to and eating out of pontoon boats; those who had eaten their ration of grain and hay were trying their teeth, with promise of success, in eating the boats. An army mule was hungrier than a soldier, and would eat anything, especially a pontoon boat or rubber blanket. The scene was a busy one. The red cap, white leggins, and baggy trousers of the Zouaves mingled with the blue uniforms and dark trimmings of the regular infantry-men, the short jackets and yellow trimmings of the cavalry, the red stripes of the artillery, and the dark blue with orange trimmings of the engineers; together with the ragged, many-colored costumes of the black laborers and teamsters, all busy at something.

One morning we broke camp and went marching up the Peninsula. The roads were very poor and muddy with recent rains, and were crowded with the indescribable material of the vast army which was slowly creeping through the mud over the flat, wooded country. It was a bright day in April—a perfect Virginia day; the grass was green beneath our feet, the buds of the trees were just unrolling into leaves under the warming sun of spring, and in the woods the birds were singing. The march was at first orderly, but under the unaccustomed burden of heavy equipments and knapsacks, and the warmth of the weather, the men straggled along the roads, mingling with the baggage-wagons, ambulances, and pontoon trains, in seeming confusion.

During our second day's march it rained, and the muddy roads, cut up and kneaded, as it were, by the teams preceding us, left them in a state of semi-liquid filth hardly possible to describe or imagine. When we arrived at Big Bethel the rain was coming down in sheets. A dozen houses of very ordinary character, scattered over an area of a third of a mile, constituted what was called the village. Just outside and west of the town was an insignificant building from which the place takes its name. It did not seem large enough or of sufficient consequence to give name to a hamlet as small as Big Bethel. Before our arrival it had evidently been occupied as officers' barracks for the enemy, and looked very little like a church.

I visited one of the dwelling-houses just outside the fortifications (if the insignificant rifle-pits could be called such) for the purpose of obtaining something more palatable than hard-tack, salt beef, or pork, which, with coffee, comprised the marching rations. The woman of the house was communicative, and expressed her surprise at the great number of Yanks who had "come down to invade our soil." She said she had a son in the Confederate army, or, as she expressed it, "in our army," and then tearfully said she should tremble for her boy every time she heard of a battle. I expressed the opinion that we should go into Richmond without much fighting. "No!" said she, with the emphasis of conviction, "you all will drink hot blood before you all get thar!"

"Why don't you get behind a tree?"

While wandering about, I came to the house of a Mrs. T——, whose husband was said to be a captain in the Confederate service and a "fire-eating" secessionist. Here some of our men were put on guard for a short time, until relieved by guards from other parts of the army as they came up, whereupon we went on. A large, good-looking woman, about forty years old, who, I learned, was Mrs. T——, was crying profusely, and I could not induce her to tell me why. One of the soldiers said her grief was caused by the fact that some of our men had helped themselves to the contents of cupboard and cellar. She was superintending the loading of an old farm-wagon, into which she was putting a large family of colored people, with numerous bundles. The only white person on the load as it started away was the mistress, who sat amid her dark chattels in desolation and tears. Returning to the house, after this exodus, I found letters, papers, and odds and ends of various kinds littering the floor; whether overturned in the haste of the mistress or by the visiting soldiers, I could only guess. No other building at Big Bethel was so devastated, and I did not see another building so treated on our whole route. The men detailed to guard it declined to protect the property of one who was in arms fighting against us.

After leaving Big Bethel we began to feel the weight of our knapsacks. Castaway overcoats, blankets, parade-coats, and shoes were scattered along the route in reckless profusion, being dropped by the overloaded soldiers, as if after plowing the roads with heavy teams they were sowing them for a harvest. I lightened my knapsack without much regret, for I could not see the wisdom of carrying a blanket or overcoat when I could pick one up almost anywhere along the march. Very likely the same philosophy actuated those who preceded me or came after. The colored people along our route occupied themselves in picking up this scattered property. They had on their faces a distrustful look, as if uncertain of the tenure of their harvest. The march up the peninsula seemed very slow, yet it was impossible to increase our speed, owing to the bad condition of the roads. I learned in time that marching on paper and the actual march made two very different impressions. I can easily understand and excuse our fire-side heroes, who fought their or our battles at home over comfortable breakfast-tables, without impediments of any kind to circumscribe their fancied operations; it is so much easier to manœuvre and fight large armies around the corner grocery, than to fight, march, and manœuvre in mud and rain, in the face of a brave and vigilant enemy.

The baggage-trains were a notable spectacle. To each baggage-wagon were attached four or six mules, driven usually by a colored man, with only one rein, or line, and that line attached to the bit of the near leading mule, while the driver rode in a saddle upon the near wheel mule. Each train was accompanied by a guard, and while the guard urged the drivers the drivers urged the mules. The drivers were usually expert, and understood well the

143

wayward, sportive natures of the creatures over whose destinies they presided. On our way to Yorktown our pontoon and baggage trains were sometimes blocked for miles, and the heaviest trains were often unloaded by the guard to facilitate their removal from the mud. It did seem at times as if there were needless delays with the trains, partly due, no doubt, to fear of danger ahead. While I was guarding our pontoon train, after leaving Big Bethel, the teams stopped all along the line. Hurrying to the front, I found one of the leading teams badly mired, but not enough to justify the stopping of the whole train. The lazy colored driver was comfortably asleep in the saddle. "Get that team out of the mud!" I yelled, bringing him to his senses. He flourished his long whip, shouted his mule lingo at the team, and the mules pulled frantically, but not together. "Can't you make your mules pull together?" I inquired. "Dem mules pull right smart!" said the driver. Cocking and capping my unloaded musket, I brought it to the shoulder and again commanded the driver, "Get that team out of the mud!" The Negro rolled his eyes wildly and woke up all over. He first patted his saddle mule, spoke to each one, and then, flourishing his long whip with a crack like a pistol, shouted, "Go 'long dar! what I feed yo' fo'!" and the mule team left the slough in a very expeditious manner.

When procuring luxuries of eggs or milk, we paid the people at first in silver, and they gave us local scrip in change; but we found on attempting to pay it out again that they were rather reluctant to receive it, even at that early stage in Confederate finance, and much preferred Yankee silver or notes.

On the afternoon of April 5th, 1862, the advance of our column was brought to a standstill, with the right in front of Yorktown, and the left by the enemy's works at Lee's mills. We pitched our camp on Wormley Creek, near the Moore house, on the York River, in sight of the enemy's water-battery and their defensive works at Gloucester Point. One of the impediments to an immediate attack on Yorktown was the difficulty of using light artillery in the muddy fields in our front, and at that time the topography of the country ahead was but little understood, and had to be learned by reconnoissance in force. We had settled down to the siege of Yorktown; began bridging the streams between us and the enemy, constructing and improving the roads for the rapid transit of supplies, and for the advance. The first parallel was opened about a mile from the enemy's fortifications, extending along the entire front of their works, which reached from the York River on the left to Warwick Creek on the right, along a line about four miles in length. Fourteen batteries and three redoubts were planted, heavily armed with ordnance.

We were near Battery No. 1, not far from the York River. On it were mounted several 200-pounder guns, which commanded the enemy's water-batteries. One day I was in a redoubt on the left, and saw General McClellan with the Prince de Joinville, examining the enemy's works through their field-glasses. They very soon drew the fire of the observant enemy, who opened with one of their heavy guns on the group, sending the first shot howling and hissing over and very close to their heads; another, quickly following it, struck in the parapet of the redoubt. The French prince, seemingly quite startled, jumped and glanced nervously around, while McClellan quietly knocked the ashes from his cigar.

Several of our war-vessels made their appearance in the York River, and occasionally threw a shot at the enemy's works; but most of them were kept busy at Hampton Roads, watching for the iron-clad *Merrimac,* which was still afloat. The firing from the enemy's lines was of little consequence, not amounting to over ten or twelve shots each day, a number of these being directed at the huge balloon which went up daily on a tour of inspection, from near General Fitz John Porter's headquarters. One day the balloon broke from its moorings of ropes and sailed majestically over the enemy's works; but fortunately for its occupants it soon met a counter-current of air which returned it safe to our lines. The month of April was a dreary one, much of the time rainy and uncomfortable. It was a common expectation among us that we were about to end the rebellion. One of my comrades wrote home to his father that we should probably finish up the war in season for him to be at home to teach the village school the following winter; in fact, I believe he partly engaged to teach it. Another wrote to his mother: "We have got them hemmed in on every side, and the only reason they don't run is because they can't." We had at last corduroyed every road and bridged every creek; our guns and mortars were in position; Battery No. 1 had actually opened on the enemy's work, Saturday, May 3d, 1862, and it was expected that our whole line would open on them in the morning. About 2 o'clock of Saturday night, or rather of Sunday morning, while on guard duty, I observed a bright illumination, as if a fire had broken out within the enemy's lines. Several guns were fired from their works during the early morning hours, but soon after daylight of May 4th it was reported that they had abandoned their works in our front, and we very quickly found the report to be true. As soon as I was relieved from guard duty, I went over on "French leave" to view our enemy's fortifications. They were prodigiously strong. A few tumble-down tents and houses and seventy pieces of heavy ordnance had been abandoned as the price of the enemy's safe retreat.

As soon as it was known that the Confederates had abandoned the works at Yorktown, the commanding general sent the cavalry and horse artillery under Stoneman in pursuit to harass the retreating column. The infantry divisions of Smith and Hooker were sent forward by two roads to support the light column. General Sumner (the officer second in rank in the Army of the Potomac) was directed to proceed to the front and assume command until McClellan's arrival. Stoneman overtook Johnston's rear-guard about noon, six miles from Williamsburg, and skirmished with the cavalry of Stuart, following sharply until 4 o'clock, when he was confronted by a line of redoubts before Williamsburg. The works consisted of a large fort (Magruder) at the junction of two roads running from Yorktown to Williamsburg, and small redoubts on each side of this, making an irregular chain of fortifications extending, with the creeks upon which they rested on either flank, across the peninsula. The Confederate brigades of Kershaw and Semmes, of Magruder's command, occupied the works when Stoneman came in front of them, and, on finding his advance stubbornly opposed, Stoneman sent his cavalry upon reconnoissances over the field, and waited for the infantry under Hooker and Smith to come to his support. These divisions marched from Yorktown on parallel roads until Smith's column was halted by a burning bridge, and compelled to turn into the road by which Hooker was advancing. Sumner accompanied Smith's column, and, immediately on the arrival before Williamsburg, formed the brigades of Hancock and Brooks for an advance through a piece of woods which screened the Confederate rifle-pits. The result is given in Sumner's official report as follows:

After entering the woods I found the underbrush much thicker than I expected, and the lines became entangled, and shortly afterward it became so dark it was impossible to advance, and I ordered the troops to halt and lie on their arms.

General Hooker was delayed on the road so long that he did not reach the field until early on the morning of May 5th, when he found himself on the left of Smith's division, and in front of Fort Magruder. The position of the Union troops then was: Smith on the right, and Hooker on the left, confronting the enemy's works, the latter having the heaviest obstacle before him, and the divisions of Kearny, Casey, and Couch struggling on toward the front, over crowded, muddy roads. General Sumner says in his report:

I had a careful reconnoissance made on the left of the enemy's works, on the morning of the 5th, and found two of their forts unoccupied. I immediately ordered General Hancock to advance with a brigade and ten pieces of artillery, and hold those works, it being my intention to force their left.

This was about 11 A. M. Meantime, at 7:30 A. M., General Hooker, on his own responsibility, had advanced his lines. In his official report he says:

Being in pursuit of a retreating army, I deemed it my duty to lose no time in making the disposition to attack, regardless of their number and position, except to accomplish the result with the least possible sacrifice of life.

Hooker sent forward Grover's brigade, and Bramhall's and Webber's batteries, and very soon all opposition on his front was silenced for a time.

Longstreet, however, ordered up reënforcements, and soon had a section of Pelham's battery, and the three fresh brigades of Wilcox, Pickett, and A. P. Hill on the ground, driving Hooker back, with the loss of all his cannon, and heavy casualties. During his desperate engagement, Hooker reported his situation to Sumner, and Kearny was promptly ordered up with his division, while Heintzelman, the proper commander of the Third Corps, was sent to the spot to take charge.

A comrade in Hooker's division gave me an account of his experiences about as follows: "Marching over the muddy road late in the afternoon, we found our farther advance prevented by a force which had preceded us, and we halted in the mud by the roadside just as it began to rain. About 5 o'clock we resumed our march by crossing over to the Hampton road, and did not halt till 11 in the evening, when we lay down in our blankets, bedraggled, wet, and tired, chewing hard-tack and the cud of reflection, the tenor of which was, 'Why did we come for a soldier?' Before daylight we were on the march, plodding in the rain through the mire. By daybreak we came out on the edge of the dense woods in front of Fort Magruder. The main fort was a strong earth-work with a bastioned front and a wide ditch. In front of this muddy-looking heap of dirt was a level plain, sprinkled plentifully with smaller earth-works; while between us and the level plain the dense forest, for a distance of a quarter of a mile, had been felled, thus forming a labyrinth of tangled abatis difficult to penetrate. A mile away lay the village of Williamsburg.

"We were soon sent out as skirmishers, with orders to advance as near the enemy's rifle-pits as possible. They immediately opened fire upon us with heavy guns from the fort, while from their rifle-pits came a hum of bullets and crackle of musketry. Their heavy shot came crashing among the tangled abatis of fallen timber, and plowed up the dirt in our front, rebounding and tearing through the branches of the woods in our rear. The constant hissing of the bullets, with their sharp *ping* or *bizz* whispering around and sometimes into us, gave me a sickening feeling and a cold perspiration. I felt weak around my knees—a sort of faintness and lack of strength in the joints of my legs, as if they would sink from under me. These symptoms did not decrease when several of my comrades were hit. The little rifle-pits in our front fairly blazed with musketry, and the continuous *snap, snap, crack, crack* was murderous. Seeing I was not killed at once, in spite of all the noise, my knees recovered from their unpleasant limpness, and my mind gradually regained its balance and composure. I never afterward felt these disturbing influences to the same degree.

"We slowly retired from stump to stump and from log to log, finally regaining the edge of the wood, and took our position near Webber's and Bramhall's batteries, which had just got into position on the right of the road, not over seven hundred yards from the hostile fort. While getting into

147

position several of the battery men were killed, as they immediately drew the artillery fire of the enemy, which opened with a noise and violence that astonished me. Our two batteries were admirably handled, throwing a number of shot and shell into the enemy's works, speedily silencing them, and by 9 o'clock the field in our front, including the rifle-pits, was completely 'cleaned out' of artillery and infantry. Shortly afterward we advanced along the edge of the wood to the left of Fort Magruder, and about 11 o'clock we saw emerging from the little ravine to the left of the fort a swarm of Confederates, who opened on us with a terrible and deadly fire. Then they charged upon us with their peculiar yell. We took all the advantage possible of the stumps and trees as we were pushed back, until we reached the edge of the wood again, where we halted and fired upon the enemy from behind all the cover the situation afforded. We were none of us too proud, not even those who had the dignity of shoulder-straps to support, to dodge behind a tree or stump. I called out to a comrade, 'Why don't you get behind a tree?' 'Confound it,' said he, 'there ain't enough for the officers.' I don't mean to accuse officers of cowardice, but we had suddenly found out that they showed the same general inclination not to get shot as privates did, and were anxious to avail themselves of the privilege of their rank by getting in our rear. I have always thought that pride was a good substitute for courage, if well backed by a conscientious sense of duty; and most of our men, officers as well as privates, were too proud to show the fear which I have no doubt they felt in common with myself. Occasionally a soldier would show symptoms which pride could not overcome. One of our men, Spinney, ran into the woods and was not seen until after the engagement. Some time afterward, when he had proved a good soldier, I asked him why he ran, and he replied that every bullet which went by his head said 'Spinney,' and he thought they were calling for him. In all the pictures of battles I had seen before I ever saw a battle, the officers were at the front on prancing steeds, or with uplifted swords were leading their followers to the charge. Of course, I was surprised to find that in a real battle the officer gets in the rear of his men, as is his right and duty—that is, if his ideas of duty do not carry him so far to the rear as to make his sword useless.

"The 'rebs' forced us back by their charge, and our central lines were almost broken. The forces withdrawn from our right had taken the infantry support from our batteries, one of which, consisting of four guns, was captured. We were tired, wet, and exhausted when supports came up, and we were allowed to fall back from under the enemy's fire, but still in easy reach of the battle. I asked one of my comrades how he felt, and his reply was characteristic of the prevailing sentiment: 'I should feel like a hero if I wasn't so blank wet.' The bullets had cut queer antics among our men. A private, who had a canteen of whisky when he went into the engagement, on endeavoring to take a drink found the canteen quite empty, a bullet having tapped it for him. Another had a part of his thumb-nail taken off. Another had a bullet pass into the toe of his boot, down between two toes, and out along the sole of his foot, without much injury. Another had a scalp-wound from a bullet, which took off a strip of hair about three inches in length from the top of his head. Two of my regiment were killed outright and fourteen badly wounded, besides quite a number slightly injured. Thus I have chronicled my first day's fight, and I don't believe any of my regiment were ambitious to 'chase the enemy' any farther just at present. Refreshed with hot coffee and hard-tack, we rested from the fight, well satisfied that we had done our duty."

On the Confederate side, according to Longstreet's account, the march of the rear column northward in retreat from the town was being delayed all day on the 5th by impassable roads, and he ordered fresh troops from time to time to countermarch to the field at Williamsburg, relieving those whose ammunition was exhausted in this unexpected engagement. After Hooker had been forced back from Fort Magruder, the threatening position of Hancock on the Confederate left was noted by the enemy, and D. H. Hill went forward with Early's brigade, Early and Hill in person leading, toward the crest where Hancock's infantry was posted.

The Confederates were met by a severe musketry fire, and at length by a counter charge, led by Hancock, in which the bayonet was used in open field. Generals Sumner, Keyes, and Smith all mentioned Hancock's victory, which was brilliant and decisive. General Smith said in his report, "The brilliancy of the plan of battle, the coolness of its execution, the seizing of the proper instant for changing from the defensive to the offensive, the steadiness of the troops engaged, and the completeness of the victory, are subjects to which I earnestly call the attention of the General-in-Chief for just praise." General Keyes wrote, "If Hancock had failed, the enemy would not have retreated."

The division of Kearny, that was coming to Hooker's aid, was delayed by crowded roads, and reached the field by brigades between 2:30 and 4 o'clock, and, taking position on Hooker's field, became engaged in a somewhat irregular fight to the extent of five regiments of the brigades of Berry and Birney. Berry's brigade made a desperate charge, recovering some of the ground yielded by Hooker earlier in the day. The heavy losses at Williamsburg fell upon Hooker and Kearny, the division of the former sustaining nearly three-fourths of the total Union loss.

After the engagement I went over the field in front of the enemy's fort. Advancing through the tangled mass of logs and stumps, I saw one of our men aiming over the branch of a fallen tree, which lay among the tangled abatis. I called to him, but he did not turn or move. Advancing nearer, I put my hand on his shoulder, looked in his face, and started back. He was dead!—shot through the brain; and so suddenly had the end come that his rigid hand grasped his musket, and he still preserved the attitude of watchfulness, liter-

149

ally occupying his post after death. At another place we came upon one of our men who had evidently died from wounds. Near one of his hands was a Testament, and on his breast lay an ambrotype picture of a group of children and another of a young woman.

The 6th of May was a beautiful morning, with birds singing among the thickets in which lay the dead. The next morning we marched through quaint, old-fashioned Williamsburg. The most substantial buildings of the town were those of William and Mary College, which were of brick. We kindled fires from that almost inexhaustible source of supply, the Virginia fences, cooked our coffee, sang, and smoked, thoughtless of the morrow.

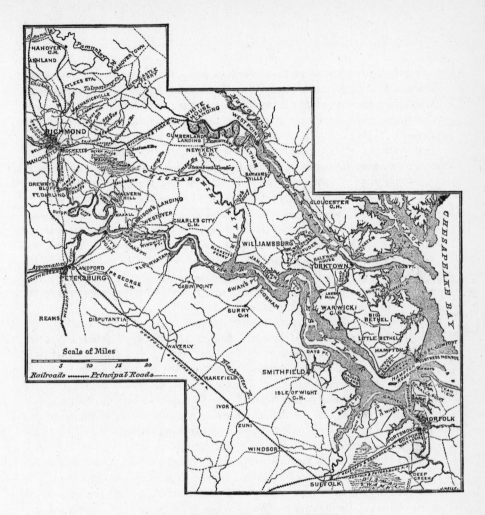

MAP OF THE PENINSULAR CAMPAIGN

In July 1861, after his successes in West Virginia, George B. McClellan was called to Washington and made general in chief. At the time it was an understandable appointment, but it was an unfortunate one. McClellan was young (thirty-four), he was lionized everywhere, and his head was turned. To his wife he wrote: "I find myself in a new and strange position here, President, cabinet, Gen. Scott and all deferring to me. By some strange operation of magic I seem to have become the power in the land." And he felt supremely qualified to exercise that power. Again he wrote: "I feel that God will give me the strength and wisdom to preserve this great nation. It is an immense task that I have on my hands, but I believe I can accomplish it . . . I can do it all." All through that fall and winter he fortified the approaches to the city, built and organized and disciplined the army, drilled and reviewed and inspected, entertained government officials at his headquarters, wrote reports. But he did not move. He seemed to have two almost pathological obsessions: that he was always outnumbered by the enemy, and that jealous officers and stupid members of the government were continually plotting his downfall.

Finally Lincoln lost patience. Late in January he issued what he called General War Order Number 1 in which he directed that on February 22 there should be a general movement of the land and naval forces against the enemy. Lincoln expected his general in chief to move on the Confederate army in northern Virginia but McClellan, finally prodded into some kind of action, proposed to approach Richmond by way of the lower Chesapeake Bay. Lincoln had reservations about the plan, particularly because it would expose Washington, but he accepted it. So early in April 1862, almost nine months after he had assumed the command, McClellan landed at Fort Monroe.

His account of the subsequent Peninsular campaign follows, and it is an interesting document. According to this report, he was plagued continually by bad weather, muddy roads, unmaneuverable country, unsafe bridges, inadequate transport, inefficiency and bad faith in Washington, the unexpected failure of others, and ever and always an enemy of overwhelming numbers (his inclination was always to accept the grossly exaggerated estimates of Confederate strength brought to him by Allen Pinkerton, the head of his intelligence service). He never considered that the enemy had similar problems to cope with and, as Lincoln remarked to John Hay, "he seemed to think, in defiance of Scripture, that Heaven sent its rain only on the just and not on the unjust." Through the next three months his army crawled up the Peninsula to within four miles of Richmond. At the end of May, Joseph E. Johnston, the Confederate commander in chief, provoked the Battle of Seven Pines which ended inconclusively but in which McClellan maintained his position. In mid-June, "Jeb" Stuart on a reconnoitering mission rode his troopers clean around the Union army, destroying $7,000,000 worth of stores. And late in June, Rob-

ert E. Lee, who had succeeded the wounded Johnston in the command, finding McClellan's forces straddling the Chickahominy River, attempted unsuccessfully to destroy the Union army in a series of savage engagements which became known as the Seven Days. McClellan did not counterattack, although he could have done so, because he was totally incapable of thinking in offensive terms and because he was oppressed with the idea that he was facing an enemy force twice the size of his own. So he withdrew to the south side of the Peninsula and the protection of the Federal gunboats. He had lost valuable material, months of time, 20,000 men—and the campaign had collapsed. Six weeks later, still afflicted with what Lincoln called "the slows," McClellan took his army off the Peninsula.

"Now we two will save the country"

BY GEORGE B. McCLELLAN, MAJOR-GENERAL, U. S. A.

IN THE following pages I purpose to give a brief sketch of the Peninsular campaign of 1862. As it is impossible, within the limits available, to describe even the most important battles, I shall confine myself to strategical considerations. But even this requires a rapid review of the circumstances under which, from a small assemblage of unorganized citizens, utterly ignorant of war and almost of the use of arms, was evolved that mighty Army of the Potomac, which, unshaken alike in victory and defeat, during a long series of arduous campaigns against an army most ably commanded and the equal in heroism of any that ever met the shock of battle, proved itself worthy to bear on its bayonets the honor and fate of the nation.

In July, 1861, after having secured solidly for the Union that part of western Virginia north of the Kanawha and west of the mountains, I was suddenly called to Washington on the day succeeding the first battle of Bull Run. Reaching the capital on the 26th, I found myself assigned to the command of that city and of the troops gathered around it.

All was chaos and despondency; the city was filled with intoxicated stragglers, and an attack was expected. The troops numbered less than fifty thou-

154

sand, many of whom were so demoralized and undisciplined that they could not be relied upon even for defensive purposes. Moreover, the term of service of a large part had already expired, or was on the point of doing so. On the Maryland side of the Potomac no troops were posted on the roads leading into the city, nor were there any intrenchments. On the Virginia side the condition of affairs was better in these respects, but far from satisfactory. Sufficient and fit material of war did not exist. The situation was difficult and fraught with danger.

The first and most pressing demand was the immediate safety of the capital and the Government. This was secured by enforcing the most rigid discipline, by organizing permanent brigades under regular officers, and by placing the troops in good defensive positions, far enough to the front to afford room for manœuvring and to enable the brigades to support each other.

The contingency of the enemy's crossing the Potomac above the city was foreseen and promptly provided for. Had he attempted this "about three months after the battle of Manassas," he would, upon reaching "the rear of Washington," have found it covered by respectable works, amply garrisoned, with a sufficient disposable force to move upon his rear and force him to "a decisive engagement." It would have been the greatest possible good fortune for us if he had made this movement at the time in question, or even some weeks earlier. It was only for a very few days after the battle of Bull Run that the movement was practicable, and every day added to its difficulty.

Two things were at once clear: first, that a large and thoroughly organized army was necessary to bring the war to a successful conclusion; second, that Washington must be so strongly fortified as to set at rest any reasonable apprehensions of its being carried by a sudden attack, in order that the active army might be free to move with the maximum strength and on any line of operations without regard to the safety of the capital.

These two herculean tasks were entered upon without delay or hesitation. They were carried to a successful conclusion, without regard to that impatient and unceasing clamor—inevitable among a people unaccustomed to war—which finally forced the hand of the general charged with their execution. He regarded their completion as essential to the salvation of his country, and determined to accomplish them, even if sacrificed in the endeavor. Nor had he, even at this distant day, and after much bitter experience, any regret that he persisted in his determination. Washington was surrounded by a line of strong detached works, armed with garrison artillery, and secure against assault. Intermediate points were occupied by smaller works, battery epaulements, infantry intrenchments, etc. The result was a line of defenses which could easily be held by a comparatively small garrison against any assault, and could be reduced only by the slow operations of a regular siege, requiring much time and material, and affording full opportunity to bring all the resources of the country to its relief. At no time during the war was the

155

enemy able to undertake the siege of Washington, nor, if respectably garrisoned, could it ever have been in danger from an assault. The maximum garrison necessary to hold the place against a siege from any and every quarter
was 34,000 troops, with 40 field-guns; this included the requisite reserves.

With regard to the formation of the Army of the Potomac, it must suffice
to say that everything was to be created from the very foundation. Raw men
and officers were to be disciplined and instructed. The regular army was too
small to furnish more than a portion of the general officers, and a very small
portion of the staff, so that the staff-departments and staff-officers were to be
fashioned mainly out of the intelligent and enthusiastic, but perfectly raw,
material furnished. Artillery, small-arms, and ammunition were to be fabri-
cated, or purchased from abroad; wagons, ambulances, bridge trains, camp
equipage, hospital stores, and all the vast *impedimenta* and material indispensable for an army in the field, were to be manufactured. So great was the
difficulty of procuring small-arms that the armament of the infantry was not
satisfactorily completed until the winter, and a large part of the field-batteries
were not ready for service until the spring of 1862. As soon as possible divisions were organized, the formation being essentially completed in November.

On the 1st of November, upon the retirement of General Winfield Scott, I
succeeded to the command of all the armies, except the Department of Virginia, which comprised the country within sixty miles of Fort Monroe. Upon
assuming the general command, I found that the West was far behind the
East in its state of preparation, and much of my time and large quantities of
material were consumed in pushing the organization of the Western armies.
Meanwhile the various coast expeditions were employed in seizing important
points of the enemy's sea-board, to facilitate the prevention of blockade-run-
ning, and to cut or threaten the lines of communication near the coast, with
reference to subsequent operations.

The plan of campaign which I adopted for the spring of 1862 was to push
forward the armies of Generals Halleck and Buell to occupy Memphis, Nashville, and Knoxville, and the line of the Memphis and Danville Railroad, so
as to deprive the enemy of that important line, and force him to adopt the
circuitous routes by Augusta, Branchville, and Charleston. It was also intended to seize Washington, North Carolina, at the earliest practicable moment, and to open the Mississippi by effecting a junction between Generals
Halleck and Butler. This movement of the Western armies was to be followed
by that of the Army of the Potomac from Urbana, on the lower Rappahannock, to West Point and Richmond, intending, if we failed to gain Richmond
by a rapid march, to cross the James and attack the city in rear, with the
James as a line of supply.

So long as Mr. Cameron was Secretary of War I received the cordial support of that department; but when he resigned, the whole state of affairs

changed. I had never met Mr. Stanton before reaching Washington, in 1861. He at once sought me and professed the utmost personal affection, the expression of which was exceeded only by the bitterness of his denunciation of the Government and its policy. I was unaware of his appointment as Secretary of War until after it had been made, whereupon he called to ascertain whether I desired him to accept, saying that to do so would involve a total sacrifice of his personal interests, and that the only inducement would be the desire to assist me in my work. Having no reason to doubt his sincerity, I desired him to accept, whereupon he consented, and with great effusion exclaimed: "Now we two will save the country."

On the next day the President came to my house to explain why he had appointed Mr. Stanton without consulting me; his reason being that he supposed Stanton to be a great friend of mine, and that the appointment would naturally be satisfactory, and that he feared that if I had known it beforehand it would be said that I had dragooned him into it.

The more serious difficulties of my position began with Mr. Stanton's accession to the War Office. It at once became very difficult to approach him, even for the transaction of ordinary current business, and our personal relations at once ceased. The impatience of the Executive immediately became extreme, and I can attribute it only to the influence of the new Secretary, who did many things to break up the free and confidential intercourse that had heretofore existed between the President and myself. The Government soon manifested great impatience in regard to the opening of the Baltimore and Ohio Railroad and the destruction of the Confederate batteries on the Potomac. The first object could be permanently attained only by occupying the Shenandoah Valley with a force strong enough to resist any attack by the Confederate army then at Manassas; the second only by a general advance of the Army of the Potomac, driving the enemy back of the Rapidan. My own view was that the movement of the Army of the Potomac from Urbana would accomplish both of these objects, by forcing the enemy to abandon all his positions and fall back on Richmond. I was therefore unwilling to interfere with this plan by a premature advance, the effect of which must be either to commit us to the overland route, or to minimize the advantages of the Urbana movement. I wished to hold the enemy at Manassas to the last moment—if possible until the advance from Urbana had actually commenced, for neither the reopening of the railroad nor the destruction of the batteries was worth the danger involved.

The positive order of the President, probably issued under the pressure of the Secretary of War, forced me to undertake the opening of the railway. For this purpose I went to Harper's Ferry in February, intending to throw over a force sufficient to occupy Winchester. To do this it was necessary to have a reliable bridge across the Potomac—to insure supplies and prompt reënforcements. The pontoon-bridge, thrown as a preliminary, could not be absolutely trusted on a river so liable to heavy freshets; therefore it was determined to construct a canal-boat bridge. It was discovered, however, when the attempt was made, that the lift-lock from the canal to the river was too narrow for the boats by some four or five inches, and I therefore decided to rebuild the railroad bridge, and content myself with occupying Charlestown until its completion, postponing to the same time the advance to Winchester. I had fully explained my intentions to the President and Secretary before leaving Washington, providing for precisely such a contingency. While at Harper's Ferry I learned that the President was dissatisfied with my action, and on reaching Washington I laid a full explanation before the Secretary, with which he expressed himself entirely satisfied, and told me that the President was already so, and that it was unnecessary for me to communicate with him on the subject. I then proceeded with the preparations necessary to force the evacuation of the Potomac batteries. On the very day appointed for the division commanders to come to headquarters to receive their final orders, the President sent for me. I then learned that he had received no explanation of the Harper's Ferry affair, and that the Secretary was not authorized to make the statement already referred to; but after my repetition of it the President became fully satisfied with my course. He then, however, said that there was another "very ugly matter" which he desired to talk about, and that was the movement by the lower Chesapeake. He said that it had been suggested that I proposed this movement with the "traitorous" purpose of leaving Washington uncovered and exposed to attack. I very promptly objected to the coupling of any such adjective with my purposes, whereon he disclaimed any intention of conveying the idea that he expressed his own opinion, as he merely repeated the suggestions of others. I then explained the purpose and effect of fortifying Washington, and, as I thought, removed his apprehensions, but informed him that the division commanders were to be at headquarters that morning, and suggested that my plans should be laid before them that they might give their opinion as to whether the capital would be endangered; I also said that in order to leave them perfectly untrammeled I would not attend the meeting. Accordingly they met on the 8th of March and approved my plans.

On the same day was issued, without my knowledge, the order forming army corps and assigning the senior general officers to their command. My own views were that, as the command of army corps involved great responsibility and demanded ability of a high order, it was safer to postpone their formation until trial in the field had shown which general officers could best perform those vital functions. An incompetent division commander could not often jeopardize the safety of an army; while an unfit corps commander could easily lose a battle and frustrate the best-conceived plan of campaign. Of the four corps commanders, one only had commanded so much as a regiment in the field prior to the Bull Run campaign. On the next day intelligence arrived that the enemy was abandoning his positions. I crossed to the Virginia side to receive information more promptly and decide upon what should be done. During the night I determined to advance the whole army, to take advantage of any opportunity to strike the enemy, to break up the permanent camps, give the troops a little experience on the march and in bivouac, get rid of extra baggage, and test the working of the staff-departments. If this were done at all, it must be done promptly, and by moving the troops by divisions, without waiting to form the army corps. Accordingly, I telegraphed to the Secretary, explaining the state of the case and asking authority to postpone the army corps formation until the completion of the movement. The reply was an abrupt and unreasonable refusal. I again telegraphed, explaining the situation and throwing the responsibility upon the Secretary, whereupon he gave way.

Meanwhile, as far back as the 27th of February, orders had been given for collecting the transportation necessary to carry out the Urbana movement. This conclusion had been reached after full discussion. On the 27th of January had been issued the President's General War Order No. 1, directing a general movement of the land and naval forces against the enemy on the 22d of February. On the 31st of January was issued the President's Special War Order No. 1, directing the Army of the Potomac to advance to the attack of Manassas on the 22d of February. The President, however, permitted me to state my objections to this order, which I did, at length, in a letter of February 3d, to the Secretary of War. As the President's order was not insisted upon, although never formally revoked, it is to be assumed that my letter produced, for a time at least, the desired effect. When Manassas had been abandoned by the enemy and he had withdrawn behind the Rapidan, the Urbana movement lost much of its promise, as the enemy was now in position to reach Richmond before we could do so. The alternative remained of making Fort Monroe and its vicinity the base of operations.

The plan first adopted was to commence the movement with the First Corps as a unit, to land north of Gloucester and move thence on West Point; or, should circumstances render it advisable, to land a little below Yorktown to turn the defenses between that place and Fort Monroe. The Navy Department were confident that we could rely upon their vessels to neutralize the *Merrimac* and aid materially in reducing the batteries on the York River, either by joining in the attack or by running by them and gaining their rear. As transports arrived very slowly, especially those for horses, and the great impatience of the Government grew apace, it became necessary to embark divisions as fast as vessels arrived, and I decided to land them at Fort Monroe, holding the First Corps to the last, still intending to move it in mass to turn Gloucester. On the 17th of March the leading division embarked at Alexandria. The campaign was undertaken with the intention of taking some 145,000 troops, to be increased by a division of 10,000 drawn from the troops

159

in the vicinity of Fort Monroe, giving a total of 155,000. Strenuous efforts were made to induce the President to take away Blenker's German division of 10,000 men. Of his own volition he at first declined, but the day before I left Washington he yielded to the non-military pressure and reluctantly gave the order, thus reducing the expected force to 145,000.

While at Fairfax Court House, on the 12th of March, I learned that there had appeared in the daily papers the order relieving me from the general command of all the armies and confining my authority to the Department of the Potomac. I had received no previous intimation of the intention of the Government in this respect. Thus, when I embarked for Fort Monroe on the 1st of April, my command extended from Philadelphia to Richmond, from the Alleghanies, including the Shenandoah, to the Atlantic; for an order had been issued a few days previous placing Fort Monroe and the Department of Virginia under my command, and authorizing me to withdraw from the troops therein ten thousand, to form a division to be added to the First Corps.

The fortifications of Washington were at this time completed and armed. I had already given instructions for the refortification of Manassas, the re-opening of the Manassas Gap Railroad, the protection of its bridges by block-houses, the intrenchment of a position for a brigade at or near the rail-road crossing of the Shenandoah, and an intrenched post at Chester Gap. I left about 42,000 troops for the immediate defense of Washington, and more than 35,000 for the Shenandoah Valley—an abundance to insure the safety of Washington and to check any attempt to recover the lower Shenandoah and threaten Maryland. Beyond this force, the reserves of the Northern States were all available.

On my arrival at Fort Monroe on the 2d of April, I found five divisions of infantry, Sykes's brigade of regulars, two regiments of cavalry, and a portion of the reserve artillery disembarked. Another cavalry regiment and a part of a fourth had arrived, but were still on shipboard; comparatively few wagons had come. On the same day came a telegram stating that the Department of Virginia was withdrawn from my control, and forbidding me to form the division of ten thousand men without General Wool's sanction. I was thus deprived of the command of the base of operations, and the ultimate strength of the army was reduced to 135,000—another serious departure from the plan of campaign. Of the troops disembarked, only four divisions, the regulars, the majority of the reserve artillery, and a part of the cavalry, could be moved, in consequence of the lack of transportation. Casey's division was unable to leave Newport News until the 16th, from the impossibility of supplying it with wagons.

The best information obtainable represented the Confederate troops around Yorktown as numbering at least fifteen thousand, with about an equal force at Norfolk; and it was clear that the army lately at Manassas, now mostly near Gordonsville, was in position to be thrown promptly to the

Peninsula. It was represented that Yorktown was surrounded by strong earthworks, and that the Warwick River, instead of stretching across the Peninsula to Yorktown—as proved to be the case—came down to Lee's Mills from the North, running parallel with and not crossing the road from Newport News to Williamsburg. It was also known that there were intrenched positions of more or less strength at Young's Mills, on the Newport News road, and at Big Bethel, Howard's Bridge, and Ship's Point, on or near the Hampton and Yorktown road, and at Williamsburg.

On my arrival at Fort Monroe, I learned, in an interview with Flag-Officer Goldsborough, that he could not protect the James as a line of supply, and that he could furnish no vessels to take an active part in the reduction of the batteries at York and Gloucester or to run by and gain their rear. He could only aid in the final attack after our land batteries had essentially silenced their fire.

I thus found myself with 53,000 men in condition to move, faced by the conditions of the problem just stated. Information was received that Yorktown was already being reënforced from Norfolk, and it was apprehended that the main Confederate army would promptly follow the same course. I therefore determined to move at once with the force in hand, and endeavor to seize a point—near the Halfway House—between Yorktown and Williamsburg, where the Peninsula is reduced to a narrow neck, and thus cut off the retreat of the Yorktown garrison and prevent the arrival of reënforcements. The advance commenced on the morning of the 4th of April, and was arranged to turn successively the intrenchment on the two roads; the result being that, on the afternoon of the 5th, the Third Corps was engaged with the enemy's outposts in front of Yorktown and under the artillery fire of the place. The Fourth Corps came upon Lee's Mills and found it covered by the unfordable line of the Warwick, and reported the position so strong as to render it impossible to execute its orders to assault. Thus, all things were brought to a stand-still, and the intended movement on the Halfway House could not be carried out. Just at this moment came a telegram, dated the 4th, informing me that the First Corps was withdrawn from my command. Thus, when too deeply committed to recede, I found that another reduction of about 43,000, including several cavalry regiments withheld from me, diminished my paper force to 92,000, instead of the 155,000 on which the plans of the campaign had been founded, and with which it was intended to operate. The number of men left behind, sick and from other causes incident to such a movement, reduced the total for duty to some 85,000, from which must be deducted all camp, depot, and train guards, escorts, and non-combatants, such as cooks, servants, orderlies, and extra-duty men in the various staff-departments, which reduced the number actually available for battle to some 67,000 or 68,000.

The order withdrawing the First Corps also broke up the Department of the Potomac, forming out of it the Department of the Shenandoah, under General Banks, and the Department of the Rappahannock, under General McDowell, the latter including Washington. I thus lost all control of the depots at Washington, as I had already been deprived of the control of the base at Fort Monroe and of the ground subsequently occupied by the depot at White House. The only territory remaining under my command was the paltry triangle between the departments of the Rappahannock and Virginia; even that was yet to be won from the enemy. I was thus relieved from the duty of providing for the safety of Washington, and deprived of all control over the troops in that vicinity. Instead of one directing head controlling operations which should have been inseparable, the region from the Alleghanies to the sea was parceled out among four independent commanders.

On the 3d of April, at the very moment of all others when it was most necessary to push recruiting most vigorously, to make good the inevitable losses in battle and by disease, an order was issued from the War Department discontinuing all recruiting for the volunteers and breaking up all their recruiting stations. Instead of a regular and permanent system of recruiting, whether by voluntary enlistment or by draft, a spasmodic system of large drafts was thereafter resorted to, and, to a great extent, the system of forming new regiments. The results were wasteful and pernicious. There were enough, or nearly enough, organizations in the field, and these should have been constantly maintained at the full strength by a regular and constant influx of recruits, who, by association with their veteran comrades, would soon have become efficient. The new regiments required much time to become useful, and endured very heavy and unnecessary losses from disease and in battle owing to the inexperience of the officers and men. A course more in accordance with the best-established military principles and the uniform experience of war would have saved the country millions of treasure and thousands of valuable lives.

Then, on the 5th of April, I found myself with 53,000 men in hand, giving less than 42,000 for battle, after deducting extra-duty men and other noncombatants. In our front was an intrenched line, apparently too strong for assault, and which I had now no means of turning, either by land or water. I now learned that 85,000 would be the maximum force at my disposal, giving only some 67,000 for battle. Of the three divisions yet to join, Casey's reached the front only on the 17th, Richardson's on the 16th, and Hooker's commenced arriving at Ship Point on the 10th. Whatever may have been said afterward, no one at the time—so far as my knowledge extended—thought an assault practicable without certain preliminary siege operations. At all events, my personal experience in this kind of work was greater than that of any officer under my command; and after personal reconnoissances more appropriate to a lieutenant of engineers than to the commanding general, I could neither discover nor hear of any point where an assault promised any chance of success. We were thus obliged to resort to siege operations in order to silence the enemy's artillery fire, and open the way to an assault. All the batteries would have been ready to open fire on the 5th, or, at latest, on the morning of the 6th of May, and it was determined to assault at various points the moment the heavy batteries had performed their allotted task; the navy was prepared to participate in the attack as soon as the main batteries were silenced; the *Galena*, under that most gallant and able officer, John Rodgers, was to take part in the attack, and would undoubtedly have run the batteries at the earliest possible moment; but during the night of the 3d and 4th of May the enemy evacuated his positions, regarding them as untenable under the impending storm of heavy projectiles.

Meanwhile, on the 22d of April, Franklin's division of McDowell's corps had joined me by water, in consequence of my urgent calls for reënforcements.

The moment the evacuation of Yorktown was known, the order was given for the advance of all the disposable cavalry and horse batteries, supported by infantry divisions, and every possible effort was made to expedite the movement of a column by water upon West Point, to force the evacuation of the lines at Williamsburg, and, if possible, cut off a portion of the enemy's force and trains.

The heavy storms which had prevailed recommenced on the afternoon of the 4th, and not only impeded the advance of troops by land, but delayed the movement by water so much that it was not until the morning of the 7th that the leading division—Franklin's—disembarked near West Point and took up a suitable position to hold its own and cover the landing of reënforcements. This division was attacked not long after it landed, but easily repulsed the enemy.

Meanwhile the enemy's rear-guard held the Williamsburg lines against our advance, except where Hancock broke through, until the night of the 5th, when they retired.

The army was now divided: a part at the mouth of the Pamunkey, a part at Williamsburg, and a part at Yorktown prepared to ascend the York River. The problem was to reunite them without giving the enemy the opportunity of striking either fraction with his whole force. This was accomplished on the 10th, when all the divisions were in communication, and the movement of concentration continued as rapidly as circumstances permitted, so that on the 15th the headquarters and the divisions of Franklin, Porter, Sykes, and Smith reached Cumberland Landing; Couch and Casey being near New Kent Court House, Hooker and Kearney near Roper's Church, and Richardson and Sedgwick near Eltham. On the 15th and 16th, in the face of dreadful weather and terrible roads, the divisions of Franklin, Porter, and Smith were advanced to White House, and a depot established. On the 18th the Fifth and Sixth Corps were formed, so that the organization of the Army of the Potomac was now as follows: Second Corps, Sumner—Divisions, Sedgwick and Richardson; Third Corps, Heintzelman—Divisions, Kearny and Hooker; Fourth Corps, Keyes—Divisions, Couch and Casey; Fifth Corps, F. J. Porter —Divisions, Morell and Sykes and the Reserve Artillery; Sixth Corps, Franklin—Divisions, Smith and Slocum.

The cavalry organization remained unchanged, and we were sadly deficient in that important arm, as many of the regiments belonging to the Army of the Potomac were among those which had been retained near Washington.

The question now arose as to the line of operations to be followed: that of the James on the one hand, and, on the other, the line from White House as a base, crossing the upper Chickahominy.

The army was admirably placed for adopting either, and my decision was to take that of the James, operating on either bank as might prove advisable, but always preferring the southern. I had urgently asked for reënforcements to come by water, as they would thus be equally available for either line of operations. The destruction of the *Merrimac* on the 11th of May had opened the James River to us, and it was only after that date that it became available. My plan, however, was changed by orders from Washington. A telegram of the 18th from the Secretary of War informed me that McDowell would advance from Fredericksburg, and directed me to extend the right of the Army of the Potomac to the north of Richmond, in order to establish communication with him. The same order required me to supply his troops from our depots at White House. Herein lay the failure of the campaign, as it necessitated the division of the army by the Chickahominy, and caused great delay in constructing practicable bridges across that stream; while if I had been able to cross to the James, reënforcements would have reached me by water rapidly and safely, the army would have been united and in no danger of having its flank turned, or its line of supply interrupted, and the attack could have been much more rapidly pushed.

I now proceeded to do all in my power to insure success on the new line of operations thus imposed upon me. On the 20th of May our light troops reached the Chickahominy at Bottom's Bridge, which they found destroyed. I at once ordered Casey's division to ford the stream and occupy the heights beyond, thus securing a lodgment on the right bank. Heintzelman was moved up in support of Keyes. By the 24th, Mechanicsville was carried, so that the enemy was now all together on the other side of the river. Sumner was near the railroad, on the left bank of the stream; Porter and Franklin were on the same bank near Mechanicsville.

It is now time to give a brief description of the Chickahominy. This river rises some fifteen miles north-westward of Richmond, and unites with the James about forty miles below that city. Our operations were on the part between Meadow and Bottom's bridges, covering the approaches to Richmond from the east. Here the river at its ordinary stage is some forty feet wide, fringed with a dense growth of heavy forest-trees, and bordered by low marshy lands, varying from half a mile to a mile in width. Within the limits above mentioned the firm ground, above high-water mark, seldom approaches the river on either bank, and in no place did the high ground come near the stream on both banks. It was subject to frequent, sudden, and great variations in the volume of water, and a single violent storm of brief duration sufficed to cause an overflow of the bottom-lands for many days, rendering the river absolutely impassable without long and strong bridges. When we reached the river it was found that all the bridges, except that at Mechanicsville, had been destroyed. The right bank, opposite New, Mechanicsville, and Meadow bridges, was bordered by high bluffs, affording the enemy commanding positions for his batteries, enfilading the approaches, and preventing the rebuilding of important bridges. We were thus obliged to select other less exposed points for our crossings. Should McDowell effect the promised junction, we could turn the head-waters of the Chickahominy, and attack Richmond from the north and north-west, still preserving our line of supply from White House. But with the force actually available such an attempt would expose the army to the loss of its communications and to destruction in detail; for we had an able and savage antagonist, prompt to take advantage of any error on our part. The country furnished no supplies, so that we could not afford a separation from our depots. All the information obtained showed that Richmond was intrenched, that the enemy occupied in force all the approaches from the east, that he intended to dispute every step of our advance, and that his army was numerically superior. Early on the 24th of May I received a telegram from the President, informing me that McDowell would certainly march on the 26th, suggesting that I should detach a force to the right to cut off the retreat of the Confederate force in front of Fredericksburg, and desiring me to march cautiously and safely. On the same day another dispatch came, informing me that, in consequence of Stonewall Jackson's advance down the Shenandoah, the movement of McDowell was suspended. Next day the President again telegraphed that the movement against General Banks seemed so general and connected as to show that the enemy could not intend a very desperate defense of Richmond; that he thought the time was near when I "must either attack Richmond or give up the job, and come back to the defense of Washington." I replied that all my information agreed that the mass of the enemy was still in the immediate vicinity of Richmond, ready to defend it, and that the object of Jackson's movement was probably to prevent reënforcements being sent to me. On the 26th General Stoneman, with my advanced guard, cut the Virginia Central Railroad in three places. On the same day I learned that a very considerable force of the enemy was in the vicinity of Hanover Court House, to our right and rear, threatening our communications, and in position to reënforce Jackson or oppose McDowell, whose advance was then eight miles south of Fredericksburg. I ordered General F. J. Porter to move next morning to dislodge them. He took with him his own old division, Warren's provisional brigade and Emory's cavalry brigade. His operations in the vicinity of Hanover Court House were entirely successful, and resulted in completely clearing our flank, cutting the railroads in several places, destroying bridges, inflicting a severe loss upon the enemy, and fully opening the way for the advance of Mc-Dowell's corps. As there was no indication of its immediate approach, and the position at Hanover Court House was too much exposed to be permanently held, General Porter's command was withdrawn on the evening of the 29th, and returned to its old position with the main army. The campaign had taken its present position in consequence of the assurance that I should be joined by McDowell's corps. As it was now clear that I could not count with certainty upon that force, I had to do the best I could with the means at hand.

The first necessity was to establish secure communications between the two parts of the army, necessarily separated by the Chickahominy. Richmond could be attacked only by troops on the right bank. As the expectation of the advance of McDowell was still held out, and that only by the land route, I could not yet transfer the base to the James, but was obliged to retain it on the Pamunkey, and therefore to keep on the left bank a force sufficient to protect our communications and cover the junction of McDowell. It was still permissible to believe that sufficient attention would be paid to the simplest principle of war to push McDowell rapidly on Jackson's heels, when he made his inevitable return march to join the main Confederate army and attack our right flank. The failure of McDowell to reach me at or before the critical moment was due to the orders he received from Washington. The bridges over the Chickahominy first built were swept away by the floods, and it became necessary to construct others more solid and with long log approaches, a slow and difficult task, generally carried on by men working in the water and under fire. The work was pushed as rapidly as possible, and on the 30th of May the corps of Heintzelman and Keyes were on the right bank of the Chickahominy, the most advanced positions being somewhat strengthened by intrenchments; Sumner's corps was on the left bank, some six miles above Bottom's Bridge; Porter's and Franklin's corps were on the left bank opposite the enemy's left. During the day and night of the 30th torrents of rain fell, inundating the whole country and threatening the destruction of our bridges.

Well aware of our difficulties, our active enemy, on the 31st of May, made a violent attack upon Casey's division, followed by an equally formidable one on Couch, thus commencing the battle of Fair Oaks or Seven Pines. Heintzelman came up in support, and during the afternoon Sumner crossed the river with great difficulty, and rendered such efficient service that the enemy was checked. In the morning his renewed attacks were easily repulsed, and the ground occupied at the beginning of the battle was more than recovered; he had failed in the purpose of the attack. The ground was now so thoroughly soaked by the rain, and the bridges were so much injured, that it was impracticable to pursue the enemy or to move either Porter or Franklin to the support of the other corps on the south bank. Our efforts were at once concentrated upon the restoration of the old and the building of new bridges.

On the 1st of June the Department of Virginia, including Fort Monroe, was placed under my command. On the 2d the Secretary telegraphed that as soon as Jackson was disposed of in the Shenandoah, another large body of troops would be at my service; on the 5th, that he intended sending a part of General McDowell's force as soon as it could return from Front Royal (in the Shenandoah Valley, near Manassas Gap, and about one hundred and fifteen miles north-west of Richmond), probably as many as I wanted; on the 11th, that McCall's force had embarked to join me on the day preceding, and that it was intended to send the residue of General McDowell's force to join me as speedily as possible, and that it was clear that a strong force was operating with Jackson for the purpose of preventing the forces there from joining me.

On the 26th the Secretary telegraphed that the forces of McDowell, Banks, and Frémont would be consolidated as the Army of Virginia, and would operate promptly in my aid by land.

Fortunately for the Army of the Potomac, however, I entertained serious doubts of the aid promised by the land route, so that, on the 18th, I ordered a number of transports, with supplies of all kinds, to be sent up the James, under convoy of the gun-boats, so that I might be free to cut loose from the Pamunkey and move over to the James, should circumstances enable me or render it desirable to do so.

The battle of Fair Oaks was followed by storms of great severity, continuing until the 20th of June, and adding vastly to the difficulties of our position, greatly retarding the construction of the bridges and of the defensive works regarded as necessary to cover us in the event of a repulse, and making the ground too difficult for the free movements of troops.

On the 19th Franklin's corps was transferred to the south side of the Chickahominy, Porter's corps, reënforced by McCall's division, being left alone on the north side.

This dangerous distribution was necessary in order to concentrate sufficient force on the south side to attack Richmond with any hope of success; and, as I was still told that McDowell would arrive by the overland route, I could not yet change the base to the James.

It was not until the 25th that the condition of the ground and the completion of the bridges and intrenchments left me free to attack. On that day the first step was taken, in throwing forward the left of our picket-line, in face of a strong opposition, to gain ground enough to enable Sumner and Heintzelman to support the attack to be made next day by Franklin on the rear of Old

167

Tavern. The successful issue of this attack would, it was supposed, drive the enemy from his positions on the heights overlooking Mechanicsville, and probably enable us to force him back into his main line of works. We would then be in position to reconnoiter the lines carefully, determine the points of attack, and take up a new base and line of supply if expedient.

During the night of the 24th information arrived confirming the anticipation that Jackson was moving to attack our right and rear, but I persisted in the operation intended for the 25th, partly to develop the strength of the enemy opposite our left and center, and with the design of attacking Old Tavern on the 26th, if Jackson's advance was so much delayed that Porter's corps would not be endangered.

Late in the afternoon of the 25th, Jackson's advance was confirmed, and it was rendered probable that he would attack next day. All hope of the advance of McDowell's corps in season to be of any service had disappeared; the dangerous position of the army had been faithfully held to the last moment. After deducting the garrisons in rear, the railroad guards, non-combatants, and extra-duty men, there were not more than 75,000 men for battle. The enemy, with a force larger than this, the strong defenses of Richmond close at hand in his rear, was free to strike on either flank. I decided then to carry into effect the long-considered plan of abandoning the Pamunkey and taking up the line of the James.

The necessary orders were given for the defense of the depots at the White House to the last moment and its final destruction and abandonment; it was also ordered that all possible stores should be pushed to the front while communications were open.

The ground to the James had already been reconnoitered with reference to this movement.

During the night of the 26th Porter's siege-guns and wagon-trains were brought over to the south side of the Chickahominy. During the afternoon of that day his corps had been attacked in its position on Beaver Dam Creek, near Mechanicsville, and the enemy repulsed with heavy losses on their part. It was now clear that Jackson's corps had taken little or no part in this attack, and that his blow would fall farther to the rear. I therefore ordered the Fifth Corps to fall back and take position nearer the bridges, where the flanks would be more secure. This was skillfully effected early on the 27th, and it was decided that this corps should hold its position until night. All the corps commanders on the south side were on the 26th directed to be prepared to send as many troops as they could spare in support of Porter on the next day. All of them thought the enemy so strong in their respective fronts as to require all their force to hold their positions.

Shortly after noon on the 27th the attack commenced upon Porter's corps, in its new position near Gaines's Mill, and the contest continued all day with great vigor.

The movements of the enemy were so threatening at many points on our center and left as to indicate the presence of large numbers of troops, and for a long time created great uncertainty as to the real point of his main attack. General Porter's first call for reënforcement and a supply of axes failed to reach me; but, upon receiving a second call, I ordered Slocum's division to cross to his support. The head of the division reached the field at 3:30 and immediately went into action. At about 5 P. M. General Porter reported his position as critical, and the brigades of French and Meagher—of Richardson's division—were ordered to reënforce him, although the fearless commander of the Second Corps, General Sumner, thought it hazardous to remove them from his own threatened front. I then ordered the reserve of Heintzelman to move in support of Sumner, and a brigade of Keyes's corps to headquarters for such use as might be required. Smith's division, left alone when Slocum crossed to the aid of Porter, was so seriously threatened that I called on Sumner's corps to send a brigade to its support.

French and Meagher reached the field before dusk, just after Porter's corps had been forced by superior numbers to fall back to an interior position nearer the bridges, and, by their steady attitude, checked all further progress of the enemy and completed the attainment of the purpose in view, which was to hold the left bank of the river until dark, so that the movement to the James might be safely commenced. The siege-guns, material, and trains on the left bank were all safe, and the right wing was in close connection with the rest of the army. The losses were heavy, but the object justified them, or rather made them necessary. At about 6 o'clock next morning the rear-guard of regulars crossed to the south side and the bridges were destroyed.

I now bent all my energies to the transfer of the army to the James, fully realizing the very delicate nature of a flank march, with heavy trains, by a single road, in face of an active enemy, but confident that I had the army well in hand and that it would not fail me in the emergency. I thought that the enemy would not anticipate that movement, but would assume that all my efforts would be directed to cover and regain the old depots; and the event proved the correctness of this supposition. It seemed certain that I could gain one or two days for the movement of the trains, while he remained uncertain as to my intentions; and that was all I required with such troops as those of the Army of the Potomac.

During the night of the 27th I assembled the corps commanders at headquarters, informed them of my intentions, and gave them their orders. Keyes's corps was ordered to move at once, with its trains, across White Oak Swamp, and occupy positions on the farther side, to cover the passage of the remainder of the army. By noon of the 28th this first step was accomplished. During the 28th Sumner, Heintzelman, and Franklin held essentially their old positions; the trains converged steadily to the White Oak Swamp and crossed as rapidly as possible, and during this day and the succeeding night

169

Porter followed the movement of Keyes's corps and took position to support it.

Early on the 28th, when Franklin's corps was drawing in its right to take a more concentrated position, the enemy opened a sharp artillery fire and made at one point a spirited attack with two Georgia regiments, which were repulsed by the two regiments on picket.

Sumner's and Heintzelman's corps and Smith's division of Franklin's were now ordered to abandon their intrenchments, so as to occupy, on the morning of the 29th, a new position in rear, shorter than the old and covering the crossing of the swamp. This new line could easily be held during the day, and these troops were ordered to remain there until dark, to cover the withdrawal of the rest of the trains, and then cross the swamp and occupy the positions about to be abandoned by Keyes's and Porter's corps. Meanwhile Slocum's division had been ordered to Savage's Station in reserve, and, during the morning, was ordered across the swamp to relieve Keyes's corps. This was a critical day; for the crossing of the swamp by the trains must be accomplished before its close, and their protection against attack from Richmond must be assured, as well as communication with the gun-boats.

A sharp cavalry skirmish on the Quaker road indicated that the enemy was alive to our movement, and might at any moment strike in force to intercept the march to the James. The difficulty was not at all with the movement of the troops, but with the immense trains that were to be moved virtually by a single road, and required the whole army for their protection. With the exception of the cavalry affair on the Quaker road, we were not troubled during this day south of the swamp, but there was severe fighting north of it. Sumner's corps evacuated their works at daylight and fell back to Allen's farm, nearly two miles west of Savage's Station, Heintzelman being on their left. Here Sumner was furiously attacked three times, but each time drove the enemy back with much loss.

Soon afterward Franklin, having only one division with him, ascertained that the enemy had repaired some of the Chickahominy bridges and was advancing on Savage's Station, whereupon he posted his division at that point and informed Sumner, who moved his corps to the same place, arriving a little after noon. About 4 P. M. Sumner and Franklin—three divisions in all —were sharply attacked, mainly by the Williamsburg road; the fighting continued until between 8 and 9 P. M., the enemy being at all times thoroughly repulsed, and finally driven from the field.

Meanwhile, through a misunderstanding of his orders, and being convinced that the troops of Sumner and Franklin at Savage's Station were ample for the purpose in view, Heintzelman withdrew his troops during the afternoon, crossed the swamp at Brackett's Ford, and reached the Charles City road with the rear of his column at 10 P. M.

Slocum reached the position of Keyes's corps early in the afternoon, and, as soon as the latter was thus relieved, it was ordered forward to the James, near Malvern Hill, which it reached, with all its artillery and trains, early on the 30th. Porter was ordered to follow this movement and prolong the line of Keyes's corps to our right. The trains were pushed on in rear of these corps and massed under cover of the gun-boats as fast as they reached the James, at Haxall's plantation. As soon as the fighting ceased with the final repulse of the enemy, Sumner and Franklin were ordered to cross the swamp; this was effected during the night, the rear-guard crossing and destroying the bridge at 5 A. M. on the 30th. All the troops and trains were now between the swamp and the James, and the first critical episode of the movement was successfully accomplished.

The various corps were next pushed forward to establish connection with Keyes and Porter, and hold the different roads by which the enemy could advance from Richmond and strike our line of march. I determined to hold the positions now taken until the trains had all reached a place of safety, and then concentrate the army near the James, where it could enjoy a brief rest after the fatiguing battles and marches through which it was passing, and then renew the advance on Richmond.

General Franklin, with Smith's division of his own corps, Richardson's of the Second, and Naglee's brigade were charged with the defense of the White Oak Swamp crossing. Slocum held the ground thence to the Charles City road; Kearny from that road to the Long Bridge road; McCall on his left; Hooker thence to the Quaker road; Sedgwick at Nelson's farm, in rear of McCall and Kearny. The Fifth Corps was at Malvern Hill, the Fourth at Turkey Bridge. The trains moved on during this day, and at 4 P. M. the last reached Malvern Hill and kept on to Haxall's, so that the most difficult part of the task was accomplished, and it only remained for the troops to hold their ground until nightfall, and then continue the march to the positions selected near Malvern Hill.

The fighting on this day (June 30th) was very severe, and extended along the whole line. It first broke out between 12 and 1, on General Franklin's command, in the shape of a fierce artillery fire, which was kept up through the day and inflicted serious losses. The enemy's infantry made several attempts to cross near the old bridge and below, but was in every case thrown back. Franklin held his position until after dark, and during the night fell back to Malvern. At half-past 2 Slocum's left was attacked in vain on the Charles City road. At about 3 McCall was attacked, and, after 5 o'clock, under the pressure of heavy masses, he was forced back; but Hooker came up from the left, and Sedgwick from the rear, and the two together not only stopped the enemy, but drove him off the field.

At about 4 P. M. heavy attacks commenced on Kearny's left, and three ineffectual assaults were made. The firing continued until after dark. About midnight Sumner's and Heintzelman's corps and McCall's division withdrew from the positions they had so gallantly held, and commenced their march to Malvern, which they reached unmolested soon after daybreak. Just after the rear of the trains reached Malvern, about 4 P. M., the enemy attacked Porter's corps, but were promptly shaken off.

Thus, on the morning of July 1st, the army was concentrated at Malvern, with the trains at Haxall's, in rear. The supplies which had been sent from White House on the 18th were at hand in the James.

After consultation with Commodore Rodgers, I decided that Harrison's Landing was a better position for the resting-place of the army, because the channel passed so close to City Point as to enable the enemy to prevent the passage of transports if we remained at Malvern. It was, however, necessary to accept battle where we were, in order to give ample time for the trains to reach Harrison's, as well as to give the enemy a blow that would check his farther pursuit.

Accordingly, the army was carefully posted on the admirable position of Malvern Hill, with the right thrown back below Haxall's. The left was the natural point of attack, and there the troops were massed and the reserve artillery placed, while full preparations were made to frustrate any attempt to turn our right. Early in the forenoon the army was concentrated and ready for battle, in a position of unusual strength—one which, with such troops as held it, could justly be regarded as impregnable. It was, then, with perfect confidence that I awaited the impending battle.

The enemy began feeling the position between 9 and 10 A. M., and at 3 P. M. made a sharp attack upon Couch's division, which remained lying on the ground until the enemy were within close range, when they rose and delivered a volley which shattered and drove back their assailants in disorder. At 4 P. M. the firing ceased for a while, and the lull was availed of to rectify the position and make every preparation for the approaching renewal of the attack. It came at 6 P. M., opened by the fire of all their artillery and followed by desperate charges of infantry advancing at a run. They were always repulsed with the infliction of fearful loss, and in several instances our infantry awaited their approach within a few yards, poured in a single volley, and then dashed forward with the bayonet. At 7 P. M. the enemy was accumulating fresh troops, and the brigades of Meagher and Sickles were sent from Sumner's and Heintzelman's corps to reënforce Porter and Couch; fresh batteries were moved forward from the reserve artillery and the ammunition was replenished.

The enemy then repeated his attacks in the most desperate style until dark, but the battle ended with his complete repulse, with very heavy losses, and without his even for one moment gaining a foothold in our position. His frightful losses were in vain. I doubt whether, in the annals of war, there was ever a more persistent and gallant attack, or a more cool and effective resistance.

172

Although the result of this bloody battle was a complete victory on our part, it was necessary, for the reasons already given, to continue the movement to Harrison's, whither the trains had been pushed during the night of the 30th of June and the day of the 1st of July. Immediately after the final repulse the orders were given for the withdrawal of the army. The movement was covered by Keyes's corps. So complete was the enemy's discomfiture, and so excellent the conduct of the rear-guard, that the last of the trains reached Harrison's after dark on the 3d, without loss and unmolested by the enemy.

This movement was now successfully accomplished, and the Army of the Potomac was at last in a position on its true line of operations, with its trains intact, no guns lost save those taken in battle, when the artillerists had proved their heroism and devotion by standing to their guns until the enemy's infantry were in the midst of them.

During the "Seven Days" the Army of the Potomac consisted of 143 regiments of infantry, 55 batteries, and less than 8 regiments of cavalry, all told. The opposing Confederate army consisted of 187 regiments of infantry, 79 batteries, and 14 regiments of cavalry. The losses of the two armies from June 25th to July 2d were:

	Killed.	Wounded.	Missing.	Total.
Confederate Army	2,823	13,703	3,223	19,749
Army of the Potomac	1,734	8,062	6,053	15,849

The Confederate losses in killed and wounded alone were greater than the total losses of the Army of the Potomac in killed, wounded, and missing.

No praise can be too great for the officers and men who passed through these seven days of battle, enduring fatigue without a murmur, successfully meeting and repelling every attack made upon them, always in the right place at the right time, and emerging from the fiery ordeal a compact army of veterans, equal to any task that brave and disciplined men can be called upon to undertake. They needed now only a few days of well-earned repose, a renewal of ammunition and supplies, and reënforcements to fill the gaps made in their ranks by so many desperate encounters, to be prepared to advance again, with entire confidence, to meet their worthy antagonists in other battles. It was, however, decided by the authorities at Washington, against my earnest remonstrances, to abandon the position on the James, and the campaign. The Army of the Potomac was accordingly withdrawn, and it was not until two years later that it again found itself under its last commander at substantially the same point on the bank of the James. It was as evident in 1862 as in 1865 that there was the true defense of Washington, and that it was on the banks of the James that the fate of the Union was to be decided.

In the South's agrarian society, almost every man could ride a horse well and, what's more, shoot from one; while it took the North half the war to develop cavalrymen from an army of shopkeepers and bank clerks. "Jeb" (for James Ewell Brown) Stuart was only one of several brilliant Confederate cavalry commanders but he was the most consistently spectacular. Horse-killing raids like that around McClellan were his specialty and one later on up in Pennsylvania was to get him and General Lee into serious trouble. But meanwhile his success in eluding the Union cavalry those three June days below Richmond made him the idol of the South—which, as usual, he acknowledged with characteristic showmanship.

When the shouting was all over, John Esten Cooke said, "That was a tight place at the river, General. If the enemy had come down on us, you would have been compelled to surrender."

"No," answered Stuart, "one other course was left."

"What was that?"

"To die game."

"Jeb" enjoyed the war.

"What's to pay? **Hell's** *to pay!"*

BY W. T. ROBINS, COLONEL, C. S. A

THE BATTLE of "Seven Pines," or "Fair Oaks," had been fought with no result. The temporary success of the Confederates early in the engagement had been more than counterbalanced by the reverses they sustained on the second day, and the two armies lay passively watching each other in front of Richmond. At this time the cavalry of Lee's army was commanded by General J. E. B. Stuart, and this restless officer conceived the idea of flanking the right wing of the Federal army near Ashland, and moving around to the rear, to cross the Chickahominy River at a place called Sycamore Ford, in New Kent County, march over to the James River, and return to the Confederate lines near Deep Bottom, in Henrico County. In carrying out this plan, Stuart would completely encircle the army of General McClellan. At the time of this movement the writer was adjutant of the 9th Virginia cavalry. When the orders were issued from headquarters directing the several commands destined to form the expedition to prepare three

175

days' rations, and the ordnance officers to issue sixty rounds of ammunition to each man, I remember the surmises and conjectures as to our destination. The officers and men were in high spirits in anticipation of a fight, and when the bugles rang out "Boots and Saddles," every man was ready. The men left behind in camp were bewailing their luck, and those forming the detail for the expedition were elated at the prospect of some excitement. "Good-bye, boys; we are going to help old Jack drive the Yanks into the Potomac," I heard one of them shout to those left behind.

On the afternoon of June 12th we went out to the Brooke turnpike, preparatory to the march. The cavalry column was the 9th Virginia, commanded by Colonel W. H. F. Lee, the 1st Virginia, led by Colonel Fitz Lee, and the Jeff Davis Legion, under Colonel Martin. A section of the Stuart Horse Artillery, commanded by Captain Pelham, accompanied the expedition. The whole numbered twelve hundred men. The first night was passed in bivouac in the vicinity of Ashland, and orders were issued enforcing strict silence and forbidding the use of fires, as the success of the expedition would depend upon secrecy and celerity. On the following morning, at the break of dawn, the troopers were mounted and the march was begun without a bugle blast, and the column headed direct for Hanover Court House, distant about two hours' ride. Here we had the first sight of the enemy. A scouting party of the 5th U. S. Cavalry was in the village, but speedily decamped when our troops were ascertained to be Confederates. One prisoner was taken after a hot chase across country. We now moved rapidly to Hawes's Shop, where a Federal picket was surprised and captured without firing a shot. Hardly had the prisoners been disarmed and turned over to the provost guard when the Confederate advance was driven in upon the main body by a squadron of Federal cavalry, sent out from Old Church to ascertain by reconnoissance whether the report of a Confederate advance was true or false. General Stuart at once ordered Colonel W. H. F. Lee, commanding the regiment leading the column, to throw forward a squadron to meet the enemy. Colonel Lee directed Captain Swann, chief of the leading squadron of his regiment, to charge with the saber. Swann moved off at a trot, and, turning a corner of the road, saw the enemy's squadron about two hundred yards in front of him. The order to charge was given, and the men dashed forward in fine style. The onset was so sudden that the Federal cavalry broke and scattered in confusion. The latter had a start of barely two hundred yards, but the Confederate yell that broke upon the air lent them wings, and only a few fell into our hands. The rest made their escape after a chase of a mile and a half. Now the road became very narrow, and the brush on either side was a place so favorable for an ambuscade that Captain Swann deemed it prudent to draw rein and sound the bugle to recall his men. Stuart, who had been marching steadily onward with the main body of the Confederate column, soon arrived at the front, and the advance-guard, which I had all along commanded, was directed to move forward again. I at once dismounted the men, and pushed forward up a hill in my front. Just beyond the hill, I ran into a force of Federal cavalry drawn up in column of fours, ready to charge. Just as my advance-guard was about to run into them, I heard their commanding officer give the order to charge. I fell back and immediately notified General Stuart of the presence of the enemy. Captain Latané, commanding a squadron of the 9th Virginia, was directed to move forward and clear the road. He moved up the hill at a trot, and when in sight of the enemy in the road gave the command to charge, and with a yell the men rushed forward. At the top of the hill, simultaneously with Latané's order to charge, a company of Federal cavalry, deployed as skirmishers in the woods on the right of the road, were stampeded, and rushed back into the woods to make good their retreat to their friends. The head of Latané's squadron, then just fairly up the hill, was in the line of their retreat and was separated from the rest of the squadron, cut off by the rush of the Federals, and borne along with them up the road toward the enemy. I was riding at the side of Latané, and just at the time when the Federal company rushed back into the road Captain Latané fell from his horse, shot dead. The rush of the Federals separated myself and six of the leading files of the squadron from our friends, and we were borne along by the flying Federals. Although the Federal cavalry both in front and rear were in full retreat, our situation was perilous in the extreme. Soon we were pushed by foes in our rear into the ranks of those in our front, and a series of hand-to-hand combats ensued. To shoot or to cut us down was the aim of every Federal as he neared us, but we did what we could to defend ourselves. Every one of my comrades was shot or cut down, and I alone escaped unhurt. After having been borne along by the retreating enemy for perhaps a quarter of a mile, I leaped my horse over the fence into the field and so got away.

Now came the rush of the Confederate column, sweeping the road clear, and capturing many prisoners. At this point my regiment was relieved by the 1st Virginia, and Colonel Lee continued the pursuit. The Federals did not attempt to make a stand until they reached Old Church. Here their officers called a halt, and made an attempt to rally to defend their camp. Fitz Lee soon swept them out, and burned their camp. They made no other attempt to stand, and we heard no more of them as an organized body, but many prisoners were taken as we passed along. We had surprised them, taken them in detail, and far outnumbered them at all points. The Federal forces, as we afterward learned, were commanded by General Philip St. George Cooke, father-in-law to General Stuart, to whom the latter sent a polite message. The casualties in this skirmish were slight—one man killed on each side, and about fifteen or twenty wounded on the Confederate side, mostly saber-cuts.

We halted for a short time at Old Church, and the people of the neighborhood, hearing of our arrival, came flocking out to greet us and wish us Godspeed. They did not come empty-handed, but brought whatever they could snatch up on the spur of the moment, rightly supposing that anything to allay hunger or thirst would be acceptable to us. Some of the ladies brought bouquets, and presented them to the officers as they marched along. One of these was given to General Stuart, who, always gallant, vowed to preserve it and take it into Richmond. He kept his promise.

We were soon far in rear of McClellan's army, which lay directly between us and Richmond. It was thought probable that the Federal cavalry was concentrating in *our* rear to cut off our retreat. We kept straight on, by Smith's store, through New Kent County to Tunstall's station, on the York River Railroad. I had been in charge of the Confederate advance-guard up to the time when Colonel Fitz Lee came to the front with the 1st Virginia, relieving the 9th of that duty. When well down in New Kent County, General Stuart sent for me again to the front. Hurrying on, I soon reached the head of the column, where I found the general, and was directed by him to take thirty men as an advance-guard, and to precede the column by about half a mile. Further, I was directed to halt at the road running from the mills to the White House long enough to cut the telegraph wire on that road; thence to proceed to Tunstall's station on the York River Railroad, at which place, the prisoners had informed the general, a company of Federal infantry was posted. At Tunstall's station I was directed to charge the infantry, disperse or capture them, cut the telegraph, and obstruct the railroad. Here was our point of danger. Once across the railroad, we were comparatively safe. But in possession of the railroad, with its rolling-stock the enemy could easily throw troops along its line to any given point. However, no timely information had been furnished to the Federal general. We moved with such celerity that we carried with us the first news of our arrival. Pushing forward at a trot, and picking up straggling prisoners every few hundred yards, the advance-guard at length reached the telegraph road. At this point we overtook an ordnance wagon, heavily loaded with canteens and Colt's revolvers. The horses had stalled in a mud-hole, and the driver, cutting them out from the wagon, made his escape. The sergeant in charge stood his ground and was captured. Here was a prize indeed, as in those days we were poorly armed. In order to save time, a man furnished with an ax was sent to cut the telegraph wire, while the rest of the party was engaged in rifling the wagon. While these operations were in progress a body of Federal cavalry, suddenly turning a bend in the road, made their appearance. As soon as the Federal officer in command saw us he called a halt, and, standing still in the road, seemed at a loss to know what to do. His men drew their sabers, as if about to charge, but they did not come on. By this time the telegraph had been cut and the wagon disposed of. Our men were hastily mounted and formed into column of fours, with drawn sabers, ready for any emergency. There we stood, eying each other, about two hundred yards apart, until the head of the main Confederate column came in sight, when the Federals retreated down the road leading to the White House. . . .

The road now being clear, we marched on briskly, and arriving near the station charged down upon it with a yell. We could see the enemy scattered about the building and lounging around before we charged them. The greater part scattered for cover, and were pursued by our people. I pushed straight for the station-house, where I found the captain of the company of infantry, with thirteen of his men, standing in front of the building, but with no arms in their hands. Only one of them seemed disposed to show fight. He ran to the platform where the muskets were stacked, and, seizing one of them, began to load. Before he could ram his cartridge home, a sweep of the saber, in close proximity to his head, made him throw down his gun, and, jumping into a ditch, he dodged under the bridge over the railroad and made his escape. I had no time to pursue him; but, turning to look after the others, met the captain, who, sword in hand, advanced and surrendered himself and his company as prisoners of war. I then proceeded to obstruct the railroad. To do this effectually, I caused a tree to be cut down which was standing on the side of the road. It fell across the railroad. In addition to this, I placed across the tracks an oak-sill about a foot square and fourteen feet long. I had barely time to do this before a train from the direction of Richmond came thundering down. At this time General Stuart, with the main body, arrived at the station. The engine driver of the coming train, probably seeing the obstructions on the track and a large force of cavalry there, suspected danger, and, being a plucky fellow, put on all steam, and came rushing down. The engine, striking the obstructions, knocked them out of the way and passed on without accident. General Stuart had dismounted a number of his men, and posted them on a high bank overlooking a cut in the road, just below the station, through which the train was about to pass. They threw in a close and effective fire upon the passing train, loaded with troops. Many of these were killed and wounded.

It was now the second night since leaving camp, and the well-filled haversacks with which we started from camp had long since been empty. The march had been so rapid that there was little opportunity of foraging for man or beast. Except a little bread and meat, brought out to the column by the country people as we passed along, we had had nothing since daybreak. The men were weary and hungry, and the horses almost exhausted by the long fast and severe exercise. As soon as a proper disposition had been made of the prisoners and of the captured horses and mules, the column moved on. Down through New Kent County, to a place called New Baltimore, we marched as rapidly as our condition would permit. I was still in the command of the advance-guard, marching some distance ahead of the column, and had orders to halt at this point, and await the coming up of the main body. Fortunately, an enterprising Yankee had established a store here, to catch the trade of all persons passing from McClellan's army to his base of supplies at the White House. He had crackers, cheese, canned fruits, sardines, and many other dainties dear to the cavalryman; and in the brief hour spent with him we of the advance were made new men. I fear little was left to cheer and to invigorate those in the rear. The main body arriving, "forward" was the order—straight down through New Kent to Sycamore Ford on the Chickahominy.

A beautiful full moon lighted our way and cast weird shadows across our path. Expecting each moment to meet the enemy, every bush in the distance looked like a sentinel, and every jagged tree bending over the road like a vidette. Marching all night, we arrived at the ford between daybreak and sunrise; and here our real troubles began. To our chagrin, we found the stream swollen by recent rains almost out of its banks, and running like a torrent. No man or horse could get over without swimming, and it happened that the entrance to the ford on our side was below the point at which we had to come out on the other side. Therefore, we had to swim against the current. Owing to the mud and mire, it was not practicable for any number of horses to approach the river at any point except by the road leading to the ford. We therefore tried it there for two long hours. The 9th Cavalry made the trial. After repeated efforts to swim the horses over we gave up, for we had crossed over only seventy-five men and horses in two hours. While we were trying to reach the opposite bank Stuart came up, and, finding crossing at this point impracticable, rode off to find another farther down the river. At a point about one mile below, known as Forge Bridge, he succeeded in throwing across one branch of the river a bridge strong enough to bear the artillery, and upon which the men, having been dismounted, could walk. Here the approach on our side was higher up stream than the point at which we would come out on the other side. So the horses were formed into a column of fours, pushed into the water, and, swimming down stream, they easily landed on the other side. After a few horses had been crossed in this manner we found no difficulty, the others following on quite readily. The column was now upon an island formed by the two branches of the Chickahominy, and to reach the mainland it was necessary to cross the other branch of that river. This was, however, accomplished, but with some difficulty. The ford at this crossing was at that time very deep, and the river out of its banks and overflowing the flats to the depth of about two feet for at least a half-mile. At this place the limber to a caisson stuck fast in the mud, and we left it.

On leaving the river, General Stuart directed me to take charge of the rearguard, and, when all had crossed, to burn the bridge. In accordance with these orders, I directed the men to collect piles of fence rails, heap them on the bridge, and set them afire. By my orders the horses had been led some distance back from the river into the brush, where they were concealed from view. The men were lounging about on the ground when the bridge fell in. I was seated under a tree on the bank of the river, and at the moment that the hissing of the burning timbers of the bridge let me know that it had fallen into the water, a rifle-shot rang out from the other side, and the whistling bullet cut off a small limb over my head, which fell into my lap. The shot was probably fired by some scout who had been following us, but who was afraid to fire until the bridge was gone. With a thankful heart for his bad aim, I at once withdrew the men, and pushed on after the column. When I came to the ford, I found it necessary to swim the horses a short distance, it having been deepened by the crossing of such a large body of horse. Soon the column was in sight, and the march across Charles City County to the James River was made as vigorously as the jaded horses were able to stand. The men, though weary and hungry, were in fine spirits, and jubilant over the successful crossing of the Chickahominy. About sunset we neared the James, at the plantation of Colonel Wilcox. Here we rested for about two hours, having marched into a field of clover, where the horses ate their fill. In the twilight, fires were lighted to cook the rations just brought in by our foragers.

We were now twenty-five miles from Richmond, on the "James River Road." Had the enemy been aware of our position, it would have been easy for him to throw a force between us and Richmond, and so cut us off. But the Federal general was not well served by his scouts, nor did his cavalry furnish him with accurate information of our movements. Relying upon the mistakes of the enemy, Stuart resolved to march straight on into Richmond by the River road on which we now lay. To accomplish this with the greater safety, it was necessary for him to march at once. Accordingly, I was ordered to take the advance-guard and move out. As soon as the cravings of hunger were appeased, sleep took possession of us. Although in the saddle and in motion, and aware that the safety of the expedition depended on great vigilance in case the enemy should be encountered, it was hard to keep awake. I was constantly falling asleep, and awaking with a start when almost off my horse. This was the condition of every man in the column. Not one had closed his eyes in sleep for forty-eight hours.

The full moon lighted us on our way as we passed along the River road, and frequently the windings of the road brought us near to and in sight of the James River, where lay the enemy's fleet. In the gray twilight of the dawn of Sunday, we passed the "Double Gates," "Strawberry Plains," and "Tighlman's gate" in succession. At "Tighlman's" we could see the masts of the fleet, not far off. Happily for us, the banks were high, and I imagine they had no lookout in the rigging, and we passed by unobserved. The sight of the enemy's fleet had aroused us somewhat, when "Who goes there?" rang out on the stillness of the early morning. The challenger proved to be a vidette of the 10th Virginia Cavalry, commanded by Colonel J. Lucius Davis, who

181

was picketing that road. Soon I was shaking hands with Colonel Davis and receiving his congratulations. Then we crossed the stream by the jug factory, up toward "New Market" heights, by the drill-house, and about a mile beyond we called halt for a little rest and food. From this point the several regiments were dismissed to their respective camps.

We lost one man killed and a few wounded, and no prisoners. The most important result was the confidence the men had gained in themselves and in their leaders. The country rang out with praises of the men who had raided entirely around General McClellan's powerful army, bringing prisoners and plunder from under his very nose. The Southern papers were filled with accounts of the expedition, none accurate, and most of them marvelous.

Once more action and reaction. At the close of the Battle of Seven Pines, McClellan screamed, as usual, for reinforcements, and Lincoln consented to send him McDowell's army from its position in northern Virginia. When Lee got wind of this movement, he decided at once that he needed a diversion—to draw off McDowell and frustrate McClellan's hopes for a union with his forces. And his diversionist was ready to hand—General Thomas J. Jackson who had earned a name by standing like a stone wall at Bull Run. Lee reinforced Jackson's small army and sent him rampaging up and down the Shenandoah Valley, routing 12,500 of the enemy, capturing $250,000 worth of supplies and property, taking 3,000 prisoners and 9,000 rifles. So the feint was multiply successful. Lincoln canceled McDowell's orders to join McClellan, and Jackson, after scattering three Union armies in the Valley, was back with Lee in time for the Seven Days.

"Jackson's foot cavalry"

STONEWALL JACKSON IN THE SHENANDOAH

BY JOHN D. IMBODEN, BRIGADIER-GENERAL, C. S. A.

SOON after the battle of Bull Run Stonewall Jackson was promoted to major-general, and the Confederate Government having on the 21st of October, 1861, organized the Department of Northern Virginia, under command of General Joseph E. Johnston, it was divided into the Valley District, the Potomac District, and Aquia District, to be commanded respectively by Major-Generals Jackson, Beauregard, and Holmes. On October 28th General Johnston ordered Jackson to Winchester to assume command of his district, and on the 6th of November the War Department ordered his old "Stonewall" brigade and six thousand troops under command of Brigadier-General W. W. Loring to report to him. These, together with Turner Ashby's cavalry, gave him a force of about ten thousand men all told.

His only movement of note in the winter of 1861–62 was an expedition at the end of December to Bath and Romney, to destroy the Baltimore and Ohio railroad and a dam or two near Hancock on the Chesapeake and Ohio canal. The weather set in to be very inclement about New Year's, with snow, rain, sleet, high winds, and intense cold. Many in Jackson's command were opposed to the expedition, and as it resulted in nothing of much military importance, but was attended with great suffering on the part of his troops, nothing but the confidence he had won by his previous services saved him from personal ruin. He and his second in command, General Loring, had a serious disagreement. He ordered Loring to take up his quarters, in January, in the exposed and cheerless village of Romney, on the south branch of the upper Potomac. Loring objected to this, but Jackson was inexorable. Loring and his principal officers united in a petition to Mr. Benjamin, Secretary of War, to order them to Winchester, or at least away from Romney. This document was sent direct to the War Office, and the Secretary, in utter disregard of "good order and discipline," granted the request without consulting Jackson. As soon as information reached Jackson of what had been done, he indignantly resigned his commission. Governor Letcher was astounded, and at once wrote Jackson a sympathetic letter, and then expostulated with Mr. Davis and his Secretary with such vigor that an apology was sent to Jackson for their obnoxious course. The orders were revoked and modified, and Jackson was induced to retain his command. This little episode gave the Confederate civil authorities an inkling of what manner of man "Stonewall" Jackson was.

In that terrible winter's march and exposure, Jackson endured all that any private was exposed to. One morning, near Bath, some of his men, having crawled out from under their snow-laden blankets, half-frozen, were cursing him as the cause of their sufferings. He lay close by under a tree, also snowed under, and heard all this; and, without noticing it, presently crawled out, too, and, shaking the snow off, made some jocular remark to the nearest men, who had no idea he had ridden up in the night and lain down amongst them. The incident ran through the little army in a few hours, and reconciled his followers to all the hardships of the expedition, and fully reëstablished his popularity.

In March Johnston withdrew from Manassas, and General McClellan collected his army of more than one hundred thousand men on the Peninsula. Johnston moved south to confront him. McClellan had planned and organized a masterly movement to capture, hold, and occupy the Valley and the Piedmont region; and if his subordinates had been equal to the task, and there had been no interference from Washington, it is probable the Confederate army would have been driven out of Virginia and Richmond captured by midsummer, 1862.

Jackson's little army in the Valley had been greatly reduced during the winter from various causes, so that at the beginning of March he did not have over 5000 men of all arms available for the defense of his district, which began to swarm with enemies all around its borders, aggregating more than ten times his own strength. Having retired up the Valley, he learned that the enemy had begun to withdraw and send troops to the east of the mountains to coöperate with McClellan. This he resolved to stop by an aggressive demonstration against Winchester, occupied by General Shields, of the Federal army, with a division of 8000 to 10,000 men.

A little after the middle of March, Jackson concentrated what troops he could, and on the 23d he occupied a ridge at the hamlet of Kernstown, four miles south of Winchester. Shields promptly attacked him, and a severe engagement of several hours ensued, ending in Jackson's repulse about dark, followed by an orderly retreat up the Valley to near Swift Run Gap in Rockingham county. The pursuit was not vigorous nor persistent. Although Jackson retired before superior numbers, he had given a taste of his fighting qualities that stopped the withdrawal of the enemy's troops from the Valley.

The result was so pleasing to the Richmond government and General Johnston that it was decided to reënforce Jackson by sending General Ewell's division to him at Swift Run Gap, which reached him about the 1st of May, thus giving Jackson an aggregate force of from 13,000 to 15,000 men to open his campaign with. At the beginning of May the situation was broadly about as follows: Milroy, with about 4087 men, was on the Staunton and Parkersburg road at McDowell, less than forty miles from Staunton, with Schenck's brigade of about 2500 near Franklin. The rest of Frémont's army in the mountain department was then about 30,000 men, of whom 20,000 were concentrating at Franklin, fifty miles north-west of Staunton, and within supporting distance of Milroy. Banks, who had fortified Strasburg, seventy miles north-east of Staunton by the great Valley turnpike, to fall back upon in an emergency, had pushed forward a force of 20,000 men to Harrisonburg, including Shields's division, 10,000 strong. General McDowell, with 34,000 men, exclusive of Shields's division, was at points east of the Blue Ridge, so as to be able to move either to Fredericksburg or to the Luray Valley and thence to Staunton. Not counting Colonel Miles's, later Saxton's, command, at Harper's Ferry, which was rapidly increased to 7000 men, sent from Washington and other points north of the Potomac, before the end of May, Jackson had about 80,000 men to take into account (including all Union forces north of the Rappahannock and east of the Ohio) and to keep from a junction with McClellan in front of Richmond. Not less than 65,000 of these enemies were in some part of the Valley under their various commanders in May and June.

Besides Ewell's division already mentioned, General Johnston could give no further assistance to Jackson, for McClellan was right in his front with superior numbers, and menacing the capital of the Confederacy with almost immediate and certain capture. Its only salvation depended upon Jackson's ability to hold back Frémont, Banks, and McDowell long enough to let Johnston try doubtful conclusions with McClellan. If he failed in this, these three commanders of an aggregate force then reputed to be, and I believe in fact, over one hundred thousand would converge and move down upon Richmond from the west as McClellan advanced from the east, and the city and its defenders would fall an easy prey to nearly, if not quite, a quarter of a million of the best-armed and best-equipped men ever put into the field by any government.

Early in May, Jackson was near Port Republic contemplating his surroundings and maturing his plans. What these latter were no one but himself knew.

Suddenly the appalling news spread through the Valley that he had fled to the east side of the Blue Ridge through Brown's and Swift Run Gaps. Only Ashby remained behind with about one thousand cavalry, scattered and moving day and night in the vicinity of McDowell, Franklin, Strasburg, Front Royal, and Luray, and reporting to Jackson every movement of the enemy. Despair was fast settling upon the minds of the people of the Valley. Jackson made no concealment of his flight, the news of which soon reached his enemies. Milroy advanced two regiments to the top of the Shenandoah Mountains, only twenty-two miles from Staunton, and was preparing to move his entire force to Staunton, to be followed by Frémont.

Jackson had collected, from Charlottesville and other stations on the Virginia Central Railroad, enough railway trains to transport all of his little army. That it was to be taken to Richmond when the troops were all embarked no one doubted. It was Sunday, and many of his sturdy soldiers were Valley men. With sad and gloomy hearts they boarded the trains at Mechum's River Station. When all were on, lo! they took a westward course, and a little after noon the first train rolled into Staunton.

News of Jackson's arrival spread like wild-fire, and crowds flocked to the station to see the soldiers and learn what it all meant. No one knew.

As soon as the troops could be put in motion they took the road leading toward McDowell, the general having sent forward cavalry to Buffalo Gap and beyond to arrest all persons going that way. General Edward Johnson, with one of Jackson's Valley brigades, was already at Buffalo Gap. The next morning, by a circuitous mountain-path, he tried to send a brigade of infantry to the rear of Milroy's two regiments on Shenandoah Mountain, but they were improperly guided and failed to reach the position in time, so that when attacked in front both regiments escaped. Jackson followed as rapidly as possible, and the following day, May 8th, on top of the Bull Pasture Mountain, three miles east of McDowell, encountered Milroy reënforced by Schenck, who commanded by virtue of seniority of commission. The conflict lasted four hours, and was severe and bloody. It was fought mainly with small-arms, the ground forbidding much use of artillery. Schenck and Milroy fled precipitately toward Franklin, to unite with Frémont. The route lay along a narrow valley hedged up by high mountains, perfectly protecting the flanks of the retreating army from Ashby's pursuing cavalry, led by Captain Sheetz. Jackson ordered him to pursue as vigorously as possible, and to guard completely all avenues of approach from the direction of McDowell or Staunton till relieved of this duty. Jackson buried the dead and rested his army, and then fell back to the Valley on the Warm Springs and Harrisonburg road.

The morning after the battle of McDowell I called very early on Jackson at the residence of Colonel George W. Hull of that village, where he had his headquarters, to ask if I could be of any service to him, as I had to go to Staunton, forty miles distant, to look after some companies that were to join my command. He asked me to wait a few moments, as he wished to prepare a telegram to be sent to President Davis from Staunton, the nearest office to McDowell. He took a seat at a table and wrote nearly half a page of foolscap; he rose and stood before the fireplace pondering it some minutes; then he tore it in pieces and wrote again, but much less, and again destroyed what he had written, and paced the room several times. He suddenly stopped, seated himself, and dashed off two or three lines, folded the paper, and said, "Send that off as soon as you reach Staunton." As I bade him "good-bye," he remarked: "I may have other telegrams to-day or to-morrow, and will send them to you for transmission. I wish you to have two or three well-mounted couriers ready to bring me the replies promptly."

I read the message he had given me. It was dated "McDowell," and read about thus: "Providence blessed our arms with victory at McDowell yesterday." That was all. A few days after I got to Staunton a courier arrived with a message to be telegraphed to the Secretary of War. I read it, sent it off, and ordered a courier to be ready with his horse, while I waited at the telegraph office for the reply. The message was to this effect: "I think I ought to attack Banks, but under my orders I do not feel at liberty to do so." In less than an hour a reply came, but not from the Secretary of War. It was from General Joseph E. Johnston, to whom I supposed the Secretary had referred General Jackson's message. I have a distinct recollection of its substance, as follows: "If you think you can beat Banks, attack him. I only intended by my orders to caution you against attacking fortifications." Banks was understood to have fortified himself strongly at Strasburg and Cedar Creek, and he had fallen back there. I started the courier with this reply, as I supposed, to McDowell, but, lo! it met Jackson only twelve miles from Staunton, to which point on the Harrisonburg and Warm Springs turnpike he had marched his little army, except part of Ashby's cavalry, which, under an intrepid leader, Captain Sheetz, he had sent from McDowell to menace Frémont, who was concentrating at Franklin in Pendleton County, where he remained in blissful ignorance that Jackson had left McDowell, till he learned by telegraph some days later that Jackson had fallen upon Banks at Front Royal and driven him through Winchester and across the Potomac.

Two hours after receiving this telegram from General Johnston, Jackson was *en route* for Harrisonburg, where he came upon the great Valley turnpike. By forced marches he reached New Market in two days. Detachments of cavalry guarded every road beyond him, so that Banks remained in total ignorance of his approach. This Federal commander had the larger part of his force well fortified at and near Strasburg, but he kept a strong detachment at Front Royal, about eight miles distant and facing the Luray or Page Valley.

From New Market Jackson disappeared so suddenly that the people of the Valley were again mystified. He crossed the Massanutten Mountain, and, passing Luray, hurried toward Front Royal. He sometimes made thirty miles in twenty-four hours with his entire army, thus gaining for his infantry the sobriquet of "Jackson's foot cavalry." Very early in the afternoon of May 23d he struck Front Royal. The surprise was complete and disastrous to the enemy, who were commanded by Colonel John R. Kenly. After a fruitless resistance they fled toward Winchester, twenty miles distant, with Jackson at their heels. A large number were captured within four miles by a splendid cavalry dash of Colonel Flournoy and Lieutenant-Colonel Watts.

News of this disaster reached Banks at Strasburg, by which he learned that Jackson was rapidly gaining his rear toward Newtown. The works Banks had constructed had not been made for defense in that direction, so he abandoned them and set out with all haste for Winchester; but, *en route*, near Newtown (May 24th), Jackson struck his flank, inflicting heavy loss, and making large captures of property, consisting of wagons, teams, camp-equipage, provisions, ammunition, and over nine thousand stand of arms, all new and in perfect order, besides a large number of prisoners.

Jackson now chased Banks's fleeing army to Winchester, where the latter made a stand, but after a sharp engagement with Ewell's division on the 25th he fled again, not halting till he had crossed the Potomac, congratulating himself and his Government in a dispatch that his army was at last safe in Maryland. General Saxton, with some 7000 men, held Harper's Ferry, 32 miles from Winchester. Jackson paid his respects to this fortified post, by marching a large part of his forces close to it, threatening an assault, long enough to allow all the captured property at Winchester to be sent away toward Staunton, and then returned to Winchester. His problem now was to escape the clutches of Frémont, knowing that that officer would be promptly advised by wire of what had befallen Banks. He could go back the way he came, by the Luray Valley, but that would expose Staunton (the most important depot in the valley) to capture by Frémont, and he had made his plans to save it.

"Jackson's foot cavalry"

I had been left at Staunton organizing my recruits. On his way to attack Banks, Jackson sent me an order from New Market to throw as many men as I could arm, and as quickly as possible, into Brock's Gap, west of Harrisonburg, and into any other mountain-pass through which Frémont could reach the valley at or south of Harrisonburg. I knew that within four miles of Franklin, on the main road leading to Harrisonburg, there was a narrow defile hemmed in on both sides by nearly perpendicular cliffs, over five hundred feet high. I sent about fifty men, well armed with long-range guns, to occupy these cliffs, and defend the passage to the last extremity.

On the 25th of May, as soon as Frémont learned of Banks's defeat and retreat to the Potomac, he put his army of about 14,000 in motion from Franklin to cut off Jackson's retreat up the valley. Ashby's men were still in his front toward McDowell, with an unknown force; so Frémont did not attempt that route, but sent his cavalry to feel the way toward Brock's Gap, on the direct road to Harrisonburg. The men I had sent to the cliffs let the head of the column get well into the defile or gorge, when, from a position of perfect safety to themselves, they poured a deadly volley into the close column. The attack being unexpected, and coming from a foe of unknown strength, the Federal column halted and hesitated to advance. Another volley and the "rebel yell" from the cliffs turned them back, never to appear again. Frémont took the road to Moorefield, and thence to Strasburg, though he had been peremptorily ordered on May 24th by President Lincoln to proceed direct to Harrisonburg. It shows how close had been Jackson's calculation of chances, to state that as his rear-guard marched up Fisher's Hill, two miles from Strasburg, Frémont's advance came in sight on the mountain-side on the road from Moorefield, and a sharp skirmish took place. Jackson continued to Harrisonburg, hotly pursued by Frémont, but avoiding a conflict.

The news of Banks's defeat created consternation at Washington, and Shields was ordered to return from east of the Blue Ridge to the Luray Valley in all haste to coöperate with Frémont. Jackson was advised of Shields's approach, and his aim was to prevent a junction of their forces till he reached a point where he could strike them in quick succession. He therefore sent cavalry detachments along the Shenandoah to burn the bridges as far as Port Republic, the river being at that time too full for fording. At Harrisonburg he took the road leading to Port Republic, and ordered me from Staunton, with a mixed battery and battalion of cavalry, to the bridge over North River near Mount Crawford, to prevent a cavalry force passing to his rear.

At Cross Keys, about six miles from Harrisonburg, he delivered battle to Frémont, on June 8th, and, after a long and bloody conflict, as night closed in he was master of the field. Leaving one division—Ewell's—on the ground, to resist Frémont if he should return next day, he that night marched the rest of his army to Port Republic, which lies in the forks of the river, and made his arrangements to attack the troops of Shields's command next morning on the Lewis farm, just below the town.

On the day of the conflict at Cross Keys I held the bridge across North River at Mount Crawford with a battalion of cavalry, four howitzers, and a Parrott gun, to prevent a cavalry flank movement on Jackson's trains at Port Republic. About 10 o'clock at night I received a note from Jackson, written in pencil on the blank margin of a newspaper, directing me to report with my command at Port Republic before daybreak. On the same slip, and as a postscript, he wrote, "Poor Ashby is dead. He fell gloriously. . . . I know you will join with me in mourning the loss of our friend, one of the noblest men and soldiers in the Confederate army." I carried that slip of paper till it was literally worn to tatters.

It was early, Sunday, June 8th, when Jackson and his staff reached the bridge at Port Republic. General E. B. Tyler, who, with two brigades of Shields's division, was near by on the east side of the river, had sent two guns and a few men under a green and inefficient officer to the bridge. They arrived about the same time as Jackson, but, his troops soon coming up, the Federal officer and his supports made great haste back to the Lewis farm, losing a gun at the bridge.

I reached Port Republic an hour before daybreak of June 9th, and sought the house occupied by Jackson; but not wishing to disturb him so early, I asked the sentinel what room was occupied by "Sandy" Pendleton, Jackson's adjutant-general. "Upstairs, first room on the right," he replied.

Supposing he meant our right as we faced the house, I went up, softly opened the door, and discovered General Jackson lying on his face across the bed, fully dressed, with sword, sash, and boots all on. The low-burnt tallow candle on the table shed a dim light, yet enough by which to recognize him. I endeavored to withdraw without waking him. He turned over, sat up on the bed, and called out, "Who is that?"

He checked my apology with "That is all right. It's time to be up. I am glad to see you. Were the men all up as you came through camp?"

"Yes, General, and cooking."

"That's right. We move at daybreak. Sit down. I want to talk to you."

I had learned never to ask him questions about his plans, for he would never answer such to any one. I therefore waited for him to speak first. He referred very feelingly to Ashby's death, and spoke of it as an irreparable loss. When he paused I said, "General, you made a glorious winding-up of your four weeks' work yesterday."

He replied, "Yes, God blessed our army again yesterday, and I hope with his protection and blessing we shall do still better to-day."

Then seating himself, for the first time in all my intercourse with him, he outlined the day's proposed operations. I remember perfectly his conversation. He said: "Charley Winder will cross the river at daybreak and attack Shields on the Lewis farm. I shall support him with all the other troops as fast as they can be put in line. General 'Dick' Taylor will move through the woods on the side of the mountain with his Louisiana brigade, and rush upon their left flank by the time the action becomes general. By 10 o'clock we shall get them on the run, and I'll now tell you what I want with you. Send the big new rifle-gun you have [a 12-pounder Parrott] to Poague [commander of the Rockbridge artillery] and let your mounted men report to the cavalry. I want you in person to take your mountain howitzers to the field, in some safe position in rear of the line, keeping everything packed on the mules, ready at any moment to take to the mountain-side. Three miles below Lewis's there is a defile on the Luray road. Shields may rally and make a stand there. If he does, I can't reach him with the field-batteries on account of the woods. You can carry your 12-pounder howitzers on the mules up the mountain-side, and at some good place unpack and shell the enemy out of the defile, and the cavalry will do the rest."

This plan of battle was carried out to the letter. I took position in a ravine about two hundred yards in rear of Poague's battery in the center of the line. General Tyler, who had two brigades of Shields's division, made a very stubborn fight, and by 9 o'clock matters began to look very serious for us. Dick Taylor had not yet come down out of the woods on Tyler's left flank.

Meanwhile I was having a remarkable time with our mules in the ravine. . . . News came up the line from the left that Winder's brigade near the river was giving way. Jackson rode down in that direction to see what it meant. As he passed on the brink of our ravine, his eye caught the scene, and, reining up a moment, he accosted me with, "Colonel, you seem to have trouble down there." I made some reply which drew forth a hearty laugh, and he said, "Get your mules to the mountain as soon as you can, and be ready to move."

Then he dashed on. He found his old brigade had yielded slightly to overwhelming pressure. Galloping up, he was received with a cheer; and, calling out at the top of his voice, "The 'Stonewall' brigade never retreats; follow me!" led them back to their original line. Taylor soon made his appearance, and the flank attack settled the work of the day. A wild retreat began. The pursuit was vigorous. No stand was made in the defile. We pursued them eight miles. I rode back with Jackson, and at sunset we were on the battlefield at the Lewis mansion. . . .

Frémont, hearing the noise of the battle, had hurried out from near Harrisonburg to help Tyler; but Jackson had burnt the bridge at Port Republic, after Ewell had held Frémont in check some time on the west side of the river and escaped, so that when Frémont came in sight of Tyler's battlefield, the latter's troops had been routed and the river could not be crossed.

The next day I returned to Staunton, and found General W. H. C. Whiting, my old commander after the fall of General Bee at Bull Run, arriving with a division of troops to reënforce Jackson. Taking him and his staff to my house as guests, General Whiting left soon after breakfast with a guide to call on Jackson at Swift Run Gap, near Port Republic, where he was resting his troops. The distance from Staunton was about twenty miles, but Whiting returned after midnight. He was in a towering passion, and declared that Jackson had treated him outrageously. I asked, "How is that possible, General, for he is very polite to every one?"

"Oh! hang him, he was polite enough. But he didn't say one word about his plans. I finally asked him for orders, telling him what troops I had. He simply told me to go back to Staunton, and he would send me orders to-morrow. I haven't the slightest idea what they will be. I believe he hasn't any more sense than my horse."

Seeing his frame of mind, and he being a guest in my house, I said little. Just after breakfast, next morning, a courier arrived with a terse order to embark his troops on the railroad trains and move to Gordonsville at once, where he would receive further orders. This brought on a new explosion of wrath. "Didn't I tell you he was a fool, and doesn't this prove it? Why, I just came through Gordonsville day before yesterday."

However, he obeyed the order; and when he reached Gordonsville he found Jackson there, and his little Valley army coming after him; a few days later McClellan was astounded to learn that Jackson was on his right flank on the Chickahominy. Shortly after the seven days' battle around Richmond, I met Whiting again, and he then said, "I didn't know Jackson when I was at your house. I have found out now what his plans were, and they were worthy of a Napoleon. But I still think he ought to have told me his plans; for if he had died McClellan would have captured Richmond. I wouldn't have known what he was driving at, and might have made a mess of it. But I take back all I said about his being a fool."

From the date of Jackson's arrival at Staunton till the battle of Port Republic was thirty-five days. He marched from Staunton to McDowell, 40 miles, from McDowell to Front Royal, about 110, from Front Royal to Winchester, 20 miles, Winchester to Port Republic, 75 miles, a total of 245 miles, fighting in the meantime 4 desperate battles, and winning them all.

On the 17th of June, leaving only his cavalry, under Brigadier-General B. H. Robertson, and Chew's battery, and the little force I was enlisting in the valley (which was now no longer threatened by the enemy), Jackson moved all his troops south-east, and on the 25th arrived at Ashland, seventeen miles from Richmond. This withdrawal from the valley was so skillfully managed that his absence from the scene of his late triumphs was unsuspected at Washington. On the contrary, something like a panic prevailed there, and the Government was afraid to permit McDowell to unite his forces with McClellan's lest it should uncover and expose the capital to Jackson's supposed movement on it.

Jackson's military operations were always unexpected and mysterious. In my personal intercourse with him in the early part of the war, before he had become famous, he often said there were two things never to be lost sight of by a military commander: "Always mystify, mislead, and surprise the enemy, if possible; and when you strike and overcome him, never let up in the pursuit so long as your men have strength to follow; for an army routed, if hotly pursued, becomes panic-stricken, and can then be destroyed by half their number. The other rule is, never fight against heavy odds, if by any possible manœuvring you can hurl your own force on only a part, and that the weakest part, of your enemy and crush it. Such tactics will win every time, and a small army may thus destroy a large one in detail, and repeated victory will make it invincible."

His celerity of movement was a simple matter. He never broke down his men by too-long-continued marching. He rested the whole column very often, but only for a few minutes at a time. I remember that he liked to see the men lie down flat on the ground to rest, and would say, "A man rests all over when he lies down."

GENERAL STONEWALL JACKSON

195

Even in the light of subsequent historical researches and interpretations, it would be difficult to summarize better than Colonel Irwin has done the conduct of President Lincoln and Secretary Stanton vis-à-vis General McClellan from July 1861 to August 1862.

"But you must act"

THE ADMINISTRATION IN THE PENINSULAR CAMPAIGN

BY RICHARD B. IRWIN, LIEUTENANT-COLONEL AND ASSISTANT
ADJUTANT-GENERAL, U. S. V.

APPOINTED on the 25th of July, 1861, immediately after Bull Run, to the command of the shattered and reduced forces then gathered about Washington, at one time not exceeding 42,000 all told, General Mc-Clellan was rapidly reënforced, until on the 15th of March, 1862, he had under his command within the division or department of the Potomac 203, 213 men present for duty. The field-artillery was increased from 30 guns to 520; to these had been added a siege train of nearly 100 heavy guns. From these materials he organized the Army of the Potomac.

In the last days of October General McClellan presented to the Secretary of War a written statement of his views as to the conduct of operations, in which, after representing the Confederate forces in his front at not less than 150,000, his own movable force as 76,285, with 228 guns, and the force re-

197

quired for active operations as 150,000 men, with 400 guns, he recommended that all operations in other quarters be confined to the defensive, and that all surplus troops be sent to reënforce the Army of the Potomac.

A vigorous employment of these means [he proceeds] will, in my opinion, enable the Army of the Potomac to assume successfully this season the offensive operations which, ever since entering upon the command, it has been my anxious desire and diligent effort to prepare for and prosecute. The advance should not be postponed beyond the 25th of November, if possible to avoid it.

Unity in councils, the utmost vigor and energy in action are indispensable. The entire military field should be grasped as a whole, and not in detached parts. One plan should be agreed upon and pursued; a single will should direct and carry out these plans. The great object to be accomplished, the crushing defeat of the rebel army (now) at Manassas, should never for one instant be lost sight of, but all the intellect and means and men of the Government poured upon that point.

On the 1st of November, 1861, the President, "with the concurrence of the entire Cabinet," designated General McClellan "to command the whole army" of the United States. No trust approaching this in magnitude had ever before been confided to any officer of the United States.

Everywhere the armies remained inactive. For seven months the Army of the Potomac was held within the defenses of Washington. Its only important movement had resulted in the disheartening disaster of Ball's Bluff. The Confederates, with headquarters at Manassas, confronted them with an army, represented by General McClellan, on the faith of his secret-service department, as numbering at least 115,500, probably 150,000, but now known to have at no time exceeded 63,000. The Potomac was closed to navigation by Confederate batteries established on its banks within twenty-three miles of the capital. Norfolk, with its navy-yard, was left untouched and unmenaced. The loyal States had furnished three-quarters of a million of soldiers, and the country had rolled up a daily increasing war debt of $600,000,000. There is no indication that General McClellan appreciated, or even perceived, the consequences that must inevitably follow the loss of confidence on the part of the people, as month after month passed without action and without success in any quarter, or the position in which, under these circumstances, he placed the President, with respect to the continued support of the people and their representatives, by withholding full information of his plans. In his "Own Story" he tells how he refused to give this information when called upon by the President in the presence of his Cabinet.

The President having, on the 31st of January, ordered the movement of all the disposable force of the Army of the Potomac, for the purpose of seizing a point on the railroad beyond Manassas Junction, General McClellan on the same day submitted his own plan for moving on Richmond by way of Urbana, on the lower Rappahannock. On the 8th of March, yielding to

198

General McClellan's views, supported by the majority of his division commanders, the President approved the Urbana movement, with certain conditions; but on the 9th the Confederates evacuated Manassas, and thus rendered the whole plan inoperative. On the 13th, upon General McClellan's recommendations, supported by the commanders of all four of the newly constituted army corps, the President authorized the movement by Fort Monroe, as it was finally made.

McClellan expected to take with him to the Peninsula 146,000 men of all arms, to be increased to 156,000 by a division to be drawn from Fort Monroe. On the 31st of March, the President informed him that he had been obliged to order Blenker's division of about 10,000 men, with 18 guns, to Frémont. "I did this with great pain," he says, "knowing that you would wish it otherwise. If you could know the full pressure of the case, I am confident you would approve."

The council of corps commanders had annexed to their approval, among other conditions, the following: "Fourth, that the force to be left to cover Washington shall be such as to give an entire feeling of security for its safety from menace. . . . NOTE.—That with the forts on the right bank of the Potomac fully garrisoned and those on the left bank occupied, a covering force in front of the Virginia line of 25,000 men would suffice (Keyes, Heintzelman, and McDowell). A total of 40,000 men for the defense of the city would suffice. (Sumner.)" Upon this point the President's orders were: "1st. Leave such a force at Manassas Junction as shall make it entirely certain that the enemy shall not repossess himself of that position and line of communication. 2d. Leave Washington secure."

On the 1st of April, as he was on the point of sailing, General McClellan reported from his headquarters on board the steamer *Commodore,* the arrangements he had made to carry out these provisions, and at once set out for Fort Monroe without knowing whether they were satisfactory to the Government or not. They were not. General McClellan had arranged to leave 7780 men at Warrenton, 10,859 at Manassas, 1350 on the Lower Potomac, and 18,000 men for the garrisons and the front of Washington, to be augmented by about 4000 new troops from New York. The President, deeming this provision wholly insufficient for the defense of the capital, ordered McDowell with his corps of 33,510 men and 68 guns to remain, and charged him with the duty of covering and defending Washington.

This led to a telegraphic correspondence, thus characterized in the President's letter to General McClellan, dated April 9th: "Your dispatches complaining that you are not properly sustained, while they do not offend me, pain me very much." Then, after again explaining the detachment of Blenker and the retention of McDowell, Mr. Lincoln concludes with these noteworthy admonitions: "I suppose the whole force which has gone forward to you is with you by this time; and if so, I think it is the precise time for you to strike a blow. By delay, the enemy will steadily gain on you—that is, he will gain faster by fortifications and reënforcements than you can by reënforcements alone.

"And once more, let me tell you, it is indispensable to *you* that you strike a blow! I am powerless to help this. You will do me the justice to remember I always insisted that going down the bay in search of a field instead of fighting at or near Manassas, was only shifting and not surmounting a difficulty; that we would find the same enemy and the same or equal intrenchments at either place. The country will not fail to note—is noting now—that the present hesitation to move upon an intrenched enemy is but the story of Manassas repeated.

"I beg to assure you that I have never written or spoken to you in greater kindness of feeling than now, nor with a fuller purpose to sustain you, so far as in my most anxious judgment I consistently can. *But you must act.*"

On the 11th of April, Franklin's division was ordered to the Peninsula, in response to General McClellan's earnest renewal of his request.

General McClellan estimates his force before Franklin's arrival at 85,000, apparently meaning fighting men, since the returns show 105,235 present for duty on the 13th of April. On the 30th, including Franklin, this number was increased to 112,392. General McClellan also estimated the Confederate forces at "probably not less than 100,000 men, and possibly more," "probably greater a good deal than my own." We now know that their total effective strength on the 30th of April was 55,633 of all arms. When the Army of the Potomac halted before the lines of the Warwick, Magruder's whole force was but 11,000. General McClellan estimated it at only 15,000, and his own, confronting it, at the same period, at 53,000.

The plan of a rapid movement up the Peninsula having resolved itself into an endeavor to take Yorktown by regular approaches in front, leaving its rear necessarily open, General McClellan thus describes the result:

Our batteries would have been ready to open on the morning of the 6th of May at latest; but on the morning of the 4th it was discovered that the enemy had already been compelled to evacuate his position during the night.

The effect of these delays on Mr. Lincoln's mind is curiously indicated by his telegram of May 1st:

Your call for Parrott guns from Washington alarms me, chiefly because it argues indefinite procrastination. Is anything to be done?

Then followed the confused and unduly discouraging battle of Williamsburg; the attempt to cut off the Confederate retreat by a landing at West Point came to nothing; and on the 20th of May, the Army of the Potomac, having moved forward 52 miles in 16 days, reached the banks of the Chickahominy. There it lay, astride of that sluggish stream, imbedded in its pestilential swamps, for thirty-nine days.

On the 31st of May, at Fair Oaks, Johnston failed, though narrowly missing success, in a well-meant attempt to crush McClellan's forces on the right bank of the swollen stream before they could be reënforced. On the 1st of June the Confederate forces were driven back in disorder upon the defenses of Richmond, but the damage suffered by the Union forces on the first day being over-estimated, and their success on the second day insufficiently appreciated, or inadequately represented, and no apparent advantage being taken of them, the general effect was to add to the discouragement already prevailing.

Reënforcements continuing to be urgently called for, Fort Monroe, with its dependencies, reporting 9277 for duty, was placed under General McClellan's orders; McCall's division, with 22 guns, was detached from McDowell, and arrived by water 9514 strong on the 12th and 13th of June; while McDowell, with the rest of his command, was ordered to march to join McClellan by land: this movement was, however, promptly brought to naught by Jackson's sudden incursion against Banks in the Shenandoah.

Meanwhile, the flow of telegrams indicated an ever-increasing tension, the Executive urging to action, the General promising to act soon, not acting, yet criticising and objecting to the President's orders to him and to others. On the 25th of May the President said: "I think the time is near when you must either attack Richmond or give up the job and come to the defense of Washington." McClellan replied: "The time is very near when I shall attack Richmond." Then, June 10th, he says : "I shall be in perfect readiness to move forward to take Richmond the moment that McCall reaches here and the ground will admit the passage of artillery." June 14th: "If I cannot control all his (McDowell's) troops I want none of them, but would prefer to fight the battle with what I have, and let others be responsible for the results." On the 18th: "After to-morrow we shall fight the rebel army as soon as Providence will permit. We shall await only a favorable condition of the earth and sky and the completion of some necessary preliminaries." While appealing to the President when some of his telegrams to the Secretary remained for a time unanswered, General McClellan allowed Mr. Stanton's cordial assurances of friendship and support to pass unnoticed.

At last, on the 25th, General McClellan advanced his picket lines on the left to within four miles of Richmond, and was apparently preparing for a further movement, though none was ordered, and the next day, as at Manassas and Yorktown and Fair Oaks, his adversary once more took the initiative out of his hands. Jackson had come from the Valley.

As soon as this was known, on the evening of the 25th, General McClellan reported it to Mr. Stanton, added that he thought Jackson would attack his right and rear, that the Confederate force was stated at 200,000, that he re-

201

gretted his great inferiority in numbers, but was in no way responsible for it, and concluded:

I will do all that a general can do with the splendid army I have the honor to command, and if it is destroyed by overwhelming numbers can at least die with it and share its fate. But if the result of the action, which will probably occur to-morrow, or within a short time, is a disaster, the responsibility cannot be thrown on my shoulders; it must rest where it belongs.

The battle of Gaines's Mill followed, where, on the 27th, one-fifth of the Union forces contended against the whole Confederate army, save Magruder's corps and Huger's division; then the retreat, or "change of base," to the James, crowned by the splendid yet unfruitful victory of Malvern; then a month of inaction and discussion at Harrison's Landing.

At 12:20 A. M., on the 28th of June, General McClellan sent a long telegram, of which these sentences strike the key-note:

Our men [at Gaines's Mill] did all that men could do . . . but they were overwhelmed by vastly superior numbers, even after I brought my last reserves into action. . . . I have lost this battle because my force is too small. . . . The Government must not and cannot hold me responsible for the result. I feel too earnestly to-night. I have seen too many dead and wounded comrades to feel otherwise than that the Government has not sustained this army. . . . If I save this army now, I tell you plainly that I owe no thanks to you *or to any other persons in Washington. You have done your best to sacrifice this army.*

On reaching the James River, General McClellan reported that he had saved his army, but it was completely exhausted and would require reënforcements to the extent of 50,000 men. On the 3d of July, he wrote more fully from Harrison's Landing, then saying that "reënforcements should be sent to me rather much over, than much less, than 100,000 men." He referred to his memorandum of the 20th of August, 1861. That memorandum called for 273,000 men. General Marcy, his chief-of-staff, who bore this dispatch to Washington, telegraphed back:

I have seen the President and Secretary of War. 10,000 men from Hunter, 10,-000 from Burnside, and 11,000 from here have been ordered to reënforce you as soon as possible. Halleck [who had been originally called on for 25,000 men which he had reported he could not spare] has been urged by the President to send you at once 10,000 men from Corinth. The President and Secretary speak very kindly of you and find no fault.

The dispatches of the President and Secretary breathe the same spirit.

Allow me to reason with you a moment [wrote Mr. Lincoln on the 2d of July, adding that he had not fifty thousand men who could be sent promptly]. If, in your frequent mention of responsibility, you have the impression that I blame you for not doing more than you can, please be relieved of such impression. I only beg that in like manner you will not ask impossibilities of me. If you think you are not strong enough to take Richmond just now, I do not ask you to try just now. Save the army, material and personal, and I will strengthen it for the offensive again as fast as I can. The governors of 18 States offer me a new levy of 300,000, which I accept.

On the 5th, Mr. Stanton wrote that he had nominated all the corps commanders for promotion.

The gallantry of every officer and man in your noble army shall be suitably acknowledged. General Marcy will take you cheering news. Be assured that you shall have the support of this Department and the Government as cordially and faithfully as ever was rendered by man to man, and if we should ever live to see each other face to face, you will be satisfied that you have never had from me anything but the most confiding integrity.

The next day Mr. Stanton followed this by a personal letter, couched in still warmer terms.

No man [he wrote] had ever a truer friend than I have been to you, and shall continue to be. You are seldom absent from my thoughts, and I am ready to make any sacrifice to aid you. Time allows me to say no more than that I pray Almighty God to deliver you and your army from all perils and lead you on to victory.

General McClellan's reply was long, cold, and formal. He reviewed their past relations, and alluded to the Secretary's official conduct toward him as "marked by repeated acts done in such manner as to be deeply offensive to my feelings, and calculated to affect me injuriously in public estimation."

After commencing the present campaign [he continued], your concurrence in the withholding of a large portion of my force, so essential to the success of my plans, led me to believe that your mind was warped by a bitter personal prejudice against me. Your letter compels me to believe that I have been mistaken in regard to your real feelings and opinions, and that your conduct, so unaccountable to my own fallible judgment, must have proceeded from views and motives which I did not understand.

The campaign had failed. The President visited Harrison's Landing to see for himself what was to be done next. Then General McClellan handed him his well-known letter "upon a civil and military policy covering the whole ground of our national trouble." He called Mr. Stanton's attention to this letter, in the reply we have just cited, and told him that for no other policy would our armies continue to fight. This must have been the last straw. On one point, however, he was in accord with the President. He wound up by recommending the appointment of a commander-in-chief of the army who should possess the President's confidence. On the 11th General Halleck was appointed.

On the 26th General Halleck arrived at General McClellan's camp. He reports that McClellan "expressed the opinion that with 30,000 reënforcements he could attack Richmond, with 'a good chance of success.' I replied that I was authorized by the President to promise only 20,000, and that if he could not take Richmond with that number we must devise some plan for withdrawing his troops from their present position to some point where they could unite with those of General Pope without exposing Washington. ... He ... the next morning informed me he would attack Richmond with the reënforcements promised. He would not say that he thought the probabilities of success were in his favor, but that there was 'a chance,' and he was 'willing to try it.'

"With regard to the force of the enemy he expressed the opinion that it was not less than 200,000."

The orders for the removal followed. "There was, to my mind," General Halleck says, "no alternative. . . . I have taken the responsibility of doing so and am to risk my reputation on it."

Upon whatever side, if upon either, of these many-sided controversies, history shall at last adjudge the right to be, upon whatever shoulders and in whatever degree the burden of blame shall finally rest, certain it is that no fair account of these operations can ever be written without taking note of these delays, whereby the initiative was transferred to the adversary; of these disasters, these unproductive victories, this ceaseless flow of telegrams, surcharged with the varying words of controversy, criticism, objection, reproach; and of the inevitable effect of all these causes combined, in weakening the confidence of the President and in undermining his authority and influence, which, however, to the last were exerted to uphold the general of his first choice at the head of his greatest army.

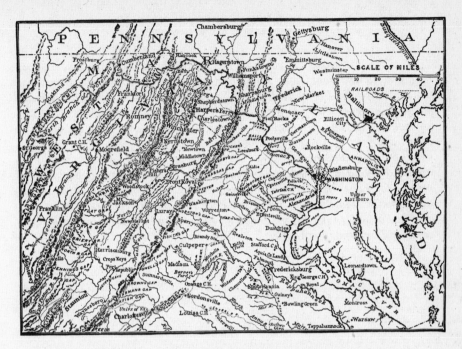

CAMPAIGN MAP OF THE SECOND BATTLE OF BULL RUN

After the disastrous campaign on the Peninsula, Lincoln continued to look for a general who would fight. John Pope, who had had some minor successes in the West, appeared to be such a man. So he was brought to Washington and placed in charge of an "Army of Virginia" comprising the commands of McDowell, Banks, and Frémont (the last promptly resigned). McClellan was to contribute part of his army to the new unit (and, as he thought, become its head) but, as usual, he was slow. Lee, no longer pinned down by McClellan around Richmond, moved north to face Pope, and that was the beginning of the end for Pope. In a series of engagements with Lee and Jackson, culminating in the Second Battle of Bull Run, Pope managed to confuse everybody including himself. In the process Bull Run was lost and Pope, relieved of his brief command, returned to the West.

"To gain time . . ."

BY JOHN POPE, MAJOR-GENERAL, U. S. A.

EARLY in June, 1862, I was in command of the army corps known as the "Army of the Mississippi," which formed the left wing of the army engaged in operations against Corinth, Miss., commanded by General Halleck. A few days after Corinth was evacuated I went to St. Louis on a short leave of absence from my command, and while there I received a telegram from Mr. Stanton, Secretary of War, requesting me to come to Washington immediately. I at once communicated the fact to General Halleck by telegraph, and received a reply from him strongly objecting to my leaving the army which was under his command. I quite concurred with him both as to his objections to my going to Washington for public reasons and as to the unadvisability of such a step on personal considerations. I was obliged, however, to go, and I went accordingly, but with great reluctance and against

207

the urgent protests of my friends in St. Louis, and subsequently of many friends in the Army of the West.

When I reached Washington the President was absent at West Point, but I reported in person to Secretary Stanton. I had never seen him before, and his peculiar appearance and manners made a vivid impression on me. He was short and stout. His long beard, which hung over his breast, was slightly tinged with gray even at that time, and he had the appearance of a man who had lost much sleep and was tired both in body and mind. Certainly, with his large eye-glasses and rather disheveled appearance, his presence was not imposing. Although he was very kind and civil to me, his manner was abrupt and his speech short and rather dictatorial. He entered at once on the business in hand, seemingly without the least idea that any one should object to, or be reluctant to agree to, his views and purposes. He was surprised, and, it seemed to me, not well pleased, that I did not assent to his plans with effusion; but went on to unfold them in the seeming certainty that they must be submitted to. He informed me that the purpose was to unite the armies under McDowell, Frémont, and Banks, all three of whom were my seniors in rank, and to place me in general command. These armies were scattered over the northern part of Virginia, with little or no communication or concert of action with one another; Frémont and Banks being at Middletown, in the Shenandoah Valley, and McDowell's corps widely separated, King's division at Fredericksburg, and Ricketts's at and beyond Manassas Junction.

The general purpose at that time was to demonstrate with the army toward Gordonsville and Charlottesville and draw off as much as possible of the force in front of General McClellan, who then occupied the line of the Chickahominy, and to distract the attention of the enemy in his front so as to reduce as far as practicable the resistance opposed to his advance on Richmond.

It became apparent to me at once that the duty to be assigned to me was in the nature of a forlorn-hope, and my position was still further embarrassed by the fact that I was called from another army and a different field of duty to command an army of which the corps commanders were all my seniors in rank. I therefore strongly urged that I be not placed in such a position, but be permitted to return to my command in the West, to which I was greatly attached and with which I had been closely identified in several successful operations on the Mississippi. It was not difficult to forecast the delicate and embarrassing position in which I should be placed, nor the almost certainly disagreeable, if not unfortunate, issue of such organization for such a purpose.

It would be tedious to relate the conversations between the President, the Secretary of War, and myself on this subject. Sufficient to say that I was finally informed that the public interests required my assignment to this command, and that it was my duty to submit cheerfully. An order from the War Department was accordingly issued organizing the Army of Virginia, to consist of the army corps of McDowell, Banks, and Frémont, and placing me in command.

One result of this order was the very natural protest of General Frémont against being placed under the command of his junior in rank, and his request to be relieved from the command of his corps.

It was equally natural that the subordinate officers and the enlisted men of those corps should have been ill-pleased at the seeming affront to their own officers, involved in calling an officer strange to them and to the country in which they were operating, and to the character of the service in which they were engaged, to supersede well-known and trusted officers who had been with them from the beginning, and whose reputation was so closely identified with their own. How far this feeling prevailed among them, and how it influenced their actions, if it did so at all, I am not able to tell; but it is only proper for me to say (and it is a pleasure as well as a duty to say it) that Generals McDowell and Banks never exhibited to me the slightest feeling on the subject either in their conversation or acts. Indeed, I think it would be hard to find officers more faithful to their duty or more deeply interested in the success of the army. To General McDowell especially is due my gratitude for his zeal and fidelity in what was and ought to have been considered a common cause, the success of the Union Army.

Knowing very well the difficulties and embarrassments certain to arise from all these sources, and the almost hopeless character of the service demanded of me, I, nevertheless, felt obliged, in deference to the wish of the President and Secretary of War, to submit; but I entered on this command with great reluctance and serious forebodings.

On the 27th of June, accordingly, I assumed command of the Army of Virginia, which consisted of the three corps above named, which numbered as follows: Frémont's corps, 11,500; Banks's corps, 8000, and McDowell's corps, 18,500—in all, 38,000 men. The cavalry numbered about 5000, but most of it was badly organized and armed, and in poor condition for service. These forces were scattered over a wide district of country, not within supporting distance of one another, and some of the brigades and divisions were badly organized and in a more or less demoralized condition. This was especially the case in the army corps of General Frémont, as shown in the report of General Sigel which was sent me when he had assumed command of it.

My first object was, therefore, to bring the three corps of the army together, or near enough together to be within supporting distance of one another, and to put them in as efficient a condition for active service as was possible with the time and means at my disposal. When I assumed this command, the troop under General Stonewall Jackson had retired from the valley of the Shenandoah to Richmond, so there was not at that time any force of the enemy of any consequence within several days' march of my command. I accordingly sent orders to General Sigel to move forward, cross the Shenandoah at Front Royal, and, pursuing the west side of the Blue Ridge to Luray, and then crossing it at Thornton's Gap, take post at Sperryville. At the same time I directed General Banks to cross the Shenandoah at Front Royal and proceed by way of Chester Gap to Little Washington. Ricketts's division of McDowell's corps, then at and beyond Manassas Junction, was ordered to move forward to Waterloo Bridge, where the turnpike from Warrenton to Sperryville crosses the Rappahannock, there known as Hedgman's River. In deference to the wishes of the Government, and much against my opinion, King's division of the same corps was kept at Fredericksburg. The wide separation of this division from the main body of the army not only deprived me of its use when, as became plain afterward, it was much needed, but left us exposed to the constant danger that the enemy might interpose between us.

The partial concentration of the corps so near to the Blue Ridge and with open communications with the Shenandoah Valley seemed to me best to fulfill the object of covering that valley from any movements from the direction of Richmond with any force less than the army under my command. The position was one also which gave most favorable facilities for the intended operations toward Gordonsville and Charlottesville.

At the date of my orders for this concentration of the army under my command, the Army of the Potomac under General McClellan occupied both banks of the Chickahominy, and it was hoped that his advance against Richmond, so long delayed, might be facilitated by vigorous use of the Army of Virginia.

During the preparation for the march of the corps of Banks and Sigel toward Sperryville and Little Washington, began the series of battles which preceded and attended the retreat of General McClellan from the Chickahominy toward Harrison's Landing.

When first General McClellan began to intimate by his dispatches that he designed making this retreat toward the James River, I suggested to the President the impolicy of such a movement, and the serious consequences that would be likely to result from it; I urged upon him that he send orders to General McClellan, if he were unable to maintain his position on the Chickahominy, and were pushed by superior forces of the enemy, to mass his whole force on the north side of that stream, even at the risk of losing some of his material of war, and endeavor to retire in the direction of Hanover Court House, but in no event to retreat farther south than the White House on the Pamunkey River. I told the President that by the movement to the James River the whole army of the enemy would be interposed between General McClellan and myself, and that they would then be able to strike in either direction as might seem most advantageous to them; that this movement would leave entirely unprotected, except so far as the small force under my command could protect it, the whole region in front of Washington, and that it would therefore be impossible to send him any of my troops without putting it in the power of the enemy to exchange Richmond for Washington; that to them the loss of Richmond would be comparatively a small loss, while to us the loss of Washington would be almost a fatal blow. I was so impressed with these opinions that I several times urged them upon the attention of the President and the Secretary of War.

The soundness of these views can be easily tested by subsequent facts. The enemy actually did choose between the danger of losing Richmond and the chance of capturing Washington. Stonewall Jackson's corps was detached from Lee's army confronting McClellan at Harrison's Landing early in July, and on the 19th of that month was concentrated at Gordonsville in my front; while Stuart's cavalry division, detached from Lee's army about the same time, was at or near Fredericksburg watching our movements from that direction. On the 13th of August Longstreet's whole corps was dispatched to join Jackson at Gordonsville, to which place he had fallen back from Cedar Mountain, and the head of Longstreet's corps had joined Jackson at that place on August 15th. These forces were commanded by Lee in person, who was at Gordonsville on that day. The first troops of the Army of the Potomac which left Harrison's Landing moved out from that place on August 14th, at which date there was nothing of Lee's army, except D. H. Hill's corps, left in front of McClellan or near to him. Hill's corps could have opposed but little effective resistance to the advance of the Army of the Potomac upon Richmond.

It seems clear, then, that the views expressed to the President and Secretary of War, as heretofore set forth, were sound, and that the enemy had left McClellan to work his will on Richmond, while they pushed forward against the small army under my command and to the capture of Washington. This movement of Lee was, in my opinion, in accordance with true military principle, and was the natural result of McClellan's retreat to Harrison's Landing, which completely separated the Army of the Potomac from the Army of Virginia and left the entire force of the enemy interposed between them.

The retreat of General McClellan to Harrison's Landing was, however, continued to the end. During these six days of anxiety and apprehension Mr. Lincoln spent much of his time in the office of the Secretary of War, most of that time reclining on a sofa or lounge. The Secretary of War was always with him, and from time to time his Cabinet officers came in. Mr. Lincoln himself appeared much depressed and wearied, though occasionally, while waiting for telegrams, he would break into some humorous remark, which seemed rather a protest against his despondent manner than any genuine expression of enjoyment. He spoke no unkind word of any one, and appeared to be anxious himself to bear all the burden of the situation; and when the final result was reported he rose with a sorrowful face and left the War Department.

A day or two after General McClellan reached the James River I was called before the President and his Cabinet to consult upon means and movements to relieve him. I do not know that it would be proper even at this day for me to state what occurred or what was said during this consultation, except so far as I was myself directly concerned. General McClellan was calling for reënforcements, and stating that "much over rather than under one hundred thousand men" were necessary before he could resume operations against Richmond. I had not under my command one-half that force.

I stated to the President and Cabinet that I stood ready to undertake any movement, however hazardous, to relieve the Army of the Potomac. Some suggestions which seemed to me impracticable were made, and much was said which under the circumstances will not bear repetition.

I stated that only on one condition would I be willing to involve the army under my command in direct operations against the enemy to relieve the Army of the Potomac. That condition was, that such peremptory orders be given to General McClellan, and in addition such measures taken in advance as would render it certain that he would make a vigorous attack on the enemy with his whole force the moment he heard that I was engaged.

In face of the extraordinary difficulties which existed and the terrible responsibility about to be thrown on me, I considered it my duty to state plainly to the President that I could not risk the destruction of my army in such a movement as was suggested if it were left to the discretion of General McClellan or any one else to withhold the vigorous use of his whole force when my attack was made.

The whole plan of campaign for the army under my command was necessarily changed by the movement of the Army of the Potomac to Harrison's Landing. A day or two after General McClellan had reached his position on James River I addressed him a letter stating to him my position, the disposition of the troops under my command, and what was required of them, and requesting him in all good faith and earnestness to write me freely and fully his views, and to suggest to me any measures which he thought desirable to enable me to coöperate with him, and offering to render any assistance in my power to the operations of the army under his command. I stated to him that I was very anxious to assist him in his operations, and that I would undertake any labor or run any risk for that purpose. I therefore requested him to feel no hesitation in communicating freely with me, as he might rest assured that any suggestions he made would meet all respect and consideration from me, and that, so far as was within my power, I would carry out his wishes with all energy and all the means at my command. In reply to this

212

communication I received a letter from General McClellan very general in its terms and proposing nothing toward the accomplishment of the purpose I suggested to him.

It became very apparent, therefore, considering the situation in which the Army of the Potomac and the Army of Virginia were placed in relation to each other and the absolute necessity of harmonious and prompt coöperation between them, that some military superior both of General McClellan and myself should be placed in general command of all the operations in Virginia, with power to enforce joint action between the two armies within that field of operations. General Halleck was accordingly called to Washington and assigned to the command-in-chief of the army, though Mr. Stanton was opposed to it and used some pretty strong language to me concerning General Halleck and my action in the matter. They, however, established friendly relations soon after General Halleck assumed command.

The reasons which induced me, in the first instance, to ask to be relieved from the command of the Army of Virginia, as heretofore set forth, were greatly intensified by the retreat of General McClellan to James River and the bitter feelings and controversies which it occasioned, and I again requested the President to relieve me from the command and permit me to return to the West. The utter impossibility of sending General McClellan anything like the reënforcements he asked for, the extreme danger to Washington involved in sending him even a fraction of the small force under my command, and the glaring necessity of concentrating these two armies in some judicious manner and as rapidly as possible, resulted in a determination to withdraw the Army of the Potomac from the James River and unite it with the Army of Virginia. The question of the command of these armies when united was never discussed in my presence, if at all, and I left Washington with the natural impression that when this junction was accomplished General Halleck would himself assume the command in the field. Under the changed condition of things brought about by General McClellan's retreat to James River, and the purpose to withdraw his army and unite it with that under my command, the campaign of the Army of Virginia was limited to the following objects:

1. To cover the approaches to Washington from any enemy advancing from the direction of Richmond, and to oppose and delay its advance to the last extremity, so as to give all the time possible for the withdrawal of the Army of the Potomac from the James River.

2. If no heavy forces of the enemy moved north, to operate on their lines of communication with Gordonsville and Charlottesville, so as to force Lee to make heavy detachments from his force at Richmond and facilitate to that extent the withdrawal of the Army of the Potomac.

Halleck was of the opinion that the junction of the two armies could be made on the line of the Rappahannock, and my orders to hold fast to my communications with Fredericksburg, through which place McClellan's army was to make its junction with the Army of Virginia, were repeated positively.

The decision of the enemy to move north with the bulk of his army was promptly made and vigorously carried out, so that it became apparent, even before General McClellan began to embark his army, that the line of the Rappahannock was too far to the front. That fact, however, was not realized by Halleck until too late for any change which could be effectively executed.

Such was the organization of the Army of Virginia, and such its objects and the difficulties with which it was embarrassed from the very beginning. This rather long preface appears to me to be essential to any sufficient understanding of the second battle of Bull Run, and why and how it was fought. It is also necessary as a reply to a statement industriously circulated at the time and repeated again and again for obvious purposes, until no doubt it is generally believed, that I had set out to capture Richmond with a force sufficient for the purpose, and that the falling back from the Rapidan was unexpected by the Government, and a great disappointment to it. The whole campaign was, and perhaps is yet, misunderstood because of the false impressions created by this statement.

Under the orders heretofore referred to, the concentration of the three corps of the Army of Virginia (except King's division of McDowell's corps) was completed, Sigel's corps being at Sperryville, Banks's at Little Washington, and Ricketts's division of McDowell's corps at Waterloo Bridge. I assumed the command in person July 29th, 1862.

As this paper is mainly concerned with the second battle of Bull Run, I shall not recount any of the military operations beyond the Rappahannock, nor give any account of the battle of Cedar Mountain and the skirmishes which followed.

It is only necessary to say that the course of these operations made it plain enough that the Rappahannock was too far to the front, and that the movements of Lee were too rapid and those of McClellan too slow to make it possible, with the small force I had, to hold that line, or to keep open communication with Fredericksburg without being turned on my right flank by Lee's whole army and cut off altogether from Washington.

On the 21st of August, being then at Rappahannock Station, my little army confronted by nearly the whole force under General Lee, which had compelled the retreat of McClellan to Harrison's Landing, I was positively assured that two days more would see me largely enough reënforced by the Army of the Potomac to be not only secure, but to assume the offensive against Lee, and I was instructed to hold on "and fight like the devil."

I accordingly held on till the 26th of August, when, finding myself to be outflanked on my right by the main body of Lee's army, while Jackson's corps having passed Salem and Rectortown the day before were in rapid march in the direction of Gainesville and Manassas Junction, and seeing that none of the reënforcements promised me were likely to arrive, I determined to abandon the line of the Rappahannock and communications with Fredericksburg, and concentrate my whole force in the direction of Warrenton and Gainesville, to cover the Warrenton pike, and still to confront the enemy rapidly marching to my right.

Stonewall Jackson's movement on Manassas Junction was plainly seen and promptly reported, and I notified General Halleck of it. He informed me on the 23d of August that heavy reënforcements would begin to arrive at Warrenton Junction on the next day (24th), and as my orders still held me to the Rappahannock I naturally supposed that these troops would be hurried forward to me with all speed. Franklin's corps especially, I asked, should be sent rapidly to Gainesville. I also telegraphed Colonel Herman Haupt, chief of railway transportation, to direct one of the strongest divisions coming forward, and to be at Warrenton Junction on the 24th, to be put in the works at Manassas Junction. A cavalry force had been sent forward to observe the Thoroughfare Gap early on the morning of the 26th, but nothing was heard from it.

On the night of August 26th Jackson's advance, having passed Thoroughfare Gap, struck the Orange and Alexandria railroad at Manassas Junction, and made it plain to me that all of the reënforcements and movements of the troops promised me had altogether failed. Had Franklin been even at Centreville, or had Cox's and Sturgis's divisions been as far west as Bull Run on that day, the movement of Jackson on Manassas Junction would not have been practicable.

As Jackson's movement on Manassas Junction marks the beginning of the second battle of Bull Run, it is essential to a clear understanding of subsequent operations to give the positions of the army under my command on the night of August 26th, as also the movements and operations of the enemy as far as we knew them.

From the 18th until the night of the 26th of August the troops had been marching and fighting almost continuously. As was to be expected under such circumstances, the effective force had been greatly diminished by death, by wounds, by sickness, and by fatigue.

Heintzelman's corps, which had come up from Alexandria, was at Warrenton Junction, and numbered, as he reported to me, less than eight thousand men, but it was without wagons, without artillery, without horses even for the field-officers, and with only forty rounds of ammunition to the man. The corps of General F. J. Porter consisted of about ten thousand men, and was by far the freshest if not the best in the army. He had made very short and deliberate marches from Fredericksburg, and his advance division, mainly troops of the regular army under Sykes, had arrived at Warrenton Junction by eleven o'clock on the morning of the 27th, Morell's division of the same corps arriving later in the same day. . . .

The troops were disposed as follows: McDowell's corps and Sigel's corps

215

were at Warrenton under general command of General McDowell, with Banks's corps at Fayetteville as a reserve. Reno's corps was directed upon the Warrenton turnpike to take post three miles east of Warrenton. Porter's corps was near Bealeton Station moving slowly toward Warrenton Junction; Heintzelman at Warrenton Junction, with very small means to move in any direction.

Up to this time I had been placed by the positive orders of General Halleck much in the position of a man tied by one leg and fighting with a person much his physical superior and free to move in any direction. The following telegrams will explain exactly the situation as heretofore indicated:

August 25th, 1862

MAJOR-GENERAL HALLECK: Your dispatch just received. Of course I shall be ready to recross the Rappahannock at a moment's notice. You will see from the positions taken that each army corps is on the best roads across the river. You wished forty-eight hours to assemble the forces from the Peninsula behind the Rappahannock, and four days have passed without the enemy yet being permitted to cross. I don't think he is yet ready to do so. In ordinarily dry weather the Rappahannock can be crossed almost anywhere, and these crossing-places are best protected by concentrating at central positions to strike at any force which attempts to cross. I had clearly understood that you wished to unite our whole forces before a forward movement was begun, and that I must take care to keep united with Burnside on my left, so that no movement to separate us could be made. This withdrew me lower down the Rappahannock than I wished to come. I am not acquainted with your views, as you seem to suppose, and would be glad to know them so far as my own position and operations are concerned. I understood you clearly that, at all hazards, I was to prevent the enemy from passing the Rappahannock. This I have done, and shall do. I don't like to be on the defensive if I can help it, but must be so as long as I am tied to Burnside's forces, not yet wholly arrived at Fredericksburg. Please let me know, if it can be done, what is to be my own command, and if I am to act independently against the enemy. I certainly understood that, as soon as the whole of our forces were concentrated, you designed to take command in person, and that, when everything was ready, we were to move forward in concert. I judge from the tone of your dispatch that you are dissatisfied with something. Unless I know what it is, of course I can't correct it. The troops arriving here come in fragments. Am I to assign them to brigades and corps? I would suppose not, as several of the new regiments coming have been assigned to army corps directly from your office. In case I commence offensive operations I must know what forces I am to take and what you wish left, and what connection must be kept up with Burnside. It has been my purpose to conform my operations to your plans, yet I was not informed when McClellan evacuated Harrison's Landing, so that I might know what to expect in that direction; and when I say these things in no complaining spirit I think that you know well that I am anxious to do everything to advance your plans of campaign. I understood that this army was to maintain the line of the Rappahannock until all the forces from the Peninsula had united behind that river. I have done so. I understood distinctly that I was not to hazard anything except for this purpose, as delay was what was wanted.

The enemy this morning has pushed a considerable infantry force up opposite Waterloo Bridge, and is planting batteries, and long lines of his infantry are moving up from Jeffersonville toward Sulphur Springs. His whole force, as far as can be ascertained, is massed in front of me, from railroad crossing of Rappahannock around to Waterloo Bridge, their main body being opposite Sulphur Springs. JOHN POPE, Major-General

U. S. MILITARY TELEGRAPH. (Received Aug. 26th, 1862, from War Dep't, 11:45 A. M.)

MAJOR-GENERAL POPE: Not the slightest dissatisfaction has been felt in regard to your operations on the Rappahannock. The main object has been accomplished in getting up troops from the Peninsula, although they have been greatly delayed by storms. Moreover, the telegraph has been interrupted, leaving us for a time ignorant of the progress of the evacuation. . . . If possible to attack the enemy in flank, do so, but the main object now is to ascertain his position. Make cavalry excursions for that purpose, especially toward Front Royal. If possible to get in his rear, pursue with vigor. H. W. HALLECK, General-in-Chief

The movements of the enemy toward my right forced me either to abandon the line of the Rappahannock and the communications with Fredericksburg, or to risk the loss of my army and the almost certain loss of Washington. Of course between these two alternatives I could not hesitate in a choice. I considered it my duty, at whatever sacrifice to my army and myself, to retard, as far as I could, the movement of the enemy toward Washington, until I was certain that the Army of the Potomac had reached Alexandria.

The movement of Jackson presented the only opportunity which had offered to gain any success over the superior forces of the enemy. I determined, therefore, on the morning of the 27th of August to abandon the line of the Rappahannock and throw my whole force in the direction of Gainesville and Manassas Junction, to crush any force of the enemy that had passed through Thoroughfare Gap, and to interpose between Lee's army and Bull Run. Having the interior line of operations, and the enemy at Manassas being inferior in force, it appeared to me, and still so appears, that with even ordinary promptness and energy we might feel sure of success.

In the meantime heavy forces of the enemy still confronted us at Waterloo Bridge, while his main body continued its march toward our right, following the course of Hedgman's River (the Upper Rappahannock). I accordingly sent orders, early on the 27th of August, to General McDowell to move rapidly on Gainesville by the Warrenton pike with his own corps, reënforced by Reynolds's division and Sigel's corps. I directed Reno, followed by Kearny's division of Heintzelman's corps, to move on Greenwich, so as to reach there that night, to report thence at once to General McDowell, and to support him in operations against the enemy which were expected near

Gainesville. With Hooker's division of Heintzelman's corps I moved along the railroad toward Manassas Junction, to reopen our communications and to be in position to coöperate with the forces along the Warrenton pike.

On the afternoon of that day a severe engagement took place between Hooker's division and Ewell's division of Jackson's corps, near Bristoe Station, on the railroad. Ewell was driven back along the railroad, but at dark still confronted Hooker along the banks of Broad Run. The loss in this action was about three hundred killed and wounded on each side. Ewell left his dead, many of his wounded, and some of his baggage on the field. . . .

The railroad had been torn up and the bridges burned in several places just west of Bristoe Station. I therefore directed General Banks, who had reached Warrenton Junction, to cover the railroad trains at that place until General Porter marched, and then to run back the trains toward Manassas as far as he could and rebuild the railroad bridges. Captain Merrill of the Engineers was also directed to repair the railroad track and bridges toward Bristoe. This work was done by that accomplished officer as far east as Kettle Run on the 27th, and the trains were run back to that point next morning.

At dark on the 27th Hooker informed me that his ammunition was nearly exhausted, only five rounds to the man being on hand. Before this time it had become apparent that Jackson, with his whole force, was south of the Warrenton pike and in the immediate neighborhood of Manassas Junction.

McDowell reached his position at Gainesville during the night of the 27th, and Kearny and Reno theirs at Greenwich. It was clear on that night that we had completely interposed between Jackson and the enemy's main body, which was still west of the Bull Run range, and in the vicinity of White Plains.

In consequence of Hooker's report, and the weakness of the small division which he commanded, and to strengthen my right wing moving in the direction of Manassas, I sent orders to Porter at dark, which reached him at 9 P. M., to move forward from Warrenton Junction at 1 A. M. night, and to report to me at Bristoe Station by daylight next morning (August 28th).

There were but two courses left to Jackson by this sudden movement of the army. He could not retrace his steps through Gainesville, as that place was occupied by McDowell with a force equal if not superior to his own. To retreat through Centreville would carry him still farther away from the main body of Lee's army. It was possible, however, to mass his whole force at Manassas Junction and assail our right (Hooker's division), which had fought a severe battle that afternoon, and was almost out of ammunition. Jackson, with A. P. Hill's division, retired through Centreville. Thinking it altogether within the probabilities that he might adopt the other alternative, I sent the orders above mentioned to General Porter. He neither obeyed them nor attempted to obey them, but afterward gave as a reason for not doing so that his men were tired, the night was too dark to march, and that there was a wagon train on the road toward Bristoe. The distance was nine miles along the railroad track, with a wagon road on each side of it most of the way; but his corps did not reach Bristoe Station until 10:30 o'clock next morning, six hours after daylight; and the moment he found that the enemy had left our front he asked to halt and rest his corps. Of his first reason for not complying with my orders, it is only necessary to say that Sykes's division had reached Warrenton Junction at 11 o'clock on the morning of the 27th, and had been in camp all day. Morell's division arrived later in the day at Warrenton Junction, and would have been in camp for at least eight hours before the time it was ordered to march. The marches of these two divisions from Fredericksburg had been extremely deliberate, and involved but little more exercise than is needed for good health. The diaries of these marches make Porter's claim of fatigue ridiculous. To compare the condition of this corps and its marches with those of any of the troops of the Army of Virginia is a sufficient answer to such a pretext. The impossibility of marching on account of the darkness of that night finds its best answer in the fact that nearly every other division of the army, and the whole of Jackson's corps, marched during the greater part of the night in the immediate vicinity of Porter's corps, and from nearly every point of the compass. The plea of darkness and of the obstruction of a wagon train along the road will strike our armies with some surprise in the light of their subsequent experience of night marches. The railroad track itself was clear and entirely practicable for the march of infantry.

According to the testimony of Colonel Myers, quartermaster in charge of the train, the train was drawn off the roads and parked after dark that night; and even if this had not been the case, it is not necessary to tell any officer who served in the war that the infantry advance could easily have pushed the wagons off the road to make way for the artillery. Colonel Myers also testified that he could have gone on with his train that night, and that he drew off the road and parked his train for rest and because of the action of Hooker's division in his front, and not because he was prevented from continuing his march by darkness or other obstacles.

At 9 o'clock on the night of the 27th, satisfied of Jackson's position, I sent orders to General McDowell at Gainesville to push forward at the earliest dawn of day upon Manassas Junction, resting his right on the Manassas Gap Railroad and extending his left to the east. I directed General Reno at the same time to march from Greenwich, also direct on Manassas Junction, and Kearny to move from the same place upon Bristoe Station. This move of Kearny was to strengthen my right at Bristoe and unite the two divisions of Heintzelman's corps.

Jackson began to evacuate Manassas Junction during the night (the 27th) and marched toward Centreville and other points of the Warrenton pike west of that place, and by 11 o'clock next morning was at and beyond Centreville and north of the Warrenton pike. I arrived at Manassas Junction shortly after the last of Jackson's force had moved off, and immediately pushed forward Hooker, Kearny, and Reno upon Centreville, and sent orders to Porter to come forward to Manassas Junction. I also wrote McDowell the situation and directed him to call back to Gainesville any part of his force which had moved in the direction of Manassas Junction, and march upon Centreville along the Warrenton pike with the whole force under his command to intercept the retreat of Jackson toward Thoroughfare Gap. With King's division in advance, McDowell, marching toward Centreville, encountered late in the afternoon the advance of Jackson's corps retreating toward Thoroughfare Gap. Late in the afternoon, also, Kearny drove the rear-guard of Jackson out of Centreville and occupied that place with his advance beyond it toward Gainesville. A very severe engagement occurred between King's division and Jackson's forces near the village of Groveton on the Warrenton pike, which was terminated by the darkness, both parties maintaining their ground. The conduct of this division in this severe engagement was admirable, and reflects the utmost credit both upon its commanders and the men under their command. That this division was not reënforced by Reynolds and Sigel seems unaccountable. The reason given, though it is not satisfactory, was the fact that General McDowell had left the command just before it encountered the enemy, and had gone toward Manassas Junction, where he supposed me to be, in order to give me some information about the immediate country in which we were operating, and with which, of course, he was much more familiar from former experience than I could be. I had left Manassas Junction, however, for Centreville. Hearing the sound of the guns indicating King's engagement with the enemy, McDowell set off to rejoin his command, but lost his way, and I first heard of him next morning at Manassas Junction. As his troops did not know of his absence, there was no one to give orders to Sigel and Reynolds.

The engagement of King's division was reported to me about 10 o'clock at night near Centreville. I felt sure then, and so stated, that there was no escape for Jackson. On the west of him were McDowell's corps (I did not then know that he had detached Ricketts), Sigel's corps, and Reynolds's division, all under command of McDowell. On the east of him, and with the advance of Kearny nearly in contact with him on the Warrenton pike, were the corps of Reno and Heintzelman. Porter was supposed to be at Manassas Junction, where he ought to have been on that afternoon.

I sent orders to McDowell (supposing him to be with his command), and also direct to General King, several times during that night and once by his own staff-officer, to hold his ground at all hazards, to prevent the retreat of Jackson toward Lee, and that at daylight our whole force from Centreville and Manassas would assail him from the east, and he would be crushed between us. I sent orders also to General Kearny at Centreville to move forward cautiously that night along the Warrenton pike; to drive in the pickets of the enemy, and to keep as closely as possible in contact with him during the night, resting his left on the Warrenton pike and throwing his right to the north, if practicable, as far as the Little River pike, and at daylight next morning to assault vigorously with his right advance, and that Hooker and Reno would certainly be with him shortly after daylight. I sent orders to General Porter, who I supposed was at Manassas Junction, to move upon Centreville at dawn, stating to him the position of our forces, and that a severe battle would be fought that morning (the 29th).

With Jackson at and near Groveton, with McDowell on the west, and the rest of the army on the east of him, while Lee, with the mass of his army, was still west of Thoroughfare Gap, the situation for us was certainly as favorable as the most sanguine person could desire, and the prospect of crushing Jackson, sandwiched between such forces, was certainly excellent. There is no doubt, had General McDowell been with his command when King's division of his corps became engaged with the enemy, he would have brought forward to its support both Sigel and Reynolds, and the result would have been to hold the ground west of Jackson at least until morning brought against him also the forces moving from the direction of Centreville.

To my great disappointment and surprise, however, I learned toward daylight the next morning (the 29th) that King's division had fallen back toward Manassas Junction, and that neither Sigel nor Reynolds had been engaged or had gone to the support of King. The route toward Thoroughfare Gap had thus been left open by the wholly unexpected retreat of King's division, due to the fact that he was not supported by Sigel and Reynolds, and an immediate change was necessary in the disposition of the troops under my command. Sigel and Reynolds were near Groveton, almost in contact with Jackson; Ricketts had fallen back toward Bristoe from Thoroughfare Gap, after offering (as might have been expected) ineffectual resistance to the passage of the Bull Run range by very superior forces; King had fallen back to Manassas Junction; Porter was at Manassas Junction or near there; Reno and Hooker near Centreville; Kearny at Centreville and beyond toward Groveton; Jackson near Groveton with his whole corps; Lee with the main army of the enemy, except three brigades of Longstreet which had passed Hopewell Gap, north of Thoroughfare Gap.

The field of battle was practically limited to the space between the old railroad grade from Sudley to Gainesville if prolonged across the Warrenton pike and the Sudley Springs road east of it. The railroad grade indicates almost exactly the line occupied by Jackson's force, our own line confronting it from left to right.

The ridge which bounded the valley of Dawkins's Branch on the west, and on which were the Hampton Cole and Monroe houses, offered from the Monroe house a full view of the field of battle from right to left, and the

221

Monroe house being on the crest of the ridge overlooked and completely commanded the approach to Jackson's right by the Warrenton turnpike. To the result of the battle this ridge was of the last importance, and, if seized and held by noon, would absolutely have prevented any reënforcement of Jackson's right from the direction of Gainesville. The northern slope of this ridge was held by our troops near the Douglass house, near which, also, the right of Jackson's line rested. The advance of Porter's corps at Dawkins's Branch was less than a mile and a half from the Monroe house, and the road in his front was one of several which converged on that point.

The whole field was free from obstacles to movement of troops and nearly so to manœuvres, with only a few eminences, and these of a nature to have been seized and easily held by our troops even against very superior numbers. The ground was gently undulating and the water-courses insignificant, while the intersecting system of roads and lanes afforded easy communication with all parts of the field. It would be difficult to find anywhere in Virginia a more perfect field of battle than that on which the second battle of Bull Run was fought.

About daylight, therefore, on the 29th of August, almost immediately after I received information of the withdrawal of King's division toward Manassas Junction, I sent orders to General Sigel, in the vicinity of Groveton, to attack the enemy vigorously at daylight and bring him to a stand if possible. He was to be supported by Reynolds's division. I instructed Heintzelman to push forward from Centreville toward Gainesville on the Warrenton pike at the earliest dawn with the divisions of Kearny and Hooker, and gave orders also to Reno with his corps to follow closely in their rear. They were directed to use all speed, and as soon as they came up with the enemy to establish communication with Sigel, and to attack vigorously and promptly. I also sent orders to General Porter at Manassas Junction to move forward rapidly with his own corps and King's division of McDowell's corps, which was there also, upon Gainesville by the direct route from Manassas Junction to that place. I urged him to make all possible speed, with the purpose that he should come up with the enemy or connect himself with the left of our line near where the Warrenton pike is crossed by the road from Manassas Junction to Gainesville.

Shortly after sending this order, I received a note from General McDowell, whom I had not been able to find during the night of the 28th, dated Manassas Junction, requesting that King's division be not taken from his command. I immediately sent a joint order, addressed to Generals McDowell and Porter, repeating the instructions to move forward with their commands toward Gainesville, and informing them of the position and movements of Sigel and Heintzelman.

Sigel attacked the enemy at daylight on the morning of the 29th about a mile east of Groveton, where he was joined by the divisions of Hooker and

Kearny. Jackson fell back, but was so closely pressed by these forces that he was obliged to make a stand. He accordingly took up his position along and behind the old railroad embankment extending along his entire front, with his left near Sudley Springs and his right just south of the Warrenton pike. His batteries, some of them of heavy caliber, were posted behind the ridges in the open ground, while the mass of his troops were sheltered by woods and the railroad embankment.

I arrived on the field from Centreville about noon, and found the opposing forces confronting each other, both considerably cut up by the severe action in which they had been engaged since daylight. Heintzelman's corps (the divisions of Hooker and Kearny) occupied the right of our line toward Sudley Springs. Sigel was on his left, with his line extending a short distance south of the Warrenton pike, the division of Schenck occupying the high ground to the left (south) of the pike. The extreme left was held by Reynolds. Reno's corps had reached the field and the most of it had been pushed forward into action, leaving four regiments in reserve behind the center of the line of battle. Immediately after I reached the ground, General Sigel reported to me that his line was weak, that the divisions of Schurz and Steinwehr were much cut up and ought to be drawn back from the front. I informed him that this was impossible, as there were no troops to replace them, and that he must hold his ground; that I would not immediately push his troops again into action, as the corps of McDowell and Porter were moving forward on the road from Manassas Junction to Gainesville, and must very soon be in a position to fall upon the enemy's right flank and possibly on his rear. I rode along the front of our line and gave the same information to Heintzelman and Reno. . . .

The troops were permitted to rest for a time, and to resupply themselves with ammunition. From 1:30 to 4 o'clock P. M. very severe conflicts occurred repeatedly all along the line, and there was a continuous roar of artillery and small-arms, with scarcely an intermission. About two o'clock in the afternoon three discharges of artillery were heard on the extreme left of our line or right of the enemy's, and I for the moment, and naturally, believed that Porter and McDowell had reached their positions and were engaged with the enemy. I heard only three shots, and as nothing followed I was at a loss to know what had become of these corps, or what was delaying them, as before this hour they should have been, even with ordinary marching, well up on our left. Shortly afterward I received information that McDowell's corps was advancing to join the left of our line by the Sudley Springs road, and would probably be up within two hours. At 4:30 o'clock I sent a peremptory order to General Porter, who was at or near Dawkins's Branch, about four or five miles distant from my headquarters, to push forward at once into action on the enemy's right, and if possible on his rear, stating to him generally the condition of things on the field in front of me. At 5:30 o'clock, when General

223

Porter should have been going into action in compliance with this order, I directed Heintzelman and Reno to attack the enemy's left. The attack was made promptly and with vigor and persistence, and the left of the enemy was doubled back toward his center. After a severe and bloody action of an hour Kearny forced the position on the left of the enemy and occupied the field of battle there.

By this time General McDowell had arrived on the field, and I pushed his corps, supported by Reynolds, forward at once into action along the Warrenton pike toward the enemy's right, then said to be falling back. This attack along the pike was made by King's division near sunset; but, as Porter made no movement whatever toward the field, Longstreet, who was pushing to the front, was able to extend his lines beyond King's left with impunity, and King's attack did not accomplish what was expected, in view of the anticipated attack which Porter was ordered to make, and should have been making at the same time. . . .

What would have been the effect of the application on the enemy's right at, or any time after, 4 o'clock that afternoon of ten or twelve thousand effective men who had not been in battle at all, I do not myself consider doubtful.

In this battle the Fifth Corps, under General F. J. Porter, took no part whatever, but remained all day in column, without even deploying into line of battle or making any effort in force to find out what was in their front. That General Porter knew of the progress of the battle on his right, and that he believed the Union army was being defeated, is shown by his own dispatches to McDowell, several times repeated during the day. That subjoined will be sufficient :

GENERALS McDOWELL AND KING: I found it impossible to communicate by crossing the woods to Groveton. The enemy are in great force on this road, and as they appear to have driven our forces back, the fire of the enemy having advanced and ours retired, I have determined to withdraw to Manassas. I have attempted to communicate with McDowell and Sigel, but my messengers have run into the enemy. They have gathered artillery and cavalry and infantry, and the advancing masses of dust show the enemy coming in force. I am now going to the head of the column to see what is passing and how affairs are going, and I will communicate with you. Had you not better send your train back?

F. J. PORTER, Major-General

Not the artillery only, but the volleys of musketry in this battle were also plainly heard on their right and front by the advance of Porter's troops much of the day. In consequence of his belief that the army on his right was being defeated, as stated in more than one of these dispatches, he informed General McDowell that he intended to retire to Manassas, and advised McDowell to send back his trains in the same direction.

For this action, or non-action, he has been on the one hand likened to

Benedict Arnold, and on the other favorably compared with George Washington. I presume he would not accept the first position, and probably would hardly lay claim to the second. Certainly I have not the inclination, even had I the power, to assign him to either or to any position between the two; and if he were alone concerned in the question, I should make no comment at all on the subject at this day. Many others than himself and the result of a battle, however, are involved in it, and they do not permit silence when the second battle of Bull Run is discussed. Without going into the merits of the case, which has been obscured and confused by so many and such varied controversies, I shall confine myself to a bare statement of the facts as they are known to me personally, or communicated officially by officers of rank and standing, and by the official reports of both armies engaged in the battle. General Porter was tried by court-martial a few months after the battle and was cashiered. The reasons given by him at the time for his failure to go into action, or take any part in the battle, were: first, that he considered himself under General McDowell's orders, who told him that they were too far to the front for a battle; and, second, that the enemy was in such heavy force in his front that he would have been defeated had he attacked. General McDowell stated before the court-martial that, so far from saying that they were too far to the front for battle, he directed General Porter before leaving him to put his corps into the action where he was, and that he (McDowell) would move farther to the right and go into the battle there. Upon Porter remarking that he could not go in there without getting into a fight, McDowell replied, "I thought that was what we came here for."

General J. E. B. Stuart, who commanded the cavalry in Lee's army, tells in his official report precisely what was in General Porter's front, and what means he took to produce upon General Porter the impression that there were heavy forces in front of him and advancing toward him. General Porter certainly made no reconnoissance in force to ascertain whether or not there was a heavy force in his front; and Stuart's report makes it quite certain that, at the time referred to by him, Porter could easily have moved forward from Dawkins's Branch and seized the ridge on which are the Hampton Cole and Monroe houses, from which he would have had a complete view of the field from right to left. Not only this, but his occupation of that ridge would have connected him closely with our left and absolutely prevented Longstreet from forming on Jackson's right until he had dislodged Porter, which would have occupied him too long to have permitted the effective use of his troops for any other purpose, and certainly for the advance which he subsequently made against our left. Longstreet now asserts that he was in front of Porter with part of his corps at some indefinite hour of the day, variously fixed, but according to him by 11 o'clock in the morning, about the time that Porter's corps reached Dawkins's Branch. He further asserts somewhat extravagantly, that if Porter had attacked he (Longstreet) would have annihilated him. He seems to have thought it a simple matter to annihilate an army corps of ten or twelve thousand men, much of which was composed of regular troops, but perhaps his statement to that effect would hardly be accepted by military men. If such an assertion made by a corps commander of one army is sufficient reason for a corps commander of the opposing army not to attack, even under orders to do so, it is hard to see how any general commanding an army could direct a battle at all; and certainly if such assertions as Longstreet's are considered reliable, there would have been no battle fought in our civil war, since they could easily have been had from either side in advance of any battle that was fought. . . .

Taking the enemy's own account of the battle that afternoon, which lasted several hours, and its result, it is not unreasonable to say that, if General Porter had attacked Longstreet's right with ten or twelve thousand men while the latter was thus engaged, the effect would have been conclusive. Porter's case is the first I have ever known, or that I find recorded in military history, in which the theory has been seriously put forth that the hero of a battle is the man who keeps out of it. With this theory in successful operation, war will be stripped of most of its terrors, and a pitched battle need not be much more dangerous to human life than a militia muster.

When the battle ceased on the 29th of August, we were in possession of the field on our right, and occupied on our left the position held early in the day, and had every right to claim a decided success. What that success might have been, if a corps of twelve thousand men who had not been in battle that day had been thrown against Longstreet's right while engaged in the severe fight that afternoon, I need not indicate. To say that General Porter's non-action during that whole day was wholly unexpected and disappointing, and that it provoked severe comment on all hands, is to state the facts mildly.

Every indication during the night of the 29th and up to 10 o'clock on the morning of the 30th pointed to the retreat of the enemy from our front. Paroled prisoners of our own army, taken on the evening of the 29th, who came into our lines on the morning of the 30th, reported the enemy retreating during the whole night in the direction of and along the Warrenton pike. Generals McDowell and Heintzelman, who reconnoitered the position held by the enemy's left on the evening of the 29th, also confirmed this statement. They reported to me the evacuation of these positions by the enemy, and that there was every indication of their retreat in the direction of Gainesville. On the morning of the 30th, as may be easily believed, our troops, who had been marching and fighting almost continuously for many days, were greatly exhausted. They had had little to eat for two days, and artillery and cavalry horses had been in harness and under the saddle for ten days, and had been almost out of forage for the last two days. It may be readily imagined how little these troops, after such severe labors and hardships, were in condition for further active marching and fighting. On the 28th I had telegraphed General Halleck our condition, and had begged of him to have rations and forage sent forward to us from Alexandria with all speed; but about daylight on the 30th I received a note from General Franklin, written by direction of General McClellan, informing me that rations and forage would be loaded into the available wagons and cars at Alexandria as soon as I should send back a cavalry escort to guard the trains. Such a letter, when we were fighting the enemy and when Alexandria was full of troops, needs no comment. Our cavalry was well-nigh broken down completely, and certainly we were in no condition to spare troops from the front, nor could they have gone to Alexandria and returned within the time by which we must have had provisions and forage or have fallen back toward supplies; nor am I able to understand of what use cavalry could be to guard railroad trains. It was not until I received this letter that I began to be hopeless of any successful issue to our operations; but I felt it to be my duty, notwithstanding the broken-down condition of the forces under my command, to hold my position. I had received no sort of information of any troops coming forward to reënforce me since the 24th, and did not expect on the morning of the 30th that any assistance would reach me from the direction of Washington, but I determined again to give battle to the enemy and delay as long as possible his farther advance toward Washington. I accordingly prepared to renew the engagement.

General Porter, with whose non-action of the day before I was naturally dissatisfied, had been peremptorily ordered that night to report to me in person with his corps, and arrived on the field early in the morning. His corps had been reënforced by Piatt's brigade of Sturgis's division, and was estimated to be about twelve thousand strong. . . .

Between 12 and 2 o'clock during the day I advanced Porter's corps, supported by King's division of McDowell's corps, and supported also on their left by Sigel's corps and Reynolds's division, to attack the enemy along the Warrenton pike. At the same time the corps of Heintzelman and Reno on our right were directed to push forward to the left and front toward the pike and attack the enemy's left flank. For a time Ricketts's division of McDowell's corps was placed in support of this movement. I was obliged to assume the aggressive or to fall back, as from want of provisions I was not able to await an attack from the enemy or the result of any other movement he might make.

Every moment of delay increased the odds against us, and I therefore pushed forward the attack as rapidly as possible. Soon after Porter advanced to attack along the Warrenton pike and the assault was made by Heintzelman and Reno on the right, it became apparent that the enemy was massing his forces as fast as they arrived on the right of Jackson, and was moving forward to force our left. General McDowell was therefore directed to recall Ricketts's division from our right, and put it so as to strengthen our left thus threatened.

Porter's corps was repulsed after some severe fighting, and began to retire, and the enemy advancing to the assault, our whole line was soon furiously engaged. The main attack of the enemy was made against our left, but was met with stubborn resistance by the divisions of Schenck and Reynolds, and the brigade of Milroy, who were soon reënforced on the left by Ricketts's division. The action was severe for several hours, the enemy bringing up heavy reserves and pouring mass after mass of his troops on our left. He was able also to present at least an equal force all along our line of battle. Porter's corps was halted and re-formed, and as soon as it was in condition it was pushed forward to the support of our left, where it rendered distinguished service, especially the brigade of regulars under Colonel (then Lieutenant-Colonel) Buchanan.

McLean's brigade of Schenck's division, which was posted in observation on our left flank, and in support of Reynolds, became exposed to the attack of the enemy on our left when Reynolds's division was drawn back to form line to support Porter's corps, then retiring from their attack, and it was fiercely assailed by Hood and Evans, in greatly superior force. This brigade was commanded in person by General Schenck, the division commander, and fought with supreme gallantry and tenacity. The enemy's attack was repulsed several times with severe loss, but he returned again and again to the assault.

It is needless for me to describe the appearance of a man so well known to the country as General R. C. Schenck. I have only to say that a more gallant and devoted soldier never lived, and to his presence and the fearless exposure of his person during these attacks is largely due the protracted resistance made by this brigade. He fell, badly wounded, in the front of his command, and his loss was deeply felt and had a marked effect on the final result in that part of the field.

Tower's brigade of Ricketts's division was pushed forward to his support, and the brigade was led by General Tower in person with conspicuous gallantry. The conduct of these two brigades and their commanders in plain view of our whole left was especially distinguished, and called forth hearty and enthusiastic cheers. Their example was of great service, and seemed to infuse new spirit into the troops that witnessed their intrepid conduct. . . .

Reno's corps was withdrawn from our right center late in the afternoon and thrown into action on our left, where the assaults of the enemy were persistent and unintermitting. Notwithstanding the disadvantages under which we labored, our troops held their ground with the utmost firmness and obstinacy. The loss on both sides was heavy. By dark our left had been forced back half or three-fourths of a mile, but still remained firm and unbroken and still held the Warrenton pike on our rear, while our right was also driven back equally far, but in good order and without confusion. At dark the enemy took possession of the Sudley Springs road, and was in position to threaten our line of communication *via* Stone Bridge. After 6 o'clock in the evening I learned, accidentally, that Franklin's corps had arrived at a point about 4 miles east of Centreville, or 12 miles in our rear, and that it was only about 8000 strong.

The result of the battle of the 30th convinced me that we were no longer able to hold our position so far to the front, and so far away from the absolute necessaries of life, suffering, as were men and horses, from fatigue and hunger, and weakened by the heavy losses in battle. About 8 o'clock in the evening, therefore, I sent written orders to the corps commanders to withdraw leisurely to Centreville, and stated to them what route each should pursue and where they should take position at and near Centreville. General Reno, with his corps, was ordered to take post to cover this movement. The withdrawal was made slowly, quietly, and in good order, no attempt whatever being made by the enemy to obstruct our movement. A division of infantry, with its batteries, was posted to cover the crossing of Cub Run.

The exact losses in this battle I am unable to give, as the reports from corps commanders only indicated the aggregate losses since August 22d, but they were very heavy.

Before leaving the field I sent orders to General Banks, at Bristoe Station, where the railroad was broken, to destroy the cars and such of the stores as he could not take off in the wagon trains, and join me at Centreville. I had previously sent him instructions to bring off from Warrenton Junction and Bristoe Station all of the ammunition and all of the sick and wounded who could bear transportation, throwing personal baggage and property out of the regimental trains, if necessary, for the purpose.

At no time during the 29th, 30th, or 31st of August was the road between Bristoe and Centreville interrupted by the enemy. The orders will show conclusively that every arrangement was made in the minutest detail for the security of our wagon train and supplies; and General Banks's subsequent report to me is positive that none of the wagons or mules were lost. I mention this matter merely to answer the wholly unfounded statements made at the time, and repeated often since, of our loss of wagons, mules, and supplies.

I arrived personally at Centreville about 9 or 10 o'clock that night [the 30th]. The next morning the various corps were posted in the old intrenchments in and around Centreville, and ammunition trains and some supplies were brought up during the day and distributed. We spent that whole day resting the men and resupplying them with ammunition and provisions as far as our means permitted.

Franklin's corps arrived at Centreville late on the afternoon of the 30th; Sumner's the next day. What was then thought by the Government of our operations up to this time is shown in the subjoined dispatch:

229

WASHINGTON, August 31st, 1862.   11 A. M.

MY DEAR GENERAL: You have done nobly. Don't yield another inch if you can avoid it. All reserves are being sent forward. . . . I am doing all I can for you and your noble army. God bless you and it. . . .

H. W. HALLECK, General-in-chief

The enemy's cavalry appeared in front of Cub Run that morning, but made no attempt to attack. Our cavalry, under Buford and Bayard, was completely broken down, and both of these officers reported to me that not five horses to the company could be forced into a trot. No horses whatever had reached us for remounts since the beginning of operations. It was impracticable, therefore, to use the cavalry as cavalry to cover our front with pickets or to make reconnoissances of the enemy's front. . . .

On the morning of the 1st of September I directed General Sumner to push forward a reconnoissance toward Little River pike, which enters the Warrenton pike at Fairfax, with two brigades, to ascertain if the enemy was making any movement toward our right by that road. The enemy was found moving again slowly toward the right, heavy columns moving along the Little River pike in the direction of Fairfax. This movement had become so developed by the afternoon of that day, and was so evidently directed to turn our right, that I made the necessary disposition of troops to fight a battle between the Little River pike and the road from Fairfax to Centreville. General Hooker was sent early in the afternoon to Fairfax Court House, and directed to concentrate all the troops in that vicinity and to push forward to Germantown with his advance. I instructed McDowell to move along the road from Centreville toward Fairfax Court House, as far as Difficult Creek, and to connect on his right with Hooker. Reno was directed to push forward north of the road to Centreville, and in the direction of Chantilly, toward the flank of the enemy's advance; Heintzelman's corps to support Reno. Just before sunset the enemy attacked us toward our right, but was met by Hooker, McDowell, and Reno, and by Kearny's division of Heintzelman's corps. A very severe action was fought in the midst of a terrific thunder-storm, and was only ended by the darkness. The enemy was driven back entirely from our front, and did not again renew his attack upon us. . . .

On the morning of the 2d of September the army was posted behind Difficult Creek from Flint Hill to the Alexandria pike. The enemy disappeared from our front, moving toward the Upper Potomac with no attempt to force our position. And here the second battle of Bull Run may be said to terminate. On that day I received orders from General Halleck to take position in the intrenchments in front of Washington, with a view to reorganizing the army and eliminating such of the discordant elements in it as had largely caused the misfortunes of the latter part of that campaign.

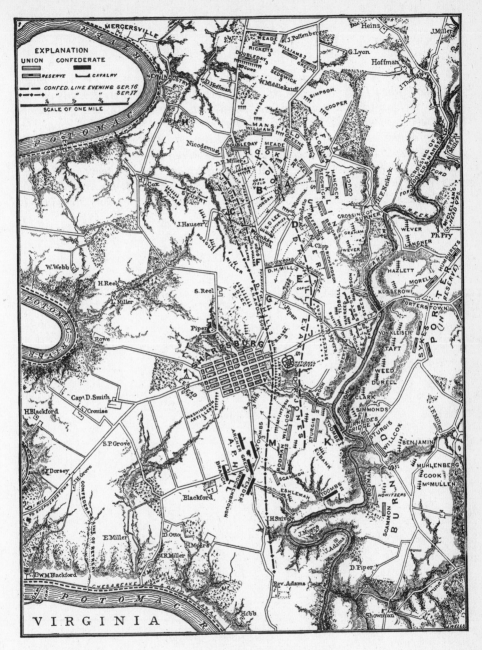

THE FIELD OF ANTIETAM

Private Thompson's notes on the march of his company into western Maryland, when Lee's first invasion of the North threatened, is remarkably modern in style. And he was a keen and sensitive observer. The Zouaves to which he belonged were made up principally of men from New York City fire companies, and their regalia—red caps and baggy trousers with white leggings—made them such ideal targets that these costumes were exchanged for regulation blue early in the war. As were the lances, with "their bright red pennons fluttering gayly from their spearheads," of certain cavalry troops. As the war became increasingly grim, any such impedimenta that risked the soldier's life had to be abandoned.

"All about us grew pennyroyal"

BY DAVID L. THOMPSON, CO. G, 9TH NEW YORK VOLUNTEERS

O N THE 5th of September, 1862, Hawkins's Zouaves, as a part of Burnside's corps, from Fredericksburg, landed at Washington to assist in the defense of the capital, then threatened by Lee's first invasion of Maryland, and, as events proved, to join in the pursuit of the invaders. Here, in pursuance of a measure for shortening the baggage train which had lately been decided on, we were deprived of our Sibley tents—those cumbersome, conical caravansaries, in which eighteen men lie upon the ground with their feet toward the center.

Shelter tents came soon to replace the "Sibleys," and with them came

233

marching orders—the army was moving west. At dusk we set up our new houses. A shelter or dog tent is like a bargain—it takes two to make it. Each man is provided with an oblong piece of thick, unbleached muslin about the length of a man—say six feet—and two-thirds as wide, bordered all round with buttons and button-holes alternately matching respectively the button-holes and buttons of his comrade's piece. To set it up, cut two crotched stakes, each about four feet long, point them at the uncrotched end, and drive them into the ground about six feet apart; cut a slender pole to lie horizontally from one crotch to the other, button the two pieces of muslin together and throw the resulting piece over the pole, drawing out the corners tight and pinning them down to the ground by means of little loops fastened in them. You will thus get a wedge-shaped structure—simply the two slopes of an ordinary roof—about three and a half feet high at its highest point, and open at both ends. This will accommodate two men, and in warm, pleasant weather is all that is needed. In rainy weather a third man is admitted. A piece of rope about four feet long is then tied to the top of one of the stakes and stretched out in the line of direction of the ridge pole, the free end being brought down to the ground and pinned there. The third man then buttons his piece of muslin to one slope of the roof, carries the other edge of the piece out around the tightened rope and brings it back to the edge of the other slope, to which it is buttoned. This third piece is shifted from one end of the tent to the other, according to the direction of the wind or storm. You thus get an extension to your tent in which knapsacks can be stored, leaving the rest of the space clear for sleeping purposes. This is large enough to accommodate three men lying side by side.

But will such a structure keep out rain? Certainly, just as your umbrella does—unless you touch it on the inside when it is soaked. If you do, the rain will come in, drop by drop, just where you have touched it. To keep the water from flowing in along the surface of the ground, dig a small trench about three inches deep all around the tent, close up, so that the rain shed from the roof will fall into it. Such a house is always with you potentially, for you carry the materials on your back and can snap your fingers at the baggage wagon. For three-fourths of the year it is all the shelter needed, as it keeps out rain, snow, and wind perfectly, being penetrable only by the cold.

We marched at last, and on the 12th of September entered Frederick, wondering all the way what the enemy meant. We of the ranks little suspected what sheaves he was gathering in at Harper's Ferry, behind the curtain of his main body. We guessed, however, as usual, and toward evening began to get our answer. He was right ahead, his rear-guard skirmishing with our advance. We came up at the close of the fight at Frederick, and, forming line of battle, went at double-quick through cornfields, potato patches, gardens, and backyards—the German washer-women of the 103d

New York regiment going in with us on the run. It was only a measure of precaution, however, the cavalry having done what little there was to do in the way of driving out of the city a Confederate rear-guard not much inclined to stay. We pitched tents at once in the outskirts, and after a hearty supper went to explore the city.

The next morning the feeling of distrust which the night before had seemed to rule the place had disappeared, and a general holiday feeling took its place. The city was abloom with flags, houses were open everywhere, trays of food were set on the window-sills of nearly all the better class of houses, and the streets were filled with women dressed in their best, walking bareheaded, singing, and testifying in every way the general joy. September 13th in Frederick City was a bright one in memory for many a month after—a pleasant topic to discuss over many a camp-fire.

The next day our regiment went on a reconnoissance to a speck of a village, rather overweighted by its name—Jefferson—about eight miles from Frederick and on our left. Far up the mountainside ahead of us we could see, in the fields confronting the edge of the woods that crowned the ridge, the scattered line of Rush's Lancers, their bright red pennons fluttering gayly from their spear heads.

We reached camp again about 10 o'clock at night, and found awaiting us marching orders for 2 o'clock the following morning. Late as it was, one of my tent-mates—an enterprising young fellow—started out on a foraging expedition, in pursuance of a vow made several days before to find something with which to vary his monotonous regimen of "hard-tack" and "salt horse." He "ran the guard"—an easy thing to do in the darkness and hubbub—and returned shortly after, struggling with a weight of miscellaneous plunder; a crock of butter, a quantity of apple-butter, some lard, a three-legged skillet weighing several pounds, and a live hen. It was a marvel how he managed to carry so much; but he was a rare gleaner always, with a comprehensive method that covered the ground. That night we had several immense flapjacks, the whole size of the pan; then, tethering the hen to one of the tent pegs, we went to sleep, to be roused an hour or so later by hearing our two-legged prize cackling and fluttering off in the darkness.

Up to the 10th the army had not marched so much as it had drifted, but from this point on our purpose seemed to grow more definite and the interest deepened steadily. There had been sporadic fighting through the day (the 13th), but it was over the hills to the west, and we heard nothing of it beyond those airy echoes that take the shape of rumor. Now, however, the ferment at the front, borne back by galloping orderlies, was swiftly leavening the mass. Occasionally, on our march we would pass a broken gun wheel or the bloated body of a slaughtered horse, and in various ways we knew that we were close upon the enemy, and that we could not now be long delayed. This would have been told us by the burden of our daily orders, always the same, to hold ourselves "in readiness to march at a moment's notice," with the stereotyped addendum, "three days' cooked rations and forty rounds." Every one lay down to sleep that night with a feeling of impending battle.

By daylight next morning we were in motion again—the whole army. The gathering of such a multitude is a swarm, its march a vast migration. It fills up every road leading in the same direction over a breadth of many miles, with long ammunition and supply trains disposed for safety along the inner roads, infantry and artillery next in order outwardly, feelers of cavalry all along its front and far out on its flanks; while behind, trailing along every road for miles (ravelings from the great square blanket which the enemy's cavalry, if active, snip off with ease), are the rabble of stragglers—laggards through sickness or exhaustion, squads of recruits, convalescents from the hospital, special duty men going up to rejoin their regiments. Each body has its route laid down for it each day, its time of starting set by watch, its place of bivouac or camp appointed, together with the hour of reaching it. If two roads come together, the corps that reaches the junction first moves on, while the other files out into the fields, stacks arms, builds fires, and boils its coffee. Stand, now, by the roadside while a corps is filing past. They march "route step," as it is called—that is, not keeping time—and four abreast, as a country road seldom permits a greater breadth, allowing for the aides and orderlies that gallop in either direction continually along the column. If the march has just begun, you hear the sound of voices everywhere, with roars of laughter in spots, marking the place of the company wag—generally some Irishman, the action of whose tongue bears out his calling. Later on, when the weight of knapsack and musket begins to tell, these sounds die out; a sense of weariness and labor rises from the toiling masses streaming by, voiced only by the shuffle of a multitude of feet, the rubbing and straining of innumerable straps, and the flop of full canteens. So uniformly does the mass move on that it suggests a great machine, requiring only its directing mind. Yet such a mass, without experience in battle, would go to pieces before a moderately effective fire. Catch up a handful of snow and throw it, it flies to fluff; pack it, it strikes like stone. Here is the secret of organization—the aim and crown of drill, to make the units one, that when the crisis comes, the missile may be thoroughly compacted. Too much, however, has been claimed for theoretic discipline—not enough for intelligent individual action. No remark was oftener on the lips of officers during the war than this: "Obey orders! *I* do your thinking for you." But that soldier is the best whose good sense tells him when to be merely a part of a machine and when not.

The premonitions of the night were not fulfilled next day. That day—the 14th of September—we crossed the Catoctin range of mountains, reaching the summit about noon, and descended its western slope into the beautiful valley of Middletown. Half-way up the valley's western side we halted for a rest, and turned to look back on the moving host. It was a scene to linger in the memory. The valley in which Middletown lies is four or five miles wide, as I remember it, and runs almost due north and south between the parallel ranges of Catoctin and South Mountains. From where we stood the landscape lay below us, the eye commanding the opposite slope of the valley almost at point-blank. An hour before, from the same spot, it had been merely a scene of quiet pastoral beauty. All at once, along its eastern edge the heads of the columns began to appear, and grew and grew, pouring over the ridge and descending by every road, filling them completely and scarring the surface of the gentle landscape with the angry welts of war. By the farthest northern road—the farthest we could see—moved the baggage wagons, the line stretching from the bottom of the valley back to the top of the ridge, and beyond, only the canvas covers of the wagons revealing their character. We knew that each dot was a heavily loaded army wagon, drawn by six mules and occupying forty feet of road at least. Now they looked like white beads on a string. So far away were they that no motion was perceptible. The constant swelling of the end of the line down in the valley, where the teams turned into the fields to park, gave evidence that, in this way, it was being slowly reeled along the way. The troops were marching by two roads farther south. The Confederates fighting on the western summit must have seen them plainly. Half a mile beyond us the column broke abruptly, filing off into line of battle, right and left, across the fields. From that point backward and downward, across the valley and up the farther slope, it stretched with scarcely a gap, every curve and zigzag of the way defined more sharply by its somber presence. Here, too, on all the distant portions of the line, motion was imperceptible, but could be inferred from the casual glint of sunlight on a musket barrel miles away. It was 3 o'clock when we resumed our march, turning our backs upon the beautiful, impressive picture—each column a monstrous, crawling, blue-black snake, miles long, quilled with the silver slant of muskets at a "shoulder," its sluggish tail writhing slowly up over the distant eastern ridge, its bruised head weltering in the roar and smoke upon the crest above, where was being fought the battle of South Mountain.

We were now getting nearer to the danger line, the rattle of musketry going on incessantly in the edges of the woods and behind the low stone fences that seamed the mountain-side. Then we came upon the fringes of the contest—slightly wounded men scattered along the winding road on their way to the hospital, and now and then a squad of prisoners, wounded and unwounded together, going under guard to the rear.

The brigade was ordered to the left of the road to support a regular battery posted at the top of a steep slope, with a cornfield on the left, and twenty yards or so in front, a thin wood. We formed behind the battery and a little down the slope—the 89th on the left, the 9th next, then the 103d. We had been in position but a few minutes when a stir in front advised us of something unusual afoot, and the next moment the Confederates burst out of the woods and made a dash at the battery. We had just obeyed a hastily given order to lie down, when the bullets whistled over our heads, and fell far down the slope behind us. Then the guns opened at short range, full-shotted with grape and canister. The force of the charge was easily broken, for though it was vigorously made it was not sustained—perhaps was not intended to be, as the whole day's battle had been merely an effort of the enemy to check our advance till he could concentrate for a general engagement. As the Confederates came out of the woods their line touched ours on the extreme left only, and there at an acute angle, their men nearly treading on those of the 89th, who were on their faces in the cornfield, before they discovered them. At that instant the situation just there was ideally, cruelly advantageous to us. The Confederates stood before us not twenty feet away, the full intention of destruction on their faces—but helpless, with empty muskets. The 89th simply rose up and shot them down.

It was in this charge that I first heard the "rebel yell"; not the deep-breasted Northern cheer, given in unison and after a struggle, to signify an advantage gained, but a high shrill yelp, uttered without concert, and kept up continually when the fighting was approaching a climax, as an incentive to further effort. This charge ended the contest for the day on that part of the line. Pickets were set well forward in the woods, and we remained some time in position, waiting. How a trivial thing will often thrust itself upon the attention in a supreme moment was well exemplified here. All about us grew pennyroyal, bruised by the tramping of a hundred feet, and the smell of it has always been associated in my memory with that battle.

Before the sunlight faded, I walked over the narrow field. All around lay the Confederate dead—undersized men mostly, from the coast district of North Carolina, with sallow, hatchet faces, and clad in "butternut"—a color running all the way from a deep, coffee brown up to the whitish brown of ordinary dust. As I looked down on the poor, pinched faces, worn with marching and scant fare, all enmity died out. There was no "secession" in those rigid forms, nor in those fixed eyes staring blankly at the sky. Clearly it was not "their war." Some of our men primed their muskets afresh with the finer powder from the cartridge-boxes of the dead. With this exception, each remained untouched as he had fallen. Darkness came on rapidly, and it grew very chilly. As little could be done at that hour in the way of burial, we unrolled the blankets of the dead, spread them over the bodies, and then sat down in line, munching a little on our cooked rations in lieu of supper, and listening to the firing, which was kept up on the right, persistently. By 9 o'clock this ceased entirely. Drawing our blankets over us, we went to sleep, lying upon our arms in line as we had stood, living Yankee and dead

Confederate side by side, and indistinguishable.—This was Sunday, the 14th of September.

The next morning, receiving no orders to march, we set to work collecting the arms and equipments scattered about the field, and burying the dead. The weather being fine, bowers were built in the woods—generally in fence corners—for such of the wounded as could not be moved with safety; others, after stimulants had been given, were helped down the mountain to the rude hospitals. Before we left the spot, some of the country people living thereabout, who had been scared away by the firing, ventured back, making big eyes at all they saw, and asking most ridiculous questions. One was, whether we were from Mexico! Those belated echoes, it seemed, were still sounding in the woods of Maryland.

After the Seven Days and Jackson's victories in the Shenandoah Valley, there was a rising clamor in the Confederacy for a full-scale invasion of the North. The Union armies seemed to be leaderless, the Confederate obviously invincible. Said the Charleston Mercury (not the most moderate of Southern journals, to be sure): "When the Government of the North shall have fled into Pennsylvania, when the public buildings in Washington shall have been razed to the ground, so as to forbid the hope of their ever again becoming the nest of Yankee despotism, then, at last, may we expect to see the hope of success vanish from the Northern mind, and reap the fruit of our bloody and long continued trials." Now, after the successful Second Bull Run campaign, General Lee agreed that the military and diplomatic interests of the South might both be well served by an invasion. Crossing the Potomac early in September he detached Jackson to take Harper's Ferry, now garrisoned again by a small Federal force, so as to keep open his lines of supply through the Valley to the South. Then he continued north. McClellan, reinstated in command to meet this threat, marched to cut Lee off. On that march, by extraordinary luck McClellan came into possession of a lost Confederate order which told him that the components of Lee's army were widely separated. He was jubilant, as well he might be, for by acting upon the intelligence this document gave him, he could drive between Lee and Jackson and destroy them separately. But again he was too slow. By the time he caught up with Lee at Sharpsburg, Jackson had captured Harper's Ferry, sent his prisoners south and was about to rejoin his chief. So McClellan was again to contend with the imagined bugbear of Lee's superior numbers. The result was Antietam, which McClellan fought timidly and badly and after which he allowed Lee's shattered forces to withdraw across the Potomac almost at their leisure. Several weeks later, after making some tentative movements southward into Virginia, he was replaced by Burnside. This time McClellan's military career was ended.

"Bloody Lane was in our hands"

BY JACOB D. COX, MAJOR-GENERAL, U. S. V.

I T WAS not till some time past noon of the 15th of September that, the way being clear for the Ninth Corps at South Mountain, we marched through Fox's gap to the Boonsboro' and Sharpsburg turnpike, and along this road till we came up in rear of Sumner's command. Hooker's corps, which was part of the right wing (Burnside's), had been in the advance, and had moved off from the turnpike to the right near Keedysville. I was with the Kanawha Division, assuming that my temporary command of the corps ended with the battle on the mountain. When we approached the line of hills bordering the Antietam, we received orders to turn off the road to the left, and halted our battalions closed in mass. It was now about 3 o'clock in the afternoon. McClellan, as it seemed, had just reached the field, and was surrounded by a group of his principal officers, most of whom I had never seen before. I rode up with General Burnside, dismounted, and was very cordially greeted by General McClellan. He and Burnside were evidently on terms of most intimate friendship and familiarity. He introduced me to the officers I had not known before, referring pleasantly to my service with him in Ohio and West Virginia, putting me upon an easy footing with them in a very agreeable and genial way.

We walked up the slope of the ridge before us, and looking westward from its crest the whole field of the coming battle was before us. Immediately in front the Antietam wound through the hollow, the hills rising gently on both sides. In the background on our left was the village of Sharpsburg, with fields inclosed by stone fences in front of it. At its right was a bit of wood (since known as the West Wood), with the little Dunker Church standing out white and sharp against it. Farther to the right and left the scene was closed in by wooded ridges with open farm lands between, the whole making as pleasing and prosperous a landscape as can easily be imagined. We made a large group as we stood upon the hill, and it was not long before we attracted the enemy's attention. A puff of white smoke from a knoll on the right of the Sharpsburg road was followed by the screaming of a shell over our heads. McClellan directed that all but one or two should retire behind the ridge, while he continued the reconnoissance, walking slowly to the right. I noted with satisfaction the cool and business-like air with which he made his examination under fire. The Confederate artillery was answered by a battery, and a lively cannonade ensued on both sides, though without any noticeable effect. The enemy's position was revealed, and he was evidently in force on both sides of the turnpike in front of Sharpsburg, covered by the undulations of the rolling ground which hid his infantry from our sight.

The examination of the enemy's position and the discussion of it continued till near the close of the day. Orders were then given for the Ninth Corps to move to the left, keeping off the road, which was occupied by other troops. We moved through fields and farm lands, an hour's march in the dusk of the evening, going into bivouac about a mile south of the Sharpsburg bridge, and in rear of the hills bordering the Antietam.

On Tuesday, September 16th, we confidently expected a battle, and I kept with my division. In the afternoon I saw General Burnside, and learned from him that McClellan had determined to let Hooker make a movement on our extreme right to turn Lee's position. Burnside's manner in speaking of this implied that he thought it was done at Hooker's solicitation and through his desire, openly evinced, to be independent in command.

I urged Burnside to assume the immediate command of the corps and allow me to lead only my own division. He objected that as he had been announced as commander of the right wing of the army composed of two corps (his own and Hooker's), he was unwilling to waive his precedence or to assume that Hooker was detached for anything more than a temporary purpose. I pointed out that Reno's staff had been granted leave of absence to take the body of their chief to Washington, and that my division staff was too small for corps duty; but he met this by saying that he would use his staff for this purpose and help me in every way he could, till the crisis of the campaign should be over.

The 16th passed without serious fighting, though there was desultory cannonading and picket firing. It was hard to restrain our men from showing themselves on the crest of the long ridge in front of us, and whenever they did so they drew the fire from some of the enemy's batteries, to which ours would respond. In the afternoon McClellan reconnoitered the line of the Antietam near us, Burnside being with him. As the result of this we were ordered to change our positions at nightfall, staff-officers being sent to guide each division to its new camp. Rodman's division went half a mile to the left, where a country road led to a ford in a great bend in the Antietam curving deeply into the enemy's side of the stream. Sturgis's division was placed on the sides of the road leading to the stone bridge, since known as Burnside's Bridge (below the Sharpsburg bridge). Willcox's was put in reserve in rear of Sturgis. My own division was divided, Scammon's brigade going with Rodman, and Crook's going with Sturgis. Crook was ordered to take the advance in crossing the bridge, in case we should be ordered to attack. This selection was made by Burnside himself, as a compliment to the division for the vigor of its assault at South Mountain. While we were moving, we heard Hooker's guns far off on the right and front, and the cannonade continued an hour or more after it became dark.

The morning of Wednesday, the 17th, broke fresh and fair. The men were astir at dawn, getting breakfast and preparing for a day of battle. The artillery opened on both sides as soon as it was fairly light, and the positions which had been assigned us in the dusk of the evening were found to be exposed in some places to the direct fire of the Confederate guns, Rodman's division suffering more than the others. Fairchild's brigade alone reported thirty-six casualties before they could find cover. It was not till 7 o'clock that orders came to advance toward the creek as far as could be done without exposing the men to unnecessary loss. Rodman was directed to acquaint himself with the situation of the ford in front of him, and Sturgis to seek the best means of approach to the stone bridge. All were then to remain in readiness to obey further orders.

When these arrangements had been made, I rode to the position Burnside had selected for himself, which was upon a high knoll north-east of the Burnside Bridge, near a hay-stack which was a prominent landmark. Near by was Benjamin's battery of 20-pounder Parrotts, and a little farther still to the right, on the same ridge, General Sturgis had sent in Durell's battery. These were exchanging shots with the enemy's guns opposite, and had the advantage in range and weight of metal.

Whatever the reason, McClellan had adopted a plan of battle which practically reduced Sumner and Burnside to the command of one corps each, while Hooker had been sent far off on the right front, followed later by Mansfield, but without organizing the right wing as a unit so that one commander could give his whole attention to handling it with vigor. In his preliminary report, made before he was relieved from command, McClellan says:

> The design was to make the main attack upon the enemy's left—at least to create a diversion in favor of the main attack, with the hope of something more, by assailing the enemy's right—and, as soon as one or both of the flank movements were fully successful, to attack their center with any reserve I might then have in hand.

McClellan's report covering his whole career in the war, dated August 4th, 1863 (and published February, 1864, after warm controversies had arisen and he had become a political character), modifies the above statement in some important particulars. It says:

> My plan for the impending general engagement was to attack the enemy's left with the corps of Hooker and Mansfield, supported by Sumner's, and if necessary by Franklin's, and as soon as matters looked favorably there to move the corps of Burnside against the enemy's extreme right upon the ridge running to the south and rear of Sharpsburg, and having carried their position, to press along the crest toward our right, and whenever either of these flank movements should be successful, to advance our center with all the forces then disposable.

The opinion I got from Burnside as to the part the Ninth Corps was to take was fairly consistent with the design first quoted, viz., that when the attack by Sumner, Hooker, and Franklin should be progressing favorably, we were "to create a diversion in favor of the main attack, with the hope of something more." It would also appear probable that Hooker's movement was at first intended to be made by his corps alone, taken up by Sumner's two corps as soon as he was ready to attack, and shared in by Franklin if he reached the field in time, thus making a simultaneous oblique attack from our right by the whole army except Porter's corps, which was in reserve, and the Ninth Corps, which was to create the "diversion" on our left and prevent the enemy from stripping his right to reënforce his left. It is hardly disputable that this would have been a better plan than the one actually carried out. Certainly the assumption that the Ninth Corps could cross the Antietam alone at the only place on the field where the Confederates had their line immediately upon the stream which must be crossed under fire by two narrow heads of columns, and could then turn to the right along the high ground occupied by the hostile army before that army had been broken or seriously shaken elsewhere, is one which would hardly be made till time had dimmed the remembrance of the actual positions of Lee's divisions upon the field.

The evidence that the plan did not originally include the wide separation of two corps to the right, to make the extended turning movement, is found in Hooker's incomplete report, and in the wide interval in time between the marching of his corps and that of Mansfield. Hooker was ordered to cross the Antietam at about 2 o'clock in the afternoon of the 16th by the bridge in front of Keedysville and the ford below it. He says that after his troops were over and in march, he rode back to McClellan, who told him that he might call for reënforcements and that when they came they should be under his command. Somewhat later McClellan rode forward with his staff to observe the progress making, and Hooker again urged the necessity of reënforcements. Yet Sumner did not receive orders to send Mansfield to support Hooker till evening, and the Twelfth Corps marched only half an hour before midnight, reaching its bivouac, about a mile and a half in rear of that of Hooker, at 2 A. M. of the 17th. Sumner was also ordered to be in readiness to march with the Second Corps an hour before day, but his orders to move did not reach him till nearly half-past 7 in the morning. By this time, Hooker had fought his battle, had been repulsed, and later in the morning was carried wounded from the field. Mansfield had fallen before his corps was deployed, and General Alpheus S. Williams who succeeded him was fighting a losing battle at all points but one—where Greene's division held the East Wood.

After crossing the Antietam, Hooker had shaped his course to the westward, aiming to reach the ridge upon which the Hagerstown turnpike runs, and which is the dominant feature of the landscape. This ridge is some two miles distant from the Antietam, and for the first mile of the way no resistance was met. However, Hooker's progress had been observed by the enemy, and Hood's two brigades were taken from the center and passed to the left of D. H. Hill. Here they occupied an open wood (since known as the East Wood), north-east of the Dunker Church. Hooker was now trying to approach the Confederate positions, Meade's division of the Pennsylvania Reserves being in the advance. A sharp skirmishing combat ensued and artillery was also brought into action on both sides, the engagement continuing till after dark. On our side Seymour's brigade had been chiefly engaged, and had felt the enemy so vigorously that Hood supposed he had repulsed a serious effort to take the wood. Hooker was, however, aiming to pass quite beyond the flank, and kept his other divisions north of the hollow beyond the wood, and upon the ridge which reaches the turnpike near the largest reëntrant bend of the Potomac, which is here only half a mile distant. Here he bivouacked upon the northern slopes of the ridge, Doubleday's division resting with its right upon the turnpike, Ricketts's division upon the left of Doubleday, and Meade covering the front of both with the skirmishers of Seymour's brigade. Between Meade's skirmishers and the ridge were the farm-house and barn of J. Poffenberger on the east of the road, where Hooker made his own quarters for the night. Half a mile farther in front was the farm of D. R. Miller, the dwelling on the east, and the barn surrounded by stacks on the west of the road. Mansfield's corps, marching as it did late in the night, kept farther to the right than Hooker's, but moved on a nearly parallel course and bivouacked upon the farm of another J. Poffenberger near the road which, branching from the Hagerstown turnpike at the Dunker Church, intersects the one running from Keedysville through Smoketown to the same turnpike about a mile north of Hooker's position.

On the Confederate side, Hood's division had been so severely handled that it was replaced by Jackson's (commanded by J. R. Jones), which, with Ewell's, had been led to the field from Harper's Ferry by Jackson, reaching Sharpsburg in the afternoon of the 16th. These divisions were formed on the left of D. H. Hill and almost at right angles to his line, crossing the turnpike and facing northward. Hood's division, on being relieved, was placed in reserve near the Dunker Church, and spent part of the night in cooking rations, of which its supply had been short for a day or two. The combatants on both sides slept upon their arms, well knowing that the dawn would bring bloody work.

When day broke on Wednesday morning, the 17th, Hooker, looking south from the Poffenberger farm along the turnpike, saw a gently rolling landscape, of which the commanding point was the Dunker Church, whose white brick walls appeared on the west side of the road backed by the foliage of the West Wood, which came toward him, filling a slight hollow which ran parallel to the turnpike, with a single row of fields between. Beyond the Miller house and barns, the ground dipped into a little depression. Beyond this was seen a large corn-field between the East Wood and the turnpike, rising again to the higher level. There was, however, another small dip beyond, which could not be seen from Hooker's position; and on the second ridge, near the church, and extending across the turnpike eastward into the East Wood, could be seen the Confederate line of gray, partly sheltered by piles of rails taken from the fences. They seemed to Hooker to be at the farther side of the corn-field and at the top of the first rise of ground beyond Miller's. It was plain that the high ground about the little white church was the key of the enemy's position, and if that could be carried Hooker's task would be well done.

The Confederates opened the engagement by a rapid fire from a battery near the East Wood as soon as it was light, and Hooker answered the challenge by an immediate order for his line to advance. Doubleday's division was in two lines, Gibbon's and Phelps's brigades in front, supported by Patrick and Hofmann. Gibbon had the right and guided upon the turnpike. Patrick held a small wood in his rear, which is upon both sides of the road a little north of Miller's house. Some of Meade's men were supposed to be in the northernmost extension of the West Wood, and thus to cover Gibbon's right flank as he advanced. Part of Battery B, 4th United States Artillery (Gibbon's own battery), was run forward to Miller's barn and stack-yard on the right of the road, and fired over the heads of the advancing regiments. Other batteries were similarly placed more to the left. The line moved swiftly forward through Miller's orchard and kitchen garden, breaking through a stout picket fence on the near side, down into the moist ground of the hollow, and up through the corn, which was higher than their heads, and shut out everything from view. At the southern side of the field they came to a low fence, beyond which was an open field, at the farther side of which was the enemy's line. But Gibbon's right, covered by the corn, had outmarched the left, which had been exposed to a terrible fire, and the direction taken had been a little oblique, so that the right wing of the 6th Wisconsin, the flanking regiment, had crossed the turnpike and was suddenly assailed by a sharp fire from the West Wood on its flank. They swung back into the road, lying down along the high, stout post-and-rail fence, keeping up their fire by shooting between the rails. Leaving this little band to protect their right, the main line, which had come up on the left, leaped the fence at the south edge of the corn-field and charged across the open at the enemy in front. But the concentrated fire of artillery and musketry was more than they could bear. Men fell by scores and hundreds, and the thinned lines gave way and ran for the shelter of the corn. They were rallied in the hollow on the north side of the field. The enemy had rapidly extended his left under cover of the West Wood, and now made a dash at the right flank and at Gibbon's exposed guns. His men on the right faced by that flank and followed him bravely, though with little order, in a dash at the Confederates, who were swarming out of the wood. The gunners double-charged the cannon with canister, and under a terrible fire of both artillery and rifles the enemy broke and sought shelter.

Patrick's brigade had come up in support of Gibbon, and was sent across the turnpike into the West Wood to cover that flank. They pushed forward, the enemy retiring, until they were in advance of the principal line in the corn-field, upon which the Confederates were now advancing. Patrick faced his men to the left, parallel to the edge of the wood and to the turnpike, and poured his fire into the flank of the enemy, following it by a charge through the field and up to the fence along the road. Again the Confederates were driven back, but only to push in again by way of these woods, forcing Patrick to resume his original line of front and to retire to the cover of a ledge at right angles to the road near Gibbon's guns.

Farther to the left Phelps's and Hofmann's brigades had had similar experience, pushing forward nearly to the Confederate lines, and being driven back with great loss when they charged over open ground against the enemy. Ricketts's division entered the edge of the East Wood; but here, at the salient angle, where D. H. Hill and Lawton joined, the enemy held the position stubbornly, and the repulse of Doubleday's division made Ricketts glad to hold even the edge of the East Wood, as the right of the line was driven back.

It was now about 7 o'clock, and Mansfield's corps (the Twelfth) was approaching, for that officer had called his men to arms at the first sound of Hooker's battle and had marched to his support. The corps consisted of two divisions, Williams's and Greene's. It contained a number of new and undrilled regiments, and in hastening to the field in columns of battalions in mass, proper intervals for deployment had not been preserved, and time was necessarily lost before the troops could be put in line. General Mansfield fell mortally wounded before the deployment was complete, and the command devolved on General Williams. Williams had only time to take the most general directions from Hooker, when the latter also was wounded. The Twelfth Corps attack seems to have been made obliquely to that of Hooker, and facing more to the westward, for General Williams speaks of the post-and-rail fences along the turnpike being a great obstruction in their front. Greene's division, on his left, moved along the ridge leading to the East Wood, taking as the guide for his extreme left the line of the burning house of Mumma, which had been set on fire by D. H. Hill's men. Doubleday, in his report, notices this change of direction of Williams's division, which had relieved him, and says Williams's brigades were swept away by a fire from their left and front, from behind rocky ledges they could not see. Our officers were deceived in part as to the extent and direction of the enemy's line by the fact that the Confederate cavalry commander, Stuart, had occupied a commanding hill west of the pike and beyond our right flank, and from this position, which, in fact, was considerably detached from the Confederate line, he used his batteries with such effect as to produce the belief that a continuous line extended from this point to the Dunker Church. Our true lines of attack were convergent ones, the right sweeping southward along the pike and through the narrow strip of the West Wood, while the division which drove the enemy from the East Wood should move upon the commanding ground around the church. This error of direction was repeated with disastrous effect a little later, when Sumner came on the ground with Sedgwick's corps.

When Mansfield's corps came on the field, Meade, who succeeded Hooker, withdrew the First Corps to the ridge north of Poffenberger's, where it had bivouacked the night before. It had suffered severely, having lost 2470 in killed and wounded, but it was still further depleted by straggling, so that Meade reported less than 7000 men with the colors that evening. Its organization was preserved, however, and the story that it was utterly dispersed was a mistake.

Greene's division, on the left of the Twelfth Corps, profited by the hard fighting of those who had preceded it, and was able to drive the enemy quite out of the East Wood and across the open fields between it and the Dunker Church. Greene even succeeded, about the time of Sumner's advance, in getting a foothold about the Dunker Church itself, which he held for some time. But the fighting of Hooker's and Mansfield's men, though lacking unity of force and of purpose, had cost the enemy dear. J. R. Jones, who commanded Jackson's division, had been wounded; Starke, who succeeded Jones, was killed; Lawton, who followed Starke, was wounded. Ewell's division, commanded by Early, had suffered hardly less. Hood was sent back into the fight to relieve Lawton, and had been reënforced by the brigades of Ripley, Colquitt, and McRae (Garland's), from D. H. Hill's division. When Greene reached the Dunker Church, therefore, the Confederates on that wing had suffered more fearfully than our own men. Nearly half their numbers were killed and wounded, and Jackson's famous "Stonewall" division was so completely disorganized that only a handful of men under Colonels Grigsby and Stafford remained and attached themselves to Early's command. Of the division under Early, his own brigade was all that retained much strength, and this, posted among the rocks in the West Wood and vigorously supported by Stuart's horse artillery on the flank, was all that covered the left of Lee's army. Could Hooker and Mansfield have attacked together—or, still better, could Sumner's Second Corps have marched before day and united with the first onset—Lee's left must inevitably have been crushed long before the Confederate divisions of McLaws, Walker, and A. P. Hill could have reached the field. It is this failure to carry out any intelligible plan which the historian must regard as the unpardonable military fault on the National side. To account for the hours between 4 and 8 on that morning, is the most serious responsibility of the National commander.

Sumner's Second Corps was now approaching the scene of action, or rather two divisions of it—Sedgwick's and French's—Richardson's being still delayed till his place could be filled by Porter's troops, the strange tardiness in sending orders being noticeable in regard to every part of the army. Sumner met Hooker, who was being carried from the field, and the few words he could exchange with the wounded general were enough to make him feel the need of haste, but not sufficient to give him any clear idea of the position.

Both Sedgwick and French marched their divisions by the right flank, in three columns, a brigade in each column, Sedgwick leading. They crossed the Antietam by Hooker's route, but did not march as far to the north-west as Hooker had done. When the center of the corps was opposite the Dunker Church, and nearly east of it, the change of direction was given; the troops faced to their proper front and advanced in line of battle in three lines, fully deployed, and 60 or 70 yards apart, Sumner himself being in rear of Sedgwick's first line, and near its left. When they approached the position held by Greene's division at Dunker Church, French kept on so as to form on

249

Greene's left, while Sedgwick, under Sumner's immediate lead, diverged somewhat to the right, passing through the East Wood, crossing the turnpike on the right of Greene and of the Dunker Church, and plunged into the West Wood. At this point there were absolutely no Confederate troops in front of them. Early was farther to the right, opposing Williams's division of the Twelfth Corps, and now made haste under cover of the woods to pass around Sedgwick's right and to get in front of him to oppose his progress. This led to a lively skirmishing fight in which Early was making as great a demonstration as possible, but with no chance of solid success. At this very moment, however, McLaws's and Walker's divisions came upon the field, marching rapidly from Harper's Ferry. Walker charged headlong upon the left flank of Sedgwick's lines, which were soon thrown into confusion, and McLaws, passing by Walker's left, also threw his division diagonally upon the already broken and retreating lines of Sumner. Taken at such a disadvantage, these had never a chance; and in spite of the heroic bravery of Sumner and Sedgwick, with most of their officers (Sedgwick being severely wounded), the division was driven off to the north with terrible losses, carrying along in the rout part of Williams's men of the Twelfth Corps, who had been holding Early at bay. All these troops were rallied at the ridge on the Poffenberger farm, where Hooker's corps had already taken position. Here some thirty batteries of both corps were concentrated, and, supported by the organized parts of all three of the corps which had fought upon this part of the field, easily repulsed all efforts of Jackson and Stuart to resume the aggressive or to pass between them and the Potomac. Sumner himself did not accompany the routed troops to this position, but as soon as it was plain that the division could not be rallied, he galloped off to put himself in communication with French and with the headquarters of the army and try to retrieve the misfortune. From the flag-station east of the East Wood he signaled to McClellan: "Reënforcements are badly wanted. Our troops are giving way." It was between 9 and 10 o'clock when Sumner entered the West Wood, and in fifteen minutes, or a little more, the one-sided combat was over.

The enemy now concentrated upon Greene at the Dunker Church, and after a stubborn resistance he too was driven back across the turnpike and the open ground to the edge of the East Wood. Here, by the aid of several batteries gallantly handled, he defeated the subsequent effort to dislodge him. French had come up on his left, and both his batteries and the numerous ones on the Poffenberger hill swept the open ground and the corn-field over which Hooker had fought, and he was able to make good his position. The enemy was content to regain the high ground near the church, and French's attack upon D. H. Hill was now attracting their attention.

The battle on the extreme right was thus ended before 10 o'clock in the morning, and there was no more serious fighting north of the Dunker Church. French advanced on Greene's left, over the open farm lands, and after a fierce combat about the Roulette and Clipp farm buildings, drove D. H. Hill's division from them. Richardson's division came up on French's left soon after, and foot by foot, field by field, from hill to hill and from fence to fence, the enemy was pressed back, till after several hours of fighting the sunken road, since known as "Bloody Lane," was in our hands, piled full of the Confederate dead who had defended it with their lives. Richardson had been mortally wounded, and Hancock had been sent from Franklin's corps to command the division. Barlow had been conspicuous in the thickest of the fight, and after a series of brilliant actions was carried off desperately wounded. On the Confederate side equal courage had been shown and a magnificent tenacity exhibited. But it is not my purpose to describe the battle in detail. I limit myself to such an outline as may make clear my interpretation of the larger features of the engagement and its essential plan.

The head of Franklin's corps (the Sixth) had arrived about 10 o'clock and taken the position near the Sharpsburg Bridge which Sumner had occupied. Before noon Smith's and Slocum's divisions were ordered to Sumner's assistance, and early in the afternoon Irwin and Brooks, of Smith, advanced to the charge and relieved Greene's division and part of French's, holding the line from Bloody Lane by the Clipp, Roulette, and Mumma houses to the East Wood and the ridge in front. Here Smith and Slocum remained till Lee retreated, Smith's division repelling a sharp attack. French and Richardson's battle may be considered as ended at 1 or 2 o'clock.

It seems to me very clear that about 10 o'clock in the morning was the great crisis in this battle. The sudden and complete rout of Sedgwick's division was not easily accounted for, and with McClellan's theory of the enormous superiority of Lee's numbers, it looked as if the Confederate general had massed overwhelming forces on our right. Sumner's notion that Hooker's corps was utterly dispersed was naturally accepted, and McClellan limited his hopes to holding on at the East Wood and the Poffenberger hill where Sedgwick's batteries were massed and supported by the troops that had been rallied there. Franklin's corps as it came on the field was detained to support the threatened right center, and McClellan determined to help it further by a demonstration upon the extreme left by the Ninth Corps. At this time, therefore (10 A. M.), he gave his order to Burnside to try to cross the Antietam and attack the enemy, thus creating a diversion in favor of our hard-pressed right. Facts within my own recollection strongly sustain this view that the hour was 10 A. M. I have mentioned the hill above the Burnside Bridge where Burnside took his position, and to which I went after the preliminary orders for the day had been issued. There I remained until the order of attack came, anxiously watching what we could see at the right, and noting the effect of the fire of the heavy guns of Benjamin's battery. From that point we could see nothing that occurred beyond the Dunker Church, for the East and West Woods, with farm-houses and orchards between, made an impenetrable screen. But as the morning wore on we saw lines of troops advancing from our right upon the other side of the Antietam, and engaging the enemy between us and the East Wood. The Confederate lines facing them now rose into view. From our position we looked, as it were, down between the opposing lines as if they had been the sides of a street, and as the fire opened we saw wounded men carried to the rear and stragglers making off. Our lines halted, and we were tortured with anxiety as we speculated whether our men would charge or retreat. The enemy occupied lines of fences and stone-walls, and their batteries made gaps in the National ranks. Our long-range guns were immediately turned in that direction, and we cheered every well-aimed shot. One of our shells blew up a caisson close to the Confederate line. This contest was going on, and it was yet uncertain which would succeed, when one of McClellan's staff rode up with an order to Burnside. The latter turned to me, saying we were ordered to make our attack. I left the hill-top at once to give personal supervision to the movement ordered, and did not return to it, and my knowledge by actual vision of what occurred on the right ceased. The manner in which we had waited, the free discussion of what was occurring under our eyes and of our relation to it, the public receipt of the order by Burnside in the usual and business-like form, all forbid the supposition that this was any reiteration of a former order. It was immediately transmitted to me without delay or discussion, further than to inform us that things were not going altogether well on the right, and that it was hoped our attack would be of assistance to that wing. If then we can determine whose troops we saw engaged, we shall know something of the time of day; for there has been a general agreement reached as to the hours of movement during the forenoon on the right. The official map settles this. No lines of our troops were engaged in the direction of Bloody Lane and the Roulette farm-house, and between the latter and our station on the hill, till French's division made its attack. We saw them distinctly on the hither side of the farm buildings, upon the open ground, considerably nearer to us than the Dunker Church or the East Wood. In number we took them to be a corps. The place, the circumstances, all fix it beyond controversy that they were French's men, or French's and Richardson's. No others fought on that part of the field until Franklin went to their assistance at noon or later. The incident of their advance and the explosion of the caisson was illustrated by the pencil of the artist, Forbes, on the spot, and placed by him at the time Franklin's head of column was approaching from Rohrersville, which was about 10 o'clock.

McClellan truly said, in his original report, that the task of carrying the bridge in front of Burnside was a difficult one. The depth of the valley and the shape of its curve made it impossible to reach the enemy's position at the bridge by artillery fire from the hill-tops on our side. Not so from the enemy's position, for the curve of the valley was such that it was perfectly enfiladed near the bridge by the Confederate batteries at the position now occupied by the national cemetery. The Confederate defense of the passage was intrusted to D. R. Jones's division of four brigades, which was the one Longstreet himself had disciplined and led till he was assigned to a larger command. Toombs's brigade was placed in advance, occupying the defenses of the bridge itself and the wooded slopes above, while the other brigades supported him, covered by the ridges which looked down upon the valley. The division batteries were supplemented by others from the reserve, and the valley, the bridge, and the ford below were under the direct and powerful fire of shot and shell from the Confederate cannon. Toombs speaks in his report in a characteristic way of his brigade holding back Burnside's corps; but his force, thus strongly supported, was as large as could be disposed of at the head of the bridge, and abundantly large for resistance to any that could be brought against it. Our advance upon the bridge could only be made by a narrow column, showing a front of eight men at most. But the front which Toombs deployed behind his defenses was three or four hundred yards both above and below the bridge. He himself says in his report :

From the nature of the ground on the other side, the enemy were compelled to approach mainly by the road which led up the river for near three hundred paces parallel with my line of battle and distant therefrom from fifty to a hundred and fifty feet, thus exposing his flank to a destructive fire the most of that distance.

Under such circumstances, I do not hesitate to affirm that the Confederate position was virtually impregnable to a direct attack over the bridge, for the column approaching it was not only exposed at pistol-range to the perfectly covered infantry of the enemy and to two batteries which were assigned to the special duty of supporting Toombs, and which had the exact range of the little valley with their shrapnel, but if it should succeed in reaching the bridge its charge across it must be made under a fire plowing through its length, the head of the column melting away as it advanced, so that, as every soldier knows, it could show no front strong enough to make an impression upon the enemy's breastworks, even if it should reach the other side. As a desperate sort of diversion in favor of the right wing, it might be justifiable; but I believe that no officer or man who knew the actual situation at that bridge thinks a serious attack upon it was any part of McClellan's original plan. Yet, in his detailed official report, instead of speaking of it as the difficult task the original report had called it, he treats it as little different from a parade or march across, which might have been done in half an hour.

Burnside's view of the matter was that the front attack at the bridge was so difficult that the passage by the ford below must be an important factor in the task; for if Rodman's division should succeed in getting across there, at the bend in the Antietam, he would come up in rear of Toombs, and either the whole of D. R. Jones's division would have to advance to meet Rodman, or Toombs must abandon the bridge. In this I certainly concurred, and Rodman was ordered to push rapidly for the ford. It is important to remember, however, that Walker's Confederate division had been posted during the earlier morning to hold that part of the Antietam line, and it was probably from him that Rodman suffered the first casualties which occurred in his ranks. But, as we have seen, Walker had been called away by Lee only an hour before, and had made the hasty march by the rear of Sharpsburg, to fall upon Sedgwick. If, therefore, Rodman had been sent to cross at 8 o'clock, it is safe to say that his column fording the stream in the face of Walker's deployed division would never have reached the farther bank—a contingency that McClellan did not consider when arguing long afterward the favorable results that might have followed an earlier attack. As Rodman died upon the field, no full report for his division was made, and we only know that he met with some resistance from both infantry and artillery; that the winding of the stream made his march longer than he anticipated, and that, in fact, he only approached the rear of Toombs's position from that direction about the time when our last and successful charge upon the bridge was made, between noon and 1 o'clock.

The attacks at Burnside's Bridge were made under my own eye. Sturgis's division occupied the center of our line, with Crook's brigade of the Kanawha Division on his right front, and Willcox's division in reserve, as I have already stated. Crook's position was somewhat above the bridge, but it was thought that by advancing part of Sturgis's men to the brow of the hill they could cover the advance of Crook, and that the latter could make a straight dash down the hill to our end of the bridge. The orders were accordingly given, and Crook advanced, covered by the 11th Connecticut (of Rodman), under Colonel Kingsbury, deployed as skirmishers. In passing over the spurs of the hills, Crook came out on the bank of the stream above the bridge and found himself under a heavy fire. He faced the enemy and returned the fire, getting such cover for his men as he could and trying to drive off or silence his opponents. The engagement was one in which the Antietam prevented the combatants from coming to close quarters, but it was none the less vigorously continued with musketry fire. Crook reported that his hands were full, and that he could not approach closer to the bridge. But later in the contest, and about the time that the successful charge at the bridge was made, he got five companies of the 28th Ohio over by a ford above. Sturgis ordered forward an attacking column from Nagle's brigade, supported and covered by Ferrero's brigade, which took position in a field of corn on one of the lower slopes of the hill opposite the head of the bridge. The whole front was carefully covered with skirmishers, and our batteries on the heights overhead were ordered to keep down the fire of the enemy's artillery. Nagle's effort was gallantly made, but it failed, and his men were forced to seek cover behind the spur of the hill from which they had advanced. We were constantly hoping to hear something from Rodman's advance by the ford, and would gladly have waited for some more certain knowledge of his progress, but at this time McClellan's sense of the necessity of relieving the right was such that he was sending reiterated orders to push the assault. Not only were these forwarded to me, but to give added weight to my instructions Burnside sent direct to Sturgis urgent messages to carry the bridge at all hazards. I directed Sturgis to take two regiments from Ferrero's brigade, which had not been engaged, and make a column by moving them by the flank, the one left in front and the other right in front, side by side, so that when they passed the bridge they could turn to left and right, forming line as they advanced on the run. He chose the 51st New York, Colonel Robert B. Potter, and the 51st Pennsylvania, Colonel John F. Hartranft (both names afterward greatly distinguished), and both officers and men were made to feel the necessity of success. At the same time Crook succeeded in bringing a light howitzer of Simmonds's mixed battery down from the hill-tops, and placed it where it had a point-blank fire on the farther end of the bridge. The howitzer was one we had captured in West Virginia, and had been added to the battery, which was partly made up of heavy rifled Parrott guns. When everything was ready, a heavy skirmishing fire was opened all along the bank, the howitzer threw in double charges of canister, the two regiments charged up the road in column with fixed bayonets, and in scarcely more time than it takes to tell it, the bridge was passed and Toombs's brigade fled through the woods and over the top of the hill. The charging regiments were advanced in line to the crest above the bridge as soon as they were deployed, and the rest of Sturgis's division, with Crook's brigade, were immediately brought over to strengthen the line. These were soon joined by Rodman's division with Scammon's brigade, which had crossed at the ford, and whose presence on that side of the stream had no doubt made the final struggle of Toombs's men less obstinate than it would otherwise have been, the fear of being taken in rear having always a strong moral effect upon even the best of troops. It was now about 1 o'clock, and nearly three hours had been spent in a bitter and bloody contest across the narrow stream. The successive efforts to carry the bridge had been made as closely following each other as possible. Each had been a fierce combat, in which the men, with wonderful courage, had not easily accepted defeat, and even when not able to cross the bridge had made use of the walls at the end, the fences, and every tree and stone as cover, while they strove to reach with their fire their well-protected and nearly concealed opponents. The lulls in the fighting had been short, and only to prepare new efforts. The severity of the work was attested by our losses, which, before the crossing was won, exceeded five hundred men and included some of our best officers, such as Colonel Kingsbury, of the 11th Connecticut; Lieutenant-Colonel Bell, of the 51st Pennsylvania, and Lieutenant-Colonel Coleman, of the 11th Ohio, two of them commanding regiments. The proportion of casualties to the number engaged was much greater than common, for the nature of the task required that comparatively few troops should be exposed at once, the others remaining under cover.

Our first task was to prepare to hold the height we had gained against the return assault of the enemy which we expected, and to reply to the destructive fire from the enemy's abundant artillery. The light batteries were brought over and distributed in the line. The men were made to lie down behind the crest to save them from the concentrated artillery fire which the enemy opened upon us as soon as Toombs's regiments succeeded in reaching their main line. But McClellan's anticipation of an overwhelming attack upon his right was so strong that he determined still to press our advance, and sent orders accordingly. The ammunition of Sturgis's and Crook's men had been nearly exhausted, and it was imperative that they should be freshly supplied before entering into another engagement. Sturgis also reported his men so exhausted by their efforts as to be unfit for an immediate advance. On this I sent to Burnside the request that Willcox's division be sent over, with an ammunition train, and that Sturgis's division be replaced by the fresh troops, remaining, however, on the west side of the stream as support to the others. This was done as rapidly as was practicable, where everything had to pass down the steep hill road and through so narrow a defile as the bridge. Still, it was 3 o'clock before these changes and further preparations could be made. Burnside had personally striven to hasten them, and had come over to the west bank to consult and to hurry matters, and took his share of personal peril, for he came at a time when the ammunition wagons were delivering cartridges, and the road where they were, at the end of the bridge, was in the range of the enemy's constant and accurate fire. It is proper to mention this because it has been said that he did not cross the stream. The criticisms made by McClellan as to the time occupied in these changes and movements will not seem forcible, if one will compare them with any similar movements on the field; such as Mansfield's to support Hooker, or Sumner's or Franklin's to reach the scene of action. About this, however, there is fair room for difference of opinion; what I personally know is that it would have been folly to advance again before Willcox had relieved Sturgis, and that as soon as the fresh troops reported and could be put in line, the order to advance was given. McClellan is in accord with all other witnesses in declaring that when the movement began, the conduct of the troops was gallant beyond criticism.

Willcox's division formed the right, Christ's brigade being north and Welsh's brigade south of the road leading from the bridge to Sharpsburg. Crook's brigade of the Kanawha Division supported Willcox. Rodman's division formed on the left, Harland's brigade having the position on the flank, and Fairchild's uniting with Willcox at the center. Scammon's brigade of the Kanawha Division was the reserve for Rodman on the extreme left. Sturgis's division remained and held the crest of the hill above the bridge. About half the batteries of the divisions accompanied the movement, the rest being in position on the hill-tops east of the Antietam. The advance necessarily followed the high ground toward Sharpsburg, and as the enemy made strongest resistance toward our right, the movement curved in that direction, the six brigades of D. R. Jones's Confederate division being deployed diagonally across our front, holding the stone fences and crests of the cross ridges and aided by abundant artillery, in which arm the enemy was particularly strong. The battle was a fierce one from the moment Willcox's men showed themselves on the open ground. Christ's brigade, taking advantage of all the cover the trees and inequalities of surface gave them, pushed on along the depression in which the road ran, a section of artillery keeping pace with them in the road. The direction of movement brought all the brigades of the first line in echelon, but Welsh soon fought his way up beside Christ, and they, together, drove the enemy successively from the fields and farm-yards till they reached the edge of the village. Upon the elevation on the right of the road was an orchard in which the shattered and diminished force of Jones made a final stand, but Willcox concentrated his artillery fire upon it, and his infantry was able to push forward and occupy it. They now partly occupied the town of Sharpsburg, and held the high ground commanding it on the south-east, where the national cemetery now is. The struggle had been long and bloody. It was half-past 4 in the afternoon, and ammunition had again run low, for the wagons had not been able to accompany the movement. Willcox paused for his men to take breath again, and to fetch up some cartridges; but meanwhile affairs were taking a serious turn on the left.

As Rodman's division went forward, he found the enemy before him seemingly detached from Willcox's opponents, and occupying ridges upon his left front, so that he was not able to keep his own connection with Willcox in the swinging movement to the right. Still, he made good progress in the face of stubborn resistance, though finding the enemy constantly developing more to his left, and the interval between him and Willcox widening. In fact his movement became practically by column of brigades. The view of the field to the south was now obstructed by fields of tall Indian corn, and under this cover Confederate troops approached the flank in line of battle. Scammon's officers in the reserve saw them as soon as Rodman's brigades echeloned, as these were toward the front and right. This hostile force proved to be A. P. Hill's division of six brigades, the last of Jackson's force to leave Harper's Ferry, and which had reached Sharpsburg since noon. Those first seen by Scammon's men were dressed in the National blue uniforms which they had captured at Harper's Ferry, and it was assumed that they were part of our own forces till they began to fire. Scammon quickly changed front to the left, drove back the enemy before him, and occupied a line of stone fences, which he held until he was withdrawn from it. Harland's brigade was partly moving in the corn-fields. One of his regiments was new, having been organized only three weeks, and the brigade had somewhat lost its order and connection when the sudden attack came. Rodman directed Colonel Harland to lead the right of the brigade, while he himself attempted to bring the left into position. In performing this duty he fell mortally wounded, and the brigade broke in confusion after a brief effort of its right wing to hold on. Fairchild, also, now received the fire on his left, and was forced to fall back and change front.

Being at the center when this break occurred on the left, I saw that it would be impossible to continue the movement to the right, and sent instant orders to Willcox and Crook to retire the left of their line, and to Sturgis to come forward into the gap made in Rodman's. The troops on the right swung back in perfect order; Scammon's brigade hung on at its stone-wall with unflinching tenacity till Sturgis had formed on the curving hill in rear of them, and Rodman's had found refuge behind. Willcox's left, then united with Sturgis and Scammon, was withdrawn to a new position on the left flank of the whole line. That these manœuvres on the field were really performed in good order is demonstrated by the fact that, although the break in Rodman's line was a bad one, the enemy was not able to capture many prisoners, the whole number of missing, out of the 2340 casualties which the Ninth Corps suffered in the battle, being 115, which includes wounded men unable to leave the field. The enemy were not lacking in bold efforts to take advantage of the check we had received, but were repulsed with severe punishment, and as the day declined were content to entrench themselves along the line of the road leading from Sharpsburg to the Potomac at the mouth of the Antietam, half a mile in our front. The men of the Ninth Corps lay that night upon their arms, the line being one which rested with both flanks near the Antietam, and curved outward upon the rolling hilltops which covered the bridge and commanded the plateau between us and the enemy. With my staff I lay upon the ground behind the troops, holding our horses by the bridles as we rested, for our orderlies were so exhausted that we could not deny them the same chance for a little broken slumber.

The conduct of the battle on the left has given rise to several criticisms, among which the most prominent has been that Porter's corps, which lay in reserve, was not put in at the same time with the Ninth Corps. McClellan answered this by saying that he did not think it prudent to divest the center of all reserve troops. No doubt a single strong division marching beyond the left flank of the Ninth Corps would have so occupied A. P. Hill's division that our movement into Sharpsburg could not have been checked, and, assisted by the advance of Sumner and Franklin on the right, apparently would have made certain the complete rout of Lee. As troops are put in reserve, not to diminish the army, but to be used in a pinch, I am deeply convinced that McClellan's refusal to use them on the left was the result of his continued conviction through all the day after Sedgwick's defeat, that Lee was overwhelmingly superior in force, and was preparing to return a crushing blow upon our right flank. He was keeping something in hand to cover a retreat, if that wing should be driven back. Except in this way, also, I am at a loss to account for the inaction of our right during the whole of our engagement on the left. Looking at our part of the battle as only a strong diversion to prevent or delay Lee's following up his success against Hooker and the rest, it is intelligible. I certainly so understood it at the time, as my report witnesses, and McClellan's preliminary report supports this view. If he had been impatient to have our attack delivered earlier, he had reason for double impatience that Franklin's fresh troops should assail Lee's left simultaneously with ours, unless he regarded action there as hopeless, and looked upon our movement as a sort of forlorn-hope to keep Lee from following up his advantages.

But even these are not all the troublesome questions requiring an answer. Couch's division had been left north-east of Maryland Heights to observe Jackson's command, supposed still to be in Harper's Ferry. Why could it not have come up on our left as well as A. P. Hill's division, which was the last of the Confederate troops to leave the Ferry, there being nothing to observe after it was gone? Couch's division, coming with equal pace with Hill's on the other side of the river, would have answered our needs as well as one from Porter's corps. Hill came, but Couch did not. Yet even then, a regiment of horse watching that flank and scouring the country as we swung it forward would have developed Hill's presence and enabled the commanding general either to stop our movement or to take the available means to support it; but the cavalry was put to no such use; it occupied the center of the whole line, only its artillery being engaged during the day. It would have been invaluable to Hooker in the morning as it would have been to us in the afternoon. McClellan had marched from Frederick City with the information that Lee's army was divided, Jackson being detached with a large force to take Harper's Ferry. He had put Lee's strength at 120,000 men. Assuming that there was still danger that Jackson might come upon our left with a large force, and that Lee had proven strong enough without Jackson to repulse three corps on our right and right center, McClellan might have regarded his own army as divided also for the purpose of meeting both opponents, and his cavalry would have been upon the flank of the part with which he was attacking Lee; Porter would have been in position to help either part in an extremity, or to cover a retreat, and Burnside would have been the only subordinate available to check Lee's apparent success. Will

259

any other hypothesis intelligibly account for McClellan's dispositions and orders? The error in the above assumption would be that McClellan estimated Lee's troops at nearly double their actual numbers, and that what was taken for proof of Lee's superiority in force on the field was a series of partial reverses which resulted directly from the piecemeal and disjointed way in which McClellan's morning attacks had been made.

The same explanation is the most satisfactory one that I can give for the inaction of Thursday, the 18th of September. Could McClellan have known the desperate condition of most of Lee's brigades he would have known that his own were in much better case, badly as they had suffered. I do not doubt that most of his subordinates discouraged the resumption of the attack, for the rooted belief in Lee's preponderance of numbers had been chronic in the army during the whole year. That belief was based upon the inconceivably mistaken reports of the secret service organization, accepted at headquarters, given to the War Department at Washington as a reason for incessant demands of reënforcements, and permeating downward through the whole organization till the error was accepted as truth by officers and men, and became a factor in their morale which can hardly be over-estimated. The result was that Lee retreated unmolested on the night of the 18th, and that what might have been a real and decisive success was a drawn battle in which our chief claim to victory was the possession of the field.

261

General Longstreet, at forty "Old Pete" to his men, was General Lee's stead-iest lieutenant and occasionally the most outspoken dissenter from his strategy, as his report of the Antietam campaign shows. The straggling he comments upon at the end of his account was, as he implies, connected to some extent with the "roasting ears" he mentions at the beginning; for the Southern sol-dier's insufficient diet accounted for much sickness and consequent straggling. Another factor is an interesting one. In some parts of the Confederacy, as in western North Carolina and eastern Tennessee, men of basic Unionist senti-ments joined Confederate armies, as they thought, to repel invasion and pro-tect their homes. When they were called upon to take part in an invasion in the other direction, some rationalized absenting themselves on moral grounds and others because such a threat to the North would strengthen the Union sol-dier's will to resist—as indeed it seemed to do both at Antietam and Gettys-burg.

"A field of blue as far as the eye could see"

BY JAMES LONGSTREET, LIEUTENANT-GENERAL, C. S. A.

WHEN the Second Bull Run campaign closed we had the most brilliant prospects the Confederates ever had. We then possessed an army which, had it been kept together, the Federals would never have dared attack. With such a splendid victory behind us, and such bright prospects ahead, the question arose as to whether or not we should go into Maryland. General Lee, on account of our short supplies, hesitated a little, but I reminded him of my experience in Mexico, where sometimes we were obliged to live two or three days on green corn. I told him we could not starve at that season of the year so long as the fields were loaded with "roasting ears." Finally he determined to go on, and accordingly crossed the river and went to Frederick City. On the 6th of September some of our cavalry, moving toward Harper's Ferry, became engaged with some of the Federal artillery near there. General Lee proposed that I should organize a force, and surround the garrison and capture it. I objected, and urged that our troops were worn with marching and were on short rations, and that it would be a bad idea to divide our forces while we were in the enemy's country, where he could get information, in six or eight hours, of any movement we might make. The Federal army, though beaten at the Second Manassas, was not disorganized, and it would certainly come out to look for us, and we should guard against being caught in such a condition. Our army consisted of a superior quality of soldiers, but it was in no condition to divide in the enemy's country. I urged that we should keep it well in hand, recruit our strength, and get up supplies, and then we could do anything we pleased. General Lee made no reply to this, and I supposed the Harper's Ferry scheme was abandoned. A day or two after we had reached Frederick City, I went up to General Lee's tent and found the front walls closed. I inquired for the general, and he, recognizing my voice, asked me to come in. I went in and found Jackson there. The two were discussing the move against Harper's Ferry, both heartily approving it. They had gone so far that it seemed useless for me to offer any further opposition, and I only suggested that Lee should use his entire army in the move instead of sending off a large portion of it to Hagerstown as he intended to do. General Lee so far changed the wording of his order as to require me to halt at Boonsboro' with General D. H. Hill; Jackson being ordered to Harper's Ferry *via* Bolivar Heights, on the south side; McLaws by the Maryland Heights on the north, and Walker, *via* Loudoun Heights, from the south-east. This was afterward changed, and I was sent on to Hagerstown, leaving D. H. Hill alone at South Mountain.

The movement against Harper's Ferry began on the 10th. Jackson made a wide, sweeping march around the Ferry, passing the Potomac at Williamsport, and moving from there on toward Martinsburg, and turning thence upon Harper's Ferry to make his attack by Bolivar Heights. McLaws made a hurried march to reach Maryland Heights before Jackson could get in position, and succeeded in doing so. With Maryland Heights in our possession the Federals could not hold their position there. McLaws put 200 or 300 men to each piece of his artillery and carried it up the heights, and was in position when Jackson came on the heights opposite. Simultaneously Walker appeared upon Loudoun Heights, south of the Potomac and east of the Shenandoah, thus completing the combination against the Federal garrison. The surrender of the Ferry and the twelve thousand Federal troops there was a matter of only a short time.

If the Confederates had been able to stop with that, they might have been well contented with their month's campaign. They had had a series of successes and no defeats; but the division of the army to make this attack on Harper's Ferry was a fatal error, as the subsequent events showed.

While a part of the army had gone toward Harper's Ferry I had moved up to Hagerstown. In the meantime Pope had been relieved and McClellan was in command of the army, and with ninety thousand refreshed troops was marching forth to avenge the Second Manassas. The situation was a very serious one for us. McClellan was close upon us. As we moved out of Frederick he came on and occupied that place, and there he came across a lost copy of the order assigning position to the several commands in the Harper's Ferry move.

This "lost order" has been the subject of much severe comment by Virginians who have written of the war. It was addressed to D. H. Hill, and they charged that its loss was due to him, and that the failure of the campaign was the result of the lost order. As General Hill has proved that he never received the order at his headquarters it must have been lost by some one else. Ordinarily, upon getting possession of such an order, the adversary would take it as a *ruse de guerre,* but it seems that General McClellan gave it his confidence, and made his dispositions accordingly. He planned his attack upon D. H. Hill under the impression that I was there with 12 brigades, 9 of which were really at Hagerstown, while R. H. Anderson's division was on Maryland Heights with General McLaws. Had McClellan exercised due diligence in seeking information from his own resources, he would have known better the situation at South Mountain and could have enveloped General D. H. Hill's division on the afternoon of the 13th, or early on the morning of the 14th, and then turned upon McLaws at Maryland Heights, before I could have reached either point. As it was, McClellan, after finding the order, moved with more confidence on toward South Mountain, where D. H. Hill was stationed as a Confederate rear-guard with five thousand men under his command. As I have stated, my command was at Hagerstown, thirteen miles farther on. General Lee was with me, and on the night of the 13th we received information that McClellan was at the foot of South Mountain with his great army. General Lee ordered me to march back to the mountain early the next morning. I suggested that, instead of meeting McClellan there, we withdraw Hill and unite my forces and Hill's at Sharpsburg, at the same time explaining that Sharpsburg was a strong defensive position from which we could strike the flank or rear of any force that might be sent to the relief of Harper's Ferry. I endeavored to show him that by making a forced march to Hill my troops would be in an exhausted condition and could not make a proper battle. Lee listened patiently enough, but did not change his plans, and directed that I should go back the next day and make a stand at the mountain. After lying down, my mind was still on the battle of the next day, and I was so impressed with the thought that it would be impossible for us to do anything at South Mountain with the fragments of a worn and exhausted army, that I rose and, striking a light, wrote a note to General Lee, urging him to order Hill away and concentrate at Sharpsburg. To that note I got no answer, and the next morning I marched as directed, leaving General Toombs, as ordered by General Lee, at Hagerstown to guard our trains and supplies.

We marched as hurriedly as we could over a hot and dusty road, and reached the mountain about 3 o'clock in the afternoon, with the troops much scattered and worn. In riding up the mountain to join General Hill I discovered that everything was in such disjointed condition that it would be impossible for my troops and Hill's to hold the mountain against such forces as McClellan had there, and wrote a note to General Lee, in which I stated that fact, and cautioned him to make his arrangements to retire that night. We got as many troops up as we could, and by putting in detachments here and there managed to hold McClellan in check until night, when Lee ordered the withdrawal to Sharpsburg.

On the afternoon of the 15th of September my command and Hill's crossed the Antietam Creek, and took position in front of Sharpsburg, my command filing into position on the right of the Sharpsburg and Boonsboro' turnpike, and D. H. Hill's division on the left. Soon after getting into position we found our left, at Dunker Church, the weak point, and Hood, with two brigades, was changed from my right to guard this point, leaving General D. H. Hill between the parts of my command.

That night, after we heard of the fall of Harper's Ferry, General Lee ordered Stonewall Jackson to march to Sharpsburg as rapidly as he could come. Then it was that we should have retired from Sharpsburg and gone to the Virginia side of the Potomac.

The moral effect of our move into Maryland had been lost by our discomfiture at South Mountain, and it was then evident we could not hope to concentrate in time to do more than make a respectable retreat, whereas by retiring before the battle we could have claimed a very successful campaign.

On the forenoon of the 15th, the blue uniforms of the Federals appeared among the trees that crowned the heights on the eastern bank of the Antietam. The number increased, and larger and larger grew the field of blue until it seemed to stretch as far as the eye could see, and from the tops of the mountains down to the edges of the stream gathered the great army of McClellan. It was an awe-inspiring spectacle as this grand force settled down in sight of the Confederates, then shattered by battles and scattered by long and tiresome marches. On the 16th Jackson came and took position with part of his command on my left. Before night the Federals attacked my left and gave us a severe fight, principally against Hood's division, but we drove them back, holding well our ground. After nightfall Hood was relieved from the position on the left, ordered to replenish his ammunition, and be ready to resume his first position on my right in the morning. General Jackson's forces, who relieved Hood, were extended to our left, reaching well back toward the Potomac, where most of our cavalry was. Toombs had joined us with two of his regiments, and was placed as guard on the bridge on my right. Hooker, who had thrown his corps against my left in the afternoon, was reënforced by the corps of Sumner and Mansfield. Sykes's division was also drawn into position for the impending battle. Burnside was over against my right, threatening the passage of the Antietam at that point. On the morning of the 17th the Federals were in good position along the Antietam, stretching up and down and across it to our left for three miles. They had a good position for their guns, which were of the most approved make and metal. Our position overcrowned theirs a little, but our guns were inferior and our ammunition was very imperfect.

Back of McClellan's line was a high ridge upon which was his signal station overlooking every point of our field. D. R. Jones's brigades of my command deployed on the right of the Sharpsburg pike, while Hood's brigades awaited orders. D. H. Hill was on the left extending toward the Hagerstown-Sharpsburg pike, and Jackson extended out from Hill's left toward the Potomac. The battle opened heavily with the attacks of the corps of Hooker, Mansfield, and Sumner against our left center, which consisted of Jackson's right and D. H. Hill's left. So severe and persistent were these attacks that I was obliged to send Hood to support our center. The Federals forced us back a little, however, and held this part of our position to the end of the day's work. With new troops and renewed efforts McClellan continued his attacks upon this point from time to time, while he brought his forces to bear against other points. The line swayed forward and back like a rope exposed to rushing currents. A force too heavy to be withstood would strike and drive in a weak point till we could collect a few fragments, and in turn force back the advance till our lost ground was recovered. A heroic effort was made by D. H. Hill, who collected some fragments and led a charge to drive back and recover our lost ground at the center. He soon found that his little band was too much exposed on its left flank and was obliged to abandon the attempt. Thus the battle ebbed and flowed with terrific slaughter on both sides.

The Federals fought with wonderful bravery and the Confederates clung to their ground with heroic courage as hour after hour they were mown down like grass. The fresh troops of McClellan literally tore into shreds the already ragged army of Lee, but the Confederates never gave back.

I remember at one time they were surging up against us with fearful numbers. I was occupying the left over by Hood, whose ammunition gave out. He retired to get a fresh supply. Soon after the Federals moved up against us in great masses.

We were under the crest of a hill occupying a position that ought to have been held by from four to six brigades. The only troops there were Cooke's regiment of North Carolina infantry, and they were without a cartridge. As I rode along the line with my staff I saw two pieces of the Washington Artillery (Miller's battery), but there were not enough men to man them. The gunners had been either killed or wounded. This was a fearful situation for the Confederate center. I put my staff-officers to the guns while I held their horses. It was easy to see that if the Federals broke through our line there, the Confederate army would be cut in two and probably destroyed, for we were already badly whipped and were only holding our ground by sheer force of desperation. Cooke sent me word that his ammunition was out. I replied that he must hold his position as long as he had a man left. He responded that he would show his colors as long as there was a man alive to hold them up. We loaded up our little guns with canister and sent a rattle of hail into the Federals as they came up over the crest of the hill.

That little battery shot harder and faster, with a sort of human energy, as though it realized that it was to hold the thousands of Federals at bay or the battle was lost. So warm was the reception we gave them that they dodged back behind the crest of the hill. We sought to make them believe we had many batteries before them. As the Federals would come up they would see the colors of the North Carolina regiment waving placidly and then would receive a shower of canister. We made it lively while it lasted. In the meantime General Chilton, General Lee's chief of staff, made his way to me and asked, "Where are the troops you are holding your line with?" I pointed to my two pieces and to Cooke's regiment, and replied, "There they are; but that regiment hasn't a cartridge."

Chilton's eyes popped as though they would come out of his head; he struck spurs to his horse and away he went to General Lee. I suppose he made some remarkable report, although I did not see General Lee again until night. After a little a shot came across the Federal front, plowing the ground in a parallel line. Another and another, each nearer and nearer their line. This enfilade fire, so distressing to soldiers, was from a battery on D. H. Hill's line, and it soon beat back the attacking column.

Meanwhile, R. H. Anderson and Hood came to our support and gave us more confidence. It was a little while only until another assault was made against D. H. Hill, and extending far over toward our left, where McLaws and Walker were supporting Jackson. In this desperate effort the lines seemed to swing back and forth for many minutes, but at last they settled down to their respective positions, the Confederates holding with a desperation which seemed to say, "We are here to die."

Meantime General Lee was over toward our right, where Burnside was trying to cross to the attack. Toombs, who had been assigned as guard at that point, did handsome service. His troops were footsore and worn from marching, and he had only four hundred men to meet the Ninth Corps. The little band fought bravely, but the Federals were pressing them slowly back. The delay that Toombs caused saved that part of the battle, however, for at the last moment A. P. Hill came in to reënforce him, and D. H. Hill discovered a good place for a battery and opened with it. Thus the Confederates were enabled to drive the Federals back, and when night settled down the army of Lee was still in possession of the field. But it was dearly bought, for thousands of brave soldiers were dead on the field and many gallant commands were torn as a forest in a cyclone. It was heart-rending to see how Lee's army had been slashed by the day's fighting.

Nearly one-fourth of the troops who went into the battle were killed or wounded. We were so badly crushed that at the close of the day ten thousand fresh troops could have come in and taken Lee's army and everything it had. But McClellan did not know it, and [apparently] feared, when Burnside was pressed back, that Sharpsburg was a Confederate victory, and that he would have to retire. As it was, when night settled down both armies were content to stay where they were. . . .

When the battle was over and night was gathering, I started to Lee's headquarters to make my report. In going through the town I passed a house that had been set afire and was still burning. The family was in great distress, and I stopped to do what I could for them. By that I was detained until after the other officers had reached headquarters and made their reports. My delay caused some apprehension on the part of General Lee that I had been hurt; in fact, such a report had been sent him. When I rode up and dismounted he seemed much relieved, and, coming to me very hurriedly for one of his dignified manner, threw his arms upon my shoulders and said:

"Here is my old war-horse at last."

When all the reports were in, General Lee decided that he would not be prepared the next day for offensive battle, and would prepare only for defense, as we had been doing.

The next day [the 18th] the Federals failed to advance, and both armies remained in position. During the day some of the Federals came over under a flag of truce to look after their dead and wounded. The following night we withdrew, passing the Potomac with our entire army. After we had crossed, the Federals made a show of pursuit, and a force of about fifteen hundred crossed the river and gave a considerable amount of trouble to the command under Pendleton. A. P. Hill was sent back with his division, and attacked the Federals who had crossed the river in pursuit of us. His lines extended beyond theirs, and he drove them back in great confusion. Some sprang over the bluffs of the river and were killed; some were drowned and others were shot.

Proceeding on our march, we went to Bunker Hill, where we remained for several days. A report was made of a Federal advance, but it turned out to be only a party of cavalry and amounted to nothing. As soon as the cavalry retired we moved back and camped around Winchester, where we remained until some time in October. Our stragglers continued to come in until November, which shows how many we had lost by severe marches.

The great mistake of the campaign was the division of Lee's army. If General Lee had kept his forces together, he could not have suffered defeat.

Here is a woman's view of Richmond at the time of the battles on the Peninsula. It is interesting not only for the pictures it paints but also for the sentimental nostalgia that runs through it. The recollection of defeat in a heroic cause, the sense of suffering intolerable wrong under fearful odds, the general drabness of life in an impoverished postwar land, the frustrated private hopes of a whole generation, the nostalgia for the better things of the past—all these combined to produce memoirs like the one which follows.

"The vast pity of it"

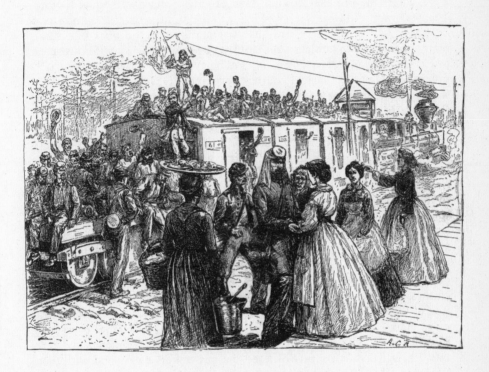

BY CONSTANCE CARY HARRISON

THE FIRST winter of the war was spent by our family in Richmond, where we found lodgings in a dismal rookery familiarly dubbed by its new occupants "The Castle of Otranto." It was the old-time Clifton Hotel, honeycombed by subterranean passages, and crowded to its limits with refugees like ourselves from country homes within or near the enemy's lines—or "'fugees," as we were all called. For want of any common sitting-room, we took possession of what had been a doctor's office, a few steps distant down the hilly street, fitting it up to the best of our ability; and there we received our friends, passing many merry hours. In rainy

271

weather we reached it by an underground passage-way from the hotel, an alley through the catacombs; and many a dignitary of camp or state will recall those "Clifton" evenings. Already the pinch of war was felt in the commissariat; and we had recourse occasionally to a contribution supper, or "Dutch treat," when the guests brought brandied peaches, boxes of sardines, French prunes, and bags of biscuit, while the hosts contributed only a roast turkey or a ham, with knives and forks. Democratic feasts those were, where major-generals and "high privates" met on an equal footing. The hospitable old town was crowded with the families of officers and members of the Government. One house was made to do the work of several, many of the wealthy citizens generously giving up their superfluous space to receive the new-comers. The only public event of note was the inauguration of Mr. Davis as President of the "Permanent Government" of the Confederate States, which we viewed by the courtesy of Mr. John R. Thompson, the State Librarian, from one of the windows of the Capitol, where, while waiting for the exercises to begin, we read "Harper's Weekly" and other Northern papers, the latest per underground express. That 22d of February was a day of pouring rain, and the concourse of umbrellas in the square beneath us had the effect of an immense mushroom-bed. As the bishop and the president-elect came upon the stand, there was an almost painful hush in the crowd. All seemed to feel the gravity of the trust our chosen leader was assuming. When he kissed the book a shout went up; but there was no elation visible as the people slowly dispersed. And it was thought ominous afterward, when the story was repeated, that, as Mrs. Davis, who had a Virginia Negro for coachman, was driven to the inauguration, she observed the carriage went at a snail's pace and was escorted by four Negro men in black clothes, wearing white cotton gloves and walking solemnly, two on either side of the equipage; she asked the coachman what such a spectacle could mean, and was answered, "Well, ma'am, you tole me to arrange everything as it should be; and this is the way we do in Richmon' at funerals and sich-like." Mrs. Davis promptly ordered the outwalkers away, and with them departed all the pomp and circumstance the occasion admitted of. In the mind of a Negro, everything of dignified ceremonial is always associated with a funeral.

About March 1st martial law was proclaimed in Richmond, and a fresh influx of refugees from Norfolk claimed shelter there. When the spring opened, as the spring does open in Richmond, with a sudden glory of green leaves, magnolia blooms, and flowers among the grass, our spirits rose after the depression of the latter months. If only to shake off the atmosphere of doubts and fears engendered by the long winter of disaster and uncertainty, the coming activity of arms was welcome! Personally speaking, there was vast improvement in our situation, since we had been fortunate enough to find a real home in a pleasant brown-walled house on Franklin street, divided from the pavement by a garden full of bounteous greenery, where it was easy to forget the discomforts of our previous mode of life. I shall not attempt to describe the rapidity with which thrilling excitements succeeded each other in our experiences in this house. The gathering of many troops around the town filled the streets with a continually moving panorama of war, and we spent our time in greeting, cheering, choking with sudden emotion, and quivering in anticipation of what was yet to follow. We had now finished other battle-flags, and one of them was bestowed upon the "Washington Artillery" of New Orleans, a body of admirable soldiers who had wakened to enthusiasm the daughters of Virginia in proportion, I dare say, to the woe they had created among the daughters of Louisiana in bidding them good-bye. One morning an orderly arrived to request that the ladies would be out upon the veranda at a given hour; and, punctual to the time fixed, the travel-stained battalion filed past our house. These were no holiday soldiers. Their gold was tarnished and their scarlet faded by sun and wind and gallant service—they were veterans now on their way to the front, where the call of duty never failed to find the flower of Louisiana. As they came in line with us, the officers saluted with their swords, the band struck up "My Maryland," the tired soldiers sitting upon the caissons that dragged heavily through the muddy street set up a rousing cheer. And there in the midst of them, taking the April wind with daring color, was our flag, dipping low until it passed us! One must grow old and cold indeed before such things are forgotten.

A few days later, on coming out of church—it is a curious fact that most of our exciting news spread over Richmond on Sunday, and just at that hour—we heard of the crushing blow of the fall of New Orleans and the destruction of our iron-clads. My brother had just reported aboard one of those splendid ships, as yet unfinished. As the news came directly from our kinsman, General Randolph, the Secretary of War, there was no doubting it; and while the rest of us broke into lamentation, Mr. Jules de St. Martin, the brother-in-law of Mr. Judah P. Benjamin, merely shrugged his shoulders, with a thoroughly characteristic gesture, making no remark.

"This must affect your interests," some one said to him inquiringly.

"I am ruined, *voilà tout!*" was the rejoinder—and this was soon confirmed.

This debonair little gentleman was one of the greatest favorites of our war society in Richmond. His cheerfulness, his wit, his exquisite courtesy, made him friends everywhere; and although his nicety of dress, after the pattern of the *boulevardier fini* of Paris, was the subject of much wonderment to the populace when he first appeared upon the streets, it did not prevent him from joining the volunteers before Richmond when occasion called, and roughing it in the trenches like a veteran. His cheerful endurance of hardship during a freezing winter of camp life became a proverb in the army later in the siege. . . .

And now we come to the 31st of May, 1862, when the eyes of the whole continent turned to Richmond. On that day Johnston assaulted the Federals who had been advanced to Seven Pines. In face of recent reverses, we in Richmond had begun to feel like the prisoner of the Inquisition in Poe's story, cast into a dungeon of slowly contracting walls. With the sound of guns, therefore, in the direction of Seven Pines, every heart leaped as if deliverance were at hand. And yet there was no joy in the wild pulsation, since those to whom we looked for succor were our own flesh and blood, barring the way to a foe of superior numbers, abundantly provided, as we were not, with all the equipments of modern warfare, and backed by a mighty nation as determined as ourselves to win. Hardly a family in the town whose father, son, or brother was not part and parcel of the defending army.

When on the afternoon of the 31st it became known that the engagement had begun, the women of Richmond were still going about their daily vocations quietly, giving no sign of the inward anguish of apprehension. There was enough to do now in preparation for the wounded; yet, as events proved, all that was done was not enough by half. Night brought a lull in the cannonading. People lay down dressed upon beds, but not to sleep, while the weary soldiers slept upon their arms. Early next morning the whole town was on the street. Ambulances, litters, carts, every vehicle that the city could produce, went and came with a ghastly burden; those who could walk limped painfully home, in some cases so black with gunpowder they passed unrecognized. Women with pallid faces flitted bareheaded through the streets searching for their dead or wounded. The churches were thrown open, many people visiting them for a sad communion-service or brief time of prayer; the lecture-rooms of various places of worship were crowded with ladies volunteering to sew, as fast as fingers could fly, the rough beds called for by the surgeons. Men too old or infirm to fight went on horseback or afoot to meet the returning ambulances, and in some cases served as escort to their own dying sons. By afternoon of the day following the battle, the streets were one vast hospital. To find shelter for the sufferers a number of unused buildings were thrown open. I remember, especially, the St. Charles Hotel, a gloomy place, where two young girls went to look for a member of their family, reported wounded. We had tramped in vain over pavements burning with the intensity of the sun, from one scene of horror to another, until our feet and brains alike seemed about to serve us no further. The cool of those vast dreary rooms of the St. Charles was refreshing; but such a spectacle! Men in every stage of mutilation lying on the bare boards, with perhaps a haversack or an army blanket beneath their heads—some dying, all suffering keenly, while waiting their turn to be attended to. To be there empty-handed and impotent nearly broke our hearts. We passed from one to the other, making such slight additions to their comfort as were possible, while looking in every upturned face in dread to find the object of our search.

This sorrow, I may add, was spared, the youth arriving at home later with a slight flesh-wound. The condition of things at this and other improvised hospitals was improved next day by the offerings from many churches of pew-cushions, which, sewn together, served as comfortable beds; and for the remainder of the war their owners thanked God upon bare benches for every "misery missed" that was "mercy gained." To supply food for the hospitals the contents of larders all over town were emptied into baskets; while cellars long sealed and cobwebbed, belonging to the old Virginia gentry who knew good Port and Madeira, were opened by the Ithuriel's spear of universal sympathy. There was not much going to bed that night, either; and I remember spending the greater part of it leaning from my window to seek the cool night air, while wondering as to the fate of those near to me. There was a summons to my mother about midnight. Two soldiers came to tell her of the wounding of one close of kin; but she was already on duty elsewhere, tireless and watchful as ever. Up to that time the younger girls had been regarded as superfluities in hospital service; but on Monday two of us found a couple of rooms where fifteen wounded men lay upon pallets around the floor, and, on offering our services to the surgeons in charge, were proud to have them accepted and to be installed as responsible nurses, under direction of an older and more experienced woman. The constant activity our work entailed was a relief from the strained excitement of life after the battle of Seven Pines. When the first flurry of distress was over, the residents of those pretty houses standing back in gardens full of roses set their cooks to work, or, better still, went themselves into the kitchen, to compound delicious messes for the wounded, after the appetizing old Virginia recipes. Flitting about the streets in the direction of the hospitals were smiling, white-jacketed Negroes, carrying silver trays with dishes of fine porcelain under napkins of thick white damask, containing soups, creams, jellies, thin biscuit, eggs *à la crême,* boiled chicken, etc., surmounted by clusters of freshly gathered flowers. A year later we had cause to pine after these culinary glories when it came to measuring out, with sinking hearts, the meager portions of milk and food we could afford to give our charges.

As an instance, however, that quality in food was not always appreciated by the patients, my mother urged upon one of her sufferers (a gaunt and soft-voiced Carolinian from the "piney woods district") a delicately served trifle from some neighboring kitchen.

"Jes ez you say, old miss," was the weary answer; "I ain't a-contradictin' you. It mout be good for me, but my stomick's kinder sot agin it. There ain't but one thing I'm sorter yarnin' arter, an' that's a dish o' greens en bacon fat, with a few molarses poured onto it."

From our patients, when they could syllable the tale, we had accounts of the fury of the fight, which were made none the less horrible by such assistance as imagination could give to the facts. I remember they told us of

275

shot thrown from the enemy's batteries, that plowed their way through lines of flesh and blood before exploding in showers of musket-balls to do still further havoc. Before these awful missiles, it was said, our men had fallen in swaths, the living closing over them to press forward in the charge.

It was at the end of one of these narrations that a piping voice came from a pallet in the corner: "They fit right smart, them Yanks did, I tell *you!*" and not to laugh was as much of an effort as it had just been not to cry.

From one scene of death and suffering to another we passed during those days of June. Under a withering heat that made the hours preceding dawn the only ones of the twenty-four endurable in point of temperature, and a shower-bath the only form of diversion we had time or thought to indulge in, to go out-of-doors was sometimes worse than remaining in our wards. But one night after several of us had been walking about town in a state of panting exhaustion, palm-leaf fans in hand, a friend persuaded us to ascend to the small platform on the summit of the Capitol, in search of fresher air. To reach it was like going through a vapor-bath, but an hour amid the cool breezes above the tree-tops of the square was a thing of joy unspeakable.

Day by day we were called to our windows by the wailing dirge of a military band preceding a soldier's funeral. One could not number those sad pageants: the coffin crowned with cap and sword and gloves, the riderless horse following with empty boots fixed in the stirrups of an army saddle; such soldiers as could be spared from the front marching after with arms reversed and crape-enfolded banners; the passers-by standing with bare, bent heads. Funerals less honored outwardly were continually occurring. Then and thereafter the green hillsides of lovely Hollywood were frequently upturned to find resting-places for the heroic dead. So much taxed for time and for attendants were those who officiated that it was not unusual to perform the last rites for the departed at night. A solemn scene was that in the July moonlight, when, in the presence of the few who valued him most, we laid to rest one of my own nearest kinsmen, of whom in the old service of the United States, as in that of the Confederacy, it was said, "He was a spotless knight."

Spite of its melancholy uses, there was no more favorite walk in Richmond than Hollywood, a picturesquely beautiful spot, where high hills sink into velvet undulations, profusely shaded with holly, pine, and cedar, as well as by trees of deciduous foliage. In spring the banks of the stream that runs through the valley were enameled with wild flowers, and the thickets were full of May-blossom and dogwood. Mounting to the summit of the bluff, one may sit under the shade of some ample oak, to view the spires and roofs of the town, with the white colonnade of the distant Capitol. Richmond, thus seen beneath her verdant foliage, "upon hills, girdled by hills," confirms what an old writer felt called to exclaim about it, "Verily, this city hath a pleasant seat." On the right, below this point, flows the rushing yellow river, making ceaseless turmoil around islets of rock whose rifts are full of birch and willow, or leaping impetuously over the bowlders of granite that strew its bed. Old-time Richmond folk used to say that the sound of their favorite James (or, to be exact, "Jeems") went with them into foreign countries, during no matter how many years of absence, haunting them like a strain of sweetest music; nor would they permit a suggestion of superiority in the flavor of any other fluid to that of a draught of its amber waters. So blent with my own memories of war is the voice of that tireless river, that I seem to hear it yet, over the tramp of rusty battalions, the short imperious stroke of the alarm-bell, the clash of passing bands, the gallop of eager horsemen, the roar of battle, the moan of hospitals, the stifled note of sorrow!

During all this time President Davis was a familiar and picturesque figure on the streets, walking through the Capitol square from his residence to the executive office in the morning, not to return until late in the afternoon, or riding just before nightfall to visit one or another of the encampments near the city. He was tall, erect, slender, and of a dignified and soldierly bearing, with clear-cut and high-bred features, and of a demeanor of stately courtesy to all. He was clad always in Confederate gray cloth, and wore a soft felt hat with wide brim. Afoot, his step was brisk and firm; in the saddle he rode admirably and with a martial aspect. His early life had been spent in the Military Academy at West Point and upon the then north-western frontier in the Black Hawk War, and he afterward greatly distinguished himself at Monterey and Buena Vista in Mexico; at the time when we knew him, everything in his appearance and manner was suggestive of such a training. He was reported to feel quite out of place in the office of President, with executive and administrative duties, in the midst of such a war; General Lee always spoke of him as the best of military advisers; his own inclination was to be with the army, and at the first tidings of sound of a gun, anywhere within reach of Richmond, he was in the saddle and off for the spot—to the dismay of his staff-officers, who were expected to act as an escort on such occasions, and who never knew at what hour of the night or of the next day they should get back to bed or to a meal. . . .

When on the 27th of June the Seven Days' strife began, there was none of the excitement that had attended the battle of Seven Pines. People had shaken themselves down, as it were, to the grim reality of a fight that must be fought. "Let the war bleed, and let the mighty fall," was the spirit of their cry.

It is not my purpose to deal with the history of those awful Seven Days. Mine only to speak of the other side of that canvas in which heroes of two armies were passing and repassing, as on some huge Homeric frieze, in the manœuvres of a strife that hung our land in mourning. The scars of war are healed when this is written, and the vast "pity of it" fills the heart that wakes the retrospect.

As in all great wars of rebellion, the Civil War was not waged across any well-defined frontiers. The lines and areas of occupation, especially in the mid-South, were fluid, changing from week to week. Civilians—some active partisans, some not—frequently crossed the lines of temporary, vague demarcation, and far behind those lines were to be found islands of dissent or actual resistance, represented by both individuals and groups. The Confederacy operated a remarkably regular courier service to the North, below Washington between the Maryland and Virginia shores. The mountain areas of the South—for example, eastern Tennessee—were solidly Unionist in their sentiments. And in the Confederate forces were men of states' rights conviction like the Pennsylvanian, Pemberton, the defender of Vicksburg; while on the Union side were loyalists like the Virginian, Farragut. All these conditions, in which no one's allegiance could be presupposed, made it possible in the spring of 1862 for twenty Union men to infiltrate the Confederate lines in Georgia, steal a railroad train and set out upon one of the most exciting adventures of the war.

"We heard the scream of a locomotive bearing down upon us"

THE LOCOMOTIVE CHASE IN GEORGIA

BY THE REV. WILLIAM PITTENGER, 2D OHIO VOLUNTEERS, ONE OF THE RAIDERS

THE railroad raid in Georgia in the spring of 1862 has always been considered to rank high among the striking and novel events of the civil war. At that time General O. M. Mitchel, under whose authority it was organized, commanded Union forces in Middle Tennessee, consisting of a division of Buell's Army. The Confederates were concentrating at Corinth, Miss., and Grant and Buell were advancing by different routes toward that point. Mitchel's orders required him to protect Nashville and the country around, but allowed him latitude in the disposition of his division, which, with detachments and garrisons, numbered nearly seventeen thousand men. His attention had long been turned toward the liberation of East Tennessee, which he knew President Lincoln also earnestly desired, and which would, if achieved, strike a most damaging blow at the resources of the Rebellion. A Union army once in possession of East Tennessee would have the inestimable advantage, found nowhere else in the South, of operating in the midst of a friendly population, and having at hand abundant supplies of all

279

kinds. Mitchel had no reason to believe that Corinth would detain the Union armies much longer than Fort Donelson had done, and was satisfied that as soon as it had been captured, the next movement would be eastward toward Chattanooga, thus throwing his own division in advance. He determined, therefore, to press into the heart of the enemy's country as far as possible, occupying strategical points before they were adequately defended.

On the 8th of April, 1862—the day after the battle of Pittsburg Landing, of which, however, Mitchel had received no intelligence—he marched swiftly southward from Shelbyville and seized Huntsville, in Alabama, on the 11th of April, and then sent a detachment westward over the Memphis and Charleston railroad to open railway communication with the Union army at Pittsburg Landing.

Another detachment, commanded by Mitchel in person, advanced on the same day 70 miles by rail directly into the enemy's territory, arriving unchecked within 30 miles of Chattanooga. In two hours' time he could have reached that point, the most important position in the West, with 2000 men. Why did he not go? The story of the railroad raid is the answer.

The night before breaking camp at Shelbyville, Mitchel sent an expedition secretly into the heart of Georgia to cut the railroad communications of Chattanooga to the south and east. The fortune of this attempt had a most important bearing upon his movements, and will now be narrated.

In the employ of General Buell was a spy, named James J. Andrews, who had rendered valuable services in the first year of the war, and had secured the confidence of the Union commanders. In March, 1862, Buell had sent him secretly with eight men to burn the bridges west of Chattanooga; but the failure of expected coöperation defeated the plan, and Andrews, after visiting Atlanta, and inspecting the whole of the enemy's lines in that vicinity and northward, had returned, ambitious to make another attempt. His plans for the second raid were submitted to Mitchel, and on the eve of the movement from Shelbyville to Huntsville, the latter authorized him to take twenty-four men, secretly enter the enemy's territory, and, by means of capturing a train, burn the bridges on the northern part of the Georgia State railroad, and also one on the East Tennessee railroad where it approaches the Georgia State line, thus completely isolating Chattanooga, which was then virtually ungarrisoned.

The soldiers for this expedition, of whom the writer was one, were selected from the three Ohio regiments belonging to General J. W. Sill's brigade, being simply told that they were wanted for secret and very dangerous service. So far as known not a man chosen declined the perilous honor. Our uniforms were exchanged for ordinary Southern dress, and all arms, except revolvers, were left in camp. On the 7th of April, by the roadside about a mile east of Shelbyville, in the late twilight, we met our leader. Taking us a little way from the road he quietly placed before us the outlines of the romantic and adventurous plan, which was: to break into small detachments of three or four, journey eastward into the mountains, and then work southward, traveling by rail after we were well within the Confederate lines, and finally meet Andrews at Marietta, Georgia, more than 200 miles away, the evening of the third day after the start. When questioned, we were to profess ourselves Kentuckians going to join the Southern army.

On the journey we were a good deal annoyed by the swollen streams and the muddy roads consequent on three days of almost ceaseless rain. Andrews was led to believe that Mitchel's column would be inevitably delayed, and as we were expected to destroy the bridges the very day that Huntsville was entered, he took the responsibility of sending word to our different groups that our attempt would be postponed one day—from Friday to Saturday, April 12th. This was a natural but a most lamentable error of judgment.

One of the men was belated and did not join us at all. Two others were very soon captured by the enemy, and though their true character was not detected, they were forced into the Southern army, and two, who reached Marietta, failed to report at the rendezvous. Thus, when we assembled, very early in the morning, in Andrews's room at the Marietta Hotel for final consultation before the blow was struck, we were but twenty, including our leader. All preliminary difficulties had been easily overcome, and we were in good spirits. But some serious obstacles had been revealed on our ride from Chattanooga to Marietta the previous evening. The railroad was found to be crowded with trains, and many soldiers were among the passengers. Then the station—Big Shanty—at which the capture was to be effected had recently been made a Confederate camp. To succeed in our enterprise it would be necessary first to capture the engine in a guarded camp, with soldiers standing around as spectators, and then to run it from 100 to 200 miles through the enemy's country, and to deceive or overpower all trains that should be met—a large contract for twenty men! Some of our party thought the chances of success so slight, under existing circumstances, that they urged the abandonment of the whole enterprise. But Andrews declared his purpose to succeed or die, offering to each man, however, the privilege of withdrawing from the attempt—an offer no one was in the least disposed to accept. Final instructions were then given, and we hurried to the ticket office in time for the northward bound mail train, and purchased tickets for different stations along the line in the direction of Chattanooga.

Our ride as passengers was but eight miles. We swept swiftly around the base of Kenesaw Mountain, and soon saw the tents of the forces camped at Big Shanty (now Kenesaw Station) gleam white in the morning mist. Here we were to stop for breakfast and attempt the seizure of the train. The morning was raw and gloomy, and a rain, which fell all day, had already begun. It was a painfully thrilling moment! We were but twenty, with an army about us and a long and difficult road before us crowded with enemies. In an instant

281

we were to throw off the disguise which had been our only protection, and trust our leader's genius and our own efforts for safety and success. Fortunately we had not time for giving way to reflections and conjectures which could only unfit us for the stern task ahead.

When we stopped, the conductor, engineer, and many of the passengers hurried to breakfast, leaving the train unguarded. Now was the moment of action! Ascertaining that there was nothing to prevent a rapid start, Andrews, our two engineers, Brown and Knight, and the fireman hurried forward, uncoupling a section of the train consisting of three empty baggage or box cars, the locomotive and tender. The engineers and fireman sprang into the cab of the engine, while Andrews, with hand on the rail and foot on the step, waited to see that the remainder of the band had gained entrance into the rear box car. This seemed difficult and slow, though it really consumed but a few seconds, for the car stood on a considerable bank, and the first who came were pitched in by their comrades, while these, in turn, dragged in the others, and the door was instantly closed. A sentinel, with musket in hand, stood not a dozen feet from the engine watching the whole proceeding, but before he or any of the soldiers and guards around could make up their minds to interfere, all was done, and Andrews, with a nod to his engineer, stepped on board. The valve was pulled wide open, and for a moment the wheels of the "General" slipped around ineffectively; then, with a bound that jerked the soldiers in the box car from their feet, the little train darted away, leaving the camp and station in the wildest uproar and confusion. The first step of the enterprise was triumphantly accomplished.

According to the time-table, of which Andrews had secured a copy, there were two trains to be met. These presented no serious hindrance to our attaining high speed, for we could tell just where to expect them. There was also a local freight not down on the time-table, but which could not be far distant. Any danger of collision with it could be avoided by running according to the schedule of the captured train until it was passed; then, at the highest possible speed, we would run to the Oostenaula and Chickamauga bridges, lay them in ashes, and pass on through Chattanooga to Mitchel, at Huntsville, or wherever eastward of that point he might be found, arriving long before the close of the day. It was a brilliant prospect, and, so far as human estimates can determine, it would have been realized had the day been Friday instead of Saturday. On Friday every train had been on time, the day dry, and the road in perfect order. Now the road was in disorder, every train far behind time, and two "extras" were approaching us. But of these unfavorable conditions we knew nothing, and pressed confidently forward.

We stopped frequently, at one point tore up the track, cut telegraph wires, and loaded on cross-ties to be used in bridge burning. Wood and water were taken without difficulty, Andrews telling, very coolly, the story to which he adhered throughout the run, namely, that he was an agent of General Beauregard's running an impressed powder train through to that officer at Corinth. We had no good instruments for track-raising, as we had intended rather to depend upon fire; but the amount of time spent in taking up a rail was not material at this stage of our journey, as we easily kept on the time of our captured train. There was a wonderful exhilaration in passing swiftly by towns and stations through the heart of an enemy's country in this manner. It possessed just enough of the spice of danger—in this part of the run—to render it thoroughly enjoyable. The slightest accident to our engine, however, or a miscarriage in any part of our programme, would have completely changed the conditions.

At Etowah Station we found the "Yonah," an old locomotive owned by an iron company, standing with steam up; but not wishing to alarm the enemy till the local freight had been safely met, we left it unharmed. Kingston, thirty miles from the starting-point, was safely reached. A train from Rome, Ga., on a branch road, had just arrived and was waiting for the morning mail— our train. We learned that the local freight would soon come also, and, taking the side track, waited for it. When it arrived, however, Andrews saw to his surprise and chagrin that it bore a red flag, indicating another train not far behind. Stepping to the conductor, he boldly asked, "What does it mean that the road is blocked in this manner when I have orders to take this powder to Beauregard without a minute's delay?" The answer was interesting but not reassuring: "Mitchel has captured Huntsville and is said to be coming to Chattanooga, and we are getting everything out of there." He was asked by Andrews to pull his train a long way down the track out of the way, and promptly obeyed.

It seemed an exceedingly long time before the expected "extra" arrived; and when it did come it bore another red flag! The reason given was that the "local," being too great for one engine, had been made up in two sections, and the second section would doubtless be along in a short time. This was terribly vexatious; yet there seemed nothing to do but wait. To start out between the sections of an extra train would be to court destruction. There were already three trains around us, and their many passengers, and others, were growing very curious about the mysterious train which had arrived on the time of the morning mail, manned by strangers. *For an hour and five minutes* from the time of arrival at Kingston, we remained in this most critical position. The sixteen of us who were shut up tightly in a box car, personating Beauregard's ammunition—hearing sounds outside, but unable to distinguish words—had perhaps the most trying position. Andrews sent us, by one of the engineers, a cautious warning to be ready to fight in case the uneasiness of the crowd around led them to make any investigation, while he himself kept near the station to prevent the sending off of any alarming telegram. So intolerable was our suspense that the order for a deadly conflict would have been felt as a relief. But the assurance of Andrews quieted the crowd until the whistle of the expected train from the north was heard; then, as it glided up to the depot, past the end of our side track, we were off without more words.

But unexpected danger had arisen behind us. Out of the panic at Big Shanty two men emerged, determined, if possible, to foil the unknown captors of their train. There was no telegraph station, and no locomotive at hand with which to follow; but the conductor of the train, W. A. Fuller, and Anthony Murphy, foreman of the Atlanta railway machine shops, who happened to be on board of Fuller's train, started on foot after us as hard as they could run! Finding a hand-car they mounted it and pushed forward till they neared Etowah, where they ran on the break we had made in the road and were precipitated down the embankment into the ditch. Continuing with more caution, they reached Etowah and found the "Yonah," which was at once pressed into service, loaded with soldiers who were at hand, and hurried with flying wheels toward Kingston. Fuller prepared to fight at that point, for he knew of the tangle of extra trains, and of the lateness of the regular trains, and did not think we would be able to pass. We had been gone only four minutes when he arrived and found himself stopped by three long, heavy trains of cars headed in the wrong direction. To move them out of the way so as to pass would cause a delay he was little inclined to afford—would indeed have almost certainly given us the victory. So, abandoning his engine, he, with Murphy, ran across to the Rome train, and, uncoupling the engine and one car, pushed forward with about forty armed men. As the Rome branch connected with the main road above the depot, he encountered no hindrance, and it was now a fair race. We were not many minutes ahead.

Four miles from Kingston we again stopped and cut the telegraph. While trying to take up a rail at this point, we were greatly startled. One end of the rail was loosened and eight of us were pulling at it, when distant, but distinct, we heard the whistle of a pursuing engine! With a frantic pull we broke the rail and all tumbled over the embankment with the effort. We moved on, and at Adairsville we found a mixed train (freight and passenger) waiting, but there was an express on the road that had not yet arrived. We could afford no more delay, and set out for the next station, Calhoun, at terrible speed, hoping to reach that point before the express, which was behind time, should arrive. The nine miles which we had to travel were left behind in less than the same number of minutes! The express was just pulling out, but, hearing our whistle, backed before us until we were able to take the side track; it stopped, however, in such a manner as completely to close up the other end of the switch. The two trains, side by side, almost touched each other, and our precipitate arrival caused natural suspicion. Many searching questions were asked which had to be answered before we could get the opportunity of proceeding. We, in the box car, could hear the altercation and were almost sure that a fight would be necessary before the conductor would consent to "pull up" in order to let us out. Here, again, our position was most critical, for the pursuers were rapidly approaching.

Fuller and Murphy saw the obstruction of the broken rail, in time to prevent wreck, by reversing their engine; but the hindrance was for the present insuperable. Leaving all their men behind, they started for a second foot-race. Before they had gone far they met the train we had passed at Adairsville and turned it back after us. At Adairsville they dropped the cars, and, with locomotive and tender loaded with armed men, they drove forward at the highest speed possible. They knew that we were not many minutes ahead, and trusted to overhaul us before the express train could be safely passed.

But Andrews had told the powder story again, with all his skill, and had added a direct request in peremptory form to have the way opened before him, which the Confederate conductor did not see fit to resist; and just before the pursuers arrived at Calhoun we were again under way. Stopping once more to cut wires and tear up the track, we felt a thrill of exhilaration to which we had long been strangers. The track was now clear before us to Chattanooga; and even west of that city we had good reason to believe that we would find no other train in the way till we had reached Mitchel's lines. If one rail could now be lifted we would be in a few minutes at Oostenaula bridge, and, that burned, the rest of the task would be little more than simple manual labor, with the enemy absolutely powerless. We worked with a will.

But in a moment the tables were turned! Not far behind we heard the scream of a locomotive bearing down upon us at lightning speed! The men on board were in plain sight and well armed! Two minutes—perhaps one— would have removed the rail at which we were toiling; then the game would have been in our own hands, for there was no other locomotive beyond that could be turned back after us. But the most desperate efforts were in vain. The rail was simply bent, and we hurried to our engine and darted away, while remorselessly after us thundered the enemy.

Now the contestants were in clear view, and a most exciting race followed. Wishing to gain a little time for the burning of the Oostenaula bridge we dropped one car, and shortly after, another; but they were "picked up" and pushed ahead to Resaca station. We were obliged to run over the high trestles and covered bridge at that point without a pause. This was the first failure in the work assigned us.

The Confederates could not overtake and stop us on the road, but their aim was to keep close behind so that we might not be able to damage the road or take in water. In the former they succeeded, but not the latter. Both engines were put at the highest rate of speed. We were obliged to cut the wire after every station passed, in order that an alarm might not be sent ahead, and we constantly strove to throw our pursuer off the track or to obstruct the road permanently in some way so that we might be able to burn the Chickamauga

285

bridges, still ahead. The chances seemed good that Fuller and Murphy would be wrecked. We broke out the end of our last box car and dropped cross-ties on the track as we ran, thus checking their progress and getting far enough ahead to take in wood and water at two separate stations. Several times we almost lifted a rail, but each time the coming of the Confederates, within rifle range, compelled us to desist and speed on. Our worst hindrance was the rain. The previous day (Friday) had been clear, with a high wind, and on such a day fire would have been easily and tremendously effective. But to-day a bridge could be burned only with abundance of fuel and careful nursing.

Thus we sped on, mile after mile, in this fearful chase, around curves and past stations in seemingly endless perspective. Whenever we lost sight of the enemy beyond a curve we hoped that some of our obstructions had been effective in throwing him from the track and that we would see him no more; but at each long reach backward the smoke was again seen, and the shrill whistle was like the scream of a bird of prey. The time could not have been so very long, for the terrible speed was rapidly devouring the distance, but with our nerves strained to the highest tension each minute seemed an hour. On several occasions the escape of the enemy from wreck seemed little less than miraculous. At one point a rail was placed across the track so skillfully on a curve that it was not seen till the train ran upon it at full speed. Fuller says that they were terribly jolted, and seemed to bounce altogether from the track, but lighted on the rails in safety. Some of the Confederates wished to leave a train which was driven at such a reckless rate, but their wishes were not gratified.

Before reaching Dalton we urged Andrews to turn and attack the enemy, laying an ambush so as to get into close quarters that our revolvers might be on equal terms with their guns. I have little doubt that if this had been carried out it would have succeeded. But Andrews—whether because he thought the chance of wrecking or obstructing the enemy still good, or feared that the country ahead had been alarmed by a telegram around the Confederacy by the way of Richmond—merely gave the plan his sanction without making any attempt to carry it into execution.

Dalton was passed without difficulty, and beyond we stopped again to cut wires and obstruct the track. It happened that a regiment was encamped not a hundred yards away, but they did not molest us. Fuller had written a dispatch to Chattanooga, and dropped a man with orders to have it forwarded instantly while he pushed on to save the bridges. Part of the message got through and created a wild panic in Chattanooga, although it did not materially influence our fortunes. Our supply of fuel was now very short, and without getting rid of our pursuer long enough to take in more, it was evident that we could not run as far as Chattanooga.

While cutting the wire we made an attempt to get up another rail, but the enemy, as usual, were too quick for us. We had no tool for this purpose except a wedge-pointed iron bar. Two or three bent iron claws for pulling out spikes would have given us such superiority, that, down to almost the last of our run, we would have been able to escape and to burn all the Chickamauga bridges. But it had not been our intention to rely on this mode of obstruction —an emergency only rendered necessary by our unexpected delay and the pouring rain.

We made no attempt to damage the long tunnel north of Dalton, as our enemies had greatly dreaded. The last hope of the raid was now staked upon an effort of a different kind. A few more obstructions were dropped on the track and our speed was increased so that we soon forged a considerable distance ahead. The side and end boards of the last car were torn into shreds, all available fuel was piled upon it, and blazing brands were brought back from the engine. By the time we approached a long covered bridge the fire in the car was fairly started. We uncoupled it in the middle of the bridge, and with painful suspense awaited the issue. Oh, for a few minutes till the work of conflagration was fairly begun! There was still steam-pressure enough in our boiler to carry us to the next wood-yard, where we could have replenished our fuel, by force if necessary, so as to run as near to Chattanooga as was deemed prudent. We did not know of the telegraph message which the pursuers had sent ahead. But, alas! the minutes were not given. Before the bridge was extensively fired the enemy was upon us. They pushed right into the smoke and drove the burning car before them to the next side-track.

With no car left, and no fuel, the last scrap having been thrown into the engine or upon the burning car, and with no obstruction to drop on the track, our situation was indeed desperate.

But it might still be possible to save ourselves if we left the train in a body and took a direct course toward the Union lines. Confederate pursuers with whom I have since conversed have agreed on two points—that we could have escaped in the manner here pointed out; and that an attack on the pursuing train would likely have been successful. But Andrews thought otherwise, at least in relation to the former plan, and ordered us to jump from the locomotive, and, dispersing in the woods, each endeavor to save himself.

The question is often asked, "Why did you not reverse your engine and thus wreck the one following?" Wanton injury was no part of our plan, and we could not afford to throw away our engine till the last extremity. When the raiders were jumping off, however, the engine was reversed and driven back, but by that time the steam was so nearly exhausted that the Confederate engine had no difficulty in reversing and receiving the shock without injury. Both were soon at a stand-still, and the Confederates, reënforced by a party from a train which soon arrived on the scene—the express passenger, which had been turned back at Calhoun—continued the chase on foot.

It is easy now to understand why Mitchel paused thirty miles west of Chattanooga. The Andrews raiders had been forced to stop eighteen miles south of the same town, and no flying train met Mitchel with tidings that all the railroad communications of Chattanooga were destroyed, and that the town was in a panic and undefended.

A few words will give the sequel to this remarkable enterprise. The hunt for the fugitive raiders was prompt, energetic, and successful. Several were captured the same day, and all but two within a week. Even these two were overtaken and brought back, when they supposed that they were virtually out of danger. Two who had reached Marietta, but had failed to board the train (J. R. Porter, Co. C, 21st Ohio, and Martin J. Hawkins, Co. A, 33d Ohio), were identified and added to the band of prisoners. Now follows the saddest part of the story. Being in citizens' dress within an enemy's lines, the whole party were held as spies. A court-martial was convened, and the leader and seven out of the remaining twenty-one were condemned and executed. The others were never brought to trial, probably because of the advance of Union forces and the consequent confusion into which the affairs of the Departments of East Tennessee and Georgia were thrown. Of the remaining fourteen, eight succeeded, by a bold effort—attacking their guard in broad daylight—in making their escape from Atlanta, Ga., and ultimately in reaching the North. The other six, who shared in this effort, but were recaptured, remained prisoners until the latter part of March, 1863, when they were exchanged through a special arrangement made by Secretary Stanton. All the survivors of this expedition received medals and promotion. The pursuers also received expressions of gratitude from their fellow Confederates, notably from the Governor and Legislature of Georgia.

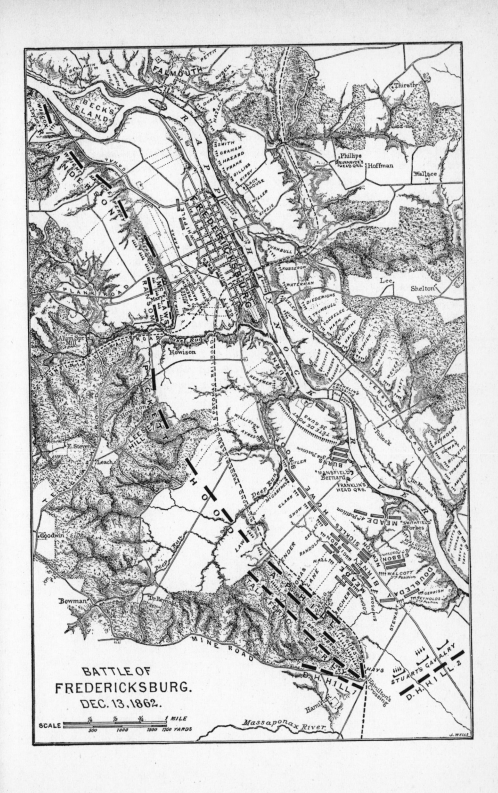

BATTLE OF
FREDERICKSBURG.
DEC. 13, 1862.

SCALE
¼   ½   ¾   1 MILE
500   1000   1500   1760 YARDS

General Ambrose E. Burnside, to whom Lincoln handed over the army "Little Mac" had largely trained and commanded so long, was one of the worst appointments Lincoln ever made. He was an amiable fellow and he did not lack courage, but he was simply not capable (as he himself protested) of operating as anything more than a subordinate commander. Nevertheless he finally took the command —some felt to keep it away from Joe Hooker—and resolved to do his best. And the best he could think of was marching down the Rappahannock to Fredericksburg, crossing the river there and driving straight down to Richmond. Unfortunately, there was another obstacle at Fredericksburg besides the river— Lee's entire army, drawn up on Marye's Heights behind the town and, even as Burnside should have been able to see, in a well-nigh impregnable position. But Burnside was undaunted. In the middle of December, after laying down one of the heaviest artillery barrages of the war, the Federal army of some 100,000 men crossed the Rappahannock, passed through the town, formed ranks and advanced in the best possible order toward the death-dealing works of the enemy. Again and again they charged, but their goal had been unobtainable from the beginning. At last Burnside ordered the retreat, but they left 15,000 on the field. Lee and his officers could hardly believe it had happened.

"A sixth time they charged"

THE BATTLE OF FREDERICKSBURG

BY JAMES LONGSTREET, LIEUTENANT-GENERAL, C. S. A.

IN THE early fall of 1862, a distance of not more than thirty miles lay between the Army of the Potomac and the Army of Northern Virginia. A state of uncertainty had existed for several weeks succeeding the battle of Sharpsburg, but the movements that resulted in the battle of Fredericksburg began to take shape when on the 5th of November the order was issued removing General McClellan from command of the Federal forces.

The order assigning General Burnside to command was received at General Lee's headquarters, then at Culpeper Court House, about twenty-four hours after it reached Warrenton, though not through official courtesy. General Lee, on receiving the news, said he regretted to part with McClellan, "for," he added, "we always understood each other so well. I fear they may continue to make these changes till they find some one whom I don't understand."

The Federal army was encamped around Warrenton, Virginia, and was soon divided into three grand divisions, whose commanders were Generals Sumner, Hooker, and Franklin.

Lee's army was on the opposite side of the Rappahannock River, divided

291

into two corps, the First commanded by myself and the Second commanded by General T. J. (Stonewall) Jackson. At that time the Confederate army extended from Culpeper Court House (where the First Corps was stationed) on its right across the Blue Ridge down the Valley of Virginia to Winchester. There Jackson was encamped with the Second Corps, except one division which was stationed at Chester Gap on the Blue Ridge Mountains.

About the 18th or 19th of November, we received information through our scouts that Sumner, with his grand division of more than thirty thousand men, was moving toward Fredericksburg. Evidently he intended to surprise us and cross the Rappahannock before we could offer resistance. On receipt of the information, two of my divisions were ordered down to meet him. We made a forced march and arrived on the hills around Fredericksburg about 3 o'clock on the afternoon of the 21st. Sumner had already arrived, and his army was encamped on Stafford Heights, overlooking the town from the Federal side. Before I reached Fredericksburg, General Patrick, provost-marshal-general, crossed the river under a flag of truce and put the people in a state of great excitement by delivering the following letter:

HEADQUARTERS OF THE ARMY OF THE POTOMAC, November 21st, 1862
To THE MAYOR AND COMMON COUNCIL OF FREDERICKSBURG. GENTLEMEN:
Under cover of the houses of your city, shots have been fired upon the troops of my command. Your mills and manufactories are furnishing provisions and the material for clothing for armed bodies in rebellion against the Government of the United States. Your railroads and other means of transportation are removing supplies to the depots of such troops. This condition of things must terminate, and by direction of General Burnside I accordingly demand the surrender of your city into my hands, as the representative of the Government of the United States, at or before 5 o'clock this afternoon. Failing in an affirmative reply to this demand by the hour indicated, sixteen hours will be permitted to elapse for the removal from the city of women and children, the sick and wounded and aged, etc., which period having expired I shall proceed to shell the town. Upon obtaining possession of the city every necessary means will be taken to preserve order and secure the protective operation of the laws and policy of the United States Government. I am, very respectfully, your obedient servant,

E. V. SUMNER,
Brevet Major-General, U. S. Army, Commanding Right Grand Division

While the people were in a state of excitement over the receipt of this demand for the surrender of their town, my troops appeared upon the heights opposite those occupied by the Federals. The alarmed non-combatants heard of my arrival and immediately sent to me the demand of the Federal general. I stated to the town authorities that I did not care to occupy the place for military purposes and that there was no reason why it should be shelled by the Federal army. We were there to protect ourselves against the advance of the enemy, and could not allow the town to be occupied by the Federals. The mayor sent to General Sumner a satisfactory statement of the situation and was notified that the threatened shelling would not take place, since the Confederates did not purpose to make the town a base of military operations.

Before my troops reached the little city, and before the people of Fredericksburg knew that any part of the Confederate army was near, there was great excitement over the demand for surrender. No people were in the place except aged and infirm men, and women and children. That they should become alarmed when the surrender of the town was demanded by the Federals was quite natural, and a number proceeded with great haste to board a train then ready to leave. As the train drew out, Sumner's batteries on Stafford Heights opened fire on it, adding to the general terror, but fortunately doing no serious damage. The spectacle was nothing, however, to what we witnessed a short time after. About the 26th or 27th it became evident that Fredericksburg would be the scene of a battle, and we advised the people who were still in the town to prepare to leave, as they would soon be in danger if they remained. The evacuation of the place by the distressed women and helpless men was a painful sight. Many were almost destitute and had nowhere to go, but, yielding to the cruel necessities of war, they collected their portable effects and turned their backs on the town. Many were forced to seek shelter in the woods and brave the icy November nights to escape the approaching assault from the Federal army.

Very soon after I reached Fredericksburg the remainder of my corps arrived from Culpeper Court House, and as soon as it was known that all the Army of the Potomac was in motion for the prospective scene of battle Jackson was drawn down from the Blue Ridge. In a very short time the Army of Northern Virginia was face to face with the Army of the Potomac.

When Jackson arrived he objected to the position, not that he feared the result of the battle, but because he thought that behind the North Anna was a point from which the most fruitful results would follow. He held that we would win a victory at Fredericksburg, but it would be a fruitless one to us, whereas at North Anna, when we drove the Federals back, we could give pursuit to advantage, which we could not do at Fredericksburg. General Lee did not entertain the proposition, however, and we continued our preparations to meet the enemy at the latter place.

At a point just above the town, a range of hills begins, extending from the river edge out a short distance and bearing around the valley somewhat in the form of a crescent. On the opposite side are the noted Stafford Heights, then occupied by the Federals. At the foot of these hills flows the Rappahannock River. On the Confederate side nestled Fredericksburg, and around it stretched the fertile bottoms from which fine crops had been gathered and upon which the Federal troops were to mass and give battle to the Confederates. On the Confederate side nearest the river was Taylor's Hill, and south of it the now famous Marye's Hill; next, Telegraph Hill, the highest of the elevations on the Confederate side (later known as Lee's Hill, because during the battle General Lee was there most of the time), where I had my headquarters in the field; next was a declination through which Deep Run Creek passed on its way to the Rappahannock River; and next was the gentle elevation at Hamilton's Crossing, not dignified with a name, upon which Stonewall Jackson massed thirty thousand men. It was upon these hills that the Confederates made their preparations to receive Burnside whenever he might choose to cross the Rappahannock. The Confederates were stationed as follows: On Taylor's Hill next the river and forming my left, R. H. Anderson's division; on Marye's Hill, Ransom's and McLaws's divisions; on Telegraph Hill, Pickett's division; to the right and about Deep Run Creek, Hood's division, the latter stretching across Deep Run Bottom.

On the hill occupied by Jackson's corps were the divisions of A. P. Hill, Early, and Taliaferro, that of D. H. Hill being in reserve on the extreme right. To the Washington Artillery, on Marye's Hill, was assigned the service of advising the army at the earliest possible moment of the Federal advance. General Barksdale, with his Mississippi brigade, was on picket duty in front of Fredericksburg on the night of the advance.

The hills occupied by the Confederate forces, although over-crowned by the heights of Stafford, were so distant as to be outside the range of effective fire by the Federal guns, and, with the lower receding grounds between them, formed a defensive series that may be likened to natural bastions. Taylor's Hill, on our left, was unassailable; Marye's Hill was more advanced toward the town, was of a gradual ascent and of less height than the others, and we considered it the point most assailable, and guarded it accordingly. The events that followed proved the correctness of our opinion on that point. Lee's Hill, near our center, with its rugged sides retired from Marye's and rising higher than its companions, was comparatively safe.

This was the situation of the 65,000 Confederates massed around Fredericksburg, and they had twenty-odd days in which to prepare for the approaching battle.

The Federals on Stafford Heights carefully matured their plans of advance and attack. General Hunt, chief of artillery, skillfully posted 147 guns to cover the bottoms upon which the infantry was to form for the attack, and at the same time play upon the Confederate batteries as circumstances would allow. Franklin and Hooker had joined Sumner, and Stafford Heights held the Federal army, 116,000 strong, watching the plain where the bloody conflict was soon to be. In the meantime the Federals had been seen along the banks of the river, looking for the most available points for crossing. President Lincoln had been down with General Halleck, and it had been suggested by the latter to cross at Hoop-pole Ferry, about 28 or 30 miles below Fredericksburg. We discovered the movement, however, and prepared to meet it, and Burnside abandoned the idea and turned his attention to Fredericksburg, under the impression that many of our troops were down at Hoop-pole, too far away to return in time for this battle.

The soldiers of both armies were in good fighting condition, and there was every indication that we would have a desperate battle. We were confident that Burnside could not dislodge us, and patiently awaited the attack.

On the morning of the 11th of December, 1862, an hour or so before daylight, the slumbering Confederates were awakened by a solitary cannon thundering on the heights of Marye's Hill. Again it boomed, and instantly the aroused Confederates recognized the signal of the Washington Artillery and knew that the Federal troops were preparing to cross the Rappahannock to give us the expected battle. The Federals came down to the river's edge and began the construction of their bridges, when Barksdale opened fire with such effect that they were forced to retire. Again and again they made an effort to cross, but each time they were met and repulsed by the well-directed bullets of the Mississippians. This contest lasted until 1 o'clock, when the Federals, with angry desperation, turned their whole available force of artillery on the little city, and sent down from the heights a perfect storm of shot and shell, crushing the houses with a cyclone of fiery metal. From our position on the heights we saw the batteries hurling an avalanche upon the town whose only offense was that near its edge in a snug retreat nestled three thousand Confederate hornets that were stinging the Army of the Potomac into a frenzy. It was terrific, the pandemonium which that little squad of Confederates had provoked. The town caught fire in several places, shells crashed and burst, and solid shot rained like hail. In the midst of the successive crashes could be heard the shouts and yells of those engaged in the struggle, while the smoke rose from the burning city and the flames leaped about, making a scene which can never be effaced from the memory of those who saw it. But, in the midst of all this fury, the little brigade of Mississippians clung to their work. At last, when I had everything in readiness, I sent a peremptory order to Barksdale to withdraw, which he did, fighting as he retired before the Federals, who had by that time succeeded in landing a number of their troops. The Federals then constructed their pontoons without molestation, and during the night and the following day the grand division of Sumner passed over into Fredericksburg.

About a mile and a half below the town, where the Deep Run empties into the Rappahannock, General Franklin had been allowed without serious opposition to throw two pontoon-bridges on the 11th, and his grand division passed over and massed on the level bottoms opposite Hamilton's Crossing, thus placing himself in front of Stonewall Jackson's corps. The 11th and 12th were thus spent by the Federals in crossing the river and preparing for battle.

Opposite Fredericksburg, the formation along the river-bank was such that the Federals were concealed in their approaches, and, availing themselves of this advantage, they succeeded in crossing and concealing the grand division

295

of Sumner and, later, a part of Hooker's grand division in the city of Fredericksburg, and so disposing of Franklin in the open plain below as to give out the impression that the great force was with the latter and about to oppose Jackson.

Before daylight on the morning of the eventful 13th I rode to the right of my line held by Hood's division. General Hood was at his post in plain hearing of the Federals south of Deep Run, who were marching their troops into position for the attack. The morning was cold and misty, and everything was obscured from view, but so distinctly did the mist bear to us the sounds of the moving Federals that Hood thought the advance was against him. He was relieved, however, when I assured him that the enemy, to reach him, would have to put himself in a pocket and be subjected to attack from Jackson on one side, Pickett and McLaws on the other, and Hood's own men in front. The position of Franklin's men on the 12th, with the configuration of the ground, had left no doubt in my mind as to Franklin's intentions. I explained all this to Hood, assuring him that the attack would be on Jackson. At the same time I ordered Hood, in case Jackson's line should be broken, to wheel around to his right and strike in on the attacking bodies, telling him that Pickett, with his division, would be ordered to join in the flank movement. These orders were given to both division generals, and at the same time they were advised that I would be attacked near my left center, and that I must be at that point to meet my part of the battle. They were also advised that my position was so well defended I could have no other need of their troops. I then returned to Lee's Hill, reaching there soon after sunrise.

Thus we stood at the eve of the great battle. Along the Stafford Heights 147 guns were turned upon us, and on the level plain below, in the town, and hidden on the opposite bank ready to cross, were assembled nearly 100,000 men, eager to begin the combat. Secure on our hills, we grimly awaited the onslaught. The valley, the mountain-tops, everything was enveloped in the thickest fog, and the preparations for the fight were made as if under cover of night. The mist brought to us the sounds of the preparation for battle, but we were blind to the movements of the Federals. Suddenly, at 10 o'clock, as if the elements were taking a hand in the drama about to be enacted, the warmth of the sun brushed the mist away and revealed the mighty panorama in the valley below.

Franklin's 40,000 men, reënforced by two divisions of Hooker's grand division, were in front of Jackson's 30,000. The flags of the Federals fluttered gayly, the polished arms shone brightly in the sunlight, and the beautiful uniforms of the buoyant troops gave to the scene the air of a holiday occasion rather than the spectacle of a great army about to be thrown into the tumult of battle. From my place on Lee's Hill I could see almost every soldier Franklin had, and a splendid array it was. But off in the distance was Jackson's ragged infantry, and beyond was Stuart's battered cavalry, with their soiled hats and yellow butternut suits, a striking contrast to the handsomely equipped troops of the Federals.

About the city, here and there, a few soldiers could be seen, but there was no indication of the heavy masses that were concealed by the houses. Those of Franklin's men who were in front of Jackson stretched well up toward Lee's Hill, and were almost within reach of our best guns, and at the other end they stretched out to the east until they came well under the fire of Stuart's horse artillery under Major John Pelham, a brave and gallant officer, almost a boy in years. As the mist rose, the Confederates saw the movement against their right near Hamilton's Crossing. Major Pelham opened fire upon Franklin's command and gave him lively work, which was kept up until Jackson ordered Pelham to retire. Franklin then advanced rapidly to the hill where Jackson's troops had been stationed, feeling the woods with shot as he progressed. Silently Jackson awaited the approach of the Federals until they were within good range, and then he opened a terrific fire which threw the Federals into some confusion. The enemy again massed and advanced, pressing through a gap between Archer and Lane. This broke Jackson's line and threatened very serious trouble. The Federals who had wedged themselves in through that gap came upon Gregg's brigade, and then the severe encounter ensued in which the latter general was mortally wounded. Archer and Lane very soon received reënforcements and, rallying, joined in the counter-attack and recovered their lost ground. The concentration of Taliaferro's and Early's divisions against this attack was too much for it, and the counter-attack drove the Federals back to the railroad and beyond the reach of our guns on the left. Some of our troops following up this repulse got too far out, and were in turn much discomfited when left to the enemy's superior numbers, and were obliged to retire in poor condition. A Federal brigade advancing under cover of Deep Run was discovered at this time and attacked by regiments of Pender's and Law's brigades, the former of A. P. Hill's and the latter of Hood's division; and, Jackson's second line advancing, the Federals were forced to retire. This series of demonstrations and attacks, the partial success and final discomfiture of the Federals, constitute the hostile movements between the Confederate right and the Federal left.

I have described, in the opening of this article, the situation of the Confederate left. In front of Marye's Hill is a plateau, and immediately at the base of the hill there is a sunken road known as the Telegraph road. On the side of the road next to the town was a stone-wall, shoulder-high, against which the earth was banked, forming an almost unapproachable defense. It was impossible for the troops occupying it to expose more than a small portion of their bodies. Behind this stone-wall I had placed about twenty-five hundred men, being all of General T. R. R. Cobb's brigade, and a portion of the brigade of

General Kershaw, both of McLaws's division. It must now be understood that the Federals, to reach what appeared to be my weakest point, would have to pass directly over this wall held by Cobb's infantry.

An idea of how well Marye's Hill was protected may be obtained from the following incident: General E. P. Alexander, my engineer and superintendent of artillery, had been placing the guns, and in going over the field with him before the battle, I noticed an idle cannon. I suggested that he place it so as to aid in covering the plain in front of Marye's Hill. He answered: "General, we cover that ground now so well that we will comb it as with a fine-tooth comb. A chicken could not live on that field when we open on it."

A little before noon I sent orders to all my batteries to open fire through the streets or at any points where the troops were seen about the city, as a diversion in favor of Jackson. This fire began at once to develop the work in hand for myself. The Federal troops swarmed out of the city like bees out of a hive, coming in double-quick march and filling the edge of the field in front of Cobb. This was just where we had expected attack, and I was prepared to meet it. As the troops massed before us, they were much annoyed by the fire of our batteries. The field was literally packed with Federals from the vast number of troops that had been massed in the town. From the moment of their appearance began the most fearful carnage. With our artillery from the front, right, and left tearing through their ranks, the Federals pressed forward with almost invincible determination, maintaining their steady step and closing up their broken ranks. Thus resolutely they marched upon the stone fence behind which quietly waited the Confederate brigade of General Cobb. As they came within reach of this brigade, a storm of lead was poured into their advancing ranks and they were swept from the field like chaff before the wind. A cloud of smoke shut out the scene for a moment, and, rising, revealed the shattered fragments recoiling from their gallant but hopeless charge. The artillery still plowed through their retreating ranks and searched the places of concealment into which the troops had plunged. A vast number went pell-mell into an old railroad cut to escape fire from the right and front. A battery on Lee's Hill saw this and turned its fire into the entire length of the cut, and the shells began to pour down upon the Federals with the most frightful destruction. They found their position of refuge more uncomfortable than the field of the assault.

Thus the right grand division of the Army of the Potomac found itself repulsed and shattered on its first attempt to drive us from Marye's Hill. Hardly was this attack off the field before we saw the determined Federals again filing out of Fredericksburg and preparing for another charge. The Confederates under Cobb reserved their fire and quietly awaited the approach of the enemy. The Federals came nearer than before, but were forced to retire before the well-directed guns of Cobb's brigade and the fire of the artillery on the heights. By that time the field in front of Cobb was thickly strewn with the dead and dying Federals, but again they formed with desperate courage and renewed the attack and again were driven off. At each attack the slaughter was so great that by the time the third attack was repulsed, the ground was so thickly strewn with dead that the bodies seriously impeded the approach of the Federals. General Lee, who was with me on Lee's Hill, became uneasy when he saw the attacks so promptly renewed and pushed forward with such persistence, and feared the Federals might break through our line. After the third charge he said to me: "General, they are massing very heavily and will break your line, I am afraid." "General," I replied, "if you put every man now on the other side of the Potomac on that field to approach me over the same line, and give me plenty of ammunition, I will kill them all before they reach my line. Look to your right; you are in some danger there, but not on my line."

I think the fourth time the Federals charged, a gallant fellow came within one hundred feet of Cobb's position before he fell. Close behind him came some few scattering ones, but they were either killed or they fled from certain death. This charge was the only effort that looked like actual danger to Cobb, and after it was repulsed I felt no apprehension, assuring myself that there were enough of the dead Federals on the field to give me half the battle. The anxiety shown by General Lee, however, induced me to bring up two or three brigades, to be on hand, and General Kershaw, with the remainder of his brigade, was ordered down to the stone-wall, rather, however, to carry ammunition than as a reënforcement for Cobb. Kershaw dashed down the declivity and arrived just in time to succeed Cobb, who, at this juncture, fell from a wound in the thigh and died in a few minutes from loss of blood.

A fifth time the Federals formed and charged and were repulsed. A sixth time they charged and were driven back, when night came to end the dreadful carnage, and the Federals withdrew, leaving the battle-field literally heaped with the bodies of their dead. Before the well-directed fire of Cobb's brigade, the Federals had fallen like the steady dripping of rain from the eaves of a house. Our musketry alone killed and wounded at least 5000; and these, with the slaughter by the artillery, left over 7000 killed and wounded before the foot of Marye's Hill. The dead were piled sometimes three deep, and when morning broke, the spectacle that we saw upon the battle-field was one of the most distressing I ever witnessed. The charges had been desperate and bloody, but utterly hopeless. I thought, as I saw the Federals come again and again to their death, that they deserved success if courage and daring could entitle soldiers to victory.

During the night a Federal strayed beyond his lines and was taken up by some of my troops. On searching him, we found on his person a memorandum of General Burnside's arrangements, and an order for the renewal of the battle the next day. This information was sent to General Lee, and immediately orders were given for a line of rifle-pits on the top of Marye's Hill for Ransom, who had been held somewhat in reserve, and for other guns to be placed on Taylor's Hill.

We were on our lines before daylight, anxious to receive General Burnside again. As the gray of the morning came without the battle, we became more anxious; yet, as the Federal forces retained position during the 14th and 15th, we were not without hope. There was some little skirmishing, but it did not amount to anything. But when the full light of the next morning revealed an abandoned field, General Lee turned to me, referring in his mind to the dispatch I had captured and which he had just re-read, and said: "General, I am losing confidence in your friend General Burnside." We then put it down as a *ruse de guerre*. Afterward, however, we learned that the order had been made in good faith but had been changed in consequence of the demoralized condition of the grand divisions in front of Marye's Hill. During the night of the 15th the Federal troops withdrew, and on the 16th our lines were reëstablished along the river.

I have heard that, referring to the attack at Marye's Hill while it was in progress, General Hooker said: "There has been enough blood shed to satisfy any reasonable man, and it is time to quit." I think myself it was fortunate for Burnside that he had no greater success, for the meeting with such discomfiture gave him an opportunity to get back safe. If he had made any progress, his loss would probably have been greater.

Such was the battle of Fredericksburg as I saw it. It has been asked why we did not follow up the victory. The answer is plain. It goes without saying that the battle of the First Corps, concluded after nightfall, could not have been changed into offensive operations. Our line was about three miles long, extending through woodland over hill and dale. An attempt at concentration to throw the troops against the walls of the city at that hour of the night would have been little better than madness. . . .

During the attack upon General Jackson, and immediately after his line was broken, General Pickett rode up to General Hood and suggested that the moment was at hand for the movement anticipated by my orders, and requested that it be executed. Hood did not agree, so the opportunity was allowed to pass. Had Hood sprung to the occasion we would have enveloped Franklin's command, and might possibly have marched it into the Confederate camp. Hood commanded splendid troops, quite fresh and eager for occasion to give renewed assurances of their mettle.

It has been reported that the troops attacking Marye's Hill were intoxicated, having been plied with whisky to nerve them to the desperate attack. That can hardly be true. I know nothing of the facts, but no sensible commander will allow his troops strong drink upon going into battle. After a battle is over, the soldier's gill is usually allowed if it is at hand. No troops could have displayed greater courage and resolution than was shown by those brought against Marye's Hill. But they miscalculated the wonderful strength of the line behind the stone fence. The position held by Cobb surpassed courage and resolution, and was occupied by those who knew well how to hold a comfortable defense.

After the retreat, General Lee went to Richmond to suggest other operations, but was assured that the war was virtually over, and that we need not harass our troops by marches and other hardships. Gold had advanced in New York to two hundred, and we were assured by those at the Confederate capital that in thirty or forty days we would be recognized and peace proclaimed. General Lee did not share in this belief.

I have been asked if Burnside could have been victorious at Fredericksburg. Such a thing was hardly possible. Perhaps no general could have accomplished more than Burnside did, and it was possible for him to have suffered greater loss. The battle of Fredericksburg was a great and unprofitable sacrifice of human life made, through the pressure from the rear, upon a general who should have known better and who doubtless acted against his judgment. If I had been in General Burnside's place, I would have asked the President to allow me to resign rather than execute his order to force the passage of the river and march the army against Lee in his stronghold.

Viewing the battle after the lapse of more than twenty years, I may say, however, that Burnside's move might have been made stronger by throwing two of his grand divisions across at the mouth of Deep Run, where Franklin crossed with his grand division and six brigades of Hooker's. Had he thus placed Hooker and Sumner, his sturdiest fighters, and made resolute assault with them in his attack on our right, he would in all probability have given us trouble. The partial success he had at that point might have been pushed vigorously by such a force and might have thrown our right entirely from position, in which event the result would have depended on the skillful handling of the forces. Franklin's grand division could have made sufficient sacrifice at Marye's Hill and come as near success as did Sumner's and two-thirds of Hooker's combined. I think, however, that the success would have been on our side, and it might have been followed by greater disaster on the side of the Federals; still they would have had the chance of success in their favor, while in the battle as it was fought it can hardly be claimed that there was even a chance.

Burnside made a mistake from the first. He should have gone from Warrenton to Chester Gap. He might then have held Jackson and fought me, or have held me and fought Jackson, thus taking us in detail. The doubt about the matter was whether or not he could have caught me in that trap before we could concentrate. At any rate, that was the only move on the board that could have benefited him at the time he was assigned to the command of the

Army of the Potomac. By interposing between the corps of Lee's army he would have secured strong ground and advantage of position. With skill equal to the occasion, he should have had success. This was the move about which we felt serious apprehension, and we were occupying our minds with plans to meet it when the move toward Fredericksburg was reported. General McClellan, in his report of August 4th, 1863, speaks of this move as that upon which he was studying when the order for Burnside's assignment to command reached him.

After the unnecessary disaster at Fredericksburg and the abortive "Mud March" the following month, Burnside's lieutenants utterly lost what little confidence they had ever had in him. Hooker was especially critical of his chief and Burnside, infuriated by "Fighting Joe's" ill-concealed hostility, went up to Washington and presented the President with the alternative of dismissing Hooker from the service or accepting his (Burnside's) resignation. This gave Lincoln an obvious choice. He not only let Burnside go but appointed Hooker to succeed him. Now General Lee had to adapt himself to still another kind of adversary.

"Oh great God! See how our men are falling!"

BY DARIUS N. COUCH, MAJOR-GENERAL, U. S. V.

O N THE evening of October 15th, 1862, a few days after McClellan
had placed me in command of the Second Corps, then at Harper's
Ferry, the commanding general sent an order for Hancock to take
his division the next morning on a reconnoissance toward Charlestown,
about ten miles distant. The division started in good season, as directed.
About 10 in the morning General McClellan reined up at my headquarters
and asked me to go out with him to see what the troops were doing. Our
people had met the enemy's outpost five miles from the Ferry, and while
artillery shots were being exchanged, both of us dismounted, walked away
by ourselves, and took seats on a ledge of rocks. After a little while Mc-

305

Clellan sent to an aide for a map of Virginia. Spreading it before us, he pointed to the strategic features of the valley of the Shenandoah, and indicated the movements he intended to make, which would have the effect of compelling Lee to concentrate in the vicinity, I think, of Gordonsville or Charlottesville, where a great battle would be fought. Continuing the conversation, he said, "But I may not have command of the army much longer. Lincoln is down on me," and, taking a paper from his pocket, he gave me my first intimation of the President's famous letter. He read it aloud very carefully, and when it was finished I told him I thought there was no ill-feeling in the tone of it. He thought there was, and quickly added, "Yes, Couch, I expect to be relieved from the Army of the Potomac, and to have a command in the West; and I am going to take three or four with me," calling off by their names four prominent officers. I queried if "so and so" would be taken along, naming one who was generally thought to be a great favorite with McClellan. His curt reply was, "No, I sha'n't have him."

This brief conversation opened a new world for me. I had never before been to any extent his confidant, and I pondered whether on a change of the commanders of the Army of the Potomac the War Department would allow him to choose the generals whose names had been mentioned. I wondered what would be the future of himself and those who followed his fortunes in that untried field. These and a crowd of other kindred thoughts quite oppressed me for several days. But as the time wore on, and preparations for the invasion of Virginia were allowed to go on without let or hindrance from Washington, I naturally and gladly inferred that McClellan's fears of hostile working against him were groundless. However, the blow came, and soon enough.

On the 8th of November, just at dark, I had dismounted, and, standing in the snow, was superintending the camp arrangements of my troops, when McClellan came up with his staff, accompanied by General Burnside. McClellan drew in his horse, and the first thing he said was:

"Couch, I am relieved from the command of the army, and Burnside is my successor."

I stepped up to him and took hold of his hand, and said, "General McClellan, I am sorry for it." Then, going around the head of his horse to Burnside, I said, "General Burnside, I congratulate you."

Burnside heard what I said to General McClellan; he turned away his head, and made a broad gesture as he exclaimed:

"Couch, don't say a word about it."

His manner indicated that he did not wish to talk about the change; that he thought it was not good policy to do so, nor the place to do it. He told me afterward that he did not like to take the command, but that he did so to keep it from going to somebody manifestly unfit for it. I assumed that he meant Hooker. Those of us who were well acquainted with Burnside knew that he was a brave, loyal man, but we did not think that he had the military ability to command the Army of the Potomac.

McClellan took leave on the 10th. Fitz John Porter sent notes to the corps commanders, informing them that McClellan was going away, and suggesting that we ride about with him. Such a scene as that leave-taking had never been known in our army. Men shed tears and there was great excitement among the troops.

I think the soldiers had an idea that McClellan would take care of them— would not put them in places where they would be unnecessarily cut up; and if a general has the confidence of his men he is pretty strong. But officers and men were determined to serve Burnside loyally.

A day or two afterward Burnside called the corps commanders together, mapped out a course that he intended to pursue; and, among other things, he said that he intended to double the army corps, and he proposed to call the three new commands—or doubles—"grand divisions." Under this arrangement my corps, the Second, and Wilcox's, the Ninth, which had been Burnside's, formed the Right Grand Division under General Sumner. When Sumner and I arrived near Falmouth, opposite Fredericksburg, November 17th, we found the enemy in small force in readiness to oppose our crossing the Rappahannock. Everybody knew that Lee would rush right in; we could see it. If the pontoons had been there, we might have crossed at once. Yet we lay there nearly a month, while they were fortifying before our eyes; besides, the weather was against us. Under date of December 7th, my diary contains this entry: "Very cold; plenty of snow. Men suffering; cold outdoors, ice indoors in my room."

Sumner's headquarters were at the Lacy House, while the Second Corps lay back of the brow of the hill behind Falmouth.

On the night of the 9th, two nights before the crossing, Sumner called a council to discuss what we were to do, the corps, division, and brigade commanders being present. The result was a plain, free talk all around, in which words were not minced, for the conversation soon drifted into a marked disapprobation of the manner in which Burnside contemplated meeting the enemy.

Sumner seemed to feel badly that the officers did not agree to Burnside's mode of advance. That noble old hero was so faithful and loyal that he wanted, even against impossibilities, to carry out everything Burnside suggested. I should doubt if his judgment concurred. It was only chivalrous attachment to Burnside, or to any commander. But there were not two opinions among the subordinate officers as to the rashness of the undertaking.

Somebody told Burnside of our views, and he was irritated. He asked us to meet him the next night at the Lacy House. He said he understood, in a general way, that we were opposed to his plans. He seemed to be rather severe on Hancock—to my surprise, for I did not think that officer had said

307

as much as myself in opposition to the plan of attack. Burnside stated that he had formed his plans, and all he wanted was the devotion of his men. Hancock made a reply in which he disclaimed any personal discourtesy, and said he knew there was a line of fortified heights on the opposite side, and that it would be pretty difficult for us to go over there and take them. I rose after him, knowing that I was the more guilty, and expressed a desire to serve Burnside, saying, among other things, that if I had ever done anything in any battle, in this one I intended to do twice as much. French came in while I was talking. He was rather late, and in his bluff way exclaimed: "Is this a Methodist camp-meeting?"

The heights on the morning of the 11th, before the bridges were thrown across, did not offer a very animated scene, because the troops were mostly hidden. The bombardment for the purpose of dislodging the sharp-shooters who under cover of the houses were delaying the bridge-making, was terrific, while the smoke settled down and veiled the scene. After the bombardment had failed to dislodge the enemy, the 7th Michigan and the 19th and the 20th Massachusetts of Howard's division sprang into the pontoons, and rowing themselves over drove away Barksdale's sharp-shooters. This gallant action enabled the engineers to complete the bridges. Howard's division was the first to cross by the upper bridge, his advance having a lively fight in the streets of Fredericksburg. Hawkins's brigade of Willcox's corps occupied the lower part of the town on the same evening, and the town was not secured without desperate fighting. I went over the next morning, Friday, the 12th, with Hancock's and French's divisions. The remainder of Willcox's corps crossed and occupied the lower part of the town. There was considerable looting. I placed a provost-guard at the bridges, with orders that nobody should go back with plunder. An enormous pile of booty was collected there by evening. But there came a time when we were too busy to guard it, and I suppose it was finally carried off by another set of spoilers. The troops of the two corps bivouacked that night in the streets and were not permitted to make fires. Late on that day we had orders to be ready to cross Hazel Run, which meant that we were to join Franklin. That was the only proper move to make, since we had done just what the enemy wanted us to do—had divided our army. The conditions were favorable for a change of position unknown to the enemy, since the night was dark and the next morning was foggy. But it would have been very difficult to make the movement. I was much worried in regard to building the necessary bridges over Hazel Run and the dangers attending a flank movement at night in the presence of the enemy. But the order to march never came. The orders that were given by Burnside showed that he had no fixed plan of battle. After getting in the face of the enemy, his intentions seemed to be continually changing.

Early the next morning, Saturday, the 13th, I received orders to make an assault in front. My instructions came from General Sumner, who did not cross the river during the fight, owing to a special understanding with which I had nothing to do, and which related to his supposed rashness. At Fair Oaks, Antietam, and on other battle-fields he had shown that he was a hard fighter. He was a grand soldier, full of honor and gallantry, and a man of great determination.

As I have said, on that Saturday morning we were enveloped in a heavy fog. At 8:15, when we were still holding ourselves in readiness to move to the left, I received the following order:

HEADQUARTERS, RIGHT GRAND DIVISION, NEAR FALMOUTH, VA.,
December 12th, 1862

MAJOR-GENERAL COUCH, Commanding Second Corps d'Armée

GENERAL: The major-general commanding directs me to say to you that General Willcox has been ordered to extend to the left, so as to connect with Franklin's right. You will extend your right so far as to prevent the possibility of the enemy occupying the upper part of the town. You will then form a column of a division for the purpose of pushing in the direction of the Plank and Telegraph roads, for the purpose of seizing the heights in rear of the town. This column will advance in three lines, with such intervals as you may judge proper, this movement to be covered by a heavy line of skirmishers in front and on both flanks. You will hold another division in readiness to advance in support of this movement, to be formed in the same manner as the leading division. Particular care and precaution must be taken to prevent collision with our own troops in the fog. The movement will not commence until you receive orders. The watchword will be, "Scott!" Very respectfully, your most obedient servant.

J. H. TAYLOR, Chief of Staff and Assistant Adjutant-General

P. S. The major-general thinks that, as Howard's division led into the town, it is proper that one of the others take the advance.

French was at once directed to prepare his division in three brigade lines for the advance, and Hancock was to follow with his division in the same order. The distance between the brigade lines was to be about 200 yards.

Toward 10 o'clock the fog began to lift; French reported that he was ready, I signaled to Sumner, and about 11 o'clock the movement was ordered to begin. French threw out a strong body of skirmishers, and his brigades filed out of town as rapidly as possible by two parallel streets, the one on the right, which was Hanover street, running into the Telegraph road, and both leading direct to Marye's Hill, the stronghold of the enemy. On the outskirts of the town the troops encountered a ditch, or canal, so deep as to be almost impassable except at the street bridges, and, one of the latter being partly torn up, the troops had to cross single file on the stringers. Once across the canal, the attacking forces deployed under the bank bordering the plain over which they were to charge. This plain was obstructed here and there by houses and fences, notably at a fork of the Telegraph road, in the narrow angles of which was a cluster of houses and gardens; and also on the parallel road just south of it, where stood a large square brick house. This cluster of houses and the brick house were the rallying-points for parts of our disordered lines of attack. The fork in the road and the brick house were less than 150 yards from the stone-wall, which covered also as much more of the plain to the left of the brick house. A little in advance of the brick house a slight rise in the ground afforded protection to men lying down, against the musketry behind the stone-wall, but not against the converging fire of the artillery on the heights. My headquarters were in the field on the edge of the town, overlooking the plain.

A few minutes after noon French's division charged in the order of Kimball's, Andrews's, and Palmer's brigades, a part of Kimball's men getting into the cluster of houses in the fork of the road. Hancock followed them in the order of Zook's, Meagher's, and Caldwell's brigades, the two former getting nearer to the stone-wall than any who had gone before, except a few of Kimball's men, and nearer than any brigade which followed them.

Without a clear idea of the state of affairs at the front, since the smoke and light fog veiled everything, I sent word to French and Hancock to carry the enemy's works by storm. Then I climbed the steeple of the court-house, and from above the haze and smoke got a clear view of the field. Howard, who was with me, says I exclaimed, "Oh, great God! see how our men, our poor fellows, are falling!" I remember that the whole plain was covered with men, prostrate and dropping, the live men running here and there, and in front closing upon each other, and the wounded coming back. The commands seemed to be mixed up. I had never before seen fighting like that, nothing approaching it in terrible uproar and destruction. There was no cheering on the part of the men, but a stubborn determination to obey orders and do their duty. I don't think there was much feeling of success. As they charged the artillery fire would break their formation and they would get mixed; then they would close up, go forward, receive the withering infantry fire, and those who were able would run to the houses and fight as best they could; and then the next brigade coming up in succession would do its duty and melt like snow coming down on warm ground.

I was in the steeple hardly ten seconds, for I saw at a glance how they were being cut down, and was convinced that we could not be successful in front, and that our only chance lay by the right. I immediately ordered Howard to work in on the right with the brigades of Owen and Hall, and attack the enemy behind the stone-wall in flank, which was done. Before he could begin this movement both Hancock and French had notified me that they must have support or they would not be responsible for the maintenance of their position. Sturgis, of Willcox's corps, who had been supporting my left, sent the brigades of Ferrero and Nagle to the fruitless charge.

"Oh great God! See how our men are falling!"

About 2 o'clock General Hooker, who was in command of the Center Grand Division (Stoneman's and Butterfield's corps), came upon the field. At an earlier hour Whipple's division of Stoneman's corps had crossed the river and relieved Howard on the right, so that the latter might join in the attack in the center, and Griffin's division of Butterfield's corps had come over to the support of Sturgis. Humphreys and Sykes, of the latter corps, came to my support. Toward 3 o'clock I received the following dispatch:

HEADQUARTERS, RIGHT GRAND DIVISION, ARMY OF THE POTOMAC, Dec. 13th, 1862—2:40 P. M. GENERAL COUCH: Hooker has been ordered to put in everything. You must hold on until he comes in. By command of Brevet Major-General SUMNER. W. G. JONES, Lieut., Aide-de-camp, etc.

Hooker was the ranking general, and as I understood that he was to take command of the whole fighting line, the putting in of his fresh men beside mine might make a success. His very coming was to me, therefore, like the breaking out of the sun in a storm. I rode back to meet him, told him what had been done, and said, "I can't carry that hill by a front assault; the only chance we have is to try to get in on the right." Hooker replied, "I will talk with Hancock." He talked with Hancock, and after a few minutes said, "Well, Couch, things are in such a state I must go over and tell Burnside it is no use trying to carry this line here"—or words to that effect—and then he went off. His going away left me again in command. Burnside was nearly two miles distant. It was not much after 2 o'clock when he went away, and it was about 4 when he returned. This was after Humphreys had made his charge and the fighting for the day was substantially finished. We were holding our lines.

Hooker left word that Humphreys, whose division was ready to advance, should take his cue from me. Butterfield also gave Humphreys orders to that effect. After a lull in the battle General Caldwell, a brigade commander under Hancock, sent word to the latter that the enemy were retreating from Marye's house. It was probably only a shifting of the enemy's troops for the relief of the front line. But, assuming that the report was true, I said, "General Humphreys, Hancock reports the enemy is falling back: now is the time for you to go in!" He was ready, and his troops around him were ready. The order had evidently been expected, and after an interval of more than twenty-five years I well recollect the grim determination which settled on the face of that gallant hero when he received the words, "Now is the time for you to go in!" Spurring to his work he led his two brigades, who charged over precisely the same ground, but who did not get quite so near to the stone-wall as some of French's and Hancock's men.

The musketry fire was very heavy, and the artillery fire was simply terrible. I sent word several times to our artillery on the right of Falmouth that

311

they were firing into us, and were tearing our own men to pieces. I thought they had made a mistake in the range. But I learned later that the fire came from the guns of the enemy on their extreme left.

Soon after 4 o'clock, or about sunset, while Humphreys was at work, Getty's division of Willcox's corps was ordered to the charge on our left by the unfinished railroad. I could see them being dreadfully cut up, although they had not advanced as far as our men. I determined to send a battery upon the plain to shell the line that was doing them so much harm; so I ordered an aide to tell Colonel Morgan to send a battery across the canal and plant it near the brick house. Morgan came to me and said: "General, a battery can't live there." I replied, "Then it must die there!"

Hazard took his battery out in gallant style and opened fire on the enemy's lines to the left of the Marye House. Men never fought more gallantly, and he lost a great many men and horses. When Hooker came he ordered Frank's battery to join Hazard. But this last effort did not last long. In the midst of it I rode to the brick house, accompanied by Colonel Francis A. Walker, Lieutenant Cushing, and my orderly, Long. The smoke lay so thick that we could not see the enemy, and I think they could not see us, but we were aware of the fact that somebody in our front was doing a great deal of shooting. I found the brick house packed with men; and behind it the dead and the living were as thick as they could be crowded together. The dead were rolled out for shelter, and the dead horses were used for breastworks. I know I tried to shelter myself behind the brick house, but found I could not, on account of the men already there. The plain thereabouts was dotted with our fallen. I started to cross to the fork of the road where our men, under Colonel John R. Brooke, were holding the cluster of houses. . . .

That night was bitter cold and a fearful one for the front line hugging the hollows in the ground, and for the wounded who could not be reached. It was a night of dreadful suffering. Many died of wounds and exposure, and as fast as men died they stiffened in the wintry air, and on the front line were rolled forward for protection to the living. Frozen men were placed for dumb sentries.

My corps again bivouacked in the town, and they were not allowed fires lest they should draw the fire of the enemy's artillery.

At 2 o'clock in the morning Burnside came to my headquarters near the center of the town. I was lying down at the time. He asked me to tell him about the battle, and we talked for about an hour. I told him everything that had occurred. "And now," I said, "General Burnside, you must know that everything that could be done by troops was done by the Second Corps." He said, "Couch, I know that; I am perfectly satisfied that you did your best." He gave no intimation of his plans for the next day. He was cheerful in his tone and did not seem greatly oppressed, but it was plain that he felt he had led us to a great disaster, and one knowing him so long and well as myself could see that he wished his body was also lying in front of Marye's Heights. I never felt so badly for a man in my life.

The next day, Sunday, the 14th, our men began digging trenches along the edge of the town. We were on the alert, for there was some fear of an assault. Of course there is no need of denying that after the battle the men became strained. The pressure of a fight carries you through, but after it is all over and you have been whipped you do not feel very pugnacious. The men, knowing that they had been unsuccessful, were in a nervous state, and officers suffered also from the reaction, the worst of it being that the mass of the army had lost confidence in its commander.

About midday of the 14th Burnside called a council of war, in which it was decided to fall back, but to hold Fredericksburg. No attack was made by us that day, though Burnside had said that he should renew the assault on Marye's Hill, with his old Ninth Corps, and that he would place himself at its head. General Getty of that corps, a very gallant officer, touched me as I passed him and said: "I understand that Burnside has given out that he intends to lead seventeen regiments to the attack." He urged me strongly to dissuade him if possible, as it would be a perfect slaughter of men.

At the council Hooker expressed himself as against the movement of retreat, saying, "We must fight those people. We are over there and we must fight them." But, as I remember, he did not advocate the plan of holding Fredericksburg if we were not to renew the fight. I urged that the army was not in a condition, after our repulse, to renew the assault, but that we ought to hold Fredericksburg at all hazards. I had an argument with General Burnside upon that point, telling him that I was willing to have him throw all the responsibility upon me; that if we held the town we should have a little something to show for the sacrifice of the day before; that the people would feel we had not failed utterly. It was agreed that Fredericksburg should be held. Then Burnside dismissed us and sent Hooker and myself to Fredericksburg to arrange for the defense. We held a council at the corner of Hanover street.

It was decided that Hooker's troops should hold the town. The question was how many men would he leave for that purpose, opinions varying from ten to eighteen thousand. My limit was ten thousand men. General Tyler turned to me and said: "Make it higher, General." We compromised on twelve thousand. We remained in the town on the 15th, and that evening my corps and the Ninth Corps recrossed the river. Next morning we found that Fredericksburg had been evacuated. When Willcox and I left, we thought, of course, it would be held. The talk was that during the night Hooker prevailed upon Burnside to evacuate the town.

Our wing of the army thought the failure of the campaign was due in part to the fact that we were put in where we ought not to have been. We were asked to achieve an impossibility. We had something to do that was not possible for us to do.

After the battle Burnside tried to regain the confidence of the army, and there is no doubt that Sumner did a good deal to help him. Burnside conceived the plan of crossing the Rappahannock a few miles above Fredericksburg, where the enemy were unprepared to receive us. The result was the "mud march" of January 20th–21st. It was Burnside's effort to redeem himself. To start off in the mud as we did with the army in its discouraged state was perfect folly. There did not seem to be anything in the move to recommend itself. If the weather had happened to turn cold, possibly he might have surprised Lee and gotten across the river, above Fredericksburg, but it was a hazardous move, with the army out of confidence with its commander and the enemy elated with brilliant success. The general demoralization that had come upon us made two or three months of rest a necessity.

When Hooker, on January 25th, was placed in command of the army, many of us were very much surprised; I think the superior officers did not regard him competent for the task. He had fine qualities as an officer, but not the weight of character to take charge of that army. Nevertheless, under his administration the army assumed wonderful vigor. I have never known men to change from a condition of the lowest depression to that of a healthy fighting state in so short a time. President Lincoln with his wife came down to spend a few days with General Hooker, and to see the different officers and talk with them. To further that, General Hooker gave a dinner party at which all the corps commanders were present, and also Mrs. Lincoln. Mr. Lincoln would talk to the officers on the subject that was uppermost in our minds—how we were to get the better of the enemy on the opposite hills. Before he went away he sent for Hooker and for me, I being second in command, and almost his last injunction was: "Gentlemen, in your next battle *put in all your men.*" Yet that is exactly what we did not do at Chancellorsville.

We had a grand review of the army in honor of the President. The Second Corps paraded with Howard's Eleventh Corps, I think, for after I had saluted at the head of my corps I rode to the side of the President, who was on horseback, and while near him General Schurz approached at the head of his division. I said: "Mr. Lincoln, that is General Schurz," pronouncing it *Shurs,* after the American fashion. Mr. Lincoln turned to me and said: "Not *Shurs,* General Couch, but *Shoortz.*" But he did it very pleasantly, and I was just a little surprised that our Western President should have the advantage of me. It was a beautiful day, and the review was a stirring sight. Mr. Lincoln, sitting there with his hat off, head bent, and seemingly meditating, suddenly turned to me and said: "General Couch, what do you suppose will become of all these men when the war is over?" And it struck me as very pleasant that somebody had an idea that the war would sometime end.

315

General Lee had a distinctive way of referring to the enemy: "those people" he was in the habit of calling them. In the following notes, he says, characteristically, "Those people have sent a flag of truce. . . ." One can only surmise that with this phrase he was trying to maintain as detached an attitude as possible toward his opponents.

"Old soldiers together"

BY W. ROY MASON, MAJOR, C. S. A.

FREDERICKSBURG was the first great battle that I saw in its entire scope. Here the situation of the country—a champaign tract inclosed in hills—offered the opportunity of seeing the troops on both sides, and the movements down the entire lines. I witnessed the magnificent charges made on our left by Meagher's Irish Brigade, and was also a sorrowful witness of the death of our noble T. R. R. Cobb of Georgia, who fell mortally wounded at the foot of the stone-wall just at the door of Mrs. Martha Stevens. This woman, the Molly Pitcher of the war, attended the wounded and the dying fearless of consequences, and refused to leave her house, al-

317

though, standing just between the advancing line of the enemy and the stone-wall, the position was one of danger. It is said that after using all the materials for bandages at her command, she tore from her person most of her garments, even on that bitter cold day, in her anxiety to administer to necessities greater than her own.

Mrs. Stevens still lives in her old home at the foot of Marye's Heights, honored by every Confederate soldier. Not long ago, hearing that she was very sick, I went out with a party of gentlemen friends who were visitors in Fredericksburg to inquire for her. Being told of our visit, she requested her son-in-law to ask me in. When jocularly asked by him if she was going to invite a gentleman into her sick-room, the old lady replied: "Yes, ask Major Mason in—we were old soldiers together."

After Burnside had withdrawn his forces across the Rappahannock, General Lee rode over to Marye's Heights, where I then was, and said to me: "Captain, those people [meaning the enemy] have sent over a flag of truce, asking permission to send a detachment to bury their dead. They have landed near your house, 'The Sentry Box.' Have you any objection to taking this reply down?" As he spoke, he handed me a sealed envelope directed to General Burnside. I accordingly rode into town and made my way down to the river-front of my residence, from which Burnside had only that morning removed his pontoons. There I found a Federal lieutenant-colonel with two soldiers in a boat, holding a flag of truce. I handed him the dispatch and at the same time asked where Burnside was. He answered, "Just up the hill across the river, under an old persimmon-tree, awaiting the dispatch." Telling him my name, I said: "Give my regards to General Burnside, and say to him that I thought he was too familiar with the surroundings of Fredericksburg to butt his brains out deliberately against our stone-walls."

"Do you know General Burnside?" inquired the officer.

"Oh, yes!" I replied, "he is an old acquaintance of mine."

"Then will you wait till I deliver your message and return? He may have something to say."

"I will wait then," was my answer.

In a very short time the flag of truce returned with a request from Burnside that I would come over in the boat to see him. I thoroughly appreciated the fact that I was running the risk of a court-martial from my own side in thus going into the enemy's lines without permission; but being that rather privileged person, a staff-officer, from whom no pass was required and of whom no questions were asked, I determined to accept this invitation and go over.

After passing the river and walking leisurely up the hill, the idle Federal soldiers, seeing a Confederate officer on their side and feeling curious about it, ran down in numbers toward the road. For the first time I was frightened by this result of my act, as I feared that our generals on the hills with their strong glasses, seeing the commotion, might inquire into it. As soon as I approached Burnside, who met me with the greatest cordiality, I expressed to him this fear. He at once sent out couriers to order the soldiers back to camp, and we then sat down on an old log, and being provided with crackers, cheese, sardines, and a bottle of brandy (all luxuries to a Confederate), we discussed this lunch as well as the situation. General Burnside seemed terribly mortified and distressed at his failure, but said that he wanted me to tell his old army friends on the other side that he was not responsible for the attack on Fredericksburg in the manner in which it was made, as he was himself under orders, and was not much more than a figure-head, or words to that effect.

We talked pleasantly for an hour about old times, Burnside asking me many questions about former friends and comrades, now on our side of the fratricidal struggle. When I expressed my wish to return, he wrapped up a bottle of brandy to give me at parting, and sent me under escort to the river. Having recrossed, I mounted my horse and rode back to Marye's Heights, but, enjoyable as this escapade had been, I said nothing, of course, about it to my army friends till long afterward.

That day I witnessed with pain the burial of many thousands of Federal dead that had fallen at Fredericksburg. The night before, the thermometer must have fallen to zero, and the bodies of the slain had frozen to the ground. The ground was frozen nearly a foot deep, and it was necessary to use pickaxes. Trenches were dug on the battle-field and the dead collected and laid in line for burial. It was a sad sight to see these brave soldiers thrown into the trenches, without even a blanket or a word of prayer, and the heavy clods thrown upon them; but the most sickening sight of all was when they threw the dead, some four or five hundred in number, into Wallace's empty ice-house, where they were found—a hecatomb of skeletons—after the war. In 1865–66 some shrewd Yankee contractors obtained government sanction to disinter all the Federal dead on the battle-fields of Fredericksburg, Chancellorsville, the Wilderness, and Spotsylvania Court House. They were to be paid *per capita.* When I went out to see the skeletons taken from the ice-house, I found the contractor provided with unpainted boxes of common pine about six feet long and twelve inches wide; but I soon saw that this scoundrel was dividing the remains so as to make as much by his contract as possible. I at once reported what I had seen to Colonel E. V. Sumner, Jr., then in command of the Sub-district of the Rappahannock. He was utterly shocked at this vandalism. I afterward heard that the contract was taken away from the fellow and given to more reliable parties.

One morning about this time I was at breakfast, when the servant, terribly frightened, announced a sergeant and file of soldiers in my porch asking for me. The ladies immediately imagined that this squad had been sent to arrest me, as they had heard more than once that charges would be pre-

ferred against me by the United States Government for extreme partisan-
ship. Going to the door, I was told by the sergeant that Colonel Sumner
had sent him to me to inquire as to the burial places of the Federal soldiers
whom I had found dead upon my lot and in my house after the battle of
Fredericksburg. I told him that I had found one Federal soldier stretched
on one of my beds. In my parlor, lying on the floor, was another whose entire form left its imprint in blood on the floor—as may be seen to this day.
In my own chamber, sitting up in an old-fashioned easy-chair, I had found
a Federal lieutenant-colonel. When I entered, I supposed him to be alive,
as the back of his head was toward me. Much startled, I approached him,
to find that he had been shot through the neck, and, probably, placed in
that upright position that he might better breathe. He was quite dead. I had
all these bodies, and five or six others found in my yard, buried in one grave
on the wharf. They had been killed, no doubt, by Barksdale's Mississippi
brigade, in their retreat from my lot. I made my report at Sumner's headquarters, after which I took the burial squad to the grave, and then returned
home to quiet the apprehensions of my family.

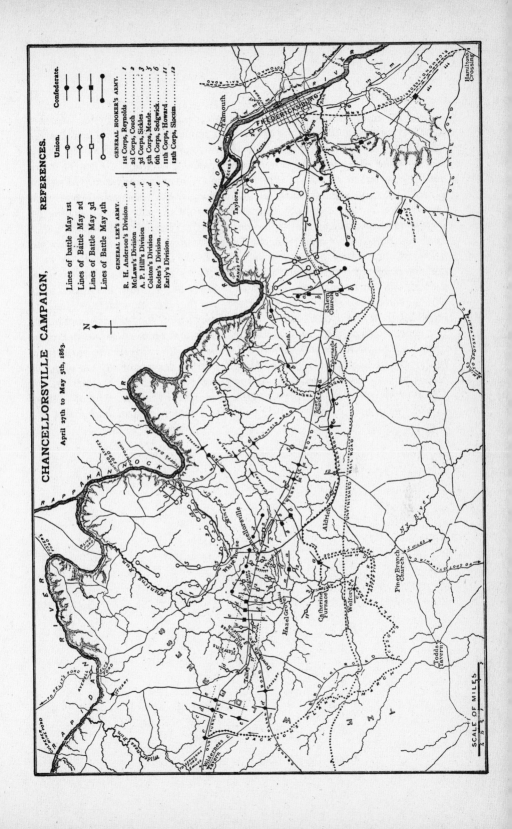

CHANCELLORSVILLE CAMPAIGN,

April 27th to May 5th, 1863.

REFERENCES.

	Union.	Confederate.
Lines of battle May 1st		
Lines of Battle May 2d		
Lines of Battle May 3d		
Lines of Battle May 4th		

GENERAL HOOKER'S ARMY.

1st Corps, Reynolds............ 1
2d Corps, Couch............ 2
3d Corps, Sickles............ 3
5th Corps, Meade............ 5
6th Corps, Sedgwick............ 6
11th Corps, Howard............ 11
12th Corps, Slocum............ 12

GENERAL LEE'S ARMY.

R. H. Anderson's Division........ a
McLaws's Division............ b
A. P. Hill's Division............ c
Colston's Division............ d
Rodes's Division............ e
Early's Division............ f

N

SCALE OF MILES

With the command of the Army of the Potomac to "Fighting Joe" Hooker went a friendly rebuke. In one of his most famous letters, President Lincoln told Hooker he had heard "in such a way as to believe it, your recently saying that both the Army and the Government needed a Dictator. Of course it was not for this, but in spite of it, that I have given you the command. Only those generals who gain successes can set up dictators. What I now ask of you is military success, and I will risk the dictatorship." Hooker's plan for military success was to move the army up the Rappahannock, effect a quick crossing and attack Lee's left flank, while a corps under Sedgwick made diversionary movements below Fredericksburg. It was a sound plan. In the last days of April, the main body of Hooker's army left its camp at Stafford's Heights as unobtrusively as possible and moved upstream. It crossed the river uneventfully and turned south with a good deal of confidence and drive—and then Lee, now alert to Hooker's intention, went into action. Instead of retreating as, in Hooker's calculations, he was supposed to do, he attacked—so vigorously that Hooker lost his nerve and drew back to the Rappahannock in a defensive position. With the initiative of battle now in Lee's hands and the Union commander personally out of action (Hooker had been stunned by a falling porch pillar at his headquarters), the Union army was beaten—recrossing the river under the command of General Couch, the writer of the following report. Another general had failed Mr. Lincoln.

"Outgeneraled by Lee"

BY DARIUS N. COUCH, MAJOR-GENERAL, U. S. V.

I N THE latter part of January, 1863, the Army of the Potomac under
Burnside was still occupying its old camps on the left bank of the Rappahannock, opposite Fredericksburg. After the failures under Burnside
it was evident that the army must have a new commander. For some days
there had been a rumor that Hooker had been fixed upon for the place, and
on the 26th of January it was confirmed. This appointment, undoubtedly,
gave very general satisfaction to the army, except perhaps to a few, mostly
superior officers, who had grown up with it, and had had abundant opportunities to study Hooker's military character; these believed that Mr. Lincoln had committed a grave error in his selection. The army, from its former
reverses, had become quite disheartened and almost sulky; but the quick,
vigorous measures now adopted and carried out with a firm hand had a
magical effect in toning up where there had been demoralization and inspiring confidence where there had been mistrust. Few changes were made

in the heads of the general staff departments, but for his chief-of-staff Hooker applied for Brigadier-General Charles P. Stone, who, through some untoward influence at Washington, was not given to him. This was a mistake of the war dignitaries, although the officer finally appointed to the office, Major-General Daniel Butterfield, proved himself very efficient. Burnside's system of dividing the army into three grand divisions was set aside, and the novelty was introduced of giving to each army corps a distinct badge, an idea which was very popular with officers and men.

Some few days after Mr. Lincoln's visit to the army in April I was again thrown with the President, and it happened in this wise. My pickets along the river were not only on speaking terms with those of the enemy on the other side of the river, but covertly carried on quite a trade in exchanging coffee for tobacco, etc. This morning it was hallooed over to our side: "You have taken Charleston," which news was sent to headquarters. Mr. Lincoln hearing of it wished me to come up and talk the matter over. I went and was ushered into a side tent, occupied only by himself and Hooker. My entrance apparently interrupted a weighty conversation, for both were looking grave. The President's manner was kindly, while the general, usually so courteous, forgot to be conventionally polite. The Charleston rumor having been briefly discussed, Mr. Lincoln remarked that it was time for him to leave. As he stepped toward the general, who had risen from his seat, as well as myself, he said: "I want to impress upon you two gentlemen in your next fight" —and turning to me he completed the sentence—"put in all of your men"— in the long run a good military maxim.

The weather growing favorable for military operations, on April 12th were commenced those suggestive preliminaries to all great battles, clearing out the hospitals, inspecting arms, looking after ammunition, shoeing animals, issuing provisions, and making every preparation necessary to an advance. The next day, the 13th, Stoneman was put in motion at the head of ten thousand finely equipped and well organized cavalry to ascend the Rappahannock and, swinging around, to attack the Confederate cavalry wherever it might be found, and "Fight! fight! fight!" At the end of two days' march Stoneman found the river so swollen by heavy rains that he was constrained to hold up, upon which Hooker suspended his advance until the 27th. This unexpected delay of the cavalry seemingly deranged Hooker's original plan of campaign. He had hoped that Stoneman would have been able to place his horsemen on the railroad between Fredericksburg and Richmond, by which Lee received his supplies, and make a wreck of the whole structure, compelling that general to evacuate his stronghold at Fredericksburg and vicinity and fall back toward Richmond.

I estimate the grand total of Hooker's seven corps at about 113,000 men ready for duty, although the data from which the conclusion is arrived at are not strictly official. This estimate does not include the cavalry corps of not less than 11,000 duty men, nor the reserve artillery, the whole number of guns in the army being 400. Lee's strength in and around Fredericksburg was placed at between 55,000 and 60,000, not including cavalry. It is not known if Hooker's information concerning the Confederate force was reliable, but Peck, operating in front of Norfolk, notified him that two of Lee's divisions under Longstreet were on the south side of the James. The hour was, therefore, auspicious for Hooker to assume the offensive, and he seized it with a boldness which argued well for his fitness to command. The aim was to transfer his army to the south side of the river, where it would have a manœuvring footing not confronted by intrenched positions. On the 27th of April the Eleventh and Twelfth corps were set in motion for Kelly's Ford, twenty-five miles up the Rappahannock, where they concentrated on the evening of the 28th, the Fifth, by reason of its shorter marching distance, moving on the 28th. The object of the expedition was unknown to the corps commanders until communicated to them after their arrival at the ford by the commanding general in person. The Eleventh Corps crossed the Rappahannock, followed in the morning by the Twelfth and Fifth corps—the two former striking for Germanna Ford, a crossing of the Rapidan, the latter for Ely's Ford, lower down the same stream. Both columns, successfully effecting crossings with little opposition from the enemy's pickets, arrived that evening, April 30th, at the point of concentration, Chancellorsville. It had been a brilliantly conceived and executed movement.

In order to confound Lee, orders were issued to assemble the Sixth, Third, and First corps under Sedgwick at Franklin's Crossing and Pollock's Mill, some three miles below Fredericksburg, on the left, before daylight of the morning of the 29th, and throw two bridges across and hold them. This was done under a severe fire of sharp-shooters. The Second Corps, two divisions, marched on the 28th for Banks's Ford, four miles to the right; the other division, Gibbon's, occupying Falmouth, near the river-bank, was directed to remain in its tents, as they were in full view of the enemy, who would readily observe their withdrawal. On the 29th the two divisions of the Second Corps reached United States Ford, held by the enemy; but the advance of the right wing down the river uncovered it, whereupon a bridge of pontoons was thrown across and the corps reached Chancellorsville the same night as the Fifth, Eleventh, and Twelfth. The same day, the 30th, Sedgwick was instructed to place a corps across the river and make a demonstration upon the enemy's right, below Fredericksburg, and the Third Corps received orders to join the right wing at Chancellorsville, where the commanding general arrived the same evening, establishing his headquarters at the Chancellor House, which, with the adjacent grounds, is Chancellorsville. All of the army lying there that night were in exuberant spirits at the success of their general in getting "on the other side" without fighting for a position. As I rode into Chancellorsville that night the general hilarity pervading the camps was particularly noticeable; the soldiers, while chopping wood and lighting fires, were singing merry songs and indulging in peppery camp jokes.

The position at Chancellorsville not only took in reverse the entire system of the enemy's river defenses, but there were roads leading from it directly to his line of communication. But in order to gain the advantages now in the commanding general's grasp he had divided his army into two wings, and the enemy, no ordinary enemy, lay between them. The line of communication connecting the wings was by way of United States Ford and twenty miles long. It was of vital importance that the line be shortened in order to place the wings within easy support of each other. The possession of Banks's Ford, foreshadowed in the instructions given to Slocum, would accomplish all that at present could be wished.

There were three roads over which the right wing could move upon Fredericksburg: the Orange turnpike, from the west, passed through Chancellorsville, and was the most direct; the United States Ford road, crossing the former at Chancellorsville, became the Plank road, bent to the left and united with the turnpike five miles or so from Chancellorsville; the third road fell back from Chancellorsville toward the Rappahannock, passed along by Banks's Ford, six miles distant, and continued to Fredericksburg. That wing was ready for the advance at an early hour in the morning of May 1st, but somehow things dragged; the order defining the movement, instead of being issued the previous night, was not received by the corps commanders, at least by me, until hours after light. Meade was finally pushed out on the left over the Banks's Ford and turnpike roads, Slocum and Howard on the right along the Plank road, the left to be near Banks's Ford by 2 P. M., the right at the junction of its line of movement with the turnpike at 12 M. No opposition was met, excepting that the division marching over the turnpike came upon the enemy two or three miles out, when the sound of their guns was heard at Chancellorsville, and General Hooker ordered me to take Hancock's division and proceed to the support of those engaged. After marching a mile and a half or so I came upon Sykes, who commanded, engaged at the time in drawing back his advance to the position he then occupied. Shortly after Hancock's troops had got into a line in front, an order was received from the commanding general "to withdraw both divisions to Chancellorsville." Turning to the officers around me, Hancock, Sykes, Warren, and others, I told them what the order was, upon which they all agreed with me that the ground should not be abandoned, because of the open country in front and the commanding position. An aide dispatched to General Hooker to this effect, came back in half an hour with positive orders to return. Nothing was to be done but carry out the command, though Warren suggested that I should disobey, and then he rode back to see the general. In the meantime Slocum, on the Plank road to my right, had been ordered in, and the enemy's advance was between that road and my right flank. Sykes was first to move back, then followed by Hancock's regiments over the same road. When all but two of the latter had withdrawn, a third order came to me, brought by one of the general's staff: "Hold on until 5 o'clock." It was then perhaps 2 P. M. Disgusted at the general's vacillation and vexed at receiving an order of such tenor, I replied with warmth unbecoming in a subordinate: "Tell General Hooker he is too late, the enemy are already on my right and rear. I am in full retreat."

The position thus abandoned was high ground, more or less open in front, over which an army might move and artillery be used advantageously; moreover, were it left in the hands of an enemy, his batteries, established on its crest and slopes, would command the position at Chancellorsville. Everything on the whole front was ordered in. General Hooker knew that Lee was apprised of his presence on the south side of the river, and must have expected that his enemy would be at least on the lookout for an advance upon Fredericksburg. But it was of the utmost importance that Banks's Ford should fall into our hands, therefore the enemy ought to have been pressed until their strength or weakness was developed; it would then have been time enough to run away.

Mott's Run, with a considerable brushy ravine, cuts the turnpike three-fourths of a mile east of Chancellorsville. Two of Hancock's regiments, under Colonel Nelson A. Miles, subsequently the Indian fighter, were directed to occupy the ravine. Continuing my way through the woods toward Chancellorsville, I came upon some of the Fifth Corps under arms. Inquiring for their commanding officer, I told him that in fifteen minutes he would be attacked. Before finishing the sentence a volley of musketry was fired into us from the direction of the Plank road. This was the beginning of the battle of Chancellorsville. Troops were hurried into position, but the observer required no wizard to tell him, as they marched past, that the high expectations which had animated them only a few hours ago had given place to disappointment. Proceeding to the Chancellor House, I narrated my operations in front to Hooker, which were seemingly satisfactory, as he said: "It is all right, Couch, I have got Lee just where I want him; he must fight me on my own ground." The retrograde movement had prepared me for something of the kind, but to hear from his own lips that the advantages gained by the successful marches of his lieutenants were to culminate in fighting a defensive battle in that nest of thickets was too much, and I retired from his presence with the belief that my commanding general was a whipped man. The army was directed to intrench itself. At 2 A. M. the corps commanders reported to General Hooker that their positions could be held; at least so said Couch, Slocum, and Howard.

Until after dark on May 1st the enemy confined his demonstrations to finding out the position of our left with his skirmishers. Then he got some guns upon the high ground which we had abandoned as before mentioned, and cannonaded the left of our line. There were not many casualties, but that day a shell severely wounded the adjutant-general of the Second Corps, now General F. A. Walker. Chancellorsville was a strategic point to an offensive or retreating army, as roads diverged from it into every part of Virginia; but for a defensive position it was bad, particularly for such an army as Hooker had under him, which prided itself upon its artillery, which was perhaps equal to any in the world. There were no commanding positions for artillery, and but little open country to operate over; in fact, the advantages of ground for this arm were mainly with the attacking party.

During the 29th and 30th the enemy lay at Fredericksburg observing Sedgwick's demonstrations on the left, entirely unconscious of Hooker's successful crossing of the right wing, until midday of the latter date, but that night Lee formed his plan of operations for checking the farther advance of the force which had not only turned the left flank of his river defenses but was threatening his line of communication with Richmond as well as the rear of his center at Fredericksburg. Stonewall Jackson, who was watching Sedgwick, received instructions to withdraw his corps, march to the left, across the front of Hooker's intrenched position, until its right flank was attained, and assault with his column of 22,000 men, while his commanding general would, with what force he could spare, guard the approaches to Fredericksburg.

On the morning of May 2d our line had become strong enough to resist a front attack unless made in great force; the enemy had also been hard at work on his front, particularly that section of it between the Plank road and turnpike. Sedgwick, the previous night, had been ordered to send the First Corps (Reynolds's) to Chancellorsville. At 7 A. M. a sharp cannonade was opened on our left, followed by infantry demonstrations of no particular earnestness. Two hours later the enemy were observed moving a mile or so to the south and front of the center, and later the same column was reported to the commander of the Eleventh Corps by General Devens, whose division was on the extreme right flank. At 9:30 A. M. a circular directed to Generals Slocum and Howard called attention to this movement and to the weakness of their flanks.

At 11 A. M. our left was furiously cannonaded by their artillery, established on the heights in front of Mott's Run, followed by sharp infantry firing on the fronts of the Second and Twelfth corps. As time flew along and no attack came from the enemy seen moving in front, Hooker conceived that Lee was retreating toward Gordonsville. There was color for this view, as the main road from Fredericksburg to that point diverged from the Plank road two miles to the left of Chancellorsville, and passed along his front at about the same distance. Hooker therefore jumped at the conclusion that the enemy's army was moving into the center of Virginia. But instead of the hostile column being on the Gordonsville road in retreat, it was Stonewall's corps moving on an interior neighborhood road, about one mile distant, and in search of our right flank and rear. At 2 P. M. I went into the Chancellor House, when General Hooker greeted me with the exclamation: "Lee is in full retreat toward Gordonsville, and I have sent out Sickles to capture his artillery." I thought, without speaking it: "If your conception is correct, it is very strange that only the Third Corps should be sent in pursuit." Sickles received orders at 1 P. M. to take two divisions, move to his front and attack, which he did, capturing some hundreds of prisoners. The country on the front being mostly wooded enabled the enemy to conceal his movements and at the same time hold Sickles in check with a rear-guard, which made such a show of strength that reënforcements were called for and furnished. In the meantime Jackson did not for a moment swerve from his purpose, but steadily moved forward to accomplish what he had undertaken.

It was about 5:30 in the evening when the head of Jackson's column found itself on the right and rear of the army, which on that flank consisted of the Eleventh Corps, the extreme right brigade receiving its first intimation of danger from a volley of musketry fired into their rear, followed up so impetuously that no efficient stand could be made by the brigades of the corps that successively attempted to resist the enemy's charge. When General Hooker found out what that terrific roar on his right flank meant he quickly mounted and flew across the open space to meet the onset, passing on his way stampeded pack-mules, officers' horses, caissons, with men and horses running for their lives. Gathering up such troops as were nearest to the scene of action, Berry's division from the Third Corps, some from the Twelfth, Hays's brigade of the Second, and a portion of the Eleventh, an effectual stand was made. Pleasonton, who was returning from the front, where he had been operating with Sickles (at the time Jackson attacked), taking in the state of things, rapidly moved his two regiments of cavalry and a battery to the head and right flank of the enemy's advance columns, when, making a charge and bringing up his own guns, with others of the Eleventh and Third Corps, he was enabled to punish them severely.

Pickets had been thrown out on Howard's flank, but not well to the right and rear. I suspect that the prime reason for the surprise was that the superior officers of the right corps had been put off their guard by adopting the conjecture of Hooker, "Lee's army is in full retreat to Gordonsville," as well as by expecting the enemy to attack precisely where ample preparations had been made to receive him. It can be emphatically stated that no corps in the army, surprised as the Eleventh was at this time, could have held its ground under similar circumstances.

At half-past two that afternoon the Second Corps' lines were assaulted by artillery and infantry. Just previous to Jackson's attack on the right a desperate effort was made by Lee's people to carry the left at Mott's Run, but the men who held it were there to stay. Hooker, desiring to know the enemy's strength in front of the Twelfth Corps, advanced Slocum into the thicket, but that officer found the hostile line too well defended for him to penetrate it and was forced to recall the attacking party. When night put an end to the fighting of both combatants, Hooker was obliged to form a new line for his right flank perpendicular to the old one and barely half a mile to the right of Chancellorsville. Sickles was retired, with the two columns, from his advanced position in the afternoon to near where Pleasonton had had his encounter, before mentioned, some distance to the left of the new line of our right flank and close up to the enemy. The situation was thought to be a very critical one by General Hooker, who had simply a strong body in front of the enemy, but without supports, at least near enough to be used for that purpose. At the same time it was a menace to Jackson's right wing or flank. Before midnight some of the latter's enterprising men pushed forward and actually cut off Sickles's line of communication. When this news was carried to Hooker it caused him great alarm, and preparations were at once made to withdraw the whole front, leaving General Sickles to his fate; but that officer showed himself able to take care of his rear, for he ordered after a little while a column of attack, and communication was restored at the point of the bayonet.

The situation of Jackson's corps on the morning of May 3d was a desperate one, its front and right flank being in the presence of not far from 25,000 men, with the left flank subject to an assault of 30,000, the corps of Meade and Reynolds, by advancing them to the right, where the thicket did not present an insurmountable obstacle. It only required that Hooker should brace himself up to take a reasonable, common-sense view of the state of things, when the success gained by Jackson would have been turned into an overwhelming defeat. But Hooker became very despondent. I think that his being outgeneraled by Lee had a good deal to do with his depression. After the right flank had been established on the morning of the 3d by Sickles getting back into position our line was more compact, with favorable positions for artillery, and the reserves were well in hand. Meade had been drawn in from the left and Reynolds had arrived with the First Corps. The engineers had been directed on the previous night to lay out a new line, its front a half mile in rear of Chancellorsville, with the flanks thrown back—the right to the Rapidan, a little above its junction with the Rappahannock, the left resting on the latter river. The Eleventh Corps, or at least that portion which formed line of battle, was withdrawn from the front and sent to the rear to reorganize and get its scattered parts together, leaving the following troops in front: one division of the Second Corps on the left from Mott's Run to Chancellorsville, the Twelfth Corps holding the center and right flank, aided by the Third Corps and one division of the Second Corps (French's), on the same flank; the whole number in front, according to my estimate, being 37,000 men. The First and Fifth corps in reserve numbered 30,000, and, placing the number of reliable men in the Eleventh Corps at 5000, it will be seen that the reserves nearly equaled those in line of battle in front.

After the day's mishaps Hooker judged that the enemy could not have spared so large a force to move around his front without depleting the defenses of Fredericksburg. Accordingly, at 9 P. M., an imperative order was sent to the commander of the left wing to cross the river at Fredericksburg, march upon Chancellorsville, and be in the vicinity of the commanding general at daylight. But Sedgwick was already across the river and three miles below Fredericksburg. It was 11 P. M., May 2d, when he got the order, and twelve or fourteen miles had to be marched over by daylight. The night was moonlight, but any officer who has had experience in making night marches with infantry will understand the vexatious delays occurring even when the road is clear; but when, in addition, there is an enemy in front, with a line of fortified heights to assault, the problem which Sedgwick had to solve will be pronounced impossible of solution. However, that officer set his column in motion by flank, leaving one division that lay opposite the enemy, who were in force to his left. The marching column, being continually harassed by skirmishers, did not arrive at Fredericksburg until daylight. The first assault upon the heights behind the town failed. Attempts to carry them by flank movements met with no success. Finally a second storming party was organized, and the series of works were taken literally at the point of the bayonet, though at heavy loss. It was then 11 A. M. The column immediately started for Chancellorsville, being more or less obstructed by the enemy until its arrival near Salem Heights, 5 or 6 miles out, where seven brigades under Early, six of which had been driven from the defenses of Fredericksburg, made a stand in conjunction with supports sent from Lee's army before Chancellorsville. This was about the middle of the afternoon, when Sedgwick in force attacked the enemy. Though at first successful, he was subsequently compelled to withdraw those in advance and look to his own safety by throwing his own flanks so as to cover Banks's Ford, the friendly proximity of which eventually saved this wing from utter annihilation.

At about 5 A. M., May 3d, fighting was begun at Chancellorsville, when the Third (Sickles's) Corps began to retire to the left of our proper right flank, and all of that flank soon became fiercely engaged, while the battle ran along the whole line. The enemy's guns on the heights to our left, as well as at every point on the line where they could be established, were vigorously used, while a full division threw itself on Miles at Mott's Run. On the right flank our guns were well handled, those of the Twelfth Corps being conspicuous, and the opposing lines of infantry operating in the thicket had almost hand-to-hand conflicts, capturing and recapturing prisoners. The

331

enemy appeared to know what he was about, for pressing the Third Corps vigorously he forced it back, when he joined or rather touched the left of Lee's main body, making their line continuous from left to right. Another advantage gained by this success was the possession of an open field, from which guns covered the ground up to the Chancellor House. Upon the south porch of that mansion General Hooker stood leaning against one of its pillars, observing the fighting, looking anxious and much careworn. After the fighting had commenced I doubt if any orders were given by him to the commanders on the field, unless, perhaps, "to retire when out of ammunition." None were received by me, nor were there any inquiries as to how the battle was going along my front. On the right flank, where the fighting was desperate, the engaged troops were governed by the corps and division leaders. If the ear of the commanding general was, as he afterward stated, strained to catch the sound of Sedgwick's guns, it could not have heard them in the continuous uproar that filled the air around him; but as Sedgwick, who was known as a fighting officer, had not appeared at the time set—daylight—nor for some hours after, it was conclusive evidence that he had met with strong opposition, showing that all of Lee's army was not at Chancellorsville, so that the moment was favorable for Hooker to try his opponent's strength with every available man. Moreover, the left wing might at that very time be in jeopardy, therefore he was bound by every patriotic motive to strike hard for its relief. If he had remembered Mr. Lincoln's injunction ("Gentlemen, in your next fight put in all of your men"), the face of the day would have been changed and the field won for the Union arms.

Not far from 8:30 A. M. the headquarters pennants of the Third and Twelfth corps suddenly appeared from the right in the open field of Chancellorsville; then the Third began to fall back, it was reported, for want of ammunition, followed by that portion of the Twelfth fighting on the same flank, and the division of the Second Corps on its right. It is not known whether any efforts were made to supply the much-needed ammunition to the Third as well as the Twelfth Corps, whose ammunition was nearly used up when it retired. My impression is that the heads of the ordnance, as well as of other important departments, were not taken into the field during this campaign, which was most unfortunate, as the commanding general had enough on his mind without charging it with details.

The open field seized by Jackson's old corps after the Third Corps drew off was shortly dotted with guns that made splendid practice through an opening in the wood upon the Chancellor House, and everything else, for that matter, in that neighborhood. Hooker was still at his place on the porch, with nothing between him and Lee's army but Geary's division of the Twelfth and Hancock's division and a battery of the Second Corps. But Geary's right was now turned, and that flank was steadily being pressed back along his intrenched line to the junction of the Plank road and the turnpike, when a cannon-shot struck the pillar against which Hooker was leaning and knocked him down. A report flew around that he was killed. I was at the time but a few yards to his left, and, dismounting, ran to the porch. The shattered pillar was there, but I could not find him or any one else. Hurrying through the house, finding no one, my search was continued through the back yard. All the time I was thinking, "If he is killed, what shall I do with this disjointed army?" Passing through the yard I came upon him, to my great joy, mounted, and with his staff also in their saddles. Briefly congratulating him on his escape—it was no time to blubber or use soft expressions—I went about my own business. This was the last I saw of my commanding general in front. The time, I reckon, was from 9:15 to 9:30 A. M., I think nearer the former than the latter. He probably left the field soon after his hurt, but he neither notified me of his going nor did he give any orders to me whatever. Having some little time before this seen that the last stand would be about the Chancellor House, I had sent to the rear for some of the Second Corps batteries, which had been ordered there by the commanding general, but word came back that they were so jammed in with other carriages that it was impossible to extricate them. General Meade, hearing of my wants, kindly sent forward the 5th Maine battery belonging to his corps. It was posted in the rear of the Chancellor House, where the United States Ford road enters the thicket. With such precision did the artillery of Jackson's old corps play upon this battery that all of the officers and most of the non-commissioned officers and men were killed or wounded. The gallant Kirby, whose guns could not be brought up, was mortally wounded in the same battery of which I had for the time placed him in command, and my horse was killed under me while I was trying to get some men to train a gun on the flank of the force then pushing Geary's division. The enemy, having 30 pieces in position on our right, now advanced some of his guns to within 500 or 600 yards of the Chancellor House, where there were only four of Pettit's Second Corps guns to oppose them, making a target of that building and taking the right of Hancock's division in reverse, a portion of which had been withdrawn from its intrenchments and thrown back to the left to meet the enemy should he succeed in forcing Mott's Run. This flank was stoutly held by Colonel Miles, who, by the bye, had been carried off the field, shot through the body. Lee by this time knew well enough, if he had not known before, that the game was sure to fall into his hands, and accordingly plied every gun and rifle that could be brought to bear on us. Still everything was firmly held excepting Geary's right, which was slowly falling to pieces, for the enemy had his flank and there was no help for it. Riding to Geary's left, I found him there dismounted, with sword swinging over his head, walking up and down, exposed to a severe infantry fire, when he said: "My division can't hold its place; what shall I do?" To which I replied: "I don't know, but do as we are doing; fight it out."

333

It was not then too late to save the day. Fifty pieces of artillery, or even forty, brought up and run in front and to the right of the Chancellor House, would have driven the enemy out of the thicket, then forcing back Geary's right, and would have neutralized the thirty guns to the right which were pounding us so hard. But it is a waste of words to write what might have been done. Hooker had made up his mind to abandon the field, otherwise he would not have allowed the Third and part of the Twelfth Corps to leave their ground for want of ammunition. A few minutes after my interview with Geary a staff-officer from General Hooker rode up and requested my presence with that general. Turning to General Hancock, near by, I told him to take care of things and rode to the rear. The Chancellor House was then burning, having been fired in several places by the enemy's shells.

At the farther side of an open field, half a mile in the rear of Chancellorsville, I came upon a few tents (three or four) pitched, around which, mostly dismounted, were a large number of staff-officers. General Meade was also present, and perhaps other generals. General Hooker was lying down I think in a soldier's tent by himself. Raising himself a little as I entered, he said: "Couch, I turn the command of the army over to you. You will withdraw it and place it in the position designated on this map," as he pointed to a line traced on a field-sketch. This was perhaps three-quarters of an hour after his hurt. He seemed rather dull, but possessed of his mental faculties. I do not think that one of those officers outside of the tent knew what orders I was to receive, for on stepping out, which I did immediately on getting my instructions, I met Meade close by, looking inquiringly as if he expected that finally he would receive the order for which he had waited all that long morning, "to go in." Colonel N. H. Davis broke out: "We shall have some fighting now." These incidents are mentioned to show the temper of that knot of officers. No time was to be lost, as only Hancock's division now held Lee's army. Dispatching Major John B. Burt with orders for the front to retire, I rode back to the thicket, accompanied by Meade, and was soon joined by Sickles, and after a little while by Hooker, but he did not interfere with my dispositions. Hancock had a close shave to withdraw in safety, his line being three-fourths of a mile long, with an exultant enemy as close in as they dared, or wished, or chose to be, firing and watching. But everything was brought off, except five hundred men of the Second Corps who, through the negligence of a lieutenant charged by Hancock with the responsibility of retiring the force at Mott's Run, were taken prisoners. However, under the circumstances, the division was retired in better shape than one could have anticipated. General Sickles assisted in getting men to draw off the guns of the Maine battery before spoken of. General Meade wished me to hold the strip of thicket in rear of Chancellorsville, some six hundred yards in front of our new line of defense. My reply was: "I shall not leave men in this thicket to be shelled out by Lee's artillery. Its possession won't give us any strength. Yonder [pointing to the rear] is the line where the fighting is to be done." Hooker heard the conversation, but made no remarks. Considerable bodies of troops of different corps that lay in the brush to the right were brought within the lines, and the battle of Chancellorsville was ended. My pocket diary, May 3d, has the following: "Sickles opened at about 5 A. M. Orders sent by me at 10 for the front to retire; at 12 M. in my new position"; the latter sentence meaning that at that hour my corps was in position on the new or second line of defense.

As to the charge that the battle was lost because the general was intoxicated, I have always stated that he probably abstained from the use of ardent spirits when it would have been far better for him to have continued in his usual habit in that respect. The shock from being violently thrown to the ground, together with the physical exhaustion resulting from loss of sleep and the anxiety of mind incident to the last six days of the campaign, would tell on any man. The enemy did not press us on the second line, Lee simply varying the monotony of watching us by an occasional cannonade from the left, a part of his army having been sent to Salem Church to resist Sedgwick. Sedgwick had difficulty in maintaining his ground, but held his own by hard fighting until after midnight, May 4th–5th, when he recrossed at Banks's Ford.

Some of the most anomalous occurrences of the war took place in this campaign. On the night of May 2d the commanding general, with 80,000 men in his wing of the army, directed Sedgwick, with 22,000, to march to his relief. While that officer was doing this on the 3d, and when it would be expected that every effort would be made by the right wing to do its part, only one-half of it was fought (or rather half-fought, for its ammunition was not replenished), and then the whole wing was withdrawn to a place where it could not be hurt, leaving Sedgwick to take care of himself.

At 12 o'clock on the night of the 4th–5th General Hooker assembled his corps commanders in council. Meade, Sickles, Howard, Reynolds, and myself were present; General Slocum, on account of the long distance from his post, did not arrive until after the meeting was broken up. Hooker stated that his instructions compelled him to cover Washington, not to jeopardize the army, etc. It was seen by the most casual observer that he had made up his mind to retreat. We were left by ourselves to consult, upon which Sickles made an elaborate argument, sustaining the views of the commanding general. Meade was in favor of fighting, stating that he doubted if we could get off our guns. Howard was in favor of fighting, qualifying his views by the remark that our present situation was due to the bad conduct of his corps, or words to that effect. Reynolds, who was lying on the ground very much fatigued, was in favor of an advance. I had similar views to those of Meade as to getting off the guns, but said I "would favor an advance if I could designate the point of attack." Upon collecting the suffrages, Meade, Reynolds, and Howard voted squarely for an advance, Sickles and myself squarely no;

upon which Hooker informed the council that he should take upon himself the responsibility of retiring the army to the other side of the river. As I stepped out of the tent Reynolds, just behind me, broke out, "What was the use of calling us together at this time of night when he intended to retreat anyhow?" . . .

In looking for the causes of the loss of Chancellorsville, the primary ones were that Hooker expected Lee to fall back without risking battle. Finding himself mistaken he assumed the defensive, and was outgeneraled and became demoralized by the superior tactical boldness of the enemy.

LEE AND JACKSON IN COUNCIL

While General Hooker lost the Battle of Chancellorsville, the Confederacy lost something of far more importance—Stonewall Jackson, struck down by a volley fired in nighttime confusion by his own men. The death of its Hannibal, its Cromwell, filled the South with lamentations. Sorrowfully General Lee said, "I know not how to replace him. God's will be done. I trust He will raise up someone in his place."

"No, no, let us pass over the river, and rest under the shade of the trees"

STONEWALL JACKSON'S LAST BATTLE

BY THE REV. JAMES POWER SMITH, CAPTAIN AND ASSISTANT ADJUTANT-GENERAL, C. S. A.

AT DAYBREAK on the morning of the 29th of April, 1863, sleeping in our tents at corps headquarters, near Hamilton's Crossing, we were aroused by Major Samuel Hale, of Early's staff, with the stirring news that Federal troops were crossing the Rappahannock on pontoons under cover of a heavy fog. General Jackson had spent the night at Mr. Yerby's hospitable mansion near by, where Mrs. Jackson had brought her infant child for the father to see. He was at once informed of the news, and promptly issued to his division commanders orders to prepare for action. At his direction I rode a mile across the fields to army headquarters, and finding General Robert E. Lee still slumbering quietly, at the suggestion of Colonel Venable, whom I found stirring, I entered the general's tent and awoke him. Turning his feet out of his cot he sat upon its side as I gave him the tidings from the front. Expressing no surprise, he playfully said: "Well, I thought I heard firing, and was beginning to think it was time some of you young fellows were coming to tell me what it was all about. Tell your good general that I am sure he knows what to do. I will meet him at the front very soon."

It was Sedgwick who had crossed, and, marching along the river front to impress us with his numbers, was now intrenching his line on the river road, under cover of Federal batteries on the north bank.

All day long we lay in the old lines of the action of December preceding, watching the operation of the enemy. Nor did we move through the next day, the 30th of April. During the forenoon of the 29th General Lee had been informed by General J. E. B. Stuart of the movement in force by General Hooker across the Rappahannock upon Chancellorsville; and during the night of Thursday, April 30th, General Jackson withdrew his corps, leaving Early and his division with Barksdale's brigade to hold the old lines from Hamilton's Crossing along the rear of Fredericksburg.

By the light of a brilliant moon, at midnight, that passed into an early dawn of dense mist, the troops were moved, by the Old Mine road, out of sight of the enemy, and about 11 A. M. of Friday, May 1st, they reached Anderson's position, confronting Hooker's advance from Chancellorsville, near the Tabernacle Church on the Plank road. To meet the whole Army of the Potomac, under Hooker, General Lee had of all arms about 60,000 men. General Longstreet, with part of his corps, was absent below Petersburg. General Lee had two divisions of Longstreet's corps, Anderson's, and McLaws's, and Jackson's corps, consisting of four divisions, A. P. Hill's, D. H. Hill's, commanded by Rodes, Trimble's, commanded by Colston, and Early's; and about 170 pieces of field-artillery. The divisions of Anderson and McLaws had been sent from Fredericksburg to meet Hooker's advance from Chancellorsville; Anderson on Wednesday, and McLaws (except Barksdale's brigade, left with Early) on Thursday. At the Tabernacle Church, about four miles east of Chancellorsville, the opposing forces met and brisk skirmishing began. On Friday, Jackson, reaching Anderson's position, took command of the Confederate advance, and urged on his skirmish line under Brigadier-General Ramseur with great vigor. How the muskets rattled along a front of a mile or two, across the unfenced fields, and through the woodlands! What spirit was imparted to the line, and what cheers rolled along its length, when Jackson, and then Lee himself, appeared riding abreast of the line along the Plank road! Slowly but steadily the line advanced, until at night-fall all Federal pickets and skirmishers were driven back upon the body of Hooker's force at Chancellorsville.

Here we reached a point, a mile and a half from Hooker's lines, where a road turns down to the left toward the old Catherine Furnace; and here at the fork of the roads General Lee and General Jackson spent the night, resting on the pine straw, curtained only by the close shadow of the pine forest. A little after night-fall I was sent by General Lee upon an errand to General A. P. Hill, on the old stone turnpike a mile or two north; and returning some time later with information of matters on our right, I found General Jackson retired to rest, and General Lee sleeping at the foot of a tree, covered with his army cloak. As I aroused the sleeper, he slowly sat up on the ground and said, "Ah, Captain, you have returned, have you? Come here and tell me what you have learned on the right." Laying his hand on me he drew me down by his side, and, passing his arm around my shoulder, drew me near to him in a fatherly way that told of his warm and kindly heart. When I had related such information as I had secured for him, he thanked me for accomplishing his commission, and then said he regretted that the young men about General Jackson had not relieved him of annoyance, by finding a battery of the enemy which had harassed our advance, adding that the young men of that day were not equal to what they were when he was a young man. Seeing immediately that he was jesting and disposed to rally me, as he often did young officers, I broke away from the hold on me which he tried to retain, and, as he laughed heartily through the stillness of the night, I went off to make a bed of my saddle-blanket, and, with my head in my saddle, near my horse's feet, was soon wrapped in the heavy slumber of a wearied soldier.

Some time after midnight I was awakened by the chill of the early morning hours, and, turning over, caught a glimpse of a little flame on the slope above me, and sitting up to see what it meant, I saw, bending over a scant fire of twigs, two men seated on old cracker boxes and warming their hands over the little fire. I had but to rub my eyes and collect my wits to recognize the figures of Robert E. Lee and Stonewall Jackson. Who can tell the story of that quiet council of war between two sleeping armies? Nothing remains on record to tell of plans discussed, and dangers weighed, and a great purpose formed, but the story of the great day so soon to follow.

It was broad daylight, and the thick beams of yellow sunlight came through the pine branches, when some one touched me rudely with his foot, saying: "Get up, Smith, the general wants you!" As I leaped to my feet the rhythmic click of the canteens of marching infantry caught my ear. Already in motion! What could it mean? In a moment I was mounted and at the side of the general, who sat on his horse by the roadside, as the long line of our troops cheerily, but in silence as directed, poured down the Furnace road. His cap was pulled low over his eyes, and, looking up from under the visor, with lips compressed, indicating the firm purpose within, he nodded to me, and in brief and rapid utterance, without a superfluous word, as though all were distinctly formed in his mind and beyond question, he gave me orders for our wagon and ambulance trains. From the open fields in our rear, at the head of the Catharpin road, all trains were to be moved upon that road to Todd's Tavern, and thence west by interior roads, so that our troops would be between them and the enemy at Chancellorsville. My orders having been delivered and the trains set in motion, I returned to the site of our night's bivouac, to find that General Jackson and his staff had followed the marching column.

Slow and tedious is the advance of a mounted officer who has to pass, in narrow wood roads through dense thickets, the packed column of marching infantry, to be recognized all along the line and good-naturedly chaffed by many a gay-spirited fellow: "Say, here's one of Old Jack's little boys, let him by, boys!" in the most patronizing tone. "Have a good breakfast this morning, sonny?" "Better hurry up, or you'll catch it for getting behind." "Tell Old Jack we're all a-comin'." "Don't let him begin the fuss till we get thar!". . .

Reaching the Orange Plank road, General Jackson himself rode with Fitz Lee to reconnoiter the position of Howard, and then sent the Stonewall brigade of Virginia troops, under Brigadier-General Paxton, to hold the point where the Germanna Plank road obliquely enters the Orange road. Leading the main column of his force farther on the Brock road to the old turnpike, the head of the column turned sharply eastward toward Chancellorsville. About a mile had been passed, when he halted and began the disposition of his forces to attack Howard. Rodes's division, at the head of the column, was thrown into line of battle, with Colston's forming the second line and A. P. Hill's the third, while the artillery under Colonel Stapleton Crutchfield moved in column on the road, or was parked in a field on the right. The well-trained skirmishers of Rodes's division, under Major Eugene Blackford, were thrown to the front. It must have been between 5 and 6 o'clock in the evening, Saturday, May 2d, when these dispositions were completed. Upon his stout-built, long-paced little sorrel, General Jackson sat, with visor low over his eyes and lips compressed, and with his watch in his hand. Upon his right sat General Robert E. Rodes, the very picture of a soldier, and every inch all that he appeared. Upon the right of Rodes sat Major Blackford.

"Are you ready, General Rodes?" said Jackson.

"Yes, sir!" said Rodes, impatient for the advance.

"You can go forward then," said Jackson.

A nod from Rodes was order enough for Blackford, and then suddenly the woods rang with the bugle call, and back came the responses from bugles on the right and left, and the long line of skirmishers, through the wild thicket of undergrowth, sprang eagerly to their work, followed promptly by the quick steps of the line of battle. For a moment all the troops seemed buried in the depths of the gloomy forest, and then suddenly the echoes waked and swept the country for miles, never failing until heard at the headquarters of Hooker at Chancellorsville—the wild "rebel yell" of the long Confederate lines.

Never was assault delivered with grander enthusiasm. Fresh from the long winter's waiting, and confident from the preparation of the spring, the troops were in fine condition and in high spirits. The boys were all back from home or sick leave. "Old Jack" was there upon the road in their midst; there could be no mistake and no failure. . . .

A little show of earth-work facing the south was quickly taken by us in reverse from the west. Flying battalions are not flying buttresses for an army's stability. Across Talley's fields the rout begins. Over at Hawkins's hill, on the north of the road, Carl Schurz makes a stand, soon to be driven into the same hopeless panic. By the quiet Wilderness Church in the vale, leaving wounded and dead everywhere, by Melzi Chancellor's, on into the deep thicket again, the Confederate lines pressed forward—now broken and all disaligned by the density of bush that tears the clothes away; now halting to load and deliver a volley upon some regiment or fragment of the enemy that will not move as fast as others. Thus the attack upon Hooker's flank was a grand success, beyond the most sanguine expectation.

The writer of this narrative, an aide-de-camp of Jackson's, was ordered to remain at the point where the advance began, to be a center of communication between the general and the cavalry on the flanks, and to deliver orders to detachments of artillery still moving up from the rear. A fine black charger, with elegant trappings, deserted by his owner and found tied to a tree, became mine only for that short and eventful night-fall; and about 8 P. M., in the twilight, thus comfortably mounted, I gathered my couriers about me and went forward to find General Jackson. The storm of battle had swept far on to the east and become more and more faint to the ear, until silence came with night over the fields and woods. As I rode along that old turnpike, passing scattered fragments of Confederates looking for their regiments, parties of prisoners concentrating under guards, wounded men by the roadside and under the trees at Talley's and Chancellor's, I had reached an open field on the right, a mile west of Chancellorsville, when, in the dusky twilight, I saw horsemen near an old cabin in the field. Turning toward them, I found Rodes and his staff engaged in gathering the broken and scattered troops that had swept the two miles of battle-field. "General Jackson is just ahead on the road, Captain," said Rodes; "tell him I will be here at this cabin if I am wanted." I had not gone a hundred yards before I heard firing, a shot or two, and then a company volley upon the right of the road, and another upon the left. A few moments farther on I met Captain Murray Taylor, an aide of A. P. Hill's, with tidings that Jackson and Hill were wounded, and some around them killed, by the fire of their own men. Spurring my horse into a sweeping gallop, I soon passed the Confederate line of battle, and, some three or four rods on its front, found the general's horse beside a pine sapling on the left, and a rod beyond a little party of men caring for a wounded officer. The story of the sad event is briefly told, and, in essentials, very much as it came to me from the lips of the wounded general himself, and in everything confirmed and completed by those who were eye-witnesses and near companions.

When Jackson had reached the point where his line now crossed the turnpike, scarcely a mile west of Chancellorsville, and not half a mile from a line of Federal troops, he had found his front line unfit for the farther and vigorous advance he desired, by reason of the irregular character of the fighting, now right, now left, and because of the dense thickets, through which it was impossible to preserve alignment. Division commanders found it more and more difficult as the twilight deepened to hold their broken brigades in hand. Regretting the necessity of relieving the troops in front, General Jackson had ordered A. P. Hill's division, his third and reserve line, to be placed in front. While this change was being effected, impatient and anxious, the general rode forward on the turnpike, followed by two or three of his staff and a number of couriers and signal sergeants. He passed the swamp depression and began the ascent of the hill toward Chancellorsville, when he came upon a line of the Federal infantry lying on their arms. Fired at by one or two muskets (two musket-balls from the enemy whistled over my head as I came to the front), he turned and came back toward his line, upon the side of the road to his left. As he rode near to the Confederate troops, just placed in position and ignorant that he was in the front, the left company began firing to the front, and two of his party fell from their saddles dead—Captain Boswell, of the Engineers, and Sergeant Cunliffe, of the Signal Corps. Spurring his horse across the road to his right, he was met by a second volley from the right company of Pender's North Carolina brigade. Under this volley, when not two rods from the troops, the general received three balls at the same instant. One penetrated the palm of his right hand and was cut out that night from the back of his hand. A second passed around the wrist of the left arm and out through the left hand. A third ball passed through the left arm half-way from shoulder to elbow. The large bone of the upper arm was splintered to the elbow-joint, and the wound bled freely. His horse turned quickly from the fire, through the thick bushes which swept the cap from the general's head, and scratched his forehead, leaving drops of blood to stain his face. As he lost his hold upon the bridle-rein, he reeled from the saddle, and was caught by the arms of Captain Wilbourn, of the Signal Corps. Laid upon the ground, there came at once to his succor General A. P. Hill and members of his staff. The writer reached his side a minute after, to find General Hill holding the head and shoulders of the wounded chief. Cutting open the coat-sleeve from wrist to shoulder, I found the wound in the upper arm, and with my handkerchief I bound the arm above the wound to stem the flow of blood. Couriers were sent for Dr. Hunter McGuire, the surgeon of the corps and the general's trusted friend, and for an ambulance. Being outside of our lines, it was urgent that he should be moved at once. With difficulty litter-bearers were brought from the line near by, and the general was placed upon the litter and carefully raised to the shoulder, I myself bearing one corner. A moment after, artillery from the Federal side was opened upon us; great broadsides thundered over the woods; hissing shells searched the dark thickets through, and shrapnels swept the road along which we moved. Two or three steps farther, and the litter-bearer at my side was struck and fell, but, as the litter turned, Major Watkins Leigh, of Hill's staff, happily caught it. But the fright of the men was so great that we were obliged to lay the litter and its burden down upon the road. As the litter-bearers ran to the cover of the trees, I threw myself by the general's side and held him firmly to the ground as he attempted to rise. Over us swept the rapid fire of shot and shell—grape-shot striking fire upon the flinty rock of the road all around us, and sweeping from their feet horses and men of the artillery just moved to the front. Soon the firing veered to the other side of the road, and I sprang to my feet, assisted the general to rise, passed my arm around him, and with the wounded man's weight thrown heavily upon me, we forsook the road. Entering the woods, he sank to the ground from exhaustion, but the litter was soon brought, and again rallying a few men, we essayed to carry him farther, when a second bearer fell at my side. This time, with none to assist, the litter careened, and the general fell to the ground, with a groan of deep pain. Greatly alarmed, I sprang to his head, and, lifting his head as a stray beam of moonlight came through clouds and leaves, he opened his eyes and wearily said: "Never mind me, Captain, never mind me." Raising him again to his feet, he was accosted by Brigadier-General Pender: "Oh, General, I hope you are not seriously wounded. I will have to retire my troops to re-form them, they are so much broken by this fire." But Jackson, rallying his strength, with firm voice said: "You must hold your ground, General Pender; you must hold your ground, sir!" and so uttered his last command on the field.

Again we resorted to the litter, and with difficulty bore it through the bush, and then under a hot fire along the road. Soon an ambulance was reached, and stopping to seek some stimulant at Chancellor's (Dowdall's Tavern), we were found by Dr. McGuire, who at once took charge of the wounded man. Passing back over the battle-field of the afternoon, we reached the Wilderness store, and then, in a field on the north, the field-hospital of our corps under Dr. Harvey Black. Here we found a tent prepared, and after midnight the left arm was amputated near the shoulder, and a ball taken from the right hand.

All night long it was mine to watch by the sufferer, and keep him warmly wrapped and undisturbed in his sleep. At 9 A. M., on the next day, when he aroused, cannon firing again filled the air, and all the Sunday through the fierce battle raged, General J. E. B. Stuart commanding the Confederates in Jackson's place. A dispatch was sent to the commanding general to announce formally his disability—tidings General Lee had received during the night with profound grief. There came back the following note:

GENERAL: I have just received your note, informing me that you were wounded. I cannot express my regret at the occurrence. Could I have directed events, I should have chosen, for the good of the country, to have been disabled in your stead. I congratulate you upon the victory which is due to your skill and energy.

Most truly yours,

R. E. LEE, GENERAL

345

When this dispatch was handed to me at the tent, and I read it aloud, General Jackson turned his face away and said, "General Lee is very kind, but he should give the praise to God."

The long day was passed with bright hopes for the wounded general, with tidings of success on the battle-field, with sad news of losses, and messages to and from other wounded officers brought to the same infirmary.

On Monday the general was carried in an ambulance, by way of Spotsylvania Court House, to most comfortable lodging at Chandler's, near Guinea's Station, on the Richmond, Fredericksburg and Potomac railroad. And here, against our hopes, notwithstanding the skill and care of wise and watchful surgeons, attended day and night by wife and friends, amid the prayers and tears of all the Southern land, thinking not of himself, but of the cause he loved, and for the troops who had followed him so well and given him so great a name, our chief sank, day by day, with symptoms of pneumonia and some pains of pleurisy, until, at 3:15 P. M. on the quiet of the Sabbath afternoon, May 10th, 1863, he raised himself from his bed, saying, "No, no, let us pass over the river, and rest under the shade of the trees"; and, falling again to his pillow, he passed away, "over the river, where, in a land where warfare is not known or feared, he rests forever 'under the trees.' "

His shattered arm was buried in the family burying-ground of the Ellwood place—Major J. H. Lacy's—near his last battle-field.

His body rests, as he himself asked, "in Lexington, in the Valley of Virginia." The spot where he was so fatally wounded in the shades of the Wilderness is marked by a large quartz rock, placed there by the care of his chaplain and friend, the Rev. Dr. B. F. Lacy, and the latter's brother, Major Lacy.

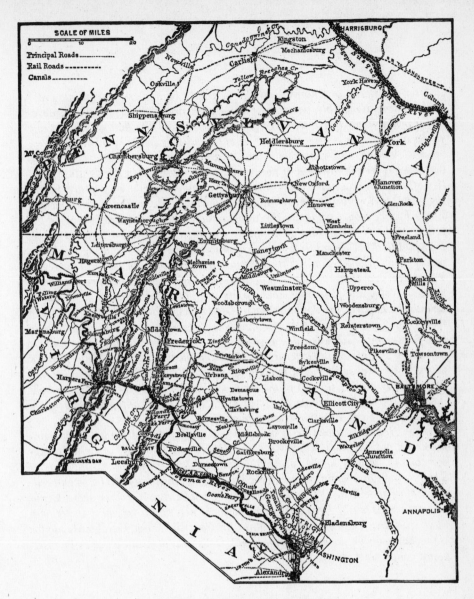

MAP OF THE GETTYSBURG CAMPAIGN

*After the Battle of Chancellorsville, General Lee had two immediate prob-
lems: finding, if possible, a successor to Jackson, and planning the future movements of the Army of Northern Virginia. It seemed to him that spring that any
primarily defensive course could only result eventually in his being pushed back
upon Richmond, and, conversely, that there were persuasive reasons for his undertaking a second invasion of the North. His confidence in the fighting qualities of his men had never been higher. If he could threaten or capture Washington after a victorious march through Pennsylvania, perhaps England and
surely France would recognize the Confederacy. Such a thrust might cause the
people of the North to lose all confidence in their leaders and demand peace.
It should make it necessary for the Union military planners to bring reinforcements from the mid-South, thus relieving the pressures on General Bragg in
Tennessee and General Pemberton at Vicksburg. Finally, Lee needed horses
for his cavalry and food and shoes for his men, and they were all to be had in
abundance north of the Potomac. All of Lee's officers favored the invasion (even
the less sanguine Longstreet acquiescing when Lee agreed the campaign "should
be offensive in strategy but defensive in tactics"); so early in June the new vast
movement began—with General "Dick" Ewell, just made a lieutenant general
to try to fill Jackson's boots, leading off up the Valley; Longstreet in his methodical way moving up east of the Blue Ridge; "Jeb" Stuart covering the right
flank but spoiling for another raid; and A. P. Hill playing cat to Hooker's mouse
at Fredericksburg. Eighty thousand men.*

*When Hooker grasped Lee's intentions, he pulled away from the Rappahan-
nock and moved slowly northward on a line roughly parallel to Lee's strung-
out column. Urging him to strike that column, Lincoln wrote, "If the head of
Lee's army is at Martinsburg and the tail of it on the plank road between Fredericksburg and Chancellorsville, the animal must be very thin somewhere. Could
you not break him?" Hooker thought he could not, and it cost him his job. On
June 27th, the President replaced him with General George Gordon Meade for
whom fate was preparing a terrible rendezvous at a pleasant place in Pennsylvania called Gettysburg.*

"There was much glory"

THE FIRST DAY AT GETTYSBURG

BY HENRY J. HUNT, BREVET MAJOR-GENERAL, U. S. A., CHIEF OF ARTILLERY OF
THE ARMY OF THE POTOMAC

T HE BATTLES of Fredericksburg and Chancellorsville raised the
confidence of the Confederate Army of Northern Virginia to such a
height as to cause its subordinate officers and soldiers to believe that,
as opposed to the Army of the Potomac, they were equal to any demand that
could be made upon them. Their belief in the superiority of the Southerner
to the Northerner as a fighter was no longer, as at the beginning of the war,
a mere provincial conceit, for it was now supported by signal successes in
the field. On each of these two occasions the Army of the Potomac had been
recently reorganized under a new general, presumably abler than his predecessor and possessing the confidence of the War Department, and the results were crowning victories for the Confederates. Yet at Fredericksburg
defeat was not owing to any lack of fighting qualities on the part of the
Federal soldiers, but rather to defective leadership.

At Chancellorsville both qualities were called in question. In none of the
previous battles between these armies had the disparity of numbers been so
great. The Federal general had taken the initiative, his plan of operations was

349

excellent, and his troops were eager for battle. The Confederates could at first oppose but a portion of their inferior force to the attack of greatly superior numbers, and the boast of the Federal commander, that "the Army of Northern Virginia was the legitimate property of the Army of the Potomac," seemed in a fair way to be justified, when at first contact the advantages already gained were thrown away by the assumption of a timid, defensive attitude. Lee's bold offensive, which followed immediately on this exhibition of weakness, the consequent rout of a Federal army-corps, and the subsequent retreat of the whole army, a large portion of which had not been engaged, confirmed the exultant Confederates in their conviction—which now became an article of faith—that both in combat and in generalship the superiority of the Southerner was fully established. The Federal soldiers returned from Chancellorsville to their camps on the northern bank of the Rappahannock, mortified and incensed at finding themselves, through no fault of their own, in the condition of having in an offensive campaign lost the battle without fighting, except when the enemy forced it upon them.

Yet in this battle the Northern soldier fought well. Under the circumstances no men could have withstood such a sudden attack as that made by "Stonewall" Jackson on the flank and rear of the Eleventh Corps; but as soon as Jackson encountered troops in condition for action, his pursuit was checked and he was brought to a stand. The panic did not extend beyond the routed corps, nor to all of that, for its artillery and so much of its infantry as could form a proper line did their duty, and the army, far from being "demoralized" by this mishap, simply ridiculed the corps which, from its supposed want of vigilance, had allowed itself to be surprised in a position in which it could not fight. The surprise itself was not the fault of the troops, and in subsequent battles the corps redeemed its reputation. Both armies were composed in the main of Americans, and there was little more difference between their men than might be found between those of either army at different periods, or under varying circumstances; for although high bounties had already brought into the Federal ranks an inferior element which swelled the muster-rolls and the number of stragglers, "bounty jumping" had not as yet become a regular business. . . .

General Lee, who felt great confidence in his own troops, and overrated the effects of successive reverses on the Federal soldiers, now resolved to assume the offensive, for he knew that to remain on the defensive would in the end force him back on Richmond. He determined, therefore, in case the Army of the Potomac could not be brought to action under favorable circumstances in Virginia, to transfer, if permitted, the field of operations to Northern soil, where a victory promptly followed up might give him possession of Baltimore or Washington, and perhaps lead to the recognition of the Confederacy by foreign powers. The valley of the Shenandoah offered a safe line of operations; the Federal troops occupying it were rather a bait than an obstacle, and to capture or destroy them seemed quite practicable to one who controlled absolutely all Confederate troops within the sphere of his operations. The sharp lesson he had administered the previous year had not been heeded by the Federal War Office; an opportunity now offered to repeat it, and he took his measures accordingly. In case his Government would not consent to a bolder offensive, he could at least clear the valley of Virginia of the enemy—a distinct operation, yet a necessary preliminary to an invasion of the North. This work was assigned to Lieutenant-General Ewell, an able officer, in every way qualified for such an enterprise.

In anticipation of the new campaign, Lee's army was strengthened and reorganized into three army-corps of three divisions each. Each division consisted of four brigades, except Rodes's and Anderson's, which had five each, and Pickett's, which had three at Gettysburg—in all, thirty-seven infantry brigades. The cavalry were the select troops of the Confederacy. Officers and men had been accustomed all their lives to the use of horses and arms, "and to the very end the best blood in the land rode after Stuart, Hampton, and the Lees." They were now organized as a division, under Major-General J. E. B. Stuart, consisting of the six brigades of Hampton, Robertson, Fitzhugh Lee, Jenkins, W. E. Jones, and W. H. F. Lee, and six batteries of horse-artillery under Major R. F. Beckham. To these should be added Imboden's command, a strong brigade of over 2000 effective horsemen and a battery of horse-artillery, which had been operating in the mountain country and was now near Staunton, awaiting orders. The artillery had recently received an excellent organization under its commandant-in-chief, General Pendleton. It consisted, besides the horse-artillery, of fifteen so-called "battalions," each of four batteries, with one lieutenant-colonel and a major. To each army-corps were attached five battalions, one for each division and two as a reserve, the whole under a colonel as chief of artillery. The total number of batteries was 69, of guns 287, of which 30 were with the cavalry. With few exceptions the batteries were of four guns each. The army was commanded by a full general, each army-corps, except the artillery, by a lieutenant-general, each division by a major-general, each brigade, except two, by brigadier-generals. Nearly all these officers were veterans of proved ability and many had served in the Mexican war.

In the Army of the Potomac the discharge of 58 regiments had reduced its strength since Chancellorsville by 25,000 effectives, partly replaced by 5 brigades numbering less than 12,000 men. At the battle of Gettysburg the 7 army-corps consisted of 19 infantry divisions, 7 of which had 2 brigades, 11 had 3, and 1 had 4; in all 51 brigades. The army and army-corps were commanded by major-generals, the divisions by 3 major-generals and 16 brigadier-generals, the infantry brigades by 22 brigadier-generals and 29 colonels. The average strength of army-corps and divisions was about half that of the Confederates, a fact that should be kept in mind, or the terms will be misleading. The cavalry had been raised under disadvantages. Men accustomed to the use of both horses and arms were comparatively few in the North and required training in everything that was necessary to make a trooper. The theater of war was not considered favorable for cavalry, and it was distributed to the various headquarters for escort duty, guards, and orderlies. It was not until 1863 that it was united under General Pleasonton in a corps consisting of three weak divisions, Buford's, D. McM. Gregg's and Duffié's, afterward consolidated into two, Stahel's cavalry, which joined at Frederick, June 28th, becoming the third division. The corps was then organized as follows: First Division, Buford: brigades, Gamble, Devin, Merritt; Second Division, Gregg: brigades, McIntosh, Huey, J. Irvin Gregg; Third Division, Kilpatrick: brigades, Farnsworth, Custer. The divisions and three of the brigades were commanded by brigadier-generals, the other five brigades by colonels. To the cavalry were attached Robertson's and Tidball's brigades of horse-artillery. Under excellent chiefs and the spirit created by its new organization, the Federal cavalry soon rivaled that of the Confederates. . . .

Early in June Lee's army began to move, and by the 8th Longstreet's and Ewell's corps had joined Stuart's cavalry at Culpeper. A. P. Hill's corps was left in observation at Fredericksburg; and so skillfully were the changes concealed that Hooker, believing that all the enemy's infantry were still near that town, ordered Pleasanton to beat up Stuart's camps at Culpeper, and get information as to the enemy's position and proposed movements. For these purposes he gave Pleasonton two small brigades of infantry, 3000 men under Generals Ames and Russell, which carried his total force to 10,981. They were echeloned along the railroad, which crosses the river at Rappahannock Station, and runs thence ten miles to Culpeper. About midway is Brandy Station a few hundred yards north of which is Fleetwood Hill. Dividing his force equally, Pleasonton ordered Buford and Ames to cross at Beverly Ford, and Gregg, Duffié, and Russell at Kelly's Ford. All were to march to Brandy Station, Duffié being thrown out to Stevensburg, seven miles east of Culpeper, to watch the Fredericksburg road. Then the whole force was to move on Culpeper. On the 8th, General Lee, having sent Jenkins's brigade as Ewell's advance into the valley, reviewed the other 5 brigades of Stuart, 10,292 combatants, on the plains near Brandy Station. After the review they were distributed in the neighborhood with a view to crossing the Rappahannock on the 9th, Stuart establishing his headquarters at Fleetwood. Accident had thus disposed his forces in the most favorable manner to meet Pleasonton's converging movements.

At daybreak Buford crossed and drove the enemy's pickets from the ford back to the main body, near St. James's church. Stuart, on the first report of the crossing, sent Robertson's brigade toward Kelly's to watch that ford, and Colonel M. C. Butler's 2d South Carolina to Brandy Station. He himself took the command at the church, where he was attacked by Buford. At Brandy Station W. H. F. Lee was wounded, and Colonel Chambliss took command of his brigade. Meantime Gregg had crossed at Kelly's Ford, and Duffié, leading, took a southerly road, by which he missed Robertson's brigade. Learning that Duffié's advance had reached Stevensburg and that Buford was heavily engaged, Gregg pushed direct for Brandy Station, sending orders to Duffié to follow his movement. Stuart, notified of his approach, had sent in haste some artillery and two of Jones's regiments to Fleetwood, and Colonel Butler started at once for Stevensburg, followed soon after by Wickham's 4th Virginia. On their approach two squadrons of the 6th Ohio, in occupation of the place, fell back skirmishing. Duffié sent two regiments to their aid, and after a severe action, mainly with the 2d South Carolina, reoccupied the village. In this action Colonel Butler lost a leg, and his lieutenant-colonel, Hampton, was killed.

On Gregg's arrival near Brandy Station the enemy appeared to be in large force, with artillery, on and about Fleetwood Hill. He promptly ordered an attack; the hill was carried, and the two regiments sent by Stuart were driven back. Buford now attacked vigorously and gained ground steadily, for Stuart had to reënforce his troops at Fleetwood from the church. In the struggles that followed, the hill several times changed masters; but as Duffié did not make his appearance, Gregg was finally overmatched and withdrew, leaving three of his guns, two of them disabled, in the enemy's hands, nearly all of their horses being killed and most of their cannoneers *hors de combat*. There were some demonstrations of pursuit, but the approach of Buford's reserve brigade stopped them. Duffié finally came up and Gregg reported to Pleasonton, informing him of the approach of Confederate infantry from Culpeper. Pleasonton, who had captured some important dispatches and orders, now considered his mission accomplished, and ordered a withdrawal of his whole command. This was effected leisurely and without molestation. Gregg recrossed at Rappahannock Station, Buford at Beverly Ford, and at sunset the river again flowed between the opposing forces. Stuart reports his losses at 485, of whom 301 were killed or wounded. Pleasonton reports an aggregate loss (exclusive of Duffié's, which would not exceed 25) of 907, of whom 421 were killed or wounded. In nearly all the previous so-called "cavalry" actions, the troops had fought as dismounted dragoons. This was in the main a true cavalry battle, and enabled the Federals to dispute the superiority hitherto claimed by, and conceded to, the Confederate cavalry. In this respect the affair was an important one. It did not, however, delay Lee's designs on the valley; he had already sent Imboden toward Cumberland to destroy the railroad and canal from that place to Martinsburg.

Milroy's Federal division, about 9000 strong, occupied Winchester, with McReynolds's brigade in observation at Berryville. Kelley's division of about 10,000 men was at Harper's Ferry, with a detachment of 1200 infantry and a battery under Colonel B. F. Smith at Martinsburg. On the night of June 11th, Milroy received instructions to join Kelley, but, reporting that he could hold Winchester, was authorized to remain there. Ewell, leaving Brandy Station June 10th, reached Cedarville *via* Chester Gap on the evening of the 12th, whence he detached Jenkins and Rodes to capture McReynolds, who, discovering their approach, withdrew to Winchester. They then pushed on to Martinsburg, and on the 14th drove out the garrison. Smith's infantry crossed the Potomac at Shepherdstown, and made its way to Maryland Heights; his artillery retreated by the Williamsport road, was pursued, and lost five guns.

Meanwhile Ewell, with Early's and Edward Johnson's divisions, marched direct on Winchester. Arriving in the neighborhood on the evening of the 13th, he ordered Early on the 14th to leave a brigade in observation on the south of the town, move his main force under cover of the hills to the north-western side, and seize the out-works which commanded the main fort. He also ordered Johnson to deploy his division on the east of the town, so as to divert attention from Early. This was so successfully done that the latter placed, unperceived, twenty guns and an assaulting column in position, and at 6 P. M., by a sudden attack, carried the outworks, driving the garrisons into the body of the place. This capture was a complete surprise, and Milroy called a council of war, which decided on an immediate retreat, abandoning the artillery and wagons. Ewell had anticipated this, and ordered Johnson to occupy with a brigade a position on the Martinsburg pike, north of Winchester. The retreat commenced at 2 A. M. of the 15th, and after proceeding three or four miles, the advance encountered Johnson's troops, attacked vigorously, and at first successfully, but, the enemy receiving reënforcements, a hard fight ensued in which the Federals lost heavily. The retreat was then continued; the troops separated in the darkness, one portion reaching Harper's Ferry, another crossing the Potomac at Hancock. On the 15th Ewell crossed the river, occupied Hagerstown and Sharpsburg, and sent Jenkins's cavalry to Chambersburg to collect supplies. On the 17th the garrison of Harper's Ferry was removed to Maryland Heights, and the valley of the Shenandoah was cleared of Federal troops. In these brilliant operations General Lee claims for Ewell the capture of 4000 prisoners and small-arms, 28 pieces of artillery, 11 colors, 300 loaded wagons, as many horses, and a considerable quantity of stores of all descriptions, the entire Confederate loss, killed, wounded, and missing, being 269.

These operations indicate on the part of General Lee either contempt for his opponent, or a belief that the chronic terror of the War Department for the safety of Washington could be safely relied upon to paralyze his movements—or both. On no other reasonable hypothesis can we account for his stretching his army from Fredericksburg to Williamsport, with his enemy concentrated on one flank, and on the shortest road to Richmond.

General Hooker's instructions were to keep always in view the safety of Washington and Harper's Ferry, and this necessarily subordinated his operations to those of the enemy. On June 5th he reported that in case Lee moved via Culpeper toward the Potomac with his main body, leaving a corps at Fredericksburg, he should consider it his duty to attack the latter, and asked if that would be within the spirit of his instructions. In reply he was warned against such a course, and its dangers to Washington and Harper's Ferry were pointed out. On June 10th, learning that Lee was in motion, and that there were but few troops in Richmond, he proposed an immediate march on that place, from which, after capturing it, he could send the disposable part of his force to any threatened point north of the Potomac, and was informed that Lee's army, and not Richmond, was his true objective. Had he taken Richmond, Peck's large force at Suffolk and Keyes's 10,000 men in the Peninsula might have been utilized, and Hooker's whole army set free for operations against Lee.

As yet an invasion of the North had not been definitely fixed upon. On June 8th, the day before the engagement at Brandy Station, Lee, in a confidential letter to Mr. Seddon, Confederate Secretary of War, stated that he was aware of the hazard of taking the aggressive, yet nothing was to be gained by remaining on the defensive; still, if the department thought it better to do so, he would adopt that course. Mr. Seddon replied, June 10th, the date of Hooker's proposal to march on Richmond, concurring in General Lee's views. He considered aggressive action indispensable, that "all attendant risks and sacrifices must be incurred," and adds, "I have not hesitated, in coöperating with your plans, to leave this city almost defenseless." General Lee now had full liberty of action, with the assured support of his Government—an immense advantage over an opponent who had neither.

As soon as Hooker learned from Pleasonton that a large infantry force was at Culpeper, he extended his right up the Rappahannock, and when informed of Ewell's move toward the valley, being forbidden to attack A. P. Hill at Fredericksburg or to spoil Lee's plans by marching to Richmond, he moved his army, on the night of June 13th, toward the line of the Orange and Alexandria Railroad, and occupied Thoroughfare Gap in advance of it. On the 15th Longstreet left Culpeper, keeping east of the Blue Ridge and so covering its gaps. Hill left Fredericksburg on the 14th, and reached Shepherdstown via Chester Gap on the 23d. Stuart's cavalry had been thrown out on Longstreet's right to occupy the passes of the Bull Run mountains and watch Hooker's army. On the 17th he encountered, near Aldie, a portion of Pleasonton's command; a fierce fight ensued, which left the Federals in possession of the field. During the four following days there was a succession of cavalry combats; those of the 19th near Middleburg, and of the 21st near Upperville, were especially well contested, and resulted in the retreat of Stuart through Ashby's Gap. Longstreet had already withdrawn

355

through the gaps and followed Hill to the Potomac. Imboden, his work of destruction completed, had taken post at Hancock. Longstreet and Hill crossed the Potomac on the 24th and 25th and directed their march on Chambersburg and Fayetteville, arriving on the 27th. Stuart had been directed to guard the mountain passes until the Federal army crossed the river, and, according to General Lee's report, "to lose no time in placing his command on the right of our [Confederate] column as soon as he should perceive the enemy moving northward," in order to watch and report his movements. According to Stuart's report, he was authorized to cross between the Federal army and Washington, and directed after crossing to proceed with all dispatch to join Early in Pennsylvania.

General Lee so far had been completely successful; his army was exultant, and he lost no time in availing himself of his advantages. On the 21st he ordered Ewell to take possession of Harrisburg; and on the 22d Ewell's whole corps was on the march, Rodes's and Johnson's division via Chambersburg to Carlisle, which they reached on the 27th, and Early via Greenwood and Gettysburg to York, with orders from Ewell to break up the Northern Central Railroad, destroy the bridge across the Susquehanna at Wrightsville, and then rejoin the main body at Carlisle. Early entered York on the 28th, and sent Gordon's brigade, not to destroy but to secure possession of the bridge, which would enable him to operate upon Harrisburg from the rear; but a small militia force under Colonel Frick, retreating from Wrightsville across the bridge, after an unsuccessful attempt to destroy one of its spans, set fire to and entirely destroyed that fine structure, Gordon's troops giving their aid to the citizens to save the town from the flames. On the 29th Ewell received orders from General Lee to rejoin the army at Cashtown; the next evening, the 30th, his reserve artillery and trains, with Johnson's division as an escort, were near Chambersburg, and Ewell with Early's and Rodes's, near Heidlersburg. Thus suddenly ended Ewell's Harrisburg expedition. One object was to collect supplies, and contributions were accordingly levied. Much damage was done to roads and bridges, but the prompt advance of the Army of the Potomac made this useless to the Confederates.

Before committing his army to an invasion of the North, General Lee recommended the proper steps to cover and support it. In a letter of June 23d, addressed to President Davis, he states that the season was so far advanced as to stop further Federal operations on the Southern coast, and that Confederate troops in that country and elsewhere were now disposable. He proposed, therefore, that an army should as soon as possible be organized at Culpeper, as "the well-known anxiety of the Northern Government for the safety of its capital would induce it to retain a large force for its defense, and thus relieve the opposition to our advance"; and suggested that General Beauregard be placed in command, "as his presence would give magnitude even to a small demonstration." On the 25th he wrote twice to Mr.

Davis urging the same views. The proposition embarrassed Mr. Davis, who could not see how, with the few troops under his hand, it could be carried out. In fact, although General Lee had pointed out the means, the proposition came too late, as the decisive battle took place much earlier than was expected. This correspondence, however, with that between Lee and Mr. Seddon, shows that Hooker's project to capture Richmond by a *coup-de-main* was feasible. It was not now a question of "swapping queens." Washington was safe, being well fortified and sufficiently garrisoned, or with available troops within reach, without drawing on Hooker; and to take Richmond and scatter the Confederate Government was the surest way to ruin Lee's army—"his true objective."

On the first appearance of danger of invasion, Pennsylvania's vigilant governor, Curtin, warned the people of the State and called out the militia. General Couch was sent to Harrisburg to organize and command them, but disbelief in the danger—due to previous false alarms—caused delays until the fugitives from Milroy's command, followed by Jenkins's cavalry, roused the country. Defensive works were then thrown up at Harrisburg and elsewhere, and local forces were raised and moved toward the enemy.

Early in June Hooker represented in strong terms the necessity of having one commander for all the troops whose operations would have an influence on those of Lee's army, and in reply was informed by Halleck that any movements he might suggest for other commands than his own would be ordered *if practicable.* Misunderstandings and confusion naturally resulted, and authority was given Hooker from time to time to exercise control over the troops of Heintzelman, commanding the Department of Washington, and of Schenck, commanding the Middle Department, followed, June 24th, by orders specifically placing the troops in Harper's Ferry and its vicinity at his disposal.

Disregarding Ewell's movements, Hooker conformed his own to those of the enemy's main body, and crossed the Potomac at Edwards's Ferry on the 25th and 26th of June. On the 27th three army-corps under Reynolds occupied Middletown and the South Mountain passes. The Twelfth Corps was near Harper's Ferry, and the three other corps at or near Frederick. Hooker now ordered the Twelfth Corps to march early on the 28th to Harper's Ferry, there to be joined by its garrison from Maryland Heights, in order to cut Lee's communications with Virginia, and in conjunction with Reynolds to operate on his rear. General Halleck, however, objected to the abandonment of the Heights, notwithstanding Hooker's representations that the position was utterly useless for any purpose; whereupon Hooker abandoned his project, and finding now that he was "not allowed to manœuvre his own army in the presence of the enemy," asked to be relieved from his command. He had encountered some of the difficulties which had beset a predecessor whom he himself mercilessly criticised, and promply succumbed to them.

357

His request was complied with, and Major-General George G. Meade was appointed his successor, this being the fifth change of commanders of the army in front of Washington in ten months. Meade was an excellent officer of long service, who had always proved equal to his position, whether as a specialist or a commander of troops. Many welcomed his advent—some regretted Hooker's departure. All thought the time for the change unfortunate, but accepted loyally, as that army ever did, the leader designated by the President, and gave Meade their hearty support. He was succeeded in the command of the Fifth Corps by Major-General George Sykes, a veteran of the Mexican war and a distinguished soldier.

When General Meade assumed command, June 28th, the best information placed Longstreet at Chambersburg, A. P. Hill between that place and Cashtown, and Ewell in occupation of Carlisle, York, and the country between them, threatening Harrisburg. Unacquainted with Hooker's plans and views, he determined at once to move on the main line from Frederick to Harrisburg, extending his wings as far as compatible with a ready concentration, in order to force Lee to battle before he could cross the Susquehanna. With this view he spent the day in ascertaining the position of his army, and brought up his cavalry, Buford to his left, Gregg to his right, and Kilpatrick to the front. Directing French to occupy Frederick with seven thousand men of the garrison of Harper's Ferry, he put his army in motion early on the morning of the 29th. Kilpatrick reached Littlestown that night; and on the morning of the 30th the rear of his division, while passing through Hanover, was attacked by a portion of Stuart's cavalry. Stuart, availing himself of the discretion allowed him, had left Robertson's and Jones's brigades to guard the passes of the Blue Ridge, and on the night of the 24th, with those of Hampton, Fitzhugh Lee, and Chambliss, had started to move round the Army of the Potomac, pass between it and Centreville into Maryland, and so rejoin Lee; but the movements of that army forced him so far east that he was compelled to ford the Potomac near Seneca [20 miles above Washington], on the night of the 27th. Next morning, learning that Hooker had already crossed the river, he marched north by Rockville, where he captured a wagon train. Paroling his prisoners and taking the train with him, he pushed on—through Westminster, where he had a sharp action with a squadron of Delaware horse—to Union Mills, and encamped there on the 29th. During the night, he learned that the Federal army was still between him and Lee on its march north, and his scouts reported its cavalry in strong force at Littlestown, barring his direct road to Gettysburg; wherefore, on the morning of the 30th he moved across country to Hanover, Chambliss in front and Hampton in rear of his long train of two hundred wagons, with Fitzhugh Lee well out on his left flank. About 10 A.M. Chambliss, reaching Hanover, found Kilpatrick passing through the town and attacked him, but was driven out before Hampton or Lee could come to his support. Stuart's men and horses were now nearly worn out; he was encumbered with a large captured train; a junction with some part of Lee's army was a necessity, and he made a night march for York, only to learn that Early had left the day before. Pushing on to Carlisle, he found that Ewell was gone, and the place occupied by a militia force under General W. F. Smith. His demand of a surrender was refused; he threw a few shells into the town and burned the Government barracks. That night he learned that Lee's army was concentrating at Gettysburg, and left for that place next day. Thus ended a raid which greatly embarrassed Lee, and by which the services of three cavalry brigades were, in the critical period of the campaign, exchanged for a few hundred prisoners and a wagon train.

Hearing nothing from Stuart, and therefore believing that Hooker was still south of the Potomac, Lee, on the afternoon of the 28th, ordered Longstreet and A. P. Hill to join Ewell at Harrisburg; but late that night one of Longstreet's scouts came in and reported that the Federal army had crossed the river, that Meade had relieved Hooker and was at Frederick. Lee thereupon changed the rendezvous of his army to Cashtown, which place Heth reached on the 29th. Next day Heth sent Pettigrew's brigade on to Gettysburg, nine miles, to procure a supply of shoes. Nearing this place, Pettigrew discovered the advance of a large Federal force and returned to Cashtown. Hill immediately notified Generals Lee and Ewell, informing the latter that he would advance next morning on Gettysburg. Buford, sending Merritt's brigade to Mechanicstown as guard to his trains, had early on the morning of the 29th crossed into and moved up the Cumberland valley via Boonsboro' and Fairfield with those of Gamble and Devin, and on the afternoon of Tuesday, June 30th, under instructions from Pleasonton, entered Gettysburg, Pettigrew's brigade withdrawing on his approach.

From Gettysburg, near the eastern base of the Green Ridge, and covering all the upper passes into the Cumberland valley, good roads lead to all important points between the Susquehanna and the Potomac. It is therefore an important strategic position. On the west of the town, distant nearly half a mile, there is a somewhat elevated ridge running north and south, on which stands the "Lutheran Seminary." This ridge is covered with open woods through its whole length, and is terminated nearly a mile and a half north of the seminary by a commanding knoll, bare on its southern side, called Oak Hill. From this ridge the ground slopes gradually to the west, and again rising forms another ridge about 500 yards from the first, upon which, nearly opposite the seminary, stand McPherson's farm buildings. The second ridge is wider, smoother, and lower than the first, and Oak Hill, their intersection, has a clear view of the slopes of both ridges and of the valley between them. West of McPherson's ridge Willoughby Run flows south into Marsh Creek. South of the farm buildings and directly opposite the seminary, a wood borders the run for about 300 yards, and stretches back to the summit of McPherson's ridge. From the town two roads run: one south-west to Hagerstown via Fairfield, the other north-westerly to Chambersburg via Cashtown. The seminary is midway between them, about 300 yards from each. Parallel to and 150 yards north of the Chambersburg pike, is the bed of an unfinished railroad, with deep cuttings through the two ridges. Directly north of the town the country is comparatively flat and open; on the east of it, Rock Creek flows south. On the south, and overlooking it, is a ridge of bold, high ground, terminated on the west by Cemetery Hill and on the east by Culp's Hill, which, bending to the south, extends half a mile or more and terminates in low grounds near Spangler's Spring. Culp's Hill is steep toward the east, is well wooded, and its eastern base is washed by Rock Creek.

Impressed by the importance of the position, Buford, expecting the early return of the enemy in force, assigned to Devin's brigade the country north, and to Gamble's that west of the town; sent out scouting parties on all the roads to collect information, and reported the condition of affairs to Reynolds. His pickets extended from below the Fairfield road, along the eastern bank of Willoughby Run, to the railroad cut, then easterly some 1500 yards north of the town, to a wooded hillock near Rock Creek.

On the night of June 30th Meade's headquarters and the Artillery Reserve were at Taneytown; the First Corps at Marsh Run, the Eleventh at Emmitsburg, Third at Bridgeport, Twelfth at Littlestown, Second at Union-town, Fifth at Union Mills, Sixth and Gregg's cavalry at Manchester, Kil-patrick's at Hanover. Lee's whole army was nearing Gettysburg, while Meade's was scattered over a wide region to the east and south of that town.

Meade was now convinced that all designs on the Susquehanna had been abandoned; but as Lee's corps were reported as occupying the country from Chambersburg to Carlisle, he ordered, for the next day's moves, the First and Eleventh corps to Gettysburg, under Reynolds, the Third to Emmitsburg, the Second to Taneytown, the Fifth to Hanover, and the Twelfth to Two Taverns, directing Slocum to take command of the Fifth in addition to his own. The Sixth Corps was left at Manchester, thirty-four miles from Gettys-burg, to await orders. But Meade, while conforming to the current of Lee's movement, was not merely drifting. The same afternoon he directed the chiefs of engineers and artillery to select a field of battle on which his army might be concentrated, whatever Lee's lines of approach, whether by Harris-burg or Gettysburg—indicating the general line of Pipe Creek as a suitable locality. Carefully drawn instructions were sent to the corps commanders as to the occupation of this line, should it be ordered; but it was added that developments might cause the offensive to be assumed from present posi-tions. These orders were afterward cited as indicating General Meade's in-tention not to fight at Gettysburg. They were, under any circumstances, wise and proper orders, and it would probably have been better had he concentrated his army behind Pipe Creek rather than at Gettysburg; but events finally controlled the actions of both leaders.

At 8 A. M., July 1st, Buford's scouts reported Heth's advance on the Cashtown road, when Gamble's brigade formed on McPherson's Ridge, from the Fairfield road to the railroad cut; one section of Calef's battery A, 2d United States, near the left of his line, the other two across the Chambersburg or Cashtown pike. Devin formed his disposable squadrons from Gamble's right toward Oak Hill, from which he had afterward to transfer them to the north of the town to meet Ewell. As Heth advanced, he threw Archer's brigade to the right, Davis's to the left of the Cashtown pike, with Pettigrew's and Brockenbrough's brigades in support. The Confederates advanced skirmishing heavily with Buford's dismounted troopers. Calef's battery, engaging double the number of its own guns, was served with an efficiency worthy of its former reputation as "Duncan's battery" in the Mexican war, and so enabled the cavalry to hold their long line for two hours. When Buford's report of the enemy's advance reached Reynolds, the latter, ordering Doubleday and Howard to follow, hastened toward Gettysburg with Wadsworth's small division and Hall's 2d Maine battery. As he approached he heard the sound of battle, and directing the troops to cross the fields toward the firing, galloped himself to the seminary, met Buford there, and both rode to the front, where the cavalry, dismounted, were gallantly holding their ground against heavy odds. After viewing the field, he sent back to hasten up Howard, and as the enemy's main line was now advancing to the attack, directed Doubleday, who had arrived in advance of his division, to look to the Fairfield road, sent Cutler with three of his five regiments north of the railroad cut, posted the other two under Colonel Fowler, of the 14th New York, south of the pike, and replaced Calef's battery by Hall's, thus relieving the cavalry. Cutler's line was hardly formed when it was struck by Davis's Confederate brigade on its front and right flank, whereupon Wadsworth, to save it, ordered it to fall back to Seminary Ridge. This order not reaching the 147th New York, its gallant major, Harney, held that regiment to its position until, having lost half its numbers, the order to retire was repeated. Hall's battery was now imperiled, and it withdrew by sections, fighting at close canister range and suffering severely. Fowler thereupon changed his front to face Davis's brigade, which held the cut, and with Dawes's 6th Wisconsin—sent by Doubleday to aid the 147th New York—charged and drove Davis from the field. The Confederate brigade suffered severely, losing all its field-officers but two, and a large proportion of its men killed and captured, being disabled for further effective service that day. In the meantime Archer's Confederate brigade had occupied McPherson's wood, and as the regiments of Meredith's "Iron Brigade" came up, they were sent forward by Doubleday, who fully recognized the importance of the position, to dislodge Archer. At the entrance of the wood they found Reynolds in person, and, animated by his presence, rushed to the charge, struck successive heavy blows, outflanked and turned the enemy's right, captured General Archer and a large portion of his brigade, and pursued the remainder across Willoughby Run. Wadsworth's small division had thus won decided successes against superior numbers, but it was at grievous cost to the army and the country, for Reynolds, while directing the operations, was killed in the wood by a sharp-shooter. It was not, however, until by his promptitude and gallantry he had determined the decisive field of the war, and had opened brilliantly a battle which required three days of hard fighting to close with a victory. To him may be applied in a wider sense than in its original one, Napier's happy eulogium on Ridge: "No man died on that field with more glory than he, yet many died, and there was much glory."

After the repulse of Davis and Archer, Heth's division was formed in line mostly south of the Cashtown pike, with Pender's in second line, Pegram's and McIntosh's artillery (nine batteries) occupying all the commanding positions west of Willoughby Run. Doubleday reëstablished his former lines, Meredith holding McPherson's wood. Soon after, Rowley's and Robinson's divisions (two brigades each) and the four remaining batteries of the corps arrived. Rowley's division was thrown forward, Stone's brigade to the interval between Meredith and Cutler, and Biddle's with Cooper's battery to occupy the ridge between the wood and the Fairfield road. Reynolds's battery replaced Hall's, and Calef's rejoined Gamble's cavalry, now in reserve. Robinson's division was halted near the base of Seminary Ridge. By this time, near noon, General Howard arrived, assumed command, and directed General Schurz, commanding the Eleventh Corps, to prolong Doubleday's line toward Oak Hill with Schimmelfennig's and Barlow's divisions and three batteries, and to post Steinwehr's division and two batteries on Cemetery Hill, as a rallying-point. By 1 o'clock, when this corps was arriving, Buford had reported Ewell's approach by the Heidlersburg road, and Howard called on Sickles at Emmitsburg and Slocum at Two Taverns for aid, to which both these officers promptly responded. It was now no longer a question of prolonging Doubleday's line, but of protecting it against Ewell whilst engaged in front with Hill. Schurz's two divisions, hardly 6000 effectives, accordingly formed line on the open plain half a mile north of the town. They were too weak to cover the ground, and a wide interval was left between the two corps, covered only by the fire of Dilger's and Wheeler's batteries (ten guns) posted behind it.

That morning, whilst on the march to Cashtown, Ewell received Hill's notice that his corps was advancing to Gettysburg, upon which he turned the heads of his own columns to that point. Reporting the change by a staff-officer to General Lee, Ewell was instructed that if the Federals were in force at Gettysburg a general battle was not to be brought on until the rest of the army was up. Approaching Gettysburg, Rodes, guided by the sounds of battle, followed the prolongation of Seminary Ridge; Iverson's, Daniel's, and Ramseur's brigades on the western, O'Neal's and Doles's on the eastern slope. Ewell, recognizing the importance of Oak Hill, ordered it to be occupied by Carter's artillery battalion, which immediately opened on both the Federal corps, enfilading Doubleday's line. This caused Wadsworth again to withdraw Cutler to Seminary Ridge, and Reynolds's battery was posted near McPherson's house, under partial cover. Stone therefore placed two of his three regiments on the Cashtown pike, so as to face Oak Hill. This left an interval between Stone and Cutler, through which Cooper and Reynolds could fire with effect, and gave to these lines a cross-fire on troops entering the angle between them. Robinson now sent his two brigades to strengthen Cutler's right. They took post behind the stone walls of a field, Paul's brigade facing west, Baxter's north. Rodes, regarding this advance as a menace, gave orders at 2:30 P. M. to attack. Iverson, sweeping round to his left, engaged Paul, who prolonged Cutler's line, and O'Neal attacked Baxter. The repulse of O'Neal soon enabled Baxter to turn upon Iverson. Cutler also attacked him in flank, and after losing 500 men killed and wounded, 3 of Iverson's regiments surrendered. General Robinson reports the capture of 1000 prisoners and 3 colors; General Paul was severely wounded, losing both eyes. Meanwhile Daniel's brigade advanced directly on Stone, who maintained his lines against this attack and also Brockenbrough's, of Hill's corps, but was soon severely wounded. Colonel Wister, who succeeded him, met the same fate, and Colonel Dana took command of the brigade. Ramseur, who followed Daniel, by a conversion to the left, now faced Robinson and Cutler with his own brigade, the remnant of Iverson's, and one regiment of O'Neal's, his right connecting with Daniel's left, and the fighting became hot. East of the ridge, Doles's brigade had been held in observation, but about 3:30 P. M., on the advance of Early, he sent his skirmishers forward and drove those of Devin—who had gallantly held the enemy's advance in check with his dismounted troopers—from their line and its hillock on Rock Creek. Barlow, considering this an eligible position for his own right, advanced his division, supported by Wilkeson's battery, and seized it. This made it necessary for Schurz to advance a brigade of Schimmelfennig's division to connect with Barlow, thus lengthening his already too extended line.

The arrival of Early's division had by this time brought an overwhelming force on the flank and rear of the Eleventh Corps. On the east of Rock Creek, Jones's artillery battalion, within easy range, enfiladed its whole line and took it in reverse, while the brigades of Gordon, Hays, and Avery in line, with Smith's in reserve, advanced about 4 P. M. upon Barlow's position, Doles, of Rodes's division, connecting with Gordon. An obstinate and bloody contest ensued, in which Barlow was desperately wounded, Wilkeson killed, and the whole corps forced back to its original line, on which, with the aid of Coster's brigade and Heckman's battery, drawn from Cemetery Hill, Schurz endeavored to rally it and cover the town. The fighting here was well sustained, but the Confederate force was overpowering in numbers, and the troops retreated to Cemetery Hill, Ewell entering the town about 4:30 P. M. These retrograde movements had uncovered the flank of the First Corps and made its right untenable.

Meanwhile, that corps had been heavily engaged along its whole line; for, on the approach of Rodes, Hill attacked with both his divisions. There were thus opposed to the single disconnected Federal line south of the Cashtown pike two solid Confederate ones which outflanked their left a quarter of a mile or more. Biddle's small command, less than a thousand men, after a severe contest, was gradually forced back. In McPherson's wood and beyond, Meredith's and Dana's brigades repeatedly repulsed their assailants, but as Biddle's retirement uncovered their left, they too fell back to successive positions from which they inflicted heavy losses, until finally all three reached the foot of Seminary Ridge, where Colonel Wainwright, commanding the corps artillery, had planted twelve guns south of the Cashtown pike, with Stewart's battery, manned in part by men of the Iron Brigade, north of it. Buford had already thrown half of Gamble's dismounted men south of the Fairfield road. Heth's division had suffered so severely that Pender's had passed to its front, thus bringing fresh troops to bear on the exhausted Federal line.

It was about 4 P. M. when the whole Confederate line advanced to the final attack. On their right Gamble held Lane's brigade for some time in check, Perrin's and Scales's suffered severely, and Scales's was broken up, for Stewart, swinging half his guns, under Lieutenant Davison, upon the Cashtown pike, raked it. The whole corps being now heavily pressed and its right uncovered, Doubleday gave the order to fall back to Cemetery Hill, which was effected in comparatively good order, the rear, covered by the 7th Wisconsin, turning when necessary to check pursuit. Colonel Wainwright, mistaking the order, had clung with his artillery to Seminary Hill, until, seeing the infantry retreating to the town, he moved his batteries down the Cashtown pike until lapped on both sides by the enemy's skirmishers, at close range, when they were compelled to abandon one gun on the road, all its horses being killed. The Eleventh Corps also left a disabled gun on the field. Of the troops who passed through the town, many, principally men of the Eleventh Corps, got entangled in the streets, lost their way, and were captured.

On ascending Cemetery Hill, the retreating troops found Steinwehr's division in position covered by stone fences on the slopes, and occupying by their skirmishers the houses in front of their line. As they arrived they were formed, the Eleventh Corps on the right, the First Corps on the left of Steinwehr. As the batteries came up, they were well posted by Colonels

Wainwright and Osborn, and soon a formidable array of artillery was ready to cover with its fire all the approaches. Buford assembled his command on the plain west of Cemetery Hill, covering the left flank and presenting a firm front to any attempt at pursuit. The First Corps found a small reënforcement awaiting it, in the 7th Indiana, part of the train escort, which brought up nearly five hundred fresh men. Wadsworth met them and led them to Culp's Hill, where, under direction of Captain Pattison of that regiment, a defensive line was marked out. Their brigade (Cutler's) soon joined them; wood and stone were plentiful, and soon the right of the line was solidly established.

Nor was there wanting other assurance to the men who had fought so long that their sacrifices had not been in vain. As they reached the hill they were received by General Hancock, who arrived just as they were coming up from the town, under orders from General Meade to assume the command. His person was well known; his presence inspired confidence, and it implied also the near approach of his army-corps. He ordered Wadsworth at once to Culp's Hill to secure that important position, and aided by Howard, by Warren who had also just arrived from headquarters, and by others, a strong line, well flanked, was soon formed.

General Lee, who from Seminary Hill had witnessed the final attack, sent Colonel Long, of his staff, a competent officer of sound judgment, to examine the position, and directed Ewell to carry it if practicable, renewing, however, his previous warning to avoid bringing on a general engagement until the army was all up. Both Ewell, who was making some preparations with a view to attack, and Long found the position a formidable one, strongly occupied and not accessible to artillery fire. Ewell's men were indeed in no condition for an immediate assault. Of Rodes's eight thousand, nearly three thousand were *hors de combat*. Early had lost over five hundred, and had but two brigades disposable, the other two having been sent on the report of the advance of Federal troops, probably the Twelfth Corps, then near by, to watch the York road. Hill's two divisions had been very roughly handled, and had lost heavily, and he withdrew them to Seminary Hill as Ewell entered the town, leaving the latter with not more than eight thousand men to secure the town and the prisoners. Ewell's absent division was expected soon, but it did not arrive until near sunset, when the Twelfth Corps and Stannard's Vermont brigade were also up, and the Third Corps was arriving. In fact an assault by the Confederates was not practicable before 5:30 P. M., and after that the position was perfectly secure. For the first time that day the Federals had the advantage of position, and sufficient troops and artillery to occupy it, and Ewell would not have been justified in attacking without the positive orders of Lee, who was present, and wisely abstained from giving them.

The field of Gettysburg was obviously not selected by Lee and all his subsequent maneuvers there were in some degree limited by that circumstance. Advance units of the Army of Northern Virginia had simply stumbled into similar units of the Army of the Potomac (who, of the two, were the better informed of their enemy's position)—and for that surprise he had "Jeb" Stuart to thank. On the 23rd of June, Stuart received orders from his chief which seemed to give him permission, in certain conditions, to "pass around [Meade's] army," which, being Stuart, he proceeded to try to do. Until the evening of July 2nd, then, the Army of Northern Virginia was blind, and when Stuart returned from his skylarking far to the east, his troopers were too exhausted to be effective the next day.

Whether Ewell should have attempted to establish himself on Cemetery Hill on July 1st has been a subject for debate ever since. Douglas Southall Freeman, after summarizing the case for Ewell, says, "The impression persists that he did not display the initiative, resolution and boldness to be expected of a good soldier." And one cannot help surmising that his predecessor, Jackson, would have performed differently.

"I proceeded to Cemetery Hill"

BY HENRY J. HUNT, BREVET MAJOR-GENERAL, U. S. A., CHIEF OF ARTILLERY A. P.

ON JUNE 30th, at Taneytown, General Meade received information that the enemy was advancing on Gettysburg, and corps commanders were at once instructed to hold their commands in readiness to march against him. The next day, July 1st, Meade wrote to Reynolds that telegraphic intelligence from Couch, and the movements reported by Buford, indicated a concentration of the enemy's army either at Chambersburg or at some point on a line drawn from that place through Heidlersburg to York. Under these circumstances, Meade informed Reynolds that he had not yet

367

decided whether it was his best policy to move to attack before he knew more definitely Lee's point of concentration. He seems, however, soon to have determined not to advance until the movements or position of the enemy gave strong assurance of success, and if the enemy took the offensive, to withdraw his own army from its actual positions and form line of battle behind Pipe Creek, between Middleburg and Manchester. The considerations probably moving him to this are not difficult to divine. Such a line would cover Baltimore and Washington in all directions from which Lee could advance, and Westminster, his base, would be immediately behind him, with short railroad communication to Baltimore. It would, moreover, save much hard marching, and restore to the ranks the thousands of stragglers who did not reach Gettysburg in time for the battle.

From Westminster—which is in Parr's Ridge, the eastern boundary of the valley of the Monocacy—good roads led in all directions, and gave the place the same strategic value for Meade that Gettysburg had for Lee. The new line could not be turned by Lee without imminent danger to his own army, nor could he afford to advance upon Baltimore or Washington, leaving the Army of the Potomac intact behind and so near him—that would be to invite the fate of Burgoyne. Meade, then, could safely select a good "offensive-defensive line" behind Pipe Creek and establish himself there, with perfect liberty of action in all directions. Without magazines or assured communications, Lee would have to scatter his army more or less in order to subsist it, and so expose it to Meade; or else keep it united, and so starve it, a course which Meade could compel by simple demonstrations. There would then be but two courses for Lee—either to attack Meade in his chosen position or to retreat without a battle. The latter, neither the temper of his army nor that of his Government would probably permit. In case of a defeat Meade's line of retreat would be comparatively short, and easily covered, whilst Lee's would be for two marches through an open country before he could gain the mountain passes. As Meade believed Lee's army to be at least equal to his own, all the elements of the problem were in favor of the Pipe Creek line. But Meade's orders for July 1st, drawing his corps toward the threatened flank, carried Reynolds to Gettysburg, and Buford's report hastened this movement. Reynolds, who probably never received the Pipe Creek circular, was eager for the conflict, and his collision with Heth assuming the dimensions of a battle, caused an immediate concentration of both armies at Gettysburg. Prior to this, the assembling of Meade's army behind Pipe Creek would have been easy, and all fears of injuring thereby the *morale* of his troops were idle; the Army of the Potomac was of "sterner stuff" than that implies. The battle of July 1st changed the situation. Overpowered by numbers, the First and Eleventh corps had, after hard fighting and inflicting as well as incurring heavy losses, been forced back to their reserve, on Cemetery Hill, which they still held. To have withdrawn them now would have been a retreat, and might have discouraged the Federal, as it certainly would have elated the Confederate troops; especially as injurious reports unjust to both the corps named had been circulated. It would have been to acknowledge a defeat when there was no defeat. Meade therefore resolved to fight at Gettysburg. An ominous dispatch from General Halleck to Meade, that afternoon, suggesting that whilst his tactical arrangements were good, his strategy was at fault, that he was too far east, that Lee might attempt to turn his left, and that Frederick was preferable as a base to Westminster, may have confirmed Meade in this decision.

In pursuance of his instructions, I had that morning (July 1st) reconnoitered the country behind Pipe Creek for a battle-ground. On my return I found General Hancock at General Meade's tent. He informed me that Reynolds was killed, that a battle was going on at Gettysburg, and that he was under orders to proceed to that place. His instructions were to examine it and the intermediate country for a suitable field, and if his report was favorable the troops would be ordered forward. Before the receipt that evening of Hancock's written report from Cemetery Hill, which was not very encouraging, General Meade received from others information as to the state of affairs at the front, set his troops in motion toward Gettysburg, afterward urged them to forced marches, and under his orders I gave the necessary instructions to the Artillery Reserve and Park for a battle there. The move was, under the circumstances, a bold one, and Meade, as we shall see, took great risks. We left Taneytown toward 11 P. M., and reached Gettysburg after midnight. Soon after, General Meade, accompanied by General Howard and myself, inspected our lines so far as then occupied, after which he directed me to examine them again in the morning, and to see that the artillery was properly posted. He had thus recognized my "command" of the artillery; indeed, he did not know it nad been suspended. I resumed it, therefore, and continued it to the end of the battle.

At the close of July 1st Johnson's and Anderson's divisions of the Confederate army were up. Ewell's corps now covered our front from Benner's Hill to the Seminary, his line passing through the town—Johnson on the left, Early in the center, Rodes on the right. Hill's corps occupied Seminary Ridge, and during the next morning extended its line from the Seminary south nearly to the Peach Orchard on the Emmitsburg road; Trimble—*vice* Pender, wounded—on the left; Anderson on the right; Pettigrew—*vice* Heth, wounded—in reserve. Of Longstreet's corps, McLaws's division and Hood's —except Law's brigade not yet up—camped that night on Marsh Creek, four miles from Gettysburg. His Reserve Artillery did not reach Gettysburg until 9 A. M. of the 2d. Pickett's division had been left at Chambersburg as rearguard, and joined the corps on the night of the 2d. . . .

A battle was a necessity to Lee, and a defeat would be more disastrous to Meade, and less so to himself, at Gettysburg than at any point east of it. With the defiles of the South Mountain range close in his rear, which could be

369

easily held by a small force, a safe retreat through the Cumberland Valley was assured, so that his army, once through these passes, would be practically on the banks of the Potomac, at a point already prepared for crossing. Any position east of Gettysburg would deprive him of these advantages. It is more probable that General Lee was influenced by cool calculation of this nature than by hot blood, or that the opening success of a chance battle had thrown him off his balance. Whatever his reasons, he decided to accept the gage of battle offered by Meade, and to attack as soon as practicable. Ewell had made arrangements to take possession of Culp's Hill in the early morning, and his troops were under arms for the purpose by the time General Meade had finished the moonlight inspection of his lines, when it was ascertained by a reconnoitering party sent out by Johnson, that the hill was occupied, and its defenders on the alert; and further, from a captured dispatch from General Sykes to General Slocum, that the Fifth Corps was on the Hanover road only four miles off, and would march at 4 A. M. for Culp's Hill. Johnson thereupon deferred his attack and awaited Ewell's instructions.

General Lee had, however, during the night determined to attack the Federal left with Longstreet's corps, and now instructed Ewell, as soon as he heard Longstreet's guns, to make a diversion in his favor, to be converted, if opportunity offered, into a real attack.

Early on the morning of July 2d, when nearly all the Confederate army had reached Gettysburg or its immediate vicinity, a large portion of the Army of the Potomac was still on the road. The Second Corps and Sykes, with two divisions of the Fifth, arrived about 7 A. M., Crawford's division not joining until noon; Lockwood's brigade—two regiments from Baltimore—at 8; De Trobriand's and Burling's brigades of the Third Corps, from Emmitsburg, at 9, and the Artillery Reserve and its large ammunition trains from Taneytown at 10:30 A. M. Sedgwick's Sixth Corps, the largest in the army, after a long night march from Manchester, thirty-four miles distant, reached Rock Creek at 4 P. M. The rapidity with which the army was assembled was creditable to it and to its commander. The heat was oppressive, the long marches, especially the night marches, were trying and had caused much straggling.

All this morning Meade was busily engaged personally or by his staff in rectifying his lines, assigning positions to the commands as they came up, watching the enemy, and studying the field, part of which we have described in general terms. Near the western base of Cemetery Hill is Ziegler's Grove. From this grove the distance nearly due south to the base of Little Round Top is a mile and a half. A well-defined ridge known as Cemetery Ridge follows this line from Ziegler's for 900 yards to another small grove, or clump of trees, where it turns sharply to the east for 200 yards, then turns south again, and continues in a direct line toward Round Top, for 700 yards, to George Weikert's. So far the ridge is smooth and open, in full view of Seminary Ridge opposite, and distant from 1400 to 1600 yards. At Weikert's, this ridge is lost in a large body of rocks, hills, and woods, lying athwart the direct line to Round Top, and forcing a bend to the east in the Taneytown road. This rough space also stretches for a quarter of a mile or more *west* of this direct line, toward Plum Run. Toward the south it sinks into low marshy ground which reaches to the base of Little Round Top, half a mile or more from George Weikert's. The west side of this broken ground was wooded through its whole extent from north to south. Between this wood and Plum Run is an open cleared space 300 yards wide—a continuation of the open country in front of Cemetery Ridge; Plum Run flows south-easterly toward Little Round Top, then makes a bend to the south-west, where it receives a small stream or "branch" from Seminary Ridge. In the angle between these streams is Devil's Den, a bold, rocky height, steep on its eastern face, and prolonged as a ridge to the west. It is 500 yards due west of Little Round Top, and 100 feet lower. The northern extremity is composed of huge rocks and bowlders, forming innumerable crevices and holes, from the largest of which the hill derives its name. Plum Run valley is here marshy but strewn with similar bowlders, and the slopes of the Round Tops are covered with them. These afforded lurking-places for a multitude of Confederate sharp-shooters whom, from the difficulties of the ground, it was impossible to dis-lodge, and who were opposed by similar methods on our part; so that at the close of the battle these hiding-places, and especially the "Den" itself, were filled with dead and wounded men. This kind of warfare was specially destructive to Hazlett's battery on Round Top, as the cannoneers had to expose themselves in firing, and in one case three were shot in quick succession, before the fourth succeeded in discharging the piece. A cross-road connecting the Taneytown and Emmitsburg roads runs along the northern base of Devil's Den. From its Plum Run crossing to the Peach Orchard is 1100 yards. For the first 400 yards of this distance, there is a wood on the north and a wheat-field on the south of the road, beyond which the road continues for 700 yards to the Emmitsburg road along Devil's Den ridge, which slopes on the north to Plum Run, on the south to Plum Branch. From Ziegler's Grove the Emmitsburg road runs diagonally across the interval between Cemetery and Seminary ridges, crossing the latter two miles from Ziegler's Grove. From Peach Orchard to Ziegler's is nearly a mile and a half. For half a mile the road runs along a ridge at right angles to that of Devil's Den, which slopes back to Plum Run. The angle at the Peach Orchard is thus formed by the intersection of two bold ridges, one from Devil's Den, the other along the Emmitsburg road. It is distant about 600 yards from the wood which skirts the whole length of Seminary Ridge and covers the movement of troops between it and Willoughby Run, half a mile beyond. South of the Round Top and Devil's Den ridge the country is open, and the principal obstacles to free movement are the fences—generally of stone—which surround the numerous fields.

As our troops came up they were assigned to places on the line: the Twelfth Corps, General A. S. Williams—*vice* Slocum, commanding the right wing—to Culp's Hill, on Wadsworth's right; Second Corps to Cemetery Ridge—Hays's and Gibbon's divisions, from Ziegler's to the clump of trees, Caldwell's to the short ridge to its left and rear. This ridge had been occupied by the Third Corps, which was now directed to prolong Caldwell's line to Round Top, relieving Geary's division, which had been stationed during the night on the extreme left, with two regiments at the base of Little Round Top. The Fifth Corps was placed in reserve near the Rock Creek crossing of the Baltimore pike; the Artillery Reserve and its large trains were parked in a central position on a cross-road from the Baltimore pike to the Taneytown road; Buford's cavalry, except Merritt's brigade (then at Emmitsburg), was near Round Top, from which point it was ordered that morning to Westminster, thus uncovering our left flank; Kilpatrick's and Gregg's divisions were well out on the right flank, from which, after a brush with Stuart on the evening of the 2d, Kilpatrick was sent next morning to replace Buford, Merritt being also ordered up to our left.

The morning was a busy and in some respects an anxious one; it was believed that the whole Confederate army was assembled, that it was equal if not superior to our own in numbers, and that the battle would commence before our troops were up. There was a gap in Slocum's line awaiting a division of infantry, and as some demonstrations of Ewell about daylight indicated an immediate attack at that point, I had to draw batteries from other parts of the line—for the Artillery Reserve was just then starting from Taneytown—to cover it until it could be properly filled. Still there was no hostile movement of the enemy, and General Meade directed Slocum to hold himself in readiness to attack Ewell with the Fifth and Twelfth, so soon as the Sixth Corps should arrive. After an examination Slocum reported the ground as unfavorable, in which Warren concurred and advised against an attack there. The project was then abandoned, and Meade postponed all offensive operations until the enemy's intentions should be more clearly developed. In the meantime he took precautionary measures. It was clearly now to his advantage to fight the battle where he was, and he had some apprehension that Lee would attempt to turn his flank and threaten his communications—just what Longstreet had been advising. In this case it might be necessary to fall back to the Pipe Creek line, if possible, or else to follow Lee's movement into the open country. In either case, or in that of a forced withdrawal, prudence dictated that arrangements should be made in advance, and General Meade gave instructions for examining the roads and communications, and to draw up an order of movement, which General Butterfield, the chief-of-staff, seems to have considered an order absolute for the withdrawal of the army without a battle.

These instructions must have been given early in the morning, for General

Butterfield states that it was on his arrival from Taneytown, which place he left at daylight. An order was drawn up accordingly, given to the adjutant-general, and perhaps prepared for issue in case of necessity to corps commanders; but it was not recorded nor issued, nor even a copy of it preserved. General Meade declared that he never contemplated the issue of such an order unless contingencies made it necessary; and his acts and dispatches during the day were in accordance with his statement. There is one circumstance pertaining to my own duties which to my mind is conclusive, and I relate it because it may have contributed to the idea that General Meade intended to withdraw from Gettysburg. He came to me that morning before the Artillery Reserve had arrived, and, therefore, about the time that the order was in course of preparation, and informed me that one of the army corps had left its whole artillery ammunition train behind it, and that others were also deficient, notwithstanding his orders on that subject. He was very much disturbed, and feared that, taking into account the large expenditure of the preceding day by the First and Eleventh corps, there would not be sufficient to carry us through the battle. This was not the first nor the last time that I was called upon to meet deficiencies under such circumstances, and I was, therefore, prepared for this, having directed General Tyler, commanding the Artillery Reserve, whatever else he might leave behind, to bring up every round of ammunition in his trains, and I knew he would not fail me. Moreover, I had previously, on my own responsibility, and unknown to General Hooker, formed a special ammunition column attached to the Artillery Reserve, carrying twenty rounds per gun, over and above the authorized amount, for every gun in the army, in order to meet such emergencies. I was, therefore, able to assure General Meade that there would be enough ammunition for the battle, but none for idle cannonades, the besetting sin of some of our commanders. He was much relieved, and expressed his satisfaction. Now, had he had at this time any intention of withdrawing the army, the first thing to get rid of would have been this Artillery Reserve and its large trains, which were then blocking the roads in our rear; and he would surely have told me of it.

Still, with the exception of occasional cannonading, and some skirmishing near the Peach Orchard, the quiet remained unbroken, although Lee had determined upon an early attack on our left. He says in his detailed report that our line extended "upon the high ground along the Emmitsburg road, with a steep ridge [Cemetery] in rear, which was also occupied"; and in a previous "outline" report he says: "In front of General Longstreet the enemy held a position [the salient angle at the Peach Orchard] from which, if he could be driven, it was thought our artillery could be used to advantage in assailing the more elevated ground beyond, and thus enable us to gain the crest of the ridge." It would appear from this that General Lee mistook the few troops on the Peach Orchard ridge in the morning for our main line, and that by taking it and sweeping up the Emmitsburg road under cover of his batteries, he expected to "roll up" our lines to Cemetery Hill. That would be an "oblique order of battle," in which the attacking line, formed obliquely to its opponent, marches directly forward, constantly breaking in the *end* of his enemy's line and gaining his rear. General Longstreet was ordered to form the divisions of Hood and McLaws on Anderson's right, so as to envelop our left and drive it in. These divisions were only three miles off at daylight, and moved early, but there was great delay in forming them for battle, owing principally to the absence of Law's brigade, for which it would have been well to substitute Anderson's fresh division, which could have been replaced by Pettigrew's, then in reserve. There seems to have been no good reason why the attack should not have been made by 8 or 9 A. M. at the latest, when the Federal Third Corps was not yet all up, nor Crawford's division, nor the Artillery Reserve, nor the Sixth Corps, and our lines were still very incomplete. This is one of the cheap criticisms after all the facts on both sides are known; but it is apt for its purpose, as it shows how great a risk Meade took in abandoning his Pipe Creek line for Gettysburg on the chances of Lee's army not yet being assembled; and also, that there was no lack of boldness and decision on Meade's part. Indeed, his course, from the hour that he took command, had been marked by these qualities.

A suggestive incident is worth recording here. In the course of my inspection of the lines that morning, while passing along Culp's Hill, I found the men hard at work intrenching, and in such fine spirits as at once to attract attention. One of them finally dropped his work, and, approaching me, inquired if the reports just received were true. On asking what he referred to, he replied that twice word had been passed along the line that General McClellan had been assigned to the command of the army, and the second time it was added that he was on the way to the field and might soon be expected. He continued, "The boys are all jubilant over it, for they know that if *he* takes command everything will go right." I have been told recently by the commander of a Fifth Corps battery that during the forced march of the preceding night the same report ran through that corps, excited great enthusiasm amongst the men, and renewed their vigor. It was probably from this corps—just arrived—that the report had spread along the line.

On my return to headquarters from this inspection General Meade told me that General Sickles, then with him, wished me to examine a new line, as he thought that assigned to him was not a good one, especially that he could not use his artillery there. I had been as far as Round Top that morning, and had noticed the unfavorable character of the ground, and, therefore, I accompanied Sickles direct to the Peach Orchard, where he pointed out the ridges, already described, as his proposed line. They commanded all the ground behind, as well as in front of them, and together constituted a favorable position for *the enemy* to hold. This was one good reason for our taking possession of it. It would, it is true, in our hands present a salient angle, which generally exposes both its sides to enfilade fires; but here the ridges were so high that each would serve as a "traverse" for the other, and reduce that evil to a minimum. On the other hand it would so greatly lengthen our line—which in any case must rest on Round Top, and connect with the left of the Second Corps—as to require a larger force than the Third Corps alone to hold it, and it would be difficult to occupy and strengthen the angle if the enemy already held the wood in its front. At my instance General Sickles ordered a reconnoissance to ascertain if the wood was occupied.

About this time a cannonade was opened on Cemetery Hill, which indicated an attack there, and as I had examined the Emmitsburg Ridge, I said I would not await the result of the reconnoissance but return to headquarters by way of Round Top, and examine that part of the proposed line. As I was leaving, General Sickles asked me if he should move forward his corps. I answered, "Not on my authority; I will report to General Meade for his instructions." I had not reached the wheat-field when a sharp rattle of musketry showed that the enemy held the wood in front of the Peach Orchard angle.

As I rode back a view from that direction showed how much farther Peach Orchard was to the front of the direct line than it appeared from the orchard itself. In fact there was a third line between them, which appeared, as seen from the orchard, to be continuous with Cemetery Ridge, but was nearly six hundred yards in front of it. This is the open ground east of Plum Run already described, and which may be called the Plum Run line. Its left where it crosses the run abuts rather on Devil's Den than Round Top; it was commanded by the much higher Peach Orchard crests, and was therefore not an eligible line to occupy, although it became of importance during the battle.

As to the other two lines, the choice between them would depend on circumstances. The direct short line through the woods, and including the Round Tops, could be occupied, intrenched, and made impregnable to a front attack. But, like that of Culp's Hill, it would be a purely defensive one, from which, owing to the nature of the ground and the enemy's commanding position on the ridges at the angle, an advance in force would be impracticable. The salient line proposed by General Sickles, although much longer, afforded excellent positions for our artillery; its occupation would cramp the movements of the enemy, bring us nearer his lines, and afford us facilities for taking the offensive. It was in my judgment tactically the better line of the two, provided it were strongly occupied, for it was the only one on the field from which we could have passed from the defensive to the offensive with a prospect of decisive results. But General Meade had not, until the arrival of the Sixth Corps, a sufficient number of troops at his disposal to risk such an extension of his lines; it would have required both the Third and the Fifth corps, and left him without any reserve. Had he known that Lee's attack would be postponed until 4 P. M., he might have occupied this line in the morning; but he did not know this, expected an attack at any moment, and, in view of the vast interests involved, adopted a defensive policy, and ordered the occupation of the *safe* line. In taking risks, it would not be for his army alone, but also for Philadelphia, Baltimore, and Washington. Gettysburg was not a good strategical position for us, and the circumstances under which our army was assembled limited us tactically to a strictly defensive battle. But even a strictly defensive battle gained here would be, in its results, almost as valuable as an offensive one with a brilliant victory, since it would necessarily be decisive as to both the campaign and the invasion, and its moral effect abroad and at home, North and South, would be of vast importance in a political as well as a military sense. The additional risks of an offensive battle were out of all proportion to the prospective gains. The decision then to fight a defensive rather than an offensive battle, to look rather to solid than to brilliant results, was wise.

After finishing my examination I returned to headquarters and briefly reported to General Meade that the proposed line was a good one in itself, that it offered favorable positions for artillery, but that its relations to other lines were such that I could not advise it, and suggested that he examine it himself before ordering its occupation. He nodded assent, and I proceeded to Cemetery Hill.

The cannonade there still continued; it had been commenced by the enemy, and was accompanied by some movements of troops toward our right. As soon as I saw that it would lead to nothing serious, I returned direct to the Peach Orchard, knowing that its occupation would require large reënforcements of artillery. I was here met by Captain Randolph, the corps chief of artillery, who informed me that he had been ordered to place his batteries on the new line. Seeing Generals Meade and Sickles, not far off, in conversation, and supposing that General Meade had consented to the occupation, I sent at once to the reserve for more artillery, and authorized other general officers to draw on the same source. This large reserve, organized by the wise forethought of General McClellan, sometimes threatened with destruction, and once actually broken up, was often, as at Malvern Hill, and now at Gettysburg, an invaluable resource in the time of greatest need. . . .

When I arrived Birney's division was already posted on the crest, from Devil's Den to the Peach Orchard, and along the Emmitsburg road, Ward's brigade on the left, Graham's at the angle, De Trobriand's connecting them by a thin line. Humphreys's division was on Graham's right, near the Emmitsburg road, Carr's brigade in the front line, about the Smith house, Brewster's in second line. Burling's, with the exception of Sewell's 5th New Jersey Regiment, then in skirmish order at the front, was sent to reënforce Birney. Seeley's battery, at first posted on the right, was soon after sent to the left of the Smith house, and replaced on the right by Turnbull's from the Artillery Reserve. Randolph had ordered Smith's battery, 4th New York, to the rocky hill at the Devil's Den; Winslow's to the wheat-field. He had placed Clark on the crest looking south, and his own ("E," 1st Rhode Island) near the angle, facing west. The whole corps was, however, too weak to cover the ground, and it was too late for Meade to withdraw it. Sykes's Fifth Corps had already been ordered up and was momentarily expected. As soon as fire opened, which was just as he arrived on the ground, General Meade also sent for Caldwell's division from Cemetery Ridge, and a division of the Twelfth Corps from Culp's, and soon after for troops from the Sixth Corps. McGilvery's artillery brigade soon arrived from the reserve, and Bigelow's, Phillips's, Hart's, Ames's, and Thompson's batteries had been ordered into position on the crests, when the enemy opened from a long line of guns, stretching down to the crossing of the Emmitsburg pike. Smith's position at Devil's Den gave him a favorable oblique fire on a part of this line, and as he did not reply I proceeded to the Den. . . . On climbing to the summit, I found that Smith had just got his guns, one by one, over the rocks and chasms, into an excellent position. After pointing out to me the advancing lines of the enemy, he opened, and very effectively. Many guns were immediately turned on him, relieving so far the rest of the line. Telling him that he would probably lose his battery, I left to seek infantry supports, very doubtful if I would find my horse, for the storm of shell bursting over the place was enough to drive any animal wild. . . . However, my horse was safe, I mounted, and in the busy excitement that followed almost forgot my scare.

It was not until about 4 P. M. that Longstreet got his two divisions into position in two lines, McLaws's on the right of Anderson's division of Hill's corps, and opposite the Peach Orchard; Hood's on the extreme Confederate right and crossing the Emmitsburg road. Hood had been ordered, keeping his left on that road, to break in the end of our line, supposed to be at the orchard; but perceiving that our left was "refused" (bent back toward Devil's Den), and noticing the importance of Round Top, he suggested to Longstreet that the latter be turned and attacked. The reply was that General Lee's orders were to attack along the Emmitsburg road. Again Hood sent his message and received the same reply, notwithstanding which he directed Law's brigade upon Round Top, in which movement a portion of Robertson's brigade joined; the rest of the division was thrown upon Devil's Den and the ridge between it and the Peach Orchard. The first assaults were repulsed, but after hard fighting, McLaws's division being also advanced, toward 6 o'clock the angle was broken in, after a resolute defense and with great loss on both sides. In the meantime three of Anderson's brigades were advancing on Humphreys, and the latter received orders from Birney, now in command of the corps (Sickles having been severely wounded soon after 6 o'clock near the Trostle house), to throw back his left, form an oblique line in his rear, and connect with the right of Birney's division, then retiring. The junction was not effected, and Humphreys, greatly outnumbered, slowly and skillfully fell back to Cemetery Ridge, Gibbon sending two regiments and Brown's Rhode Island battery to his support. But the enemy was strong and covered the whole Second Corps front, now greatly weakened by detachments. Wilcox's, Perry's, and Wright's Confederate brigade pressed up to the ridge, outflanking Humphreys's right and left, and Wright broke through our line and seized the guns in his front, but was soon driven out, and not being supported they all fell back, about dusk, under a heavy artillery fire.

As soon as Longstreet's attack commenced, General Warren was sent by General Meade to see to the condition of the extreme left. The duty could not have been intrusted to better hands. Passing along the lines he found Little Round Top, the key of the position, unoccupied except by a signal station. The enemy at the time lay concealed, awaiting the signal for assault, when a shot fired in their direction caused a sudden movement on their part which, by the gleam of reflected sunlight from their bayonets, revealed their long lines outflanking the position. Fully comprehending the imminent danger, Warren sent to General Meade for a division. The enemy was already advancing when, noticing the approach of the Fifth Corps, Warren rode to meet it, caused Weed's and Vincent's brigades and Hazlett's battery to be detached from the latter and hurried them to the summit. The passage of the six guns through the roadless woods and amongst the rocks was marvelous. Under ordinary circumstances it would have been considered an impossible feat, but the eagerness of the men to get into action with their comrades of the infantry, and the skillful driving, brought them without delay to the very summit, where they went immediately into battle. They were barely in time, for the enemy were also climbing the hill. A close and bloody hand-to-hand struggle ensued, which left both Round Tops in our possession. Weed and Hazlett were killed, and Vincent was mortally wounded—all young men of great promise. . . .

The enemy, however, clung to the woods and rocks at the base of Round Top, carried Devil's Den and its woods, and captured three of Smith's guns, who, however, effectively deprived the enemy of their use by carrying off all the implements.

The breaking in of the Peach Orchard angle exposed the flanks of the batteries on its crests, which retired firing, in order to cover the retreat of the infantry. Many guns of different batteries had to be abandoned because of the destruction of their horses and men; many were hauled off by hand; all the batteries lost heavily. Bigelow's 9th Massachusetts made a stand close by the Trostle house in the corner of the field through which he had retired fighting with prolonges fixed. Although already much cut up, he was directed by McGilvery to hold that point at all hazards until a line of artillery could be formed in front of the wood beyond Plum Run; that is, on what we have called the "Plum Run line." This line was formed by collecting the serviceable batteries, and fragments of batteries, that were brought off, with which, and Dow's Maine battery fresh from the reserve, the pursuit was checked. Finally some twenty-five guns formed a solid mass, which unsupported by infantry, held this part of the line, aided General Humphreys's movements, and covered by its fire the abandoned guns until they could be brought off, as all were, except perhaps one. When, after accomplishing its purpose, all that was left of Bigelow's battery was withdrawn, it was closely pressed by Colonel Humphreys's 21st Mississippi, the only Confederate regiment which succeeded in crossing the run. His men had entered the battery and fought hand-to-hand with the cannoneers; one was killed whilst trying to spike a gun, and another knocked down with a handspike whilst endeavoring to drag off a prisoner. The battery went into action with 104 officers and men. Of the four battery officers one was killed, another mortally, and a third, Captain Bigelow, severely wounded. Of 7 sergeants, 2 were killed and 4 wounded; or a total of 28 men, including 2 missing; and 65 out of 88 horses were killed or wounded. As the battery had sacrificed itself for the safety of the line, its work is specially noticed as typical of the service that artillery is not infrequently called upon to render, and did render in other instances at Gettysburg besides this one.

When Sickles was wounded General Meade directed Hancock to take command of the Third as well as his own corps, which he again turned over to Gibbon. About 7:15 P. M. the field was in a critical condition. Birney's division was now broken up; Humphreys's was slowly falling back, under cover of McGilvery's guns; Anderson's line was advancing. On its right, Barksdale's brigade, except the 21st Mississippi, was held in check only by McGilvery's artillery, to whose support Hancock now brought up Willard's brigade of the Second Corps. Placing the 39th New York in reserve, Willard with his other three regiments charged Barksdale's brigade and drove it back nearly to the Emmitsburg road, when he was himself repulsed by a heavy artillery and infantry fire, and fell back to his former position near the sources of Plum Run. In this affair Willard was killed and Barksdale mortally wounded. Meanwhile the 21st Mississippi crossed the run from the neighborhood of the Trostle house, and drove out the men of Watson's battery ("I," 5th United States), on the extreme left of McGilvery's line, but was in turn driven off by the 39th New York, led by Lieutenant Peeples of the battery, musket in hand, who thus recovered his guns, Watson being severely wounded.

Birney's division once broken, it was difficult to stem the tide of defeat. Hood's and McLaws's divisions—excepting Barksdale's brigade—compassed the Devil's Den and its woods, and as the Federal reënforcements from other corps came piecemeal, they were beaten in detail until by successive accretions they greatly outnumbered their opponents, who had all the advantages of position, when the latter in turn retired, but were not pursued. This fighting was confined almost wholly to the woods and wheat-field between the Peach Orchard and Little Round Top, and the great number of brigade and regimental commanders, as well as of inferior officers and soldiers, killed and wounded on both sides, bears testimony to its close and desperate character. General Meade was on the ground active in bringing up and putting in reenforcements, and in doing so had his horse shot under him. At the close of the day the Confederates held the base of the Round Tops, Devil's Den, its woods, and the Emmitsburg road, with skirmishers thrown out as far as the Trostle house; the Federals had the two Round Tops, the Plum Run line, and Cemetery Ridge. During the night the Plum Run line, except the wood on its left front (occupied by McCandless's brigade, Crawford's division, his other brigade being on Big Round Top), was abandoned; the Third Corps was massed to the left and rear of Caldwell's division, which had reoccupied its short ridge, with McGilvery's artillery on its crest. The Fifth Corps remained on and about Round Top, and a division [Ruger's] which had been detached from the Twelfth Corps returned to Culp's Hill.

When Longstreet's guns were heard, Ewell opened a cannonade, which after an hour's firing was overpowered by the Federal artillery on Cemetery Hill. Johnson's division then advanced, and found only one brigade— Greene's—of the Twelfth Corps in position, the others having been sent to the aid of Sickles at the Peach Orchard. Greene fought with skill and determination for two or three hours, and, reënforced by seven or eight hundred men of the First and Eleventh corps, succeeded in holding his own intrenchments, the enemy taking possession of the abandoned works of Geary and Ruger. This brought Johnson's troops near the Baltimore pike, but the darkness prevented their seeing or profiting by the advantage then within their reach. When Ruger's division returned from Round Top, and Geary's from Rock Creek, they found Johnson in possession of their intrenchments, and immediately prepared to drive him out at daylight.

It had been ordered that when Johnson engaged Culp's Hill, Early and Rodes should assault Cemetery Hill. Early's attack was made with great spirit, by Hoke's and Avery's brigades, Gordon's being in reserve; the hill was ascended through the wide ravine between Cemetery and Culp's hills, a line of infantry on the slopes was broken, and Wiedrich's Eleventh Corps and Ricketts's reserve batteries near the brow of the hill were overrun; but the excellent position of Stevens's 12-pounders at the head of the ravine, which enabled him to sweep it, the arrival of Carroll's brigade sent unasked by Hancock—a happy inspiration, as this line had been weakened to send supports both to Greene and Sickles—and the failure of Rodes to coöperate with Early, caused the attack to miscarry. The cannoneers of the two batteries, so summarily ousted, rallied and recovered their guns by a vigorous attack —with pistols by those who had them, by others with handspikes, rammers, stones, and even fence-rails—the "Dutchmen" showing that they were in no way inferior to their "Yankee" comrades, who had been taunting them ever since Chancellorsville. After an hour's desperate fighting the enemy was driven out with heavy loss, Avery being among the killed. At the close of this second day a consultation of corps commanders was held at Meade's headquarters. I was not present, although summoned, but was informed that the vote was unanimous to hold our lines and to await an attack for at least one day before taking the offensive, and Meade so decided.

Because Gettysburg marked Lee's deepest penetration of the North, and because the fortunes of the Confederacy ebbed more perceptibly after it than before, the notion is quite general that this particular engagement represented the so-called High Watermark of the Confederacy. (The guides on the field today will even pinpoint that turning of the tide at the Bloody Angle.) Actually, as such authorities as Bruce Catton agree, there is little evidence to support this view. If it is desirable to select a High Watermark Battle, Antietam is a far better candidate. In fact not long after the War, Longstreet, a qualified observer, wrote that at Antietam "was sprung the arch upon which the Confederate cause rested."

"Indescribably grand"

BY HENRY J. HUNT, BREVET MAJOR-GENERAL, U. S. A., CHIEF OF ARTILLERY, A. P.

IN VIEW of the successes gained on the second day, General Lee resolved to renew his efforts. These successes were:

1st. *On the right,* the lodgment at the bases of the Round Tops, the possession of Devil's Den and its woods, and the ridges on the Emmitsburg road, which gave him the coveted positions for his artillery.

2d. *On the left,* the occupation of part of the intrenchments of the Twelfth Corps, with an outlet to the Baltimore pike, by which all our lines could be taken in reverse.

3d. *At the center,* the partial success of three of Anderson's brigades in penetrating our lines, from which they were expelled only because they lacked proper support. It was thought that better concert of action might have made good a lodgment here also.

Both armies had indeed lost heavily, but the account in that respect seemed in favor of the Confederates, or at worst, balanced. Pickett's and Edward Johnson's divisions were fresh, as were Posey's and Mahone's brigades of R. H. Anderson's, and William Smith's brigade of Early's division. These could be depended upon for an assault; the others could be used as supports, and to follow up a success. The artillery was almost intact. Stuart had arrived with his cavalry, excepting the brigades of Jones and Robertson,

383

guarding the communications; and Imboden had also come up. General Lee, therefore, directed the renewal of operations both on the right and left. Ewell had been ordered to attack at daylight on July 3d, and during the night reënforced Johnson with Smith's, Daniel's, and O'Neal's brigades. Johnson had made his preparations, and was about moving, when at dawn Williams's artillery opened upon him, preparatory to an assault by Geary and Ruger for the recovery of their works. The suspension of this fire was followed by an immediate advance by both sides. A conflict ensued which lasted with varying success until near 11 o'clock, during which the Confederates were driven out of the Union intrenchments by Geary and Ruger, aided by Shaler's brigade of the Sixth Corps. They made one or two attempts to regain possession, but were unsuccessful, and a demonstration to turn Johnson's left caused him to withdraw his command to Rock Creek. At the close of the war the scene of this conflict was covered by a forest of dead trees, leaden bullets proving as fatal to them as to the soldiers whose bodies were thickly strewn beneath them.

Longstreet's arrangements had been made to attack Round Top, and his orders issued with a view to turning it, when General Lee decided that the assault should be made on Cemetery Ridge by Pickett's and Pettigrew's divisions, with part of Trimble's. Longstreet formed these in two lines—Pickett on the right, supported by Wilcox; Pettigrew on the left, with Lane's and Scales's brigades under Trimble in the second line. Hill was ordered to hold his line with the remainder of his corps—six brigades—give Longstreet assistance if required, and avail himself of any success that might be gained. Finally a powerful artillery force, about one hundred and fifty guns, was ordered to prepare the way for the assault by cannonade. The necessary arrangements caused delay, and before notice of this could be received by Ewell, Johnson, as we have seen, was attacked, so that the contest was over on the left before that at the center was begun. The hoped-for concert of action in the Confederate attacks was lost from the beginning.

On the Federal side Hancock's corps held Cemetery Ridge with Robinson's division, First Corps, on Hays's right in support, and Doubleday's at the angle between Gibbon and Caldwell. General Newton, having been assigned to the command of the First Corps, *vice* Reynolds, was now in charge of the ridge held by Caldwell. Compactly arranged on its crest was McGilvery's artillery, forty-one guns, consisting of his own batteries, reënforced by others from the Artillery Reserve. Well to the right, in front of Hays and Gibbon, was the artillery of the Second Corps under its chief, Captain Hazard. Woodruff's battery was in front of Ziegler's Grove; on his left, in succession, Arnold's Rhode Island, Cushing's United States, Brown's Rhode Island, and Rorty's New York. In the fight of the preceding day the two last-named batteries had been to the front and suffered severely. Lieutenant T. Fred Brown was severely wounded, and his command devolved on

Lieutenant Perrin. So great had been the loss in men and horses that they were now of four guns each, reducing the total number in the corps to twenty-six. Daniel's battery of horse artillery, four guns, was at the angle. Cowan's 1st New York battery, six rifles, was placed on the left of Rorty's soon after the cannonade commenced. In addition, some of the guns on Cemetery Hill, and Rittenhouse's on Little Round Top, could be brought to bear, but these were offset by batteries similarly placed on the flanks of the enemy, so that on the Second Corps line, within the space of a mile, were 77 guns to oppose nearly 150. They were on an open crest plainly visible from all parts of the opposite line. Between 10 and 11 A. M., everything looking favorable at Culp's Hill, I crossed over to Cemetery Ridge, to see what might be going on at other points. Here a magnificent display greeted my eyes. Our whole front for two miles was covered by batteries already in line or going into position. They stretched—apparently in one unbroken mass— from opposite the town to the Peach Orchard, which bounded the view to the left, the ridges of which were planted thick with cannon. Never before had such a sight been witnessed on this continent, and rarely, if ever, abroad. What did it mean? It might possibly be to hold that line while its infantry was sent to aid Ewell, or to guard against a counter-stroke from us, but it most probably meant an assault on our center, to be preceded by a cannonade in order to crush our batteries and shake our infantry; at least to cause us to exhaust our ammunition in reply, so that the assaulting troops might pass in good condition over the half mile of open ground which was beyond our effective musketry fire. With such an object the cannonade would be long and followed immediately by the assault, their whole army being held in readiness to follow up a success. From the great extent of ground occupied by the enemy's batteries, it was evident that all the artillery on our west front, whether of the army corps or the reserve, must concur as a *unit,* under the chief of artillery, in the defense. This is provided for in all well-organized armies by special rules, which formerly were contained in our own army regulations, but they had been condensed in successive editions into a few short lines, so obscure as to be virtually worthless, because, like the rudimentary toe of the dog's paw, they had become, from lack of use, mere survivals—unintelligible except to the specialist. It was of the first importance to subject the enemy's infantry, from the first moment of their advance, to such a cross-fire of our artillery as would break their formation, check their impulse, and drive them back, or at least bring them to our lines in such condition as to make them an easy prey. There was neither time nor necessity for reporting this to General Meade, and beginning on the right, I instructed the chiefs of artillery and battery commanders to withhold their fire for fifteen or twenty minutes after the cannonade commenced, then to concentrate their fire with all possible accuracy on those batteries which were most destructive to us—but slowly, so that when the enemy's ammunition was exhausted, we should have sufficient left to meet the assault. I had just given these orders to the last battery on Little Round Top, when the signal-gun was fired, and the enemy opened with all his guns. From that point the scene was indescribably grand. All their batteries were soon covered with smoke, through which the flashes were incessant, whilst the air seemed filled with shells, whose sharp explosions, with the hurtling of their fragments, formed a running accompaniment to the deep roar of the guns. Thence I rode to the Artillery Reserve to order fresh batteries and ammunition to be sent up to the ridge as soon as the cannonade ceased; but both the reserve and the train had gone to a safer place. Messengers, however, had been left to receive and convey orders, which I sent by them; then I returned to the ridge. Turning into the Taneytown pike, I saw evidence of the necessity under which the reserve had "decamped," in the remains of a dozen exploded caissons, which had been placed under cover of a hill, but which the shells had managed to search out. In fact, the fire was more dangerous behind the ridge than on its crest, which I soon reached at the position occupied by General Newton behind McGilvery's batteries, from which we had a fine view as all our own guns were now in action.

Most of the enemy's projectiles passed overhead, the effect being to sweep all the open ground in our rear, which was of little benefit to the Confederates—a mere waste of ammunition, for everything here could seek shelter. And just here an incident already published may be repeated, as it illustrates a peculiar feature of civil war. Colonel Long, who was at the time on General Lee's staff, had a few years before served in my mounted battery expressly to receive a course of instruction in the use of field-artillery. At Appomattox we spent several hours together, and in the course of conversation I told him I was not satisfied with the conduct of this cannonade which I had heard was under his direction, inasmuch as he had not done justice to his instruction; that his fire, instead of being concentrated on the point of attack, as it ought to have been, and as I expected it would be, was scattered over the whole field. He was amused at the criticism and said: "I remembered my lessons at the time, and when the fire became so scattered, wondered what you would think about it!" . . .

The Confederate approach was magnificent, and excited our admiration; but the story of that charge is so well known that I need not dwell upon it further than as it concerns my own command. The steady fire from McGilvery and Rittenhouse, on their right, caused Pickett's men to "drift" in the opposite direction, so that the weight of the assault fell upon the positions occupied by Hazard's batteries. I had counted on an artillery cross-fire that would stop it before it reached our lines, but, except a few shots here and there, Hazard's batteries were silent until the enemy came within canister range. They had unfortunately exhausted their long range projectiles during the cannonade, under the orders of their corps commander, and it was too late to replace them. Had my instructions been followed here, as they were by McGilvery, I do not believe that Pickett's division would have reached our line. We lost not only the fire of one-third of our guns, but the resulting cross-fire, which would have doubled its value. The prime fault was in the obscurity of our army regulations as to the artillery, and the absence of all regulations as to the proper relations of the different arms of service to one another. On this occasion it cost us much blood, many lives, and for a moment endangered the integrity of our line if not the success of the battle. Soon after Pickett's repulse, Wilcox's, Wright's, and Perry's brigades were moved forward, but under the fire of the fresh batteries in Gibbon's front, of McGilvery's and Rittenhouse's guns and the advance of two regiments of Stannard's Vermont brigade, they soon fell back. The losses in the batteries of the Second Corps were very heavy. Of the five battery commanders and their successors on the field, Rorty, Cushing, and Woodruff were killed, and Milne was mortally and Sheldon severely wounded at their guns. So great was the destruction of men and horses, that Cushing's and Woodruff's United States, and Brown's and Arnold's Rhode Island batteries were consolidated to form two serviceable ones.

The advance of the Confederate brigades to cover Pickett's retreat showed that the enemy's line opposite Cemetery Ridge was occupied by infantry. Our own line on the ridge was in more or less disorder, as the result of the conflict, and in no condition to advance a sufficient force for a counter-assault. The largest bodies of organized troops available were on the left, and General Meade now proceeded to Round Top and pushed out skirmishers to feel the enemy in its front. An advance to the Plum Run line, of the troops behind it, would have brought them directly in front of the numerous batteries which crowned the Emmitsburg Ridge, commanding that line and all the intervening ground; a farther advance, to the attack, would have brought them under additional heavy flank fires. McCandless's brigade, supported by Nevin's, was, however, pushed forward, under cover of the woods, which protected them from the fire of all these batteries; it crossed the Wheatfield, cleared the woods, and had an encounter with a portion of Benning's brigade, which was retiring. Hood's and McLaws's divisions were falling back under Longstreet's orders to their strong position, resting on Peach Orchard and covering Hill's line. Our troops on the left were locked up. As to the center, Pickett's and Pettigrew's assaulting divisions had formed no part of A. P. Hill's line, which was virtually intact. The idea that there must have been "a gap of at least a mile" in that line, made by throwing forward these divisions, and that a prompt advance from Cemetery Ridge would have given us the line, or the artillery in front of it, was a delusion. A prompt counter-charge after a combat between two small bodies of men is one thing; the change from the defensive to the offensive of an army, after an engagement at a single *point,* is quite another. *This* was not a "Waterloo defeat"

387

with a fresh army to follow it up, and to have made such a change to the offensive, on the assumption that Lee had made no provision against a reverse, would have been rash in the extreme. An advance of 20,000 men from Cemetery Ridge in the face of the 140 guns then in position would have been stark madness; an immediate advance from any point, in force, was simply impracticable, and before due preparation could have been made for a change to the offensive, the favorable moment—had any resulted from the repulse—would have passed away.

Whilst the main battle was raging, sharp cavalry combats took place on both flanks of the army. On the left the principal incident was an attack made by order of General Kilpatrick on infantry and artillery in woods and behind stone fences, which resulted in considerable losses, and especially in the death of General Farnsworth, a gallant and promising officer who had but a few days before been appointed brigadier-general and had not yet received his commission. On the right an affair of some magnitude took place between Stuart's command of four and Gregg's of three brigades; but Jenkins's Confederate brigade was soon thrown out of action from lack of ammunition, and two only of Gregg's were engaged. Stuart had been ordered to cover Ewell's left and was proceeding toward the Baltimore pike, where he hoped to create a diversion in aid of the Confederate infantry, and in case of Pickett's success to fall upon the retreating Federal troops. From near Cress's Ridge, two and a half miles east of Gettysburg, Stuart commanded a view of the roads in rear of the Federal lines. On its northern wooded end he posted Jackson's battery, and took possession of the Rummel farm-buildings, a few hundred yards distant. Hampton and Fitzhugh Lee were on his left, covered by the wood, Jenkins and Chambliss on the right, along the ridge. Half a mile east on a low parallel ridge, the southern part of which bending west toward Cress's Ridge furnished excellent positions for artillery, was the Federal cavalry brigade of McIntosh, who now sent a force toward Rummel's, from which a strong body of skirmishers was thrown to meet them, and the battery opened. McIntosh now demanded reënforcements, and Gregg, then near the Baltimore pike, brought him Custer's brigade and Pennington's and Randol's batteries. The artillery soon drove the Confederates out of Rummel's, and compelled Jackson's Virginia battery to leave the ridge. Both sides brought up reënforcements and the battle swayed from side to side of the interval. Finally the Federals were pressed back, and Lee and Hampton, emerging from the wood, charged, sword in hand, facing a destructive artillery fire—for the falling back of the cavalry had uncovered our batteries. The assailants were met by Custer's and such other mounted squadrons as could be thrown in; a *mêlée* ensued, in which Hampton was severely wounded and the charge repulsed. Breathed's and McGregor's Confederate batteries had replaced Jackson's, a sharp artillery duel took place, and at nightfall each side held substantially its original ground. Both sides claim to have held the Rummel house. The advantage was decidedly with the Federals, who had foiled Stuart's plans. Thus the battle of Gettysburg closed as it had opened, with a very creditable cavalry battle.

General Lee now abandoned the attempt to dislodge Meade, intrenched a line from Oak Hill to Peach Orchard, started all his *impedimenta* to the Potomac in advance, and followed with his army on the night of July 4th, via Fairfield. . . .

But the hopes and expectations excited by the victory of Gettysburg were as unreasonable as the fears that had preceded it; and great was the disappointment that followed the "escape" of Lee's army. It was promptly manifested, too, and in a manner which indicates how harshly and unjustly the Army of the Potomac and its commanders were usually judged and treated; and what trials the latter had to undergo whilst subjected to the meddling and hectoring of a distant superior, from which they were not freed until the general-in-chief accompanied them in the field. On the day following Lee's withdrawal, before it was possible that all the circumstances could be known, three dispatches passed between the respective headquarters.

First. Halleck to Meade July 14th (in part):

I need hardly say to you that the escape of Lee's army without another battle has created great dissatisfaction in the mind of the President, and it will require an active and energetic pursuit on your part to remove the impression that it has not been sufficiently active heretofore.

Second. Meade to Halleck July 14th:

Having performed my duty conscientiously and to the best of my ability, the censure of the President conveyed in your dispatch of 1 P. M. this day, is, in my judgment, so undeserved that I feel compelled most respectfully to ask to be immediately relieved from the command of this army.

Third. Halleck to Meade July 14th:

My telegram stating the disappointment of the President at the escape of Lee's army was not intended as a censure, but as a stimulus to an active pursuit. It is not deemed a sufficient cause for your application to be relieved.

Whatever the object of these dispatches of General Halleck, they are perfectly consistent with a determination on the part of the War Department to discredit under all circumstances the Army of the Potomac and any commander identified with it—and that was the effect in this case.

General Longstreet always thought Gettysburg was lost because Lee, contrary to their agreement at the beginning of the campaign, carried the fight to the enemy instead of making the enemy carry it to him. And at Gettysburg, surely, he seems to have been more of a military realist than his commander. He was, for example, dead set against Pickett's charge and, as General Alexander reveals in the following report, he delayed as long as possible the order to Pickett to begin it. As that now famous charge swept toward the Union lines, Colonel Freemantle, a British observer who was watching it with Longstreet, said, "I wouldn't have missed this for anything." And Longstreet replied, "The devil you wouldn't! I would like to have missed it very much." The conclusion seems inescapable now that General Lee did not fight Gettysburg well, but that from his point of view, everything that could go wrong those three days did go wrong.

"Pickett's division swept out of the wood"

THE GREAT CHARGE AND ARTILLERY FIGHTING AT GETTYSBURG

BY E. PORTER ALEXANDER, BRIGADIER-GENERAL, C. S. A.

W E MARCHED quite steadily, with a good road and a bright moon, until about 7 A. M. on the 2d, when we halted in a grassy open grove about a mile west of Seminary Ridge, and fed and watered. Here, soon afterward, I was sent for by General Longstreet, and, riding forward, found him with General Lee on Seminary Ridge. Opposite, about a mile away, on Cemetery Ridge, overlooking the town, lay the enemy, their batteries making considerable display, but their infantry, behind stone walls and ridges, scarcely visible. In between us were only gentle rolling slopes of pasture and wheat-fields, with a considerable body of woods to the right and front. The two Round Tops looked over everything, and a signal-flag was visible on the highest. Instinctively the idea arose, "If we could only take position here and have them attack us through this open ground!" But I soon learned that we were in no such luck—the boot, in fact, being upon the other foot.

It was explained to me that our corps was to assault the enemy's left flank, and I was directed to reconnoiter it and then to take charge of all the artillery of the corps and direct it in the attack, leaving my own battalion to the command of Major Huger. I was particularly cautioned, in moving the artillery, to keep it out of sight of the signal-station upon Round Top. . . .

We waited quite a time for the infantry, and I think it was about 4 o'clock when at last the word was given for Hood's division to move out and endeavor to turn the enemy's left, while McLaws awaited the development of Hood's attack, ready to assault the Peach Orchard. Henry's battalion moved out with Hood and was speedily and heavily engaged; Cabell was ready to support him, and at once went into action near Snyder's house, about seven hundred yards from the Peach Orchard.

The Federal artillery was ready for us and in their usual full force and good practice. The ground at Cabell's position gave little protection, and he suffered rapidly in both men and horses. To help him I ran up Huger with 18 guns of my own 26, to Warfield's house, within 500 yards of the Peach Orchard, and opened upon it. This made fifty-four guns in action, and I hoped they would crush that part of the enemy's line in a very short time, but the fight was longer and hotter than I expected. So accurate was the enemy's fire, that two of my guns were fairly dismounted, and the loss of men was so great that I had to ask General Barksdale, whose brigade was lying down close behind in the wood, for help to handle the heavy 24-pounder howitzers of Moody's battery. He gave me permission to call for volunteers, and in a minute I had eight good fellows, of whom, alas! we buried two that night, and sent to the hospital three others mortally or severely wounded. At last I sent for my other two batteries, but before they arrived McLaws's division charged past our guns, and the enemy deserted their line in confusion. Then I believed that Providence was indeed "taking the proper view," and that the war was very nearly over. Every battery was limbered to the front, and the two batteries from the rear coming up, all six charged in line across the plain and went into action again at the position the enemy had deserted. I can recall no more splendid sight, on a small scale—and certainly no more inspiriting moment during the war—than that of the charge of these six batteries. An artillerist's heaven is to follow the routed enemy, after a tough resistance, and throw shells and canister into his disorganized and fleeing masses. Then the explosions of the guns sound louder and more powerful, and the very shouts of the gunners, ordering "Fire!" in rapid succession, thrill one's very soul. There is no excitement on earth like it. It is far prettier shooting than at a compact, narrow line of battle, or at another battery. Now we saw our heaven just in front, and were already breathing the very air of victory. Now we would have our revenge, and make them sorry they had staid so long. Everything was in a rush. The ground was generally good, and pieces and caissons went at a gallop, some cannoneers mounted, and some running by the sides—not in regular line, but a general race and scramble to get there first.

But we only had a moderately good time with Sickles's retreating corps after all. They fell back upon fresh troops in what seemed a strong position extending along the ridge north of Round Top. Hood's troops under Law gained the slope of Little Round Top, but were driven back to its base. Our infantry lines had become disjoined in the advance, and the fighting became a number of isolated combats between brigades. The artillery took part wherever it could, firing at everything in sight, and a sort of pell-mell fighting lasted until darkness covered the field and the fuses of the flying shells looked like little meteors in the air. But then both musketry and artillery slackened off, and by 9 o'clock the field was silent. . . .

Early in the morning General Lee came around, and I was then told that we were to assault Cemetery Hill, which lay rather to our left. This necessitated a good many changes of our positions, which the enemy did not altogether approve of, and they took occasional shots at us, though we shifted about, as inoffensively as possible, and carefully avoided getting into bunches. But we stood it all meekly, and by 10 o'clock, Dearing having come up, we had seventy-five guns in what was virtually one battery, so disposed as to fire on Cemetery Hill and the batteries south of it, which would have a fire on our advancing infantry. Pickett's division had arrived, and his men were resting and eating. Along Seminary Ridge, a short distance to our left, were sixty-three guns of A. P. Hill's corps, under Colonel R. L. Walker. As their distance was a little too great for effective howitzer fire, General Pendleton offered me the use of nine howitzers belonging to that corps. I accepted them, intending to take them into the charge with Pickett; so I put them in a hollow behind a bit of wood, with no orders but to wait there until I sent for them. About 11, some of Hill's skirmishers and the enemy's began fighting over a barn between the lines, and gradually his artillery and the enemy's took part, until over a hundred guns were engaged, and a tremendous roar was kept up for quite a time. But it gradually died out, and the whole field became as silent as a churchyard until 1 o'clock. The enemy, aware of the strength of his position, simply sat still and waited for us. It had been arranged that when the infantry column was ready, General Longstreet should order two guns fired by the Washington Artillery. On that signal all our guns were to open on Cemetery Hill and the ridge extending toward Round Top, which was covered with batteries. I was to observe the fire and give Pickett the order to charge. I accordingly took position, about 12, at the most favorable point, just on the left of the line of guns and with one of Pickett's couriers with me. Soon after I received the following note from Longstreet:

COLONEL: If the artillery fire does not have the effect to drive off the enemy or greatly demoralize him, so as to make our efforts pretty certain, I would prefer that you should not advise General Pickett to make the charge. I shall rely a great deal on your good judgment to determine the matter, and shall expect you to let General Pickett know when the moment offers.

This note rather startled me. If that assault was to be made on General Lee's judgment it was all right, but I did not want it made on mine. I wrote back to General Longstreet to the following effect:

GENERAL : I will only be able to judge of the effect of our fire on the enemy by his return fire, for his infantry is but little exposed to view and the smoke will obscure the whole field. If, as I infer from your note, there is any alternative to this attack, it should be carefully considered before opening our fire, for it will take all the artillery ammunition we have left to test this one thoroughly, and, if the result is unfavorable, we will have none left for another effort. And even if this is entirely successful, it can only be so at a very bloody cost.

To this presently came the following reply:

COLONEL: The intention is to advance the infantry if the artillery has the desired effect of driving the enemy's off, or having other effect such as to warrant us in making the attack. When the moment arrives advise General Pickett, and of course advance such artillery as you can use in aiding the attack.

I hardly knew whether this left me discretion or not, but at any rate it seemed decided that the artillery must open. I felt that if we went that far we could not draw back, but the infantry must go too. General A. R. Wright, of Hill's corps, was with me looking at the position when these notes were received, and we discussed them together. Wright said, "It is not so hard to *go* there as it looks; I was nearly there with my brigade yesterday. The trouble is to *stay* there. The whole Yankee army is there in a bunch."

I was influenced by this, and somewhat by a sort of camp rumor which I had heard that morning, that General Lee had said that he was going to send every man he had upon that hill. At any rate, I assumed that the question of supports had been well considered, and that whatever was possible would be done. But before replying I rode to see Pickett, who was with his division a short distance in the rear. I did not tell him my object, but only tried to guess how he felt about the charge. He seemed very sanguine, and thought himself in luck to have the chance. Then I felt that I could not make any delay or let the attack suffer by any indecision on my part. And, that General Longstreet might know my intention, I wrote him only this: "GENERAL: When our artillery fire is at its best, I shall order Pickett to charge."

Then, getting a little more anxious, I decided to send for the nine howitzers and take them ahead of Pickett up nearly to musket range, instead of following close behind him as at first intended; so I sent a courier to bring them up in front of the infantry, but under cover of the wood. The courier could not find them. He was sent again, and only returned after our fire was opened, saying they were gone. I afterward learned that General Pendleton had sent for a part of them, and the others had moved to a neighboring hollow to get out of the line of the enemy's fire at one of Hill's batteries during the artillery duel they had had an hour before.

At exactly 1 o'clock by my watch the two signal-guns were heard in quick succession. In another minute every gun was at work. The enemy were not slow in coming back at us, and the grand roar of nearly the whole artillery of both armies burst in on the silence, almost as suddenly as the full notes of an organ would fill a church.

The artillery of Ewell's corps, however, took only a small part, I believe, in this, as they were too far away on the other side of the town. Some of them might have done good service from positions between Hill and Ewell, enfilading the batteries fighting us. The opportunity to do that was the single advantage in our having the exterior line, to compensate for all its disadvantages. But our line was so extended that all of it was not well studied, and the officers of the different corps had no opportunity to examine each other's ground for chances to coöperate.

The enemy's position seemed to have broken out with guns everywhere, and from Round Top to Cemetery Hill was blazing like a volcano. The air seemed full of missiles from every direction. . . .

Before the cannonade opened I had made up my mind to give Pickett the order to advance within fifteen or twenty minutes after it began. But when I looked at the full development of the enemy's batteries, and knew that his infantry was generally protected from our fire by stone walls and swells of the ground, I could not bring myself to give the word. It seemed madness to launch infantry into that fire, with nearly three-quarters of a mile to go at midday under a July sun. I let the 15 minutes pass, and 20, and 25, hoping vainly for something to turn up. Then I wrote to Pickett: "If you are coming at all you must come at once, or I cannot give you proper support; but the enemy's fire has not slackened at all; at least eighteen guns are still firing from the cemetery itself." Five minutes after sending that message, the enemy's fire suddenly began to slacken, and the guns in the cemetery limbered up and vacated the position.

We Confederates often did such things as that to save our ammunition for use against infantry, but I had never before seen the Federals withdraw their guns simply to save them up for the infantry fight. So I said, "If he does not run fresh batteries in there in five minutes, this is our fight." I looked anxiously with my glass, and the five minutes passed without a sign of life on the deserted position, still swept by our fire, and littered with dead men and horses and fragments of disabled carriages. Then I wrote Pickett, urgently: "For God's sake, come quick. The eighteen guns are gone; come quick, or my ammunition won't let me support you properly."

I afterward heard from others what took place with my first note to Pickett.

Pickett took it to Longstreet, Longstreet read it, and said nothing. Pickett said, "General, shall I advance?" Longstreet, knowing it had to be, but unwilling to give the word, turned his face away. Pickett saluted and said, "I am going to move forward, sir," galloped off to his division and immediately put it in motion.

Longstreet, leaving his staff, came out alone to where I was. It was then about 1:40 P.M. I explained the situation, feeling then more hopeful, but afraid our artillery ammunition might not hold out for all we would want. Longstreet said, "Stop Pickett immediately and replenish your ammunition." I explained that it would take too long, and the enemy would recover from the effect our fire was then having, and we had, moreover, very little to replenish with. Longstreet said, "I don't want to make this attack. I would stop it now but that General Lee ordered it and expects it to go on. I don't see how it can succeed."

I listened, but did not dare offer a word. The battle was lost if we stopped. Ammunition was far too low to try anything else, for we had been fighting three days. There was a chance, and it was not my part to interfere. While Longstreet was still speaking, Pickett's division swept out of the wood and showed the full length of its gray ranks and shining bayonets, as grand a sight as ever a man looked on. Joining it on the left, Pettigrew stretched farther than I could see. General Dick Garnett, just out of the sick ambulance, and buttoned up in an old blue overcoat, riding at the head of his brigade passed us and saluted Longstreet. Garnett was a warm personal friend, and we had not met before for months. We had served on the plains together before the war. I rode with him a short distance, and then we wished each other luck and a good-bye, which was our last.

Then I rode down the line of guns, selecting such as had enough ammunition to follow Pickett's advance, and starting them after him as fast as possible. I got, I think, fifteen or eighteen in all, in a little while, and went with them. Meanwhile, the infantry had no sooner debouched on the plain than all the enemy's line, which had been nearly silent, broke out again with all its batteries. The eighteen guns were back in the cemetery, and a storm of shell began bursting over and among our infantry. All of our guns—silent as the infantry passed between them—reopened over their heads when the lines had got a couple of hundred yards away, but the enemy's artillery let us alone and fired only at the infantry. No one could have looked at that advance without feeling proud of it.

But, as our supporting guns advanced, we passed many poor, mangled victims left in its trampled wake. A terrific infantry fire was now opened upon Picket, and a considerable force of the enemy moved out to attack the right flank of his line. We halted, unlimbered, and opened fire upon it. Pickett's men never halted, but opened fire at close range, swarmed over the fences and among the enemy's guns—were swallowed up in smoke, and that was the last of them. The conflict hardly seemed to last five minutes before they were melted away, and only disorganized stragglers pursued by a moderate fire were coming back. Just then, Wilcox's brigade passed by us, moving to Pickett's support. There was no longer anything to support, and with the keenest pity at the useless waste of life, I saw them advance. The men, as they passed us, looked bewildered, as if they wondered what they were expected to do, or why they were there. However, they were soon halted and moved back. They suffered some losses, and we had a few casualties from canister sent at them at rather long range.

From the position of our guns the sight of this conflict was grand and thrilling, and we watched it as men with a life-and-death interest in the result. If it should be favorable to us, the war was nearly over; if against us, we each had the risks of many battles yet to go through. And the event culminated with fearful rapidity. Listening to the rolling crashes of musketry, it was hard to realize that they were made up of single reports, and that each musket-shot represented nearly a minute of a man's life in that storm of lead and iron. It seemed as if 100,000 men were engaged, and that human life was being poured out like water. As soon as it appeared that the assault had failed, we ceased firing in order to save ammunition in case the enemy should advance. But we held our ground as boldly as possible, though we were entirely without support, and very low in ammunition. The enemy gave us an occasional shot for a while and then, to our great relief, let us rest. About that time General Lee, entirely alone, rode up and remained with me for a long time. He then probably first appreciated the full extent of the disaster as the disorganized stragglers made their way back past us. The Comte de Paris, in his excellent account of this battle, remarks that Lee, as a soldier, must at this moment have foreseen Appomattox—that he must have realized that he could never again muster so powerful an army, and that for the future he could only delay, but not avert, the failure of his cause. However this may be, it was certainly a momentous thing to him to see that superb attack end in such a bloody repulse. But, whatever his emotions, there was no trace of them in his calm and self-possessed bearing. I thought at the time his coming there very imprudent, and the absence of all his staff-officers and couriers strange. It could only have happened by his express intention. I have since thought it possible that he came, thinking the enemy might follow in pursuit of Pickett, personally to rally stragglers about our guns and make a desperate defense. He had the instincts of a soldier within him as strongly as any man. Looking at Burnside's dense columns swarming through the fire of our guns toward Marye's Hill at Fredericksburg, he had said: "It is well war is so terrible or we would grow too fond of it." No soldier could have looked on at Pickett's charge and not burned to be in it. To have a personal part in a close and desperate fight at that moment would, I believe, have been at heart a great pleasure to General Lee, and possibly he was looking for one. We were here joined by Colonel Fremantle of Her Majesty's Coldstream Guards, who was visiting our army. He afterward published an excellent account of the battle in "Blackwood," and described many little incidents that took place here, such as General Lee's encouraging the retreating stragglers to rally as soon as they got back to cover, and saying that the failure was his fault, not theirs. Colonel Fremantle especially noticed that General Lee reproved an officer for spurring a foolish horse, and advised him to use only gentle measures. The officer was Lieutenant F. M. Colston of my staff, whom General Lee had requested to ride off to the right and try to discover the cause of a great cheering we heard in the enemy's lines. We thought it might mean an advance upon us, but it proved to be only a greeting to some general officer riding along the line.

That was the end of the battle. . . . Night came very slowly, but came at last; and about 10 the last gun was withdrawn to Willoughby Run, whence we had moved to the attack the afternoon before.

Of Pickett's three brigadiers, Garnett and Armistead were killed and Kemper dangerously wounded. Fry, who commanded Pettigrew's brigade, which adjoined Garnett on the left, and in the charge was the brigade of direction for the whole force, was also left on the field desperately wounded. Of all Pickett's field-officers in the three brigades only one major came out unhurt. The men who made the attack were good enough: the only trouble was, there were not enough of them.

PICKETT'S CHARGE. LOOKING DOWN THE UNION LINES GENERAL HANCOCK
AND STAFF ARE SEEN IN THE LEFT CENTER. FROM THE CYCLORAMA OF GETTYS-
BURG

The prisoner is a peculiar tragedy of war, one minute a useful member of a familiar group—the next a man without dignity or status, purposeless, an inhabitant of limbo. In the Civil War, prisoners were exchanged in wholesale lots until Grant became Commander in Chief. Then he, realizing that every captured Confederate was literally irreplaceable while his men were not, decided the North should hold all the rebel soldiers it could gather in. It was a shrewd military move which undoubtedly hastened the end of the war; but it also helped to produce prisons and stockades like Libby and Andersonville which killed the bodies and the spirits of thousands of brave but luckless men.

"My sight left me and I threw myself down on the roadside to die"

A PRISONER'S MARCH FROM GETTYSBURG TO STAUNTON

BY JOHN L. COLLINS, 8TH PENNSYLVANIA CAVALRY

ON THE 4th, when Lee's movement of withdrawal became known, the cavalry was ordered to throw itself between the Confederate army and the Potomac. To do this the different divisions were headed for the gaps and passes through which the trains sent under escort in advance were escaping over the mountains to Williamsport.

The regiment to which I belonged was in Gregg's division, but having become detached with the rest of the brigade during the three days of the battle, it united with two other brigades under General Kilpatrick and made an attack upon a Confederate train near Monterey. The fight took place before midnight the first day of the march, the train was burned, the guard was made prisoners, and then our command pushed on after another train that was reported ahead of the one we destroyed. A few whose horses were killed or disabled were ordered back to the division for a remount, instead of being mounted upon the enemy's horses. I disobeyed the orders, and hoping to get one of the enemy's horses I led my own and followed on foot.

401

I soon lost sight of the brigade, however, but toiled along the dark and rough road, until my horse, which at first could walk with only the weight of the saddle, refused to go any farther. As the day was breaking, I was examining and washing the poor creature's wounded shoulder, when I was surprised by about 150 Confederate cavalry, whose approach I had hailed as that of friends. At a motion from their colonel three men dismounted, the foremost of whom held out his hand to me and cheerfully said: "Good morning, sir! I am sorry to say you are a prisoner." The other two went toward my arms, which were piled on the saddle on the roadside, and, holding them up, exclaimed, "What splendid arms he has!" Surprise and the novelty of the first man's greeting kept me from realizing my position until I saw them take my carbine, saber, and pistol. Then my heart sank.

Those "splendid arms" had been my companions for two years, and two months previously I had been publicly commended for bringing them with me through the enemy's ranks when my horse was shot inside their lines as we charged upon Jackson's men at Chancellorsville. But such is war, and I bade them a sorrowful adieu, as I looked from them to the faces of my captors, some of which showed sympathy, some indifference, while all seemed manly and soldierly. The commander alone took no notice of me or my arms; he gazed up the road through the gray light of the morning as if bent on some bold manœuvre, and then said to one of his men in a loud voice: "Tell General Lee (Fitzhugh) that there is a regiment of Yankee cavalry half a mile up the road, and ask him if I shall charge them."

The man galloped back, and without waiting for General Lee's orders, the colonel wheeled his men and galloped after him—such a piece of cheap braggadocio as I had seen displayed by some of our own colonels. I was left in the care of two men to put the saddle on my horse and follow at a walk. My guards were frank, and in answer to my question told me that they belonged to General William E. Jones's brigade, that they had been captured in the fight just mentioned, and had escaped during the night from Kilpatrick who was more intent in overtaking larger bodies than in watching the few hundred he had taken. Between midnight and daybreak the colonel and about 150 men came together in the woods and fell in with General Fitzhugh Lee, who was then slipping out between two divisions of our cavalry.

About noon I was introduced to about thirty of those who had been sent back for horses to the division, and had shared my fate. We were with General Stuart's headquarters, as he was moving in the center of his brigades—they being pushed out in every direction, trying to keep a road clear for their infantry and artillery.

A young Virginian about my own age, but with much more suavity and self-complacency than I could claim, introduced himself to me and told me that he belonged to the "King and Queen" cavalry (1st Virginia, I think), and said that they knew my regiment well, and considered it a "rough one to deal with." He asked me if I remembered all the skirmishes we had as we advanced from New Kent Court House to the Chickahominy, which I did well, and then when we had become quite well acquainted, asked me if I would have any objections to exchanging saddles with him. I had not the least, as I never expected to sit on mine again, and when we stopped on the roadside to make the exchange I walked back into the ranks without my horse, as I saw no reason why I should bother leading him along for my captors to ride, if he should ever get well. Fresh prisoners were added all the time, mostly cavalry, and we marched along through the mountains the entire day. Stuart and his staff rode in our midst—rather an imprudent thing, I thought, for many of the men observed him closely with reference to a future meeting. I know it was in my mind every time I looked at him, though I had no malice and nothing to complain of in regard to my treatment. Within a year he fell by the carbine of a cavalryman whose regiment was at this time well represented among the prisoners.

The day was a hard one for me, used to fatigue and fasting though I was. The roads were the roughest and narrowest that could be found, and I had eaten nothing since the previous day, having lost my haversack during the night. I was at last compelled to tell one of the guards that I was very hungry, and he apologized for having nothing to give me, but promised to see that I got something before we went much farther. He left the ranks soon and shortly afterward returned with some bread and butter, which he divided with me. Later in the afternoon foragers brought us in rations collected from the farm-houses.

Just before sunset, as we were going through a gap, a rapid exchange of shots was heard ahead of us, and both prisoners and captors became excited. A few moments later we were near enough to look out into the plain beyond; we saw the Confederates in front of us dismounting and deploying as skirmishers, and my heart bounded as I saw my own regiment drawn up for a charge about five hundred yards away! I began to cry like a child; I thought that I would be free again in about ten minutes, with my friends; that I would be armed and mounted as twenty-four hours before. The question, How did I know my regiment? naturally comes, and is as easily answered. I could distinguish the companies by the color of their horses, and knew the order of the squadrons in the line. The black horses of troop C and the light bays of H formed the first squadron, the sorrel horses of E and the dark bays of G formed the next, and so on. The troops changed squadron often to suit the seniority of the captains, and the squadrons changed positions in the regiment for the same reason, but the combination of companies before me now had been that of the regiment for a week at least.

A call was made for sharp-shooters, and those who dismounted and presented themselves were supplied with cartridges and sent into the corn-field in front of us. But my regiment seemed disinclined to charge, and merely threw out skirmishers to meet them. Some of the Confederates enthusiastically cried, "My! won't the sharp-shooters make it hot for that cavalry!"

Though the firing became brisk, it wearied me; I wanted the charge, because I was sure that a vigorous attack would send our guards fleeing without us in less than five minutes. . . .

Now is the time for a charge, I thought. General Stuart had not more than three hundred men, encumbered by as many prisoners, and the regiment in front had five hundred in line. But while their commander hesitated, General Stuart, whose genius and courage had gotten him out of many a difficulty, proved himself equal to the present emergency. While his skirmishers were firing their last cartridges he made us fall in by fours, and marched us two or three times across the opening. We were mistaken in the twilight for Confederate infantry coming up, and then his whole column was moved along the edge of the corn-field, keeping the skirmishers between us and my regiment, which moved parallel with us, until darkness shut them out from my view.

The next morning Stuart's men were gone, and we were guarded toward the Potomac by Pickett's division. I regretted the change, the rank and file of the cavalry were so different from what I had expected to find the Southern soldiers. They were quiet, courteous, and considerate; they all seemed young, of light build with fair or sandy complexions predominant; and, better than all, they had more by far than the average share of intelligence. The infantry that took their place were nearer my conception of the Southern soldier. But I must not blame the poor fellows if they had not the kindness and elasticity of the cavalry. They were out of heart—a large part of their division had been left on the field on the 3d of July, and besides the commander of the division there was only one officer above the rank of captain left in it.

We were halted by the roadside often during the day to let Confederate troops hurry past us. In one of these halts General Longstreet was pointed out to me with evident pride by a staff-officer who had turned aside to make some courteous remarks to me. I told the officer as politely as I could that I thought they were badly beaten, and would hardly get across the Potomac. He laughed and said that they were not trying to get across—that Baltimore was their objective point just then; from there, he explained, it was but a forced march to Washington, and once there they could conquer a peace in thirty days. His hopes amused me; I remembered that when retreating from the Chickahominy and from Chancellorsville *I* did not know anything of defeat, but thought I was marching to victory by another road.

The next time we were halted I was not so pleasantly entertained. I sat on a high bank watching the various regiments and batteries go by, when a haughty young officer rode up, looking at the prisoners' feet, as if he wanted a pair of boots. Several of the men concealed theirs by drawing them up, but I did not; the soles of mine were coming off, for two days' march over rough roads was something the contractor for cavalry boots had not contemplated. The officer pulled up in front of me, however, and said in an overbearing manner, "I want those spurs." I merely looked at them and nodded. "Hand them to me," he said sternly. "They were given to me for the United States service, not for rebel service," I said, stung by his manner. "Oh!" he scornfully remarked, "I suppose you know you are a prisoner?" "Yes, I have been nearly two days without food; that convinces me." "And when a soldier is taken, his horse, his arms, and equipments are his captor's?" "Yes, mine are all gone." "And his spurs, too?" "Yes, and his boots sometimes." "Hand me your spurs, then." "Take them, if you want them, I won't hand them to you." He took out his pistol and raised it, but controlling himself lowered it and moved away. Then he turned his horse and demanded them again. The same answer, and the same arguments were repeated; the pistol was pointed at me, but his soldierly qualities triumphed over his temper as before. There seemed no way out of the difficulty; he was determined to have the spurs, but too proud to dismount and unbuckle them, and I was too stubborn to yield. At last one of Pickett's men came up and took them off, and the officer rode away with them.

Before I left the spot I kicked off my boots, for they seemed made only to carry spurs, and went barefoot the rest of the way to Richmond. The prisoners who on the first day had numbered only about 300, mostly cavalry, were now increased to nearly as many thousands, as the men taken at Gettysburg were added to us. Besides these, fresh cavalry prisoners were brought in every day. From them we heard of the extent of the victory, and the fighting that was still in progress, and we were assured by them that neither we nor our guards could ever reach the Potomac. This helped to restore the self-respect that a soldier partly loses when his arms are taken from him, and which continued captivity almost entirely destroys.

We were marched past a handsome house which had attracted our attention on our way to Gettysburg by the number of United States flags and the gayly dressed ladies waving handkerchiefs to us. They were waving them as boldly to the Confederates now, and the stars and stripes had been transformed into the stars and bars.

Some of the newly captured were badly wounded, but had no attention given them, except such crude service as their fellow-prisoners could do for them. None of our surgeons were captured, and I suppose those of the enemy had plenty to do among their own. One poor fellow of the 5th New York Cavalry had seventeen wounds which he got from the 11th Virginia. He was cut and slashed at every angle, and when we had gotten some bandages and patched him up he looked ludicrously odd. . . .

At Williamsport all was crowded and in confusion. The Confederates were throwing up weak defenses in expectation of an attack. Our cavalry had cut their way in and destroyed the only bridge that Lee had left in his rear. Some of the poor fellows that must always get left on such occasions cheered us by telling us how they did it. Three regiments charged in—one fought to the right, another to the left, while the third, supplied with straw and turpentine, dashed at the bridge, set fire to it, then cut it loose from its moorings and let it float down the river, a burning wreck. "Score another for the cavalry," we cried.

My hopes rose with the river, which was a seething flood, boiling over its banks; it seemed impossible to get us across the Potomac now. Rigging up a rope ferry, and getting the prisoners across on flat-boats was the work of two or three days, and then they encamped us on a hill a few days more, waiting for their army to follow. I think they feared an advance by Harper's Ferry and Martinsburg. The cavalry and flying artillery came from that direction; Imboden's men told us so, and I never gave up hope until we had passed Winchester. A brigade composed of infantry, cavalry, and artillery under General Imboden guarded us from this point to Staunton, a distance of over 120 miles, I think. It seemed five hundred miles to me, for I was barefooted and the pike had been recently repaired.

The mode of marching us was now for the first time systematic. We numbered at least four thousand men, and were divided into divisions, marching by columns of fours. The cavalry and artillery marched *en masse* between the divisions, while the infantry marched in two files, one at each side of the column. Imboden's brigade did not seem to have seen much hard service, at least I thought so because their clothes were new, yet the general had a new suit of gray on, and certainly he had seen plenty of hard service. The men were as kind to us as could be expected; only one unpleasant affair came under my observation all the way. In the heat of a discussion a guard clubbed his musket and struck a wounded man on the head. I have no doubt that the latter had his tongue to blame for it; but he was a prisoner and a wounded man, and the guard was promptly placed under arrest.

I have said nothing so far of the commissary arrangements simply because there was nothing to be said. I do not now remember getting anything to eat until we crossed the Potomac, except from Stuart's cavalry the first day of my captivity. But my memory must fail me, for I could not have lived unless I had gotten something occasionally. After we left Williamsport the arrangements were regular—in their meagerness, too regular. We got about a pint of flour every other day, and with it now and then a piece of rusty flitch. Some of the men tried to make bread of the flour as we camped, but the greater number stirred it up in water, and drank the paste, saying that "it stuck to their ribs longer" that way. We got an extra ration at Martinsburg, that, out of compliment to the ladies, I ought not to forget. As we marched through the town the whole populace turned out to greet us, not as enemies but as friends and sympathizers. They cried out to us, to cheer up—not to be downhearted—that we had won a great victory at Gettysburg, and though we were being marched to prison we were already avenged by the thousands of rebels that were left dead or prisoners in Pennsylvania. They appeared to be well posted by the Northern newspapers, and right in the teeth of the guards they upbraided the Confederates for theft and violence north of the Potomac. It must have been very galling to Imboden's command to be reviled that way by their country-women, but they bore it with cast-down heads, and made no reply. We could not have done it, I fear, had we been the guards, and in Pennsylvania. At last some of our men, in reply to questions on the subject, said they did not give us anything to eat. There was a sudden rush for the houses, and in a few seconds the street was lined with women with dishes of cake, bread, and everything they could lay hands on with so short a notice.

The sight of the food threw our column into disorder. Some men tried to break out of the ranks, and this being resisted, the women tried to break in. In the confusion that followed a few women were pushed back to the street-curb and fell down. The falls were, I think, accidental; but the prisoners became furious when they saw them fall, they struck at the guards right and left, and overpowered many of them, bearing them to the ground. It looked for the moment as if there would be a general fight, which must result in the death of many prisoners and the escape of others; but this was prevented by the prompt action of the cavalry and artillery, marching near the scene of the revolt. Then the general, or some one for him, promised the people and the prisoners that the latter would be halted outside the town to receive the contributions. In an open wood by the roadside we were halted, and the guards themselves soon brought us the coveted food. The sly rascals must have tossed the dainties up in the blankets as they brought them along so that every man of us at a single grab could get a sample of all they sent. I got one good handful only, but it was a mixture of ginger-bread, cookies, cake, corn-bread, and everything else that the people of Martinsburg ate. It was here that the Barbara Frietchies lived. After the battle of Antietam these women had laid planks on a torn up bridge for us, so that we could cross and drive Stuart's cavalry out of the town.

But notwithstanding this extra food at Martinsburg the low diet and the sharp stones soon told on my strength. My feet were sore, and my stomach was faint beyond endurance, and the climax was reached one day when my sight left me, and I threw myself down on the roadside to die. The rallying cry of "A cavalry charge" had no more effect on me; I knew they could not approach us now, and I gave up in despair as soon as I found I was blind. The guards tried to make me get up, but I listened with indifference to their threats to shoot me. The rear-guard of each division passed me with the same result for their efforts to rouse me, until at last the rear-guard of all came up; the officer in command assured me that it was his duty to kill me rather than leave me behind, and though I believed him I could not move, and merely told him so. At last he told a man to "run me through" with his bayonet, but I suppose there was a saving sign that I did not see, for after a pause I heard him tell the man to stay with me until a wagon came along and I could be taken and given something to eat. I never saw that officer, but I hope God saw his act of forbearance and humanity and rewarded him for it. There have been miserable cowards in either army who bullied and mistreated unfortunate prisoners when they had the power to do so, but the true soldier never did, and I never saw anything but kindness shown to the prisoners that my regiment took, and I never experienced anything but kindness from the men who guarded me from Gettysburg to Staunton.

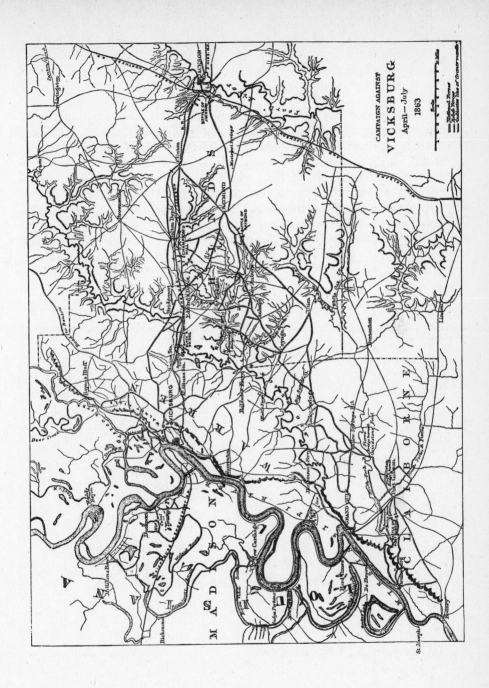

CAMPAIGN AGAINST
VICKSBURG
April — July
1863

Scale

409

In the summer of 1863, President Lincoln had more than one military campaign to worry about. The previous November, General Grant had begun an operation against Vicksburg and eight months later he was still at it. Then on July 7th, after a terrible siege, a delayed dispatch announced the surrender of Vicksburg on the Fourth of July. Lincoln was beside himself—the news, temporarily at least, driving out his disappointment at Meade's failure to pursue the retreating Lee. His jubilation was justified. Grant had eliminated an entire army, opened the Mississippi River, given the country the most clear-cut victory of the war so far—and he had done it all operating a thousand miles from his base. This man Grant looked like a soldier who might even take the measure of Robert Lee.

"Well, Yank, when are you coming into town?"

BY ULYSSES S. GRANT, GENERAL, U. S. A.

IT IS generally regarded as an axiom in war that all great armies moving in an enemy's country should start from a base of supplies, which should be fortified and guarded, and to which the army is to fall back in case of disaster. The first movement looking to Vicksburg and the force defending it as an objective was begun early in November, 1862, and conformed to this axiom. It followed the line of the Mississippi Central Railroad, with Columbus, Kentucky, as a base, and soon after it started, a coöperating column was moved down the Mississippi River on transports, with Memphis as its base. Both these movements failing, the entire Army of the Tennessee was transferred to the neighborhood of Vicksburg, and landed on the opposite or western bank of the river at Milliken's Bend. The Mississippi flows through a low alluvial bottom many miles in width, and is very tortuous in its course, running to all points of the compass, some-

411

times within a few miles. This valley is bounded on the east side by a range of high land rising in some places more than two hundred feet above the bottom. At points the river runs up to the bluffs, washing their base. Vicksburg is built on the first high land on the eastern bank below Memphis, and four hundred miles from that place by the windings of the river.

The winter of 1862–63 was unprecedented for continuous high water in the Mississippi, and months were spent in ineffectual efforts to reach high land above Vicksburg from which we could operate against that stronghold, and in making artificial waterways through which a fleet might pass, avoiding the batteries to the south of the town, in case the other efforts should fail.

In early April, 1863, the waters of the Mississippi having receded sufficiently to make it possible to march an army across the peninsula opposite Vicksburg, I determined to adopt this course, and moved my advance to a point below the town. It was necessary, however, to have transports below, both for the purpose of ferrying troops over the river and to carry supplies. These had necessarily to run the batteries. Under the direction of Admiral Porter this was successfully done. On the 29th, Grand Gulf, the first bluff south of Vicksburg on the east side of the river, and about fifty miles below, was unsuccessfully attacked by the navy. The night of the same day the batteries of that place were run by the navy and transports, again under the direction of Admiral Porter, and on the following day the river was crossed by the troops, and a landing effected at Bruinsburg, some nine miles below.

I was now in the enemy's country, with a vast river and the stronghold of Vicksburg between me and my base of supplies. I had with me the Thirteenth Corps, General McClernand commanding, and two brigades of Logan's division of the Seventeenth Corps, General McPherson commanding; in all not more than twenty thousand men to commence the campaign with. These were soon reënforced by the remaining brigade of Logan's division and by Crocker's division of the Seventeenth Corps. On the 7th of May I was further reënforced by Sherman with two divisions of his, the Fifteenth Corps. My total force was then about thirty-three thousand men. The enemy occupied Grand Gulf, Vicksburg, Haynes's Bluff, and Jackson, with a force of nearly sixty thousand men. My first problem was to capture Grand Gulf to use as a base, and then if possible beat the enemy in detail outside the fortifications of Vicksburg. Jackson is fifty miles east of Vicksburg, and was connected with it by a railroad. Haynes's Bluff is eleven miles north, and on the Yazoo River, which empties into the Mississippi some miles above the town.

Bruinsburg is two miles from high ground. The bottom at that point is higher than most of the low land in the valley of the Mississippi, and a good road leads to the bluff. It was natural to expect the garrison from Grand

Gulf to come out to meet us, and prevent, if they could, our reaching this solid base. Bayou Pierre enters the Mississippi just above Bruinsburg; and as it is a navigable stream, and was high at the time, in order to intercept us they had to go by Port Gibson, the nearest point where there was a bridge to cross upon. This more than doubled the distance from Grand Gulf to the high land back of Bruinsburg. No time was to be lost in securing this foothold. Our transportation was not sufficient to move all the army across the river at one trip or even two. But the landing of the Thirteenth Corps and one division of the Seventeenth was effected during the day, April 30th, and early evening. McClernand was advanced as soon as ammunition and two days' rations (to last five) could be issued to his men. The bluffs were reached an hour before sunset, and McClernand was pushed on, hoping to reach Port Gibson and save the bridge spanning the Bayou Pierre before the enemy could get there; for crossing a stream in the presence of an enemy is always difficult. Port Gibson, too, is the starting-point of roads to Grand Gulf, Vicksburg, and Jackson.

McClernand's advance met the enemy about five miles south of Port Gibson at Thompson's plantation. There was some firing during the night, but nothing rising to the dignity of a battle until daylight. The enemy had taken a strong natural position with most of the Grand Gulf garrison, numbering about seven or eight thousand men, under General Bowen. His hope was to hold me in check until reënforcements under Loring could reach him from Vicksburg; but Loring did not come in time to render much assistance south of Port Gibson. Two brigades of McPherson's corps followed McClernand as fast as rations and ammunition could be issued, and were ready to take position upon the battle-field whenever the Thirteenth Corps could be got out of the way.

The country in this part of Mississippi stands on edge, as it were, the roads running along the ridges except when they occasionally pass from one ridge to another. Where there are no clearings, the sides of the hills are covered with a very heavy growth of timber, and with undergrowth, and the ravines are filled with vines and canebrakes, almost impenetrable. This makes it easy for an inferior force to delay, if not defeat, a far superior one.

Near the point selected by Bowen to defend, the road to Port Gibson divides, taking two ridges, which do not diverge more than a mile or two at the widest point. These roads unite just outside the town. This made it necessary for McClernand to divide his force. It was not only divided, but it was separated by a deep ravine of the character above described. One flank could not reënforce the other except by marching back to the junction of the roads. McClernand put the divisions of Hovey, Carr, and A. J. Smith upon the right-hand branch, and Osterhaus on the left. I was on the field by 10 A. M., and inspected both flanks in person. On the right the enemy, if not being pressed back, was at least not repulsing our advance. On the left, however,

Osterhaus was not faring so well. He had been repulsed, with some loss. As soon as the road could be cleared of McClernand's troops I ordered up Mc-Pherson, who was close upon the rear of the Thirteenth Corps with two brigades of Logan's division. This was about noon. I ordered him to send one brigade (General John E. Smith's was selected) to support Osterhaus, and to move to the left and flank the enemy out of his position. This movement carried the brigade over a deep ravine to a third ridge, and when Smith's troops were seen well through the ravine Osterhaus was directed to renew his front attack. It was successful and unattended by heavy loss. The enemy was sent in full retreat on their right, and their left followed before sunset. . . .

We started next morning [May 2d] for Port Gibson as soon as it was light enough to see the road. We were soon in the town, and I was delighted to find that the enemy had not stopped to contest our crossing further at the bridge, which he had burned. The troops were set to work at once to construct a bridge across the South Fork of the Bayou Pierre. At this time the water was high, and the current rapid. What might be called a raft-bridge was soon constructed from material obtained from wooden buildings, stables, fences, etc., which sufficed for carrying the whole army over safely. Colonel James H. Wilson, a member of my staff, planned and superintended the construction of this bridge, going into the water and working as hard as any one engaged. Officers and men generally joined in this work. When it was finished the army crossed, and marched eight miles beyond to the North Fork that day. One brigade of Logan's division was sent down the stream to occupy the attention of a rebel battery which had been left behind, with infantry supports, to prevent our repairing the burnt railroad bridge. Two of his brigades were sent up the bayou to find a crossing, and to reach the North Fork to repair the bridge there. The enemy soon left when he found we were building a bridge elsewhere. Before leaving Port Gibson we were reënforced by Crocker's division, McPherson's corps, which had crossed the Mississippi at Bruinsburg and come up without stopping, except to get two days' rations. McPherson still had one division west of the Mississippi River guarding the road from Milliken's Bend to the river below until Sherman's command should relieve it. . . .

It was necessary to have transportation for ammunition. Provisions could be taken from the country; but all the ammunition that can be carried on the person is soon exhausted when there is much fighting. I directed therefore, immediately on landing, that all the vehicles and draught animals, whether horses, mules, or oxen, in the vicinity should be collected and loaded to their capacity with ammunition. Quite a train was collected during the 30th, and a motley train it was. In it could be found fine carriages, loaded nearly to the tops with boxes of cartridges that had been pitched in promiscuously, drawn by mules with plow-harness, straw-collars, rope lines, etc.; long-coupled wagons, with racks for carrying cotton bales, drawn by oxen, and everything that could be found in the way of transportation on a plantation, either for use or pleasure. The making out of provision returns was stopped for the time. No formalities were to retard our progress until a position was secured, when time could be spared to observe them.

During the night of the 2d of May the bridge over the North Fork was repaired, and the troops commenced crossing at 5 the next morning. Before the leading brigade was over, it was fired upon by the enemy from a commanding position; but they were soon driven off. It was evident that the enemy was covering a retreat from Grand Gulf to Vicksburg. Every commanding position from this crossing to Hankinson's Ferry, over the Big Black, was occupied by the retreating foe to delay our progress. McPherson, however, reached Hankinson's Ferry before night, seized the ferry-boat, and sent a detachment of his command across and several miles north on the road to Vicksburg. When the junction of the road going to Vicksburg with the road from Grand Gulf to Raymond and Jackson was reached, Logan, with his division, was turned to the left toward Grand Gulf. I went with him a short distance from this junction. McPherson had encountered the largest force yet met since the battle of Port Gibson, and had a skirmish nearly approaching a battle; but the road Logan had taken enabled him to come up on the enemy's right flank, and they soon gave way. McPherson was ordered to hold Hankinson's Ferry, and the road back to Willow Springs, with one division; General McClernand who was now in the rear was to join in this, as well as to guard the line back down the bayou. I did not want to take the chances of having an enemy lurking in our rear.

On the way from the junction to Grand Gulf, where the road comes into the one from Vicksburg to the same place, six or seven miles out, I learned that the last of the enemy had retreated past that place on their way to Vicksburg. I left Logan to make the proper disposition of his troops for the night, while I rode into the town with an escort of about twenty cavalry. Admiral Porter had already arrived with his fleet. The enemy had abandoned his heavy guns and evacuated the place.

When I reached Grand Gulf, May 3d, I had not been with my baggage since the 27th of April, and, consequently, had had no change of underclothing, no meal except such as I could pick up sometimes at other headquarters, and no tent to cover me. The first thing I did was to get a bath, borrow some fresh underclothing from one of the naval officers, and get a good meal on the flag-ship. Then I wrote letters to the general-in-chief informing him of our present position, dispatches to be telegraphed from Cairo, orders to General Sullivan, commanding above Vicksburg, and gave orders to all my corps commanders. About 12 o'clock at night I was through my work, and started for Hankinson's Ferry, arriving there before daylight. While at Grand Gulf I heard from Banks, who was on the Red River, and he said that he could not be at Port Hudson before the 10th of May, and then with only fifteen thousand men. Up to this time my intention had been to secure Grand Gulf as a base of supplies, detach McClernand's corps to Banks, and coöperate with him in the reduction of Port Hudson.

The news from Banks forced upon me a different plan of campaign from the one intended. To wait for his coöperation would have detained me at least a month. The reënforcements would not have reached 10,000 men, after deducting casualties and necessary river-guards, at all high points close to the river, for over 300 miles. The enemy would have strengthened his position and been reënforced by more men than Banks could have brought. I therefore determined to move independently of Banks, cut loose from my base, destroy the rebel force in rear of Vicksburg, and invest or capture the city.

Grand Gulf was accordingly given up as a base, and the authorities at Washington were notified. I knew well that Halleck's caution would lead him to disapprove this course; but it was the only one that gave any chance of success. The time it would take to communicate with Washington and get a reply would be so great that I could not be interfered with until it was demonstrated whether my plan was practicable. Even Sherman, who afterward ignored bases of supplies other than what were afforded by the country while marching through four States of the Confederacy, with an army more than twice as large as mine at this time, wrote me from Hankinson's Ferry, advising me of the impossibility of supplying our army over a single road. He urged me to "stop all troops till your army is partially supplied with wagons, and then act as quick as possible; for this road will be jammed, as sure as life." To this I replied, "I do not calculate upon the possibility of supplying the army with full rations from Grand Gulf. I know it will be impossible without constructing additional roads. What I do expect is to get up what rations of hard bread, coffee, and salt we can, and make the country furnish the balance." We started from Bruinsburg with an average of about two days' rations, and received no more from our own supplies for some days; abundance was found in the meantime. A delay would give the enemy time to reënforce and fortify.

McClernand's and McPherson's commands were kept substantially as they were on the night of the 2d, awaiting supplies to give them three days' rations in haversacks. Beef, mutton, poultry, and forage were found in abundance. Quite a quantity of bacon and molasses was also secured from the country, but bread and coffee could not be secured in quantity sufficient for all the men. Every plantation, however, had a run of stone, propelled by mule-power, to grind corn for the owners and their slaves. All these were kept running while we were stopping day and night, and when we were marching, during the night, at all plantations covered by the troops. But the product was taken by the troops nearest by; so that the majority of the command was destined to go without bread until a new base was established on the Yazoo, above Vicksburg.

While the troops were awaiting the arrival of rations, I ordered reconnoissances made by McClernand and McPherson, with a view of leading the enemy to believe that we intended to cross the Big Black and attack the city at once.

On the 6th Sherman arrived at Grand Gulf, and crossed his command that night and the next day. . . .

Up to this point our movements had been made without serious opposition. My line was now nearly parallel with the Jackson and Vicksburg Railroad, and about seven miles south of it. The right was at Raymond, eighteen miles from Jackson, McPherson commanding; Sherman in the center on Fourteen Mile Creek, his advance thrown across; McClernand to the left, also on Fourteen Mile Creek, advance across, and his pickets within two miles of Edwards's Station, where the enemy had concentrated a considerable force, and where they undoubtedly expected us to attack. McClernand's left was on the Big Black. In all our moves, up to this time, the left had hugged the Big Black closely, and all the ferries had been guarded to prevent the enemy throwing a force on our rear.

McPherson encountered the enemy, 5000 strong, with 2 batteries, under General Gregg, about 2 miles out of Raymond. This was about 2 P. M. Logan was in advance with one of his brigades. He deployed and moved up to engage the enemy. McPherson ordered the road in rear to be cleared of wagons, and the balance of Logan's division, and Crocker's, which was still farther in rear, to come forward with all dispatch. The order was obeyed with alacrity. Logan got his division in position for assault before Crocker could get up, and attacked with vigor, carrying the enemy's position easily, sending Gregg flying from the field, not to appear against our front again until we met at Jackson.

In this battle McPherson lost 66 killed, 339 wounded, and 37 missing—nearly or quite all from Logan's division. The enemy's loss was 100 killed, 305 wounded, besides 415 taken prisoners. . . .

When the news reached me of McPherson's victory at Raymond about sundown, my position was with Sherman. I decided at once to turn the whole column toward Jackson and capture that place without delay.

Accordingly, all previous orders given during the day for movements on the 13th were annulled by new ones. McPherson was ordered at daylight to move on Clinton, ten miles from Jackson. Sherman was notified of my determination to capture Jackson and work from there westward. He was ordered to start at four in the morning and march to Raymond. McClernand was ordered to march with three divisions by Dillon's to Raymond. One was left to guard the crossing of the Big Black. On the 10th I received a letter from Banks, on the Red River, asking reënforcements. Porter had gone to his assistance, with a part of his fleet, on the 3d, and I now wrote to him describing my position and declining to send any troops. I looked upon side

417

movements, as long as the enemy held Port Hudson and Vicksburg, as a waste of time and material. General Joseph E. Johnston arrived at Jackson in the night of the 13th, from Tennessee, and immediately assumed command of all the Confederate troops in Mississippi. I knew he was expecting reënforcements from the south and east. On the 6th I had written to General Halleck, "Information from the other side leaves me to believe the enemy are bringing forces from Tullahoma."

Up to this time my troops had been kept in supporting distances of each other as far as the nature of the country would admit. Reconnoissances were constantly made from each corps to enable them to acquaint themselves with the most practicable routes from one to another in case a union became necessary.

McPherson reached Clinton with the advance early on the 13th, and immediately set to work destroying the railroad. Sherman's advance reached Raymond before the last of McPherson's command had got out of the town. McClernand withdrew from the front of the enemy, at Edwards's Station, with much skill and without loss, and reached his position for the night in good order. On the night of the 13th McPherson was ordered to march at early dawn upon Jackson, only fifteen miles away. Sherman was given the same order; but he was to move by the direct road from Raymond to Jackson, which is south of the road McPherson was on, and does not approach within two miles of it at the point where it crossed the line of intrenchments which at that time defended the city. McClernand was ordered to move one division of his command to Clinton, one division a few miles beyond Mississippi Springs—following Sherman's line—and a third to Raymond. He was also directed to send his siege-guns, four in number, with the troops going by Mississippi Springs. McClernand's position was an advantageous one, in any event. With one division at Clinton, he was in position to reënforce McPherson at Jackson rapidly if it became necessary. The division beyond Mississippi Springs was equally available to reënforce Sherman. The one at Raymond could take either road. He still had two other divisions farther back now that Blair had come up, available within a day at Jackson. If this last command should not be wanted at Jackson, they were already one day's march from there on their way to Vicksburg, and on three different roads leading to the latter city. But the most important consideration in my mind was to have a force confronting Pemberton if he should come out to attack my rear. . . .

I notified General Halleck that I should attack the State capital on the 14th. A courier carried the dispatch to Grand Gulf, through an unprotected country.

Sherman and McPherson communicated with each other during the night, and arranged to reach Jackson at the same hour. It rained in torrents during the night of the 13th and the fore part of the day of the 14th. The roads were intolerable, and in some places on Sherman's line, where the land was low, they were covered more than a foot deep with water. But the troops never murmured. By 9 o'clock Crocker, of McPherson's corps, who was now in advance, came upon the enemy's pickets and speedily drove them in upon the main body. They were outside of the intrenchments, in a strong position, and proved to be the troops that had been driven out of Raymond. Johnston had been reënforced during the night by Georgia and South Carolina regiments, so that his force amounted to eleven thousand men, and he was expecting still more.

Sherman also came upon the rebel pickets some distance out from the town, but speedily drove them in. He was now on the south and south-west of Jackson, confronting the Confederates behind their breastworks; while McPherson's right was nearly two miles north, occupying a line running north and south across the Vicksburg Railroad. Artillery was brought up and reconnoissances made preparatory to an assault. McPherson brought up Logan's division, while he deployed Crocker's for the assault. Sherman made similar dispositions on the right. By 11 A. M. both were ready to attack. Crocker moved his division forward, preceded by a strong skirmish line. These troops at once encountered the enemy's advance and drove it back on the main body, when they returned to their proper regiment, and the whole division charged, routing the enemy completely and driving him into this main line. This stand by the enemy was made more than two miles outside of his main fortifications. McPherson followed up with his command until within range of the guns of the enemy from their intrenchments, when he halted to bring his command into line, and reconnoiter to determine the next move. It was now about noon.

While this was going on, Sherman was confronting a rebel battery which enfiladed the road on which he was marching—the Mississippi Springs road —and commanded a bridge spanning the stream over which he had to pass. By detaching right and left the stream was forced, and the enemy flanked and speedily driven within the main line. This brought our whole line in front of the enemy's line of works, which was continuous on the north, west, and south sides, from the Pearl River north of the city to the same river south. I was with Sherman. He was confronted by a sufficient force to hold us back. Appearances did not justify an assault where we were. I had directed Sherman to send a force to the right, and to reconnoiter as far as to the Pearl River. This force—Tuttle's division—not returning, I rode to the right with my staff, and soon found that the enemy had left that part of the line. Tuttle's movement or McPherson's pressure had, no doubt, led Johnston to order a retreat, leaving only the men at the guns to retard us while he was getting away. Tuttle had seen this, and, passing through the lines without resistance, came up in rear of the artillerists confronting Sherman, and captured them, with ten pieces of artillery. I rode immediately to the State

House, where I was soon followed by Sherman. About the same time Mc-Pherson discovered that the enemy was leaving his front, and advanced Crocker, who was so close upon the enemy that they could not move their guns or destroy them. He captured seven guns, and, moving on, hoisted the National flag over the Confederate capital of Mississippi. Stevenson's brigade was sent to cut off the Confederate retreat, but was too late or not expeditious enough.

Our loss in this engagement was: McPherson, 36 killed, 229 wounded, 3 missing; Sherman, 6 killed, 22 wounded, and 4 missing. The enemy lost 845 killed, wounded, and captured. Seventeen guns fell into our hands, and the enemy destroyed by fire their storehouses, containing a large amount of commissary stores. On this day Blair reached New Auburn and joined McClernand's Fourth Division. He had with him two hundred wagons loaded with rations, the only commissary supplies received during the entire campaign. I slept that night in the room that Johnston had occupied the night before.

About 4 in the afternoon I sent for the corps commanders, and directed the disposition to be made of their troops. Sherman was to remain in Jackson until he destroyed that place as a railroad center and manufacturing city of military supplies. He did the work most effectually. . . .

On the night of the 13th Johnston sent the following dispatch to Pemberton at Edwards's Station:

I have lately arrived, and learn that Major-General Sherman is between us with four divisions at Clinton. It is important to establish communication, that you may be reënforced. If practicable, come up in his rear at once. To beat such a detachment would be of immense value. All the troops you can quickly assemble should be brought. Time is all-important.

This dispatch was sent in triplicate by different messengers. One of the messengers happened to be a loyal man, who had been expelled from Memphis some months before, by Hurlbut, for uttering disloyal and threatening sentiments. There was a good deal of parade about this expulsion, ostensibly as a warning to those who entertained the sentiments he expressed; but Hurlbut and the expelled man understood each other. He delivered his copy of Johnston's dispatch to McPherson, who forwarded it to me.

Receiving this dispatch on the 14th, I ordered McPherson to move promptly in the morning back to Bolton, the nearest point where Johnston could reach the road. Bolton is about twenty miles west of Jackson. I also informed McClernand of the capture of Jackson, and sent him the following orders:

It is evidently the design of the enemy to get north of us and cross the Big Black, and beat us into Vicksburg. We must not allow them to do this. Turn all your forces toward Bolton Station, and make all dispatch in getting there. Move troops by the most direct road from wherever they may be on the receipt of this order.

"Well, Yank, when are you coming into town?"

And to Blair I wrote:

Their design is evidently to cross the Big Black and pass down the peninsula between the Big Black and Yazoo rivers. We must beat them. Turn your troops immediately to Bolton; take all the trains with you. Smith's division, and any other troops now with you, will go to the same place. If practicable, take parallel roads, so as to divide your troops and trains.

Johnston stopped on the Canton road, only six miles north of Jackson, the night of the 14th. He sent from there to Pemberton dispatches announcing the loss of Jackson, and the following dispatch:

Can he [Grant] supply himself from the Mississippi? Can you not cut him off from it, and above all, should he be compelled to fall back for want of supplies, beat him? As soon as the reënforcements are all up, they must be united to the rest of the army. I am anxious to see a force assembled that may be able to inflict a heavy blow upon the enemy.

The concentration of my troops was easy, considering the character of the country. McPherson moved along the road parallel with and near the railroad. Of McClernand's command one division (Hovey's) was on the road McPherson had to take, but with a start of four miles; one (Osterhaus's) was at Raymond, on a converging road that intersected the other near Champion's Hill; one (Carr's) had to pass over the same road with Osterhaus's, but, being back at Mississippi Springs, would not be detained thereby; the fourth (Smith's, with Blair's division) was near Auburn, with a different road to pass over. McClernand faced about and moved promptly. His cavalry from Raymond seized Bolton by half-past 9 in the morning, driving out the enemy's pickets and capturing several men.

The night of the 15th Hovey was at Bolton; Carr and Osterhaus were about three miles south, but abreast, facing west; Smith was north of Raymond, with Blair in his rear.

McPherson's command, with Logan in front, had marched at 7 o'clock, and by 4 reached Hovey and went into camp. Crocker bivouacked just in Hovey's rear on the Clinton road. Sherman, with two divisions, was in Jackson, completing the destruction of roads, bridges, and military factories. I rode in person out to Clinton. On my arrival I ordered McClernand to move early in the morning on Edwards's Station, cautioning him to watch for the enemy, and not to bring on an engagement unless he felt very certain of success.

I naturally expected that Pemberton would endeavor to obey the orders of his superior, which I have shown were to attack us at Clinton. This, indeed, I knew he could not do, but I felt sure he would make the attempt to reach that point. It turned out, however, that he had decided his superior's plans

421

were impracticable, and consequently determined to move south from Edwards's Station, and get between me and my base. I, however, had no base, having abandoned it more than a week before. On the 15th Pemberton had actually marched south from Edwards's Station; but the rains had swollen Baker's Creek, which he had to cross, so much that he could not ford it, and the bridges were washed away. This brought him back to the Jackson road, on which there was a good bridge over Baker's Creek. Some of his troops were marching until midnight to get there. Receiving here early on the 16th a repetition of his order to join Johnston at Clinton, he concluded to obey, and sent a dispatch to his chief, informing him of the route by which he might be expected.

About 5 o'clock in the morning (16th) two men who had been employed on the Jackson and Vicksburg Railroad were brought to me. They reported that they had passed through Pemberton's army in the night, and that it was still marching east. They reported him to have 80 regiments of infantry and 10 batteries; in all about 25,000 men.

I had expected to leave Sherman at Jackson another day in order to complete his work. But, getting the above information, I sent him orders to move with all dispatch to Bolton, and to put one division, with an ammunition train, on the road at once, with directions to its commander to march with all possible speed until he came up to our rear. Within an hour after receiving this order, Steele's division was on the road. At the same time I dispatched to Blair, who was near Auburn, to move with all speed to Edwards's Station. McClernand was directed to embrace Blair in his command for the present. Blair's division was a part of the Fifteenth Army Corps (Sherman's); but as it was on its way to join its corps, it naturally struck our left first, now that we had faced about and were moving west. The Fifteenth Corps, when it got up, would be on our extreme right. McPherson was directed to get his trains out of the way of the troops, and to follow Hovey's division as closely as possible. McClernand had two roads, about three miles apart, converging at Edwards's Station, over which to march his troops. Hovey's division of his corps had the advance on a third road (the Clinton) still farther north. McClernand was directed to move Blair's and A. J. Smith's divisions by the southernmost of these roads, and Osterhaus and Carr by the middle road. Orders were to move cautiously, with skirmishers in the front to feel for the enemy. Smith's division, on the most southern road, was the first to encounter the enemy's pickets, who were speedily driven in. Osterhaus, on the middle road, hearing the firing, pushed his skirmishers forward, found the enemy's pickets, and forced them back to the main line. About the same time Hovey encountered the enemy on the northern or direct wagon road from Jackson to Vicksburg. McPherson was hastening up to join Hovey, but was embarrassed by Hovey's trains occupying the roads. I was still back at Clinton. McPherson sent me word of the situation and expressed the wish that I was up. By 7:30 I was on the road and proceeded rapidly to the front, ordering all trains that were in front of troops off the road. When I arrived Hovey's skirmishing amounted almost to a battle.

McClernand was in person on the middle road, and had a shorter distance to march to reach the enemy's position than McPherson. I sent him word by a staff-officer to push forward and attack. These orders were repeated several times without apparently expediting McClernand's advance.

Champion's Hill, where Pemberton had chosen his position to receive us, whether taken by accident or design, was well selected. It is one of the highest points in that section, and commanded all the ground in range. On the east side of the ridge, which is quite precipitous, is a ravine, running first north, then westerly, terminating at Baker's Creek. It was grown up thickly with large trees and undergrowth, making it difficult to penetrate with troops, even when not defended. The ridge occupied by the enemy terminated abruptly where the ravine turns westerly. The left of the enemy occupied the north end of this ridge. The Bolton and Edwards's Station road turns almost due south at this point, and ascends the ridge, which it follows for about a mile, then, turning west, descends by a gentle declivity to Baker's Creek, nearly a mile away. On the west side the slope of the ridge is gradual, and is cultivated from near the summit to the creek. There was, when we were there, a narrow belt of timber near the summit, west of the road.

From Raymond there is a direct road to Edwards's Station, some three miles west of Champion's Hill. There is one also to Bolton. From this latter road there is still another, leaving it about three and a half miles before reaching Bolton, and leading direct to the same station. It was along these two roads that three divisions of McClernand's corps, and Blair, of Sherman's, temporarily under McClernand, were moving. Hovey, of McClernand's command, was with McPherson, farther north on the road from Bolton, direct to Edwards's Station. The middle road comes into the northern road at the point where the latter turns to the west, and descends to Baker's Creek; the southern road is still several miles south and does not intersect the others until it reaches Edwards's Station. Pemberton's lines covered all these roads and faced east. Hovey's line, when it first drove in the enemy's pickets, was formed parallel to that of the enemy, and confronted his left.

By eleven o'clock the skirmishing had grown into a hard-contested battle. Hovey alone, before other troops could be got to assist him, had captured a battery of the enemy. But he was not able to hold his position, and had to abandon the artillery. McPherson brought up his troops as fast as possible— Logan in front—and posted them on the right of Hovey and across the flank of the enemy. Logan reënforced Hovey with one brigade from his division; with his other two he moved farther west to make room for Crocker, who was coming up as rapidly as the roads would admit. Hovey was still being heavily pressed, and was calling on me for more reënforcements. I ordered Crocker, who was now coming up, to send one brigade from his division. McPherson ordered two batteries to be stationed where they nearly enfiladed the enemy's line, and they did good execution.

From Logan's position now a direct forward movement would carry him over open fields in rear of the enemy and in a line parallel with them. He did make exactly this move, attacking, however, the enemy through the belt of woods covering the west slope of the hill for a short distance. Up to this time I had kept my position near Hovey, where we were the most heavily pressed; but about noon I moved with a part of my staff by our right, around, until I came up with Logan himself. I found him near the road leading down to Baker's Creek. He was actually in command of the only road over which the enemy could retreat; Hovey, reënforced by two brigades from McPherson's command, confronted the enemy's left; Crocker, with two brigades, covered their left flank; McClernand, two hours before, had been within two and a half miles of their center with two divisions, and two divisions— Blair's and A. J. Smith's—were confronting the rebel right; Ransom, with a brigade of McArthur's division, of the Seventeenth Corps (McPherson's), had crossed the river at Grand Gulf a few days before and was coming up on their right flank. Neither Logan nor I knew that we had cut off the retreat of the enemy. Just at this juncture a messenger came from Hovey, asking for more reënforcements. There were none to spare. I then gave an order to move McPherson's command by the left flank around to Hovey. This uncovered the Confederate line of retreat, which was soon taken advantage of by the enemy.

During all this time Hovey, reënforced as he was by a brigade from Logan and another from Crocker, and by Crocker gallantly coming up with two other brigades on his right, had made several assaults, the last one about the time the road was opened to the rear. The enemy fled precipitately. This was between 3 and 4 o'clock. I rode forward, or rather back, to where the middle road intersects the north road, and found the skirmishers of Carr's division just coming in. Osterhaus was farther south, and soon after came up with skirmishers advanced in like manner. Hovey's division, and Mc-Pherson's two divisions with him, had marched and fought from early dawn, and were not in the best condition to follow the retreating foe. I sent orders to Osterhaus to pursue the enemy, and to Carr, whom I saw personally, I explained the situation, and directed him to pursue vigorously as far as the Big Black, and to cross it if he could, Osterhaus to follow him. The pursuit was continued until after dark.

The battle of Champion's Hill lasted about four hours of hard fighting, preceded by two or three hours of skirmishes, some of which rose almost to the dignity of battle. Every man of Hovey's division and of McPherson's two divisions was engaged during the battle. No other part of my command was engaged at all, except that (as described before). Osterhaus's and A. J. Smith's had encountered the rebel advanced pickets as early as 7:30. Their positions were admirable for advancing upon the enemy's line. McClernand, with two divisions, was within a few miles of the battle-field long before noon, and in easy hearing. I sent him repeated orders by staff-officers fully competent to explain to him the situation. These traversed the road separating us, without escort, and directed him to push forward, but he did not come. Instead of this he sent orders to Hovey, who belonged to his corps, to join on to his right flank. Hovey was bearing the brunt of the battle at the time. To obey the order he would have had to pull out from the front of the enemy and march back as far as McClernand had to advance to get into battle, and substantially over the same ground. Of course, I did not permit Hovey to obey the order of his intermediate superior.

We had in this battle about fifteen thousand men actually engaged. This excludes those that did not get up—all of McClernand's command except Hovey. Our loss was 410 killed, 1844 wounded, and 187 missing. Hovey alone lost twelve hundred killed, wounded, and missing—one-third of his division.

Had McClernand come up with reasonable promptness, or had I known the ground as I did afterward, I cannot see how Pemberton could have escaped with any organized force. As it was he lost over 3000 killed and wounded, and about 3000 captured in battle and in pursuit. Loring's division, which was the right of Pemberton's line, was cut off from the retreating army, and never got back into Vicksburg. Pemberton himself fell back that night to the Big Black River. His troops did not stop before midnight, and many of them left before the general retreat commenced, and no doubt a good part of them returned to their homes. Logan alone captured 1300 prisoners and 11 guns. Hovey captured 300, under fire, and about 700 in all, exclusive of 500 sick and wounded, whom he paroled, thus making 1200.

McPherson joined in the advance as soon as his men could fill their cartridge-boxes, leaving one brigade to guard our wounded. The pursuit was continued as long as it was light enough to see the road. The night of the 16th of May found McPherson's command bivouacked from two to six miles west of the battle-field, along the line of the road to Vicksburg. Carr and Osterhaus were at Edwards's Station, and Blair was about three miles south-east. Hovey remained on the field where his troops had fought so bravely and bled so freely. Much war material abandoned by the enemy was picked up on the battle-field, among it thirty pieces of artillery. I pushed through the advancing column with my staff, and kept in advance until after night. Finding ourselves alone we stopped and took possession of a vacant house. As no troops came up we moved back a mile or more, until we met the head of the column just going into bivouac on the road. We had no tents, so we occupied the porch of a house which had been taken for a rebel hospital, and which was filled with wounded and dying who had been brought from the battle-field we had just left.

While a battle is raging one can see his enemy mowed down by the thousand and the ten thousand, with great composure. But after the battle these scenes are distressing, and one is naturally disposed to do as much to alleviate the suffering of an enemy as of a friend.

We were now assured of our position between Johnston and Pemberton, without the possibility of a junction of their forces. Pemberton might indeed have made a night march to the Big Black, crossed the bridge there, and, by moving north on the west side, have eluded us, and finally returned to Johnston. But this would have given us Vicksburg. It would have been his proper move, however, and the one Johnston would have made had he been in Pemberton's place. In fact, it would have been in conformity with Johnston's orders to Pemberton.

Sherman left Jackson with the last of his troops about noon on the 16th, and reached Bolton, twenty miles west, before halting. His rear-guard did not get in until 2 A. M. the 17th, but renewed their march by daylight. He paroled his prisoners at Jackson, and was forced to leave his own wounded—in care of surgeons and attendants however. At Bolton he was informed of our victory. He was directed to commence the march early next day, and to diverge from the road he was on, to Bridgeport, on the Big Black River, some eleven miles above where we expected to find the enemy. Blair was ordered to join him there with the pontoon train as early as possible.

This movement brought Sherman's corps together, and at a point where I hoped a crossing of the Big Black might be effected, and Sherman's corps used to flank the enemy out of his position in our front, and thus open a crossing for the remainder of the army. I informed him that I would endeavor to hold the enemy in my front while he crossed the river.

The advanced division, Carr's (McClernand's corps), resumed the pursuit at 3:30 A.M. on the 17th, followed closely by Osterhaus; McPherson bringing up the rear with his corps. As I expected, the enemy was found in position on the Big Black. The point was only six miles from that where my advance had rested for the night, and was reached at an early hour. Here the river makes a turn to the west, and has washed close up to the high land. The east side is a low bottom, sometimes overflowed at very high water, but was cleared and in cultivation. A bayou runs irregularly across this low land, the bottom of which, however, is above the surface of the Big Black at ordinary stages. When the river is full, water runs through it, converting the point of land into an island. The bayou was grown up with timber, which the enemy had felled into the ditch. All this time there was a foot or two of water in it. The rebels had constructed a parapet along the inner bank of this bayou, by using cotton bales from the plantation close by and throwing dirt over them. The whole was thoroughly commanded from the height west of the river. At the upper end of the bayou there was a strip of uncleared land, which afforded a cover for a portion of our men. Carr's divi-

426

sion was deployed on our right, Lawler's brigade forming his extreme right, and reaching through these woods to the river above. Osterhaus's division was deployed to the left of Carr, and covered the enemy's entire front. Mc-Pherson was in column on the road, the head close by, ready to come in whenever he could be of assistance.

While the troops were standing as here described, an officer from Banks's staff came up and presented me with a letter from General Halleck, dated the 11th of May. It had been sent by the way of New Orleans to Banks to forward to me. It ordered me to return to Grand Gulf, and to coöperate from there with Banks, against Port Hudson, and then to return with our combined forces to besiege Vicksburg. I told the officer that the order came too late, and that Halleck would not give it then if he knew our position. The bearer of the dispatch insisted that I ought to obey the order, and was giving arguments to support his position, when I heard great cheering to the right of our line, and, looking in that direction, saw Lawler, in his shirt-sleeves, leading a charge upon the enemy. I immediately mounted my horse and rode in the direction of the charge, and saw no more of the officer who delivered the dispatch, I think not even to this day.

The assault was successful. But little resistance was made. The enemy fled from the west bank of the river, burning the bridge behind them, leaving the men and guns on the east side to fall into our hands. Many tried to escape by swimming the river. Some succeeded and some were drowned in the attempt. Eighteen guns were captured, and 1751 prisoners. Our loss was 39 killed, 237 wounded, and 3 missing. The enemy probably lost but few men except those captured and drowned. But for the successful and complete destruction of the bridge, I have but little doubt that we should have followed the enemy so closely as to prevent his occupying his defenses around Vicksburg.

As the bridge was destroyed and the river was high, new bridges had to be built. It was but little after 9 o'clock A. M. when the capture took place. As soon as work could be commenced, orders were given for the construction of three bridges. One was taken charge of by Lieutenant Peter C. Hains, of the Engineer Corps, one by General McPherson himself, and one by General Ransom, a most gallant and intelligent volunteer officer. My recollection is that Hains built a raft-bridge; McPherson a pontoon, using cotton bales in large numbers for pontoons; and that Ransom felled trees on opposite banks of the river, cutting only on one side of the tree, so that they would fall with their tops interlacing in the river, without the trees being entirely severed from their stumps. A bridge was then made with these trees to support the roadway. Lumber was taken from buildings, cotton-gins, and wherever found, for this purpose. By 8 o'clock on the morning of the 18th all three bridges were complete and the troops were crossing.

Sherman reached Bridgeport about noon of the 17th, and found Blair with the pontoon train already there. A few of the enemy were intrenched on the

427

west bank, but they made little resistance, and soon surrendered. Two divisions were crossed that night, and the third the following morning.

On the 18th I moved along the Vicksburg road in advance of the troops, and as soon as possible joined Sherman. My first anxiety was to secure a base of supplies on the Yazoo River above Vicksburg. Sherman's line of march led him to the very point on Walnut Hills occupied by the enemy the December before, when he was repulsed. Sherman was equally anxious with myself. Our impatience led us to move in advance of the column, and well up with the advanced skirmishers. There were some detached works along the crest of the hill. These were still occupied by the enemy, or else the garrison from Haynes's Bluff had not all got past on their way to Vicksburg. At all events, the bullets of the enemy whistled by thick and fast for a short time. In a few minutes Sherman had the pleasure of looking down from the spot coveted so much by him the December before—on the ground where his command lay so helpless for offensive action [Chickasaw Bayou]. He turned to me, saying that up to this minute he had felt no positive assurance of success. This, however, he said, was the end of one of the greatest campaigns in history, and I ought to make a report of it at once. Vicksburg was not yet captured, and there was no telling what might happen before it was taken; but whether captured or not, this was a complete and successful campaign. I do not claim to quote Sherman's language, but the substance only. My reason for mentioning this incident will appear farther on.

McPherson, after crossing the Big Black, came into the Jackson and Vicksburg road which Sherman was on, but to his rear. He arrived at night near the lines of the enemy, and went into camp. McClernand moved by the direct road near the railroad to Mount Albans, and then turned to the left, and put his troops on the road from Baldwin's Ferry to Vicksburg. This brought him south of McPherson. I now had my three corps up to the works built for the defense of Vicksburg on three roads—one to the north, one to the east, and one to the south-east of the city. By the morning of May 19th the investment was as complete as my limited number of troops would allow. Sherman was on the right and covered the high ground from where it overlooked the Yazoo as far south-east as his troops would extend. McPherson joined on to his left, and occupied ground on both sides of the Jackson road. McClernand took up the ground to his left, and extended as far toward Warrenton as he could, keeping a continuous line.

On the 19th there was constant skirmishing with the enemy while we were getting into better position. The enemy had been much demoralized by his defeats at Champion's Hill and the Big Black, and I believed would not make much effort to hold Vicksburg. Accordingly at 2 o'clock I ordered an assault. It resulted in securing more advanced positions for all our troops, where they were fully covered from the fire of the enemy.

The 20th and 21st were spent in strengthening our position, and in making roads in rear of the army, from Yazoo River, or Chickasaw Bayou. Most of the army had now been for three weeks with only five days' rations issued by the commissary. They had an abundance of food, however, but began to feel the want of bread. I remember, that in passing around to the left of the line on the 21st, a soldier, recognizing me, said in rather a low voice, but yet so that I heard him, *"Hard-tack."* In a moment the cry was taken up all along the line, *"Hard-tack! Hard-tack!"* I told the men nearest to me that we had been engaged ever since the arrival of the troops in building a road over which to supply them with everything they needed. The cry was instantly changed to cheers. By the night of the 21st all the troops had full rations issued to them. The bread and coffee were highly appreciated.

I now determined on a second assault. Johnston was in my rear, only fifty miles away, with an army not much inferior in numbers to the one I had with me, and I knew he was being reënforced. There was danger of his coming to the assistance of Pemberton, and, after all, he might defeat my anticipations of capturing the garrison, if, indeed, he might not prevent the capture of the city. The immediate capture of Vicksburg would save sending me the reënforcements, which were so much wanted elsewhere, and would set free the army under me to drive Johnston from the State. But the first consideration of all was: the troops believed they could carry the works in their front, and would not have worked so patiently in the trenches if they had not been allowed to try.

The attack was ordered to commence on all parts of the line at 10 o'clock A. M. on the 22d with a furious cannonading from every battery in position. All the corps commanders set their time by mine, so that all might open the engagement at the same minute. The attack was gallant, and portions of each of the three corps succeeded in getting up to the very parapets of the enemy, and in planting their battle-flags upon them; but at no place were we able to enter. General McClernand reported that he had gained the enemy's intrenchments at several points, and wanted reënforcements. I occupied a position from which I believed I could see as well as he what took place in his front, and I did not see the success he reported. But his request for reënforcements being repeated, I could not ignore it, and sent him Quinby's division of the Seventeenth Corps. Sherman and McPherson were both ordered to renew their assaults as a diversion in favor of Mc-Clernand. This last attack only served to increase our casualties, without giving any benefit whatever. As soon as it was dark, our troops that had reached the enemy's line and had been obliged to remain there for security all day, were withdrawn, and thus ended the last assault on Vicksburg.

I now determined upon a regular siege—to "out-camp the enemy," as it were, and to incur no more losses. The experience of the 22d convinced officers and men that this was best, and they went to work on the defenses and approaches with a will. With the navy holding the river the investment of Vicksburg was complete. As long as we could hold our position, the enemy was limited in supplies of food, men, and munitions of war, to what they had on hand. These could not last always.

The crossing of troops at Bruinsburg commenced April 30th. On the 18th of May the army was in rear of Vicksburg. On the 19th, just twenty days after the crossing, the city was completely invested and an assault had been made: five distinct battles—besides continuous skirmishing—had been fought and won by the Union forces; the capital of the State had fallen, and its arsenals, military manufactories, and everything useful for military purposes had been destroyed; an average of about 180 miles had been marched by the troops engaged; but 5 days' rations had been issued, and no forage; over 6000 prisoners had been captured, and as many more of the enemy had been killed or wounded; 27 heavy cannon and 61 field-pieces had fallen into our hands; 250 miles of the river, from Vicksburg to Port Hudson, had become ours. The Union force that had crossed the Mississippi River up to this time was less than 43,000 men. One division of these—Blair's—only arrived in time to take part in the battle of Champion's Hill, but was not engaged there; and one brigade—Ransom's—of McPherson's corps reached the field after the battle. The enemy had at Vicksburg, Grand Gulf, Jackson, and on the roads between these places, over sixty thousand men. They were in their own country, where no rear-guards were necessary. The country is admirable for defense, but difficult to conduct an offensive campaign in. All their troops had to be met. We were fortunate, to say the least, in meeting them in detail: at Port Gibson, 7000 or 8000; at Raymond, 5000; at Jackson, from 8000 to 11,000; at Champion's Hill, 25,000; at the Big Black, 4000. A part of those met at Jackson were all that were left of those encountered at Raymond. They were beaten in detail by a force smaller than their own, upon their own ground. . . .

After the unsuccessful assault on the 22d, the work of the regular siege began. Sherman occupied the right, starting from the river above Vicksburg; McPherson the center (McArthur's division now with him); and McClernand the left, holding the road south to Warrenton. Lauman's division arrived at this time and was placed on the extreme left of the line.

In the interval between the assaults of the 19th and 22d, roads had been completed from the Yazoo River and Chickasaw Bayou, around the rear of the army, to enable us to bring up supplies of food and ammunition; ground had been selected and cleared, on which the troops were to be encamped, and tents and cooking utensils were brought up. The troops had been without these from the time of crossing the Mississippi up to this time. All was now ready for the pick and spade. With the two brigades brought up by McArthur, which reached us in rear of Vicksburg, and Lauman's division brought from Memphis, and which had just arrived, we had now about forty thousand men for the siege. Prentiss and Hurlbut were ordered to send forward every man that could be spared. Cavalry especially was wanted to watch the fords along the Big Black, and to observe Johnston. I knew that Johnston was receiving reënforcements from Bragg, who was confronting Rosecrans in Tennessee. Vicksburg was so important to the enemy that I believed he would make the most strenuous efforts to raise the siege, even at the risk of losing ground elsewhere.

My line was more than fifteen miles long, extending from Haynes's Bluff to Vicksburg, thence south to Warrenton. The line of the enemy was about seven. In addition to this, having an enemy at Canton and Jackson, in our rear, who was being constantly reënforced, we required a second line of defense facing the other way. I had not troops enough under my command to man these. But General Halleck appreciated the situation, and, without being asked, forwarded reënforcements with all possible dispatch.

The ground about Vicksburg is admirable for defense. On the north it is about two hundred feet above the Mississippi River at the highest point, and very much cut up by the washing rains; the ravines were grown up with cane and underbrush, while the sides and tops were covered with a dense forest. Farther south the ground flattens out somewhat, and was in cultivation. But here, too, it was cut by ravines and small streams. The enemy's line of defense followed the crest of a ridge, from the river north of the city, eastward, then southerly around to the Jackson road, full three miles back of the city; thence in a south-westerly direction to the river. Deep ravines of the description given lay in front of these defenses.

As there is a succession of gullies, cut out by rains, along the side of the ridge, the line was necessarily very irregular. To follow each of these spurs with intrenchments, so as to command the slopes on either side, would have lengthened their line very much. Generally, therefore, or in many places, their line would run from near the head of one gully nearly straight to the head of another, and an outer work, triangular in shape, generally open in the rear, was thrown up on the point; with a few men in this outer work they commanded the approaches to the main line completely.

The work to be done to make our position as strong against the enemy as his was against us, was very great. The problem was also complicated by our wanting our lines as near that of the enemy as possible. We had but four engineer officers with us. . . .

We had no siege-guns except six 32-pounders, and there were none in the West to draw from. Admiral Porter, however, supplied us with a battery of navy-guns, of large caliber, and with these, and the field-artillery used in the campaign, the siege began. The first thing to do was to get the artillery in batteries, where they would occupy commanding positions; then establish the camps, under cover from the fire of the enemy, but as near up as possible; and then construct rifle-pits and covered ways, to connect the entire command by the shortest route. The enemy did not harass us much

431

while we were constructing our batteries. Probably their artillery ammunition was short; and their infantry was kept down by our sharp-shooters, who were always on the alert and ready to fire at a head whenever it showed itself above the rebel works.

In no place were our lines more than six hundred yards from the enemy. It was necessary, therefore, to cover our men by something more than the ordinary parapet. To give additional protection sand-bags, bullet-proof, were placed along the tops of the parapets, far enough apart to make loop-holes for musketry. On top of these, logs were put. By these means the men were enabled to walk about erect when off duty, without fear of annoyance from sharp-shooters. The enemy used in their defense explosive musket-balls, thinking, no doubt, that, bursting over the men in the trenches, they would do some execution; but I do not remember a single case where a man was injured by a piece of one of the shells. When they were hit, and the ball exploded, the wound was terrible. In these cases a solid ball would have hit as well. Their use is barbarous, because they produce increased suffering without any corresponding advantage to those using them.

The enemy could not resort to the method we did to protect their men, because we had an inexhaustible supply of ammunition to draw upon, and used it freely. Splinters from the timber would have made havoc among the men behind.

There were no mortars with the besiegers, except what the navy had in front of the city; but wooden ones were made by taking logs of the toughest wood that could be found, boring them out for six or twelve pounder shells, and binding them with strong iron bands. These answered as coehorns, and shells were successfully thrown from them into the trenches of the enemy.

The labor of building the batteries and intrenching was largely done by the pioneers, assisted by Negroes who came within our lines and who were paid for their work, but details from the troops had often to be made. The work was pushed forward as rapidly as possible, and when an advanced position was secured and covered from the fire of the enemy, the batteries were advanced. By the 30th of June there were 220 guns in position, mostly light field-pieces, besides a battery of heavy guns belonging to, manned, and commanded by the navy. We were now as strong for defense against the garrison of Vicksburg as they were against us. But I knew that Johnston was in our rear, and was receiving constant reënforcements from the east. He had at this time a larger force than I had prior to the battle of Champion's Hill. . . .

On the 26th of May I sent Blair's division up the Yazoo to drive out a force of the enemy supposed to be between the Big Black and the Yazoo. The country was rich, and full of supplies of both fruit and forage. Blair was instructed to take all of it. The cattle were to be driven in for the use of our army, and the food and forage to be consumed by our troops or destroyed by fire; all bridges were to be destroyed, and the roads rendered as nearly impassable as possible. Blair went forty-five miles, and was gone almost a week. His work was effectually done. I requested Porter at this time to send the Marine brigade—a floating nondescript force which had been assigned to his command, and which proved very useful—up to Haynes's Bluff to hold it until reënforcements could be sent.

On the 26th I also received a letter from Banks, asking me to reënforce him with ten thousand men at Port Hudson. Of course I could not comply with his request, nor did I think he needed them. He was in no danger of an attack by the garrison in his front, and there was no army organizing in his rear to raise the siege. On the 3d of June a brigade from Hurlbut's command arrived, General Nathan Kimball commanding. It was sent to Mechanicsburg, some miles north-east of Haynes's Bluff, and about midway between the Big Black and the Yazoo. A brigade of Blair's division and twelve hundred cavalry had already, on Blair's return from up the Yazoo, been sent to the same place—with instructions to watch the crossings of the Big Black River, to destroy the roads in his (Blair's) front, and to gather or destroy all supplies.

On the 7th of June our little force of colored and white troops across the Mississippi, at Milliken's Bend, were attacked by about three thousand men from Richard Taylor's Trans-Mississippi command. With the aid of the gunboats these were speedily repelled. I sent Mower's brigade over with instructions to drive the enemy beyond the Tensas bayou; and we had no further trouble in that quarter during the siege. This was the first important engagement of the war in which colored troops were under fire. These were very raw, having all been enlisted since the beginning of the siege, but they behaved well.

On the 8th of June a full division arrived from Hurlbut's command, under General Sooy Smith. It was sent immediately to Haynes's Bluff, and General C. C. Washburn was assigned to the general command at that point.

On the 11th a strong division arrived from the Department of the Missouri under General Herron, which was placed on our left. This cut off the last possible chance of communication between Pemberton and Johnston, as it enabled Lauman to close up on McClernand's left, while Herron intrenched from Lauman to the water's edge. At this point the water recedes a few hundred yards from the high land. Through this opening, no doubt, the Confederate commanders had been able to get messengers under cover of night.

On the 14th General Parke arrived with two divisions of Burnside's corps, and was immediately dispatched to Haynes's Bluff. These latter troops—Herron's and Parke's—were the reënforcements already spoken of, sent by Halleck in anticipation of their being needed. They arrived none too soon.

433

I now had about seventy-one thousand men. More than half were disposed of across the peninsula, between the Yazoo, at Haynes's Bluff, and the Big Black, with the division of Osterhaus watching the crossings of the latter river farther south and west, from the crossing of the Jackson road to Baldwin's Ferry, and below.

There were eight roads leading into Vicksburg, along which and the immediate sides of which our work was specially pushed and batteries advanced; but no commanding point within range of the enemy was neglected.

On the 17th I received a letter from General Sherman and on the 18th one from McPherson, saying that their respective commands had complained to them of a fulsome congratulatory order published by General McClernand to the Thirteenth Corps, which did great injustice to the other troops engaged in the campaign.

This order had been sent north and published, and now papers containing it had reached our camps. The order had not been heard of by me, and certainly not by troops outside of McClernand's command, until brought in this way. I at once wrote McClernand, directing him to send me a copy of this order. He did so, and I at once relieved him from the command of the Thirteenth Army Corps, and ordered him back to Springfield, Illinois. The publication of his order in the press was in violation of War Department orders and also of mine.

On the 22d of June positive information was received that Johnston had crossed the Big Black River for the purpose of attacking our rear, to raise the siege and release Pemberton. The correspondence between Johnston and Pemberton shows that all expectation of holding Vicksburg had by this time passed from Johnston's mind. I immediately ordered Sherman to the command of all the forces from Haynes's Bluff to the Big Black River. This amounted now to quite half the troops about Vicksburg. Besides these, Herron's and A. J. Smith's divisions were ordered to hold themselves in readiness to reënforce Sherman. Haynes's Bluff had been strongly fortified on the land side, and on all commanding points from there to the Big Black, at the railroad crossing, batteries had been constructed. The work of connecting by rifle-pits, where this was not already done, was an easy task for the troops that were to defend them.

We were now looking west, besieging Pemberton, while we were also looking east to defend ourselves against an expected siege by Johnston. But as against the garrison of Vicksburg we were as substantially protected as they were against us. When we were looking east and north we were strongly fortified, and on the defensive. Johnston evidently took in the situation and wisely, I think, abstained from making an assault on us, because it would simply have inflicted loss on both sides without accomplishing any result.

We were strong enough to have taken the offensive against him; but I did not feel disposed to take any risk of loosing our hold upon Pemberton's army, while I would have rejoiced at the opportunity of defending ourselves against an attack by Johnston.

From the 23d of May the work of fortifying and pushing forward our position nearer to the enemy had been steadily progressing. At three points on the Jackson road in front of Ransom's brigade a sap was run up to the enemy's parapet, and by the 25th of June we had it undermined and the mine charged. The enemy had countermined, but did not succeed in reaching our mine. At this particular point the hill on which the rebel work stands rises abruptly. Our sap ran close up to the outside of the enemy's parapet. In fact, this parapet was also our protection. The soldiers of the two sides occasionally conversed pleasantly across this barrier; sometimes they exchanged the hard bread of the Union soldiers for the tobacco of the Confederates; at other times the enemy threw over hand-grenades, and often our men, catching them in their hands, returned them.

Our mine had been started some distance back down the hill, consequently when it had extended as far as the parapet it was many feet below it. This caused the failure of the enemy in his search to find and destroy it. On the 25th of June, at 3 o'clock, all being ready, the mine was exploded. A heavy artillery fire all along the line had been ordered to open with the explosion. The effect was to blow the top of the hill off and make a crater where it stood. The breach was not sufficient to enable us to pass a column of attack through. In fact, the enemy, having failed to reach our mine, had thrown up a line farther back, where most of the men guarding that point were placed. There were a few men, however, left at the advance line, and others working in the counter-mine, which was still being pushed to find ours. All that were there were thrown into the air, some of them coming down on our side, still alive. I remember one colored man, who had been under-ground at work, when the explosion took place, who was thrown to our side. He was not much hurt, but was terribly frightened. Some one asked him how high he had gone up. "Dunno, Massa, but t'ink 'bout t'ree mile," was the reply. General Logan commanded at this point, and took this colored man to his quarters, where he did service to the end of the siege. . . .

At this time an intercepted dispatch from Johnston to Pemberton informed me that Johnston intended to make a determined attack upon us, in order to relieve the garrison of Vicksburg. I knew the garrison would make no forcible effort to relieve itself. The picket lines were so close to each other—where there was space enough between the lines to post pickets— that the men could converse. On the 21st of June I was informed, through this means, that Pemberton was preparing to escape, by crossing to the Louisiana side under cover of night; that he had employed workmen in making boats for that purpose; that the men had been canvassed to ascertain if they would make an assault on the "Yankees" to cut their way out; that they had refused, and almost mutinied, because their commander would not surrender

435

and relieve their sufferings, and had only been pacified by the assurance that boats enough would be finished in a week to carry them all over. The rebel pickets also said that houses in the city had been pulled down to get material to build these boats with. Afterward this story was verified. On entering the city we found a large number of very rudely constructed boats.

All necessary steps were at once taken to render such an attempt abortive. Our pickets were doubled; Admiral Porter was notified so that the river might be more closely watched; material was collected on the west bank of the river to be set on fire and light up the river if the attempt was made; and batteries were established along the levee crossing the peninsula on the Louisiana side. Had the attempt been made, the garrison of Vicksburg would have been drowned or made prisoners on the Louisiana side. General Richard Taylor was expected on the west bank to coöperate in this movement, I believe, but he did not come, nor could he have done so with a force sufficient to be of service. The Mississippi was now in our possession from its source to its mouth, except in the immediate front of Vicksburg and Port Hudson. We had nearly exhausted the country, along a line drawn from Lake Providence to opposite Bruinsburg. The roads west were not of a character to draw supplies over for any considerable force.

By the 1st of July our approaches had reached the enemy's ditch at a number of places. At ten points we could move under cover to within from five to 100 yards of the enemy. Orders were given to make all preparations for assault on the 6th of July. The debouches were ordered widened, to afford easy egress, while the approaches were also to be widened to admit the troops to pass through four abreast. Plank and sand-bags, the latter filled with cotton packed in tightly, were ordered prepared, to enable the troops to cross the ditches.

On the night of the 1st of July Johnston was between Brownsville and the Big Black, and wrote Pemberton from there that about the 7th of the month an attempt would be made to create a diversion to enable him to cut his way out. Pemberton was a prisoner before this message reached him.

On July 1st Pemberton, seeing no hope of outside relief, addressed the following letter to each of his four division commanders:

Unless the siege of Vicksburg is raised, or supplies are thrown in, it will become necessary very shortly to evacuate the place. I see no prospect of the former, and there are many great, if not insuperable, obstacles in the way of the latter. You are, therefore, requested to inform me with as little delay as possible as to the condition of your troops, and their ability to make the marches and undergo the fatigues necessary to accomplish a successful evacuation.

Two of his generals suggested surrender, and the other two practically did the same; they expressed the opinion that an attempt to evacuate would fail. Pemberton had previously got a message to Johnston suggesting that he should try to negotiate with me for a release of the garrison with their arms. Johnston replied that it would be a confession of weakness for him to do so; but he authorized Pemberton to use his name in making such an arrangement.

On the 3d, about 10 o'clock A. M., white flags appeared on a portion of the rebel works. Hostilities along that part of the line ceased at once. Soon two persons were seen coming toward our lines bearing a white flag. They proved to be General Bowen, a division commander, and Colonel Montgomery, aide-de-camp to Pemberton, bearing the following letter to me:

I have the honor to propose an armistice for —— hours, with the view to arranging terms for the capitulation of Vicksburg. To this end, if agreeable to you, I will appoint three commissioners, to meet a like number to be named by yourself, at such place and hour to-day, as you may find convenient. I make this proposition to save the further effusion of blood, which must otherwise be shed to a frightful extent, feeling myself fully able to maintain my position for a yet indefinite period. This communication will be handed you, under a flag of truce, by Major-General John S. Bowen.

It was a glorious sight to officers and soldiers on the line where these white flags were visible, and the news soon spread to all parts of the command. The troops felt that their long and weary marches, hard fighting, ceaseless watching by night and day in a hot climate, exposure to all sorts of weather, diseases, and, worst of all, to the gibes of many Northern papers that came to them, saying all their suffering was in vain, Vicksburg would never be taken, were at last at an end, and the Union sure to be saved.

Bowen was received by General A. J. Smith, and asked to see me. I had been a neighbor of Bowen's in Missouri, and knew him well and favorably before the war; but his request was refused. He then suggested that I should meet Pemberton. To this I sent a verbal message saying that if Pemberton desired it I would meet him in front of McPherson's corps, at 3 o'clock that afternoon. I also sent the following written reply to Pemberton's letter:

Your note of this date is just received, proposing an armistice for several hours, for the purpose of arranging terms of capitulation through commissioners to be appointed, etc. The useless effusion of blood you propose stopping by this course can be ended at any time you may choose, by the unconditional surrender of the city and garrison. Men who have shown so much endurance and courage as those now in Vicksburg will always challenge the respect of an adversary, and I can assure you will be treated with all the respect due to prisoners of war. I do not favor the proposition of appointing commissioners to arrange the terms of capitulation, because I have no terms other than those indicated above.

At 3 o'clock Pemberton appeared at the point suggested in my verbal message, accompanied by the same officers who had borne his letter of the morning. Generals Ord, McPherson, Logan, A. J. Smith, and several officers of my staff accompanied me. Our place of meeting was on a hill-side within a few hundred feet of the rebel lines. Near by stood a stunted oak-tree, which was made historical by the event. It was but a short time before the last vestige of its body, root, and limb had disappeared, the fragments being taken as trophies. Since then the same tree has furnished as many cords of wood, in the shape of trophies, as "The True Cross."

Pemberton and I had served in the same division during a part of the Mexican war. I knew him very well, therefore, and greeted him as an old acquaintance. He soon asked what terms I proposed to give his army if it surrendered. My answer was the same as proposed in my reply to his letter. Pemberton then said, rather snappishly, "The conference might as well end," and turned abruptly as if to leave. I said, "Very well." General Bowen, I saw, was very anxious that the surrender should be consummated. His manners and remarks while Pemberton and I were talking showed this. He now proposed that he and one of our generals should have a conference. I had no objection to this, as nothing could be made binding upon me that they might propose. Smith and Bowen accordingly had a conference, during which Pemberton and I, moving some distance away toward the enemy's lines, were in conversation. After a while Bowen suggested that the Confederate army should be allowed to march out, with the honors of war, carrying their small-arms and field-artillery. This was promptly and unceremoniously rejected. The interview here ended, I agreeing, however, to send a letter giving final terms by 10 o'clock that night. I had sent word to Admiral Porter soon after the correspondence with Pemberton had commenced, so that hostilities might be stopped on the part of both army and navy. It was agreed on my parting with Pemberton that they should not be renewed until our correspondence should cease.

When I returned to my headquarters I sent for all the corps and division commanders with the army immediately confronting Vicksburg. (Half the army was from eight to twelve miles off, waiting for Johnston.) I informed them of the contents of Pemberton's letters, of my reply, and the substance of the interview, and was ready to hear any suggestion; but would hold the power of deciding entirely in my own hands. This was the nearest to a "council of war" I ever held. Against the general and almost unanimous judgment of the council I sent the following letter:

In conformity with agreement of this afternoon I will submit the following proposition for the surrender of the city of Vicksburg, public stores, etc. On your accepting the terms proposed I will march in one division as a guard, and take possession at 8 A. M. to-morrow. As soon as rolls can be made out and paroles be signed by officers and men, you will be allowed to march out of our lines, the officers taking with them their side-arms and clothing; and the field, staff, and cavalry officers one horse each. The rank and file will be allowed all their clothing, but no other property. If these conditions are accepted, any amount of rations you may deem necessary can be taken from the stores you now have, and also the necessary cooking-utensils for preparing them. Thirty wagons also, counting two-horse or mule teams as one, will be allowed to transport such articles as cannot be carried along. The same conditions will be allowed to all sick and wounded officers and soldiers as fast as they become able to travel. The paroles for these latter must be signed, however, whilst officers present are authorized to sign the roll of prisoners.

By the terms of the cartel then in force, prisoners captured by either army were required to be forwarded, as soon as possible, to either Aiken's Landing below Dutch Gap, on the James River, or to Vicksburg, there to be exchanged, or paroled until they could be exchanged. There was a Confederate Commissioner at Vicksburg, authorized to make the exchange. I did not propose to take him prisoner, but to leave him free to perform the functions of his office. Had I insisted upon an unconditional surrender, there would have been over thirty-odd thousand men to transport to Cairo, very much to the inconvenience of the army on the Mississippi; thence the prisoners would have had to be transported by rail to Washington or Baltimore; thence again by steamer to Aiken's—all at very great expense. At Aiken's they would have to be paroled, because the Confederates did not have Union prisoners to give in exchange. Then again Pemberton's army was largely composed of men whose homes were in the south-west; I knew many of them were tired of the war and would get home just as soon as they could. A large number of them had voluntarily come into our lines during the siege and requested to be sent north where they could get employment until the war was over and they could go to their homes.

Late at night I received the following reply to my last letter:

I have the honor to acknowledge the receipt of your communication of this date, proposing terms of capitulation for this garrison and post. In the main, your terms are accepted; but, in justice both to the honor and spirit of my troops manifested in the defense of Vicksburg, I have to submit the following amendments, which, if acceded to by you, will perfect the agreement between us. At 10 o'clock A. M. to-morrow I propose to evacuate the works in and around Vicksburg, and to surrender the city and garrison under my command, by marching out with my colors and arms, stacking them in front of my present lines, after which you will take possession. Officers to retain their side-arms and personal property, and the rights and property of citizens to be respected.

This was received after midnight; my reply was as follows:

I have the honor to acknowledge the receipt of your communication of 3d July. The amendment proposed by you cannot be acceded to in full. It will be necessary to furnish every officer and man with a parole signed by himself, which, with the completion of the roll of prisoners, will necessarily take some time. Again, I can make no stipulations with regard to the treatment of citizens and their private property. While I do not propose to cause them any undue annoyance or loss, I cannot consent to leave myself under any restraint by stipulations. The property which officers will be allowed to take with them will be as stated in my proposition of last evening; that is, officers will be allowed their private baggage and side-arms, and mounted officers one horse each. If you mean by your proposition for each brigade to march to the front of the lines now occupied by it, and stack arms at 10 o'clock A. M., and then return to the inside and there remain as prisoners until properly paroled, I will make no objection to it. Should no notification be received of your acceptance of my terms by 9 o'clock A. M., I shall regard them as having been rejected, and shall act accordingly. Should these terms be accepted, white flags should be displayed along your lines to prevent such of my troops as may not have been notified from firing upon your men.

Pemberton promptly accepted these terms.

During the siege there had been a good deal of friendly sparring between the soldiers of the two armies, on picket and where the lines were close together. All rebels were known as "Johnnies"; all Union troops as "Yanks." Often "Johnny" would call, "Well, Yank, when are you coming into town?" The reply was sometimes: "We propose to celebrate the 4th of July there." Sometimes it would be: "We always treat our prisoners with kindness and do not want to hurt them"; or, "We are holding you as prisoners of war while you are feeding yourselves." The garrison, from the commanding general down, undoubtedly expected an assault on the 4th. They knew from the temper of their men it would be successful when made, and that would be a greater humiliation than to surrender. Besides it would be attended with severe loss to them.

The Vicksburg paper, which we received regularly through the courtesy of the rebel pickets, said prior to the 4th, in speaking of the "Yankee" boast that they would take dinner in Vicksburg that day, that the best receipt for cooking rabbit was, "First ketch your rabbit." The paper at this time, and for some time previous, was printed on the plain side of wall paper. The last was issued on the 4th and announced that we had "caught our rabbit."

I have no doubt that Pemberton commenced his correspondence on the 3d for the twofold purpose; first, to avoid an assault, which he knew would be successful, and second, to prevent the capture taking place on the great national holiday—the anniversary of the Declaration of American Independence. Holding out for better terms, as he did, he defeated his aim in the latter particular.

At the 4th, at the appointed hour, the garrison of Vicksburg marched out of their works, and formed line in front, stacked arms, and marched back in good order. Our whole army present witnessed this scene without cheering.

Logan's division, which had approached nearest the rebel works, was the first to march in, and the flag of one of the regiments of his division was soon floating over the court-house. Our soldiers were no sooner inside the lines than the two armies began to fraternize. Our men had had full rations from the time the siege commenced to the close. The enemy had been suffering, particularly toward the last. I myself saw our men taking bread from their haversacks and giving it to the enemy they had so recently been engaged in *starving out.* It was accepted with avidity and with thanks. . . .

On the 3d, as soon as negotiations were commenced, I notified Sherman, and directed him to be ready to take the offensive against Johnston, drive him out of the State, and destroy his army if he could. Steele and Ord were directed at the same time to be in readiness to join Sherman as soon as the surrender took place. Of this Sherman was notified.

I rode into Vicksburg with the troops, and went to the river to exchange congratulations with the navy upon our joint victory. At that time I found that many of the citizens had been living under-ground. The ridges upon which Vicksburg is built, and those back to the Big Black, are composed of a deep yellow clay, of great tenacity. Where roads and streets are cut through, perpendicular banks are left, and stand as well as if composed of stone. The magazines of the enemy were made by running passage-ways into this clay at places where there were deep cuts. Many citizens secured places of safety for their families by carving out rooms in these embankments. A door-way in these cases would be cut in a high bank, starting from the level of the road or street, and after running in a few feet a room of the size required was carved out of the clay, the dirt being removed by the door-way. In some instances I saw where two rooms were cut out, for a single family, with a doorway in the clay wall separating them. Some of these were carpeted and furnished with considerable elaboration. In these the occupants were fully secure from the shells of the navy, which were dropped into the city, night and day, without intermission.

I returned to my old headquarters outside in the afternoon, and did not move them into the town until the 6th. On the afternoon of the 4th I sent Captain William M. Dunn, of my staff, to Cairo, the nearest point where the telegraph could be reached, with a dispatch to the general-in-chief. It was as follows:

The enemy surrendered this morning. The only terms allowed is their parole as prisoners of war. This I regard as a great advantage to us at this moment. It saves, probably, several days in the capture, and leaves troops and transports ready for immediate service. Sherman, with a large force, moves immediately on Johnston, to drive him from the State. I will send troops to the relief of Banks, and return the Ninth Army Corps to Burnside.

At the same time I wrote to General Banks informing him of the fall, and sending him a copy of the terms, also saying I would send him all the troops he wanted to insure the capture of the only foothold the enemy now had on the Mississippi River. General Banks had a number of copies of this letter printed, or at least a synopsis of it, and very soon a copy fell into the hands of General Gardner, who was then in command of Port Hudson. Gardner at once sent a letter to the commander of the National forces, saying that he had been informed of the surrender of Vicksburg and telling how the information reached him. He added that if this was true it was useless for him to hold out longer. General Banks gave him assurances that Vicksburg had been surrendered, and General Gardner surrendered unconditionally on the 9th of July. Port Hudson, with nearly 6000 prisoners, 51 guns, and 5000 small-arms and other stores, fell into the hands of the Union Forces. From that day on, the river remained under National control. . . .

At Vicksburg 31,600 prisoners were surrendered, together with 172 cannon, about 60,000 muskets, and a large amount of ammunition. The small-arms of the enemy were far superior to the bulk of ours. Up to this time our troops at the west had been limited to the old United States flint-lock muskets changed into percussion, or the Belgian musket imported early in the war—almost as dangerous to the person firing it as to the one aimed at—and a few new and improved arms. These were of many different calibers, a fact that caused much trouble in distributing ammunition during an engagement. The enemy had generally new arms, which had run the blockade, and were of uniform caliber. After the surrender I authorized all colonels, whose regiments were armed with inferior muskets, to place them in the stack of captured arms, and replace them with the latter. A large number of arms, turned in to the ordnance department as captured, were these arms that had really been used by the Union army in the capture of Vicksburg. . . .

The navy, under Porter, was all it could be, during the entire campaign. Without its assistance the campaign could not have been successfully made with twice the number of men engaged. It could not have been made at all, in the way it was, with any number of men, without such assistance. The most perfect harmony reigned between the two arms of the service. There never was a request made, that I am aware of, either of the flag-officer or any of his subordinates, that was not promptly complied with.

The campaign of Vicksburg was suggested and developed by circumstances. The elections of 1862 had gone against the prosecution of the war: voluntary enlistments had nearly ceased, and the draft had been resorted to; this was resisted, and a defeat, or backward movement, would have made its execution impossible. A forward movement to a decisive victory was necessary. Accordingly I resolved to get below Vicksburg, unite with Banks against Port Hudson, and make New Orleans a base; and, with that base and Grand Gulf as a starting-point, move our combined forces against Vicksburg.

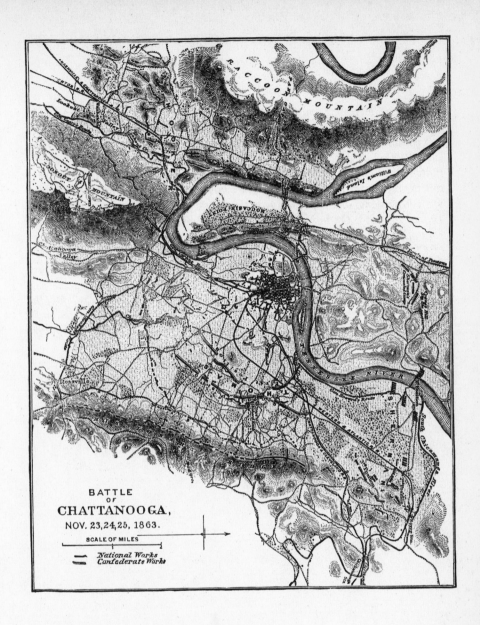

BATTLE
OF
CHATTANOOGA,
NOV. 23, 24, 25, 1863.

SCALE OF MILES

National Works
Confederate Works

443

Between Gettysburg and Vicksburg there was another vast battleground, eastern Tennessee, where North and South contended for the control of Chattanooga and its railroads stretching east, west, south. The Confederate commander there was Braxton Bragg, the Union commander William S. Rosecrans—ideally matched for each was vain, sensitive, irascible, and not in the least eager to test the other. Finally they were pushed into an engagement by Lincoln acting upon Rosecrans, and the result was the Battle of Chickamauga on September 19 and 20, 1863. On the second day a tactical blunder by Rosecrans led to the rout of half his forces and, thinking the battle lost, he galloped to the shelter of Chattanooga. But General George H. Thomas kept his head, held his men on the field, and turned back the rebels in an afternoon of fighting so savage that they said the stream there ran red with human blood. Thomas the Virginian, ever after the "Rock of Chickamauga." He brought what was left of the army back to Chattanooga in good order and there became its commander under Grant, the new head of all the Union forces between the Alleghanies and the River.

"We will hold the town till we starve"

BY ULYSSES S. GRANT, GENERAL, U. S. A.

AFTER the fall of Vicksburg I urged strongly upon the Government the propriety of a movement against Mobile. General Rosecrans had been at Murfreesboro', Tennessee, with a large and well-equipped army from early in the year 1863, with Bragg confronting him with a force quite equal to his own at first, considering that it was on the defensive. But after the investment of Vicksburg, Bragg's army was largely depleted to strengthen Johnston, in Mississippi, who was being reënforced to raise the siege. I frequently wrote to General Halleck suggesting that Rosecrans should move against Bragg. By so doing he would either detain the latter's troops where they were, or lay Chattanooga open to capture. General Halleck strongly approved the suggestion, and finally wrote me that he had repeatedly ordered Rosecrans to advance, but that the latter had constantly failed to comply with the order, and at last, after having held a council of war, replied, in effect, that it was a military maxim "not to fight two decisive battles at the same time." If true, the maxim was not applicable in this case. It would be bad to be defeated in two decisive battles fought the same day, but it would not be bad to win them. I, however, was fighting no battle, and the

445

siege of Vicksburg had drawn from Rosecrans's front so many of the enemy that his chances of victory were much greater than they would be if he waited until the siege was over, when these troops could be returned. Rosecrans was ordered to move against the army that was detaching troops to raise the siege. Finally, on the 24th of June, he did move, but ten days afterward Vicksburg surrendered, and the troops sent from Bragg were free to return. It was at this time that I recommended to the general-in-chief the movement against Mobile. I knew the peril the Army of the Cumberland was in, being depleted continually not only by ordinary casualties, but also by having to detach troops to hold its constantly extending line over which to draw supplies, while the enemy in front was as constantly being strengthened. Mobile was important to the enemy, and, in the absence of a threatening force, was guarded by little else than artillery. If threatened by land and from the water at the same time, the prize would fall easily, or troops would have to be sent to its defense. Those troops would necessarily come from Bragg.

My judgment was overruled, however, and the troops under my command were dissipated over other parts of the country where it was thought they could render the most service. Four thousand were sent to Banks, at New Orleans; five thousand to Schofield, to use against Price, in Arkansas; the Ninth Corps back to Kentucky; and finally, in August, the whole of the Thirteenth Corps to Banks. I also sent Ransom's brigade to Natchez, to occupy that point, and to relieve Banks from guarding any part of the river above what he had guarded before the fall of Port Hudson. Ransom captured a large amount of ammunition and about five thousand beef cattle that were crossing the river going east for the rebel armies. At this time the country was full of deserters from Pemberton's army, and it was reported that many had also left Johnston. These avowed they would never go back to fight against us again. Many whose homes were west of the river went there, and others went North to remain until they could return with security.

Soon it was discovered in Washington that Rosecrans was in trouble and required assistance. The emergency was now too immediate to allow us to give this assistance by making an attack in the rear of Bragg upon Mobile. It was, therefore, necessary to reënforce directly, and troops were sent from every available point. On the 13th of September Halleck telegraphed me to send all available forces to Memphis, and thence east along the Memphis and Charleston railroad to coöperate with Rosecrans. This instruction was repeated two days later, but I did not get even the first until the 23d of the month. As fast as transports could be provided all the troops except a portion of the Seventeenth Corps were forwarded under Sherman, whose services up to this time demonstrated his superior fitness for a separate command. I also moved McPherson, with most of the troops still about Vicksburg, eastward, to compel the enemy to keep back a force to meet him. Meanwhile Rosecrans had very skillfully manœuvred Bragg south of the Tennessee River, and through and beyond Chattanooga. If he had stopped and intrenched, and made himself strong there, all would have been right, and the mistake of not moving earlier partially compensated. But he pushed on, with his forces very much scattered, until Bragg's troops from Mississippi began to joint him. Then Bragg took the initiative. Rosecrans had to fall back in turn, and was able to get his army together at Chickamauga, some miles south-east of Chattanooga, before the main battle was brought on. The battle was fought on the 19th and 20th of September, and Rosecrans was badly defeated, with a heavy loss in artillery, and some sixteen thousand men killed, wounded, and captured. The corps under Major-General George H. Thomas stood its ground, while Rosecrans, with Crittenden and McCook, returned to Chattanooga. Thomas returned also, but later, and with his troops in good order. Bragg followed and took possession of Missionary Ridge, overlooking Chattanooga. He also occupied Lookout Mountain, west of the town, which Rosecrans had abandoned, and with it his control of the river and river road as far back as Bridgeport. The National troops were now strongly intrenched in Chattanooga Valley, with the Tennessee River behind them, the enemy occupying commanding heights to the east and west, with a strong line across the valley, from mountain to mountain, and Chattanooga Creek for a large part of the way in front of their line.

On the 29th of September Halleck telegraphed me the above results, and directed all the forces that could be spared from my department to be sent to Rosecrans, suggesting that a good commander like Sherman or McPherson should go with the troops; also that I should go in person to Nashville to superintend the movement. Long before this dispatch was received Sherman was already on his way, and McPherson also was moving east with most of the garrison of Vicksburg. I at once sent a staff-officer to Cairo, to communicate, in my name, directly with the Government, and to forward me any and all important dispatches without the delays that had attended the transmission of previous ones. On the 3d of October a dispatch was received at Cairo ordering me to move with my staff and headquarters to that city, and report from there my arrival. This dispatch reached me on the 10th. I left Vicksburg the same day, reached Columbus *en route* for Cairo on the 16th, and reported my arrival at once. The reply to my telegram from Cairo, announcing my arrival at that point, came on the morning of the 17th, directing me to proceed immediately to the Galt House, Louisville, Kentucky, where I would meet an officer of the War Department with my instructions. I left Cairo within an hour after the receipt of this dispatch, going by rail by the way of Indianapolis, Indiana. Just as the train I was on was starting out of the depot at Indianapolis, a messenger came running up to stop it, saying the Secretary of War was coming into the station and wanted to see me. I had never met Mr. Stanton up to that time, though we had held frequent conversations over the wires, the year before, when I was in Tennessee. Occasionally, at night, he would order the wires between the War Department and my headquarters to be connected, and we would hold a conversation for an hour or two. On

447

this occasion the secretary was accompanied by Governor Brough, of Ohio, whom I had never met, though he and my father had been old acquaintances. Mr. Stanton dismissed the special train that had brought him to Indianapolis and accompanied me to Louisville.

Up to this time no hint had been given me of what was wanted after I left Vicksburg, except the suggestion in one of Halleck's dispatches that I had better go to Nashville and superintend the operation of the troops sent to relieve Rosecrans. Soon after we had started, the secretary handed me two orders, saying that I might take my choice of them. The two were identical in all but one particular. Both created the Military Division of the Mississippi, giving me the command, composed of the Departments of the Ohio, the Cumberland, and the Tennessee, and all the territory from the Alleghanies to the Mississippi River, north of Banks's command in the south-west. One order left the department commanders as they were, while the other relieved Rosecrans and assigned Thomas to his place. I accepted the latter. We reached Louisville after night, and, if I remember rightly, in a cold, drizzling rain. The Secretary of War told me afterward that he caught a cold on that occasion from which he never expected to recover.

A day was spent in Louisville, the secretary giving me the military news at the capital, and talking about the disappointment at the results of some of the campaigns. By the evening of the day after our arrival all matters of discussion seemed exhausted, and I left the hotel to spend the evening away, both Mrs. Grant (who was with me) and myself having relations living in Louisville. In the course of the evening Mr. Stanton received a dispatch from Mr. C. A. Dana [an officer of the War Department], then in Chattanooga, informing him that unless prevented Rosecrans would retreat, and advising peremptory orders against his doing so. A retreat at that time would have been a terrible disaster. It would not only have been the loss of a most important strategic position to us, but it would have been attended with the loss of all the artillery still left with the Army of the Cumberland, and the annihilation of that army itself, either by capture or demoralization.

All supplies for Rosecrans had to be brought from Nashville. The railroad between this base and the army was in possession of the Government up to Bridgeport, the point at which the road crosses to the south side of the Tennessee River; but Bragg, holding Lookout and Raccoon mountains west of Chattanooga, commanded the railroad, the river, and the shortest and best wagon roads both south and north of the Tennessee, between Chattanooga and Bridgeport. The distance between these two places is but twenty-six miles by rail; but owing to this position of Bragg all supplies for Rosecrans had to be hauled by a circuitous route, north of the river, and over a mountainous country, increasing the distance to over sixty miles. This country afforded but little food for his animals, nearly ten thousand of which had already starved, and none were left to draw a single piece of artillery or even the ambulances to convey the sick. The men had been on half rations of hard bread for a considerable time, with but few other supplies, except beef driven from Nashville across the country. The region along the road became so exhausted of food for the cattle that by the time they reached Chattanooga they were much in the condition of the few animals left alive there, "on the lift." Indeed, the beef was so poor that the soldiers were in the habit of saying, with a faint facetiousness, that they were living on half rations of hard bread and "beef dried on the hoof." Nothing could be transported but food, and the troops were without sufficient shoes or other clothing suitable for the advancing season. What they had was well worn. The fuel within the Federal lines was exhausted, even to the stumps of trees. There were no teams to draw it from the opposite bank, where it was abundant. The only means for supplying fuel, for some time before my arrival, had been to cut trees from the north bank of the river, at a considerable distance up the stream, form rafts of it, and float it down with the current, effecting a landing on the south side, within our lines, by the use of paddles or poles. It would then be carried on the shoulders of the men to their camps. If a retreat had occurred at this time it is not probable that any of the army would have reached the railroad as an organized body, if followed by the enemy.

On the receipt of Mr. Dana's dispatch Mr. Stanton sent for me. Finding that I was out, he became nervous and excited, inquiring of every person he met, including guests of the house, whether they knew where I was, and bidding them find me and send me to him at once. About 11 o'clock I returned to the hotel, and on my way, when near the house, every person met was a messenger from the secretary, apparently partaking of his impatience to see me. I hastened to the room of the secretary and found him pacing the floor rapidly, in a dressing-gown. Saying that the retreat must be prevented, he showed me the dispatch. I immediately wrote an order assuming command of the Military Division of the Mississippi, and telegraphed it to General Rosecrans. I then telegraphed to him the order from Washington assigning Thomas to the command of the Army of the Cumberland; and to Thomas that he must hold Chattanooga at all hazards, informing him at the same time that I would be at the front as soon as possible. A prompt reply was received from Thomas, saying, "We will hold the town till we starve." I appreciated the force of this dispatch later when I witnessed the condition of affairs which prompted it. It looked, indeed, as if but two courses were open: one to starve, the other to surrender or be captured.

On the morning of the 20th of October I started by train with my staff, and proceeded as far as Nashville. At that time it was not prudent to travel beyond that point by night, so I remained in Nashville until the next morning. Here I met for the first time Andrew Johnson, Military Governor of Tennessee. He delivered a speech of welcome. His composure showed that it was by no means his maiden effort. It was long, and I was in torture while he was delivering it, fearing something would be expected from me in response. I was relieved, however, the people assembled having apparently heard enough. At all events they commenced a general hand-shaking, which, although trying where there is so much of it, was a great relief to me in this emergency.

From Nashville I telegraphed to Burnside, who was then at Knoxville, that important points in his department ought to be fortified, so that they could be held with the least number of men; to Porter at Cairo, that Sherman's advance had passed Eastport, Miss., and that rations were probably on their way from St. Louis by boat for supplying his army, and requesting him to send a gun-boat to convoy them; and to Thomas, suggesting that large parties should be put at work on the wagon road then in use back to Bridgeport.

On the morning of the 21st we took the train for the front, reaching Stevenson, Alabama, after dark. Rosecrans was there on his way north. He came into my car, and we held a brief interview in which he described very clearly the situation at Chattanooga, and made some excellent suggestions as to what should be done. My only wonder was that he had not carried them out. We then proceeded to Bridgeport, where we stopped for the night. From here we took horses and made our way by Jasper and over Waldron's Ridge to Chattanooga. There had been much rain and the roads were almost impassable from mud knee-deep in places, and from washouts on the mountainsides. I had been on crutches since the time of my fall in New Orleans, and had to be carried over places where it was not safe to cross on horseback. The roads were strewn with the debris of broken wagons and the carcasses of thousands of starved mules and horses. At Jasper, some ten or twelve miles from Bridgeport, there was a halt. Howard had his headquarters there. From this point I telegraphed Burnside to make every effort to secure 500 rounds of ammunition for his artillery and small-arms. We stopped for the night at a little hamlet some ten or twelve miles farther on. The next day we reached Chattanooga, a little before dark. I went directly to Thomas's headquarters, and remained there a few days until I could establish my own.

During the evening most of the general officers called in to pay their respects and to talk about the condition of affairs. They pointed out on the maps the line marked with a red or blue pencil which Rosecrans had contemplated falling back upon. If any of them had approved the move, they did not say so to me. I found General W. F. Smith occupying the position of chief engineer of the Army of the Cumberland. I had known Smith as a cadet at West Point, but had no recollection of having met him after my graduation, in 1843, up to this time. He explained the situation of the two armies and the topography of the country so plainly that I could see it without an inspection. I found that he had established a saw-mill on the banks of the river, by utilizing an old engine found in the neighborhood; and by rafting logs from the north side of the river above had got out the lumber and completed pontoons and roadway plank for a second bridge, one flying-bridge being there already. He was also rapidly getting out the materials for constructing the boats for a third bridge. In addition to this he had far under way a steamer for plying between Chattanooga and Bridgeport whenever he might get possession of the river. This boat consisted of a scow made of the plank sawed out at the mill, housed in, with a stern-wheel attached which was propelled by a second engine taken from some shop or factory.

I telegraphed to Washington this night, notifying Halleck of my arrival, and asking to have Sherman assigned to the command of the Army of the Tennessee, headquarters in the field. The request was at once complied with.

The next day, the 24th, I started out to make a personal inspection, taking Thomas and Smith with me, besides most of the members of my personal staff. We crossed to the north side of the river, and, moving to the north of detached spurs of hills, reached the Tennessee, at Brown's Ferry, some three miles below Lookout Mountain, unobserved by the enemy. Here we left our horses back from the river and approached the water on foot. There was a picket station of the enemy, on the opposite side, of about twenty men, in full view, and we were within easy range. They did not fire upon us nor seem to be disturbed by our presence. They must have seen that we were all commissioned officers. But, I suppose, they looked upon the garrison of Chattanooga as prisoners of war, feeding or starving themselves, and thought it would be inhuman to kill any of them except in self-defense. That night I issued orders for opening the route to Bridgeport—a "cracker line," as the soldiers appropriately termed it. They had been so long on short rations that my first thought was the establishment of a line over which food might reach them.

Chattanooga is on the south bank of the Tennessee, where that river runs nearly due west. It is at the northern end of a valley five or six miles in width through which runs Chattanooga Creek. To the east of the valley is Missionary Ridge, rising from five to eight hundred feet above the creek, and terminating somewhat abruptly a half-mile or more before reaching the Tennessee. On the west of the valley is Lookout Mountain, 2200 feet above tide-water. Just below the town, the Tennessee makes a turn to the south and runs to the base of Lookout Mountain, leaving no level ground between the mountain and river. The Memphis and Charleston railroad passes this point, where the mountain stands nearly perpendicular. East of Missionary Ridge flows the South Chickamauga River; west of Lookout Mountain is Lookout Creek; and west of that, the Raccoon Mountain. Lookout Mountain at its northern end rises almost perpendicularly for some distance, then breaks off in a gentle slope of cultivated fields to near the summit, where it ends in a palisade thirty or more feet in height. On the gently sloping ground, between the upper and lower palisades, there is a single farm-house, which is reached by a wagon road from the valley to the east.

The intrenched line of the enemy commenced on the north end of Missionary Ridge and extended along the crest for some distance south, thence across Chattanooga Valley to Lookout Mountain. Lookout Mountain was also fortified and held by the enemy, who also kept troops in Lookout Valley and on Raccoon Mountain, with pickets extending down the river so as to command the road on the north bank and render it useless to us. In addition to this there was an intrenched line in Chattanooga Valley extending from the river east of the town to Lookout Mountain, to make the investment complete. Besides the fortifications on Missionary Ridge there was a line at the base of the hill, with occasional spurs of rifle-pits half-way up the front. The enemy's pickets extended out into the valley toward the town, so far that the pickets of the two armies could converse. At one point they were separated only by the narrow creek which gives its name to the valley and town, and from which both sides drew water. The Union lines were shorter than those of the enemy.

Thus the enemy, with a vastly superior force, was strongly fortified to the east, south, and west, and commanded the river below. Practically the Army of the Cumberland was besieged. The enemy, with his cavalry north of the river, had stopped the passing of a train loaded with ammunition and medical supplies. The Union army was short of both, not having ammunition enough for a day's fighting.

Long before my coming into this new field, General Halleck had ordered parts of the Eleventh and Twelfth corps, commanded respectively by Generals Howard and Slocum, Hooker in command of the whole, from the Army of the Potomac, to reënforce Rosecrans. It would have been folly to have sent them to Chattanooga to help eat up the few rations left there. They were consequently left on the railroad, where supplies could be brought them. Before my arrival Thomas ordered their concentration at Bridgeport.

General W. F. Smith had been so instrumental in preparing for the move which I was now about to make, and so clear in his judgment about the manner of making it, that I deemed it but just to him that he should have command of the troops detailed to execute the design, although he was then acting as a staff-officer, and was not in command of troops.

On the 24th of October, after my return to Chattanooga, the following details were made: General Hooker, who was now at Bridgeport, was ordered to cross to the south side of the Tennessee and march up by Whiteside's and Wauhatchie to Brown's Ferry. General Palmer, with a division of the Fourteenth Corps, Army of the Cumberland, was ordered to move down the river on the north side, by a back road, until opposite Whiteside's, then cross and hold the road in Hooker's rear after he had passed. Four thousand men were at the same time detailed to act under General Smith directly from Chattanooga. Eighteen hundred of them, under General Hazen, were to take sixty pontoon-boats and, under cover of night, float by the pickets of the enemy at the north base of Lookout, down to Brown's Ferry, then land on the south side and capture or drive away the pickets at that point. Smith was to march with the remainder of the detail, also under cover of night, by the north bank of the river, to Brown's Ferry, taking with him all the material for laying the bridge, as soon as the crossing was secured.

On the 26th Hooker crossed the river at Bridgeport and commenced his eastward march. At 3 o'clock on the morning of the 27th Hazen moved into the stream with his sixty pontoons and eighteen hundred brave and well-equipped men. Smith started enough in advance to be near the river when Hazen should arrive. There are a number of detached spurs of hills north of the river at Chattanooga, back of which is a good road parallel to the stream, sheltered from view from the top of Lookout. It was over this road Smith marched. At 5 o'clock Hazen landed at Brown's Ferry, surprised the picket-guard and captured most of it. By 7 o'clock the whole of Smith's force was ferried over and in possession of a height commanding the ferry. This was speedily fortified while a detail was laying the pontoon-bridge. By 10 o'clock the bridge was laid, and our extreme right, now in Lookout Valley, was fortified and connected with the rest of the army. The two bridges over the Tennessee River—a flying one at Chattanooga and the new one at Brown's Ferry—with the road north of the river, covered from both the fire and the view of the enemy, made the connection complete. Hooker found but slight obstacles in his way, and on the afternoon of the 28th emerged into Lookout Valley at Wauhatchie. Howard marched on to Brown's Ferry, while Geary, who commanded a division in the Twelfth Corps, stopped three miles south. The pickets of the enemy on the river below were cut off and soon came in and surrendered.

The river was now open to us from Lookout Valley to Bridgeport. Between Brown's Ferry and Kelley's Ferry the Tennessee runs through a narrow gorge in the mountains, which contracts the stream so much as to increase the current beyond the capacity of an ordinary steamer to stem. To get up these rapids, steamers must be cordelled, that is, pulled up by ropes from the shore. But there is no difficulty in navigating the stream from Bridgeport to Kelley's Ferry. The latter point is only eight miles from Chattanooga, and connected with it by a good wagon road, which runs through a low pass in the Raccoon Mountain on the south side of the river to Brown's Ferry, thence on the north side to the river opposite Chattanooga. There were several steamers at Bridgeport, and abundance of forage, clothing, and provisions.

On the way to Chattanooga I had telegraphed back to Nashville for a good supply of vegetables and small rations, which the troops had been so long deprived of. Hooker had brought with him from the east a full supply of land transportation. His animals had not been subjected to hard work on bad roads without forage, but were in good condition. In five days from my arrival at Chattanooga the way was open to Bridgeport, and, with the aid of steamers and Hooker's teams, in a week the troops were receiving full rations. It is hard for any one not an eye-witness to realize the relief this brought. The men were soon reclothed and well fed; an abundance of ammunition was brought up, and a cheerfulness prevailed not before enjoyed in many weeks. Neither officers nor men looked upon themselves any longer as doomed. The weak and languid appearance of the troops, so visible before, disappeared at once. I do not know what the effect was on the other side, but assume it must have been correspondingly depressing. Mr. Davis had visited Bragg but a short time before, and must have perceived our condition to be about as Bragg described it in his subsequent report. "These dispositions," he said, "faithfully sustained, insured the enemy's speedy evacuation of Chattanooga, for want of food and forage. Possessed of the shortest route to his depot and the one by which reënforcements must reach him, we held him at our mercy, and his destruction was only a question of time." But the dispositions were not "faithfully sustained," and I doubt not that thousands of men engaged in trying to "sustain" them now rejoice that they were not.

There was no time during the rebellion when I did not think, and often say, that the South was more to be benefited by defeat than the North. The latter had the people, the institutions, and the territory to make a great and prosperous nation. The former was burdened with an institution abhorrent to all civilized peoples not brought up under it, and one which degraded labor, kept it in ignorance, and enervated the governing class. With the outside world at war with this institution, they could not have extended their territory. The labor of the country was not skilled, nor allowed to become so. The whites could not toil without becoming degraded, and those who did were denominated "poor white trash." The system of labor would have soon exhausted the soil and left the people poor. The non-slaveholders would have left the country, and the small slaveholder must have sold out to his more fortunate neighbors. Soon the slaves would have outnumbered the masters, and, not being in sympathy with them, would have risen in their might and exterminated them. The war was expensive to the South as well as to the North, both in blood and treasure; but it was worth all it cost.

The enemy was surprised by the movement which secured to us a line of supplies. He appreciated its importance, and hastened to try to recover the line from us. His strength on Lookout Mountain was not equal to Hooker's command in the valley below. From Missionary Ridge we had to march twice the distance we had from Chattanooga, in order to reach Lookout Valley. But on the night of the 28th–29th [of October] an attack was made on Geary, at Wauhatchie, by Longstreet's corps. When the battle commenced, Hooker ordered Howard up from Brown's Ferry. He had three miles to march to reach Geary. On his way he was fired upon by rebel troops from a foot-hill to the left of the road, and from which the road was commanded. Howard turned to the left, and charged up the hill, and captured it before the enemy had time to intrench, taking many prisoners. Leaving sufficient men to hold this height, he pushed on to reënforce Geary. Before he got up, Geary had been engaged for about three hours against a vastly superior force. The night was so dark that the men could not distinguish one another except by the light of the flashes of their muskets. In the darkness and uproar Hooker's teamsters became frightened, and deserted their teams. The mules also became frightened, and, breaking loose from their fastenings, stampeded directly toward the enemy. The latter no doubt took this for a charge, and stampeded in turn. By 4 o'clock in the morning the battle had entirely ceased, and our "cracker line" was never afterward disturbed.

In securing possession of Lookout Valley, Smith lost one man killed and four or five wounded. The enemy lost most of his pickets at the ferry by capture. In the night engagement of the 28th–29th Hooker lost 416 killed and wounded. I never knew the loss of the enemy, but our troops buried over 150 of his dead, and captured more than 100.

Having got the Army of the Cumberland in a comfortable position, I now began to look after the remainder of my new command. Burnside was in about as desperate a condition as the Army of the Cumberland had been, only he was not yet besieged. He was a hundred miles from the nearest possible base, Big South Fork of the Cumberland River, and much farther from any railroad we had possession of. The roads back were over mountains, and all supplies along the line had long since been exhausted. His animals, too, had been starved, and their carcasses lined the road from Cumberland Gap, and far back toward Lexington, Kentucky. East Tennessee still furnished supplies of beef, bread, and forage, but it did not supply ammunition, clothing, medical supplies, or small rations, such as coffee, sugar, salt, and rice.

Stopping to organize his new command, Sherman had started from Memphis for Corinth on the 11th of October. His instructions required him to repair the road in his rear in order to bring up supplies. The distance was about 330 miles through a hostile country. His entire command could not have maintained the road if it had been completed. The bridges had all been destroyed by the enemy and much other damage done; a hostile community lived along the road; guerrilla bands infested the country, and more or less of the cavalry of the enemy was still in the west. Often Sherman's work was destroyed as soon as completed, though he was only a short distance away.

The Memphis and Charleston road strikes the Tennessee River at Eastport, Mississippi. Knowing the difficulty Sherman would have to supply himself from Memphis, I had previously ordered supplies sent from St. Louis on small steamers, to be convoyed by the navy, to meet him at Eastport. These he got. I now ordered him to discontinue his work of repairing roads, and to move on with his whole force to Stevenson, Alabama, without delay. This order was borne to Sherman by a messenger who paddled down the Tennessee in a canoe, and floated over Muscle Shoals; it was delivered at Iuka on the 27th. In this Sherman was notified that the rebels were moving a force toward Cleveland, east Tennessee, and might be going to Nashville, in which

455

event his troops were in the best position to beat them there. Sherman, with his characteristic promptness, abandoned the work he was engaged upon and pushed on at once. On the 1st of November he crossed the Tennessee at Eastport, and that day was in Florence, Alabama, with the head of column, while his troops were still crossing at Eastport, with Blair bringing up the rear.

Sherman's force made an additional army, with cavalry, artillery, and trains, all to be supplied by the single-track road from Nashville. All indications pointed also to the probable necessity of supplying Burnside's command, in east Tennessee, 25,000 more, by the same road. A single track could not do this. I therefore gave an order to Sherman to halt General G. M. Dodge's command of eight thousand men at Athens, and subsequently directed the latter to arrange his troops along the railroad from Decatur, north toward Nashville, and to rebuild that road. The road from Nashville to Decatur passes over a broken country, cut up with innumerable streams, many of them of considerable width, and with valleys far below the road-bed. All the bridges over these had been destroyed and the rails taken up and twisted by the enemy. All the locomotives and cars not carried off had been destroyed as effectually as they knew how to destroy them. All bridges and culverts had been destroyed between Nashville and Decatur, and thence to Stevenson, where the Memphis and Charleston and the Nashville and Chattanooga roads unite. The rebuilding of this road would give us two roads as far as Stevenson over which to supply the army. From Bridgeport, a short distance farther east, the river supplements the road.

General Dodge, besides being a most capable soldier, was an experienced railroad builder. He had no tools to work with except those of the pioneers —axes, picks, and spades. With these he was able to intrench his men and protect them against surprises by small parties of the enemy. As he had no base of supplies until the road could be completed back to Nashville, the first matter to consider, after protecting his men, was the getting in of food and forage from the surrounding country. He had his men and teams bring in all the grain they could find, or all they needed, and all the cattle for beef, and such other food as could be found. Millers were detailed from the ranks to run the mills along the line of the army; when these were not near enough to the troops for protection, they were taken down and moved up to the line of the road. Blacksmith shops, with all the iron and steel found in them, were moved up in like manner. Blacksmiths were detailed and set to work making the tools necessary in railroad and bridge building. Axemen were put to work getting out timber for bridges, and cutting fuel for the locomotives when the road should be completed; car-builders were set to work repairing the locomotives and cars. Thus every branch of railroad-building, making tools to work with, and supplying the workingmen with food, was all going on at once, and without the aid of a mechanic or laborer except what the command itself furnished. But rails and cars the men could not make without material, and

456

there was not enough rolling stock to keep the road we already had worked to its full capacity. There were no rails except those in use. To supply these deficiencies I ordered eight of the ten engineers General McPherson had at Vicksburg to be sent to Nashville, and all the cars he had, except ten. I also ordered the troops in west Tennessee to points on the river and on the Memphis and Charleston road, and ordered the cars, locomotives, and rails from all the railroads, except the Memphis and Charleston, to Nashville. The military manager of railroads, also, was directed to furnish more rolling stock, and, as far as he could, bridge material. General Dodge had the work assigned him finished within forty days after receiving his orders. The number of bridges to rebuild was 182, many of them over deep and wide chasms. The length of road repaired was 182 miles.

The enemy's troops, which it was thought were either moving against Burnside or were going to Nashville, went no farther than Cleveland. Their presence there, however, alarmed the authorities at Washington, and on account of our helpless condition at Chattanooga caused me much uneasiness. Dispatches were constantly coming, urging me to do something for Burnside's relief; calling attention to the importance of holding east Tennessee; saying the President was much concerned for the protection of the loyal people in that section, etc. We had not at Chattanooga animals to pull a single piece of artillery, much less a supply train. Reënforcements could not help Burnside, because he had neither supplies nor ammunition sufficient for them; hardly indeed bread and meat for the men he had. There was no relief possible for him, except by expelling the enemy from Missionary Ridge and about Chattanooga.

On the 4th of November Longstreet left our front with about 15,000 troops, besides Wheeler's cavalry, 5000 more, to go against Burnside. The situation seemed desperate, and was more exasperating because nothing could be done until Sherman should get up. The authorities at Washington were now more than ever anxious for the safety of Burnside's army, and plied me with dispatches faster than ever, urging that something should be done for his relief. On the 7th, before Longstreet could possibly have reached Knoxville, I ordered Gen. Thomas peremptorily to attack the enemy's right so as to force the return of the troops that had gone up the valley. I directed him to take mules, officers' horses, or animals wherever he could get them, to move the necessary artillery. But he persisted in the declaration that he could not move a single piece of artillery, and could not see how he could possibly comply with the order. Nothing was left to be done but to answer Washington dispatches as best I could, urge Sherman forward, although he was making every effort to get forward, and encourage Burnside to hold on, assuring him that in a short time he would be relieved. All of Burnside's dispatches showed the greatest confidence in his ability to hold his position as long as his ammunition should hold out. He even suggested the propriety of

457

abandoning the territory he held south and west of Knoxville, so as to draw the enemy farther from his base, and to make it more difficult for him to get back to Chattanooga when the battle should begin. Longstreet had a railroad as far as Loudon; but from there to Knoxville he had to rely on wagon trains. Burnside's suggestion, therefore, was a good one, and it was adopted. On the 14th I telegraphed him:

Sherman's advance has reached Bridgeport. His whole force will be ready to move from there by Tuesday at furthest. If you can hold Longstreet in check until he gets up, or, by skirmishing and falling back, can avoid serious loss to yourself, and gain time, I will be able to force the enemy back from here, and place a force between Longstreet and Bragg that must inevitably make the former take to the mountain-passes by every available road, to get to his supplies. Sherman would have been here before this but for the high water in Elk River driving him some thirty miles up the river to cross.

Longstreet, for some reason or other, stopped at Loudon until the 13th. That being the terminus of his railroad communications, it is probable he was directed to remain there awaiting orders. He was in a position threatening Knoxville, and at the same time where he could be brought back speedily to Chattanooga. The day after Longstreet left Loudon, Sherman reached Bridgeport in person, and proceeded on to see me that evening, the 14th, and reached Chattanooga the next day.

My orders for the battle were all prepared in advance of Sherman's arrival, except the dates, which could not be fixed while troops to be engaged were so far away. The possession of Lookout Mountain was of no special advantage to us now. Hooker was instructed to send Howard's corps to the north side of the Tennessee, thence up behind the hills on the north side, and to go into camp opposite Chattanooga; with the remainder of the command Hooker was, at a time to be afterward appointed, to ascend the western slope between the upper and lower palisades, and so get into Chattanooga Valley.

The plan of battle was for Sherman to attack the enemy's right flank, form a line across it, extend our left over South Chickamauga River, so as to threaten or hold the railroad in Bragg's rear, and thus force him either to weaken his lines elsewhere or lose his connection with his base at Chickamauga Station. Hooker was to perform like service on our right. His problem was to get from Lookout Valley to Chattanooga Valley in the most expeditious way possible; cross the latter valley rapidly to Rossville, south of Bragg's line on Missionary Ridge, form line there across the ridge, facing north, with his right flank extended to Chickamauga Valley east of the ridge, thus threatening the enemy's rear on that flank and compelling him to reën-force this also. Thomas, with the Army of the Cumberland, occupied the center, and was to assault while the enemy was engaged with most of his forces on his two flanks.

458

To carry out this plan, Sherman was to cross the Tennessee at Brown's Ferry and move east of Chattanooga to a point opposite the north end of Missionary Ridge, and to place his command back of the foot-hills out of sight of the enemy on the ridge. There are two streams called Chickamauga emptying into the Tennessee River east of Chattanooga: North Chickamauga, taking its rise in Tennesee, flowing south and emptying into the river some seven or eight miles east; while the South Chickamauga, which takes its rise in Georgia, flows northward, and empties into the Tennessee some three or four miles above the town. There were now 116 pontoons in the North Chickamauga River, their presence there being unknown to the enemy.

At night a division was to be marched up to that point, and at 2 o'clock in the morning moved down with the current, thirty men in each boat. A few were to land east of the mouth of the South Chickamauga, capture the pickets there, and then lay a bridge connecting the two banks of the river. The rest were to land on the south side of the Tennessee, where Missionary Ridge would strike it if prolonged, and a sufficient number of men to man the boats were to push to the north side to ferry over the main body of Sherman's command, while those left on the south side intrenched themselves. Thomas was to move out from his lines facing the ridge, leaving enough of Palmer's corps to guard against an attack down the valley. Lookout Valley being of no present value to us, and being untenable by the enemy if we should secure Missionary Ridge, Hooker's orders were changed. His revised orders brought him to Chattanooga by the established route north of the Tennessee. He was then to move out to the right to Rossville.

The next day after Sherman's arrival I took him, with Generals Thomas and Smith and other officers, to the north side of the river and showed them the ground over which Sherman had to march, and pointed out generally what he was expected to do. I, as well as the authorities in Washington, was still in a great state of anxiety for Burnside's safety. Burnside himself, I believe, was the only one who did not share in this anxiety. Nothing could be done for him, however, until Sherman's troops were up. As soon, therefore, as the inspection was over, Sherman started for Bridgeport to hasten matters, rowing a boat himself, I believe, from Kelley's Ferry. Sherman had left Bridgeport the night of the 14th, reached Chattanooga the evening of the 15th, made the above-described inspection the morning of the 16th, and started back the same evening to hurry up his command, fully appreciating the importance of time.

His march was conducted with as much expedition as the roads and season would admit of. By the 20th he was himself at Brown's Ferry with head of column, but many of his troops were far behind, and one division, Ewing's, was at Trenton, sent that way to create the impression that Lookout was to be taken from the south. Sherman received his orders at the ferry, and was asked if he could not be ready for the assault the following morning. News

459

had been received that the battle had been commenced at Knoxville. Burnside had been cut off from telegraphic communication. The President, the Secretary of War, and General Halleck were in an agony of suspense. My suspense was also great, but more endurable, because I was where I could soon do something to relieve the situation. It was impossible to get Sherman's troops up for the next day. I then asked him if they could not be got up to make the assault on the morning of the 22d, and ordered Thomas to move on that date. But the elements were against us. It rained all the 20th and 21st. The river rose so rapidly that it was difficult to keep the pontoons in place.

General Orlando B. Willcox, a division commander under Burnside, was at this time occupying a position farther up the valley than Knoxville—about Maynardsville—and was still in telegraphic communication with the North. A dispatch was received from him, saying that he was threatened from the east. The following was sent in reply:

If you can communicate with General Burnside, say to him that our attack on Bragg will commence in the morning. If successful, such a move will be made as, I think, will relieve east Tennessee, if he can hold out. Longstreet passing through our lines to Kentucky need not cause alarm. He would find the country so bare that he would lose his transportation and artillery before reaching Kentucky, and would meet such a force before he got through that he could not return.

Meantime Sherman continued his crossing, without intermission, as fast as his troops could be got up. The crossing had to be effected in full view of the enemy on the top of Lookout Mountain. Once over, the troops soon disappeared behind the detached hills on the north side, and could not come to view again, either to watchmen on Lookout Mountain or Missionary Ridge, until they emerged between the hills to strike the bank of the river. But when Sherman's advance reached a point opposite the town of Chattanooga, Howard, who, it will be remembered, had been concealed behind the hills on the north side, took up his line of march to join the troops on the south side. His crossing was in full view both from Missionary Ridge and the top of Lookout, and the enemy, of course, supposed these troops to be Sherman's. This enabled Sherman to get to his assigned position without discovery.

On the 20th, when so much was occurring to discourage—rains falling so heavily as to delay the passage of troops over the river at Brown's Ferry, and threatening the entire breaking of the bridge; news coming of a battle raging at Knoxville; of Willcox being threatened by a force from the east—a letter was received from Bragg which contained these words:

As there may still be some non-combatants in Chattanooga, I deem it proper to notify you that prudence would dictate their early withdrawal.

Of course I understood that this was a device intended to deceive; but I did not know what the intended deception was. On the 22d, however, a deserter came in who informed me that Bragg was leaving our front, and on that day Buckner's division was sent to reënforce Longstreet, at Knoxville, and another division started to follow, but was recalled. The object of Bragg's letter no doubt was in some way to detain me until Knoxville could be captured, and his troops there be returned to Chattanooga.

During the night of the 21st the rest of the pontoon-boats, completed, one hundred and sixteen in all, were carried up to and placed in North Chickamauga. The material for the roadway over these was deposited out of view of the enemy within a few hundred yards of the bank of the Tennessee where the north end of the bridge was to rest.

Hearing nothing from Burnside, and hearing much of the distress in Washington on his account, I could no longer defer operations for his relief. I determined therefore to do on the 23d, with the Army of the Cumberland, what had been intended to be done on the 24th.

The position occupied by the Army of the Cumberland had been made very strong for defense during the months it had been besieged. The line was about a mile from the town, and extended from Citico Creek, a small stream running near the base of Missionary Ridge and emptying into the Tennessee about two miles below the mouth of the South Chickamauga, on the left, to Chattanooga Creek on the right. All commanding points on the line were well fortified and well equipped with artillery. The important elevations within the line had all been carefully fortified and supplied with a proper armament. Among the elevations so fortified was one to the east of the town, named Fort Wood. It owed its importance chiefly to the fact that it lay between the town and Missionary Ridge, where most of the strength of the enemy was. Fort Wood had in it twenty-two pieces of artillery, most of which would reach the nearer points of the enemy's line. On the morning of the 23d Thomas, according to instructions, moved Granger's corps of two divisions, Sheridan and T. J. Wood commanding, to the foot of Fort Wood, and formed them into line as if going on parade—Sheridan on the right, Wood to the left, extending to or near Citico Creek. Palmer, commanding the Fourteenth Corps, held that part of our line facing south and south-west. He supported Sheridan with one division, Baird's, while his other division, under [R. W.] Johnson, remained in the trenches, under arms, ready to be moved to any point. Howard's corps was moved in rear of the center. The picket lines were within a few hundred yards of each other. At 2 o'clock in the afternoon all were ready to advance. By this time the clouds had lifted so that the enemy could see from his elevated position all that was going on. The signal for advance was given by a booming of cannon from Fort Wood and other points on the line. The rebel pickets were soon driven back upon the main guards, which occupied minor and detached heights between the main ridge and our

461

lines. These too were carried before halting, and before the enemy had time to reënforce their advance guards. But it was not without loss on both sides. This movement secured to us a line fully a mile in advance of the one we occupied in the morning, and one which the enemy had occupied up to this time. The fortifications were rapidly turned to face the other way. During the following night they were made strong. We lost in this preliminary action about eleven hundred killed and wounded, while the enemy probably lost quite as heavily, including the prisoners that were captured. With the exception of the firing of artillery, kept up from Missionary Ridge and Fort Wood until night closed in, this ended the fighting for the day.

The advantage was greatly on our side now, and if I could only have been assured that Burnside could hold out ten days longer I should have rested more easy. But we were doing the best we could for him and the cause.

By the night of the 23d Sherman's command was in a position to move, though one division (Osterhaus's) had not yet crossed the river at Brown's Ferry. The continuous rise in the Tennessee had rendered it impossible to keep the bridge at that point in condition for troops to cross; but I was determined to move that night, even without this division. Accordingly, orders were sent to Osterhaus to report to Hooker if he could not cross by 8 o'clock on the morning of the 24th. Because of the break in the bridge, Hooker's orders were again changed, but this time only back to those first given to him.

General W. F. Smith had been assigned to duty as chief engineer of the military division. To him was given the general direction of moving troops by the boats from North Chickamauga, laying the bridge after they reached their position, and, generally, all the duties pertaining to his office of chief engineer. During the night General Morgan L. Smith's division was marched to the point where the pontoons were, and the brigade of Giles A. Smith was selected for the delicate duty of manning the boats and surprising the enemy's pickets on the south bank of the river. During this night, also, General J. M. Brannan, chief of artillery, moved forty pieces of artillery belonging to the Army of the Cumberland, and placed them on the north side of the river so as to command the ground opposite, to aid in protecting the approach to the point where the south end of the bridge was to rest. He had to use Sherman's artillery horses for this purpose, Thomas having none.

At 2 o'clock in the morning, November 24th, Giles A. Smith pushed out from the North Chickamauga with his 116 boats, each loaded with 30 brave and well-armed men. The boats, with their precious freight, dropped down quietly with the current to avoid attracting the attention of any one who could convey information to the enemy, until arriving near the mouth of South Chickamauga. Here a few boats were landed, the troops debarked, and a rush was made upon the picket-guard known to be at that point. The guard was surprised, and twenty of their number captured. The remainder of the troops effected a landing at the point where the bridge was to start, with equally good results. The work of ferrying over Sherman's command from the north side of the Tennessee was at once commenced, using the pontoons for the purpose. A steamer was also brought up from the town to assist. The rest of M. L. Smith's division came first, then the division of John E. Smith. The troops as they landed were put to work intrenching their position. By daylight the two entire divisions were over, and well covered by the works they had built.

The work of laying the bridge on which to cross the artillery and cavalry was now begun. The ferrying over the infantry was continued with the steamer and the pontoons, taking the pontoons, however, as fast as they were wanted to put in their place in the bridge. By a little past noon the bridge was completed, as well as one over the South Chickamauga, connecting the troops left on that side with their comrades below, and all the infantry and artillery were on the south bank of the Tennessee.

Sherman at once formed his troops for assault on Missionary Ridge. By 1 o'clock he started, with M. L. Smith on his left, keeping nearly the course of Chickamauga River; J. E. Smith next, to the right and a little in the rear; then Ewing, still farther to the right, and also a little to the rear of J. E. Smith's command, in column ready to deploy to the right if an enemy should come from that direction. A good skirmish line preceded each of these columns. Soon the foot of the hill was reached; the skirmishers pushed directly up, followed closely by their supports. By half-past 3 Sherman was in possession of the height, without having sustained much loss. A brigade from each division was now brought up, and artillery was dragged to the top of the hill by hand. The enemy did not seem to have been aware of this movement until the top of the hill was gained. There had been a drizzling rain during the day, and the clouds were so low that Lookout Mountain and the top of Missionary Ridge were obscured from the view of persons in the valley. But now the enemy opened fire upon their assailants, and made several attempts with their skirmishers to drive them away, but without avail. Later in the day a more determined attack was made, but this, too, failed, and Sherman was left to fortify what he had gained.

Sherman's cavalry took up its line of march soon after the bridge was completed, and by half-past three the whole of it was over both bridges, and on its way to strike the enemy's communications at Chickamauga Station. All of Sherman's command was now south of the Tennessee. During the afternoon General Giles A. Smith was severely wounded and carried from the field.

Thomas having done on the 23d what was expected of him on the 24th, there was nothing for him to do this day, except to strengthen his position. Howard, however, effected a crossing of Citico Creek and a junction with Sherman, and was directed to report to him. With two or three regiments of his command, he moved in the morning along the banks of the Tennessee and reached the point where the bridge was being laid. He went out on the bridge as far as it was completed from the south end, and saw Sherman su-

463

perintending the work from the north side, moving himself south as fast as an additional boat was put in and the roadway put upon it. Howard reported to his new chief across the chasm between them, which was now narrow and in a few minutes was closed.

While these operations were going on to the east of Chattanooga, Hooker was engaged on the west. He had three divisions: Osterhaus's, of the Fifteenth Corps, Army of the Tennessee; Geary's, Twelfth Corps, Army of the Potomac; and Cruft's Fourteenth Corps, Army of the Cumberland. Geary was on the right at Wauhatchie, Cruft at the center, and Osterhaus near Brown's Ferry. These troops were all west of Lookout Creek. The enemy had the east bank of the creek strongly picketed and intrenched, and three brigades of troops in the rear to reënforce them if attacked. These brigades occupied the summit of the mountain. General Carter L. Stevenson was in command of the whole. Why any troops except artillery, with a small infantry guard, were kept on the mountain-top, I do not see. A hundred men could have held the summit—which is a palisade for more than thirty feet down—against the assault of any number of men from the position Hooker occupied.

The side of Lookout Mountain confronting Hooker's command was rugged, heavily timbered, and full of chasms, making it difficult to advance with troops, even in the absence of an opposing force. Farther up the ground becomes more even and level, and was in cultivation. On the east side the slope is much more gradual, and a good wagon road, zigzagging up it, connects the town of Chattanooga with the summit.

Early in the morning of the 24th Hooker moved Geary's division, supported by a brigade of Cruft's, up Lookout Creek, to effect a crossing. The remainder of Cruft's division was to seize the bridge over the creek, near the crossing of the railroad. Osterhaus was to move up to the bridge and cross it. The bridge was seized by Grose's brigade after a slight skirmish with the picket guarding it. This attracted the enemy so that Geary's movement farther up was not observed. A heavy mist obscured him from the view of the troops on the top of the mountain. He crossed the creek almost unobserved, and captured the picket of over forty men on guard near by. He then commenced ascending the mountain directly in his front. By this time the enemy was seen coming down from their camp on the mountain slope, and filing into their rifle-pits to contest the crossing of the bridge. By 11 o'clock the bridge was complete. Osterhaus was up, and after some sharp skirmishing the enemy was driven away, with considerable loss in killed and captured.

While the operations at the bridge were progressing, Geary was pushing up the hill over great obstacles, resisted by the enemy directly in his front, and in face of the guns on top of the mountain. The enemy, seeing their left flank and rear menaced, gave way and were followed by Cruft and Osterhaus. Soon these were up abreast of Geary, and the whole command pushed up the hill, driving the enemy in advance. By noon Geary had gained the open

464

ground on the north slope of the mountain with his right close up to the base of the upper palisade, but there were strong fortifications in his front. The rest of the command coming up, a line was formed from the base of the upper palisade to the mouth of Chattanooga Creek.

Thomas and I were on the top of Orchard Knob. Hooker's advance now made our line a continuous one. It was in full view extending from the Tennessee River, where Sherman had crossed, up Chickamauga River to the base of Missionary Ridge, over the top of the north end of the ridge, to Chattanooga Valley, then along parallel to the ridge a mile or more, across the valley to the mouth of Chattanooga Creek, thence up the slope of Lookout Mountain to the foot of the upper palisade. The day was hazy, so that Hooker's operations were not visible to us except at moments when the clouds would rise. But the sound of his artillery and musketry was heard incessantly. The enemy on his front was partially fortified, but was soon driven out of his works. At 2 o'clock the clouds, which had so obscured the top of Lookout all day as to hide whatever was going on from the view of those below, settled down and made it so dark where Hooker was as to stop operations for the time. At 4 o'clock Hooker reported his position as impregnable. By a little after 5, direct communication was established, and a brigade of troops was sent from Chattanooga to reënforce him. These troops had to cross Chattanooga Creek, and met with some opposition, but soon overcame it, and by night the commander, General Carlin, reported to Hooker and was assigned to his left. I now telegraphed to Washington:

The fight to-day progressed favorably. Sherman carried the end of Missionary Ridge, and his right is now at the tunnel, and his left at Chickamauga Creek. Troops from Lookout Valley carried the point of the mountain, and now hold the eastern slope and a point high up. Hooker reports two thousand prisoners taken, besides which a small number have fallen into our hands, from Missionary Ridge.

The next day the President replied:

Your dispatches as to fighting on Monday and Tuesday are here. Well done. Many thanks to all. Remember Burnside.

Halleck also telegraphed:

I congratulate you on the success thus far of your plans. I fear that Burnside is hard pushed, and that any further delay may prove fatal. I know you will do all in your power to relieve him.

The division of Jefferson C. Davis, Army of the Cumberland, had been sent to the North Chickamauga to guard the pontoons as they were deposited in the river, and to prevent all ingress or egress by citizens. On the night of the

465

24th his division, having crossed with Sherman, occupied our extreme left, from the upper bridge over the plain to the north base of Missionary Ridge. Firing continued to a late hour in the night, but it was not connected with an assault at any point.

At 12 o'clock at night, when all was quiet, I began to give orders for the next day, and sent a dispatch to Willcox to encourage Burnside. Sherman was directed to attack at daylight. Hooker was ordered to move at the same hour, and endeavor to intercept the enemy's retreat, if he still remained; if he had gone, then to move directly to Rossville and operate against the left and rear of the force on Missionary Ridge. Thomas was not to move until Hooker had reached Missionary Ridge. As I was with him on Orchard Knob, he would not move without further orders from me.

The morning of the 25th opened clear and bright, and the whole field was in full view from the top of Orchard Knob. It remained so all day. Bragg's headquarters were in full view, and officers—presumably staff-officers—could be seen coming and going constantly.

The point of ground which Sherman had carried on the 24th was almost disconnected from the main ridge occupied by the enemy. A low pass, over which there is a wagon road crossing the hill, and near which there is a railroad tunnel, intervenes between the two hills. The problem now was to get to the latter. The enemy was fortified on the point, and back farther, where the ground was still higher, was a second fortification commanding the first. Sherman was out as soon as it was light enough to see, and by sunrise his command was in motion. Three brigades held the hill already gained. Morgan L. Smith moved along the east base of Missionary Ridge; Loomis along the west base, supported by two brigades of John E. Smith's division; and Corse with his brigade was between the two, moving directly toward the hill to be captured. The ridge is steep and heavily wooded on the east side, where M. L. Smith's troops were advancing, but cleared and with a more gentle slope on the west side. The troops advanced rapidly and carried the extreme end of the rebel works. Morgan L. Smith advanced to a point which cut the enemy off from the railroad bridge and the means of bringing up supplies by rail from Chickamauga Station, where the main depot was located. The enemy made brave and strenuous efforts to drive our troops from the position we had gained, but without success. The contest lasted for two hours. Corse, a brave and efficient commander, was badly wounded in this assault. Sherman now threatened both Bragg's flank and his stores, and made it necessary for him to weaken other points of his line to strengthen his right. From the position I occupied I could see column after column of Bragg's forces moving against Sherman; every Confederate gun that could be brought to bear upon the Union forces was concentrated upon him. J. E. Smith, with two brigades, charged up the west side of the ridge to the support of Corse's command, over open ground, and in the face of a heavy fire of both artillery and musketry, and reached the very parapet of the enemy. He lay here for a time, but the enemy coming with a heavy force upon his right flank, he was compelled to fall back, followed by the foe. A few hundred yards brought Smith's troops into a wood, where they were speedily reformed, when they charged and drove the attacking party back to his intrenchments.

Seeing the advance, repulse, and second advance of J. E. Smith from the position I occupied, I directed Thomas to send a division to reënforce him. Baird's division was accordingly sent from the right of Orchard Knob. It had to march a considerable distance, directly under the eyes of the enemy, to reach its position. Bragg at once commenced massing in the same direction. This was what I wanted. But it had now got to be late in the afternoon, and I had expected before this to see Hooker crossing the ridge in the neighborhood of Rossville, and compelling Bragg to mass in that direction also.

The enemy had evacuated Lookout Mountain during the night, as I expected he would. In crossing the valley he burned the bridges over Chattanooga Creek, and did all he could to obstruct the roads behind him. Hooker was off bright and early, with no obstructions in his front but distance and the destruction above named. He was detained four hours in crossing Chattanooga Creek, and thus was lost the immediate advantages I expected from his forces. His reaching Bragg's flank and extending across it was to be the signal for Thomas's assault of the ridge. But Sherman's condition was getting so critical that the assault for his relief could not be delayed any longer.

Sheridan's and Wood's divisions had been lying under arms from early in the morning, ready to move the instant the signal was given. I now directed Thomas to order the charge at once. I watched eagerly to see the effect, and became impatient at last that there was no indication of any charge being made. The center of the line which was to make the charge was near where Thomas and I stood together, but concealed from our view by the intervening forest. Turning to Thomas to inquire what caused the delay, I was surprised to see General Thomas J. Wood, one of the division commanders who were to make the charge, standing talking to him. I spoke to General Wood, asking him why he had not charged, as ordered an hour before. He replied very promptly that this was the first he had heard of it, but that he had been ready all day to move at a moment's notice. I told him to make the charge at once. He was off in a moment, and in an incredibly short time loud cheering was heard, and he and Sheridan were driving the enemy's advance before them toward Missionary Ridge. The Confederates were strongly intrenched on the crest of the ridge in front of us, and had a second line half-way down and another at the base. Our men drove the troops in front of the lower line of rifle-pits so rapidly, and followed them so closely, that rebel and Union troops went over the first line of works almost at the same time. Many rebels were captured and sent to the rear under the fire of their own friends higher up the hill. Those that were not captured retreated, and were pursued. The retreating hordes being between friends and pursuers, caused the enemy to fire high, to avoid killing their own men. In fact, on that occasion the Union soldier nearest the enemy was in the safest position. Without awaiting further orders or stopping to re-form, on our troops went to the second line of works; over that and on for the crest—thus effectually carrying out my orders of the 18th for the battle and of the 24th for this charge. I watched their progress with intense interest. The fire along the rebel line was terrific. Cannon and musket balls filled the air; but the damage done was in small proportion to the ammunition used. The pursuit continued until the crest was reached, and soon our men were seen climbing over the Confederate barrier at different points in front of both Sheridan's and Wood's divisions. The retreat of the enemy along most of his line was precipitate, and the panic so great that Bragg and his officers lost all control over their men. Many were captured and thousands threw away their arms in their flight.

Sheridan pushed forward until he reached the Chickamauga River at a point above where the enemy had crossed. He met some resistance from troops occupying a second hill in rear of Missionary Ridge, probably to cover the retreat of the main body and of the artillery and trains. It was now getting dark, but Sheridan, without halting on that account, pushed his men forward up this second hill slowly and without attracting the attention of the men placed to defend it, while he detached to the right and left to surround the position. The enemy discovered the movement before these dispositions were complete, and beat a hasty retreat, leaving artillery, wagon trains, and many prisoners in our hands. To Sheridan's prompt movement the Army of the Cumberland and the nation are indebted for the bulk of the capture of prisoners, artillery, and small-arms that day. Except for his prompt pursuit, so much in this way would not have been accomplished.

While the advance up Missionary Ridge was going forward, General Thomas, with his staff, General Gordon Granger, commander of the corps, making the assault, and myself and staff, occupied Orchard Knob, from which the entire field could be observed. The moment the troops were seen going over the last line of rebel defenses I ordered Granger to join his command, and mounting my horse I rode to the front. General Thomas left about the same time. Sheridan, on the extreme right, was already in pursuit of the enemy east of the ridge. Wood, who commanded the division to the left of Sheridan, accompanied his men on horseback, but did not join Sheridan in the pursuit. To the left, in Baird's front, where Bragg's troops had massed against Sherman, the resistance was more stubborn, and the contest lasted longer. I ordered Granger to follow the enemy with Wood's division, but he was so much excited, and kept up such a roar of musketry, in the direction the enemy had taken, that by the time I could stop the firing the enemy had got well out of the way. The enemy confronting Sherman, now seeing everything to their left giving away, fled also. Sherman, however, was not aware of the extent of our success until after nightfall, when he received orders to pursue at daylight in the morning.

Hooker, as stated, was detained at Chattanooga Creek by the destruction of the bridges at that point. He got his troops over, with the exception of the artillery, by fording the stream, at a little after 3 o'clock. Leaving his artillery to follow when the bridges should be reconstructed, he pushed on with the remainder of his command. At Rossville he came upon the flank of a division of the enemy, which soon commenced a retreat along the ridge. This threw them on Palmer. They could make but little resistance in the position they were caught in, and as many of them as could do so escaped. Many, however, were captured. Hooker's position during the night of the 25th was near Rossville, extending east of the ridge. Palmer was on his left, on the road to Graysville.

During the night I telegraphed to Willcox that Bragg had been defeated, and that immediate relief would be sent to Burnside if he could hold out; to Halleck I sent an announcement of our victory, and informed him that forces would be sent up the valley to relieve Burnside.

Before the battle of Chattanooga opened I had taken measures for the relief of Burnside the moment the way should be clear. Thomas was directed to have the little steamer that had been built at Chattanooga loaded to its capacity with rations and ammunition. Granger's corps was to move by the south bank of the Tennessee River to the mouth of the Holston, and up that to Knoxville, accompanied by the boat. In addition to the supplies transported by boat, the men were to carry forty rounds of ammunition in their cartridge-boxes, and four days' rations in haversacks.

In the battle of Chattanooga, troops from the Army of the Potomac, from the Army of the Tennessee, and from the Army of the Cumberland participated. In fact, the accidents growing out of the heavy rains and the sudden rise in the Tennessee River so mingled the troops that the organizations were not kept together, under their respective commanders, during the battle. Hooker, on the right, had Geary's division of the Twelfth Corps, Army of the Potomac; Osterhaus's division of the Fifteenth Corps, Army of the Tennessee; and Cruft's division of the Army of the Cumberland. Sherman had three divisions of his own army, Howard's corps from the Army of the Potomac, and Jeff. C. Davis's division of the Army of the Cumberland. There was no jealousy—hardly rivalry. Indeed I doubt whether officers or men took any note at the time of this intermingling of commands. All saw a defiant foe surrounding them, and took it for granted that every move was intended to dislodge him, and it made no difference where the troops came from so that the end was accomplished.

The victory at Chattanooga was won against great odds, considering the advantage the enemy had of position; and was accomplished more easily than was expected by reason of Bragg's making several grave mistakes: first, in sending away his ablest corps commander, with over 20,000 troops; second, in sending away a division of troops on the eve of battle; third, in placing so much of a force on the plain in front of his impregnable position.

It was known that Mr. Davis had visited Bragg on Missionary Ridge a short time before my reaching Chattanooga. It was reported and believed that he had come out to reconcile a serious difference between Bragg and Longstreet, and finding this difficult to do planned the campaign against Knoxville, to be conducted by the latter general. I had known both Bragg and Longstreet before the war, the latter very well. We had been three years at West Point together, and, after my graduation, for a time in the same regiment. Then we served together in the Mexican war. I had known Bragg in Mexico, and met him occasionally subsequently. I could well understand how there might be an irreconcilable difference between them.

Bragg was a remarkably intelligent and well-informed man, professionally and otherwise. He was also thoroughly upright. But he was possessed of an irascible temper, and was naturally disputatious. A man of the highest moral character and the most correct habits, yet in the old army he was in frequent trouble. As a subordinate he was always on the lookout to catch his commanding officer infringing upon his prerogatives; as a post commander he was equally vigilant to detect the slightest neglect, even of the most trivial order.

I heard in the old army an anecdote characteristic of General Bragg. On one occasion, when stationed at a post of several companies, commanded by a field-officer, he was himself commanding one of the companies and at the same time acting post quartermaster and commissary. He was a first lieutenant at the time, but his captain was detached on other duty. As commander of the company he made a requisition upon the quartermaster—himself—for something he wanted. As quartermaster he declined to fill the requisition, and indorsed on the back of it his reason for so doing. As company commander he responded to this, urging that his requisition called for nothing but what he was entitled to, and that it was the duty of the quartermaster to fill it. As quartermaster he still persisted that he was right. In this condition of affairs Bragg referred the whole matter to the commanding officer of the post. The latter, when he saw the nature of the matter referred, exclaimed: "My God, Mr. Bragg, you have quarreled with every officer in the army, and now you are quarreling with yourself."

Longstreet was an entirely different man. He was brave, honest, intelligent, a very capable soldier, subordinate to his superior, just and kind to his subordinates, but jealous of his own rights, which he had the courage to maintain. He was never on the lookout to detect a slight, but saw one as soon as anybody when intentionally given.

It may be that Longstreet was not sent to Knoxville for the reason stated, but because Mr. Davis had an exalted opinion of his own military genius, and thought he saw a chance of "killing two birds with one stone." On several occasions during the war he came to the relief of the Union army by means of his *superior military genius.*

I speak advisedly when I say Mr. Davis prided himself on his military capacity. He says so himself virtually, in his answer to the notice of his nomination to the Confederate Presidency. Some of his generals have said so in their writings since the downfall of the Confederacy. Whatever the cause or whoever is to blame, grave mistakes were made at Chattanooga, which enabled us, with the undaunted courage of the troops engaged, to gain a great victory, under the most trying circumstances presented during the war, much more easily than could otherwise have been attained. If Chattanooga had been captured, east Tennessee would have followed without a struggle. It would have been a victory to have got the army away from Chattanooga safely. It was manifold greater to defeat, and nearly destroy, the besieging army.

In this battle the Union army numbered in round figures about 60,000 men; we lost 752 killed, and 4713 wounded and 350 captured or missing. The rebel loss was much greater in the aggregate, as we captured, and sent North to be rationed there, over 6100 prisoners. Forty pieces of artillery, over seven thousand stand of small-arms, and many caissons, artillery wagons, and baggage wagons fell into our hands. The probabilities are that our loss in killed was the heavier, as we were the attacking party. The enemy reported his loss in killed at 361; but as he reported his missing at 4146, while we held over 6000 of them as prisoners, and there must have been hundreds, if not thousands, who deserted, but little reliance can be placed in this report. There was certainly great dissatisfaction with Bragg, on the part of the soldiers, for his harsh treatment of them, and a disposition to get away if they could. Then, too, Chattanooga following in the same half-year with Gettysburg in the East, and Vicksburg in the West, there was much the same feeling in the South at this time that there had been in the North the fall and winter before. If the same license had been allowed the people and the press in the South that was allowed in the North, Chattanooga would probably have been the last battle fought for the preservation of the Union.

Bragg's army now being in full retreat, the relief of Burnside's position at Knoxville was a matter for immediate consideration. Sherman marched with a portion of the Army of the Tennessee, and one corps of the Army of the Cumberland, toward Knoxville; but his approach caused Longstreet to abandon the siege long before these troops reached their destination. Knoxville was now relieved; the anxiety of the President was removed, and the loyal portion of the North rejoiced over the double victory: the raising of the siege of Knoxville and the victory at Chattanooga.

After Chattanooga the rank of Lieutenant General was revived (Washington had been the last to hold it) and bestowed by a grateful Congress upon Ulysses Grant, along with the supreme command of all the Union armies. Turning his Military Division of the Mississippi over to General Sherman, he hurried to Washington, for it was March with the campaigning season at hand. There he issued orders for the simultaneous advance of all the key Union armies: Sherman toward Atlanta and the forces of Joe Johnston, who had succeeded Bragg; Ben Butler up the Peninsula toward Richmond; Sigel down the Shenandoah Valley to deprive Lee of that granary; Banks toward Mobile; and Meade, with Grant himself, toward Richmond and the Army of Northern Virginia. Banks could not disengage himself from the Red River campaign in time, and Sigel suffered an early setback in the Valley. But the other three Federal armies moved on schedule—the first time in the war that Union movements had been coördinated.

Early in May, Grant and Meade crossed the Rapidan River with the Army of the Potomac and slid around Lee's right flank, provoking the first of a month-long series of battles near the place where Hooker had been turned back the previous year almost to the day. Some of these battles were among the bloodiest of the war, provoking at the time considerable criticism of Grant's tactics in both North and South. But as subsequent events revealed, they decimated Lee's ranks, which could no longer be refilled by conscription or otherwise; and they took a terrible toll in general officers—including the hard-fighting "Jeb" Stuart. In that one month alone, Freeman tells us, Lee lost twenty-two generals out of the fifty-eight originally present in his command—over 36 per cent! Such men were well-nigh irreplaceable. Although the North grumbled and the South reviled the new commander in chief, one of Lee's own officers acknowledged that in his plodding and pounding "we began to understand that Grant had taken hold of the problem of destroying the Confederate strength in the only way that the strength of such an army, so commanded, could be destroyed."

"A half-dozen take the place of every one we kill"

FROM THE WILDERNESS TO COLD HARBOR

BY E. M. LAW, MAJOR-GENERAL, C. S. A.

O N THE 2d of May, 1864, a group of officers stood at the Confederate signal station on Clark's Mountain, Virginia, south of the Rapidan, and examined closely through their field-glasses the position of the Federal army then lying north of the river in Culpeper county. The central figure of the group was the commander of the Army of Northern Virginia, who had requested his corps and division commanders to meet him there. Though some demonstrations had been made in the direction of the upper fords, General Lee expressed the opinion that the Federal army would cross the river at Germanna or Ely's. Thirty-six hours later General Meade's army, General Grant, now commander-in-chief, being with it, commenced its march to the crossings indicated by General Lee.

The Army of the Potomac, which had now commenced its march toward Richmond, was more powerful in numbers than at any previous period of the war. It consisted of three corps: the Second (Hancock's), the Fifth (Warren's), and the Sixth (Sedgwick's); but the Ninth (Burnside's) acted with

473

Meade throughout the campaign. Meade's army was thoroughly equipped, and provided with every appliance of modern warfare. On the other hand, the Army of Northern Virginia had gained little in numbers during the winter just passed, and had never been so scantily supplied with food and clothing. The equipment as to arms was well enough for men who knew how to use them, but commissary and quartermasters' supplies were lamentably deficient. A new pair of shoes or an overcoat was a luxury, and full rations would have astonished the stomachs of Lee's ragged Confederates. But they took their privations cheerfully, and complaints were seldom heard. I recall an instance of one hardy fellow whose trousers were literally "worn to a frazzle" and would no longer adhere to his legs even by dint of the most persistent patching. Unable to buy, beg, or borrow another pair, he wore instead a pair of thin cotton drawers. By nursing these carefully he managed to get through the winter. Before the campaign opened in the spring a small lot of clothing was received, and he was the first man of his regiment to be supplied.

I have often heard expressions of surprise that these ragged, barefooted, half-starved men would fight at all. But the very fact that they remained with their colors through such privations and hardships was sufficient to prove that they would be dangerous foes to encounter upon the line of battle. The *morale* of the army at this time was excellent, and it moved forward confidently to the grim death-grapple in the wilderness of Spotsylvania with its old enemy, the Army of the Potomac.

General Lee's headquarters were two miles north-east of Orange Court House; of his three corps, Longstreet's was at Gordonsville, Ewell's was on and near the Rapidan, above Mine Run, and Hill's on his left, higher up the stream. When the Federal army was known to be in motion, General Lee prepared to move upon its flank with his whole force as soon as his opponent should clear the river and begin the march southward. The route selected by General Grant led entirely around the right of Lee's position on the river above. Grant's passage of the Rapidan was unopposed, and he struck boldly out on the direct road to Richmond. Two roads lead from Orange Court House down the Rapidan toward Fredericksburg. They follow the general direction of the river, and are almost parallel to each other, the "Old turnpike" nearest the river, and the "Plank road" a short distance south of it. The route of the Federal army lay directly across these two roads, along the western borders of the famous Wilderness.

About noon on the 4th of May, Ewell's corps was put in motion on and toward the Orange turnpike, while A. P. Hill, with two divisions, moved parallel with him on the Orange Plank road. The two divisions of Longstreet's corps encamped near Gordonsville were ordered to move rapidly across the country and follow Hill on the Plank road. Ewell's corps was the first to find itself in the presence of the enemy. As it advanced along the turnpike on the morning of the 5th, the Federal column was seen crossing it from the direction of Germanna Ford. Ewell promptly formed line of battle across the turnpike, and communicated his position to General Lee, who was on the Plank road with Hill. Ewell was instructed to regulate his movements by the head of Hill's column, whose progress he could tell by the firing in its front, and not to bring on a general engagement until Longstreet should come up. The position of Ewell's troops, so near the flank of the Federal line of march, was anything but favorable to a preservation of the peace, and a collision soon occurred which opened the campaign in earnest.

General Warren, whose corps was passing when Ewell came up, halted, and turning to the right made a vigorous attack upon Edward Johnson's division, posted across the turnpike. J. M. Jones's brigade, which held the road, was driven back in confusion. Steuart's brigade was pushed forward to take its place. Rodes's division was thrown in on Johnson's right, south of the road, and the line, thus reëstablished, moved forward, reversed the tide of battle, and rolled back the Federal attack. The fighting was severe and bloody while it lasted. At some points the lines were in such close proximity in the thick woods which covered the battle-field that when the Federal troops gave way several hundred of them, unable to retreat without exposure to almost certain death, surrendered themselves as prisoners.

Ewell's entire corps was now up—Johnson's division holding the turnpike, Rodes's division on the right of it, and Early's in reserve. So far Ewell had been engaged only with Warren's corps, but Sedgwick's soon came up from the river and joined Warren on his right. Early's division was sent to meet it. The battle extended in that direction, with steady and determined attacks upon Early's front, until nightfall. The Confederates still clung to their hold on the Federal flank against every effort to dislodge them.

When Warren's corps encountered the head of Ewell's column on the 5th of May, General Meade is reported to have said: "They have left a division to fool us here, while they concentrate and prepare a position on the North Anna." If the stubborn resistance to Warren's attack did not at once convince him of his mistake, the firing that announced the approach of Hill's corps along the Plank road, very soon afterward, must have opened his eyes to the bold strategy of the Confederate commander. General Lee had deliberately chosen this as his battle-ground. He knew this tangled wilderness well, and appreciated fully the advantages such a field afforded for concealing his great inferiority of force and for neutralizing the superior strength of his antagonist. General Grant's bold movement across the lower fords into the Wilderness, in the execution of his plan to swing past the Confederate army and place himself between it and Richmond, offered the expected opportunity of striking a blow upon his flank while his troops were stretched out on the line of march. The wish for such an opportunity was doubtless in a measure "father to the thought" expressed by General Lee three days before, at the signal station on Clark's Mountain.

Soon after Ewell became engaged on the Old turnpike, A. P. Hill's advance struck the Federal outposts on the Plank road at Parker's store, on the outskirts of the Wilderness. These were driven in and followed up to their line of battle, which was so posted as to cover the junction of the Plank road with the Stevensburg and Brock roads, on which the Federal army was moving toward Spotsylvania. The fight began between Getty's division of the Sixth Corps and Heth's division, which was leading A. P. Hill's column. Hancock's corps, which was already on the march for Spotsylvania by way of Chancellorsville, was at once recalled, and at 4 o'clock in the afternoon was ordered to drive Hill "out of the Wilderness." Cadmus Wilcox's division went to Heth's support, and Poague's battalion of artillery took position in a little clearing on the north side of the Plank road, in rear of the Confederate infantry. But there was little use for artillery on such a field. After the battle was fairly joined in the thickets in front, its fire might do as much damage to friend as to foe; so it was silent. It was a desperate struggle between the infantry of the two armies, on a field whose physical aspects were as grim and forbidding as the struggle itself. It was a battle of brigades and regiments rather than of corps and divisions. Officers could not see the whole length of their commands, and could tell whether the troops on their right and left were driving or being driven only by the sound of the firing. It was a fight at close quarters too, for as night came on, in those tangled thickets of stunted pine, sweet-gum, scrub-oak, and cedar, the approach of the opposing lines could be discerned only by the noise of their passage through the underbrush or the flashing of their guns. The usually silent Wilderness had suddenly become alive with the angry flashing and heavy roar of the musketry, mingled with the yells of the combatants as they swayed to and fro in the gloomy thickets. . . .

When the battle closed at 8 o'clock, General Lee sent an order to Longstreet to make a night march, so as to arrive upon the field at daylight the next morning. The latter moved at 1 A. M. of the 6th, but it was already daylight when he reached the Plank road at Parker's store, three miles in rear of Hill's battle-field. During the night the movements of troops and preparations for battle could be heard on the Federal line, in front of Heth's and Wilcox's divisions, which had so far sustained themselves against every attack by six divisions under General Hancock. But Heth's and Wilcox's men were thoroughly worn out. Their lines were ragged and irregular, with wide intervals, and in some places fronting in different directions. In the expectation that they would be relieved during the night, no effort was made to rearrange and strengthen them to meet the storm that was brewing.

As soon as it was light enough to see what little could be seen in that dark forest, Hancock's troops swept forward to the attack. The blow fell with greatest force upon Wilcox's troops south of the Orange Plank road. They made what front they could and renewed the fight, until, the attacking column overlapping the right wing, it gave way, and the whole line "rolled up" from the right and retired in disorder along the Plank road as far as the position of Poague's artillery, which now opened upon the attacking force. The Federals pressed their advantage and were soon abreast of the artillery on the opposite side, their bullets flying across the road among the guns where General Lee himself stood. For a while matters looked very serious for the Confederates. General Lee, after sending a messenger to hasten the march of Longstreet's troops and another to prepare the trains for a movement to the rear, was assisting in rallying the disordered troops and directing the fire of the artillery, when the head of Longstreet's corps appeared in double column, swinging down the Orange Plank road at a trot. In perfect order, ranks well closed, and no stragglers, those splendid troops came on, regardless of the confusion on every side, pushing their steady way onward like "a river in the sea" of confused and troubled human waves around them. Kershaw's division took the right of the road, and, coming into line under a heavy fire, moved obliquely to the right (south) to meet the Federal left, which had "swung round" in that direction. The Federals were checked in their sweeping advance and thrown back upon their front line of breastworks, where they made a stubborn stand. But Kershaw, urged on by Longstreet, charged with his whole command, swept his front, and captured the works.

Nearly at the same moment Field's division took the left of the road, with Gregg's brigade in front, Benning's behind it, Law's next, and Jenkins's following. As the Texans in the front line swept past the batteries where General Lee was standing, they gave a rousing cheer for "Marse Robert," who spurred his horse forward and followed them in the charge. When the men became aware that he was "going in" with them, they called loudly to him to go back. "We won't go on unless you go back," was the general cry. One of the men dropped to the rear, and taking the bridle turned the general's horse around, while General Gregg came up and urged him to do as the men wished. At that moment a member of his staff (Colonel Venable) directed his attention to General Longstreet, whom he had been looking for, and who was sitting on his horse near the Orange Plank road. With evident disappointment General Lee turned off and joined General Longstreet.

The ground over which Field's troops were advancing was open for a short distance, and fringed on its farther edge with scattered pines, beyond which began the Wilderness. The Federals were advancing through the pines with apparently resistless force, when Gregg's eight hundred Texans, regardless of numbers, flanks, or supports, dashed directly upon them. There was a terrific crash, mingled with wild yells, which settled down into a steady roar

477

of musketry. In less than ten minutes one-half of that devoted eight hundred were lying upon the field dead or wounded; but they had delivered a staggering blow and broken the force of the Federal advance. Benning's and Law's brigades came promptly to their support, and the whole swept forward together. The tide was flowing the other way. It ebbed and flowed many times that day, strewing the Wilderness with human wrecks. . . .

About 10 o'clock it was ascertained that the Federal left flank rested only a short distance south of the Orange Plank road, which offered a favorable opportunity for a turning movement in that quarter. General Longstreet at once moved Mahone's, Wofford's, Anderson's, and Davis's brigades, the whole under General Mahone, around this end of the Federal line. Forming at right angles to it, they attacked in flank and rear, while a general advance was made in front. So far the fight had been one of anvil and hammer. But this first display of tactics at once changed the face of the field. The Federal left wing was rolled up in confusion toward the Plank road and then back upon the Brock road.

This partial victory had been a comparatively easy one. The signs of demoralization and even panic among the troops of Hancock's left wing, who had been hurled back by Mahone's flank attack, were too plain to be mistaken by the Confederates, who believed that Chancellorsville was about to be repeated. General Longstreet rode forward and prepared to press his advantage. Jenkins's fresh brigade was moved forward on the Plank road to renew the attack, supported by Kershaw's division, while the flanking column was to come into position on its right. The latter were now in line south of the road and almost parallel to it. Longstreet and Kershaw rode with General Jenkins at the head of his brigade as it pressed forward, when suddenly the quiet that had reigned for some moments was broken by a few scattering shots on the north of the road, which were answered by a volley from Mahone's line on the south side. The firing in their front, and the appearance of troops on the road whom they failed to recognize as friends through the intervening timber, had drawn a single volley, which lost to them all the fruits of the splendid work they had just done. General Jenkins was killed and Longstreet seriously wounded by our own men. The troops who were following them faced quickly toward the firing and were about to return it; but when General Kershaw called out, "They are friends!" every musket was lowered, and the men dropped upon the ground to avoid the fire.

The head of the attack had fallen, and for a time the movements of the Confederates were paralyzed. Lee came forward and directed the dispositions for a new attack, but the change of commanders after the fall of Longstreet, and the resumption of the thread of operations, occasioned a delay of several hours, and then the tide had turned, and we received only hard knocks instead of victory. When at 4 o'clock an attack was made upon the

Federal line along the Brock road, it was found strongly fortified and stubbornly defended. The log breastworks had taken fire during the battle, and at one point separated the combatants by a wall of fire and smoke which neither could pass. Part of Field's division captured the works in their front, but were forced to relinquish them for want of support. Meanwhile Burnside's corps, which had reënforced Hancock during the day, made a vigorous attack on the north of the Orange Plank road. Law's (Alabama) and Perry's (Florida) brigades were being forced back, when, Heth's division coming to their assistance, they assumed the offensive, driving Burnside's troops beyond the extensive line of breastworks constructed previous to their advance.

The battles fought by Ewell on the Old turnpike and by A. P. Hill on the Plank road, on the 5th of May, were entirely distinct, no connected line existing between them. Connection was established with Ewell's right by Wilcox's division, after it had been relieved by Longstreet's troops on the morning of the 6th. While the battle was in progress on the Orange Plank road, on the 6th, an unsuccessful attempt was made to turn Ewell's left next the river, and heavy assaults were made upon the line of Early's division. So persistent were these attacks on the front of Pegram's brigade, that other troops were brought up to its support, but the men rejected the offer of assistance.

Late in the day General Ewell ordered a movement against the Federal right wing, similar to that by which Longstreet had "doubled up" Hancock's left in the morning. Two brigades, under General John B. Gordon, moved out of their works at sunset, and lapping the right of Sedgwick's corps made a sudden and determined attack upon it. Taken by surprise, the Federals were driven from a large portion of their works with the loss of six hundred prisoners—among them Generals Seymour and Shaler. Night closed the contest, and with it the battle of the Wilderness.

When Lee's army appeared on the flank of the Federal line of march on the 5th of May, General Grant had at once faced his adversary and endeavored to push him out of the way. Grant's strongest efforts had been directed to forcing back the Confederate advance on the Orange Plank road, which, if successful, would have enabled him to complete his plan of "swinging past" that army and placing himself between it and Richmond. On the other hand, Lee's principal effort had been to strike the head of Grant's column a crushing blow where it crossed the Plank road, in order to force it from its route and throw it in confusion back into the Wilderness. Both attempts had failed. What advantages had been gained by the two days' fighting remained with the Confederates. They held a position nearer the Federal line of march than when the battle began, and had inflicted losses incomparably heavier than they had themselves sustained. Both sides were now strongly intrenched, and neither could well afford to attack. And so the 7th of May

479

was spent in skirmishing, each waiting to see what the other would do. That night the race for Spotsylvania began. General Lee had been informed by "Jeb" Stuart of the movement of the Federal trains southward during the afternoon. After dark the noise of moving columns along the Brock road could be heard, and it was at once responded to by a similar movement on the part of Lee. The armies moved in parallel columns separated only by a short interval. Longstreet's corps (now commanded by R. H. Anderson) marched all night and arrived at Spotsylvania at 8 o'clock on the morning of the 8th, where the ball was already in motion. Stuart had thrown his cavalry across the Brock road to check the Federal advance, and as the Federal cavalry had failed to dislodge him, Warren's corps had been pushed forward to clear the way. Kershaw's, Humphreys's, and Law's brigades were at once sent to Stuart's assistance. The head of Warren's column was forced back and immediately commenced intrenching. Spotsylvania Court House was found occupied by Federal cavalry and artillery, which retired without a fight. The Confederates had won the race.

The troops on both sides were now rapidly arriving. Sedgwick's corps joined Warren's, and in the afternoon was thrown heavily against Anderson's right wing, which, assisted by the timely arrival of Ewell's corps, repulsed the attack with great slaughter. Hill's corps (now under command of General Early) did not arrive until the next morning, May 9th. General Lee's line now covered Spotsylvania Court House, with its left (Longstreet's corps) resting on the Po River, a small stream which flows on the south-west; Ewell's corps in the center, north of the Court House, and Hill's on the right, crossing the Fredericksburg road. These positions were generally maintained during the battles that followed, though brigades and divisions were often detached from their proper commands and sent to other parts of the field to meet pressing emergencies.

No engagement of importance took place on the 9th, which was spent in intrenching the lines and preparing places of refuge from the impending storm. But the 10th was "a field-day." Early in the morning it was found that Hancock's corps had crossed the Po above the point where the Confederate left rested, had reached the Shady Grove road, and was threatening our rear, as well as the trains which were in that direction on the Old Court House road leading to Louisa Court House. General Early was ordered from the right with Mahone's and Heth's divisions, and, moving rapidly to the threatened quarter, attacked Hancock's rear division as it was about to recross the Po—driving it, with severe loss, through the burning woods in its rear, back across the river.

Meanwhile General Grant was not idle elsewhere. He had commenced his efforts to break through the lines confronting him. The first assault was made upon Field's division of Longstreet's corps and met with a complete and bloody repulse. Again at 3 o'clock in the afternoon, the blue columns pressed forward to the attack, and were sent back torn and bleeding, leaving the ground covered with their dead and wounded. Anticipating a renewal of the assaults, many of our men went out in front of their breastworks, and, gathering up the muskets and cartridge-boxes of the dead and wounded, brought them in and distributed them along the line. If they did not have repeating-rifles, they had a very good substitute—several loaded ones to each man. They had no reserves, and knew that if they could not sufficiently reduce the number of their assailants to equalize matters somewhat before they reached the works, these might become untenable against such heavy and determined attacks.

A lull of several hours succeeded the failure of the second attack, but it was only a breathing spell preparatory to the culminating effort of the day. Near sunset our skirmishers were driven in and the heavy, dark lines of attack came into view, one after another, first in quick time, then in a trot, and then with a rush toward the works. The front lines dissolved before the pitiless storm that met them, but those in the rear pressed forward, and over their dead and dying comrades reached that portion of the works held by the Texas brigade. These gallant fellows, now reduced to a mere handful by their losses in the Wilderness, stood manfully to their work. Their line was bent backward by the pressure, but they continued the fight in rear of the works with bayonets and clubbed muskets. Fortunately for them, Anderson's brigade had cleared its own front, and a portion of it turned upon the flank of their assailants, who were driven out, leaving many dead and wounded inside the works.

While this attack was in progress on Field's line, another, quite as determined, was made farther to the right, in front of Rodes's division of Ewell's corps. Doles's brigade was broken and swept out of its works with the loss of three hundred prisoners. But as the attacking force poured through the gap thus made, Daniel's brigade on one side and Steuart's on the other drew back from their lines and fell upon its flanks, while Battle's and Johnston's brigades were hurried up from the left and thrown across its front. Assailed on three sides at once, the Federals were forced back to the works, and over them, whereupon they broke in disorderly retreat to their own lines.

The next day was rainy and disagreeable, and no serious fighting took place. There were movements, however, along the Federal lines during the day that indicated a withdrawal from the front of Longstreet's corps. Late in the afternoon, under the impression that General Grant had actually begun another flanking movement, General Lee ordered that all the artillery on the left and center that was "difficult of access" should be withdrawn from the lines, and that everything should be in readiness to move during the night if necessary. Under this order, General Long, Ewell's chief of artillery, removed all but two batteries from the line of General Edward Johnson's division, for the reason given, that they were "difficult of access."

481

Johnson's division held an elevated point somewhat advanced from the general line, and known as "the salient" [or "Bloody Angle"], the breastworks there making a considerable angle, with its point toward the enemy. This point had been held because it was a good position for artillery, and if occupied by the enemy would command portions of our line. Such projections on a defensive line are always dangerous if held by infantry alone, as an attack upon the point of the angle can only be met by a diverging fire; or if attacked on either face, the troops holding the other face, unless protected by traverses or by works in rear (as were some of the Confederates), are more exposed than those on the side attacked. But with sufficient artillery, so posted as to sweep the sides of the angle, such a position may be very strong. To provide against contingencies, a second line had been laid off and partly constructed a short distance in rear, so as to cut off this salient.

After the artillery had been withdrawn on the night of the 11th, General Johnson discovered that the enemy was concentrating in his front, and, convinced that he would be attacked in the morning, requested the immediate return of the artillery that had been taken away. The men in the trenches were kept on the alert all night and were ready for the attack, when at dawn on the morning of the 12th a dense column emerged from the pines half a mile in the front of the salient and rushed to the attack. They came on, to use General Johnson's words, "in great disorder, with a narrow front, but extending back as far as I could see." Page's battalion of artillery, which had been ordered back to the trenches at 4 o'clock in the morning, was just arriving and was not in position to fire upon the attacking column, which offered so fair a mark for artillery. The guns came only in time to be captured. The infantry in the salient fought as long as fighting was of any use; but deprived of the assistance of the artillery, which constituted the chief strength of the position, they could do little to check the onward rush of the Federal column, which soon overran the salient, capturing General Johnson himself, 20 pieces of artillery, and 2800 men—almost his entire division. The whole thing happened so quickly that the extent of the disaster could not be realized at once. Hancock's troops, who made the assault, had recovered their formation, and, extending their lines across the works on both sides of the salient, had resumed their advance, when Lane's brigade of Hill's corps, which was immediately on the right of the captured works, rapidly drew back to the unfinished line in rear, and poured a galling fire upon Hancock's left wing, which checked its advance and threw it back with severe loss. General Gordon, whose division (Early's) was in reserve and under orders to support any part of the line about the salient, hastened to throw it in front of the advancing Federal column. As the division was about to charge, General Lee rode up and joined General Gordon, evidently intending to go forward with him. Gordon remonstrated, and the men, seeing his intention, cried out, "General Lee to the rear!" which was taken up all along the line. One of the men respectfully but firmly took hold of the general's bridle and led his horse to the rear, and the charge went on. The two moving lines met in the rear of the captured works, and after a fierce struggle in the woods the Federals were forced back to the base of the salient. But Gordon's division did not cover their whole front. On the left of the salient, where Rodes's division had connected with Johnson's, the attack was still pressed with great determination. General Rodes drew out Ramseur's brigade from the left of his line, and sent it to relieve the pressure on his right and restore the line between himself and Gordon. Ramseur swept the trenches the whole length of his brigade, but did not fill the gap, and his right was exposed to a terrible fire from the works still held by the enemy. Three brigades from Hill's corps were ordered up. Perrin's, which was the first to arrive, rushed forward through a fearful fire and recovered a part of the line on Gordon's left. General Perrin fell dead from his horse just as he reached the works. General Daniel had been killed, and Ramseur painfully wounded, though remaining in the trenches with his men. Rodes's right being still hard pressed, Harris's (Mississippi) and McGowan's (South Carolina) brigades were ordered forward and rushed through the blinding storm into the works on Ramseur's right. The Federals still held the greater part of the salient, and though the Confederates were unable to drive them out, the Federals could get no farther. Hancock's corps, which had made the attack, had been reënforced by Russell's and Wheaton's divisions of the Sixth Corps and one-half of Warren's corps, as the battle progressed. Artillery had been brought up on both sides, the Confederates using every piece that could be made available upon the salient. Before 10 o'clock General Lee had put in every man that could be spared for the restoration of his broken center. It then became a matter of endurance with the men themselves. All day long and until far into the night the battle raged with unceasing fury, in the space covered by the salient and the adjacent works. Every attempt to advance on either side was met and repelled from the other. The hostile battle-flags waved over different portions of the same works, while the men fought like fiends for their possession.

During the day diversions were made on both sides, to relieve the pressure in the center. An attack upon Anderson's (Longstreet's) corps by Wright's Sixth Corps (Sedgwick having been killed on the 9th) was severely repulsed, while, on the other side of the salient, General Early, who was moving with a part of Hill's corps to strike the flank of the Federal force engaged there, met and defeated Burnside's corps, which was advancing at the same time to attack Early's works.

WHILE the battle was raging at the salient, a portion of Gordon's division was busily engaged in constructing in rear of the old line of intrenchments a new and shorter one, to which Ewell's corps retired before daylight on the

483

13th. Never was respite more welcome than the five days of comparative rest that followed the terrible battle of the 12th to our wearied men, who had been marching and fighting almost without intermission since the 4th of May. Their comfort was materially enhanced, too, by the supply of coffee, sugar, and other luxuries to which they had long been strangers, obtained from the haversacks of the Federal dead. It was astonishing into what close places a hungry Confederate would go to get something to eat. Men would sometimes go out under a severe fire, in the hope of finding a full haversack. It may seem a small matter to the readers of war history; but to the *makers* of it who were in the trenches, or on the march, or engaged in battle night and day for weeks without intermission, the supply of the one article of coffee, furnished by the Army of the Potomac to the Army of Northern Virginia, was *not* a small matter, but did as much as any other material agency to sustain the spirits and bodily energies of the men, in a campaign that taxed both to their utmost limit. Old haversacks gave place to better ones, and tin cups now dangled from the accouterments of the Confederates, who at every rest on the march or interval of quiet on the lines could be seen gathered around small fires, preparing the coveted beverage.

In the interval from the 12th to the 18th our army was gradually moving east to meet corresponding movements on the other side. Longstreet's corps was shifted from the left to the extreme right, beyond the Fredericksburg road. Ewell's corps still held the works in rear of the famous salient, when on the morning of the 18th a last effort was made to force the lines of Spotsylvania at the only point where previous efforts had met with even partial success. This was destined to a more signal failure than any of the others. Under the fire of thirty pieces of artillery, which swept all the approaches to Ewell's line, the attacking force was broken and driven back in disorder before it came well within reach of the muskets of the infantry. After the failure of this attack, the "sidling" movement, as the men expressed it, again began, and on the afternoon of the 19th Ewell's corps was thrown round the Federal left wing to ascertain the extent of this movement. After a severe engagement, which lasted until night, Ewell withdrew, having lost about nine hundred men in the action. This seemed a heavy price to pay for information that might have been otherwise obtained, but the enemy had suffered more severely, and General Grant was delayed in his turning movement for twenty-four hours. He however got the start in the race for the North Anna; Hancock's corps, leading off on the night of the 20th, was followed rapidly by the remainder of his army.

On the morning of the 21st Ewell's corps moved from the left to the right of our line, and later on the same day it was pushed southward on the Telegraph road, closely followed by Longstreet's corps. A. P. Hill brought up the rear that night, after a sharp "brush" with the Sixth Corps, which was in the act of retiring from its lines. Lee had the inside track this time, as the

Telegraph road on which he moved was the direct route, while Grant had to swing round on the arc of a circle of which this was the chord. About noon on the 22d the head of our column reached the North Anna, and that night Lee's army lay on the south side of the river. We had won the second heat and secured a good night's rest besides, when the Federal army appeared on the other side in the forenoon of the 23d.

Warren's corps crossed the river that afternoon without opposition at Jericho Ford, four miles above the Chesterfield bridge on the Telegraph road; but as it moved out from the river it met Cadmus Wilcox's division of Hill's corps, and a severe but indecisive engagement ensued, the confronting lines intrenching as usual. Meanwhile a small earth-work, that had been built the year before, covering the approaches to the bridge on the Telegraph road and now held by a small detachment from Kershaw's division, was attacked and carried by troops of Hancock's corps, the Confederates retiring across the river with the loss of a few prisoners.

It did not seem to be General Lee's purpose to offer any serious resistance to Grant's passage of the river at the points selected. His lines had been retired from it at both these points, but touched it at Ox Ford, a point intermediate between them. Hancock's corps, having secured the Chesterfield bridge, crossed over on the morning of the 24th, and, extending down the river, moved out until it came upon Longstreet's and Ewell's corps in position and ready for battle. The Sixth Corps (General Wright) crossed at Jericho Mill and joined Warren. The two wings of Grant's army were safely across the river, but there was no connection between them. Lee had only thrown back his flanks and let them in on either side, while he held the river between; and when General Grant attempted to throw his center, under Burnside, across between the ford and the bridge, it was very severely handled and failed to get a foothold on the south side. A detachment from Warren's corps was sent down on the south side to help Burnside across, but was attacked by Mahone's division, and driven back with heavy loss, narrowly escaping capture. General Grant found himself in what may be called a military dilemma. He had cut his army in two by running it upon the point of a wedge. He could not break the point, which rested upon the river, and the attempt to force it out of place by striking on its sides must of necessity be made without much concert of action between the two wings of his army, neither of which could reënforce the other without crossing the river twice; while his opponent could readily transfer his troops, as needed, from one wing to the other, across the narrow space between them.

The next two days were consumed by General Grant in fruitless attempts to find a vulnerable point in our lines. The skirmishers were very active, often forcing their way close up to our works. The line of my brigade crossed the Richmond and Fredericksburg railroad. It was an exposed point, and the men stationed there, after building their log breastwork, leant their mus-

485

kets against it and moved out on one side, to avoid the constant fire that was directed upon it. . . .

On the morning of May 27th General Grant's army had disappeared from our front. During the night it had "folded its tents like the Arab and as quietly stolen away," on its fourth turning movement since the opening of the campaign. The Army of the Potomac was already on its march for the Pamunkey River at Hanovertown, where the leading corps crossed on the morning of the 27th. Lee moved at once to head off his adversary, whose advance column was now eight miles nearer Richmond than he was. In the afternoon of the 28th, after one of the severest cavalry engagements of the war, in which Hampton and Fitz Lee opposed the advance of Sheridan at Hawes's Shop, the infantry of both armies came up and again confronted each other along the Totopotomoy. Here the Confederate position was found too strong to be attacked in front with any prospect of success, and again the "sidling" movements began—this time toward Cold Harbor.

Sheridan's cavalry had taken possession of Cold Harbor on the 31st, and had been promptly followed up by two corps of infantry. Longstreet's and a part of Hill's corps, with Hoke's and Breckinridge's divisions, were thrown across their front. The fighting began on the Cold Harbor line, late in the afternoon of the 1st of June, by a heavy attack upon the divisions of Hoke and Kershaw. Clingman's brigade on Hoke's left gave way, and Wofford's on Kershaw's right, being turned, was also forced back; but the further progress of the attack was checked and the line partly restored before night. By the morning of the 2d of June the opposing lines had settled down close to each other, and everything promised a repetition of the scenes at Spotsylvania.

Three corps of Grant's army (General W. F. Smith's Eighteenth Corps having arrived from Drewry's Bluff) now confronted the Confederate right wing at Cold Harbor, while the other two looked after Early's (Ewell's) corps near Bethesda Church. In the afternoon of June 2d, General Early, perceiving a movement that indicated a withdrawal of the Federal force in his front, attacked Burnside's corps while it was in motion, striking also the flank of Warren's corps, and capturing several hundred prisoners. This was accomplished with small loss, and had the effect of preventing the coöperation of these two corps in the attack at Cold Harbor the next day.

Early in the morning of the 2d I was ordered to move with my own and Anderson's brigades, of Field's division, "to reënforce the line on the right," exercising my own discretion as to the point where assistance was most needed. After putting the troops in motion I rode along the line, making a personal inspection as I went. Pickett's division, the first on our right, held a strong position along the skirt of a wood, with open fields in front, and needed no strengthening. The left of Kershaw's division, which was the next in order, was equally strong; but on calling at General Kershaw's quarters

I was informed of the particulars of the attack upon his own and Hoke's divisions the evening before, and requested by him to place my troops as a support to his right wing, which had been thrown back by the attack. On examining the line I found it bent sharply back at almost a right angle, the point of which rested upon a body of heavy woods. The works were in open ground and were ill-adapted to resist an attack. The right face of the angle ran along a slope, with a small marshy stream behind and higher ground in front. The works had evidently been built just where the troops found themselves at the close of the fight the previous evening.

Convinced that under such assaults as we had sustained at Spotsylvania our line would be broken at that point, I proposed to cut off the angle by building a new line across its base, which would throw the marshy ground in our front and give us a clear sweep across it with our fire from the slope on the other side. This would not only strengthen but shorten the line considerably, and I proposed to General Kershaw to build and occupy it with my two brigades that night.

Meanwhile the enemy was evidently concentrating in the woods in front, and every indication pointed to an early attack. Nothing could be done upon the contemplated line during the day, and we waited anxiously the coming of night. The day passed without an attack. I was as well satisfied that it would come at dawn the next morning as if I had seen General Meade's order directing it. That no mistake should be made in the location of the works, I procured a hatchet, and accompanied by two members of my staff, each with an armful of stakes, went out after dark, located the line, and drove every stake upon it. The troops were formed on it at once, and before morning the works were finished. Artillery was placed at both ends of the new line, abreast of the infantry. General Kershaw then withdrew that portion of his division which occupied the salient, the men having leveled the works as far as possible before leaving them.

Our troops were under arms and waiting, when with the misty light of early morning the scattering fire of our pickets, who now occupied the abandoned works in the angle, announced the beginning of the attack. As the assaulting column swept over the old works a loud cheer was given, and it rushed on into the marshy ground in the angle. Its front covered little more than the line of my own brigade of less than a thousand men; but line followed line until the space inclosed by the old salient became a mass of writhing humanity, upon which our artillery and musketry played with cruel effect. I had taken position on the slope in rear of the line and was carefully noting the firing of the men, which soon became so heavy that I feared they would exhaust the cartridges in their boxes before the attack ceased. Sending an order for a supply of ammunition to be brought into the lines, I went down to the trenches to regulate the firing. On my way I met a man, belonging to the 15th Alabama regiment of my brigade, running to the rear through the storm of bullets that swept the hill. He had left his hat behind in his retreat, was crying like a big baby, and was the bloodiest man I ever saw. "Oh, General," he blubbered out, "I am dead! I am killed! Look at this!" showing his wound. He was a broad, fat-faced fellow, and a minie-ball had passed through his cheek and the fleshy part of his neck, letting a large amount of blood. Finding it was only a flesh-wound, I told him to go on; he was not hurt. He looked at me doubtfully for a second as if questioning my veracity or my surgical knowledge, I don't know which; then, as if satisfied with my diagnosis, he broke into a broad laugh, and, the tears still running down his cheeks, trotted off, the happiest man I saw that day.

On reaching the trenches, I found the men in fine spirits, laughing and talking as they fired. There, too, I could see more plainly the terrible havoc made in the ranks of the assaulting column. I had seen the dreadful carnage in front of Marye's Hill at Fredericksburg, and on the "old railroad cut" which Jackson's men held at the Second Manassas; but I had seen nothing to exceed this. It was not war; it was murder. When the fight ended, more than a thousand men lay in front of our works either killed or too badly wounded to leave the field. Among them were some who were not hurt, but remained among the dead and wounded rather than take the chances of going back under that merciless fire. Most of these came in and surrendered during the day, but were fired on in some instances by their own men (who still held a position close in our front) to prevent them from doing so. The loss in my command was fifteen or twenty, most of them wounded about the head and shoulders, myself among the number. Our artillery was handled superbly during the action. Major Hamilton, chief of artillery of Kershaw's division, not only coöperated with energy in strengthening our line on the night of June 2d, but directed the fire of his guns with great skill during the attack on the 3d, reaching not only the front of the attacking force, but its flanks also, as well as those of the supporting troops.

While we were busy with the Eighteenth Corps on the center of the general line, the sounds of battle could be heard both on the right and left, and we knew from long use what that meant. It was a general advance of Grant's whole army. Early's corps below Bethesda Church was attacked without success. On our right, where the line extended toward the Chickahominy, it was broken at one point, but at once restored by Finegan's (Florida) brigade, with heavy loss to Hancock's troops who were attacking there. The result of the action in the center, which has been described, presents a fair picture of the result along the entire line—a grand advance, a desperate struggle, a bloody and crushing repulse. Before 8 o'clock A. M. on the 3d of June the battle of Cold Harbor was over, and with it Grant's "overland campaign" against Richmond. . . .

The results of the "overland campaign" against Richmond, in 1864, cannot be gauged simply by the fact that Grant's army found itself within a few

miles of the Confederate capital when it ended. It might have gotten there
in a much shorter time and without any fighting at all. Indeed, one Federal
army under General Butler was already there, threatening Richmond, which
was considered by the Confederates much more secure after the arrival of
the Armies of Lee and Grant than it had been before. Nor can these results
be measured only by the losses of the opposing armies on the battle-field,
except as they affected the *morale* of armies themselves; for their losses were
about proportional to their relative strength. So far as the Confederates were
concerned, it would be idle to deny that they (as well as General Lee himself)
were disappointed at the result of their efforts in the Wilderness on the 5th
and 6th of May, and that General Grant's constant "hammering" with his
largely superior force had, to a certain extent, a depressing effect upon both
officers and men. "It's no use killing these fellows; a half-dozen take the place
of every one we kill," was a common remark in our army. We knew that our
resources of men were exhausted, and that the vastly greater resources of the
Federal Government, if brought fully to bear, even in this costly kind of warfare, must wear us out in the end. The question with us (and one often asked
at the time) was, "How long will the people of the North, and the army itself,
stand it?" We heard much about the demoralization of Grant's army, and of
the mutterings of discontent at home with the conduct of the campaign, and
we verily believed that their patience would soon come to an end.

As the Army of the Potomac crossed the Rapidan and plunged into the Wilderness early in May 1864, Sherman at the head of three Union armies struck south from Tennessee, his destination Atlanta, major rail and industrial center of the Confederacy. The invasion, opposed by Johnston with an army whose morale was high and equipment good, went rapidly at first, then slowed to a crawl as it approached its goal—as the enemy's resistance stiffened and the maintenance of lines of supply and communication back to Chattanooga became more complicated. It was not until September 2d, in fact, that Sherman could telegraph Lincoln: "Atlanta is ours, and fairly won."

The North, growing increasingly critical of Grant's undramatic campaign in Virginia and increasingly despondent over its losses and the apparent stalemate there, badly needed the Atlanta victory. As Lincoln needed it also in the election two months later when the people gave him a handsome margin over McClellan and the radical peace-at-any-price advocates, thus endorsing the conduct and further prosecution of the war.

"The very woods seemed to moan and groan"

THE STRUGGLE FOR ATLANTA

BY OLIVER O. HOWARD, MAJOR-GENERAL, U. S. A.

THE FORCES under General Grant after his appointment as general-in-chief were, the Army of the Potomac, under Meade; that of the Ohio, near Knoxville, under Schofield; that of the Cumberland, under Thomas, near Chattanooga; that of the Tennessee, under McPherson, scattered from Huntsville, Alabama, to the Mississippi; that of the Gulf, under Banks, in Louisiana; besides subordinate detachments, under Steele and others, in Arkansas and farther west.

Grant took the whole field into his thought. He made three parts to the long, irregular line of armies, which extended from Virginia to Texas. He gave to Banks the main work in the south-west; to Sherman the middle part, covering the hosts of McPherson, Thomas, Schofield, and Steele; and reserved to himself the remainder. The numbers were known, at least on paper; the plan, promptly adopted, was simple and comprehensive: To break and

491

keep broken the connecting links of the enemy's opposing armies, beat them one by one, and unite for a final consummation. Sherman's part was plain. Grant's plan, flexible enough to embrace his own, afforded Sherman "infinite satisfaction." It looked like "enlightened war." He rejoiced at "this verging to a common center." "Like yourself," he writes to Grant, "you take the biggest load, and from me you shall have thorough and hearty coöperation."

Sherman made his calculations so as to protect most faithfully our line of supply which ran through Louisville, Nashville, and Chattanooga, guarding it against enemies within and without his boundaries, and against accidents. He segregated the men of all arms for this protection. Block-houses and intrenchments were put at bridges and tunnels along the railway. Locomotives and freight cars were gathered in, and a most energetic force of skilled railroad men was put at work or held in reserve under capable chiefs.

Besides an equal number of guards of his large depots and long line of supply, Sherman had an effective field force of 100,000—50,000 with Thomas, 35,000 with McPherson, 15,000 with Schofield.

Sherman was gratified at the number of his force; for two years before, he had been held up as worthy of special distrust because he had declared to Secretary Cameron that before they were done with offensive operations on the line from the Big Sandy to Paducah, 200,000 men would be required.

A few changes of organization were made. Slocum's corps, the Twelfth, and mine, the Eleventh, were consolidated, making a new Twentieth, and Hooker was assigned to its command. I went at once to Loudon, east Tennessee, to take the Fourth Corps and relieve General Gordon Granger to enable him to have a leave of absence. Slocum was sent to Vicksburg, Mississippi, to watch the great river from that quarter; while Hooker, Palmer, and myself, under Thomas, were to control the infantry and artillery of the Army of the Cumberland. In a few days I moved Wagner's (afterward Newton's) division and T. J. Wood's of my new corps to Cleveland, east Tennessee. Rations, clothing, transportation, and ammunition came pouring in with sufficient abundance, so that when orders arrived for the next movement, on the 3d of May, 1864, my division commanders, Stanley, Newton, and Wood, reported everything ready. This very day Schofield's column, coming from Knoxville, made its appearance at Cleveland. There was now the thrill of preparation, a new life everywhere. Soldiers and civilians alike caught the inspiration.

Ringgold and Catoosa Springs, Georgia, were the points of concentration for Thomas's three corps. We of his army were all in that neighborhood by the 4th of May. It took till the 7th for McPherson to get into Villanow, a few miles to the south of us. Schofield meanwhile worked steadily southward from Cleveland, east Tennessee, through Red Clay, toward Dalton, Georgia. The three railway lines uniting Chattanooga, Cleveland, and Dalton form an almost equilateral triangle. Dalton, its south-east vertex, was the center of the Confederate army, under Joseph E. Johnston. Pushing out from Dalton toward us at Catoosa Springs, Johnston occupied the famous pass through Taylor's Ridge, Buzzard-Roost Gap, and part of the ridge itself; and held, for his extreme outpost in our direction, Tunnel Hill, near which our skirmish-line and his first exchanged shots. His northern lines ran along the eastern side of the triangle, between Dalton and Red Clay.

Johnston, according to his official return for April, had a force of 52,992. At Resaca, a few days later, after the corps of Polk had joined him, it numbered 71,235. Our three field armies aggregated then, in officers and men, 98,797, with 254 pieces of artillery. The Confederate commander had about the same number of cannon. McPherson had thus far brought to Sherman but 24,465 men.

When the Army of the Cumberland was in line, facing the enemy, its left rested near Catoosa Springs, its center at Ringgold, the railway station, and its right at Leet's Tan-yard. My corps formed the left. Catoosa Springs was a Georgia watering-place, where there were several large buildings, hotel and boarding-houses, amid undulating hills, backed by magnificent mountain scenery. Here, on the morning of the 6th, I met Thomas and Sherman. Sherman had a habit of dropping in and explaining in a happy way what he purposed to do. At first he intended that Thomas and Schofield should simply breast the enemy and skirmish with him on the west and north, while McPherson, coming from Alabama, was to strike the Atlanta railroad at least ten miles below Resaca. McPherson, failing in getting some of his troops back from furlough, was not now deemed strong enough to operate alone; hence he was brought to Chattanooga instead, and sent thence to Villanow, soon after to pass through the Snake Creek Gap of Taylor's Ridge, all the time being kept near enough the other armies to get help from them in case of emergency. By this it was ardently hoped by Sherman that McPherson might yet succeed in getting upon Johnston's communications near Resaca. Thomas here urged his own views, which were to give Schofield and McPherson the skirmishing and demonstrations, while he (Thomas), with his stronger army, should pass through Snake Creek Gap and seize Johnston's communications. He felt sure of victory. Sherman, however, hesitated to put his main army twenty miles away beyond a mountain range on the enemy's line, lest he should thereby endanger his own. He could not yet afford an exchange of base. Still, in less than a week, as we shall see, he ran even a greater risk.

Early in the day, May 7th, the Fourth Corps, arranged for battle, was near a small farm-house in sight of Tunnel Hill. Two divisions, Stanley's and Newton's, abreast in long, wavy lines, and the other, Wood's, in the rear, kept on the *qui vive* to prevent surprises, particularly from the sweep of country to the north of us. The front and the left of the moving men were well protected by infantry skirmishers. It was a beautiful picture—that army corps, with arms glistening in the morning light, ascending the slope. By 8 o'clock the few rifle-shots had become a continuous rattle. First we saw far off, here and there, puffs of smoke, and then the gray horsemen giving back and passing the crest. Suddenly there was stronger resistance, artillery and musketry rapidly firing upon our advance. At 9 o'clock the ridge of Tunnel Hill bristled with Confederates, mounted and dismounted. A closer observation from Stanley's field-glass showed them to be only horse artillery and cavalry supports. In a few moments Stanley's and Newton's men charged the hill at a run and cleared the ridge, and soon beheld the enemy's artillery and cavalry galloping away. "The ball is opened," Stanley called out, as I took my place by his side to study Taylor's Ridge and its "Rocky Face." . . .

Thomas's three corps, Palmer occupying the middle and Hooker the right, were now marched forward till my men received rifle-shots from the heights, Palmer's a shower of them from the defenders of the gap, and Hooker's a more worrisome fusillade from spurs of the ridge farther south. Thomas could not sit down behind this formidable wall and do nothing. How could he retain before him the Confederate host? Only by getting into closer contact.

On the 8th I sent Newton some two miles northward, where the ascent was not so abrupt. He succeeded by rushes in getting from cover to cover, though not without loss, till he had wrested at least one-third of the "knife edge" from those resolute men of gray. Quickly the observers of this sharp contest saw the bright signal flags up there in motion. Stanley and Wood gave Newton all possible support by their marksmen and by their efforts to land shells on the ridge. The enemy's signals were near Newton. He tried hard to capture them, but failed. In the night two pieces of artillery, after much toil, reached the top, and soon cleared away a few hundred yards more of this territory in bloody dispute. On May 9th Thomas put forth a triple effort to get nearer his foe. First, Stanley's division reconnoitered Buzzard-Roost Gap into the very "jaws of death," till it drew the fire from newly discovered batteries, and set whole lines of Confederate musketry-supports ablaze. At this time I had a narrow escape. Stanley, Captain G. C. Kniffin of his staff, several other officers, and myself were in a group, watching a reconnoissance. All supposed there were no Confederate sharp-shooters near enough to do harm, when *whiz* came a bullet which passed through the group; Kniffin's hat was pierced, three holes were made in my coat, and a neighboring tree was struck.

Thomas now made a second effort. Palmer sent Morgan's brigade up one of the spurs south of the gap. It encountered the hottest fire, and suffered a considerable loss in killed and wounded. One regiment drove back the enemy's first line, and, like Newton's men, came within speaking distance of their opponents. Here arose the story to the effect that a witty corporal proposed to read to them the President's Emancipation Proclamation, and that they kept from firing while he did so. Still farther south, with Hooker's Twentieth Corps, and almost beyond our hearing, Thomas made his third push. In this action fifty were reported killed, and a larger number wounded; among them every regimental commander engaged. Similarly, but with easier approaches than ours, Schofield kept Johnston's attention at the east and north. Such was the demonstration, while McPherson was making his long détour through Villanow, Snake Creek Gap, and out into Sugar Valley. He found the gap unoccupied; and so, with Kilpatrick's small cavalry detachment ahead, followed closely by Dodge's Sixteenth Corps, with Logan's Fifteenth well closed up, he emerged from the mountains on the morning of the 9th, at the eastern exit.

Immediately there was excitement—the cavalry advance stumbled upon Confederate cavalry, which had run out from Resaca to watch this doorway. Our cavalry followed up the retreating Confederates with dash and persistency, till they found shelter behind the deep-cut works and guns at Resaca. In plain view of these works, though on difficult ground, Logan and Dodge pressed up their men, under orders from McPherson "to drive back the enemy and break the railroad." And pray, why were not these plain orders carried out? McPherson answers in a letter that night sent to Sherman: "They [probably Polk's men] displayed considerable force and opened on us with artillery. After skirmishing [among the gulches and thickets] till nearly dark, and finding that I could not succeed in cutting the railroad before dark, or in getting to it, I decided to withdraw the command and take up a position for the night between Sugar Valley and the entrance to the gap." At the first news Sherman was much vexed, and declared concerning McPherson's failure to break the enemy's main artery: "Such an opportunity does not occur twice in a single life . . . still he was perfectly justified by his orders."

Our commander, believing that Johnston would now speedily fall back to Resaca, at once changed his purpose. Leaving me at Rocky Face with the Fourth Corps and Stoneman's small division of cavalry to hold our line of supply, Sherman pressed after McPherson the armies of Thomas and Schofield. But Johnston was not in a hurry. He terrified me for two days by his tentative movements, till our skirmishing amounted at times almost to a battle. But the night of the 12th of May he made off in one of his clean retreats. At dawn of the 13th the formidable Buzzard-Roost Gap was open and safe, and our men passed through. Stoneman rushed into the village of Dalton from the north, and the Fourth Corps, eager and rapid, kept close to the chasing cavalry. Not far south of Dalton we came upon a bothersome Confederate rear-guard, which made our marching all that long day slow and spasmodic, yet before dark my command had skirted the eastern slope of Taylor's Ridge for eighteen miles and joined skirmishers with Sherman, who was already, with McPherson, abreast of Resaca. Thus we ended the combats of Tunnel Hill and Dalton, and opened up Resaca.

As soon as Johnston reached the little town of Resaca he formed a horseshoe-shaped line, something like ours at Gettysburg. He rested Polk's corps on the Oostenaula River; placed Hardee's next, running up Milk Creek; and then curved Hood's back to strike the Connasauga River. After the Confederates had thrown up the usual intrenchments, and put out one or two small advanced forts with cannon, the position was as strong as Marye's Heights had been against direct attack. We spent a part of the 14th of May creeping up among the bushes, rocks, and ravines.

Early that morning, while this was going on, Sherman, who had worked all night, was sitting on a log, with his back against a tree, fast asleep. Some men marching by saw him, and one fellow ended a slurring remark by: "A pretty way we are commanded!" Sherman, awakened by the noise, heard the last words. "Stop, my man," he cried; "while you were sleeping, last night, I was planning for you, sir; and now I was taking a nap." Thus, familiarly and kindly, the general gave reprimands and won confidence.

McPherson rested his right upon the Oostenaula River, opposite Polk. Thomas, with the corps of Palmer and Hooker, came next; and then that brave young officer, Cox, commanding the Twenty-third Corps, against a storm of bullets and shells swung his divisions round to follow the bend in the enemy's line. I watched the operation, so as to close upon his left. T. J. Wood's division moved up in a long line, with skirmishers well out, and then Stanley's carried us to the railway. Stanley's chief-of-artillery arranged two or three batteries to keep the enemy from walking around our unprotected left. The air was full of screeching shells and whizzing bullets, coming uncomfortably near, while line after line was adjusting itself for the deadly conflict. Our fighting at Resaca did not effect much. There might possibly have been as much accomplished if we had used skirmish-lines alone. In McPherson's front Logan had a battery well placed, and fired till he had silenced the troublesome foes on a ridge in his front; then his brave men, at a run, passed the ravine and secured the ridge. Here Logan intrenched his corps; and Dodge, abreast of him, did the same. Afterward, McPherson seized another piece of ground across Camp Creek, and held it. During the evening of the 14th a vigorous effort was made by Polk to regain this outpost, but he was repulsed with loss.

The detailed account gives great credit to Generals Charles R. Woods, Giles A. Smith, and J. A. J. Lightburn. One hundred prisoners and 1300 Confederates *hors de combat* were on Logan's list. This work forced Johnston to lay a new bridge over the Oostenaula. The divisions of Absalom Baird, R. W. Johnson, Jefferson C. Davis, and John Newton plunged into the thickets and worked their way steadily and bravely into the reëntrant angles on Hardee's front. Schofield's right division, under Judah, had a fearful struggle, losing six hundred men; the others, coming to its help, captured and secured a part of the enemy's intrenchments. Hood assailed my left after 3 P. M. The front attack was repulsed, but heavy columns came surging around Stanley's left.

Everybody, battery men and supporting infantry, did wonders; still, but for help promptly rendered, Sherman's whole line, like the left of Wellington's at Waterloo, would soon have been rolled up and displaced. But Colonel Morgan of my staff, who had been sent in time, brought up Williams's division from Hooker's corps as quickly as men could march. Stanley's brave artillerymen were thus succored before they were forced to yield their ground, and Hood, disappointed, returned to his trenches. The next day, the 15th, came Hooker's attack. He advanced in a column of deployed brigades. Both armies watched with eager excitement this passage-at-arms. The divisions of Generals Butterfield, Williams, and Geary seized some trenches and cheered, but were stopped before a sort of lunette holding four cannon. The Confederates were driven from their trenches; but our men, meeting continuous and deadly volleys, could not get the guns till night. A color-bearer named Hess, of Colonel Benjamin Harrison's brigade, while his comrades were retiring a few steps for better cover, being chagrined at the defiant yell behind him, unfurled his flag and swung it to the breeze. He was instantly killed. A witness says: "There were other hands to grasp the flag, and it came back, only to return and wave from the very spot where its former bearer fell."

While the main battle was in progress, Dodge had sent a division under the one-armed Sweeny, to Lay's Ferry, a point below Resaca. Under the chief engineer, Captain Reese, he laid a bridge and protected it by a small force. Sweeny, being threatened by some Confederates crossing the river above him, and fearing that he might be cut off from the army, suddenly drew back about a mile beyond danger. On the 15th, however, he made another attempt and was more successful; formed a bridge-head beyond the river; threw over his whole force; and fought a successful battle against Martin's Confederate cavalry, before Walker's infantry, which was hastily sent against him from Calhoun, could arrive. Besides Sweeny's division, Sherman dispatched a cavalry force over the pontoons, instructing them to make a wider détour. The operations in this quarter being successful, there was nothing left to the Confederate commander but to withdraw his whole army from Resaca. This was effected during the night of the 15th, while our weary men were sound asleep. At the first peep of dawn Newton's skirmishers sprang over the enemy's intrenchments to find them abandoned. . . .

Our enemy made a brief stand on the 17th of May at Adairsville, and fortified. About 4 P. M. Newton and Wood, of my corps, Wood on the right, found the resistance constantly increasing as they advanced, till Newton's skirmishers, going at double-time through clumps of trees, awakened a heavy opposing fire. . . . In fact, both parties, though desiring to avoid a general battle, nevertheless reënforced, till the firing amounted to an engagement. It was not till after 9 o'clock that the rattling of the musketry had diminished to the ordinary skirmish, and the batteries had ceased, except an occasional shot, as if each were trying to have the last gun. The losses in my command in this combat were about two hundred killed and wounded. The morning of the 18th found the works in front of Adairsville with few reminders that an army had been there the night before. Hooker and Schofield had done the work. Johnston's scouts during the night brought him word that a large Federal force was already far beyond his right near Cassville, threatening his main crossing of the Etowah; and also that McPherson was camping below him at McGuire's Cross-roads, and that our infantry was already in sight of the little town of Rome, where, under a weak guard, were foundries and important mills. We began now to perceive slight evidences of our opponent's demoralization. I captured a regiment and quite a large number of detached prisoners. The whole number taken, including many commissioned officers, was about four thousand.

The rapidity with which the badly broken railroad was repaired seemed miraculous. We had hardly left Dalton before trains with ammunition and other supplies arrived. While our skirmishing was going on at Calhoun, the locomotive whistle sounded in Resaca. The telegraphers were nearly as rapid: the lines were in order to Adairsville on the morning of the 18th. While we were breaking up the State arsenal at Adairsville, caring for the wounded and bringing in Confederate prisoners, word was telegraphed from Resaca that bacon, hard-bread, and coffee were already there at our service.

Johnston, by his speedy night-work, passed on through Kingston, and formed an admirable line of battle in the vicinity of Cassville, with his back to the Etowah River, protecting the selected crossing.

This was his final halt north of that river, so difficult with its mountain banks. Johnston remained here to obstruct and dispute our way one day only, for Schofield and Hooker had penetrated the forests eastward of him so far that Hood, still on Johnston's right, insisted that the Yankees were already beyond him and in force.

Upon this report, about which there has since been much controversy, Johnston ordered a prompt withdrawal. The morning of the 21st of May, bright and clear, showed us a country picturesque in its natural features, with farm and woodland as quiet and peaceful as if there had been no war. So Sherman, taking up his headquarters at Kingston, a little hamlet on the railway, gave his armies three days' rest. . . .

Johnston was holding the region south of the Etowah, including the pass of Allatoona, and extended his army along the ridge of Allatoona Creek toward the south-west. He was picketing a parallel ridge in front of his line, along another creek, the Pumpkin Vine. This is substantially where we found this able and careful commander; but he pushed a little to the left and forward as we came on, till Hardee was at Dallas and Hood at New Hope Church. Our march was resumed on the morning of the 24th of May, Thomas crossing on his own pontoons south of Kingston; Hooker, contrary to the plan, went in advance of Schofield's column over a bridge at Milan's, east of

Kingston; Davis, being at Rome, went straight forward from that place, and McPherson did the same from his position, laying his bridges so as to take the road to Van Wert. Stoneman's cavalry covered the left; Garrard's division was near McPherson and Davis, while McCook's cleared the front for the center. The whole country between the Etowah and the Chattahoochee presented a desolate appearance, with few openings and very few farms, and those small and poor; other parts were covered with trees and dense underbrush, which the skirmishers had great difficulty in penetrating. Off the ordinary "hog-backs" one plunged into deep ravines or ascended abrupt steeps. There was much loose, shifting soil on the hills, and many lagoons and small streams bordered with treacherous quicksands.

Very soon on May 24th the usual skirmishing with the cavalry began, but there was not much delay. Hooker, coming into Thomas's road the next morning, the 25th, led our column, taking the direct road toward Dallas. It was showery all day, and the weather and bad roads had a disheartening effect on men and animals. To relieve the situation as much as possible Thomas had my corps take advantage of country roads to the right, that would bring us into Dallas by the Van Wert route. McPherson and Davis had already come together at Van Wert. Now, suddenly, Geary's division found a bridge over Pumpkin Vine Creek on fire, and hostile cavalry behind it. The cavalry soon fled, and the bridge was repaired. Hooker, thinking there was more force in that quarter, pushed up the road toward New Hope Church. He had gone but a short distance before he ran upon one of Hood's brigades. It was an outpost of Stewart's division, put there to create delay. Hooker soon dislodged this outpost and moved on, driving back the brigade through the woods, till he came upon the enemy's main line.

The sound of cannon speedily drew Sherman to the point of danger. He immediately ordered the necessary changes. Williams's division, having passed on, faced about and came back. Butterfield's hastened up. The two divisions, each forming in parallel lines, promptly assaulted Hood's position. Again and again Hooker's brave men went forward through the forest only to run upon log-barricades thoroughly manned and protected by well-posted artillery. During these charges occurred a thunder-storm, the heaviest shower of the day. I turned to the left by the first opportune road, and deployed Newton's division to the right of Hooker by 6 P. M. The remainder of my command came up over roads deep with mud and obstructed by wagons. In the morning all the troops were at hand. On that terrible night the nearest house to the field was filled with the wounded. Torch-lights and candles lighted up dimly the incoming stretchers and the surgeons' tables and instruments. The very woods seemed to moan and groan with the voices of sufferers not yet brought in.

McPherson, with Davis for his left, took position at Dallas, having Logan on his right, and Garrard's cavalry still beyond. There must have been a gap of three miles between McPherson and us. Schofield was badly injured by the fall of his horse in that black forest while finding his way during the night to Sherman's bivouac, so that for a few days Cox took his command. Cox, with his Twenty-third Corps, and Palmer with the Fourteenth, swung in beyond me, as my men were moving up carefully into their usual positions in line of battle. Now the enemy kept strengthening his trench-barricades, which were so covered by thickets that at first we could scarcely detect them. As he did, so did we. No regiment was long in front of Johnston's army without having virtually as good a breastwork as an engineer could plan. There was a ditch before the embankment and a strong log revetment behind it, and a heavy "top-log" to shelter the heads of the men. I have known a regiment to shelter itself completely against musketry and artillery with axes and shovels, in less than an hour after it reached its position.

It would only weary the reader's patience to follow up the struggle step by step from New Hope Church to the Chattahoochee. Still, these were the hardest times which the army experienced. It rained continuously for seventeen days; the roads, becoming as broad as the fields, were a series of quagmires. And, indeed, it was difficult to bring enough supplies forward from Kingston to meet the needs of the army. Sherman began to pass his armies to the left. First, I was sent with two divisions to attempt to strike Johnston's right. I marched thither Wood's division, supported by R. W. Johnson's, and connected with the army by Cox on my right. At Pickett's Mill, believing I had reached the extreme of the Confederate line, at 6 P. M. of the 27th I ordered the assault. Wood encountered just such obstructions as Hooker had found at New Hope Church, and was similarly repulsed, suffering much loss. R. W. Johnson's division was hindered by a side-thrust from the hostile cavalry, so that we did not get the full benefit of his forward push. We believed that otherwise we should have lodged at least a brigade beyond Hindman's Confederate division. But we did what was most important: we worked our men all that weary night in fortifying. The Confederate commander was ready at daylight to take the offensive against us at Pickett's Mill, but he did not do so, because he found our position and works too strong to warrant the attempt. With a foot bruised by the fragment of a shell, I sat that night among the wounded in the midst of a forest glade, while Major Howard of my staff led regiments and brigades into the new position chosen for them. General R. W. Johnson had been wounded, Captain Stinson of my staff had been shot through the lungs, and a large number lay there, on a sideling slope by a faint camp-fire, with broken limbs or disfigured faces.

The next day, the 28th, McPherson made an effort to withdraw from Dallas, so as to pass beyond my left; but as Hardee at the first move quickly assailed him with great fury, he prudently advised further delay. This battle was the reverse of mine at Pickett's Mill. The enemy attacked mainly in columns of deployed regiments along the front of Dodge's and Logan's corps, and was repulsed with a dreadful loss, which Logan estimated at two thousand. Now, necessity pressing him in every direction, Sherman, mixing divisions somewhat along the line, gradually bore his armies to the left. The 1st of June put Stoneman into Allatoona, and on the 3d Schofield's infantry was across the railroad near Ackworth, having had a severe and successful combat *en route.*

Being now far beyond Johnston's right, and having seized and secured the Allatoona Creek from its mouth to Ackworth, Sherman was ready, from Allatoona as a new base, to push forward and strike a new and heavy blow, when, to his chagrin, in the night of the 4th of June Johnston abandoned his works and fell back to a new line. This line ran from Brush Mountain to Lost Mountain, with "Pine Top" standing out in a salient near the middle. He also held an outpost in front of Gilgal Church abreast of Pine Top. Slowly, with skirmishes and small combats, for the most part in dense woods, we continuously advanced. On my front we seized the skirmish-holes of the enemy, made epaulements for batteries there, and little by little extended our deep ditches or log-barricades close up to Johnston's. As we settled down to steady work again, McPherson was near Brush Mountain, having pushed down the railroad. F. P. Blair's corps from Huntsville, Alabama, had now joined him, making up for our losses, which were already, from all causes, upward of nine thousand. This accession gave heart to us all. Thomas was next, advancing and bearing away toward Pine Top, and Schofield coming up against the salient angle near Gilgal Church. To tell the work of these two opposing hosts in their new position is a similar story to the last. There was gallant fighting here and there all along the lines. Here it was that my batteries, opening fire under the direct instruction of Sherman, drove back the enemy from the exposed intrenchments on Pine Top. It was at this time that General Polk was killed. McPherson, by overlapping Hood, skirmished heavily, and captured the 40th Alabama regiment entire. Schofield, brushing away the cavalry, penetrated between Lost Mountain and Gilgal Church, put his artillery on a prominent knoll, and, with rapid discharges, took Hardee in reverse.

That night, the 16th of June, Johnston again went back to a new line, already prepared, just behind Mud Creek. Our troops, being on the alert, followed at once with great rapidity. Just where the old lines joined the new (for Johnston's right wing was unchanged), I saw a feat the like of which never elsewhere fell under my observation. Baird's division, in a comparatively open field, put forth a heavy skirmish-line, which continued such a rapid fire of rifles as to keep down a corresponding hostile line behind its well-constructed trenches, while the picks and shovels behind the skirmishers fairly flew, till a good set of works was made four hundred yards distant from the enemy's and parallel to it. One of my brigades (Harker's), by a

501

rush, did also a brave and unusual thing in capturing an intrenched and well-defended line of the enemy's works and taking their defenders captive. Again, another (Kirby's brigade), having lost Bald Hill in a skirmish, re-took it by a gallant charge in line, under a hot fire of artillery and infantry, and intrenched and kept it.

Hood, who had been massed opposite McPherson, made a forced night-march, and suddenly appeared on the other flank fronting Schofield and Hooker. With his known method of charging and firing, he delivered there a desperate attack on the 22d of June. After a hard battle he was repulsed with heavy loss. This was the "Battle of Culp's Farm." . . .

Again, by the gradual pressure against Johnston's right and left, Sherman forced him to a new contraction of his lines. This time it was the famous Kenesaw position that he assumed. With his right still at Brush Mountain, he extended a light force over the crest of the Kenesaws, and placed a heavier one along the southern slope, reaching far beyond the Dallas and Marietta road. He drew back his left and fortified. The whole line was stronger in arti-ficial contrivances and natural features than the cemetery at Gettysburg. The complete works, the slashings in front, and the difficulties of the slope toward us under a full sweep of cross-fire made the position almost impregnable.

For reasons similar to those which influenced Lee to strike twice for Little Round Top, Sherman ordered an assault here with the hope of carrying the southern slope of Kenesaw, or of penetrating Johnston's long front at some weak point. Schofield, well southward, advanced and crossed Olley's Creek, and kept up enough fire and effort to hold a large force in his front. Mc-Pherson, on the left, did the same, a serious engagement being sustained by Logan's corps advancing straight against the mountain. Logan lost heavily from the trenches in his front, and from artillery that raked his men as they advanced. Seven regimental commanders fell, killed or wounded. But the dreadful battle, hard to describe, was left to Thomas. He commanded two attacks, one opposite the Confederate General Loring's left, the other in front of Cheatham. Newton's division led my attack, and Davis that of Palmer. Like Pickett's charge at Gettysburg, the movement was preceded by a heavy cannonade. Then our skirmishers sprang forward and opened; and quickly the enemy's skirmish-line was drawn back to their main work. Harker, commanding one brigade, led his column rapidly over the open ground. Wagner did the same on Harker's left, and Kimball put his brigade in close support. The enemy's fire was terrific. Our men did not stop till they had gained the edge of the felled trees; a few penetrated, to fall close to the enemy's parapet; but most sought shelter behind logs and rocks, in rifle-holes, or depressions. Harker, moving with them, cheered on his men; when they were forced to stop, he rallied them again and made a second vigorous effort, in which he fell mortally wounded. Davis's effort was like Newton's; he met the same withering fire from rifle-balls and shells. But his men managed to make a shelter, which they kept, close up to the hostile works. Here they staid and intrenched. Our losses in this assault were heavy indeed, and our gain was nothing. We realized now, as never before, the futility of direct assaults upon intrenched lines already well prepared and well manned.

Plainly there was now nothing left for Sherman to do but to send his left army (McPherson's) to follow up the right (Schofield's) across Olley's Creek, and force his cavalry to Sandtown and the Chattahoochee far below Johnston's force. The first sign, namely, McPherson's starting, and Schofield's boldness, set the Confederates again in motion. On the morning of the 3d of July Sherman turned his spy-glass to the Kenesaw crest, and saw our pickets "crawling up the hill cautiously." The strong works were found vacant. Johnston had made new breastworks six miles below, at Smyrna Camp Ground, and another complete set, by the labor of slaves and new levies, where the railway crosses the Chattahoochee. Thomas, taking up the pursuit, followed his enemy through Marietta and beyond. My command skirmished up to the Smyrna works during the 3d. The next day Sherman paid us a Fourth of July visit. He could not at first believe that Johnston would make another stand north of the river. "Howard," he said to me, "you are mistaken; there is no force in your front; they are laughing at you!" We were in a thinnish grove of tall trees, in front of a farm-house. "Well, General," I replied, "let us see." I called Stanley, whose division held the front. "General, double your skirmishers and press them." At once it was done. The lines sped forward, capturing the outlying pits of the enemy, and took many prisoners; but a sheet of lead instantly came from the hidden works in the edge of the wood beyond us, and several unseen batteries hurled their shot across our lines, some of them reaching our grove and forcing us to retire. Sherman, as he rode away, said that I had been correct in my report. While we kept the Confederates busy by skirmishing and battery firing, a set of demonstrations to the north and south of us finally resulted in gaining crossings of the river at Roswell, Soap Creek, Powers's and Paice's ferries. Schofield effected the first crossing by pushing out from Soap Creek boats loaded with men, crossing quickly, and surprising the Confederate cavalry and cannon in his front. This was done on the 9th of July. As soon as Johnston knew of it, he left his excellent works near the Chattahoochee, burned his bridges, and hastened his retreat to Atlanta. The weather had become good, and there was great animation and manifest joy on our side. It was gratifying to escape from such fastnesses and dismal forests as those which had hampered us for over a month, and we now firmly believed that the end of the campaign was sure.

Our armies made a right wheel—Thomas, on the pivot, taking the shortest line to Atlanta; McPherson, on the outer flank, coming by Roswell to Decatur, with Schofield between.

As the several columns were crossing the famous Peach Tree Creek my corps was divided. . . .

Just at this time, much to our comfort and to his surprise, Johnston was removed, and Hood placed in command of the Confederate army. Johnston had planned to attack Sherman at Peach Tree Creek, expecting just such a division between our wings as we made.

Hood endeavored to carry out the plan. A. P. Stewart now had Polk's corps, and Cheatham took Hood's. Hardee on the right and Stewart on his left, in lines that overlapped Newton's position, at 3 o'clock of the 20th of July, struck the blow. They came surging on through the woods, down the gentle slope, with noise and fury like Stonewall Jackson's men at Chancellorsville. As to our men, some of them were protected by piles of rails, but the most had not had time to barricade.

Stewart's masses advanced successively from his right, so Newton was first assailed. His rifles and cannon, firing incessantly and with utmost steadiness, soon stopped and repulsed the front attack; but whole battalions went far east of him into the gap before described. Thomas, behind the creek, was watching; he turned some reserved batteries upon those Confederate battalions, and fired his shells into the thickets that bordered the deep creek, sweeping the creek's valley as far as the cannon could reach. This was sufficient; in his own words, "it relieved the hitch." The hostile flankers broke back in confusion. . . .

The battle of the 20th did not end till Gresham's division, on McPherson's left, had gone diagonally toward Atlanta, sweeping the hostile cavalry of Wheeler before it past the Augusta railroad, and skirmishing up against an open knob denominated Bald Hill. . . . The Bald Hill was an important outpost.

The 21st, a fearfully hot day, was spent by all in readjustment. Thomas brought his three corps forward, near to the enemy. The gap in my lines was closed as we neared the city. Schofield filled the space between the Fourth (mine) and Logan's corps. McPherson, to get a better left, ordered Blair to seize Bald Hill. General Force, of Leggett's division, supported by Giles A. Smith, who now had Gresham's place, charged the hill and carried it, though with a heavy loss. No time ran to waste till this point was manned with batteries protected by thick parapets and well secured by infantry supports.

Atlanta appeared to us like a well-fortified citadel with outer and inner works. After Thomas had beaten him, Hood resolved to give up the Peach Tree line; so, after dark, he drew back two corps into those outer works.

Hardee, however, was destined to a special duty. About midnight he gathered his four divisions into Atlanta: Bate led the way; Walker came next; Cleburne, having now left the vicinity of Bald Hill (for he was soon to go beyond it), followed; then came Maney in rear. They pushed out far south and around Gresham's sleeping soldiers; they kept on eastward till Hardee's advance was within two miles of Decatur, and his rear was nearly past Sherman's extreme left. There, facing north, he formed his battle front; then he halted on rough ground, mostly covered by forest and thicket. He had made a blind night-march of fifteen miles; so he rested his men for a sufficient time, when, slowly and confidently, the well-disciplined Confederates in line took up their forward movement. Success was never more assured, for was not Sherman's cavalry well out of the way, breaking a railroad and burning bridges at and beyond Decatur? And thus far no Yankee except a chance prisoner had discovered this Jacksonian march! The morning showed us empty trenches from Bald Hill to the right of Thomas. We quickly closed again on Atlanta, skirmishing as we went. McPherson's left was, however, near enough already, only a single valley lying between Blair's position and the outer defensive works of the city. The Sixteenth Corps (Dodge), having sent a detachment under General Sprague to hold Decatur, to support the cavalry and take care of sundry army wagons—a thing successfully accomplished—had marched, on the 21st, toward Atlanta. Dodge remained for the night with head of column a mile or more in rear of Blair's general line. Fuller's division was nearest Blair's left, and Sweeny's not far from the Augusta railroad, farther to the north. McPherson spent the night with Sweeny. His hospitals and main supply trains were between Sweeny and the front. About midday McPherson, having determined to make a stronger left, had set Dodge's men in motion. They marched, as usual, by fours, and were in long column pursuing their way nearly parallel to Hardee's battle front, which was hidden by the thick trees. Now danger threatened: at the first skirmish shots Dodge's troops halted and faced to the left and were in good line of battle. The Confederate divisions were advancing; fortunately for Dodge, after the firing began Hardee's approaching lines nearing him had to cross some open fields. McPherson was then paying a brief visit to Sherman near the Howard house. The attack was sudden, but Dodge's veterans, not much disturbed, went bravely to their work. It is easy to imagine the loud roar of artillery and the angry sounds of musketry that came to Sherman and McPherson when the sudden assault culminated and extended from Dodge to Blair's left. McPherson mounted, and galloped off toward the firing. He first met Logan and Blair near the railway; then the three separated, each to hasten to his place on the battle-line. McPherson went at once to Dodge; saw matters going well there; sent off aides and orderlies with dispatches, till he had but a couple of men left with him. He then rode forward to pass to Blair's left through the thick forest interval. Cheatham's division was just approaching. The call was made, "Surrender!" But McPherson, probably without a thought save to escape from such a trap, turned his horse toward his command. He was instantly slain, and fell from his horse. . . . Logan immediately took the Army of the Tennessee, giving his corps to Morgan L. Smith. As soon as Hood, from a prominent point in front of Atlanta, beheld Hardee's lines emerging from the thickets of Bald Hill, and knew by the smoke and

505

sound that the battle was fully joined, he hurried forward Cheatham's division to attack Logan all along the east front of Atlanta. At the time, I sat beside Schofield and Sherman near the Howard house, and we looked upon such parts of the battle as our glasses could compass. Before long we saw the line of Logan broken, with parts of two batteries in the enemy's hands. Sherman put in a cross-fire of cannon, a dozen or more, and Logan organized an attacking force that swept away the bold Confederates by a charge in double-time. Blair's soldiers repulsed the front attack of Cheatham's and Maney's divisions, and then, springing over their parapets, fought Bate's and Maney's men from the other side. The battle continued till night, when Hood again yielded the field to Sherman and withdrew. The losses on both sides in this battle of Atlanta were probably nearly even—about four thousand each. Our gain was in morale.

Sherman now drew his half-circle closer and closer, and began to manœuvre with a view to get upon the railways proceeding southward. The Army of the Tennessee (late McPherson's) was assigned to me by the President, and I took command on the 27th of July, while it was marching around by the rear of Schofield and Thomas, in order to throw itself forward close to Atlanta on the south-west side, near Ezra Church. Skirmishing briskly, Dodge was first put into line facing the city; next Blair, beside him; last, Logan, on the right, making a large angle with Blair. He was not at night quite up to the crest of the ridge that he was to occupy. In the morning of the 28th he was moving slowly and steadily into position. About 8 o'clock Sherman was riding with me through the wooded region in rear of Logan's forces, when the skirmishing began to increase, and an occasional shower of grape cut through the tree-tops and struck the ground beyond us. I said: "General, Hood will attack me here." "I guess not—he will hardly try it again," Sherman replied. I said that I had known Hood at West Point, and that he was indomitable. As the signs increased, Sherman went back to Thomas, where he could best help me should I need reënforcement. Logan halted his line, and the regiments hurriedly and partially covered their front with logs and rails, having only a small protection while kneeling or lying down. It was too late for intrenching. With a terrifying yell, Hood's men charged through the forest. They were met steadily and repulsed. But in the impulse a few Confederate regiments passed beyond Logan's extreme right. To withstand them four regiments came from Dodge; Inspector-General Strong led thither two from Blair, armed with repeating-rifles; and my chief-of-artillery placed several batteries so as to sweep that exposed flank. These were brought in at the exact moment, and after a few rapid discharges, the repeating-rifles being remarkable in their execution, all the groups of flankers were either cut down or had sought safety in flight. This battle was prolonged for hours. We expected help from Morgan's division of Palmer's corps, coming back from Turner's Ferry; but the Confederate cavalry kept it in check. Our troops here exhibited nerve and persistency; Logan was cheerful and hearty and full of enthusiasm. He stopped stragglers and sent them back, and gave every needed order. Blair was watchful and helpful, and so was Dodge. After the last charge had been repelled I went along my lines, and felt proud and happy to be intrusted with such brave and efficient soldiers. Hood, having again lost three times as many as we, withdrew within his fortified lines. Our skirmishers cleared the field, and the battle of Ezra Church was won; and with this result I contented myself. . . .

For a month Hood kept to a defensive attitude, and, like a long storm, the siege operations set in. Sherman worked his right, with block after block, eastward and southward. Schofield and part of Thomas's command had passed beyond me, digging as they halted. Every new trench found a fresh one opposite. The lines were near together. Many officers and men were slain and many were wounded and sent back to the hospitals. Dodge, while reconnoitering, was badly hurt; T. E. G. Ransom took his corps, and J. M. Corse a division in it. . . .

Sherman now having his supplies well up, beginning on the night of the 25th of August, intrenched Slocum's strong corps across his railroad communication to defend it; then made another grand wheel of his armies. Schofield this time clung to the pivot. My command described an arc of 25 miles radius aiming at Jonesboro', while Thomas followed the middle course. Both southern railways were to be seized, and the stations and road destroyed.

Preceded by Kilpatrick, we made the march rapidly enough, considering the endless plague of the enemy's horse artillery supported by Wheeler's cavalry, and the time it took us to break up the West Point railroad. At Renfro Place we were to encamp on the night of the 30th of August. Finding no water there, and also hoping to secure the Flint River Bridge, six miles ahead, I called to Kilpatrick for a squadron. He sent me a most energetic young man, Captain Estes, and the horsemen needed. I asked Estes if he could keep the enemy in motion. He gave a sanguine reply, and galloped off at the head of his men. Wheeler's rear-guard was surprised, and hurried toward the river. Hazen's infantry followed, forgetting their fatigue in the excitement of pursuit. We reached the bridge as it was burning, extinguished the fire, crossed over in the dusk of the evening under an increasing fire from hostile cavalry and infantry, but did not stop till Logan had reached the wooded ridge beyond, near Jonesboro'. The command was soon put into position, and worked all night and during the next morning to intrench, and build the required bridges. Hood had sent Hardee by rail, with perhaps half of his command, to hold Jonesboro'. My Confederate classmate, S. D. Lee, who had had the immediate assault at Ezra Church, here appeared again, commanding Cheatham's corps. At 3 P. M. on the 31st the Confederates came on with the usual vigor, but were met by Logan and Ransom, and thoroughly repulsed. Hood now abandoned Atlanta, and united

507

with Hardee in the vicinity of Jonesboro', near Lovejoy's Station. Thomas, joining my left flank, fought mainly the battle of September 1st. During the rest that followed, Blair and Logan went home on leave of absence; the field-force of the Army of the Tennessee was consolidated into two corps, Osterhaus temporarily commanding the Fifteenth, and Ransom the Seventeenth. Thomas went to Chattanooga to defend the communications with Sherman's army. Wagner's division was sent to Chattanooga, and Corse's division to Rome. Colonel John E. Tourtellotte had a detachment garrisoning the works at Allatoona Pass.

Hood had been threatening for some time to break Sherman's long line of communication and supply. Sherman could not divine where the blow would fall. He was already arranging for a campaign southward; but he wanted Grant's formal sanction, and he wished to make proper provision for Hood.

At last, on the 2d of October, Hood had passed on his way back beyond the Chattahoochee. Sherman had waited for this till he was sure that the first attempt against his line would be south of the Etowah. Now, leaving one corps, Slocum's, at Atlanta, he followed Hood with the remainder of his force. Hood stopped near Dallas, and sent French's division to take the garrison of Allatoona and the depots there. From the top of Kenesaw, Sherman communicated with Corse, who had joined Tourtellotte at Allatoona, and taken command. The popular hymn, "Hold the Fort," was based upon the messages between these chiefs and the noble defense that the garrison successfully made against a whole Confederate division. Sherman was coming, and French, several times repulsed with great loss, withdrew and joined Hood at New Hope Church.

Taking up his northward march, Hood avoided Rome and aimed for Resaca. Schofield was warned, and got ready to defend Chattanooga, while Sherman now made forced marches so as to overtake his enemy and force him to battle. Finding us on his heels, Hood, picking up two or three small garrisons, but leaving untouched those that showed great pluck, like that of the resolute Colonel Clark R. Wever at Resaca, rushed through Sugar Valley and Snake Creek Gap, choking it behind him with trees. My command, following rapidly through the pass (October 16th), cut away or threw the gap obstructions to the right and left, and camped close up to Hood's rear-guard. He again refused battle, and we pursued him beyond Gaylesville, Alabama. Between Rome and Gaylesville, General Ransom, the gallant and promising young officer before mentioned, died from over-work, and exposure due to our forced marches. Taking advantage of a rich country, Sherman recuperated his men and moved slowly back to the Chattahoochee. Now, with the full consent of Grant, he hastened his preparations for his grand march to the sea.

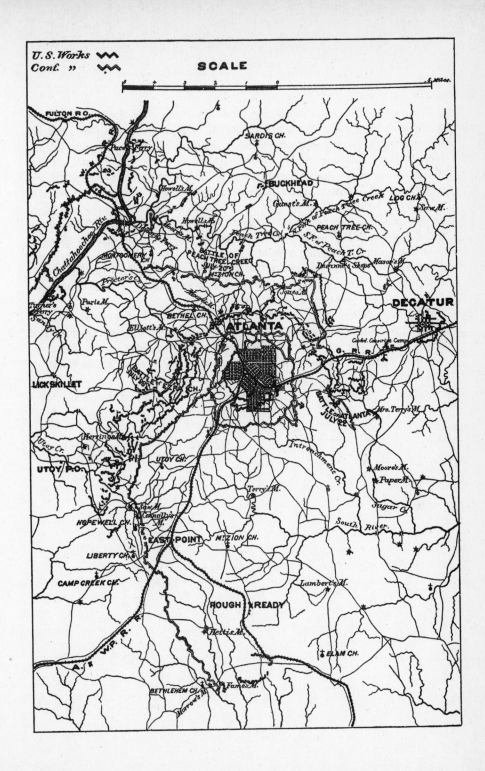

In July when Sherman finally crossed the Chattahoochee, the last natural obstacle before Atlanta, Jefferson Davis got the most pleasure out of the situation he could by relieving Johnston, whom he disliked. In Johnston's place he put John B. Hood, a veteran of Lee's army who had given the Confederacy an arm at Gettysburg and a leg at Chickamauga. When the news of the change of command reached Sherman, he asked General Schofield, a West Point classmate of Hood's, about the new commander. "Bold even unto rashness and courageous in the extreme," was Schofield's report, which pleased Sherman because it meant Hood would probably abandon Johnston's defensive policy and fight. Less pleased were the officers and men of the Army of Tennessee. There the soldiers were used to Johnston and liked him, the officers distrusting Hood's ability to cope with an independent command—and there is considerable evidence that their doubts were well founded.

After Atlanta fell, Hood marched north hoping Sherman would follow; and although for a time he threatened central Tennessee—"The gallant Hood of Texas played hell in Tennessee," his men were still able to sing—his army was demolished and dispersed by Thomas in mid-December in the Battle of Nashville.

"It was painful yet strange to mark how expert grew the old men, women, and children in building their underground forts"

THE DEFENSE OF ATLANTA

BY JOHN B. HOOD, GENERAL, C. S. A.

ABOUT 11 o'clock on the night of the 17th of July, 1864, I received a telegram from the War Office directing me to assume command of the Army of Tennessee. It is difficult to imagine a commander placed at the head of an army under more embarrassing circumstances than those against which I was left to contend. I was comparatively a stranger to the Army of Tennessee. The troops of the Army of Tennessee had for such length of time been subjected to the ruinous policy pursued from Dalton to Atlanta that they were unfitted for united action in pitched battle. They had, in other words, been so long habituated to security behind breastworks that they had become wedded to the "timid defensive" policy, and naturally regarded with distrust a commander likely to initiate offensive operations. The senior corps commander [Hardee] considered he had been supplanted

511

through my promotion and thereupon determined to resign. In consequence, I have no doubt, of my application to President Davis to postpone the order transferring to me the command of the army, he, however, altered his decision, and concluded to remain with his corps.

The evening of the 18th of July found General Johnston comfortably quartered at Macon, whilst McPherson's and Schofield's corps were tearing up the Georgia railroad between Stone Mountain and Decatur; Thomas's army was hastening preparations to cross Peach Tree Creek, within about six miles of Atlanta; and I was busily engaged in hunting up the positions of, and establishing communication with, Stewart's and Hardee's corps.

After having established communication with the corps and the cavalry of the army during the forepart of the night, I found myself upon the morning of the 19th in readiness to fulfill the grave duties devolving upon me.

Our troops had awakened in me heartfelt sympathy, as I had followed their military career with deep interest from early in May of that year. I had witnessed their splendid condition at that period; had welcomed with pride the fine body of reënforcements under General Polk; but, with disappointment, I had seen them, day after day, turn their back upon the enemy, and lastly cross the Chattahoochee River on the night of the 9th of July with one-third of their number lost—the men downcast, dispirited, and demoralized. Stragglers and deserters, the captured and killed, could not now, however, be replaced by recruits, because all the recruiting depots had been drained to reënforce either Lee or Johnston. I could, therefore, but make the best dispositions in my power with the reduced numbers of the army, which opposed a force of 106,000 Federals, buoyant with success and hope, and who were fully equal to 140,000 such troops as confronted Johnston at Dalton, by reason of their victorious march of a hundred miles into the heart of the Confederacy.

Accordingly, on the night of the 18th and morning of the 19th I formed line of battle facing Peach Tree Creek; the left rested near Pace's Ferry road, and the right covered Atlanta. I was informed on the 19th that Thomas was building bridges across Peach Tree Creek; that McPherson and Schofield were well over toward, and even on, the Georgia railroad, near Decatur. I perceived at once that the Federal commander had committed a serious blunder in separating his corps or armies by such distance as to allow me to concentrate the main body of our army upon his right wing, whilst his left was so far removed as to be incapable of rendering timely assistance. General Sherman's violation of the established maxim that an army should always be held well within hand, or its detachments within easy supporting distance, afforded one of the most favorable occasions for complete victory which could have been offered; especially as it presented an opportunity, after crushing his right wing, to throw our entire force upon his left. In fact, such a blunder affords a small army the best, if not the sole, chance of success when contending with a vastly superior force.

Line of battle having been formed, Stewart's corps was in position on the left, Hardee's in the center, and Cheatham's [formerly Hood's] on the right. Orders were given to Generals Hardee and Stewart to observe closely and report promptly the progress of Thomas in the construction of bridges across Peach Tree Creek and the passage of troops. General Cheatham was directed to reconnoiter in front of his left; to erect, upon that part of his line, batteries so disposed as to command the entire space between his left and Peach Tree Creek, in order to completely isolate McPherson's and Schofield's forces from those of Thomas; and, finally, to intrench his line thoroughly. This object accomplished, and Thomas having partially crossed the creek and made a lodgment on the east side within the pocket formed by Peach Tree Creek and the Chattahoochee River, I determined to attack him with two corps—Hardee's and Stewart's, which constituted the main body of the Confederate army—and thus, if possible, crush Sherman's right wing, as we drove it into the narrow space between the creek and the river.

Major-General G. W. Smith's Georgia State troops were posted on the right of Cheatham, and it was impossible for Schofield or McPherson to assist Thomas without recrossing Peach Tree Creek in the vicinity of Decatur, and making on the west side a détour which necessitated a march of not less than ten or twelve miles, in order to reach Thomas's bridges across this creek. I immediately assembled the three corps commanders, Hardee, Stewart, and Cheatham, together with Major-General G. W. Smith, commanding Georgia State troops, for the purpose of giving orders for battle on the following day, the 20th of July.

The three corps commanders, together with General G. W. Smith, were assembled not only for the purpose of issuing to them orders for battle, but with the special design to deliver most explicit instructions in regard to their respective duties. I sought to "make assurance doubly sure" by direct interrogatory; each was asked whether or not he understood his orders. All replied in the affirmative. I was very careful in this respect, inasmuch as I had learned from long experience that no measure is more important, upon the eve of battle, than to make certain, in the presence of the commanders, that each thoroughly comprehends his orders. The usual discretion allowed these officers in no manner diminishes the importance of this precaution.

I also deemed it of equal moment that each should fully appreciate the imperativeness of the orders then issued, by reason of the certainty that our troops would encounter hastily constructed works, thrown up by the Federal troops which had been foremost to cross Peach Tree Creek. Although a portion of the enemy would undoubtedly be found under cover of temporary breastworks, it was equally certain a larger portion would be caught in the act of throwing up such works, and in just the state of confusion to enable our forces to rout them by a bold and persistent attack. With these convictions, I timed the assault at 1 P. M., so as to surprise the enemy in their unsettled condition.

513

The charge was unfortunately not made till about 4 o'clock P. M., on account of General Hardee's failure to obey my specific instructions in regard to the extension of the one-half division front to the right, in order to afford General Cheatham an advantageous position to hold in check McPherson and Schofield. The result was not, however, materially affected by this delay, since the Federals were completely taken by surprise.

General Stewart carried out his instructions to the letter; he moreover appealed in person to his troops before going into action, and informed them that orders were imperative they should carry everything, at all hazards, on their side of Peach Tree Creek; he impressed upon them that they should not halt before temporary breastworks, but charge gallantly over every obstacle and rout the enemy. It was evident that, after long-continued use of intrenchments, General Stewart deemed a personal appeal to his soldiers expedient.

General Stewart and his troops nobly performed their duty in the engagement of the 20th. At the time of the attack his corps moved boldly forward, drove the enemy from his works, and held possession of them until driven out by an enfilade fire of batteries placed in position by General Thomas.

Unfortunately, the corps on Stewart's right, although composed of the best troops in the army, virtually accomplished nothing. In lieu of moving promptly, attacking as ordered, and supporting Stewart's gallant assault, the troops of Hardee—as their losses on that day indicate—did nothing more than skirmish with the enemy. Instead of charging down upon the foe as Sherman represents Stewart's men to have done, many of the troops, when they discovered that they had come into contact with breastworks, lay down, and, consequently, this attempt at pitched battle proved abortive.

The failure on the 20th rendered urgent the most active measures, in order to save Atlanta even for a short period. Through the vigilance of General Wheeler I received information, during the night of the 20th, of the exposed position of McPherson's left flank; it was standing out in air, near the Georgia railroad between Decatur and Atlanta, and a large number of the enemy's wagons had been parked in and around Decatur. The roads were in good condition, and ran in the direction to enable a large body of our army to march, under cover of darkness, around this exposed flank and attack in rear.

I determined to make all necessary preparations for a renewed assault; to attack the extreme left of the Federals in rear and flank, and endeavor to bring the entire Confederate army into united action.

Accordingly, Hardee's and Stewart's corps resumed their former positions. Colonel Presstman, chief engineer, was instructed to examine at once the partially completed line of works toward Peach Tree Creek, which General Johnston had ordered to be constructed for the defense of Atlanta, and to report, at the earliest moment, in regard to their fitness to be occupied by Stewart's and Cheatham's corps, together with the Georgia State troops, under General G. W. Smith. The report was received early on the morning of the 21st, to the effect that the line established by Johnston was not only too close to the city and located upon too low ground, but was totally inadequate for the purpose designed; that Sherman's line, which extended from the vicinity of Decatur almost to the Dalton railroad, north of Atlanta, rendered necessary the construction of an entirely new line, and upon more elevated ground.

The chief engineer was thereupon directed to prepare and stake off a new line, and to employ his entire force, in order that the troops might occupy the works soon after dark on the night of the 21st, and have time to aid in strengthening their position before dawn of next morning. This task was soon executed through the skill and energy of Colonel Presstman and his assistants. Generals Stewart, Cheatham, and G. W. Smith were instructed to order their division and brigade commanders to examine before dark the ground to be occupied by their respective troops, so as to avoid confusion or delay at the time of the movement.

General Hardee, who commanded the largest corps, and whose troops were comparatively fresh, as they had taken but little part in the attack of the previous day, was ordered to hold his forces in readiness to move promptly at dark that night—the 21st. I selected Hardee for this duty, because Cheatham had, at that time, but little experience as a corps commander, and Stewart had been heavily engaged the day previous.

The position of the enemy during the 21st remained, I may say, unchanged, with the exception that Schofield and McPherson had advanced slightly toward Atlanta. To transfer after dark our entire line from the immediate presence of the enemy to another line around Atlanta, and to throw Hardee, the same night, entirely to the rear and flank of McPherson—as Jackson was thrown, in a similar movement, at Chancellorsville and Second Manassas—and to initiate the offensive at daylight, required no small effort upon the part of the men and officers. I hoped, however, that the assault would result not only in a general battle, but in a signal victory to our arms.

It was absolutely necessary these operations should be executed that same night, since a delay of even twenty-four hours would allow the enemy time to intrench further, and afford Sherman a chance to rectify, in a measure, his strange blunder in separating Thomas so far from Schofield and McPherson.

I well knew he would seek to retrieve his oversight at the earliest possible moment; therefore I determined to forestall his attempt and to make another effort to defeat the Federal army. No time was to be lost in taking advantage of this second unexpected opportunity to achieve victory and relieve Atlanta.

I was convinced that McPherson and Schofield intended to destroy not only the Georgia railroad, but likewise our main line of communication, the railroad to Macon. It is now evident the blow on the 20th checked the reckless manner of moving, which had so long been practiced by the enemy, without fear of molestation, during the Dalton-Atlanta campaign. The rap of warning received by Thomas, on Peach Tree Creek, must have induced the Federal commander to alter his plan.

Thus was situated the Federal army at the close of night, on the 21st: it was but partially intrenched; Schofield and McPherson were still separated from Thomas, and at such distance as to compel them to make a détour of about twelve miles, in order to reach the latter in time of need.

The Confederate army occupied the same position, at dark, as prior to the attack of the 20th. The new line around the city, however, had been chosen; each corps commander fully advised of the ground assigned to him, and the special duty devolving upon him; working parties had been detailed in advance from the corps of Stewart and Cheatham, and from the Georgia State troops; rations and ammunition had been issued, and Hardee's corps instructed to be in readiness to move at a moment's warning.

The demonstrations of the enemy upon our right, and which threatened to destroy the Macon railroad—our main line for receiving supplies—rendered it imperative that I should check, immediately, his operations in that direction; otherwise Atlanta was doomed to fall at a very early day. Although the attack of the 20th had caused Sherman to pause and reflect, I do not think he would have desisted extending his left toward our main line of communications had not the events occurred which I am about to narrate.

As already stated, every preparation had been carefully made during the day of the 21st. I had summoned, moreover, to my headquarters the three corps commanders, Hardee, Stewart, and Cheatham, together with Major-General Wheeler, commanding cavalry corps, and Major-General G. W. Smith, commanding Georgia State troops. The following minute instructions were given in the presence of all assembled, in order that each might understand not only his own duty, but likewise that of his brother corps commanders. By this means I hoped each officer would know what support to expect from his neighbor in the hour of battle.

Stewart, Cheatham, and G. W. Smith were ordered to occupy soon after dark the positions assigned them in the new line round the city, and to intrench as thoroughly as possible. General Shoup, chief-of-artillery, was ordered to mass artillery on our right. General Hardee was directed to put his corps in motion soon after dusk; to move south on the McDonough road, across Entrenchment Creek at Cobb's Mills, and *completely* to turn the left of McPherson's army and attack at daylight, or as soon thereafter as possible. He was furnished guides from Wheeler's cavalry, who were familiar with the various roads in that direction; was given clear and positive orders to detach his corps, to swing away from the main body of the army, and to march entirely around and to the rear of McPherson's left flank, even if he was forced to go to or beyond Decatur, which is only about six miles from Atlanta.

Major-General Wheeler was ordered to move on Hardee's right with all the cavalry at his disposal, and to attack with Hardee at daylight. General Cheatham, who was in line of battle on the right and around the city, was instructed to take up the movement from his right as soon as Hardee succeeded in forcing back, or throwing into confusion, the Federal left, and to assist in driving the enemy down and back upon Peach Tree Creek, from right to left. General G. W. Smith would, thereupon, join in the attack. General Stewart, posted on the left, was instructed not only to occupy and keep a strict watch upon Thomas, in order to prevent him from giving aid to Schofield and McPherson, but to engage the enemy the instant the movement became general, *i. e.*, as soon as Hardee and Cheatham succeeded in driving the Federals down Peach Tree Creek and near his right.

Thus orders were given to attack from right to left, and to press the Federal army down and against the deep and muddy stream in their rear. These orders were carefully explained again and again, till each officer present gave assurance that he fully comprehended his duties.

At dawn on the morning of the 22d, Cheatham, Stewart, and G. W. Smith had, by alternating working parties during the night previous, not only strongly fortified their respective positions, but had kept their men comparatively fresh for action, and were in readiness to act as soon as the battle was initiated by Hardee, who was supposed to be at that moment in rear of the adversary's flank.

I took my position at daybreak near Cheatham's right, whence I could observe the left of the enemy's intrenchments, which seemed to be thrown back a short distance on their extreme left. After awaiting nearly the entire morning, I heard, about 10 or 11 o'clock, skirmishing going on directly opposite the left of the enemy, which was in front of Cheatham's right and Shoup's artillery. A considerable time had elapsed when I discovered, with astonishment and bitter disappointment, a line of battle composed of one of Hardee's divisions advancing directly against the intrenched flank of the enemy. I at once perceived that Hardee had not only failed to turn McPherson's left, according to positive orders, but had thrown his men against the enemy's breastworks, thereby occasioning unnecessary loss to us, and rendering doubtful the great result desired. In lieu of completely turning the Federal left and taking the intrenched line of the enemy in reverse, he attacked the retired wing of their flank, having his own left almost within gunshot of our main line around the city. I then began to fear that his disregard of the fixed rule in war, that one danger in rear is more to be feared than ten in front—in other words, that one thousand men in rear are equal to ten thousand in front—would cause us much embarrassment, and place his corps at great disadvantage, notwithstanding he had held success within

517

easy grasp. It had rested in his power to rout McPherson's army by simply moving a little further to the right, and attacking in rear and flank instead of assaulting an intrenched flank. I hoped, nevertheless, this blunder would be remedied, at least in part, by the extreme right of his line lapping round, during the attack, to the rear of McPherson.

I anxiously awaited tidings from the scene of action while listening attentively to what seemed a spirited engagement upon that part of the field. This sound proceeded from the guns of the gallant Wheeler, in the direction of Decatur, whence I hoped, momentarily, to hear a continuous roar of musketry, accompanied by the genuine Confederate shout from Hardee's entire corps, as it advanced and drove the enemy down Peach Tree Creek between our general line of battle and that formidable stream. Although the troops of Hardee fought, seemingly, with determination and spirit, there were indications that the desired end was not being accomplished. The roar of musketry occurring only at intervals strengthened this impression, and a staff-officer was dispatched to General Hardee to know the actual result.

During the early afternoon I received information that the attack had been, in part, successful, but had been checked in consequence of our troops coming in contact with different lines of intrenchments, several of which they had carried and held. Fearing a concentration of the enemy upon Hardee, I commanded General Cheatham, about 3 P. M., to move forward with his corps and attack the position in his front, so as to, at least, create a diversion. The order was promptly and well executed, and our troops succeeded in taking possession of the enemy's defenses in that part of the field. A heavy enfilade fire, however, forced Cheatham to abandon the works he had captured.

Major-General G. W. Smith, perceiving that Cheatham had moved out on his left, and having thoroughly comprehended all the orders relative to the battle, moved gallantly forward with his State troops in support of Cheatham's attack, but was eventually forced to retire on account of superiority of numbers in his front.

Hardee bore off as trophies eight guns and thirteen stand of colors, and, having rectified his line, remained in the presence of the enemy. Cheatham captured five guns and five or six stand of colors.

Notwithstanding the non-fulfillment of the brilliant result anticipated, the partial success of that day was productive of much benefit to the army. It greatly improved the *morale* of the troops, infused new life and fresh hopes, arrested desertions, which had hitherto been numerous, defeated the movement of McPherson and Schofield upon our communications in that direction, and demonstrated to the foe our determination to abandon no more territory without at least a manful effort to retain it.

It became apparent almost immediately after the battle of the 22d that Sherman would make an attack upon our left, in order to destroy the Macon railroad; and, from that moment, I may say, began the siege of Atlanta. The battles of the 20th and 22d checked the enemy's reckless manner of moving, and illustrated effectually to Sherman the danger of stretching out his line in such a manner as to form extensive gaps between his corps or armies as he admits he did at Rocky Face Ridge and New Hope Church.

On the 26th of July the Federals were reported to be moving to our left. This movement continued during the 27th, when I received the additional information that their cavalry was turning our right, in the direction of Flat Rock, with the intention, as I supposed, of interrupting our main line of communication, the Macon railroad. We had lost the road to Augusta previous to the departure of General Johnston on the 18th, and, by the 22d, thirty miles or more thereof had been utterly destroyed. . . .

The holding of Atlanta—unless some favorable opportunity offered itself to defeat the Federals in battle—depended upon our ability to hold intact the road to Macon.

General Wheeler started on the 27th of July in pursuit of the Federal cavalry which had moved around our right; and General [W. H.] Jackson, with the brigades of [Thomas] Harrison and [L. S.] Ross, was ordered, the following day, to push vigorously another body of the enemy's cavalry which was reported to have crossed the river, at Campbellton, and to be moving, via Fairburn, in the direction of the Macon road. On the 28th it was apparent that Sherman was also moving in the same direction with his main body. Lieutenant-General S. D. Lee was instructed to move out with his corps upon the Lick-Skillet road, and to take the position most advantageous to prevent or delay the extension of the enemy's right flank. This officer promptly obeyed orders, and in the afternoon, unexpectedly, came in contact with the Federals in the vicinity of Ezra Church, where a spirited engagement ensued. The enemy was already in possession of a portion of the ground Lee desired to occupy, and the struggle grew to such dimensions that I sent Lieutenant-General Stewart to his support. The contest lasted till near sunset without any material advantage having been gained by either opponent. Our troops failed to dislodge the enemy from their position, and the Federals likewise to capture the position occupied by the Confederates.

Whilst these operations were in progress, Wheeler and Jackson were in hot pursuit of the Federal cavalry; General Lewis's infantry brigade having been sent to Jonesboro', the point about which I supposed the raiders would strike our communications.

At an early hour on the 29th dispatches were received from various points upon the Macon road to the effect that General Wheeler had successfully checked the enemy at Latimer's, and was quietly awaiting developments. On our left, the Federals succeeded in eluding our cavalry, for a time, by skirmishing with our main body, whilst their main force moved round to the rear and cut the telegraph lines at Fairburn and Palmetto. General Jackson, however, soon discovered the ruse, and marched rapidly toward Fayetteville and Jonesboro', the direction in which the Federals had moved. The enemy succeeded in destroying a wagon-train at the former place, in capturing one or two quartermasters who afterward made their escape, and in striking the Macon road about four miles below Jonesboro', when the work of destruction was begun in earnest.

General Lewis, within three hours after receiving the order, had placed his men on the cars and was in Jonesboro' with his brigade ready for action. Meantime Jackson was coming up with his cavalry, when the Federals became alarmed and abandoned their work, but not without having destroyed about a mile and a half of the road, which was promptly repaired.

While Jackson followed in pursuit and Lewis returned to Atlanta, Wheeler moved across from Latimer's, with a portion of his command, in rear of this body of the enemy, leaving General Iverson to pursue General Stoneman, who, after somewhat further damaging the Augusta road and burning the bridges across Walnut Creek and the Oconee River, had moved against Macon.

These operations had been ordered by General Sherman upon a grand scale; picked men and horses had been placed under the command of Generals McCook and Stoneman, with the purpose to destroy our sole line of communication, and to release, at Andersonville, 34,000 Federal prisoners.

These raiders, under McCook, came in contact with General Roddey's cavalry at Newnan, and were there held in check till Wheeler's and Jackson's troops came up; whereupon the combined forces, directed by General Wheeler, attacked the enemy with vigor and determination, and finally routed them. Whilst these operations were progressing in the vicinity of Newnan, General Cobb was gallantly repelling the assault of Stoneman at Macon, when Iverson came up and engaged the enemy with equal spirit and success.

The flanks of the Federal army were at this juncture so well protected by the Chattahoochee and the deep ravines which run down into the river, that my antagonist was enabled to throw his entire force of cavalry against the Macon road; and but for the superiority of the Confederate cavalry he might have succeeded to such an extent as to cause us great annoyance and subject our troops to short rations for a time.

After the utter failure of this experiment General Sherman perceived that his mounted force, about twelve thousand in number, in concert with a corps of infantry as support, could not so effectually destroy our main line of communication as to compel us to evacuate Atlanta.

Wheeler and Iverson having thus thoroughly crippled the Federal cavalry, I determined to detach all the troops of that arm that I could possibly spare, and expedite them, under the command of Wheeler, against Sherman's railroad to Nashville; at the same time to request of the proper authorities that General Maury, commanding at Mobile, be instructed to strike with small bodies the line at different points, in the vicinity of the Tennessee River, and also that Forrest be ordered, with the whole of his available force, into Tennessee for the same object.

General Wheeler, with 4500 men, began operations at once. He succeeded in burning the bridge over the Etowah; recaptured Dalton and Resaca; destroyed about 35 miles of railroad in the vicinity, and captured about 300 mules and 1000 horses; he destroyed in addition about 50 miles of railroad in Tennessee. General Forrest, with his usual energy, struck shortly afterward the Federal line of supplies in this State, and inflicted great damage upon the enemy. Forrest and Wheeler accomplished all but the impossible with their restricted numbers, and the former, finally, was driven out of Tennessee by superior forces.

So vast were the facilities of the Federal commander to reënforce his line of skirmishers, extending from Nashville to Atlanta, that we could not bring together a sufficient force of cavalry to accomplish the desired object. I thereupon became convinced that no sufficiently effective number of cavalry could be assembled in the Confederacy to interrupt the enemy's line of supplies to an extent to compel him to retreat. . . .

On the 7th General Cleburne's division was transferred to our extreme left, and the 9th was made memorable by the most furious cannonade which the city sustained during the siege. Women and children fled into cellars, and were forced to seek shelter a greater length of time than at any period of the bombardment.

The 19th, nigh two weeks after Wheeler's departure with about one-half of our cavalry force, General Sherman took advantage of the absence of these troops, and again attempted a lodgment on the Macon road with cavalry. At 3:30 A. M. General Kilpatrick was reported to be moving, via Fairburn, in the direction of Jonesboro'. General Jackson quickly divined his object, moved rapidly in pursuit, overtook him at an early hour, attacked and forced him to retreat after sustaining considerable loss in killed, wounded, and prisoners. The Federals had previously destroyed a mile and a half of the Macon road, and they had cut the wires and burned the depot at Jonesboro'.

Our cavalry also drove a brigade of the enemy from the Augusta road on the 22d, which affair, together with the happy results obtained in the engagement with Kilpatrick, demonstrated conclusively that, the absence of one-half of our mounted force notwithstanding, we had still a sufficient number, with Jackson, to protect not only the flanks of the army, but likewise our communications against similar raids, and, moreover, to defend our people against pillaging expeditions.

The severe handling by Wheeler and Iverson of the troops under Stoneman and McCook, together with Jackson's success, induced me not to recall Wheeler's 4500 men, who were still operating against the railroad to Nashville. I had, moreover, become convinced that our cavalry was able to

521

compete successfully with double their number. Our cavalry were not cavalrymen *proper,* but were mounted riflemen, trained to dismount and hold in check or delay the advance of the enemy, and who had learned by experience that they could without much difficulty defeat the Federal cavalry.

The bombardment of the city continued till the 25th of August; it was painful, yet strange, to mark how expert grew the old men, women, and children in building their little underground forts, in which to fly for safety during the storm of shell and shot. Often 'mid the darkness of night were they constrained to seek refuge in these dungeons beneath the earth; albeit, I cannot recall one word from their lips expressive of dissatisfaction or willingness to surrender.

Sherman had now been over one month continuously moving toward our left and thoroughly fortifying, step by step, as he advanced in the direction of the Macon railroad. On the night of the 25th he withdrew from our immediate front; his works, which at an early hour the following morning we discovered to be abandoned, were occupied at a later hour by the corps of Stewart and Lee.

On the 27th General G. W. Smith's division was ordered to the left to occupy the position of Stevenson's division which, together with Maury's command, was held in reserve. Early the following morning the enemy were reported by [F. C.] Armstrong in large force at Fairburn, on the West Point road. It became at once evident that Sherman was moving with his main body to destroy the Macon road, and that the fate of Atlanta depended upon our ability to defeat this movement.

Reynolds's and Lewis's brigades were dispatched to Jonesboro' to coöperate with Armstrong. General Adams, at Opelika, was directed to guard the defenses of that place with renewed vigilance, while General Maury was requested to render him assistance, if necessary. The chief quartermaster, ordnance officer, and commissary were given most explicit instructions in regard to the disposition of their respective stores. All surplus property, supplies, etc., were ordered to the rear, or to be placed on cars in readiness to move at any moment the railroad became seriously threatened. Armstrong was instructed to establish a line of couriers to my headquarters, in order to report every hour, if requisite, the movements of the enemy. In fact, every precaution was taken not only to hold our sole line of communication unto the last extremity, but also, in case of failure, to avoid loss or destruction of stores and material.

On the 29th the Federals marched slowly in the direction of Rough and Ready and Jonesboro'. A portion of Brown's division was directed to take position at the former place and fortify thoroughly, in order to afford protection to the road at that point. General Hardee, who was at this juncture in the vicinity of East Point, was instructed to make such disposition of his troops as he considered most favorable for defense; and, in addition, to hold his corps in readiness to march at the word of command. Jackson and Armstrong received orders to report the different positions of the corps of the enemy at dark every night.

The morning of the 30th found our general line extended farther to the left —Hardee being in the vicinity of Rough and Ready with Lee's corps on his right, near East Point. Information from our cavalry clearly indicated that the enemy would strike our road at Jonesboro'. After consultation with the corps commanders, I determined upon the following operations as the last hope of holding on to Atlanta.

A Federal corps crossed Flint River, at about 6 P. M., near Jonesboro', and made an attack upon Lewis's brigade, which was gallantly repulsed. This action became the signal for battle. General Hardee was instructed to move rapidly with his troops to Jonesboro', whither Lieutenant-General Lee, with his corps, was ordered to follow during the night. Hardee was to attack with the entire force early on the morning of the 31st, and drive the enemy, at all hazards, into the river in their rear. In the event of success, Lee and his command were to be withdrawn that night back to Rough and Ready; Stewart's corps, together with Major-General G. W. Smith's State troops, were to form line of battle on Lee's right, near East Point, and the whole force move forward the following morning, attack the enemy in flank, and drive him down Flint River and the West Point railroad. In the meantime the cavalry was to hold in check the corps of the enemy, stationed at the railroad bridge across the Chattahoochee, near the mouth of Peach Tree Creek, whilst Hardee advanced from his position near Jonesboro', or directly on Lee's left.

Such were the explicit instructions delivered. I impressed upon General Hardee that the fate of Atlanta rested upon his ability, with the aid of two corps, to drive the Federals across Flint River, at Jonesboro'. I also instructed him in the event of failure—which would necessitate the evacuation of the city—to send Lee's corps, at dark, back to or near Rough and Ready, in order to protect our retreat to Lovejoy's Station.

The attack was not made till about 2 P. M., and then resulted in our inability to dislodge the enemy. The Federals had been allowed time, by the delay, to strongly intrench; whereas had the assault been made at an early hour in the morning the enemy would have been found but partially protected by works.

General Hardee transmitted to me no official report at that period, nor subsequently, of his operations whilst under my command. I find, however, from the diary in my possession that his corps succeeded in gaining a portion of the Federal works; the general attack, notwithstanding, must have been rather feeble, as the loss incurred was only about 1400 in killed and wounded—a small number in comparison to the forces engaged.

This failure gave to the Federal army the control of the Macon road, and thus necessitated the evacuation of Atlanta at the earliest hour possible.

I was not so much pained by the fall of Atlanta as by the *recurrence* of

523

retreat, which I full well knew would further demoralize the army and renew desertions. The loss of over 4000, sustained from this same cause during the change from Kenesaw Mountain to and across the Chattahoochee,
augmented my great reluctance to order the army to again turn its back to
the foe. Howbeit, the presence of 34,000 Federal prisoners at Andersonville
rendered it absolutely incumbent to place the army between Sherman and
that point, in order to prevent the Federal commander from turning loose
this large body. . . . Thus the proximity of these prisoners to Sherman's army
not only forced me to remain in a position to guard the country against the
fearful calamity aforementioned, but also thwarted my design to move north,
across Peach Tree Creek and the Chattahoochee, back to Marietta, where I
would have destroyed the enemy's communications and supplies, and then
have taken position near the Alabama line, with the Blue Mountain railroad in rear, by which means the Confederate army could, with ease, have
been provisioned.

.In lieu of the foregoing operations, the battle of Jonesboro' was fought,
and on the following day, September 1st, at 2 A. M., Lieutenant-General Lee,
with his corps, marched from Jonesboro' to the vicinity of Rough and Ready,
and so posted his troops as to protect our flank, whilst we marched out of Atlanta at 5 P. M. the same day, on the McDonough road, in the direction of
Lovejoy's Station. Generals Morgan and Scott, stationed at East Point, received similar orders to protect our flank during the retreat. . . .

On the 6th the Federals withdrew from our immediate front and moved
off in the direction of Atlanta. General Sherman published orders stating
that his army would retire to East Point, Decatur, and Atlanta, and repose
after the fatigue of the campaign through which it had passed. We were apprised of these instructions soon after their issuance—as well as of nigh every
important movement of the enemy—through the vigilance of our cavalry,
spies, and scouts, and from information received through Federal prisoners.
Upon this date it may be justly considered that the operations round Atlanta
ceased. We had maintained a defense, during forty-six days, of an untenable
position, and had battled almost incessantly, day and night, with a force of
about 45,000 against an army of 106,000 effectives, flushed with victory upon
victory from Dalton to Atlanta.

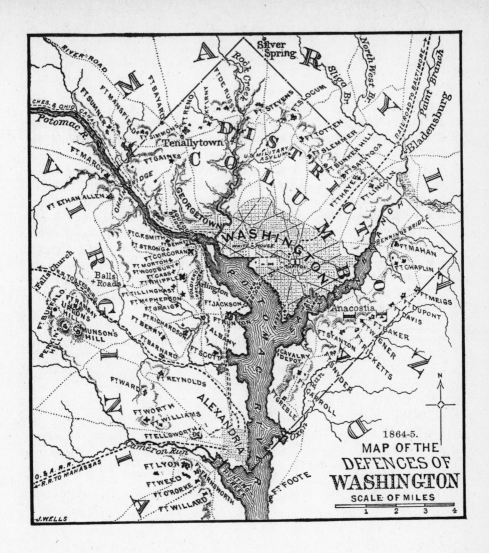

1864-5.

MAP OF THE
DEFENCES OF
WASHINGTON

SCALE OF MILES

J.WELLS

Of all the Confederate generals, Jubal Early (his men called him "Old Jube" or "Old Jubilee") got closest to Washington—in June 1864 while Lee and Grant were sparring around Richmond. And considering the condition of his men, it was one of the most remarkable feats of the war. In his official report, he says sedately that while he had to abandon hopes of capturing Washington, he had undoubtedly "given the Federal authorities a terrible fright." One of his officers remembered that Early expressed his regret more colorfully. As they rode away south, "Old Jube" said to him, "Major, we haven't taken Washington, but we've scared Abe Lincoln like hell!" What Early probably didn't imagine as he sat his horse in front of Fort Stevens, appraising its strength, was that Lincoln had come out to see the fighting and was right there on the parapets. Those who were with the President later reported him cool under fire —"with grave and passive countenance."

"In sight of the dome of the Capitol"

EARLY'S MARCH TO WASHINGTON IN 1864

BY JUBAL A. EARLY, LIEUTENANT-GENERAL, C. S. A.

O N THE 12th of June, 1864, while the Second Corps (Ewell's) of the Army of Northern Virginia was lying near Gaines's Mill, in rear of Hill's line at Cold Harbor, I received orders from General Lee to move the corps, with two of the battalions of artillery attached to it, to the Shenandoah Valley; to strike Hunter's force in the rear and, if possible, destroy it; then to move down the valley, cross the Potomac near Leesburg, in Loudoun County, or at or above Harper's Ferry, as I might find most practicable, and threaten Washington city. I was further directed to communicate with General Breckinridge, who would coöperate with me in the attack on Hunter and the expedition into Maryland.

The Second Corps now numbered a little over eight thousand muskets for duty. It had been on active and arduous service in the field for forty

527

days. Divisions were not stronger than brigades ought to have been, nor brigades than regiments. On the morning of the 13th, at 2 o'clock, we commenced the march, and on the 16th arrived at the Rivanna River, near Charlottesville, having marched over eighty miles in four days. At Charlottesville I received a telegram from Breckinridge, dated at Lynchburg, informing me that Hunter was then in Bedford County about twenty miles from that place and moving on it. The railroad and telegraph between Charlottesville and Lynchburg had been, fortunately, but slightly injured by the enemy's cavalry, and had been repaired. I ordered all the trains of the two roads to be sent to me with all dispatch, for the purpose of transporting my troops to Lynchburg. The trains were not in readiness to take the troops on board until sunrise on the morning of the 17th, and then only enough were furnished to transport about half my infantry. I accompanied Ramseur's division, going on the front train; but the road and rolling stock were in such bad condition that I did not reach Lynchburg until about 1 o'clock in the afternoon, and the other trains were much later.

As General Breckinridge was in bed, suffering from an injury received near Cold Harbor, at his request General D. H. Hill, who happened to be in town, had made arrangements for the defense of the city with such troops as were at hand. Slight works had been hastily thrown up on College Hill, covering the turnpike and Forest roads from Liberty, manned by Breckinridge's infantry and the dismounted cavalry of the command [Jones's and Vaughn's brigades] which had been with Jones at Piedmont. The reserves, invalids from the hospitals, and the cadets from the Military Institute at Lexington occupied other parts of the line. My troops, as they arrived, had been ordered in front of the works to bivouac, and I immediately sent orders for them to move out on the turnpike, and two brigades of Ramseur's division arrived just in time to be thrown across the road at a redoubt about two miles from the city as Imboden's command was driven back by vastly superior numbers. These brigades, with two pieces of artillery in the redoubt, arrested the progress of the enemy, and Ramseur's other brigade, and the part of Gordon's division which had arrived, took position on the same line. The enemy opened a heavy fire of artillery on us, but as night soon came on he went into camp on our front.

Orders had been given for the immediate return of the trains for the rest of my infantry, but it did not get to Lynchburg until late in the afternoon of the 18th, and meanwhile I contented myself with acting on the defensive. There was artillery firing and skirmishing along the line, and in the afternoon an attack was made to the right of the turnpike, which was handsomely repulsed with considerable loss to the enemy. A demonstration of the enemy's cavalry on the Forest road was checked by part of Breckinridge's infantry under Wharton, and McCausland's cavalry. As soon as the remainder of my infantry arrived by the railroad, though none of my artillery had gotten up, arrangements were made for attacking Hunter at daylight on the 19th; but after midnight it was discovered that he was moving, and at light it was observed that he was in retreat, and pursuit commenced. The enemy's rear was overtaken at Liberty, twenty-five miles from Lynchburg, just before night, and driven through that place, after a brisk skirmish, by Ramseur's division. The day's march on the old turnpike, which was very rough, had been terrible. The pursuit was resumed early on the morning of the 20th, and the enemy was pursued into the mountains at Buford's Gap, but he had taken possession of the crest of the Blue Ridge, and put batteries in position commanding a gorge through which the road passes. On the 21st the pursuit was resumed very shortly after sunrise. The enemy had turned off from Salem toward Lewisburg, and McCausland had struck his column and captured ten pieces of artillery, but was compelled to fall back, carrying off, however, the prisoners and also a part of the artillery, and disabling the rest. As the enemy had got into the mountains, where nothing useful could be accomplished by pursuit, I did not deem it proper to continue it farther. A great part of my command had had nothing to eat for the last two days, except a little bacon which was obtained at Liberty. It had marched sixty miles in the three days' pursuit, over very rough roads. I determined, therefore, to rest on the 22d, so as to enable the wagons and artillery to get up, and prepare the men for the long march before them.

At Lynchburg I had received a telegram from General Lee, directing me, after disposing of Hunter, either to return to his army or to carry out the original plan, as I might deem most expedient. After the pursuit had ceased I received another dispatch from him, submitting it to my judgment whether the condition of my troops would permit the expedition across the Potomac to be carried out, and I determined to take the responsibility of continuing it. On the 23d the march was resumed, and we reached Buchanan that night. On the 26th I reached Staunton in advance of the troops, and the latter came up next day, which was spent in reducing transportation and getting provisions from Waynesboro'. The official reports at this place showed about two thousand mounted men for duty in the cavalry, which was composed of four small brigades, to wit: Imboden's, McCausland's, Jackson's, and Jones's (now Johnson's). The official reports of the infantry showed ten thousand muskets for duty, including Vaughn's dismounted cavalry. Besides Breckinridge's own infantry division, under Elzey (now under Vaughn, afterward under Echols), Gordon's division of the Second Corps was assigned to General Breckinridge, in order to give him a command commensurate with his proper one. Nearly half the troops were barefoot, or nearly so, and shoes were sent for. But without waiting for them the march was resumed on the 28th, with five days' rations in the wagons and two days' in haversacks. Imboden was sent through Brock's Gap to the South Branch of the Potomac to destroy the railroad bridge over that stream, and all the bridges on the

Baltimore and Ohio Railroad from that point to Martinsburg. On the 2d of July we reached Winchester, and here I received a dispatch from General Lee, directing me to remain in the lower valley until everything was in readiness to cross the Potomac, and to destroy the Baltimore and Ohio Railroad and the Chesapeake and Ohio Canal as far as possible. This was in accordance with my previous determination, and its policy was obvious. My provisions were nearly exhausted, and if I had moved through Loudoun it would have been necessary for me to halt and thresh wheat and have it ground, as neither bread nor flour could be otherwise obtained; which would have caused much greater delay than was required on the other route, where we could take provisions from the enemy. Moreover, unless the Baltimore and Ohio Railroad was torn up the enemy would have been able to move troops from the West over that road to Washington.

On the morning of the 3d Sigel, with a considerable force, after slight skirmishing, evacuated Martinsburg, leaving considerable stores in our hands. McCausland burned the bridge over Back Creek, capturing the guard at North Mountain depot, and succeeded in reaching Hainesville; but Bradley T. Johnson, after driving Mulligan, with hard fighting at Leetown, across the railroad, was himself forced back, when Sigel united with Mulligan, upon Rodes's and Ramseur's divisions, which arrived at Leetown after a march of twenty-four miles. During the night Sigel retreated across the Potomac at Shepherdstown to Maryland Heights.

During the night of the 4th the enemy evacuated Harper's Ferry, burning the railroad and pontoon bridges across the Potomac. It was not possible to occupy the town of Harper's Ferry, except with skirmishers, as it was thoroughly commanded by the heavy guns on Maryland Heights; and the 5th was spent by Rodes's and Ramseur's divisions in demonstrating at that place. In the afternoon Breckinridge's command moved to Shepherdstown and crossed the Potomac, followed by Rodes's and Ramseur's divisions early on the 6th. Gordon's division advanced toward Maryland Heights, and drove the enemy into his works. Working parties were employed in destroying the aqueduct of the canal over the Antietam, and the locks and canal-boats. On the 7th Rodes moved through Rohrersville on the road to Crampton's Gap in South Mountain, and skirmished with a small force of the enemy, while Breckinridge demonstrated against Maryland Heights. McCausland had occupied Hagerstown and levied a contribution of $20,000, and Boonsboro' had been occupied by Johnson's cavalry. A letter from General Lee had informed me that an effort would be made to release the prisoners at Point Lookout, and directing me to take steps to unite them with my command. My desire had been to manœuvre the enemy out of Maryland Heights, so as to move directly to Washington; but he had taken refuge in his strongly fortified works, and I therefore determined to move through the gaps of South Mountain north of the Heights. On the 7th the greater portion of the cavalry was sent in the direction of Frederick; and that night the expected shoes arrived and were distributed.

Early on the morning of the 8th the whole force moved: Rodes through Crampton's Gap to Jefferson; Breckinridge through Fox's Gap; and Ramseur, with the trains, through Boonsboro' Gap, followed by Lewis's brigade, which had started from Harper's Ferry the night before, after burning the trestle-work on the railroad and the stores which had not been brought off. Early on the 9th Johnson, with his brigade of cavalry and a battery of horse artillery, moved to the north of Frederick, with orders to strike the railroads from Baltimore to Harrisburg and Philadelphia, burn the bridges over the Gunpowder, also to cut the railroad between Washington and Baltimore, and threaten the latter place; and then to move toward Point Lookout for the purpose of releasing the prisoners, if we should succeed in getting into Washington. The other troops also moved forward toward Monocacy Junction, and Ramseur's division passed through Frederick, driving a force of skirmishers before it.

The enemy in considerable force, under General Lew Wallace, was found strongly posted on the eastern bank of the Monocacy, near the junction, with an earth-work, and two block-houses commanding both the railroad bridge and the bridge on the Georgetown pike. McCausland, crossing the river with his brigade, dismounted his men and advanced rapidly against the enemy's left flank, which he threw into confusion, but he was then gradually forced back. McCausland's movement, which was very brilliantly executed, solved the problem for me, and orders were sent to Breckinridge to move up rapidly with Gordon's division to McCausland's assistance, and, striking the enemy's left, to drive him from the positions commanding the crossings in Ramseur's front, so that the latter might cross. This division crossed under the personal superintendence of General Breckinridge, and while Ramseur skirmished with the enemy in front, the attack was made by Gordon in gallant style, and with the aid of several pieces of King's artillery, which had been crossed over, and Nelson's artillery from the opposite side, he threw the enemy into great confusion and forced him from his position. Ramseur immediately crossed on the railroad bridge and pursued the enemy's flying forces, and Rodes crossed on the left and joined in the pursuit. Between 600 and 700 unwounded prisoners fell into their hands, and the enemy's loss in killed and wounded was very heavy. Our loss in killed and wounded was about 700. The action closed about sunset, and we had marched about fourteen miles before it commenced. All the troops and trains were crossed over the Monocacy that night, so as to resume the march early the next day. During the operations at Monocacy, a contribution of $200,000 in money was levied on the city of Frederick, and some much-needed supplies were obtained.

On the 10th the march was resumed at daylight, and we bivouacked four miles from Rockville, on the Georgetown pike, having marched twenty miles. McCausland, moving in front, drove a body of the enemy's cavalry before him, and had a brisk engagement at Rockville, where he encamped after defeating and driving off the enemy.

We moved at daylight on the 11th, McCausland on the Georgetown pike, while the infantry, preceded by Imboden's cavalry under Colonel Smith, turned to the left at Rockville, so as to reach the 7th street pike which runs by Silver Springs into Washington. Jackson's cavalry moved on the left flank. The previous day had been very warm, and the roads were exceedingly dusty, as there had been no rain for several weeks. The heat during the night had been very oppressive, and but little rest had been obtained. This day was an exceedingly hot one, and there was no air stirring. While marching, the men were enveloped in a suffocating cloud of dust, and many of them fell by the way from exhaustion. Our progress was therefore very much impeded, but I pushed on as rapidly as possible, hoping to get into the fortifications around Washington before they could be manned. Smith drove a small body of cavalry before him into the works on the 7th street pike, and dismounted his men and deployed them as skirmishers. I rode ahead of the infantry, and arrived in sight of Fort Stevens on this road a short time after noon, when I discovered that the works were but feebly manned.

Rodes, whose division was in front, was immediately ordered to bring it into line as rapidly as possible, throw out skirmishers, and move into the works if he could. My whole column was then moving by flank, which was the only practicable mode of marching on the road we were on, and before Rodes's division could be brought up we saw a cloud of dust in the rear of the works toward Washington, and soon a column of the enemy filed into them on the right and left, and skirmishers were thrown out in front, while an artillery fire was opened on us from a number of batteries. This defeated our hopes of getting possession of the works by surprise, and it became necessary to reconnoiter.

Rodes's skirmishers were thrown to the front, driving those of the enemy to the cover of the works, and we proceeded to examine the fortifications in order to ascertain if it was practicable to carry them by assault. They were found to be exceedingly strong, and consisted of what appeared to be inclosed forts for heavy artillery, with a tier of lower works in front of each, pierced for an immense number of guns, the whole being connected by curtains with ditches in front, and strengthened by palisades and abatis. The timber had been felled within cannon range all around and left on the ground, making a formidable obstacle, and every possible approach was raked by artillery. On the right was Rock Creek, running through a deep ravine which had been rendered impassable by the felling of the timber on each side, and beyond were the works on the Georgetown pike which had been reported to be the strongest of all. On the left, as far as the eye could reach, the works appeared to be of the same impregnable character. This reconnoissance consumed the balance of the day.

The rapid marching and the losses at Harper's Ferry, Maryland Heights, and Monocacy had reduced my infantry to about 8000 muskets. Of these a very large number were greatly exhausted by the last two days' marching, some having fallen by sunstroke, and not more than one-third of my force could have been carried into action. I had about forty pieces of artillery, of which the largest were 12-pounder Napoleons, besides a few pieces of horse-artillery with the cavalry. McCausland reported the works on the Georgetown pike too strongly manned for him to assault. After dark on the 11th I held a consultation with Major-Generals Breckinridge, Rodes, Gordon, and Ramseur, in which I stated to them the necessity of doing something immediately, as the passes of South Mountain and the fords of the Upper Potomac would soon be closed against us. After interchanging views with them, I determined to make an assault on the enemy's works at daylight next morning. But during the night a dispatch was received from General Bradley T. Johnson from near Baltimore, that two corps had arrived from General Grant's army, and that his whole army was probably in motion. As soon as it was light enough to see, I rode to the front, and found the parapet lined with troops. I had, therefore, reluctantly to give up all hopes of capturing Washington, after I had arrived in sight of the dome of the Capitol, and given the Federal authorities a terrible fright.

Even a year earlier, before Gettysburg, the Federal Cavalry had found it could hold its own with the troopers of Stuart, Hampton, Wheeler and Company. Now, in the summer of 1864, it had an unlimited supply of splendid mounts and the men to handle them. What's more, it had developed several resourceful commanders, at least one of whom, General Philip H. Sheridan, was turning into a soldier with a grasp of broad military strategy and the ability to manage large bodies of fighters mounted or unmounted. His exploits in the Shenandoah Valley in the last half of 1864 were reminiscent of Jackson's in the same theater two years before; but this time they had more meaning because, as reflective men North and South could already tell, they were prelude to the final act of the insane drama that was the Civil War.

"Destroying, burning . . . "

BY WESLEY MERRITT, MAJOR-GENERAL, U. S. V., BRIGADIER-GENERAL, U. S. A.

U P to the summer of 1864 the Shenandoah Valley had not been to the Union armies a fortunate place either for battle or for strategy. A glance at the map will go far toward explaining this. The Valley has a general direction from south-west to north-east. The Blue Ridge Mountains, forming its eastern barrier, are well defined from the James River above Lynchburg to Harper's Ferry on the Potomac. Many passes (in Virginia called "gaps") made it easy of access from the Confederate base of operations; and, bordered by a fruitful country filled with supplies, it offered a tempting highway for an army bent on a flanking march on Washington or the invasion of Maryland or Pennsylvania. For the Union armies, while it was an equally practicable highway, it led away from the objective, Rich-

535

mond, and was exposed to flank attacks through the gaps from vantage-ground and perfect cover.

It was not long after General Grant completed his first campaign in Virginia, and while he was in front of Petersburg, that his attention was called to this famous seat of side issues between Union and Confederate armies. With quick military instinct he saw that the Valley was not useful to the Government for aggressive operations. He decided that it must be made untenable for either army. In doing this he reasoned that the advantage would be with us, who did not want it as a source of supplies, nor as a place of arms, and against the Confederates, who wanted it for both. Accordingly, instructions were drawn up for carrying on a plan of devastating the Valley in a way least injurious to the people. These instructions, which were intended for Hunter, were destined to be carried out by another, and how well this was accomplished it is my purpose to recount.

Hunter's failure to capture Lynchburg in the spring of 1864 and his retreat by a circuitous line opened the Valley to General Early, who had gone to the relief of Lynchburg. Marching down the Valley and taking possession of it without serious opposition, Early turned Harper's Ferry, which was held by a Union force under Sigel, and crossed into Maryland at Shepherdstown. The governors of New York, Pennsylvania, and Massachusetts were called on for hundred-days men to repel the invasion, and later the Army of the Potomac supplied its quota of veterans as a nucleus around which the new levies could rally. General Early marched on Washington, and on the 11th of July was in front of the gates of the capital. The following day, after a severe engagement in which the guns of Fort Stevens took part, he withdrew his forces through Rockville and Poolesville, and, crossing the Potomac above Leesburg, entered the Valley of Virginia through Snicker's Gap. Afterward, crossing the Shenandoah at the ferry of the same name, he moved to Berrysville, and there awaited developments.

After the immediate danger to Washington had passed it became a question with General Grant and the authorities in Washington to select an officer who, commanding in the Valley, would prevent further danger from invasion. After various suggestions, Major-General Philip H. Sheridan was selected temporarily for this command. . . .

Naturally, on assuming command, Sheridan moved with caution. He was incited to this by his instructions, and inclined to it by his unfamiliarity with the country, with the command, and with the enemy he had to deal with. On the other hand, Early, who had nothing of these to learn, save the mettle of his new adversary, was aggressive, and at once manœuvred with a bold front, seemingly anxious for a battle. The movements of the first few days showed, however, that Early was not disposed to give battle unless he could do so on his own conditions.

On the morning of the 10th of August Sheridan, who had massed his army at Halltown, in front of Harper's Ferry, marched toward the enemy's communications, his object being to occupy Early's line of retreat and force him to fight before reënforcements could reach him. The march of my cavalry toward the Millwood-Winchester road brought us in contact with the enemy's cavalry on that road, and it was driven toward Kernstown. At the same time a brigade under Custer, making a reconnoissance on the Berryville-Winchester road, came on the enemy holding a defile of the highway while "his trains and infantry were marching toward Strasburg." As soon as the retreat of the enemy was known to General Sheridan the cavalry was ordered to pursue and harass him. Near White Post, Devin came upon a strongly posted force, which, after a sharp fight, he drove from the field, and the division took position on the Winchester-Front Royal pike. The same day my division had a severe affair with infantry near Newtown, in which the loss to my Second Brigade was considerable.

On the 12th of August, the enemy having retired the night before, the cavalry pursued to Cedar Creek, when it came up with Early's rear-guard and continued skirmishing until the arrival of the head of the infantry column. The day following, the reconnoissance of a brigade of cavalry discovered the enemy strongly posted at Fisher's Hill. About this time Early received his expected reënforcements. General Sheridan, being duly informed of this, made preparations to retire to a position better suited for defense and adapted to the changed conditions of the strength of the two armies.

On the 13th of August General Devin's brigade of the First Division was ordered to Cedarville on the Front Royal pike, and on the 14th I marched with the rest of my division to the same point, Gibbs taking position near Nineveh. On the arrival of his reënforcements Early had requested General R. H. Anderson, in command, to take station at Front Royal, it being a convenient point from which to make a flank movement in case of attack on Sheridan's command, which Early undoubtedly contemplated. At the same time it constituted a guard to the Luray Valley.

About 2 P. M. on the 16th an attack was made by this command on the First Cavalry Division, which resulted in the battle of Cedarville. A force of cavalry under Fitz Lee, supported by a brigade of Kershaw's division, made a descent on Devin's brigade. General Fitz Lee drove in the cavalry pickets and attacked Devin with great violence. This force was scarcely repulsed when a brigade of infantry was discovered moving on the opposite bank of the Shenandoah River toward the left of the cavalry position. One regiment of Custer's brigade, dismounted, was moved up to the crest of a hill near the river-bank to meet this force, while the rest of the brigade, mounted, was stationed to the right of the hill. At the same time the Reserve Brigade under General Gibbs was summoned to the field. The enemy advanced boldly, wading the river, and when within short carbine range was met by a murderous volley from the dismounted men, while the remainder

537

of the command charged mounted. The Confederates were thrown into confusion and retreated, leaving 300 prisoners, together with two stand of colors. Anderson hurried reënforcements to his beaten brigades, but no further attempt to cross the river was made. The loss to the Union cavalry was about 60 in killed and wounded. The loss to the enemy was not less than 500.

These affairs between the Union cavalry and the enemy's infantry were of more importance than might appear at first glance. They gave the cavalry increased confidence, and made the enemy correspondingly doubtful even of the ability of its infantry, in anything like equal numbers, to contend against our cavalry in the open fields of the Valley.

On the night of the 16th Sheridan withdrew toward his base, and on the following day the cavalry marched, driving all the cattle and live stock in the Valley before it, and burning the grain from Cedar Creek to Berryville. No other private property was injured, nor were families molested.

On the afternoon of the 17th the Third Division of cavalry, under General James H. Wilson, reported to General Torbert, chief-of-cavalry, who with it and Lowell's brigade and the Jersey brigade (Penrose's) of the Sixth Corps was ordered to cover the flank of the army which marched and took position near Berryville. General Early, who on the morning of the 17th discovered the withdrawal of Sheridan's force, pursued rapidly, Anderson advancing from Front Royal with his command. Early struck Torbert's force with such vigor and with such overwhelming numbers as completely to overthrow it, with considerable loss, and drive it from Winchester. In this affair Penrose's brigade lost about 300 men in killed, wounded, and prisoners, and Wilson's cavalry lost in prisoners some 50 men. At this time, information having reached Sheridan that the reënforcements that had come to Early under Anderson were only part of what might be expected, Sheridan concluded still further to solidify his lines. On the 21st of August Early moved with his army to attack Sheridan. His own command marched through Smithfield toward Charlestown, and Anderson on the direct road through Summit Point. Rodes's and Ramseur's infantry were advanced to the attack, and heavy skirmishing was continued for some time with a loss to the Sixth Corps, principally Getty's division, of 260 killed and wounded. In the meantime Anderson was so retarded by the Union cavalry that he did not reach the field, and night overtaking him at Summit Point, he there went into camp. That night Sheridan drew in the cavalry, and, carrying out the resolution already formed, withdrew his army to Halltown. During the three days following the Confederates demonstrated in front of Sheridan's lines, but to little purpose except to skirmish with Crook's and Emory's pickets. On the 25th, leaving Anderson's force in front of Sheridan, Early moved with his four divisions and Fitzhugh Lee's cavalry to Leetown, from which place he dispatched Lee toward Williamsport while he crossed the railroad at Kearneysville and moved toward Shepherdstown. Between Kearneysville and Leetown he was met by Torbert with the cavalry. A sharp fight followed, in the first shock of which Early's advance, consisting of Wharton's division, was driven back in confusion, but upon discovering the strength of the enemy, Torbert withdrew in good order, though Custer's brigade was pressed so closely that he was forced to cross the Potomac. A charge on the flank of the pursuing infantry relieved Custer from danger, and the next morning he returned, as ordered, via Harper's Ferry to the army at Halltown. Early's movement ended with this affair, and during the following two days he returned to the vicinity of Winchester.

During the absence of Early, R. H. Anderson's position was reconnoitered by Crook with two divisions and Lowell's cavalry brigade, who carried Anderson's lines, driving two brigades from their earth-works and capturing a number of officers and men, after which Anderson withdrew from Sheridan's front.

In a dispatch to Halleck Sheridan said: "I have thought it best to be prudent, everything considered." Grant commended Sheridan's conduct of affairs in general terms, and predicted the withdrawal from the Valley of all of Early's reënforcements. This the pressure of Grant's lines at Petersburg finally accomplished.

On the 28th of August Sheridan moved his army forward to Charlestown. My division of cavalry marched to Leetown, and drove the enemy's cavalry to Smithfield and across the Opequon. The next day Early's infantry, in turn, drove my division from Smithfield; whereupon Sheridan, advancing with Ricketts's division, repulsed the enemy's infantry, which retired to the west bank of the Opequon. On this day the cavalry had some severe fighting with Early's infantry, but not until in hand-to-hand fighting the Confederate cavalry had been driven from the field.

On the 3d of September Rodes's Confederate division proceeded to Bunker Hill, and in conjunction with Lomax's cavalry made a demonstration which was intended to cover the withdrawal of Anderson's force from the Valley. But on marching toward the gap of the Blue Ridge, via Berryville, Anderson came upon Crook's infantry just taking station there. The meeting was a surprise to both commands and resulted in a sharp engagement which continued till nightfall. On the following morning Early moved with part of his infantry to Anderson's assistance, and demonstrating toward the right of Sheridan's lines, he made show of giving battle, but only long enough to extricate Anderson and his trains, when the entire command retired to the country near Winchester. On the 14th Anderson withdrew from Early's army, and this time unmolested pursued his march through the Blue Ridge to Culpeper Court House. Fitzhugh Lee's cavalry remained with Early.

About this time General Grant visited the Valley and found everything to his satisfaction. Sheridan was master of the situation, and he was not slow in showing it to his chief. On the 12th of September Sheridan had telegraphed Grant to the effect that it was exceedingly difficult to attack Early in his position behind the Opequon, which constituted a formidable barrier; that the crossings, though numerous, were deep, and the banks abrupt and difficult for an attacking force; and, in general, that he was waiting for the chances to change in his favor, hoping that Early would either detach troops or take some less defensible position. His caution was fortunate at this time, and his fearlessness and hardihood were sufficiently displayed thereafter. In the light of criticisms, then, it is curious that the world is now inclined to call Sheridan reckless and foolhardy.

At 2 A. M. of September 19th Sheridan's army was astir under orders to attack Early in front of Winchester. My cavalry was to proceed to the fords of the Opequon, near the railroad crossing, and, if opposed only by cavalry, was to cross at daylight and, turning to the left, attack Early's left flank. Wilson's division was to precede the infantry and clear the crossing of the Opequon, on the Berryville road, leading to Winchester. The infantry of the army, following Wilson, was to cross the Opequon, first Wright and then Emory, while Crook's command, marching across country, was to take position in reserve, or be used as circumstances might require. South of Winchester, running nearly east and emptying into the Opequon, is Abraham's Creek, and nearly parallel to it, on the north of Winchester, is Red Bud Creek. These two tributaries flanked the usual line of the Confederates, when in position, covering Winchester, and on this line, across the Berryville-Winchester road, Ramseur was stationed with his infantry, when Sheridan's forces debouched from the defile and deployed for attack. Sheridan's plan was to attack and overthrow this part of Early's force before the rest of the army, which a day or two before was known to be scattered to the north as far as Martinsburg, could come to its assistance. At daylight Wilson advanced across the Opequon, and carried the earth-work which covered the defile and captured part of the force that held it. The infantry followed—Wright's corps first, with Getty leading, and Emory next. Between two and three miles from the Opequon, Wright came up with Wilson, who was waiting in the earth-work he had captured. There the country was suitable for the deployment of the column, which commenced forming line at once. Ramseur, with the bulk of the Confederate artillery, immediately opened on Wright's troops, and soon the Union guns were in position to reply. Wilson took position on the left of the Sixth Corps. Then followed a delay that thwarted the part of the plan which contemplated the destruction of Early's army in detail. Emory's command was crowded off the road in its march, and so delayed by the guns and trains of the Sixth Corps that it was slow getting on the field, and it was hours before the lines were formed. This delay gave the Confederates time to bring up the infantry of Gordon and Rodes. Gordon, who first arrived, was posted on Ramseur's left near the Red Bud, and when Rodes arrived with three of his four brigades, he was given the center. This change in the situation, which necessitated fighting Early's army in his chosen position, did not disconcert the Union commander. He had come out to fight, and though chafing at the unexpected delay, fight he would to the bitter end.

In the meantime the cavalry, which had been ordered to the right, had not been idle. Moving at the same time as did the rest of the army, my division reached the fords of the Opequon near the railroad crossing at early dawn. Here I found a force of cavalry supported by Breckinridge's infantry. After sharp skirmishing the stream was crossed at three different points, but the enemy contested every foot of the way beyond. The cavalry, however, hearing Sheridan's guns, and knowing the battle was in progress, was satisfied with the work it was doing in holding from Early a considerable force of infantry. The battle here continued for some hours, the cavalry making charges on foot or mounted according to the nature of the country, and steadily though slowly driving the enemy's force toward Winchester. Finally Breckinridge, leaving one brigade to assist the cavalry in retarding our advance, moved to the help of Early, arriving on the field about 2 P. M.

It was 11:30 A. M. before Sheridan's lines were ready to advance. When they moved forward Early, who had gathered all his available strength, met them with a front of fire, and the battle raged with the greatest fury. The advance was pressed in the most resolute manner, and the resistance by the enemy being equally determined and both sides fighting without cover, the casualties were very great. Wright's infantry forced Ramseur and Rodes steadily to the rear, while Emory on the right broke the left of the enemy's line and threw it into confusion. At this time the Confederate artillery opened with canister at short range, doing fearful execution. This, coupled with the weakening of the center at the junction between Emory and Wright, and with a charge delivered on this junction of the lines by a part of Rodes's command, just arrived on the field, drove back the Union center. At this critical moment Russell's division of Wright's corps moved into the breach on Emory's left, and, striking the flank of the Confederate troops who were pursuing Grover, restored the lines and stayed the Confederate advance. . . .

A lull in the battle now followed, which General Sheridan improved to restore his lines and to bring up Crook, who had not yet been engaged. It had been the original purpose to use Crook on the left to assist Wilson's cavalry in cutting off Early's retreat toward Newtown. But the stress of battle compelled Sheridan to bring his reserve in on the line, and accordingly Crook was ordered up on Emory's right, one brigade extending to the north of Red Bud Creek. At the same time Early re-formed his lines, placing Breckinridge's command in reserve. At this time Merritt, who with his cavalry had followed Breckinridge closely to the field, approached on the left rear of the Confederates, driving their flying and broken cavalry through the infantry lines. The cavalry then charged repeatedly into Early's infantry, first striking it in the rear, and afterward face to face as it changed front to repel the attack. These attacks were made by the cavalry without any knowledge of the state of the battle except what was apparent to the eye. First Devin charged with his brigade, returning to rally, with three battle-flags and over three hundred prisoners. Next Lowell charged with his brigade, capturing flags, prisoners, and two guns. After this the entire division was formed and charged to give the final coup.

At the time of this last charge the Union infantry advanced along the entire line and the enemy fled in disorder from the field, and night alone (for it was now dark) saved Early's army from capture.

At daylight on the morning of the 20th the army moved rapidly up the main Valley road in pursuit of the enemy. Early had not stopped on the night of the battle until he reached the shelter of Fisher's Hill. This is admirably situated for defense for an army resisting a movement south. Here the Valley is obstructed by the Massanutten Mountains and its width virtually reduced to four or five miles. In this position Early's right was protected by impassable mountains and by the north fork of the Shenandoah, and he at once took means to protect his left artificially.

"On the evening of the 20th," reports Sheridan, "Wright and Emory went into position on the heights of Strasburg, Crook north of Cedar Creek, the cavalry on the right and rear of Emory, extending to the back road."

On the 21st Sheridan occupied the day in examining the enemy's lines and improving his own. Accompanied by General Wright, he directed changes in the lines of the Sixth Corps, so that it occupied the high lands to the north of Tumbling Run. Wright did not secure this vantage-ground without a severe struggle, in which Warner's brigade was engaged, finally holding the heights after a brilliant charge. Sheridan decided on turning Early's impregnable position by a movement on the Little North Mountain. On the night of the 21st he concealed Crook's command in the timber north of Cedar Creek. In making his disposition Sheridan did not attempt to cover the entire front, it being his intention to flank the enemy by Crook's march, and then, by advancing the right of Wright's and Emory's line, to form connection and make his line continuous. On the morning of the 22d, Crook, being still concealed, was marched to the timber near Little North Mountain and massed in it. . . .

Not long before sundown Crook's infantry, which had not yet been discovered by the enemy, struck Early's left and rear so suddenly as to cause his army to break in confusion and flee. The rout was complete, the whole of Sheridan's troops uniting in the attack. That night, though the darkness made the marching difficult, Sheridan followed Early as far as Woodstock, some fifteen miles, and the following day up to Mount Jackson, where he drove the enemy, now to some extent reorganized, from a strong position on the opposite bank of the river. From this point the enemy retreated in line of battle. But every effort to make him fight failed. No doubt Sheridan in this pursuit regretted the absence of his cavalry, which, with Torbert, was striving, by a circuitous and obstructed march, to reach the enemy's rear.

A few miles beyond New Market Early abandoned the main road, which leads on through Harrisonburg; turning to the east, he pursued the road that leads thence to Port Republic. This direction was taken to receive the reënforcements which were to reach him through one of the gaps of the Blue Ridge. For it appears that Kershaw and his command had not proceeded beyond Culpeper in his march to Lee's army before he was ordered to return to Early, the news of whose overthrow at Winchester, and afterward at Fisher's Hill, had reached the authorities at Richmond.

On the 25th of September Torbert with the cavalry rejoined General Sheridan, and was at once put to work doing what damage was possible to the Central Railway. After proceeding to Staunton and destroying immense quantities of army stores, Torbert moved to Waynesboro', destroying the railway track, and after burning the railway bridges toward the Blue Ridge, and on being threatened by Early's forces, which had moved thither to attack him, he retired to Bridgewater.

Naturally a question now arose between Sheridan, the authorities in Washington, and General Grant as to the future theater of the campaign and the line of operations. Sheridan was opposed to the proposition submitted by the others, which was to operate against Central Virginia from his base in the Valley. The general reasons for his opposition were the distance from the base of supplies, the lines of communication, which in a country infested by guerrillas it would take an army to protect, and the nearness, as the campaign progressed, if successful, to the enemy's base, from which large reënforcements could easily and secretly be hurried and the Union army be overwhelmed. But before the plan was finally adopted a new turn was given to affairs, and the plan originally formed was delayed in its execution if not changed altogether.

When the army commenced its return march, the cavalry was deployed across the Valley, burning, destroying, or taking away everything of value, or likely to become of value, to the enemy. . . . There is little doubt, however, that enough was left in the country for the subsistence of the people, for this, besides being contemplated by orders, resulted of necessity from the fact that, while the work was done hurriedly, the citizens had ample time to secrete supplies, and did so.

The movement north was conducted without interruption for two days, except that the enemy's cavalry, made more bold by the accession to its strength of a command under General T. L. Rosser, followed our cavalry, dispersed across the Valley as already described. On the 8th of October the enemy's cavalry harassed Custer's division on the back road during the day, taking from him some battery-forges and wagons. The cavalry also showed itself on the main road upon which Merritt was retiring, but dispersed upon being charged by a brigade which was sent to develop their strength. That night Sheridan gave orders to his chief-of-cavalry, Torbert, to attack and beat the enemy's cavalry the following day "or to get whipped himself," as it was expressed.

On the morning of the 9th Torbert's cavalry moved out to fight that of the enemy under Generals Rosser and Lomax. Merritt's division moved on the pike and extended across to the back road where Custer was concentrated. A stubborn cavalry engagement commenced the day, but it was not long before the Confederate cavalry was broken and routed, and from that time till late in the day it was driven a distance of twenty-six miles, losing everything on wheels, except one gun, and this at one time was in possession of a force too weak to hold it. . . .

In reporting the result of the cavalry battle of October 9th, Early says:

This is very distressing to me, and God knows I have done all in my power to avert the disasters which have befallen this command; but the fact is the enemy's cavalry is so much superior to ours, both in numbers and equipment, and the country is so favorable to the operations of cavalry, that it is impossible for ours to compete with his.

He further says in this same connection:

Lomax's cavalry is armed entirely with rifles and has no sabers, and the consequence is they cannot fight on horseback, and in this open country they cannot successfully fight on foot against large bodies of cavalry.

On the return of the army after the pursuit of the scattered remnants of Early's force, General Sheridan placed it in position on Cedar Creek north of the Shenandoah, Crook on the left, Emory in the center, and Wright in reserve. The cavalry was placed on the flanks. The occupation of Cedar Creek was not intended to be permanent; there were many serious objections to it as a position for defense. The approaches from all points of the enemy's stronghold at Fisher's Hill were through wooded ravines in which the growth and undulations concealed the movement of troops, and for this reason and its proximity to Fisher's Hill the pickets protecting its front could not be thrown, without danger of capture, sufficiently far to the front to give ample warning of the advance of the enemy. We have already seen how Sheridan took advantage of like conditions at Fisher's Hill. Early was now contemplating the surprise of his antagonist.

On the 12th of October Sheridan received a dispatch from Halleck saying that Grant wished a position taken far enough south to serve as a base for operations upon Gordonsville and Charlottesville. On the 13th and the 16th he received dispatches from the Secretary of War and from General Halleck pressing him to visit Washington for consultation.

On the 15th General Sheridan, taking with him Torbert with part of the cavalry, started for Washington, the design being to send the cavalry on a raid to Gordonsville and vicinity. The first camp was made near Front Royal, from which point the cavalry was returned to the army, it being considered safer to do so in consequence of a dispatch intercepted by our signal officers from the enemy's station on Three Top Mountain, and forwarded to General Sheridan by General Wright. This dispatch was as follows:

To LIEUTENANT-GENERAL EARLY: Be ready to move as soon as my forces join you, and we will crush Sheridan.—LONGSTREET, Lieutenant-General.

In sending back the cavalry General Sheridan wrote to General Wright, directing caution on his part, so that he might be duly prepared to resist the attack in case the above dispatch was genuine. Sheridan continued to Washington, and the cavalry resumed its station in the line of defense at Cedar Creek. At this time everything was quiet—suspiciously so.

On the 16th Custer made a reconnoissance in his front on the back road, but found no enemy outside the lines at Fisher's Hill. This absence of the enemy's cavalry was accounted for the next morning just before daylight by the appearance of Rosser in the rear of Custer's picket line with his cavalry and one brigade of infantry. Rosser carrying the infantry behind his cavalry troopers had made a march of thirty-two miles to capture an exposed brigade of Custer's division on the right; but a change in the arrangements of the command (the return of Torbert) thwarted the scheme, and it resulted only in the capture of a picket guard. On the 18th reconnoissances on both flanks discovered no sign of a movement by the enemy.

The result of the destruction of supplies in the Valley was now being felt by Early's troops. About this time he writes: "I was now compelled to move back for want of provisions and forage, or attack the enemy in his position with the hope of driving him from it; and I determined to attack." From reports made by General Gordon and a staff-officer who ascended Three Top Mountain to reconnoiter the Union position, and the result of a reconnoissance made at the same time by General Pegram toward the right flank of the Union army, General Early concluded to attack by secretly moving a force to turn Sheridan's left flank at Cedar Creek.

The plan of this attack was carefully made; the routes the troops were to pursue, even after the battle had commenced, were carefully designated. The attack was made at early dawn. The surprise was complete. Crook's camp, and afterward Emory's, were attacked in flank and rear and the men and officers driven from their beds, many of them not having the time to hurry into their clothes, except as they retreated half awake and terror-stricken from the overpowering numbers of the enemy. Their own artillery, in conjunction with that of the enemy, was turned on them, and long before it was light enough for their eyes, unaccustomed to the dim light, to distinguish friend from foe, they were hurrying to our right and rear intent only on their safety. Wright's infantry, which was farther removed from the point of attack, fared somewhat better, but did not offer more than a spasmodic resistance. The cavalry on the right was on the alert. The rule that in the immediate presence of the enemy the cavalry must be early prepared for attack resulted in the whole First Division being up with breakfast partly finished, at the time the attack commenced. A brigade sent on reconnoissance to the right had opened with its guns some minutes before the main attack on the left, for it had met cavalry sent by Early to make a demonstration on our right.

The disintegration of Crook's command did not occupy many minutes. With a force of the enemy passing through its camp of sleeping men, and another powerful column well to their rear, it was not wonderful that the men as fast as they were awakened by the noise of battle thought first and only of saving themselves from destruction. The advance of Gordon deflected this fleeing throng from the main road to the rear, and they passed over to the right of the army and fled along the back road. Emory made an attempt to form line facing along the main road, but the wave of Gordon's advance on his left, and the thunders of the attack along the road from Strasburg, rendered the position untenable, and he was soon obliged to withdraw to save his lines from capture.

At this time there were hundreds of stragglers moving off by the right to the rear, and all efforts to stop them proved of no avail. A line of cavalry was stretched across the fields on the right, which halted and formed a respectable force of men, so far as numbers were concerned, but these fled and disappeared to the rear as soon as the force which held them was withdrawn. By degrees the strength of the battle died away. The infantry of the Sixth Corps made itself felt on the advance of the enemy, and a sort of confidence among the troops which had not fled from the field was being restored. A brigade of cavalry was ordered to the left to intercept the enemy's advance to Winchester. Taylor's battery of artillery, belonging to the cavalry, moved to the south, and, taking position with the infantry which was retiring, opened on the enemy. The artillery with the cavalry was the only artillery left to the army. The other guns had either been captured or sent to the rear. This battery remained on the infantry lines and did much toward impeding the enemy's advance until the cavalry changed position to the Winchester-Strasburg road. This change took place by direction of General Torbert about 10 o'clock. In making it the cavalry marched through the broken masses of infantry direct to a point on the main road north-east of Middletown. The enemy's artillery fire was terrific. Not a man of the cavalry left the ranks unless he was wounded, and everything was done with the precision and quietness of troops on parade. General Merritt informed Colonel Warner of Getty's division, near which the cavalry passed, and which was at that time following the general retreat of the army, of the point where the cavalry would take position and fight, and Warner promised to notify General Getty, and no doubt did so, for that division of the Sixth Corps advanced to the position on the cavalry's right. Then Devin and Lowell charged and drove back the advancing Confederates. Lowell dismounted his brigade and held some stone walls whose position was suited to defense. Devin held on to his advance ground. Here the enemy's advance was checked for the first time, and beyond this it did not go.

The enemy's infantry sheltered themselves from our cavalry attacks in the woods to the left, and in the inclosures of the town of Middletown. But they opened a devastating fire of artillery. This was the state of affairs when Sheridan arrived.

Stopping at Winchester over night on the 18th, on his way from Washington, General Sheridan heard the noise of the battle the following morning, and hurried to the field. His coming restored confidence. A cheer from the cavalry, which awakened the echoes of the valley, greeted him and spread the good news of his coming over the field.

He rapidly made the changes necessary in the lines, and then ordered an advance. The cavalry on the left charged down on the enemy in their front, scattering them in all directions. The infantry, not to be outdone by the mounted men, moved forward in quick time and charged impetuously the lines of Gordon, which broke and fled. It took less time to drive the enemy from the field than it had for them to take it. They seemed to feel the changed conditions in the Union ranks, for their divisions broke one after another and disappeared toward their rear. The cavalry rode after them and over them, until night fell and ended the fray at the foot of Fisher's Hill. Three battle-flags and twenty-two guns were added to the trophies of the cavalry that day. Early lost almost all his artillery and trains, besides everything that was captured from the Union army in the morning. . . .

The victory was a fitting sequel to Winchester, a glorious prelude to Five Forks and Appomattox.

After the costly Union repulse at Cold Harbor, it became evident to Grant that on this field at least the enemy would not abandon his defensive tactics and that further attempts to storm his position would be suicidal. Consequently, early in June he determined to make still another flanking movement to his left, pulling away from Lee's army as quietly as possible and crossing first the swamps of the Chickahominy River, then the James River, and investing Richmond from the south. The transfer was performed successfully—one of the few times General Lee seems to have been surprised by a movement of his adversary—but through a series of errors and miscalculations, its first object, the quick capture of Petersburg, failed. And because the Confederate forces there, already well entrenched, were promptly reinforced, the Army of the Potomac had no choice but to settle down to what was to become a protracted siege.

The final act of the drama was about to begin, coincidentally with the chief character of its opening in a leading role—Beauregard, still planning on a large scale, still defiant, still sanguine of ultimate success. But in Richmond food was becoming desperately scarce, with the Shenandoah Valley and other important sources of supply now in the hands of the Federals, and for the first time General Lee and his lieutenants were beset by the ugly problem of wholesale desertions from the ranks. Soldiers as well as civilians were beginning to doubt now, and to express it quietly to each other, that there could ever be an independent Confederate States of America.

"To hold on at all hazards!"

FOUR DAYS OF BATTLE AT PETERSBURG

BY G. T. BEAUREGARD, GENERAL, C. S. A.

THE movement of the Army of the Potomac to the south side of the James began on the evening of the 12th of June, and Smith's corps (the Eighteenth) was at Bermuda Hundred in the early afternoon of the 14th. From Point of Rocks it crossed the river that night and was pushed forward without delay against Petersburg. Kautz's cavalry and Hinks's command of colored troops had been added to it.

It was with a view to thwart General Grant in the execution of such a plan that I proposed to the War Department [June 9th] the adoption—should the emergency justify it, and I thought it did—of the bold and, to me, safer plan of concentrating all the forces we could readily dispose of to give battle to

Grant, and thus decide at once the fate of Richmond and of the cause we were fighting for, while we still possessed a comparatively compact, well-disciplined, and enthusiastic army in the field.

From Swift Creek, early on June 14th, I telegraphed to General Bragg: "Movement of Grant's across Chickahominy and increase of Butler's force render my position here critical. With my present forces I cannot answer for consequences. Cannot my troops sent to General Lee be returned at once? . . ." No answer came. Late in the evening of the same day, having further reason to believe that one corps at least of General Grant's army was already within Butler's lines, I telegraphed to General Lee: "A deserter from the enemy reports that Butler has been reënforced by the Eighteenth and a part of the Tenth Army Corps." To this dispatch, likewise, there came no response. But, as prompt and energetic action became more and more imperative, and as I could no longer doubt the presence of Smith's corps with Butler's forces, I sent one of my aides, Colonel Samuel B. Paul, to General Lee with instructions to explain to him the exact situation. General Lee's answer to Colonel Paul was not encouraging. He said that I must be in error in believing the enemy had thrown a large force on the south side of the James; that the troops referred to by me could be but a few of Smith's corps going back to Butler's lines. Strange to say, at the very time General Lee was thus expressing himself to Colonel Paul, the whole of Smith's corps was actually assaulting the Petersburg lines. But General Lee finally said that he had already issued orders for the return of Hoke's division; that he would do all he could to aid me, and even come himself should the necessity arise.

The Confederate forces opposed to Smith's corps on the 15th of June consisted of the 26th, 34th, and 46th Virginia regiments, the 64th Georgia, the 23d South Carolina, Archer's militia, Battle's and Wood's battalions, Sturdivant's battery, Dearing's small command of cavalry, and some other transient forces, having a real effective for duty of 2200 only. These troops occupied the Petersburg line on the left from Battery No. 1 to what was called Butterworth's Bridge, toward the right, and had to be so stationed as to allow but one man for every 4½ yards. From that bridge to the Appomattox—a distance of fully 4½ miles—the line was defenseless.

Early in the morning—at about 7 o'clock—General Dearing, on the Broadway and City Point roads, reported his regiment engaged with a large force of the enemy. The stand made by our handful of cavalry, near their breastworks, was most creditable to themselves and to their gallant commander, and the enemy's ranks, at that point, were much thinned by the accurate firing of the battery under Graham. But the weight of numbers soon produced its almost inevitable result, and, in spite of the desperate efforts of our men, the cavalry breastworks were flanked and finally abandoned by us, with the loss of one howitzer. Still, Dearing's encounter with the enemy, at that moment and on that part of the field, was of incalculable advantage to the defenders of our line, inasmuch as it afforded time for additional preparation and the distribution of new orders by Wise.

At 10 o'clock A. M. the skirmishing had assumed very alarming proportions. To the urgent demands of General Wise for reënforcements, I was enabled at last to answer that part of Hoke's division was on the way from Drewry's Bluff and would be in time to save the day, if our men could stand their ordeal, hard as it was, a little while longer. Then all along the line, from one end to the other, the order was given "to hold on at all hazards!" It was obeyed with the resolute fortitude of veterans, though many of the troops thus engaged, with such odds against them, had hardly been under fire before. At 12 M., and as late as 2 P. M., our center was vigorously pressed, as though the Norfolk and Petersburg Railroad were the immediate object of the onset. General Wise now closed the line from his right to strengthen Colonel J. T. Goode and, with him, the 34th Virginia; while, at the same time and with equal perspicacity, he hurried Wood's battalion toward the left in support of Colonel P. R. Page and his command.

The enemy, continuing to mass his columns toward the center of our line, pressed it more and more and concentrated his heaviest assaults upon Batteries Nos. 5, 6, and 7. Thinned out and exhausted as they were, General Wise's heroic forces resisted still, with such unflinching stubbornness as to equal the veterans of the Army of Northern Virginia. I was then on the field and only left it when darkness set in. Shortly after 7 P. M. the enemy entered a ravine between Batteries 6 and 7, and succeeded in flanking Battery No. 5.

But just then very opportunely appeared, advancing at double-quick, Hagood's gallant South Carolina brigade, followed soon afterward by Colquitt's, Clingman's, and, in fact, by the whole of Hoke's division. They were shown their positions, on a new line selected at that very time by my orders, a short distance in the rear of the captured works, and were kept busy the greatest part of the night throwing up a small epaulement for their additional protection.

Strange to say, General Smith contented himself with breaking into our lines, and attempted nothing further that night. All the more strange was this inaction on his part, since General Hancock, with his strong and well-equipped Second Army Corps, had also been hurried to Petersburg, and was actually there, or in the immediate vicinity of the town, on the evening of the 15th. He had informed General Smith of the arrival of his command and of the readiness of two of his divisions—Birney's and Gibbon's—to give him whatever assistance he might require. Petersburg at that hour was clearly at the mercy of the Federal commander, who had all but captured it, and only failed of final success because he could not realize the fact of the unparalleled disparity between the two contending forces. Although the result of the fighting of the 15th had demonstrated that 2200 Confederates successfully withheld nearly a whole day the repeated assaults of at least 18,000

551

Federals, it followed, none the less, that Hancock's corps, being now in our front, with fully 28,000 men—which raised the enemy's force against Petersburg to a grand total of 46,000—our chance of resistance, the next morning and in the course of the next day, even after the advent of Hoke's division, was by far too uncertain to be counted on, unless strong additional reënforcements could reach us in time.

Without awaiting an answer from the authorities at Richmond to my urgent representations, I ordered General Bushrod R. Johnson to evacuate the lines in front of Bermuda Hundred at the dawn of day on the 16th, leaving pickets and skirmishers to cover the movement until daylight, or later if necessary, and to march as rapidly as possible with his entire force to the assistance of Petersburg. The emergency justified this action. I had previously [1:45 P. M.] communicated with General Bragg upon this point, and had asked the War Department to elect between the Bermuda Hundred line and Petersburg, as, under the present circumstances, I could no longer hold both. The War Department had given me no answer, clearly intending that I should assume the responsibility of the measure, which I did. Scarcely two hours after Johnson's division had abandoned its position at Bermuda Hundred, Butler's forces drove off the Confederate pickets left there, as already stated, and took full possession of the lines.

By the 16th of June three Federal corps—Smith's, Hancock's, and Burnside's—aggregating about 66,000 men, confronted our lines. Opposed to them I had, after the arrival of Johnson's division, about 10 A. M., an effective of not more than 10,000 men of all arms.

Through a sense of duty I addressed the following telegram, June 16th, 7:45 A. M., to General Lee: "Prisoner captured this A. M. reports that he belongs to Hancock's corps (Second), and that it crossed day before yesterday and last night from Harrison's Landing. Could we not have more reënforcements here?"

No direct answer was received to the above. But in reply to another dispatch of mine, June 16th, 4 P. M., relative to tugs and transports of the enemy reported to have been seen that day by Major Terrell, General Lee sent this message: "The transports you mention have probably returned Butler's troops. Has Grant been seen crossing James River?" This shows that Lee was still uncertain as to his adversary's movements, and, notwithstanding the information already furnished him, could not realize that the Federals had crossed the James, and that three of their corps were actually assaulting the Petersburg lines.

General Hancock, the ranking Federal officer present, had been instructed by General Meade not to begin operations before the arrival of Burnside's command. Hence the tardiness of the enemy's attack, which was not made till after 5 o'clock P. M., though Burnside had reached Petersburg, according to his own report, at 10 o'clock A. M.

552

The engagement lasted fully three hours, much vigor being displayed by the Federals, while the Confederates confronted them with fortitude, knowing that they were fighting against overwhelming odds, constantly increasing. Birney's division of Hancock's corps finally broke into part of our line and effected a lodgment. The contest, with varying results, was carried on until after nightfall, with advantage to us on the left and some serious loss on the right. It then slackened and gradually came to an end. In the meantime Warren's corps, the Fifth, had also come up, but too late to take a part in the action of the day. Its presence before our lines swelled the enemy's aggregate to about 90,000, against which stood a barrier of not even 10,000 exhausted, half-starved men, who had gone through two days of constant hard fighting and many sleepless nights in the trenches.

Hostilities began early on the 17th. I here quote from "Military Operations of General Beauregard," Vol. II., p. 232:

Three times were the Federals driven back, but they as often resumed the offensive and held their ground. About dusk a portion of the Confederate lines was wholly broken and the troops in that quarter were about to be thrown into a panic, which might have ended in irreparable disaster, when happily, as General Beauregard, with his staff, was endeavoring to rally and re-form the troops, Gracie's brigade, of Johnson's division, consisting of about twelve hundred men —the return of which to his command General Beauregard had been urgently asking—came up from Chaffin's Bluff, whence, at last, the War Department had ordered it to move. It was promptly and opportunely thrown into the gap on the lines and drove back the Federals, capturing about two thousand prisoners. The conflict raged with great fury until after 11 o'clock at night.

Anticipating the inevitable result of such a pressure upon our weak defenses, and knowing that at any moment they might be irrevocably lost to us, I had—accompanied by Colonel D. B. Harris, of the Engineers—selected the site of another and shorter line, near Taylor's Creek, at a convenient distance toward the rear. I caused it to be carefully staked out during the battle, and shown to the adjutants, quartermasters, and other staff-officers of Hoke's and Johnson's divisions, and through them to all the available regimental adjutants on the field; so that each command, at the appointed hour, even at dead of night, might easily retire upon the new line with order and precision, and unperceived by the enemy. Meanwhile, the order to "hold on at any cost" remained unchanged all down the line. There was no reason to hope for assistance of any kind. The Army of Northern Virginia was yet far distant, and I had failed to convince its distinguished commander of the fact that I was then fighting Grant's whole army with less than eleven thousand men. On the 17th, from Clay's House, at 12 o'clock M., General Lee answered as follows one of my telegrams of that morning: "Telegram of 9 A. M. received. Until I can get more definite information of Grant's move-

553

ments, I do not think it prudent to draw more troops to this side of the river." And, acting on the desire for additional information, at 3:30 P. M., on the same day, he telegraphed W. H. F. Lee, then at Malvern Hill, as follows: "Push after the enemy, and endeavor to ascertain what has become of Grant's army." Later on—*i. e.,* at 4:30 P. M., on the same day—he sent this message to A. P. Hill, at Riddle's shop: "General Beauregard reports large numbers of Grant's troops crossed James River, above Fort Powhatan, yesterday. If you have nothing contradictory of this, move to Chaffin's Bluff." Just at that time, however [5 P. M.], I sent another telegram to General Lee, reiterating my former assertions, with the addition of other particulars:

Prisoners just taken represent themselves as belonging to Second, Ninth, and Eighteenth corps. They state that Fifth and Sixth corps are behind coming on. Those from Second and Eighteenth came here yesterday, and arrived first. Others marched night and day from Gaines's Mill, and arrived yesterday evening. The Ninth crossed at Turkey Bend, where they have a pontoon-bridge. They say Grant commanded on the field yesterday. All are positive that they passed him on the road seven miles from here.

The firing lasted, on the 17th, until a little after 11 o'clock P. M. Just before that time I had ordered all the camp-fires to be brightly lighted, with sentinels well thrown forward and as near as possible to the enemy's. Then, at about 12:30 A. M., on the 18th, began the retrograde movement, which, notwithstanding the exhaustion of our troops and their sore disappointment at receiving no further reënforcements, was safely and silently executed, with uncommonly good order and precision, though the greatest caution had to be used in order to retire unnoticed from so close a contact with so strong an adversary.

The digging of trenches was begun by the men as soon as they reached their new position. Axes, as well as spades; bayonets and knives, as well as axes—in fact, every utensil that could be found—were used. And when all was over, or nearly so, with much anxiety still, but with comparative relief, nevertheless, I hurried off this telegram to General Lee [18th, 12:40 A. M.]: "All quiet at present. I expect renewal of attack in morning. My troops are becoming much exhausted. Without immediate and strong reënforcements, results may be unfavorable. Prisoners report Grant on the field with his whole army."

But General Lee, although not wholly convinced even at that hour that the Army of the Potomac was already on the south side of the James, long before the dawn of day, on the 18th, and immediately after his conference with Major Cooke, sent me this message: "Am not yet satisfied as to General Grant's movements; but upon your representations will move at once to Petersburg." And, in fact, even previous to that hour, on the same night, he had concluded to send Kershaw's division to my assistance. The next step taken by General Lee was to endeavor to procure sufficient means for the immediate transportation of his troops. The same morning he communicated with General Early [at Lynchburg], who had not yet returned from his Shenandoah campaign: "Strike as quick as you can, and, if circumstances authorize, carry out the original plan, or move upon Petersburg without delay." Late as had been the credence given by General Lee to my representations of Grant's movements, it was, fortunately, not yet too late, by prompt and energetic action, to save Petersburg—and, therefore, Richmond.

General Kershaw's division, which proved to be the vanguard of General Lee's army, reached Petersburg early Saturday morning, June 18th; it numbered about 5000 men, and, by my orders, was placed on the new line already occupied by our forces with its right on or near the Jerusalem plank-road, extending across the open field and bending back toward the front of the cemetery. Field's division, of about equal strength, came in some two hours after Kershaw's. It had not yet been assigned to its place on the line when Lee in person arrived at 11:30 o'clock A. M. on that day.

When, early in the morning, the enemy was pushed forward to make the "grand attack ordered for 4 A. M. on the 18th," the retirement of our forces on the previous night from their first positions to the new line of defenses selected by me, as already explained, had so much surprised the assaulting columns as to induce their immediate commanders to additional prudence in their advance and to a complete halt in their operations.

On that morning the troops arrayed against us consisted of Hancock's, Burnside's, and Warren's corps, with the larger portion of Smith's under General Martindale, and finally Neill's division from Wright's corps (the Sixth), strengthened by its whole artillery. This gave the enemy an aggregate of over 90,000 effectives. We had on our side, after Kershaw's arrival, but 15,000 men, no deduction being made for the casualties of the three preceding days. It was only later on, somewhere between 12 M. and 1 P. M., that Field's command was put in position on the line, and from that moment to the end of the day our grand total amounted to about 20,000 men. At noon—or thereabout—the predetermined "grand attack" was renewed, although partial disconnected assaults had been made before that hour on several parts of our line, but with no tangible result of any kind. This renewed attack was mainly led by Gibbon's division of Hancock's corps. It proved to be entirely ineffectual. And still another grand attempt was made at 4 P. M., with at least three full Federal corps coöperating: Hancock's on the right, Burnside's in the center, and Warren's on the left. General Meade, in his report, says it was "without success." And he adds these words: "Later in the day attacks were made by the Fifth and Ninth corps with no better results." The truth is that, despite the overwhelming odds against us, every Federal assault, on the 18th, was met with most signal defeat, "attended," says Mr. Swinton, the Federal historian, "with another mournful loss of life." This was, in fact, very heavy, and exceeded ours in the proportion of nine to one.

My welcome to General Lee was most cordial. He was at last where I had, for the past three days, so anxiously hoped to see him—within the limits of Petersburg! Two of his divisions had preceded him there, and his whole army would be in by evening of the next day, namely, the 19th of June. I felt sure, therefore, that, for the present at least, Petersburg and Richmond were safe. Not that our forces would be numerically equal to those of the enemy, even after the arrival of the last regiment of the Army of Northern Virginia; but I was aware that our defensive line would now count more than one man per every four and a half yards of its length; and I felt relieved to know that, at last, the whole of our line—not portions of it only, as heretofore—would be guarded by veteran troops, alike, if not superior, in mettle to the veteran troops opposing them. . . .

The evening of the 18th was quiet. There was no further attempt on the part of General Meade to assault our lines. He was "satisfied," as he said in his report, that there was "nothing more to be gained by direct attacks." The spade took the place of the musket, and the regular siege was begun. It was only raised April 2, 1865.

The two mines which had been sunk and exploded by the assaulters at Vicks-burg had accomplished nothing—unless they had relieved the ennui of the be-siegers. And perhaps it was because of this experience that Grant was only luke-warm to the mining of the Confederate earthworks at Petersburg, except for the same reason. When Burnside submitted the plan to him and Meade, he says in his Memoirs *that they both "approved of it as a means of keeping the men busy." While the operation undoubtedly disturbed the Confederate soldiers in the lines as well as the residents of the town behind, for they both knew it was going for-ward, the powder keg they imagined they were sitting on proved to be a fiasco— which Grant afterward attributed to ineptitude on Burnside's part and cowardice and inefficiency on the part of the divisional commanders. After the battle of the crater, the two armies resumed their prolonged duel of mortars and sharpshoot-ers while climactic military activities were taking place in other theaters of the war.*

"All in the crater who could hang on by their elbows and toes . . ."

THE BATTLE OF THE PETERSBURG CRATER

BY WILLIAM H. POWELL, MAJOR, U. S. A.

B Y THE assaults of June 17th and 18th, 1864, on the Confederate works at Petersburg, the Ninth Corps, under General Burnside, gained an advanced position beyond a deep cut in the railroad, within 130 yards of the enemy's main line and confronting a strong work called by the Confederates Elliott's Salient, and sometimes Pegram's Salient. In rear of that advanced position was a deep hollow. A few days after gaining this position Lieutenant-Colonel Henry Pleasants, who had been a mining engineer and who belonged to the 48th Pennsylvania Volunteers, composed for the most part of miners from the upper Schuylkill coal region, suggested to his division commander, General Robert B. Potter, the possibility of running a mine under one of the enemy's forts in front of the deep hollow. This proposition was submitted to General Burnside, who approved of the measure, and work was commenced on the 25th of June. If ever a man labored under

559

disadvantages, that man was Colonel Pleasants. In his testimony before the Committee on the Conduct of the War, he said:

My regiment was only about four hundred strong. At first I employed but a few men at a time, but the number was increased as the work progressed, until at last I had to use the whole regiment—non-commissioned officers and all. The great difficulty I had was to dispose of the material got out of the mine. I found it impossible to get any assistance from anybody; I had to do all the work myself. I had to remove all the earth in old cracker-boxes; I got pieces of hickory and nailed on the boxes in which we received our crackers, and then iron-clad them with hoops of iron taken from old pork and beef barrels. . . . Whenever I made application I could not get anything, although General Burnside was very favorable to it. The most important thing was to ascertain how far I had to mine, because if I fell short of or went beyond the proper place, the explosion would have no practical effect. Therefore I wanted an accurate instrument with which to make the necessary triangulations. I had to make them on the farthest front line, where the enemy's sharp-shooters could reach me. I could not get the instrument I wanted, although there was one at army headquarters, and General Burnside had to send to Washington and get an old-fashioned theodolite, which was given to me. . . . General Burnside told me that General Meade and Major Duane, chief engineer of the Army of the Potomac, said the thing could not be done—that it was all clap-trap and nonsense; that such a length of mine had never been excavated in military operations, and could not be; that I would either get the men smothered, for want of air, or crushed by the falling of the earth; or the enemy would find it out and it would amount to nothing. I could get no boards or lumber supplied to me for my operations. I had to get a pass and send two companies of my own regiment, with wagons, outside of our lines to rebel saw-mills, and get lumber in that way, after having previously got what lumber I could by tearing down an old bridge. I had no mining picks furnished me, but had to take common army picks and have them straightened for my mining picks. . . . The only officers of high rank, so far as I learned, that favored the enterprise were General Burnside, the corps commander, and General Potter, the division commander.

On the 23d of July Colonel Pleasants had the whole mine ready for the placing of the powder. With proper tools and instruments it could have been done in one-third or one-fourth of the time. The greatest delay was occasioned by taking out the material, which had to be carried the whole length of the gallery. Every night the pioneers of Colonel Pleasant's regiment had to cut bushes to cover the fresh dirt at the mouth of the gallery; otherwise the enemy could have observed it from trees inside his own lines.

The main gallery was 510 feet in length. The left lateral gallery was thirty-seven feet in length and the right lateral thirty-eight feet. The magazines, eight in number, were placed in the lateral galleries—two at each end a few feet apart in branches at nearly right angles to the side galleries, and two more in each of the side galleries similarly placed by pairs, situated equidistant from each other and the end of the galleries.

It had been the intention of General Grant to make an assault on the enemy's works in the early part of July; but the movement was deferred in consequence of the work on the mine, the completion of which was impatiently awaited. As a diversion Hancock's corps and two divisions of cavalry had crossed to the north side of the James at Deep Bottom and had threatened Richmond. A part of Lee's army was sent from Petersburg to checkmate this move, and when the mine was ready to be sprung Hancock was recalled in haste to Petersburg. When the mine was ready for the explosives General Meade requested General Burnside to submit a plan of attack. This was done in a letter dated July 26th, 1864, in which General Burnside said:

. . . It is altogether probable that the enemy are cognizant of the fact that we are mining, because it is mentioned in their papers, and they have been heard at work on what are supposed to be shafts in close proximity to our galleries. But the rain of night before last has, no doubt, much retarded their work. We have heard no sound of workmen in them either yesterday or to-day; and nothing is heard by us in the mine but the ordinary sounds of work on the surface above. This morning we had some apprehension that the left lateral gallery was in danger of caving in from the weight of the batteries above it and the shock of their firing. But all possible precautions have been taken to strengthen it, and we hope to preserve it intact. The placing of the charges in the mine will not involve the necessity of making a noise. It is therefore probable that we will escape discovery if the mine is to be used within two or three days. It is, nevertheless, highly important, in my opinion, that the mine should be exploded at the earliest possible moment consistent with the general interests of the campaign. . . . But it may not be improper for me to say that the advantages reaped from the work would be but small if it were exploded without any coöperative movement.

My plan would be to explode the mine just before daylight in the morning or at about 5 o'clock in the afternoon; mass the two brigades of the colored division in rear of my first line, in columns of division—"double-columns closed in mass"—the head of each brigade resting on the front line, and, as soon as the explosion has taken place, move them forward, with instructions for the divisions to take half distance, and as soon as the leading regiments of the two brigades pass through the gap in the enemy's line, the leading regiment of the right brigade to come into line perpendicular to the enemy's line by the "right companies on the right into line, wheel," the left companies on the right into line, and proceed at once down the line of the enemy's works as rapidly as possible; and the leading regiment of the left brigade to execute the reverse movement to the left, moving up the enemy's line. The remainder of the columns to move directly toward the crest in front as rapidly as possible, diverging in such a way as to enable them to deploy into column of regiments, the right column making as nearly as possible for Cemetery Hill; these columns to be followed by the other divisions of the corps as soon as they can be thrown in. This would involve the

561

necessity of relieving these divisions by other troops before the movement, and of holding columns of other troops in readiness to take our place on the crest, in case we gain it, and sweep down it. It would, in my opinion, be advisable, if we succeed in gaining the crest, to throw the colored division right into the town. There is a necessity for the coöperation, at least in the way of artillery, by the troops on our right and left. Of the extent of this you will necessarily be the judge. I think our chances of success, in a plan of this kind, are more than even. . . .

With a view of making the attack, the division of colored troops, under General Edward Ferrero, had been drilling for several weeks, General Burnside thinking that they were in better condition to head a charge than either of the white divisions. They had not been in any very active service. On the other hand, the white divisions had performed very arduous duties since the beginning of the campaign, and before Petersburg had been in such proximity to the enemy that no man could raise his head above the parapets without being fired at. They had been in the habit of using every possible means of covering themselves from the enemy's fire.

General Meade objected to the use of the colored troops, on the ground, as he stated, that they were a new division and had never been under fire, while this was an operation requiring the very best troops. General Burnside, however, insisted upon his programme, and the question was referred to General Grant, who confirmed General Meade's views, although he subsequently said in his evidence before the Committee on the Conduct of the War:

General Burnside wanted to put his colored division in front, and I believe if he had done so it would have been a success. Still I agreed with General Meade as to his objections to that plan. General Meade said that if we put the colored troops in front (we had only one division) and it should prove a failure, it would then be said, and very properly, that we were shoving these people ahead to get killed because we did not care anything about them. But that could not be said if we put white troops in front.

The mine was charged with only 8000 pounds of powder, instead of 14,000, as asked for, the amount having been reduced by order of General Meade; and while awaiting the decision of General Grant on the question of the colored troops, precise orders for making and supporting the attack were issued by General Meade.

In the afternoon of the 29th of July, Generals Potter and O. B. Willcox met together at General Burnside's headquarters, to talk over the plans of the attack, based upon the idea that the colored troops would lead the charge, and while there the message was received from General Meade that General Grant disapproved of that plan, and that General Burnside must detail one of his white divisions to take the place of the colored division. This was the first break in the original plan. There were then scarcely twelve hours, and half of these at night, in which to make this change—and no possible time in which the white troops could be familiarized with the duties expected of them in connection with the assault.

General Burnside was greatly disappointed by this change; but he immediately sent for General Ledlie, who had been in command of the First Division only about six weeks. Upon his arrival General Burnside determined that the three commanders of his white divisions should "pull straws," and Ledlie was (as he thought) the unlucky victim. He, however, took it good-naturedly, and, after receiving special instructions from General Burnside, proceeded with his brigade commanders to ascertain the way to the point of attack. This was not accomplished until after dark on the evening before the explosion.

The order of attack, as proposed by General Burnside, was also changed by direction of General Meade with the approval of General Grant. Instead of moving down to the right and left of the crater of the mine, for the purpose of driving the enemy from their intrenchments, and removing to that extent the danger of flank attacks, General Meade directed that the troops should push at once for the crest of Cemetery Hill.

The approaches to the Union line of intrenchments at this particular point were so well covered by the fire of the enemy that they were cut up into a network of covered ways almost as puzzling to the uninitiated as the catacombs of Rome.

Upon General Ledlie's return from the front orders were issued, and the division was formed at midnight. Shortly afterward it advanced through the covered ways, and was in position some time before daybreak, behind the Union breastworks, and immediately in front of the enemy's fort, which was to be blown up. The orders were that Ledlie's division should advance first, pass over the enemy's works, and charge to Cemetery Hill, four hundred yards to the right, and approached by a slope comparatively free from obstacles; as soon as the First Division should leave the works, the next division (Willcox's) was to advance to the left of Cemetery Hill, so as to protect the left flank of the First Division; and the next division (Potter's) was to move in the same way to the right of Cemetery Hill. The Ninth Corps being out of the way, it was intended that the Fifth and Eighteenth corps should pass through and follow up the movement.

At 3:30 A. M. Ledlie's division was in position, the Second Brigade, Colonel E. G. Marshall, in front, and that of General W. F. Bartlett behind it, the men and officers in a feverish state of expectancy, the majority of them having been awake all night. Daylight came slowly, and still they stood with every nerve strained prepared to move forward the instant an order should be given. Four o'clock arrived, officers and men began to get nervous, having been on their feet four hours; still the mine had not been exploded. General Ledlie then directed me to go to General Burnside and report to him that the command had been in readiness to move since 3:30 A. M., and to inquire the cause of the delay of the explosion. I found General Burnside in rear of the fourteen-gun battery, delivered my message, and received the reply from the general information that there was some trouble with the fuse dying out, but that an officer had gone into the gallery to ignite it again, and that the explosion would soon take place.

I returned immediately, and just as I arrived in rear of the First Division the mine was sprung. It was a magnificent spectacle, and as the mass of earth went up into the air, carrying with it men, guns, carriages, and timbers, and spread out like an immense cloud as it reached its altitude, so close were the Union lines that the mass appeared as if it would descend immediately upon the troops waiting to make the charge. This caused them to break and scatter to the rear, and about ten minutes were consumed in re-forming for the attack. Not much was lost by this delay, however, as it took nearly that time for the cloud of dust to pass off. The order was then given for the advance. As no part of the Union line of breastworks had been removed (which would have been an arduous as well as hazardous undertaking), the troops clambered over them as best they could. This in itself broke the ranks, and they did not stop to re-form, but pushed ahead toward the crater, about 130 yards distant, the débris from the explosion having covered up the abatis and *chevaux-de-frise* in front of the enemy's works.

Little did these men anticipate what they would see upon arriving there: an enormous hole in the ground about 30 feet deep, 60 feet wide, and 170 feet long, filled with dust, great blocks of clay, guns, broken carriages, projecting timbers, and men buried in various ways—some up to their necks, others to their waists, and some with only their feet and legs protruding from the earth. One of these near me was pulled out, and proved to be a second lieutenant of the battery which had been blown up. The fresh air revived him, and he was soon able to walk and talk. He was very grateful and said that he was asleep when the explosion took place, and only awoke to find himself wriggling up in the air; then a few seconds afterward he felt himself descending, and soon lost consciousness.

The whole scene of the explosion struck every one dumb with astonishment as we arrived at the crest of the débris. It was impossible for the troops of the Second Brigade to move forward in line, as they had advanced; and, owing to the broken state they were in, every man crowding up to look into the hole, and being pressed by the First Brigade, which was immediately in rear, it was equally impossible to move by the flank, by any command, around the crater. Before the brigade commanders could realize the situation, the two brigades became inextricably mixed, in the desire to look into the hole.

However, Colonel Marshall yelled to the Second Brigade to move forward, and the men did so, jumping, sliding, and tumbling into the hole, over the débris of material, and dead and dying men, and huge blocks of solid clay. They were followed by General Bartlett's brigade. Up on the other side of the crater they climbed, and while a detachment stopped to place two of the dismounted guns of the battery in position on the enemy's side of the crest of the crater, a portion of the leading brigade passed over the crest and attempted to re-form. In doing so, members of these regiments were killed by musket-shots from the rear, fired by the Confederates who were still occupying the traverses and intrenchments to the right and left of the crater. These men had been awakened by the noise and shock of the explosion, and during the interval before the attack had recovered their equanimity, and when the Union troops attempted to re-form on the enemy's side of the crater, they had faced about and delivered a fire into the backs of our men. This coming so unexpectedly caused the forming line to fall back into the crater.

Had General Burnside's original plan, providing that two regiments should sweep down inside the enemy's line to the right and left of the crater, been sanctioned, the brigades of Colonel Marshall and General Bartlett could and would have re-formed and moved on to Cemetery Hill before the enemy realized fully what was intended; but the occupation of the trenches to the right and left by the enemy prevented re-formation, and there being no division, corps, or army commander present to give orders to other troops to clear the trenches, a formation under fire from the rear was something no troops could accomplish.

After falling back into the crater a partial formation was made by General Bartlett and Colonal Marshall with some of their troops, but owing to the precipitous walls the men could find no footing except by facing inward, digging their heels into the earth, and throwing their backs against the side of the crater, or squatting in a half-sitting, half-standing posture, and some of the men were shot even there by the fire from the enemy in the traverses. It was at this juncture that Colonel Marshall requested me to go to General Ledlie and explain the condition of affairs, which he knew that I had seen and understood perfectly well. This I did immediately.

While the above was taking place the enemy had not been idle. He had brought a battery from his left to bear upon the position, and as I started on my errand the crest of the crater was being swept with canister. Special attention was given to this battery by our artillery, but for some reason or other the enemy's guns could not be silenced. Passing to the Union lines under this storm of canister, I found General Ledlie and a part of his staff ensconced in a protected angle of the works. I gave him Colonel Marshall's message, explained to him the situation, and Colonel Marshall's reasons for not being able to move forward. General Ledlie then directed me to return at once and say to Colonel Marshall and General Bartlett that it was General Burnside's order that they should move forward immediately. This message

565

was delivered. But the firing on the crater now was incessant, and it was as heavy a fire of canister as was ever poured continuously upon a single objective point. It was as utterly impracticable to re-form a brigade in that crater as it would be to marshal bees into line after upsetting the hive; and equally as impracticable to re-form outside of the crater, under the severe fire in front and rear, as it would be to hold a dress parade in front of a charging enemy. Here, then, was the second point of advantage lost by the fact that there was no person present with authority to change the programme to meet the circumstances. Had a prompt attack of the troops to the right and left of the crater been made as soon as the leading brigade had passed into the crater, or even fifteen minutes afterward, clearing the trenches and diverting the fire of the enemy, success would have been inevitable, and particularly would this have been the case on the left of the crater, as the small fort immediately in front of the Fifth Corps was almost, if not entirely, abandoned for a while after the explosion of the mine, the men running away from it as if they feared that it was to be blown up also.

Whether General Ledlie informed General Burnside of the condition of affairs as reported by me I do not know; but I think it likely, as it was not long after I had returned to the crater that a brigade of the Second Division (Potter's) under the command of Brigadier-General S. G. Griffin advanced its skirmishers and followed them immediately, directing its course to the right of the crater. General Griffin's line, however, overlapped the crater on the left, where two or three of his regiments sought shelter in the crater. Those on the right passed over the trenches, but owing to the peculiar character of the enemy's works, which were not single, but complex and involuted and filled with pits, traverses, and bomb-proofs, forming a labyrinth as difficult of passage as the crater itself, the brigade was broken up, and, meeting the severe fire of canister, also fell back into the crater, which was then full to suffocation. Every organization melted away, as soon as it entered this hole in the ground, into a mass of human beings clinging by toes and heels to the almost perpendicular sides. If a man was shot on the crest he fell and rolled to the bottom of the pit.

From the actions of the enemy, even at this time, as could be seen by his moving columns in front, he was not exactly certain as to the intentions of the Union commander; he appeared to think that possibly the mine explosion was but a feint and that the main attack would come from some other quarter. However, he massed some of his troops in a hollow in front of the crater, and held them in that position.

Meantime General Potter, who was in rear of the Union line of intrenchments, being convinced that something ought to be done to create a diversion and distract the enemy's attention from this point, ordered Colonel Zenas R. Bliss, commanding his First Brigade, to send two of his regiments to support General Griffin, and with the remainder to make an attack on the right. Subsequently it was arranged that the two regiments going to the support of General Griffin should pass into the crater, turn to the right, and sweep down the enemy's lines. Colonel Bliss was partly successful, and obtained possession of some 200 or 300 yards of the line, and one of the regiments advanced to within 20 or 30 yards of the battery whose fire was so severe on the troops; but it could make no further headway for lack of support—its progress being impeded by slashed timber, while an unceasing fire of canister was poured into the men. They therefore fell back to the enemy's traverses and intrenchments.

At the time of ordering forward Colonel Bliss's command General Potter wrote a dispatch to General Burnside, stating that it was his opinion, from what he had seen, and from the reports he had received from subordinate officers, that too many men were being forced in at this one point; that the troops there were in confusion, and it was absolutely necessary that an attack should be made from some other point of the line, in order to divert the enemy's attention and give time to straighten out our line. To that dispatch he never received an answer. Orders were, however, being constantly sent to the three division commanders of the white troops to push the men forward as fast as could be done, and this was, in substance, about all the orders that were received by them during the day up to the time of the order for the withdrawal.

When General Willcox came with the Third Division to support the First, he found the latter and three regiments of his own, together with the regiments of Potter's Second Division which had gone in on the right, so completely filling up the crater that no more troops could be got in there, and he therefore ordered an attack with the remainder of his division on the works of the enemy to the left of the crater. This attack was successful, so far as to carry the intrenchments for about 150 yards; but they were held only for a short time.

Previous to this last movement I had again left the crater and gone to General Ledlie, and had urged him to try to have something done on the right and left of the crater—saying that every man who got into the trenches to the right or left of it used them as a means of escape to the crater, and the enemy was reoccupying them as fast as our men left. All the satisfaction I received was an order to go back and tell the brigade commanders to get their men out and press forward to Cemetery Hill. This talk and these orders, coming from a commander sitting in a bomb-proof inside the Union lines, were disgusting. I returned again to the crater and delivered the orders, which I knew beforehand could not possibly be obeyed; and I told General Ledlie so before I left him. Upon my return to the crater I devoted my attention to the movements of the enemy, who was evidently making dispositions for an assault.

About two hours after the explosion of the mine (7 o'clock) and after I had returned to the crater for the third time, General Edward Ferrero, commanding the colored division of the Ninth Corps, received an order to advance his division, pass the white troops which had halted, and move on to carry the crest of Cemetery Hill at all hazards. General Ferrero did not think it advisable to move his division in, as there were three divisions of white troops already huddled together, and he so reported to Colonel Charles G. Loring, of General Burnside's staff. Loring requested Ferrero to wait until he could report to General Burnside. General Ferrero declined to wait, and then Colonel Loring gave him an order, in General Burnside's name, to halt without passing over the Union works, which order he obeyed. Colonel Loring went off to report to General Burnside, came back, and reported that the order was peremptory for the colored division to advance at all hazards.

The division then started in, moved by the left flank, under a most galling fire, passed around the crater on the crest on the débris, and all but one regiment passed beyond the crater. The fire upon them was incessant and severe, and many acts of personal heroism were done here by officers and men. Their drill for this object had been unquestionably of great benefit to them, and had they led the attack, fifteen or twenty minutes from the time the débris of the explosion had settled would have found them at Cemetery Hill, before the enemy could have brought a gun to bear on them.

But the leading brigade struck the enemy's force, which I had previously reported as massed in front of the crater, and in a sharp little action the colored troops captured some two hundred prisoners and a stand of colors, and recaptured a stand of colors belonging to a white regiment of the Ninth Corps. In this almost hand-to-hand conflict the colored troops became somewhat disorganized, and some twenty minutes were consumed in re-forming; then they made the attempt to move forward again. But, unsupported, subjected to a galling fire from batteries on the flanks, and from infantry fire in front and partly on the flank, they broke up in disorder and fell back to the crater, the majority passing on to the Union line of defenses, carrying with them a number of the white troops who were in the crater and in the enemy's intrenchments.

Had any one in authority been present when the colored troops made their charge, and had they been supported, even at that late hour in the day, there would have been a possibility of success; but when they fell back and broke up in disorder, it was the closing scene of the tragedy. The rout of the colored troops was followed up by a feeble attack from the enemy, more in the way of a reconnoissance than a charge; but the attack was repulsed by the troops in the crater and in the intrenchments connected therewith, and the Confederates retired.

It was now evident that the enemy did not fear a demonstration from any other quarter, as they began to collect their troops for a decisive assault. On observing this I left the crater and reported to General Ledlie, whom I found seated in a bomb-proof with General Ferrero, that some means ought to be devised for withdrawing the mass of men from the crater without exposing them to the terrific fire which was kept up by the enemy; that if some shovels and picks could be found, the men in an hour could open a covered way by which they could be withdrawn; that the enemy was making every preparation for a determined assault on the crater, and, disorganized as the troops were, they could make no permanent resistance. Not an implement of any kind could be found; indeed, the proposition was received with disfavor. Matters remained *in statu quo* until about 2 P. M., when the enemy's anticipated assault was made.

About 9:30 A. M. General Meade had given positive orders to have the troops withdrawn from the crater. To have done so under the severe fire of the enemy would have produced a stampede, which would have endangered the Union lines, and might possibly have communicated itself to the troops that were massed in rear of the Ninth Corps. General Burnside thought, for these and other reasons, that it would be possible to leave his command there until nightfall, and then withdraw it. There was no means of getting food or water to them, for which they were suffering. The midsummer sun caused waves of moisture produced by the exhalation from this mass to rise above the crater. Wounded men died there begging piteously for water, and soldiers extended their tongues to dampen their parched lips until their tongues seemed to hang from their mouths. Finally, the enemy, having taken advantage of our inactivity to mass his troops, was seen to emerge from the swale between the hill on which the crater was situated and that of the cemetery. On account of this depression they could not be seen by our artillery, and hence no guns were brought to bear upon them. The only place where they could be observed was from the crater. But there was no serviceable artillery there, and no infantry force sufficiently organized to offer resistance when the enemy's column pressed forward. All in the crater who could possibly hang on by their elbows and toes lay flat against its conical wall and delivered their fire; but not more than a hundred men at a time could get into position, and these were only armed with muzzle-loading guns, and in order to re-load they were compelled to face about and place their backs against the wall.

The enemy's guns suddenly ceased their long-continued and uninterrupted fire on the crater, and the advancing column charged in the face of feeble resistance offered by the Union troops. At this stage they were perceived by our artillery, which opened a murderous fire, but too late. Over the crest and into the crater they poured, and a hand-to-hand conflict ensued. It was of short duration, however; crowded as our troops were, and without organization, resistance was vain. Many men were bayoneted at that time—some probably that would not have been, except for the excitement of battle.

569

About 87 officers and 1652 men of the Ninth Corps were captured, the remainder retiring to our own lines, to which the enemy did not attempt to advance. . . .

In this affair the several efforts made to push troops forward to Cemetery Hill were as futile in their results as the dropping of handfuls of sand into a running stream to make a dam. With the notable exception of General Robert B. Potter, there was not a division commander in the crater or connecting lines, nor was there a corps commander on the immediate scene of action; the result being that the subordinate commanders attempted to carry out the orders issued prior to the commencement of the action, when the first attack developed the fact that a change of these plans was absolutely necessary.

GENERAL ULYSSES S. GRANT

The degree of participation of Negroes in the war effort was a thorny problem for both North and South. In the Confederacy at the outbreak of hostilities, many free Negroes came forward and spontaneously volunteered their services to the seceded states, and these and large numbers of slaves were generally used, unarmed, as laborers of various kinds throughout the war. In the North, it was felt for a long time that making soldiers of colored men would do their cause more harm than good and, furthermore, that they would not stand up under fire. Finally, though, Governor John A. Andrew of Massachusetts, a leader in the movement to arm the Negro, was authorized by the Secretary of War to organize a colored regiment to serve three years. Eventually, the North armed over 180,000 Negro troops in all, while at the war's end 25 per cent of her Navy personnel consisted of Negro volunteers. By the time the Petersburg crater explosion was touched off, Negro troops had already experienced fierce fighting and acquitted themselves with honor. At Fort Wagner, Port Hudson, Milliken's Bend, in the engagement between the Alabama *and the* Kearsarge, *Negro fighters had proved that when well officered they could hold their own with white men of North or South, and that they were ready to die if need be for the freedom of their race.*

"We looks like men a-marchin' on,
We looks like men er war"

THE COLORED TROOPS AT PETERSBURG

BY HENRY GODDARD THOMAS, BREVET MAJOR-GENERAL, U. S. V.

EAST of Petersburg, on high ground, protruding like the ugly horn of a rhinoceros, stood the Confederate earth-work, fortified as a battery, which we undermined and exploded July 30th, 1864. It did a good deal of goring before we destroyed it. Its position enabled the garrison to throw a somewhat enfilading fire into our lines, under which many fell, a few at a time.

For some time previous to the explosion of the mine it was determined by General Burnside that the colored division should lead the assault. The general tactical plan had been given to the brigade commanders (Colonel Sigfried and myself), with a rough outline map of the ground, and directions to study the front for ourselves. But this latter was impracticable except in momentary glimpses. The enemy made a target of every head that appeared above the work, and their marksmanship was good. The manner of studying the ground was this: Putting my battered old hat on a ramrod and lifting it above the rampart just enough for them not to discover that

573

no man was under it, I drew their fire; then stepping quickly a few paces one side, I took a hasty observation.

We were all pleased with the compliment of being chosen to lead in the assault. Both officers and men were eager to show the white troops what the colored division could do. We had acquired confidence in our men. They believed us infallible. We had drilled certain movements, to be executed in gaining and occupying the crest. It is an axiom in military art that there are times when the ardor, hopefulness, and enthusiasm of new troops, not yet rendered doubtful by reverses or chilled by defeat, more than compensate, in a dash, for training and experience. General Burnside, for this and other reasons, most strenuously urged his black division for the advance. Against his most urgent remonstrance he was overruled. About 11 P. M., July 29th, a few hours before the action, we were officially informed that the plan had been changed, and our division would not lead.

We were then bivouacking on our arms in rear of our line, just behind the covered way leading to the mine. I returned to that bivouac dejected and with an instinct of disaster for the morrow. As I summoned and told my regimental commanders, their faces expressed the same feeling.

Any striking event or piece of news was usually eagerly discussed by the white troops, and in the ranks military critics were as plenty and perhaps more voluble than among the officers. Not so with the blacks; important news such as that before us, after the bare announcement, was usually followed by long silence. They sat about in groups, "studying," as they called it. They waited, like the Quakers, for the spirit to move; when the spirit moved, one of their singers would uplift a mighty voice, like a bard of old, in a wild sort of chant. If he did not strike a sympathetic chord in his hearers, if they did not find in his utterance the exponent of their idea, he would sing it again and again, altering sometimes the words, more often the music. If his changes met general acceptance, one voice after another would chime in; a rough harmony of three parts would add itself; other groups would join his, and the song would become the song of the command.

The night we learned that we were to lead the charge the news filled them too full for ordinary utterance. The joyous Negro guffaw always breaking out about the camp-fire ceased. They formed circles in their company streets and were sitting on the ground intently and solemnly "studying." At last a heavy voice began to sing,

> *"We-e looks li-ike me-en a-a-marchin' on,*
> *We looks li-ike men-er-war."*

Over and over again he sang it, making slight changes in the melody. The rest listened to him intently; no sign of approval or disapproval escaped their lips or appeared on their faces. All at once, when his refrain had struck the right response in their hearts, his group took it up, and shortly half a thousand voices were upraised extemporizing a half dissonant middle part and bass. It was a picturesque scene—these dark men, with their white eyes and teeth and full red lips, crouching over a smoldering camp-fire, in dusky shadow, with only the feeble rays of the lanterns of the first sergeants and the lights of the candles dimly showing through the tents. The sound was as weird as the scene, when all the voices struck the low E (last note but one), held it, and then rose to A with a *portamento* as sonorous as it was clumsy. Until we fought the battle of the crater they sang this every night to the exclusion of all other songs. After that defeat they sang it no more.

About 3 A. M. the morning of the battle we were up after a short sleep under arms. Then came the soldiers' hasty breakfast. "Never fight on an empty stomach" was a proverb more honored in that army than any of Solomon; for the full stomach helps the wounded man to live through much loss of blood. This morning our breakfast was much like that on other mornings when we could not make fires: two pieces of hard-tack with a slice of raw, fat salt pork between—not a dainty meal, but solid provender to fight on. By good fortune I had a bottle of cucumber pickles. These I distributed to the officers about me. They were gratefully accepted, for nothing cuts the fat of raw salt pork like a pickle. We moistened our repast with black coffee from our canteens. The privates fared the same, barring the luxury of the pickle.

We had been told that the mine would be fired at 3:45 A. M. But 4 o'clock arrived, and all was quiet. Not long after that came a dull, heavy thud, not at all startling; it was a heavy, smothered sound, not nearly so distinct as a musket-shot. Could this be the mine? No; impossible. There was no charging, no yells—neither the deep-mouthed bass growl of the Union troops, nor the sharp, shrill, fox-hunting cry of the Confederates. Here was a mine blown up, making a crater from 150 to 200 feet long, 60 wide, and 30 deep, and the detonation and the concussion were so inconsiderable to us, not over a third of a mile away, that we could hardly believe the report of a staff-officer, back from the line, that the great mine had been exploded.

At about 5:30 A. M. a fairly heavy musketry fire from the enemy had opened. Shortly after, as we lay upon our arms awaiting orders, a quiet voice behind me said, "Who commands this brigade?" "I do," I replied. Rising, and turning toward the voice, I saw General Grant. He was in his usual dress: a broad-brimmed felt hat and the ordinary coat of a private. He wore no sword. Colonel Horace Porter, his aide-de-camp, and a single orderly accompanied him. "Well," said the general, slowly and thoughtfully, as if communing with himself rather than addressing a subordinate, "why are you not in?" Pointing to the First Brigade just in my front, I replied, "My orders are to follow that brigade." Feeling that golden opportunities might be slipping away from us, I added, "Will you give me the order to go in now?" After a moment's hesi-

575

tation he answered in the same slow and ruminating manner, "No, you may keep the orders you have." Then, turning his horse's head, he rode away at a walk.

Fifteen minutes later an aide to the division commander gave us the order, and we moved into the covered way, my brigade following Sigfried's. This was about 6 A. M. For an hour or more we lay here inactive, the musketry growing quicker and sharper all the time. A heavy cannonading opened. We sat down at first, resting against the walls of the covered way. Soon, however, we had to stand to make room for the constantly increasing throng of wounded who were being brought past us to the rear. Some few, with flesh-wounds merely, greeted us with such jocularity as, "I'm all right, boys! This is good for a thirty days' sick-leave." Others were plucky and silent, their pinched faces telling the effort they were making to suppress their groans; others, with the ashy hue of death already gathering on their faces, were largely past pain. Many, out of their senses through agony, were moaning or bellowing like wild beasts. We stood there over an hour with this endless procession of wounded men passing. There could be no greater strain on the nerves. Every moment changed the condition from that of a forlorn hope to one of forlorn hopelessness. Unable to strike a blow, we were sickened with the contemplation of revolting forms of death and mutilation.

Finally, about 7:30 A. M., we got the order for the colored division to charge. My brigade followed Sigfried's at the double-quick. Arrived at the crater, a part of the First Brigade entered. The crater was already too full; that I could easily see. I swung my column to the right and charged over the enemy's rifle-pits connecting with the crater on our right. These pits were different from any in our lines—a labyrinth of bomb-proofs and magazines, with passages between. My brigade moved gallantly on right over the bomb-proofs and over the men of the First Division. As we mounted the pits, a deadly enfilade from eight guns on our right and a murderous cross-fire of musketry met us. Among the officers, the first to fall was the gallant Fessenden of the 23d Regiment. Ayres and Woodruff of the 31st dropped within a few yards of Fessenden, Ayres being killed, and Woodruff mortally wounded. Liscomb of the 23d then fell to rise no more; and then Hackhiser of the 28th and Flint and Aiken of the 29th. Major Rockwood of the 19th then mounted the crest and fell back dead, with a cheer on his lips. Nor were these all; for at that time hundreds of heroes "carved in ebony" fell. These black men commanded the admiration and respect of every beholder.

The most advantageous point for the purpose, about eight hundred feet from the crater, having been reached, we leaped from the works and endeavored to make a rush for the crest. Captain Marshall L. Dempcy, and Lieutenant Christopher Pennell, of my staff, and four white orderlies with the brigade guidon accompanied me, closely followed by Lieutenant-Colonel

Ross, leading the 31st Regiment. At the instant of leaving the works Ross was shot down; the next officer in rank, Captain Wright, was shot as he stooped over him. The men were largely without leaders, and their organization was destroyed. Two of my four orderlies were wounded: one, flag in hand; the remaining two sought shelter when Lieutenant Pennell, rescuing the guidon, hastened down the line outside the pits. With his sword uplifted in his right hand and the banner in his left, he sought to call out the men along the whole line of the parapet. In a moment, a musketry fire was focused upon him, whirling him round and round several times before he fell. Of commanding figure, his bravery was so conspicuous that, according to Colonel Weld's testimony, a number of his (Weld's) men were shot because, spell-bound, they forgot their own shelter in watching this superb boy, who was an only child of an old Massachusetts clergyman, and to me as Jonathan was to David. . . .

The men of the 31st making the charge were being mowed down like grass, with no hope of any one reaching the crest, so I ordered them to scatter and run back. The fire was such that Captain Dempcy and myself were the only officers who returned, unharmed, of those who left the works for that charge.

We were not long back within the honeycomb of passages and bomb-proofs near the crater before I received this order from the division commander: "Colonels Sigfried and Thomas, if you have not already done so, you will immediately proceed to take the crest in your front." My command was crowded into the pits, already too full, and were sandwiched, man for man, against the men of the First Division. They were thus partly sheltered from the fire that had reduced them coming up; but their organization was almost lost. I had already sent word to General Burnside by Major James L. Van Buren, of his staff, that unless a movement simultaneous with mine was made to the right, to stop the enfilading fire, I thought not a man would live to reach the crest; but that I would try another charge in about ten minutes, and I hoped to be supported. I then directed the commanders of the 23d, 28th, and 29th regiments to get their commands as much together and separated from the others as possible in that time, so that each could have a regimental following, for we were mixed up with white troops, and with one another to the extent of almost paralyzing any effort. We managed to make the charge, however, Colonel Bross of the 29th leading. The 31st had been so shattered, was so diminished, so largely without officers, that I got what was left of them out of the way of the charging column as much as possible. This column met the same fate in one respect as the former. As I gave the order, Lieutenant-Colonel John A. Bross, taking the flag into his own hands, was the first man to leap from the works into the valley of death below. He had attired himself in full uniform, evidently with the intent of inspiring his men. He had hardly reached the ground outside the works before he fell to rise no more. He was conspicuous and magnificent in his gal-

577

lantry. The black men followed into the jaws of death, and advanced until met by a charge in force from the Confederate lines.

The report of the Confederate General Bushrod R. Johnson (commanding the opposing forces at that point), to which I have had access, says that the Confederate troops in this charge were the First Brigade of Mahone's division, with the 25th and 49th North Carolina and the 26th and part of the 17th South Carolina regiments. It was no discredit to what was left of three regiments that they were repulsed by a force like that.

I lost in all 36 officers and 877 men—total, 913. The 23d Regiment entered the charge with eighteen officers; it came out with seven. The 28th entered with eleven officers, and came out with four. The 31st had but two officers for duty that night. . . .

Nor was the giving way a willing movement on the part of the colored troops. One little band, after my second charge was repulsed, defended the intrenchments we had won from the enemy, exhibiting fighting qualities that I never saw surpassed in the war. This handful stood there without the slightest organization of company or regiment, each man for himself, until the enemy's banners waved in their very faces. Then they made a dash for our own lines, and that at my order. Speaking of this stand, General Burnside says in his official report: "But not all of the colored troops retired; some held the pits behind which they had advanced, severely checking the enemy until they were nearly all killed."

The summer of 1864 was a black period for both North and South. Both armies were weary—one discouraged by the plodding pace of the war, the other literally approaching exhaustion. Then the spirits of one of the contestants was suddenly raised by a sea battle in the English Channel off the harbor of Cherbourg. For almost a year the Confederate raider Alabama—built in a British yard, equipped with British armament, manned largely by a British crew—had been cruising the sea lanes of the Atlantic and Indian Oceans preying on ships of the United States. Finally it became necessary for the rebel skipper, Admiral Raphael Semmes, to seek a neutral port for repairs, and he chose Cherbourg because the government of Napoleon III had been, if possible, even more hopeful for the success of Confederate arms than the government of Queen Victoria. There Semmes decided to risk an encounter with the U.S.S. Kearsarge, and with disastrous results. In a little over an hour, the nemesis of some sixty-six Union ships was no more. Mrs. Mary Chesnut commented in her Journal, "Admiral Semmes, of whom we have been so proud, is a fool after all. He risked the Alabama in a sort of duel of ships, and now he has lowered the flag of the famous Alabama to the Kearsarge. Forgive who may, I cannot!"

Later in that otherwise dark season, the Union Navy gave the North another lift and a slogan when Admiral Farragut sank and scattered the Confederate warships in Mobile Bay, reduced the forts there and took the town, thus closing the Confederacy's last door to the Gulf. The slogan came from the commander himself. When one of his captains reported torpedoes off his bow, Farragut megaphoned back, "Damn the torpedoes! Full Speed ahead!" It was just the kind of order the Union needed in August 1864.

"For God's sake, do what you can to save them!"

THE DUEL BETWEEN THE "ALABAMA" AND THE "KEARSARGE"

BY JOHN M. BROWNE, SURGEON OF THE "KEARSARGE"

O N SUNDAY, the 12th of June, 1864, the *Kearsarge,* Captain John A. Winslow, was lying at anchor in the Scheldt, off Flushing, Holland. The cornet suddenly appeared at the fore, and a gun was fired. These were unexpected signals that compelled absent officers and men to return to the ship. Steam was raised, and as soon as we were off, and all hands called, Captain Winslow gave the welcome news of a telegram from Mr. Dayton, our minister to France, announcing that the *Alabama* had arrived the day previous at Cherbourg; hence the urgency of departure, the probability of an encounter, and the expectation of her capture or destruction. The crew responded with cheers. The succeeding day witnessed the arrival of the *Kearsarge* at Dover for dispatches, and the day after (Tuesday) her appearance off

581

Cherbourg, where we saw the Confederate flag flying within the breakwater. As we approached, officers and men gathered in groups on deck, and looked intently at the "daring rover" that had been able for two years to escape numerous foes and to inflict immense damage on our commerce. She was a beautiful specimen of naval architecture. The surgeon went on shore and obtained *pratique* (permission to visit the port) for boats. Owing to the neutrality limitation, which would not allow us to remain in the harbor longer than twenty-four hours, it was inexpedient to enter the port. We placed a vigilant watch by turns at each of the harbor entrances, and continued it to the moment of the engagement.

On Wednesday Captain Winslow paid an official visit to the French admiral commanding the maritime district, and to the United States commercial agent, bringing on his return the unanticipated news that Captain Semmes had declared his intention to fight. At first the assertion was barely credited, the policy of the *Alabama* being regarded as opposed to a conflict, and to escape rather than to be exposed to injury, perhaps destruction; but the doubters were half convinced when the so-called challenge was known to read as follows:

C. S. S. "ALABAMA," CHERBOURG, June 14th, 1864

To A. BONFILS, ESQ., CHERBOURG. SIR: I hear that you were informed by the U. S. Consul that the *Kearsarge* was to come to this port solely for the prisoners landed by me, and that she was to depart in twenty-four hours. I desire you to say to the U. S. Consul that my intention is to fight the *Kearsarge* as soon as I can make the necessary arrangements. I hope these will not detain me more than until to-morrow evening, or after the morrow morning at furthest. I beg she will not depart before I am ready to go out.

I have the honor to be, very respectfully,

Your obedient servant,

R. SEMMES, Captain

This communication was sent by Mr. Bonfils, the Confederate States Commercial Agent, to Mr. Liais, the United States Commercial Agent, with a request that the latter would furnish a copy to Captain Winslow for his guidance. There was no other challenge to combat. The letter that passed between the commercial agents *was* the challenge about which so much has been said. Captain Semmes informed Captain Winslow through Mr. Bonfils of his intention to fight; Captain Winslow informed Captain Semmes through Mr. Liais that he came to Cherbourg to fight, and had no intention of leaving. He made no other reply.

Captain Winslow assembled the officers and discussed the expected battle. It was probable the two ships would engage on parallel lines, and the *Alabama* would seek neutral waters in event of defeat; hence the necessity of beginning the action several miles from the breakwater. It was determined not to surrender, but to fight until the last, and, if need be, to go down with colors flying. Why Captain Semmes should imperil his ship was not understood, since he would risk all and expose the cause of which he was a selected champion to a needless disaster, while the *Kearsarge,* if taken or destroyed, could be replaced. It was therefore concluded that he would fight because he thought he would be the victor.

Preparations were made for battle, with no relaxation of the watch. Thursday passed; Friday came; the *Kearsarge* waited with ports down, guns pivoted to starboard, the whole battery loaded, and shell, grape, and canister ready to use in any mode of attack or defense; yet no *Alabama* appeared. French pilots came on board and told of unusual arrangements made by the enemy, such as the hurried taking of coals, the transmission of valuable articles to the shore, such as captured chronometers, specie, and the bills of ransomed vessels; and the sharpening of swords, cutlasses, and boarding-pikes. It was reported that Captain Semmes had been advised not to give battle; that he replied he would prove to the world that his ship was not a privateer, intended only for attack upon merchant vessels, but a true man-of-war; further, that he had consulted French officers, who all asserted that in his situation they would fight. Certain newspapers declared that he ought to improve the opportunity afforded by the presence of the enemy to show that his ship was not a "corsair," to prey upon defenseless merchantmen, but a real ship-of-war, able and willing to fight the "Federal" waiting outside the harbor. It was said the *Alabama* was swift, with a superior crew, and it was known that the ship, guns, and ammunition were of English make. . . .

Sunday, the 19th, came; a fine day, atmosphere somewhat hazy, little sea, light westerly wind. At 10 o'clock the *Kearsarge* was near the buoy marking the line of shoals to the eastward of Cherbourg, at a distance of about three miles from the entrance. The decks had been holystoned, the bright work cleaned, the guns polished, and the crew were dressed in Sunday suits. They were inspected at quarters and dismissed to attend divine service. Seemingly no one thought of the enemy; so long awaited and not appearing, speculation as to her coming had nearly ceased. At 10:20 the officer of the deck reported a steamer approaching from Cherbourg—a frequent occurrence, and consequently it created no surprise. The bell was tolling for service when some one shouted, "She's coming, and heading straight for us!" Soon, by the aid of a glass, the officer of the deck made out the enemy and shouted, "The *Alabama!*" and calling down the ward-room hatch repeated the cry, "The *Alabama!*" The drum beat to general quarters; Captain Winslow put aside the prayer-book, seized the trumpet, ordered the ship about, and headed seaward. The ship was cleared for action, with the battery pivoted to starboard.

The *Alabama* approached from the western entrance, escorted by the

583

French iron-clad frigate *Couronne,* flying the pennant of the commandant of the port, followed in her wake by a small fore-and-aft-rigged steamer, the *Deerhound,* flying the flag of the Royal Mersey Yacht Club. The commander of the frigate had informed Captain Semmes that his ship would escort him to the limit of the French waters. The frigate, having convoyed the *Alabama* three marine miles from the coast, put down her helm, and steamed back into port without delay.

The steam-yacht continued on, and remained near the scene of action.

Captain Winslow had assured the French admiral that in the event of an engagement the position of the ship should be far enough from shore to prevent a violation of the law of nations. To avoid a question of jurisdiction, and to avert an escape to neutral waters in case of retreat, the *Kearsarge* steamed to sea, followed by the enemy, giving the appearance of running away and being pursued. Between six and seven miles from the shore the *Kearsarge,* thoroughly ready, at 10:50 wheeled, at a distance of one and a quarter miles from her opponent, presented the starboard battery, and steered direct for her, with the design of closing or of running her down. The *Alabama* sheered and presented her starboard battery. More speed was ordered, the *Kearsarge* advanced rapidly, and at 10:57 received a broadside of solid shot at a range of about eighteen hundred yards. This broadside cut away a little of the rigging, but the shot mostly passed over or fell short. It was apparent that Captain Semmes intended to fight at long range.

The *Kearsarge* advanced with increased speed, receiving a second and part of a third broadside, with similar effect. Captain Winslow wished to get at short range, as the guns were loaded with five-second shell. Arrived within nine hundred yards, the *Kearsarge,* fearing a fourth broadside, and apprehensive of a raking, sheered and broke her silence with the starboard battery. Each ship was now pressed under a full head of steam, the position being broadside, both employing the starboard guns.

Captain Winslow, fearful that the enemy would make for the shore, determined with a port helm to run under the *Alabama's* stern for raking, but was prevented by her sheering and keeping her broadside to the *Kearsarge,* which forced the fighting on a circular track, each ship, with a strong port helm, steaming around a common center, and pouring its fire into its opponent a quarter to half a mile away. There was a current setting to westward three knots an hour.

The action was now fairly begun. The *Alabama* changed from solid shot to shell. A shot from an early broadside of the *Kearsarge* carried away the spanker-gaff of the enemy, and caused his ensign to come down by the run. This incident was regarded as a favorable omen by the men, who cheered and went with increased confidence to their work. The fallen ensign reappeared at the mizzen. The *Alabama* returned to solid shot, and soon after fired both shot and shell to the end. The firing of the *Alabama* was rapid and wild, getting better near the close; that of the *Kearsarge* was deliberate, accurate, and almost from the beginning productive of dismay, destruction, and death. The *Kearsarge* gunners had been cautioned against firing without direct aim, and had been advised to point the heavy guns below rather than above the water-line, and to clear the deck of the enemy with the lighter ones. Though subjected to an incessant storm of shot and shell, they kept their stations and obeyed instructions.

The effect upon the enemy was readily perceived, and nothing could restrain the enthusiasm of our men. Cheer succeeded cheer; caps were thrown in the air or overboard; jackets were discarded; sanguine of victory, the men were shouting, as each projectile took effect: "That is a good one!" "Down, boys!" "Give her another like the last!" "Now we have her!" and so on, cheering and shouting to the end.

After the *Kearsarge* had been exposed to an uninterrupted cannonade for eighteen minutes, a 68-pounder Blakely shell passed through the starboard bulwarks below the main rigging, exploded upon the quarter-deck, and wounded three of the crew of the after pivot-gun. With these exceptions, not an officer or man received serious injury. The three unfortunate men were speedily taken below, and so quietly was the act done that at the termination of the fight a large number of the men were unaware that any of their comrades were wounded. Two shots entered the ports occupied by the thirty-twos, where several men were stationed, one taking effect in the hammock-netting, the other going through the opposite port, yet none were hit. A shell exploded in the hammock-netting and set the ship on fire; the alarm calling for fire-quarters was sounded, and men who had been detailed for such an emergency put out the fire, while the rest staid at the guns.

It is wonderful that so few casualties occurred on board the *Kearsarge,* considering the number on the *Alabama*—the former having fired 173 shot and shell, and the latter nearly double that number. The *Kearsarge* concentrated her fire, and poured in the 11-inch shells with deadly effect. One penetrated the coal-bunker of the *Alabama,* and a dense cloud of coal-dust arose. Others struck near the water-line between the main and mizzen masts, exploded within board, or, passing through, burst beyond. Crippled and torn, the *Alabama* moved less quickly and began to settle by the stern, yet did not slacken her fire, but returned successive broadsides without disastrous result to us.

Captain Semmes witnessed the havoc made by the shells, especially by those of our after pivot-gun, and offered a reward to any one who would silence it. Soon his battery was turned upon this particular offending gun. It was in vain, for the work of destruction went on. We had completed the seventh rotation on the circular track and had begun the eighth, when the *Alabama,* now settling, sought to escape by setting all available sail (fore-trysail and two jibs), left the circle amid a shower of shot and shell, and headed for the French waters; but to no purpose. In winding, the *Alabama* presented the port battery, with only two guns bearing, and showed gaping sides, through which the water washed. The *Kearsarge* pursued, keeping on a line nearer the shore, and with a few well-directed shots hastened the sinking. Then the *Alabama* was at our mercy. Her colors were struck, and the *Kearsarge* ceased firing. I was told by our prisoners that two of the junior officers swore they would never surrender, and in a mutinous spirit rushed to the two port guns and opened fire upon the *Kearsarge*. Captain Winslow, amazed at this extraordinary conduct of an enemy who had hauled down his flag in token of surrender, exclaimed, "He is playing us a trick; give him another broadside." Again the shot and shell went crashing through her sides, and the *Alabama* continued to settle by the stern. The *Kearsarge* was laid across her bows for raking, and in position to use grape and canister.

A white flag was then shown over the stern of the *Alabama* and her ensign was half-masted, union down. Captain Winslow for the second time gave orders to cease firing. Thus ended the fight, after a duration of one hour and two minutes. Captain Semmes, in his report, says: "Although we were now but four hundred yards from each other, the enemy fired upon me five times after my colors had been struck. It is charitable to suppose that a ship-of-war of a Christian nation could not have done this intentionally." He is silent as to the renewal by the *Alabama* of the fight after his surrender—an act which, in Christian warfare, would have justified the *Kearsarge* in continuing the fire until the *Alabama* had sunk beneath the waters.

Boats were now lowered from the *Alabama.* Her master's-mate, Fullam, an Englishman, came alongside the *Kearsarge* with a few of the wounded, reported the disabled and sinking condition of his ship, and asked for assistance. Captain Winslow inquired, "Does Captain Semmes surrender his ship?" "Yes," was the reply. Fullam then solicited permission to return with his boat and crew to assist in rescuing the drowning, pledging his word of honor that when this was done he would come on board and surrender. Captain Winslow granted the request. With less generosity he could have detained the officer and men, supplied their places in the boat from his ship's company, secured more prisoners, and afforded equal aid to the distressed. The generosity was abused, as the sequel shows. Fullam pulled to the midst of the drowning, rescued several officers, went to the yacht *Deerhound,* and cast his boat adrift, leaving a number of men struggling in the water.

It was now seen that the *Alabama* was settling fast. The wounded, and the boys who could not swim, were sent away in the quarter-boats, the waist-boats having been destroyed. Captain Semmes dropped his sword into the sea and jumped overboard with the remaining officers and men.

Coming under the stern of the *Kearsarge* from the windward, the *Deerhound* was hailed, and her commander requested by Captain Winslow to run down and assist in picking up the men of the sinking ship. Or, as her owner, Mr. John Lancaster, reported: "The fact is, that when we passed the *Kearsarge* the captain cried out, 'For God's sake, do what you can to save them'; and that was my warrant for interfering in any way for the aid and succor of his enemies." The *Deerhound* was built by the Lairds at the same time and in the same yard with the *Alabama*. Throughout the action she kept about a mile to the windward of the contestants. After being hailed she steamed toward the *Alabama,* which sank almost immediately after. This was at 12:24. The *Alabama* sank in forty-five fathoms of water, at a distance of about four and a half miles from the breakwater, off the west entrance. She was severely hulled between the main and mizzen masts, and settled by the stern; the mainmast, pierced by a shot at the very last, broke off near the head and went over the side, the bow lifted high from the water, and then came the end. Suddenly assuming a perpendicular position, caused by the falling aft of the battery and stores, straight as a plumb-line, stern first, she went down, the jib-boom being the last to appear above water. Thus sank the terror of merchantmen, riddled through and through, and as she disappeared to her last resting-place there was no cheer; all was silent. . . .

The *Kearsarge* received twenty-eight shot and shell, of which thirteen were in the hull, the most efficient being abaft the mainmast. A 100-pounder rifle shell entered at the starboard quarter and lodged in the stern-post. The blow shook the ship from stem to stern. Luckily the shell did not explode, otherwise the result would have been serious, if not fatal. A 32-pounder shell entered forward of the forward pivot port, crushing the waterways, raising the gun and carriage, and lodged, but did not explode, else many of the gun's crew would likely have been injured by the fragments and splinters. The smoke-pipe was perforated by a rifle shell, which exploded inside and tore a ragged hole nearly three feet in diameter, and carried away three of the chain guys. Three boats were shattered. The cutting away of the rigging was mostly about the mainmast. The spars were left in good order. A large number of pieces of burst shell were gathered from the deck and thoughtlessly thrown overboard. During the anchorage in Cherbourg harbor no assistance was received from shore except that rendered by a boiler-maker in patching up the smoke-stack, every other repair being made by our own men.

Captain Semmes in his official report says:

At the end of the engagement it was discovered, by those of our officers who went alongside the enemy's ship with the wounded, that her midship section on both sides was thoroughly iron-coated. The planking had been ripped off in every direction by our shot and shell, the chain broken and indented in many places, and forced partly into the ship's side. The enemy was heavier than myself, both in ship, battery, and crew; but I did not know until the action was over that she was also iron-clad.

The ships were well matched in size, speed, armament, and crew, showing a likeness rarely seen in naval battles. The number of the ship's company of the *Kearsarge* was 163. That of the *Alabama,* from the best information, was estimated at 150.

The chain plating was made of one hundred and twenty fathoms of sheet-chains of one and seven-tenths inch iron, covering a space amidships of forty-nine and one-half feet in length by six feet two inches in depth, stopped up and down to eye-bolts with marlines, secured by iron dogs, and employed for the purpose of protecting the engines when the upper part of the coal-bunkers was empty, as happened during the action. The chains were concealed by one-inch deal-boards as a finish. The chain plating was struck by a 32-pounder shot in the starboard gangway, which cut the chain and bruised the planking; and by a 32-pounder shell, which broke a link of the chain, exploded, and tore away a portion of the deal covering. Had the shot been from the 100-pounder rifle the result would have been different, though without serious damage, because the shot struck five feet above the water-line, and if sent through the side would have cleared the machinery and boilers. It is proper therefore to assert that in the absence of the chain armor the result would have been nearly the same, notwithstanding the common opinion at the time that the *Kearsarge* was an "iron-clad" contending with a wooden ship. The chains were fastened to the ship's sides more than a year previous to the fight, while at the Azores. It was the suggestion of the executive officer, Lieutenant-Commander James S. Thornton, to hang the sheet-chain (or spare anchor-cable) over the sides, so as to protect the midship section, he having served with Admiral Farragut in passing the forts to reach New Orleans, and having observed its benefit on that occasion. The work was done in three days, at a cost for material not exceeding seventy-five dollars. In our visit to European ports, the use of sheet-chains for protective purposes had attracted notice and caused comment. It is strange that Captain Semmes did not know of the chain armor; supposed spies had been on board and had been shown through the ship, as there was no attempt at concealment; the same pilot had been employed by both ships, and had visited each during the preparation for battle. The *Alabama* had bunkers full of coal, which brought her down in the water. The *Kearsarge* was deficient in seventy tons of coal of her proper supply, but the sheet-chains stowed outside gave protection to her partly-filled bunkers.

The battery of the *Kearsarge* consisted of seven guns: two 11-inch pivots, smooth bore, one 30-pounder rifle, and four light 32-pounders; that of the *Alabama* of eight guns: one 68-pounder pivot, smooth bore, one 100-pounder pivot rifle, and six heavy 32-pounders. Five guns were fought by the *Kearsarge* and seven by the *Alabama,* each with the starboard battery. Both ships had made thirteen knots an hour under steam; at the time of the battle the *Alabama* made ten knots. The masts of the *Kearsarge* were low and small; she never carried more than top-sail yards, depending upon her engines for speed. The greater size and height of the masts of the *Alabama* and the heaviness of her rig (barque) gave the appearance of a larger vessel than her antagonist. . . .

The contest was decided by the superiority of the 11-inch Dahlgrens, especially the after-pivot, together with the coolness and accuracy of aim of the gunners of the *Kearsarge,* and notably by the skill of William Smith, the captain of the after-pivot, who in style and behavior was like Long Tom Coffin in Cooper's "Pilot." . . .

This Sunday naval duel was fought in the presence of more than 15,000 spectators, who, upon the heights of Cherbourg, the breakwater, and rigging of men-of-war, witnessed "the last of the *Alabama.*" Among them were the captains, their families, and crews of two merchant ships burnt by the daring cruiser a few days before her arrival at Cherbourg, where they were landed in a nearly destitute condition. Many spectators were provided with spy-glasses and camp-stools. The *Kearsarge* was burning Newcastle coals, and the *Alabama* Welsh coals, the difference in the amount of smoke enabling the movements of each ship to be distinctly traced. An excursion train from Paris arrived in the morning, bringing hundreds of pleasure-seekers, who were unexpectedly favored with the spectacle of a sea-fight. A French gentleman at Boulogne-sur-Mer assured me that the fight was the conversation of Paris for more than a week.

THE *Kearsarge* GETTING INTO POSITION TO RAKE THE *Alabama*

589

As the months passed, General Sherman became an advocate of "total war." The rebels, he could see, wanted him to detach a division here, a brigade there, to protect their families and property while they were fighting; and this he called a one-sided game of war. After the fall of Atlanta, Sherman convinced Grant (not without difficulty) that he could cut all his links with the North, take his army of 62,000 eastward across the heart of the Confederacy, desolating the country in a fifty- or sixty-mile belt, and in a month come out at Savannah. "This may not be war but rather statesmanship," he wrote Grant. "Nevertheless it is overwhelming to my mind that there ~re thousands of people abroad and in the South who reason thus: If the North can march an army right through the South, it is proof positive that the North can prevail." It was a brilliant plan —if it worked.

On November 15, Sherman's men, the bulk of them from the states west of the Appalachians, turned their backs on the smoking ruins of Atlanta and marched toward the sea. It was one of the most dramatic maneuvers of the war and for weeks the whole world speculated on its outcome. The British Army and Navy Gazette cautiously observed, "If Sherman has really left his army in the air and started off without a base to march from Georgia to South Carolina, he has done one of the most brilliant or one of the most foolish things ever performed by a military leader. The data on which he goes and the plan on which he acts must really place him among the great Generals or the very little ones." On December 13th, to the North's delight, Sherman's army reached the sea, almost immediately taking Fort McAllister, a few miles below Savannah. Nine days later the Confederate defenders of Savannah had withdrawn and Sherman was in the city.

In reply to Sherman's telegraphed pleasantry to Mr. Lincoln ("I beg to present you as a Christmas gift, the city of Savannah. . . . "), the President expressed his relief at hearing the great news and asked, "But what next? I suppose it will be safe if I leave General Grant and yourself to decide." The next move, again at Sherman's urging and Grant's acquiescence, developed into the march northward through South Carolina, with the object of uniting with Grant but meanwhile destroying the rebels' will to resist—a movement the Union soldiers undertook with a special enthusiasm since, clearly to them, the Palmetto State bore the chief guilt for bringing on the war more than three long years before.

"A howling waste . . ."

MARCHING THROUGH GEORGIA AND THE CAROLINAS

BY DANIEL OAKEY, CAPTAIN, 2D MASSACHUSETTS VOLUNTEERS

TO US of the Twelfth Corps who had gone West with the Eleventh Corps from the Army of the Potomac, the distant thunder of "the battle of the clouds" was the first sound of conflict in the new field. Some of our "Potomac airs," which had earned us the name of "Kid gloves and paper collars," began to wear away as we better understood the important work to be done by the great army organizing around us, and of which we were to form a considerable part. A most interesting feature of these preparations was the reënlistment of the old three-years regiments. The two Potomac corps were consolidated, and we of the Twelfth who wore "the bloody star" were apprehensive lest different insignia should be adopted; but the star became the badge of the new (Twentieth) corps, the crescent men amiably dropping their Turkish emblem. . . .

We observed in the Western troops an air of independence hardly consistent with the nicest discipline; but this quality appeared to some purpose at the battle of Resaca, where we saw our Western companions deliberately leave the line, retire out of range, clean their guns, pick up ammunition from the wounded, and return again to the fight. This cool self-reliance excited our admiration. On we went in a campaign of continual skirmishes and battles that ended in the capture of Atlanta. The morale of the troops had been visibly improved by this successful campaign.

On my way to army headquarters at Atlanta to call upon a staff friend, I met General Sherman, who acknowledged my salute with a familiar "How do you do, Captain." Scrutinizing the insignia on my cap, he continued, "Second Massachusetts? Ah, yes, I know your regiment; you have very fine parades over there in the park."

Sherman could be easily approached by any of his soldiers, but no one could venture to be familiar. His uniform coat, usually wide open at the throat, displayed a not very military black cravat and linen collar, and he generally wore low shoes and one spur. On the march he rode with each column in turn, and often with no larger escort than a single staff-officer and an orderly. In passing us on the march he acknowledged our salutations as if he knew us all, but hadn't time to stop. On "the march to the sea" a soldier called out to Sherman, "Uncle Billy, I guess Grant's waiting for us at Richmond." Sherman's acquaintance among his officers was remarkable, and of great advantage, for he learned the character of every command, even of regiments, and could assign officers to special duties, with knowledge of those who were to fill the vacancies so made. The army appreciated these personal relations, and every man felt in a certain sense that Sherman had his eye on him.

Before the middle of November, 1864, the inhabitants of Atlanta, by Sherman's orders, had left the place. Serious preparations were making for the march to the sea. Nothing was to be left for the use or advantage of the enemy. The sick were sent back to Chattanooga and Nashville, along with every pound of baggage that could be dispensed with. The army was reduced, one might say, to its fighting weight, no man being retained who was not capable of a long march. Our communications were then abandoned by destroying the railroad and telegraph. There was something intensely exciting in this perfect isolation.

The engineers had peremptory orders to avoid any injury to dwellings, but to apply gunpowder and the torch to public buildings, machine-shops, depots, and arsenals. Sixty thousand of us witnessed the destruction of Atlanta, while our post band and that of the 33d Massachusetts played martial airs and operatic selections. It was a night never to be forgotten. Our regular routine was a mere form, and there could be no "taps" amid the brilliant glare and excitement.

The throwing away of superfluous conveniences began at daybreak. The old campaigner knows what to carry and what to throw away. Each group of messmates decided which hatchet, stew-pan, or coffee-pot should be taken. The single wagon allowed to a battalion carried scarcely more than a grip-sack and blanket, and a bit of shelter tent about the size of a large towel, for each officer, and only such other material as was necessary for regimental business. Transportation was reduced to a minimum, and fast marching was to be the order of the day. Wagons to carry the necessary ammunition in the contingency of a battle, and a few days' rations in case of absolute need, composed the train of each army corps, and with one wagon and one ambulance for each regiment made very respectable "impedimenta," averaging about eight hundred wagons to a corps.

At last came the familiar "Fall in"; the great "flying column" was on the march, and the last regiment in Atlanta turned its back upon the smoking ruins. Our left wing (the Fourteenth and Twentieth corps under Slocum) seemed to threaten Macon, while the right wing (the Fifteenth and Seventeenth corps under Howard) bent its course as if for Augusta. Skirmishers were in advance, flankers were out, and foraging parties were ahead gathering supplies from the rich plantations. We were all old campaigners, so that a brush with the militia now and then or with Hardee's troops made no unusual delay; and Wheeler's cavalry was soon disposed of. We were expected to make fifteen miles a day; to corduroy the roads where necessary; to destroy such property as was designated by our corps commander, and to consume everything eatable by man or beast.

Milledgeville proved to be Sherman's first objective, and both wings came within less than supporting distance in and around the capital of the State. Our colored friends, who flocked to us in embarrassing numbers, told many stories about the fear and flight of the inhabitants at the approach of Sherman.

Cock-fighting became one of the pastimes of the "flying column." Many fine birds were brought in by our foragers. Those found deficient in courage and skill quickly went to the stew-pan in company with the modest barn-yard fowl, but those of redoubtable valor won an honored place and name, and were to be seen riding proudly on the front seat of an artillery caisson, or carried tenderly under the arm of an infantry soldier.

Our next objective was Savannah. Hazen's capture of Fort McAllister opened the gates of that beautiful city, while Hardee managed to escape with his little army; and Sherman, in a rather facetious dispatch, presented the city to Mr. Lincoln as a Christmas gift. Flushed with the success of our march, we settled down for a rest. Our uniforms were the worse for wear, but the army was in fine condition and fully prepared for the serious work ahead.

In the middle of December in the neighborhood of Savannah, after Hardee's troops had nearly exhausted the country, which was now mainly under water, there was little opportunity for the foragers to exercise their talents, and some of them returned to the ranks. The troops bivouacked here and there in comparatively dry spots, while picket duty had to be performed at many points in the water. In going from Sister's Ferry to Robertsville, where my regiment was in bivouac, I waded for a mile and a half in water knee-deep. At Purysburg the pickets were all afloat in boats and scows and on rafts, and the crestfallen foragers brought in nothing but rice, which became unpalatable when served three times a day for successive weeks. At length, when we left Savannah and launched cheerily into the untrodden land of South Carolina, the foragers began to assume their wonted spirit. We were proud of our foragers. They constituted a picked force from each regiment, under an officer selected for the command, and were remarkable for intelligence, spirit, and daring. Before daylight, mounted on horses captured on the plantations, they were in the saddle and away, covering the country sometimes seven miles in advance. Although I have said "in the saddle," many a forager had nothing better than a bit of carpet and a rope halter; yet this simplicity of equipment did not abate his power of carrying off hams and sweet-potatoes in the face of the enemy. The foragers were also important as a sort of advance guard, for they formed virtually a curtain of mounted infantry screening us from the inquisitive eyes of parties of Wheeler's cavalry, with whom they did not hesitate to engage when it was a question of a rich plantation.

When compelled to retire, they resorted to all the tricks of infantry skirmishers, and summoned reënforcements of foragers from other regiments to help drive the "Johnnies" out. When success crowned their efforts, the plantation was promptly stripped of live stock and eatables. The natives were accustomed to bury provisions, for they feared their own soldiers quite as much as they feared ours. These subterranean stores were readily discovered by the practiced "Yankee" eye. The appearance of the ground and a little probing with a ramrod or a bayonet soon decided whether to dig. Teams were improvised; carts and vehicles of all sorts were pressed into the service and loaded with provisions. If any antiquated militia uniforms were discovered, they were promptly donned, and a comical procession escorted the valuable train of booty to the point where the brigade was expected to bivouac for the night. The regimentals of the past, even to those of revolutionary times, were often conspicuous.

On an occasion when our brigade had the advance, several parties of foragers, consolidating themselves, captured a town from the enemy's cavalry, and occupied the neighboring plantations. Before the arrival of the main column hostilities had ceased; order had been restored, and mock arrangements were made to receive the army. Our regiment in the advance was confronted by a picket dressed in continental uniform, who waved his plumed hat in response to the gibes of the men, and galloped away on his bareback mule to apprise his comrades of our approach. We marched into the town and rested on each side of the main street. Presently a forager, in ancient militia uniform indicating high rank, debouched from a side street to do the honors of the occasion. He was mounted on a raw-boned horse with a bit of carpet for a saddle. His old plumed chapeau in hand, he rode with gracious dignity through the street, as if reviewing the brigade. After him came a family carriage laden with hams, sweet-potatoes, and other provisions, and drawn by two horses, a mule, and a cow, the two latter ridden by postilions. . . .

The march through Georgia has been called a grand military promenade, all novelty and excitement. But its moral effect on friend and foe was immense. It proved our ability to lay open the heart of the Confederacy, and left the question of what we might do next a matter of doubt and terror. It served also as a preliminary training for the arduous campaign to come. Our work was incomplete while the Carolinas, except at a few points on the seacoast, had not felt the rough contact of war. But their swamps and rivers, swollen and spread into lakes by winter floods, presented obstructions almost impracticable to an invading army, if opposed by even a very inferior force.

The task before us was indeed formidable. It involved exposure and indefatigable exertion. To succeed, our forward movement had to be continuous, for even the most productive regions would soon be exhausted by our 60,000 men and more, and 13,000 animals.

Although we were fully prepared, with our great trains of ammunition, to fight a pitched battle, our mission was not to fight, but to consume and destroy. Our inability to care properly for the wounded, who must necessarily be carried along painfully in jolting ambulances to die on the way from exhaustion and exposure, was an additional and very serious reason for avoiding collision with the enemy. But where he could not be evaded, his very presence across our path increased the velocity of our flying column. We repelled him by a decisive blow and without losing our momentum.

The beginning of our march in South Carolina was pleasant, the weather favorable, and the country productive. Sometimes at the midday halt a stray pig that had cunningly evaded the foragers would venture forth in the belief of having escaped "the cruel war," and would find his error, alas! too late, by encountering our column. Instantly an armed mob would set upon him, and his piercing shrieks would melt away in the scramble for fresh pork. But the midday sport of the main column and the happy life of the forager were sadly interrupted. The sun grew dim, and the rain came and continued. A few of our excellent foragers were reported captured by Wheeler's cavalry, while we sank deeper and deeper in the mud as we approached the Salkehatchie Swamp, which lay between us and the Charleston and Augusta railroad. As the heads of column came up, each command knew what it had to do. Generals Mower and G. A. Smith got their divisions across by swimming, wading, and floating, and effected lodgments in spite of the enemy's fire. An overwhelming mass of drenched and muddy veterans swept away the enemy, while the rest of our force got the trains and artillery over by corduroying, pontooning, and bridging. It seemed a grand day's work to have accomplished, as we sank down that night in our miry bivouac. . . .

We destroyed about forty miles of the Charleston and Augusta railroad, and, by threatening points beyond the route we intended to take, we deluded the enemy into concentrating at Augusta and other places, while we marched rapidly away, leaving him well behind, and nothing but Wade Hampton's cavalry, and the more formidable obstacle of the Saluda River and its swamps, between us and Columbia, our next objective. As the route of our column lay west of Columbia, I saw nothing of the oft-described and much-discussed burning of that city.

During the hasty removal of the Union prisoners from Columbia two Massachusetts officers managed to make their escape. Exhausted and almost naked, they found their way to my command. My mess begged for the privilege of caring for one of them. We gave him a mule to ride with a comfortable saddle, and scraped together an outfit for him, although our clothes were in the last stages. Our guest found the mess luxurious, as he sat down with us at the edge of a rubber blanket spread upon the ground for a table-cloth, and set with tin cups and platters. Stewed fighting-cock and bits of fried turkey were followed by fried corn-meal and sorghum. Then came our coffee and pipes, and we lay down by a roaring fire of pine-knots, to hear our guest's story of life in a rebel prison. Before daybreak the tramp of horses reminded us that our foragers were sallying forth. The red light from the countless camp-fires melted away as the dawn stole over the horizon, casting its wonderful gradations of light and color over the masses of sleeping soldiers, while the smoke from burning pine-knots befogged the chilly morning air. Then the bugles broke the impressive stillness, and the roll of drums was heard on all sides. Soon the scene was alive with blue coats and the hubbub of roll-calling, cooking, and running for water to the nearest spring or stream. The surgeons looked to the sick and footsore, and weeded from the ambulances those who no longer needed to ride.

It was not uncommon to hear shots at the head of the column. The foragers would come tumbling back, and ride alongside the regiment, adding to the noisy talk their account of what they had seen, and dividing among their comrades such things as they had managed to bring away in their narrow escape from capture. A staff-officer would gallop down the roadside like a man who had forgotten something which must be recovered in a hurry. At the sound of the colonel's ringing voice, silence was instant and absolute. Sabers flashed from their scabbards, the men brought their guns to the "carry," and the battalion swung into line at the roadside; cats, fighting-cocks, and frying-pans passed to the rear rank; officers and sergeants buzzed round their companies to see that the guns were loaded and the men ready for action. The color-sergeant loosened the water-proof cover of the battle-flag, a battery of artillery flew past on its way to the front, following the returning staff-officer, and we soon heard the familiar bang of shells. Perhaps it did not amount to much after all, and we were soon swinging into "route step" again.

At times when suffering from thirst it was hard to resist the temptation of crystal swamp water, as it rippled along the side of a causeway, a tempting sight for the weary and unwary. In spite of oft-repeated cautions, some contrived to drink it, but these were on their backs with malarial disease at the end of the campaign, if not sooner. . . .

We marched into Cheraw with music and with colors flying. Stacking arms in the main street, we proceeded to supper, while the engineers laid the pontoons across the Pedee River. The railing of the town pump, and the remains of a buggy, said to belong to Mr. Lincoln's brother-in-law, Dr. Todd, were quickly reduced to kindling-wood to boil the coffee. The necessary destruction of property was quickly accomplished, and on we went. A mile from the Lumber River the country, already flooded ankle-deep, was rendered still more inhospitable by a steady down-pour of rain. The bridges had been partly destroyed by the enemy, and partly swept away by the flood. An attempt to carry heavy army wagons and artillery across this dreary lake might have seemed rather foolhardy, but we went to work without loss of time. The engineers were promptly floated out to the river, to direct the rebuilding of bridges, and the woods all along the line of each column soon rang with the noise of axes. Trees quickly became logs, and were brought to the submerged roadway. No matter if logs disappeared in the floating mud; thousands more were coming from all sides. So, layer upon layer, the work went bravely on. Soon the artillery and wagons were jolting over our wooden causeway.

As my regiment was the rear-guard for the day, we had various offices to perform for the train, and it was midnight before we saw the last wagon over the bridge by the light of our pine torches. It seemed as if that last wagon was never to be got over. It came bouncing and bumping along, its six mules smoking and blowing in the black, misty air. The teamster, mounted on one of the wheelers, guided his team with a single rein and addressed each mule by name, reminding the animal of his faults, and accusing him of having, among other peculiarities, "a black military heart." Every sentence of his oath-adorned rhetoric was punctuated with a dexterous whip-lash. At last, drenched to the skin and covered with mud, I took my position on the bridge, seated in a chair which one of my men had presented to me, and waited for the command to "close up." . . .

As we advanced into the wild pine regions of North Carolina the natives seemed wonderfully impressed at seeing every road filled with marching troops, artillery, and wagon trains. They looked destitute enough as they stood in blank amazement gazing upon the "Yanks" marching by. The scene before us was very striking; the resin pits were on fire, and great columns of black smoke rose high into the air, spreading and mingling together in gray clouds, and suggesting the roof and pillars of a vast temple. All traces of habitation were left behind, as we marched into that grand forest with its beautiful carpet of pine-needles. The straight trunks of the pine-tree shot up to a great height, and then spread out into a green roof, which kept us in perpetual shade. As night came on, we found that the resinous sap in the cavities cut in the trees to receive it, had been lighted by "bummers" in our advance. The effect of these peculiar watch-fires on every side, several feet above the ground, with flames licking their way up the tall trunks, was peculiarly striking and beautiful. But it was sad to see this wanton destruction of property, which, like the firing of the resin pits, was the work of "bummers," who were marauding through the country committing every sort of outrage. There was no restraint except with the column or the regular foraging parties. We had no communications, and could have no safeguards. The country was necessarily left to take care of itself, and became a "howling waste." The "coffee-coolers" of the Army of the Potomac were archangels compared to our "bummers," who often fell to the tender mercies of Wheeler's cavalry, and were never heard of again, earning a fate richly deserved.

On arriving within easy distance of the Cape Fear River, where we expected to communicate with the navy, detachments were sent in rapid advance to secure Fayetteville. Our division, after a hard day of corduroying in various spots over a distance of twelve miles, went into camp for supper, and then, taking the plank-road for Fayetteville, made a moonlight march of nine miles in three hours, but our friends from the right wing arrived there before us.

Hardee retired to a good position at Averysboro', where Kilpatrick found him intrenched and too strong for the cavalry to handle unassisted. It was the turn of our brigade to do special duty, so at about 8 o'clock in the evening we were ordered to join the cavalry. We were not quite sure it rained, but everything was dripping. The men furnished themselves with pine-knots, and our weapons glistened in the torch-light, a cloud of black smoke from the torches floating back over our heads. The regimental wits were as ready as ever, and amid a flow of lively badinage we toiled on through the mud. . . .

The clear wintry dawn disclosed a long line of blue-coats spread over the ground in motionless groups. This was the roaring torch-light brigade of the night before. The orders "Fall in!" "Forward!" in gruff tones broke upon the chilly air, and brought us shivering to our feet. We moved to the edge of the woods with the cavalry. The skirmish line, under Captain J. I. Grafton, had already disappeared into the opposite belt of woods, and evidently were losing no time in developing the enemy and ascertaining his force. They were drawing his fire from all points, indicating a force more than double that of our brigade. Dismounted cavalry were now sent forward to prolong the skirmish-line. Captain Grafton was reported badly wounded in the leg, but still commanding with his usual coolness. Suddenly he appeared staggering out of the wood into the open space in our front, bareheaded, his face buried in his hands, his saber hanging by the sword-knot from his wrist, one leg bound up with a handkerchief, his uniform covered with blood; in a moment he fell toward the colors. Officers clustered about him in silence, and a gloom spread through the brigade as word passed that Grafton was dead.

The main column was now arriving, and as the troops filed off to the right and left of the road, and the field-guns galloped into battery, we moved forward to the attack. The enemy gave us a hot reception, which we returned with a storm of lead. It was a wretched place for a fight. At some points we had to support our wounded until they could be carried off, to prevent their falling into the swamp water, in which we stood ankle-deep. Here and there a clump of thick growth in the black mud broke the line as we advanced. No ordinary troops were in our front. They would not give way until a division of Davis's corps was thrown upon their right, while we pressed them closely. As we passed over their dead and wounded, I came upon the body of a very young officer, whose handsome, refined face attracted my attention. While the line of battle swept past me I knelt at his side for a moment. His buttons bore the arms of South Carolina. Evidently we were fighting the Charleston chivalry. Sunset found us in bivouac on the Goldsboro' road, and Hardee in retreat.

As we trudged on toward Bentonville, distant sounds told plainly that the head of the column was engaged. We hurried to the front and went into action, connecting with Davis's corps. Little opposition having been expected, the distance between our wing and the right wing had been allowed to increase beyond supporting distance in the endeavor to find easier roads for marching as well as for transporting the wounded. The scope of this paper precludes a description of the battle of Bentonville, which was a combination of mistakes, miscarriages, and hard fighting on both sides. It ended in Johnston's retreat, leaving open the road to Goldsboro', where we arrived ragged and almost barefoot. While we were receiving letters from home, getting new clothes, and taking our regular doses of quinine, Lee and Johnston surrendered, and the great conflict came to an end.

On April 1, 1865, the Battle of Five Forks broke the Confederate line below Petersburg, opening the city to Grant's forces after a siege that had begun almost ten months before. At the same time, in an atmosphere of great disorder, Richmond was also largely evacuated. The end of the long war was at hand. Lee's army of starving, weary men pulled away to the west, hoping for a junction somewhere with Joe Johnston's small command then in North Carolina, but it was pursued promptly by Grant's well-fed infantrymen and harried on the flanks by his now greatly superior cavalry under Sheridan.

At points along the line of march where rations were to have been waiting for the retreating men, provision trains failed to appear. The country through which they were passing was too poor to yield to foraging. And they could not pause for that purpose anyhow lest Grant's eager foot soldiers overtake them. Many of the men simply dropped from utter exhaustion. Many quietly slipped away never to return. Many shuffled onward in a daze. "My God! has the army dissolved?" cried Lee. And although he was assured there were still men left to do their duty, the Army of Northern Virginia *was* actually dissolving. Although neither of them knew it, Lee and Grant had an appointment to keep on April 9th at a crossroads village called Appomattox—in a house owned by a Mr. McLean, whose place in northern Virginia had been Beauregard's headquarters during the first great battle of the war and who had sold out and moved south to get away from the path of the armies!

"Lee . . . facing Grant"

THE SURRENDER AT APPOMATTOX COURT HOUSE

BY HORACE PORTER, BREVET BRIGADIER-GENERAL, U. S. A.

A LITTLE before noon on the 7th of April, 1865, General Grant, with his staff, rode into the little village of Farmville, on the south side of the Appomattox River, a town that will be memorable in history as the place where he opened the correspondence with Lee which led to the surrender of the Army of Northern Virginia. He drew up in front of the village hotel, dismounted, and established headquarters on its broad piazza. News came in that Crook was fighting large odds with his cavalry on the north side of the river, and I was directed to go to his front and see what was necessary to be done to assist him. I found that he was being driven back, the enemy (Munford's and Rosser's cavalry divisions under Fitzhugh Lee) having made a bold stand north of the river. Humphreys was also on the north side, isolated from the rest of our infantry, confronted by a large portion of Lee's army, and having some very heavy fighting. On my return to general headquarters that evening Wright's corps was ordered to cross

601

the river and move rapidly to the support of our troops there. Notwithstanding their long march that day, the men sprang to their feet with a spirit that made every one marvel at their pluck, and came swinging through the main street of the village with a step that seemed as elastic as on the first day of their toilsome tramp. It was now dark, but they spied the general-in-chief watching them with evident pride from the piazza of the hotel.

Then was witnessed one of the most inspiring scenes of the campaign. Bonfires were lighted on the sides of the street, the men seized straw and pine knots, and improvised torches; cheers arose from throats already hoarse with shouts of victory, bands played, banners waved, arms were tossed high in air and caught again. The night march had become a grand review, with Grant as the reviewing officer.

Ord and Gibbon had visited the general at the hotel, and he had spoken with them as well as with Wright about sending some communication to Lee that might pave the way to the stopping of further bloodshed. Dr. Smith, formerly of the regular army, a native of Virginia and a relative of General Ewell, now one of our prisoners, had told General Grant the night before that Ewell had said in conversation that their cause was lost when they crossed the James River, and he considered that it was the duty of the authorities to negotiate for peace then, while they still had a right to claim concessions, adding that now they were not in condition to claim anything. He said that for every man killed after this somebody would be responsible, and it would be little better than murder. He could not tell what General Lee would do, but he hoped he would at once surrender his army. This statement, together with the news that had been received from Sheridan saying that he had heard that General Lee's trains of provisions which had come by rail were at Appomattox, and that he expected to capture them before Lee could reach them, induced the general to write the following communication:

> HEADQUARTERS, ARMIES OF THE U. S.
> 5 P. M., April 7th, 1865
>
> GENERAL R. E. LEE, Commanding C. S. A.:
>
> The results of the last week must convince you of the hopelessness of further resistance on the part of the Army of Northern Virginia in this struggle. I feel that it is so, and regard it as my duty to shift from myself the responsibility of any further effusion of blood by asking of you the surrender of that portion of the Confederate States army known as the Army of Northern Virginia.
>
> U. S. GRANT, Lieutenant-General

This he intrusted to General Seth Williams, adjutant-general, with directions to take it to Humphreys's front, as his corps was close up to the enemy's rear-guard, and have it sent into Lee's lines. The general decided to remain all night at Farmville and await the reply from Lee, and he was shown to a room in the hotel in which, he was told, Lee had slept the night before. Lee wrote the following reply within an hour after he received General Grant's letter, but it was brought in by rather a circuitous route and did not reach its destination till after midnight:

April 7th, 1865

GENERAL: I have received your note of this date. Though not entertaining the opinion you express of the hopelessness of further resistance on the part of the Army of Northern Virginia, I reciprocate your desire to avoid useless effusion of blood, and therefore, before considering your proposition, ask the terms you will offer on condition of its surrender.

R. E. LEE, General

LIEUTENANT-GENERAL U. S. GRANT, Commanding Armies of the U. S.

The next morning before leaving Farmville the following reply was given to General Williams, who again went to Humphreys's front to have it transmitted to Lee:

April 8th, 1865

GENERAL R. E. LEE, Commanding C. S. A.:

Your note of last evening in reply to mine of the same date, asking the conditions on which I will accept the surrender of the Army of Northern Virginia, is just received. In reply I would say that, peace being my great desire, there is but one condition I would insist upon—namely, that the men and officers surrendered shall be disqualified for taking up arms against the Government of the United States until properly exchanged. I will meet you, or will designate officers to meet any officers you may name for the same purpose, at any point agreeable to you, for the purpose of arranging definitely the terms upon which the surrender of the Army of Northern Virginia will be received.

U. S. GRANT, Lieutenant-General

There turned up at this time a rather hungry-looking gentleman in gray, in the uniform of a colonel, who proclaimed himself the proprietor of the hotel. He said his regiment had crumbled to pieces, he was the only man left in it, and he thought he might as well "stop off" at home. His story was significant as indicating the disintegrating process that was going on in the ranks of the enemy.

General Grant had been marching most of the way with the columns that were pushing along south of Lee's line of retreat; but expecting that a reply would be sent to his last letter and wanting to keep within easy communication with Lee, he decided to march this day with the portion of the Army of the Potomac that was pressing Lee's rear-guard. After issuing some further instructions to Ord and Sheridan, he started from Farmville, crossed to the north side of the Appomattox, conferred in person with Meade, and rode with his columns. Encouraging reports came in all day, and that night headquarters were established at Curdsville in a large white farm-house, a few hundred yards from Meade's camp. The general and several of the staff had cut loose from the headquarters trains the night he started to meet Sheridan at Jetersville, and had neither baggage nor camp-equipage. The general did not even have his sword with him. This was the most advanced effort yet made at moving in "light marching order," and we billeted ourselves at night in farm-houses, or bivouacked on porches, and picked up meals at any camp that seemed to have something to spare in the way of rations. This night we sampled the fare of Meade's hospitable mess and once more lay down with full stomachs.

General Grant had been suffering all the afternoon from a severe headache, the result of fatigue, anxiety, scant fare, and loss of sleep, and by night it was much worse. He had been induced to bathe his feet in hot water and mustard, and apply mustard plasters to his wrists and the back of his neck, but these remedies afforded little relief. The dwelling we occupied was a double house. The general threw himself upon a sofa in the sitting-room on the left side of the hall, while the staff-officers bunked on the floor of the room opposite to catch what sleep they could. About midnight we were aroused by Colonel Charles A. Whittier of Humphreys's staff, who brought another letter from Lee. Rawlins at once took it in to General Grant's room. It was as follows:

April 8th, 1865

GENERAL: I received at a late hour your note of to-day. In mine of yesterday I did not intend to propose the surrender of the Army of Northern Virginia, but to ask the terms of your proposition. To be frank, I do not think the emergency has arisen to call for the surrender of this army, but, as the restoration of peace should be the sole object of all, I desired to know whether your proposals would lead to that end. I cannot, therefore, meet you with a view to surrender the Army of Northern Virginia; but as far as your proposal may affect the Confederate States forces under my command, and tend to the restoration of peace, I should be pleased to meet you at 10 A. M. to-morrow on the old stage road to Richmond, between the picket-lines of the two armies.

R. E. LEE, General

LIEUTENANT-GENERAL U. S. GRANT

General Grant had been able to get but very little sleep. He now sat up and read the letter, and after making a few comments upon it to General Rawlins lay down again on the sofa.

About 4 o'clock on the morning of the 9th I rose and crossed the hall to ascertain how the general was feeling. I found his room empty, and upon going out of the front door saw him pacing up and down in the yard holding both hands to his head. Upon inquiring how he felt, he replied that he had had very little sleep, and was still suffering the most excruciating pain. I said: "Well, there is one consolation in all this, General: I never knew you to be ill that you did not receive some good news. I have become a little superstitious regarding these coincidences, and I should not be surprised if some good fortune overtook you before night." He smiled and said: "The best thing that can happen to me to-day is to get rid of the pain I am suffering." We were soon joined by some others of the staff, and the general was induced to go over to Meade's headquarters with us and get some coffee, in the hope that it would do him good. He seemed to feel a little better now, and after writing the following letter to Lee and dispatching it he prepared to move forward. The letter was as follows:

April 9th, 1865

GENERAL: Your note of yesterday is received. I have no authority to treat on the subject of peace. The meeting proposed for 10 A. M. to-day could lead to no good. I will state, however, that I am equally desirous for peace with yourself, and the whole North entertains the same feeling. The terms upon which peace can be had are well understood. By the South laying down their arms, they would hasten that most desirable event, save thousands of human lives, and hundreds of millions of property not yet destroyed. Seriously hoping that all our difficulties may be settled without the loss of another life, I subscribe myself, etc.

U. S. GRANT, Lieutenant-General

GENERAL R. E. LEE

It was proposed to him to ride during the day in a covered ambulance which was at hand, instead of on horseback, so as to avoid the intense heat of the sun, but this he declined to do, and soon after mounted "Cincinnati" and struck off toward New Store. From that point he went by way of a cross-road to the south side of the Appomattox with the intention of moving around to Sheridan's front. While riding along the wagon road that runs from Farmville to Appomattox Court House, at a point eight or nine miles east of the latter place, Lieutenant Charles E. Pease of Meade's staff overtook him with a dispatch. It was found to be a reply from Lee, which had been sent in to our lines on Humphreys's front. It read as follows:

April 9th, 1865

GENERAL: I received your note of this morning on the picket-line, whither I had come to meet you and ascertain definitely what terms were embraced in your proposal of yesterday with reference to the surrender of this army. I now ask an interview, in accordance with the offer contained in your letter of yesterday, for that purpose.

R. E. LEE, General

LIEUTENANT-GENERAL U. S. GRANT

Pease also brought a note from Meade, saying that at Lee's request he had read the communication addressed to General Grant and in consequence of it had granted a short truce.

The general, as soon as he had read these letters, dismounted, sat down on the grassy bank by the roadside, and wrote the following reply to Lee:

April 9th, 1865

GENERAL R. E. LEE, Commanding C. S. Army:

Your note of this date is but this moment (11:50 A. M.) received, in consequence of my having passed from the Richmond and Lynchburg road to the Farmville and Lynchburg road. I am at this writing about four miles west of Walker's Church, and will push forward to the front for the purpose of meeting you. Notice sent to me on this road where you wish the interview to take place will meet me.

U. S. GRANT, Lieutenant-General

He handed this to Colonel Babcock of the staff, with directions to take it to General Lee by the most direct route. Mounting his horse again the general rode on at a trot toward Appomattox Court House. When five or six miles from the town, Colonel Newhall, Sheridan's adjutant-general, came riding up from the direction of Appomattox and handed the general a communication. This proved to be a duplicate of the letter from Lee that Lieutenant Pease had brought in from Meade's lines. Lee was so closely pressed that he was anxious to communicate with Grant by the most direct means, and as he could not tell with which column Grant was moving he sent in one copy of his letter on Meade's front and one on Sheridan's. Colonel Newhall joined our party, and after a few minutes' halt to read the letter we continued our ride toward Appomattox. On the march I had asked the general several times how he felt. To the same question now he said, "The pain in my head seemed to leave me the moment I got Lee's letter." The road was filled with men, animals, and wagons, and to avoid these and shorten the distance we turned slightly to the right and began to "cut across lots"; but before going far we spied men conspicuous in gray, and it was seen that we were moving toward the enemy's left flank, and that a short ride farther would take us into his lines. It looked for a moment as if a very awkward condition of things might possibly arise, and Grant become a prisoner in Lee's lines instead of Lee in his. Such a circumstance would have given rise to an important cross-entry in the system of campaign book-keeping. There was only one remedy —to retrace our steps and strike the right road, which was done without serious discussion. About 1 o'clock the little village of Appomattox Court House, with its half-dozen houses, came in sight, and soon we were entering its single street. It is situated on some rising ground, and beyond the country slopes down into a broad valley. The enemy was seen with his columns and wagon trains covering the low ground. Our cavalry, the Fifth Corps, and part of Ord's command were occupying the high ground to the south and west of the enemy, heading him off completely. Generals Sheridan and Ord, with a group of officers around them, were seen in the road, and as our party came up General Grant said: "How are you, Sheridan?" "First-rate, thank you;

606

how are you?" cried Sheridan, with a voice and look that seemed to indicate that on his part he was having things all his own way. "Is Lee over there?" asked General Grant, pointing up the street, having heard a rumor that Lee was in that vicinity. "Yes, he is in that brick house," answered Sheridan. "Well, then, we'll go over," said Grant.

The general-in-chief now rode on, accompanied by Sheridan, Ord, and some others, and soon Colonel Babcock's orderly was seen sitting on his horse in the street in front of a two-story brick house, better in appearance than the rest of the houses. He said General Lee and Colonel Babcock had gone into this house a short time before, and he was ordered to post himself in the street and keep a lookout for General Grant, so as to let him know where General Lee was. Babcock told me afterward that in carrying General Grant's last letter he passed through the enemy's lines and found General Lee a little more than half a mile beyond Appomattox Court House. He was lying down by the roadside on a blanket which had been spread over a few fence rails on the ground under an apple-tree, which was part of an orchard. This circumstance furnished the only ground for the widespread report that the surrender occurred under an apple-tree. Babcock dismounted upon coming near, and as he approached on foot, Lee sat up, with his feet hanging over the roadside embankment. The wheels of the wagons in passing along the road had cut away the earth of this embankment and left the roots of the tree projecting. Lee's feet were partly resting on these roots. One of his staff-officers came forward, took the dispatch which Babcock handed him and gave it to General Lee. After reading it, the general rose and said he would ride forward on the road on which Babcock had come, but was apprehensive that hostilities might begin in the meantime, upon the termination of the temporary truce, and asked Babcock to write a line to Meade informing him of the situation. Babcock wrote accordingly, requesting Meade to maintain the truce until positive orders from General Grant could be received. To save time it was arranged that a Union officer, accompanied by one of Lee's officers, should carry this letter through the enemy's lines. This route made the distance to Meade nearly ten miles shorter than by the roundabout way of the Union lines. Lee now mounted his horse and directed Colonel Charles Marshall, his military secretary, to accompany him. They started for Appomattox Court House in company with Babcock and followed by a mounted orderly. When the party reached the village they met one of its residents, named Wilmer McLean, who was told that General Lee wanted to occupy a convenient room in some house in the town. McLean ushered them into the sitting-room of one of the first houses he came to, but upon looking about and finding it quite small and meagerly furnished, Lee proposed finding something more commodious and better fitted for the occasion. McLean then conducted the party to his own house, about the best one in the town, where they awaited General Grant's arrival.

The house had a comfortable wooden porch with seven steps leading up to it. A hall ran through the middle from front to back, and on each side was a room having two windows, one in front and one in rear. Each room had two doors opening into the hall. The building stood a little distance back from the street, with a yard in front, and to the left was a gate for carriages and a roadway running to a stable in rear. We entered the grounds by this gate and dismounted. In the yard were seen a fine large gray horse, which proved to be General Lee's, and a good-looking mare belonging to Colonel Marshall. An orderly in gray was in charge of them, and had taken off their bridles to let them nibble the grass.

General Grant mounted the steps and entered the house. As he stepped into the hall Colonel Babcock, who had seen his approach from the window, opened the door of the room on the left, in which he had been sitting with General Lee and Colonel Marshall awaiting General Grant's arrival. The general passed in, while the members of the staff, Generals Sheridan and Ord, and some general officers who had gathered in the front yard, remained outside, feeling that he would probably want his first interview with General Lee to be, in a measure, private. In a few minutes Colonel Babcock came to the front door and, making a motion with his hat toward the sitting-room, said: "The general says, come in." It was then about half-past one of Sunday, the 9th of April. We entered, and found General Grant sitting at a marble-topped table in the center of the room, and Lee sitting beside a small oval table near the front window, in the corner opposite to the door by which we entered, and facing General Grant. Colonel Marshall, his military secretary, was standing at his left. We walked in softly and ranged ourselves quietly about the sides of the room, very much as people enter a sick-chamber when they expect to find the patient dangerously ill. Some found seats on the sofa and the few chairs which constituted the furniture, but most of the party stood.

The contrast between the two commanders was striking, and could not fail to attract marked attention as they sat ten feet apart facing each other. General Grant, then nearly forty-three years of age, was five feet eight inches in height, with shoulders slightly stooped. His hair and full beard were a nut-brown, without a trace of gray in them. He had on a single-breasted blouse, made of dark-blue flannel, unbuttoned in front, and showing a waistcoat underneath. He wore an ordinary pair of top-boots, with his trousers inside, and was without spurs. The boots and portions of his clothes were spattered with mud. He had had on a pair of thread gloves, of a dark-yellow color, which he had taken off on entering the room. His felt "sugar-loaf" stiff-brimmed hat was thrown on the table beside him. He had no sword, and a pair of shoulder-straps was all there was about him to designate his rank. In fact, aside from these, his uniform was that of a private soldier.

Lee, on the other hand, was fully six feet in height, and quite erect for one of his age, for he was Grant's senior by sixteen years. His hair and full beard were a silver-gray, and quite thick, except that the hair had become a little thin in front. He wore a new uniform of Confederate gray, buttoned up to the throat, and at his side he carried a long sword of exceedingly fine workmanship, the hilt studded with jewels. It was said to be the sword that had been presented to him by the State of Virginia. His top-boots were comparatively new, and seemed to have on them some ornamental stitching of red silk. Like his uniform, they were singularly clean, and but little travel-stained. On the boots were handsome spurs, with large rowels. A felt hat, which in color matched pretty closely that of his uniform, and a pair of long buckskin gauntlets lay beside him on the table. We asked Colonel Marshall afterward how it was that both he and his chief wore such fine toggery, and looked so much as if they had turned out to go to church, while with us our outward garb scarcely rose to the dignity even of the "shabby-genteel." He enlightened us regarding the contrast, by explaining that when their headquarters wagons had been pressed so closely by our cavalry a few days before, and it was found they would have to destroy all their baggage, except the clothes they carried on their backs, each one, naturally, selected the newest suit he had, and sought to propitiate the god of destruction by a sacrifice of his second-best.

General Grant began the conversation by saying: "I met you once before, General Lee, while we were serving in Mexico, when you came over from General Scott's headquarters to visit Garland's brigade, to which I then belonged. I have always remembered your appearance, and I think I should have recognized you anywhere." "Yes," replied General Lee, "I know I met you on that occasion, and I have often thought of it and tried to recollect how you looked, but I have never been able to recall a single feature." After some further mention of Mexico, General Lee said: "I suppose, General Grant, that the object of our present meeting is fully understood. I asked to see you to ascertain upon what terms you would receive the surrender of my army." General Grant replied: "The terms I propose are those stated substantially in my letter of yesterday—that is, the officers and men surrendered to be paroled and disqualified from taking up arms again until properly exchanged, and all arms, ammunition, and supplies to be delivered up as captured property." Lee nodded an assent, and said: "Those are about the conditions which I expected would be proposed." General Grant then continued: "Yes, I think our correspondence indicated pretty clearly the action that would be taken at our meeting; and I hope it may lead to a general suspension of hostilities and be the means of preventing any further loss of life."

Lee inclined his head as indicating his accord with this wish, and General Grant then went on to talk at some length in a very pleasant vein about the prospects of peace. Lee was evidently anxious to proceed to the formal work of the surrender, and he brought the subject up again by saying:

609

"I presume, General Grant, we have both carefully considered the proper steps to be taken, and I would suggest that you commit to writing the terms you have proposed, so that they may be formally acted upon."

"Very well," replied General Grant, "I will write them out." And calling for his manifold order-book, he opened it on the table before him and proceeded to write the terms. The leaves had been so prepared that three impressions of the writing were made. He wrote very rapidly, and did not pause until he had finished the sentence ending with "officers appointed by me to receive them." Then he looked toward Lee, and his eyes seemed to be resting on the handsome sword that hung at that officer's side. He said afterward that this set him to thinking that it would be an unnecessary humiliation to require the officers to surrender their swords, and a great hardship to deprive them of their personal baggage and horses, and after a short pause he wrote the sentence: "This will not embrace the side-arms of the officers, nor their private horses or baggage." When he had finished the letter he called Colonel (afterward General) Ely S. Parker, one of the military secretaries on the staff, to his side and looked it over with him and directed him as they went along to interline six or seven words and to strike out the word "their," which had been repeated. When this had been done, he handed the book to General Lee and asked him to read over the letter. It was as follows:

APPOMATTOX CT. H., VA., April 9, 1865

GENERAL R. E. LEE, Commanding C. S. A.

GENERAL: In accordance with the substance of my letter to you of the 8th inst., I propose to receive the surrender of the Army of Northern Virginia on the following terms, to wit: Rolls of all the officers and men to be made in duplicate, one copy to be given to an officer to be designated by me, the other to be retained by such officer or officers as you may designate. The officers to give their individual paroles not to take up arms against the Government of the United States until properly [exchanged], and each company or regimental commander to sign a like parole for the men of their commands. The arms, artillery, and public property to be parked, and stacked, and turned over to the officers appointed by me to receive them. This will not embrace the side-arms of the officers, nor their private horses or baggage. This done, each officer and man will be allowed to return to his home, not to be disturbed by the United States authorities so long as they observe their paroles, and the laws in force where they may reside. Very respectfully,

U. S. GRANT, Lieutenant-General

Lee took it and laid it on the table beside him, while he drew from his pocket a pair of steel-rimmed spectacles and wiped the glasses carefully with his handkerchief. Then he crossed his legs, adjusted the spectacles very slowly and deliberately, took up the draft of the letter, and proceeded to read it attentively. It consisted of two pages. When he reached the top line of the second page, he looked up, and said to General Grant: "After the words 'until properly,' the word 'exchanged' seems to be omitted. You doubtless intended to use that word."

"Why, yes," said Grant; "I thought I had put in the word 'exchanged.'"

"I presumed it had been omitted inadvertently," continued Lee, "and with your permission I will mark where it should be inserted."

"Certainly," Grant replied.

Lee felt in his pocket as if searching for a pencil, but did not seem to be able to find one. Seeing this and happening to be standing close to him, I handed him my pencil. He took it, and laying the paper on the table noted the interlineation. During the rest of the interview he kept twirling this pencil in his fingers and occasionally tapping the top of the table with it. When he handed it back it was carefully treasured by me as a memento of the occasion. When Lee came to the sentence about the officers' side-arms, private horses, and baggage, he showed for the first time during the reading of the letter a slight change of countenance, and was evidently touched by this act of generosity. It was doubtless the condition mentioned to which he particularly alluded when he looked toward General Grant as he finished reading and said with some degree of warmth in his manner: "This will have a very happy effect upon my army."

General Grant then said: "Unless you have some suggestions to make in regard to the form in which I have stated the terms, I will have a copy of the letter made in ink and sign it."

"There is one thing I would like to mention," Lee replied after a short pause. "The cavalrymen and artillerists own their own horses in our army. Its organization in this respect differs from that of the United States." This expression attracted the notice of our officers present, as showing how firmly the conviction was grounded in his mind that we were two distinct countries. He continued: "I would like to understand whether these men will be permitted to retain their horses?"

"You will find that the terms as written do not allow this," General Grant replied; "only the officers are permitted to take their private property."

Lee read over the second page of the letter again, and then said:

"No, I see the terms do not allow it; that is clear." His face showed plainly that he was quite anxious to have this concession made, and Grant said very promptly and without giving Lee time to make a direct request:

"Well, the subject is quite new to me. Of course I did not know that any private soldiers owned their animals, but I think this will be the last battle of the war—I sincerely hope so—and that the surrender of this army will be followed soon by that of all the others, and I take it that most of the men in the ranks are small farmers, and as the country has been so raided by the two armies, it is doubtful whether they will be able to put in a crop to carry themselves and their families through the next winter without the aid of the horses they are now riding, and I will arrange it in this way: I will not change the terms as now written, but I will instruct the officers I shall appoint to receive the paroles to let all the men who claim to own a horse or mule take the animals home with them to work their little farms." (This expression has been quoted in various forms and has been the subject of some dispute. I give the exact words used.)

Lee now looked greatly relieved, and though anything but a demonstrative man, he gave every evidence of his appreciation of this concession, and said, "This will have the best possible effect upon the men. It will be very gratifying and will do much toward conciliating our people." He handed the draft of the terms back to General Grant, who called Colonel T. S. Bowers of the staff to him and directed him to make a copy in ink. Bowers was a little nervous, and he turned the matter over to Colonel (afterward General) Parker, whose handwriting presented a better appearance than that of any one else on the staff. Parker sat down to write at the table which stood against the rear side of the room. Wilmer McLean's domestic resources in the way of ink now became the subject of a searching investigation, but it was found that the contents of the conical-shaped stoneware inkstand which he produced appeared to be participating in the general breaking up and had disappeared. Colonel Marshall now came to the rescue, and pulled out of his pocket a small boxwood inkstand, which was put at Parker's service, so that, after all, we had to fall back upon the resources of the enemy in furnishing the stage "properties" for the final scene in the memorable military drama.

Lee in the meantime had directed Colonel Marshall to draw up for his signature a letter of acceptance of the terms of surrender. Colonel Marshall wrote out a draft of such a letter, making it quite formal, beginning with "I have the honor to reply to your communication," etc. General Lee took it, and, after reading it over very carefully, directed that these formal expressions be stricken out and that the letter be otherwise shortened. He afterward went over it again and seemed to change some words, and then told the colonel to make a final copy in ink. When it came to providing the paper, it was found we had the only supply of that important ingredient in the recipe for surrendering an army, so we gave a few pages to the colonel. The letter when completed read as follows:

HEADQUARTERS, ARMY OF NORTHERN VIRGINIA, April 9th, 1865
GENERAL: I received your letter of this date containing the terms of the surrender of the Army of Northern Virginia as proposed by you. As they are substantially the same as those expressed in your letter of the 8th inst., they are accepted. I will proceed to designate the proper officers to carry the stipulations into effect.

R. E. LEE, General

LIEUTENANT-GENERAL U. S. GRANT

While the letters were being copied, General Grant introduced the general officers who had entered, and each member of the staff, to General Lee. The General shook hands with General Seth Williams, who had been his adjutant when Lee was superintendent at West Point, some years before the war, and gave his hand to some of the other officers who had extended theirs, but to most of those who were introduced he merely bowed in a dignified and formal manner. He did not exhibit the slightest change of features during this ceremony until Colonel Parker of our staff was presented to him. Parker was a full-blooded Indian, and the reigning Chief of the Six Nations. When Lee saw his swarthy features he looked at him with evident surprise, and his eyes rested on him for several seconds. What was passing in his mind probably no one ever knew, but the natural surmise was that he at first mistook Parker for a Negro, and was struck with astonishment to find that the commander of the Union armies had one of that race on his personal staff.

Lee did not utter a word while the introductions were going on, except to Seth Williams, with whom he talked quite cordially. Williams at one time referred in rather jocose a manner to a circumstance which occurred during their former service together, as if he wanted to say something in a good-natured way to break up the frigidity of the conversation, but Lee was in no mood for pleasantries, and he did not unbend, or even relax the fixed sternness of his features. His only response to the allusion was a slight inclination of the head. General Lee now took the initiative again in leading the conversation back into business channels. He said:

"I have a thousand or more of your men as prisoners, General Grant, a number of them officers whom we have required to march along with us for several days. I shall be glad to send them into your lines as soon as it can be arranged, for I have no provisions for them. I have, indeed, nothing for my own men. They have been living for the last few days principally upon parched corn, and we are badly in need of both rations and forage. I telegraphed to Lynchburg, directing several train-loads of rations to be sent on by rail from there, and when they arrive I shall be glad to have the present wants of my men supplied from them."

At this remark all eyes turned toward Sheridan, for he had captured these trains with his cavalry the night before, near Appomattox Station. General Grant replied: "I should like to have our men sent within our lines as soon as possible. I will take steps at once to have your army supplied with rations, but I am sorry we have no forage for the animals. We have had to depend upon the country for our supply of forage. Of about how many men does your present force consist?"

"Indeed, I am not able to say," Lee answered after a slight pause. "My losses in killed and wounded have been exceedingly heavy, and, besides, there have been many stragglers and some deserters. All my reports and public papers, and, indeed, my own private letters, had to be destroyed on the march, to prevent them from falling into the hands of your people. Many companies are entirely without officers, and I have not seen any returns for several days; so that I have no means of ascertaining our present strength."

General Grant had taken great pains to have a daily estimate made of the enemy's forces from all the data that could be obtained, and, judging it to be about 25,000 at this time, he said: "Suppose I send over 25,000 rations, do you think that will be a sufficient supply?" "I think it will be ample," remarked Lee, and added with considerable earnestness of manner, "and it will be a great relief, I assure you."

General Grant now turned to his chief commissary, Colonel (now General) M. R. Morgan, who was present, and directed him to arrange for issuing the rations. The number of officers and men surrendered was over 28,000. As to General Grant's supplies, he had ordered the army on starting out to carry twelve days' rations. This was the twelfth and last day of the campaign.

Grant's eye now fell upon Lee's sword again, and it seemed to remind him of the absence of his own, and by way of explanation he said to Lee:

"I started out from my camp several days ago without my sword, and as I have not seen my headquarters baggage since, I have been riding about without any side-arms. I have generally worn a sword, however, as little as possible, only during the actual operations of a campaign." "I am in the habit of wearing mine most of the time," remarked Lee; "I wear it invariably when I am among my troops, moving about through the army."

General Sheridan now stepped up to General Lee and said that when he discovered some of the Confederate troops in motion during the morning, which seemed to be a violation of the truce, he had sent him (Lee) a couple of notes protesting against this act, and as he had not had time to copy them he would like to have them long enough to make copies. Lee took the notes out of the breast-pocket of his coat and handed them to Sheridan with a few words expressive of regret that the circumstance had occurred, and intimating that it must have been the result of some misunderstanding.

After a little general conversation had been indulged in by those present, the two letters were signed and delivered, and the parties prepared to separate. Lee before parting asked Grant to notify Meade of the surrender, fearing that fighting might break out on that front and lives be uselessly lost. This request was complied with, and two Union officers were sent through the enemy's lines as the shortest route to Meade—some of Lee's officers accompanying them to prevent their being interfered with. At a little before 4 o'clock General Lee shook hands with General Grant, bowed to the other officers, and with Colonel Marshall left the room. One after another we followed, and passed out to the porch. Lee signaled to his orderly to bring up his horse, and while the animal was being bridled the general stood on the lowest step and gazed sadly in the direction of the valley beyond where his army lay—now an army of prisoners. He smote his hands together a number of times in an absent sort of a way; seemed not to see the group of Union officers in the yard who rose respectfully at his approach, and appeared unconscious of everything about him. All appreciated the sadness that overwhelmed him, and he had the personal sympathy of every one who beheld him at this supreme moment of trial. The approach of his horse seemed to recall him from his reverie, and he at once mounted. General Grant now stepped down from the porch, and, moving toward him, saluted him by raising his hat. He was followed in this act of courtesy by all our officers present; Lee raised his hat respectfully, and rode off to break the sad news to the brave fellows whom he had so long commanded.

General Grant and his staff then mounted and started for the headquarters camp, which, in the meantime, had been pitched near by. The news of the surrender had reached the Union lines, and the firing of salutes began at several points, but the general sent orders at once to have them stopped, and used these words in referring to the occurrence: "The war is over, the rebels are our countrymen again, and the best sign of rejoicing after the victory will be to abstain from all demonstrations in the field." . . .

About 9 o'clock on the morning of the 10th General Grant with his staff rode out toward the enemy's lines, but it was found upon attempting to pass through that the force of habit is hard to overcome, and that the practice which had so long been inculcated in Lee's army of keeping Grant out of his lines was not to be overturned in a day, and he was politely requested at the picket-lines to wait till a message could be sent to headquarters asking for instructions. As soon as Lee heard that his distinguished opponent was approaching, he was prompt to correct the misunderstanding at the picket-line, and rode out at a gallop to receive him. They met on a knoll that overlooked the lines of the two armies, and saluted respectfully, by each raising his hat. The officers present gave a similar salute, and then grouped themselves around the two chieftains in a semicircle, but withdrew out of earshot. General Grant repeated to us that evening the substance of the conversation, which was as follows:

Grant began by expressing a hope that the war would soon be over, and Lee replied by stating that he had for some time been anxious to stop the further effusion of blood, and he trusted that everything would now be done to restore harmony and conciliate the people of the South. He said the emancipation of the Negroes would be no hindrance to the restoring of relations between the two sections of the country, as it would probably not be the desire of the majority of the Southern people to restore slavery then, even if the question were left open to them. He could not tell what the other armies would do or what course Mr. Davis would now take, but he believed it would be best for their other armies to follow his example, as nothing could be gained by further resistance in the field. Finding that he entertained these sentiments, General Grant told him that no one's influence in the South was so great as his, and suggested to him that he should advise the surrender of the remaining armies and thus exert his influence in favor of immediate peace. Lee said he could not take such a course without consulting President Davis first. Grant then proposed to Lee that he should do so, and urge the hastening of a result which was admitted to be inevitable. Lee, however, was averse to stepping beyond his duties as a soldier, and said the authorities would doubtless soon arrive at the same conclusion without his interference. There was a statement put forth that Grant asked Lee to see Mr. Lincoln and talk with him as to the terms of reconstruction, but this was erroneous. I asked General Grant about it when he was on his deathbed, and his recollection was distinct that he had made no such suggestion. I am of opinion that the mistake arose from hearing that Lee had been requested to go and see the "President" regarding peace, and thinking that this expression referred to Mr. Lincoln, whereas it referred to Mr. Davis. After the conversation had lasted a little more than half an hour and Lee had requested that such instructions be given to the officers left in charge to carry out the details of the surrender, that there might be no misunderstanding as to the form of paroles, the manner of turning over the property, etc., the conference ended. The two commanders lifted their hats and said good-bye. Lee rode back to his camp to take a final farewell of his army, and Grant returned to McLean's house, where he seated himself on the porch until it was time to take his final departure. During the conference Ingalls, Sheridan, and Williams had asked permission to visit the enemy's lines and renew their acquaintance with some old friends, classmates, and former comrades in arms who were serving in Lee's army. They now returned, bringing with them Cadmus M. Wilcox, who had been General Grant's groomsman when he was married; Longstreet, who had also been at his wedding; Heth, who had been a subaltern with him in Mexico, besides Gordon, Pickett, and a number of others. They all stepped up to pay their respects to General Grant, who received them very cordially and talked with them until it was time to leave. The hour of noon had now arrived, and General Grant, after shaking hands with all present who were not to accompany him, mounted his horse, and started with his staff for Washington without having entered the enemy's lines. Lee set out for Richmond, and it was felt by all that peace had at last dawned upon the land. The charges were now withdrawn from the guns, the camp-fires were left to smolder in their ashes, the flags were tenderly furled—those historic banners, battle-stained, bullet-riddled, many of them but remnants of their former selves, with scarcely enough left of them on which to imprint the names of the battles they had seen—and the Army of the Union and the Army of Northern Virginia turned their backs upon each other for the first time in four long, bloody years.

In the Union camps at Appomattox, the surrender brought relief and jubilation—with toasts, cheers, and music the order of the day. Around the Confederate campfires, the news was received with occasional defiance but for the most part in bewilderment and with numb resignation. In this hour, as men recalled their successes at Manassas, Cedar Mountain, Chancellorsville, their condition seemed incredible, a bad dream. Yet their great commander had confirmed the incredible. As General Lee rode away from the McLean house late that afternoon, in his new uniform with sword, sash, and gold spurs, they had clustered about him, many in tears, asking, "General, are we surrendered?" And with head bowed and in a voice filled with emotion, he had told them they were all paroled and were now to go to their homes. It was Palm Sunday, 1865. After four years lacking three days, to all intents and purposes the Civil War had come to an end.

"An affectionate farewell"

THE following account of the preparation of the Farewell Address of General Lee to his army is taken from a letter written by Lieutenant-Colonel Charles Marshall, of General Lee's staff, to General Bradley T. Johnson, dated Sept. 27th, 1887:

"General Lee's order to the Army of Northern Virginia at Appomattox Court House was written the day after the meeting at McLean's house, at which the terms of the surrender were agreed upon. That night the general sat with several of us at a fire in front of his tent, and after some conversation about the army, and the events of the day, in which his feelings toward his men were strongly expressed, he told me to prepare an order to the troops.

"The next day it was raining, and many persons were coming and going, so that I was unable to write without interruption until about 10 o'clock, when General Lee, finding that the order had not been prepared, directed me to get into his ambulance, which stood near his tent, and placed an orderly to prevent any one from approaching me.

"I sat in the ambulance until I had written the order, the first draft of which (in pencil) contained an entire paragraph that was omitted by General Lee's direction. He made one or two verbal changes, and I then made a copy of the order as corrected, and gave it to one of the clerks in the adjutant-general's office to write in ink. I took the copy, when made by the clerk, to the general, who signed it, and other copies were then made for transmission to the corps commanders and the staff of the army. All these copies were signed by the general, and a good many persons sent other copies which they had made or procured, and obtained his signature. In this way many copies of the order had the general's name signed as if they were originals, some of which I have seen."

The text of the order as issued was as follows:

"HEADQUARTERS, ARMY OF NORTHERN VIRGINIA, April 10th, 1865. After four years of arduous service, marked by unsurpassed courage and fortitude, the Army of Northern Virginia has been compelled to yield to overwhelming numbers and resources. I need not tell the survivors of so many hard-fought battles, who have remained steadfast to the last, that I have consented to this result from no distrust of them, but, feeling that valor and devotion could accomplish nothing that could compensate for the loss that would have attended the continuation of the contest, I have determined to avoid the useless sacrifice of those whose past services have endeared them to their countrymen.

"By the terms of the agreement, officers and men can return to their homes, and remain there until exchanged. You will take with you the satisfaction that proceeds from the consciousness of duty faithfully performed; and I earnestly pray that a merciful God will extend to you his blessing and protection.

"With an increasing admiration for your constancy and devotion to your country, and a grateful remembrance of your kind and generous consideration of myself, I bid you an affectionate farewell. R. E. LEE, General."

Major battles and campaigns—in addition to their listing under the names of these leaders—may be found in the Table of Contents.

Abbreviations used in this index are as follows: U for Union or federal and C for Confederate to indicate to which side the entry belonged; the designation in either case covers regular and enlisted officers and men, all forces supplied by the States, and volunteers. In addition to the usual abbreviations for the States, "Chat." stands for Chattanooga, "Pen." for Peninsular, and "Shen." for Shenandoah. The rank given in each entry is the eventual rank achieved, not necessarily the rank held at the time of the action listed; in addition to the usual abbreviations for rank, "b'v't" stands for Brevet, "cdr." for Commander (naval), and "com." for Commodore. Other abbreviations are: "art'y" for artillery, "bat'y" for battery, "cav." for cavalry, "cam." for campaign, "cd." for command, and "exped." for expedition.